Insights

A Selection of Creative Literature
About Childhood

INSIGHTS

A Selection of Creative Literature About Childhood

Selected and Edited by the
Child Study Association of America
With an Introduction and Comment by
Anna W. M. Wolf

**Jason Aronson
New York**

COPYRIGHT © 1973 BY
JASON ARONSON, INC.

Library of Congress Catalog Card Number: 73-17745
ISBN: 0-87668-116-X

Manufactured in the United States of America

Copyright © 1963 by The Child Study Association of America

A Death in the Family by James Agee. Copyright 1938, 1956 by The James Agee Trust. Selections reprinted by permission of Ivan Obolensky, Inc.

The Door of Life by Enid Bagnold. Copyright 1928 by Enid Bagnold Jones. Published by William Morrow & Company. Selections reprinted by permission of the author.

Memoirs of a Dutiful Daughter by Simone de Beauvoir, translated by James Kirkup. Copyright © 1957 by The World Publishing Co. Selections reprinted by permission of the World Publishing Co. Canada, by permission of Weidenfeld & Nicholson, Ltd.

"Coming Home" from *Early Stories* by Elizabeth Bowen. Copyright, 1950, by Elizabeth Bowen. Reprinted by permission of Alfred A. Knopf, Inc.

"First Love and Other Sorrows" by Harold Brodkey. Copyright © 1957 The New Yorker Magazine, Inc. Reprinted by permission.

My Father, Charlie Chaplin by Charles Chaplin, Jr. with N. and M. Rau. Copyright © 1960 by Charles Chaplin, Jr. Selection reprinted by permission of Random House, Inc.

A Roving Commission by Winston Churchill, now published in The Scribner Library as *My Early Life* by Winston Churchill. Copyright 1930 by Charles Scribner's Sons. Renewal copyright © 1958 by Winston Churchill. Selections reprinted by permission of Charles Scribner's Sons. Canada by permission of Odhams Press, Ltd. and Winston S. Churchill.

The Blue Cup and Other Stories by B. J. Chute. Published 1957 by E. P. Dutton & Co., Inc. Selection "The Legacy" copyright © 1952 by The Crowell-Collier Publishing Company. Reprinted by permission of E. P. Dutton & Co., Inc.

My Mother's House and Sido by Colette. Copyright 1953 by Farrar, Straus & Young, Inc. Selections reprinted by permission of Farrar, Straus & Cudahy, Inc. Canada by permission of Martin Secker & Warburg, Ltd.

Life with Father by Clarence Day. Copyright 1934, 1935 by Clarence Day. Selection "Father Opens My Mail" reprinted by permission of Alfred A. Knopf, Inc. Originally in *The New Yorker*.

My Family and Other Animals by Gerald Durrell. Copyright © 1957 by Gerald Durrell. Selection reprinted by permission of The Viking Press, Inc. Canada by permission of Rupert-Hart Davis, Ltd.

My Little Boy, Sections III and VIII, by Carl Ewald. Translated by Alexander Teizeria DeMattos. Reprinted by permission of Charles Scribner's Sons.

"Two Soldiers," by William Faulkner. Copyright 1942 by The Curtis Publishing Co. Reprinted from *Collected Stories of William Faulkner* by permission of Random House, Inc.

"Sex Education" by Dorothy Canfield Fisher. Copyright 1945 by Dorothy Canfield Fisher. Reprinted by permission of Harcourt, Brace & World, Inc.

Anne Frank: The Diary of a Young Girl by Anne Frank. Copyright 1952 by Otto H. Frank. Selections reprinted by permission of Doubleday & Co., Inc. Canada by permission of Vallentine, Mitchell & Co., Ltd.

Promise at Dawn by Romain Gary. Copyright © 1961 by Romain Gary. Selection reprinted by permission of Harper & Row, Publishers.

"Love and Like," Part 4, by Herbert Gold. Reprinted from *Love and Like*. Copyright © 1958, 1960 by Herbert Gold. Used with permission of the publisher, The Dial Press, Inc.

Dream Days by Kenneth Grahame. Selection reprinted by permission of Dodd, Mead & Company.

Act One by Moss Hart. Copyright © 1959 by Catherine Carlisle Hart and Joseph M. Hyman, Trustees. Selection reprinted by permission of Random House, Inc.

"To Telemachus" from *Breakfast in Mycenae* by Lee Hatfield. Copyright 1961 and reprinted by permission of Clarke & Way, publishers.

A High Wind in Jamaica by Richard Hughes. Copyright 1929 by Richard Hughes. Selection reprinted by permission of Harper & Row, Publishers.

"A Night Visitor" from *The Sunnier Side* by Charles Jackson. Copyright 1939, 1944, 1949, 1950 by Charles Jackson. Reprinted by permission of Farrar, Straus & Cudahy, Inc.

"How to Perfect Maternal Feelings of Guilt" from *Special Delivery* by Shirley Jackson. Copyright © 1959, 1960 by the McCall Corporation. Selection reprinted by permission of Little, Brown & Co. Originally in *Redbook* Magazine.

Dubliners by James Joyce. Selection "An Encounter" reprinted by permission of The Viking Press, Inc. All rights reserved. Canada by permission of Jonathan Cape, Ltd., and the Executors of the James Joyce Estate.

A Walker in the City by Alfred Kazin. Copyright 1951 by Alfred Kazin. Selection reprinted by permission of Harcourt, Brace & World, Inc.

"True Adventures of the Boy Reader" by Laurie Lee. Reprinted by permission of *The New York Times Book Review* and the Author.

"Ballade of Lost Objects" from *Times Three* by Phyllis McGinley. Copyright 1953 by Phyllis McGinley. Originally published in *The New Yorker*. Reprinted by permission of The Viking Press, Inc.

"Disorder and Early Sorrow" from *Stories of Three Decades* by Thomas Mann. Copyright 1936 by Alfred A. Knopf, Inc. Reprinted by permission of Alfred A. Knopf, Inc.

"At the Bay" from *The Short Stories of Katherine Mansfield*. Copyright 1922, 1937 by Alfred A. Knopf, Inc. Selection reprinted by permission of Alfred A. Knopf, Inc. Canada by permission of The Society of Authors as literary representative of the Estate of the late Miss Katherine Mansfield.

"Shoe the Horse and Shoe the Mare" by Astrid Meighan. Copyright © 1943 The New Yorker Magazine, Inc. Reprinted by permission.

"A Bit of Hiraeth" by Derek Morgan. Copyright 1961, The Reporter Magazine Company. Selections reprinted by permission.

"Birdies, Don't Make Me Laugh." Copyright, 1935 by the Curtis Publishing Company. From *Verses From 1929 On* by Ogden Nash. Reprinted by permission of Little, Brown & Co.

"My Oedipus Complex" from *The Stories of Frank O'Connor* by Frank O'Connor, copyright 1950, 1952 by Frank O'Connor. Reprinted by permission of Alfred A. Knopf, Inc. Canada by permission of Harold Matson Company.

"Such, Such were the Joys," by George Orwell. Copyright 1945, 1952, 1953, by Sonia Brownell Orwell. Selections reprinted by permission of Harcourt, Brace & World, Inc. Canada by permission of A. M. Heath & Co., Ltd.

"The Downward Path to Wisdom" by Katherine Anne Porter. Copyright 1939 by Katherine Anne Porter. Reprinted from *The Leaning Tower and Other Stories* by Katherine Anne Porter, by permission of Harcourt, Brace & World, Inc.

"Swann's Way" by Marcel Proust. Copyright 1928 and renewed 1956 by The Modern Library, Inc. Selections reprinted from *Remembrance of Things Past* by Marcel Proust, translated by C. K. Scott-Moncrieff by permission of Random House, Inc. Canada by permission of Chatto & Windus, Ltd.

Period Piece by Gwen Raverat. Copyright 1952 by Gwendolen Mary Raverat. Selections reprinted by permission of W. W. Norton & Company, Inc. Canada by permission of Faber & Faber, Ltd.

This Is My Story by Eleanor Roosevelt. Copyright 1937 by Anna Eleanor Roosevelt. Selections reprinted by permission of Harper & Row, Publishers.

Always the Young Strangers by Carl Sandburg. Copyright 1952, 1953 by Carl Sandburg. Selection reprinted by permission of Harcourt, Brace & World, Inc.

"The Summer of the Beautiful White Horse" from *My Name Is Aram* by William Saroyan. Copyright 1937, 1938, 1939, 1940, by William Saroyan. Reprinted by permission of Harcourt, Brace & World, Inc.

"Mrs. Levine's House" by Lore Groszmann Segal. © 1961 The New Yorker Magazine, Inc. Reprinted by permission of the author. First published in *The New Yorker*.

"The Gift" by Peter Shrubb. Copyright © 1961 The New Yorker Magazine, Inc. Reprinted by permission.

"Those Friends of His" by Cornelia Otis Skinner. Copyright © 1950 The New Yorker Magazine, Inc. Reprinted by permission.

"A Miserable Merry Christmas" from *The Autobiography of Lincoln Steffens*. Copyright 1931 by Harcourt, Brace & World, Inc. and reprinted with their permission.

"His Oceanic Majesty's Goldfish" by Austin Strong. Copyright 1944 by The Atlantic Monthly Company. Reprinted by permission of Brandt & Brandt.

"The Centaur" from *A Cage of Spines* by May Swenson. Copyright © 1956, 1958 by May Swenson. Reprinted by permission of Holt, Rinehart and Winston, Inc.

"With Child" from *Collected Poems* by Genevieve Taggard. Copyright 1938 by Harper & Row, Publishers, Inc. Reprinted by permission of the publishers.

"'Tis a Fond Ambush" by E. W. Tedlock, Jr. Copright 1959 by the University of New Mexico Press. Reprinted by permission of the *New Mexico Quarterly*.

"Strong Man" by Niccolò Tucci. Copyright © 1947 The New Yorker Magazine, Inc. Reprinted by permission.

"Wife Wooing" from *Pigeon Feathers and Other Stories* by John Updike. Copyright 1960, 1962 by John Updike. Reprinted by permission of Alfred A. Knopf, Inc. Originally in *The New Yorker*.

"House of Many Rooms" by Robin White. Harper & Brothers. Copyright © 1956, 1957, 1958 by Robin White. Selection reprinted by permission of Brandt & Brandt.

"A Game of Catch" by Richard Wilbur. Copyright © 1953 The New Yorker Magazine, Inc. Reprinted by permission.

Black Boy by Richard Wright. Copyright 1945 by Richard Wright. Selection reprinted by permission of Harper & Row, Publishers.

CONTENTS

Introduction   *11*

PART ONE: *In The Beginning*   *15*

    GENEVIEVE TAGGARD   *With Child*   19
    SHIRLEY JACKSON   *How to Perfect Maternal Feelings of Guilt*   20
    ENID BAGNOLD from *The Door of Life*   25
    E. W. TEDLOCK, JR.   *'Tis a Fond Ambush*   32
    FRANK O'CONNOR   *My Oedipus Complex*   34
    LEE HATFIELD   *To Telemachus*   44
    NICCOLÒ TUCCI   *Strong Man*   45
    KATHERINE MANSFIELD from *At the Bay*   48
    MARCEL PROUST from *Swann's Way*   51
    ELEANOR ROOSEVELT from *This is My Story*   61
    OGDEN NASH   *Birdies, Don't Make Me Laugh*   70
    CARL EWALD from *My Little Boy*   72
    LEO TOLSTOI   *First Recollections*   78
    THOMAS MANN   *Disorder and Early Sorrow*   82

PART TWO: *The World Widens*   *108*

    WINSTON CHURCHILL from *A Roving Commission*   112
    GEORGE ORWELL from *Such, Such Were the Joys*   118
    CORNELIA OTIS SKINNER   *Those Friends of His*   126
    MOSS HART from *Act One*   131
    SIMONE DE BEAUVOIR from *Memoirs of a Dutiful Daughter*   133
    ROMAIN GARY from *Promise at Dawn*   141
    LORE GROSZMANN SEGAL   *Mrs. Levine's House*   145
    HENRY ADAMS from *The Education of Henry Adams*   158

ALFRED KAZIN from *A Walker in the City* 161
GERALD DURRELL from *My Family and Other Animals* 169
WILLIAM FAULKNER *Two Soldiers* 176

PART THREE: *Fun, Fantasy and Adventure*   *189*

WILLIAM SAROYAN *The Summer of the Beautiful White Horse* 192
SAMUEL CLEMENS from *Adventures of Huckleberry Finn* 198
GWEN RAVERAT from *Period Piece* 201
CARL SANDBURG from *Always the Young Strangers* 206
AUSTIN STRONG *His Oceanic Majesty's Goldfish* 212
CHARLES DICKENS *Gone Astray* 219
CHARLES CHAPLIN, JR. AND N. & M. RAU from *My Father, Charlie Chaplin* 227
LINCOLN STEFFENS *A Miserable, Merry Christmas* 229
RICHARD WILBUR *A Game of Catch* 234
MAY SWENSON *The Centaur* 238
DEREK MORGAN from *A Bit of Hiraeth* 241
KENNETH GRAHAME from *Dream Days* 246
OLIVER WENDELL HOLMES from *The Autocrat of the Breakfast-Table* 251

PART FOUR: *Growing Up*   *254*

PHYLLIS MCGINLEY *Ballade of Lost Objects* 258
RICHARD HUGHES from *A High Wind in Jamaica* 260
LAURIE LEE *True Adventures of the Boy Reader* 263
HAROLD BRODKEY *First Love and Other Sorrows* 267
WILLIAM SHAKESPEARE from *Romeo and Juliet* 291
B. J. CHUTE *The Legacy* 295
CHARLES JACKSON *A Night Visitor* 308
CLARENCE DAY *Father Opens My Mail* 320
DOROTHY CANFIELD FISHER *Sex Education* 325
COLETTE *The Abduction* 335
COLETTE *Laughter* 338
ANNE FRANK from *The Diary of a Young Girl* 341
PETER SHRUBB *The Gift* 355

PART FIVE: *The Discovery of Ambiguity*   *365*

JOHN UPDIKE *Wife-Wooing* 369
CHARLES DICKENS from *David Copperfield* 373
JAMES JOYCE *An Encounter* 385

KATHERINE ANNE PORTER *The Downward Path to
    Wisdom* 392
ELIZABETH BOWEN *Coming Home* 408
RICHARD WRIGHT from *Black Boy* 414
HERBERT GOLD from *Love and Like, Part 4* 421
ASTRID MEIGHAN *Shoe the Horse and Shoe the Mare* 425
JAMES AGEE from *A Death in the Family* 431
ROBIN WHITE from *House of Many Rooms* 449

Introduction

THIS COLLECTION of insightful stories about childhood will have a deep appeal for all those who work and live with children. Parents, teachers, and mental health professionals will welcome the chance to explore and ponder these perceptions of creative writers.

The artist is a thinker whose approach is intuitive. At his best, he reveals in a flash that carries a special kind of beauty what the theorist expounds and analyzes at length. Sometimes he is not fully aware of the extent of what he is revealing, his vision welling up from the depths almost unbidden. Often, indeed, his insights are as ambiguous as life itself. Which of us can say with certainty just which life experiences will result in this or that character? Or what the outcome for the individual human being is bound to be.

In these stories, the artist-writer does of course indicate directions. But in some cases he also bids us beware of facile conclusions. So, while they offer insights, the stories may also be used as takeoff points for discussion groups where interpretations may vary. They are literature from which to learn and to teach.

And they are enjoyable—a treat that cannot fail to add to our pleasure in children and to challenge us anew as we struggle with the whole complicated, strenuous, painful, joyful business of growing up. Pausing to read about children often adds another dimension to how we have perceived them for we are all in danger of running in grooves with our boys and girls. Seeing them as we do day after day, we need something to jolt us out of old habits of thought, a source of refreshment. And children have a wonderful way of responding to deepened understanding.

The stories that follow will, we hope, be a delight to read, evoking laughter, poignant memories and sometimes tears. For these selections are not all pleasurable in the usual sense. Some are sad or painful, even tragic. Yet in each, there are deep satisfactions—the sudden illumination of the more shadowy places of the child soul; or a truth about themselves, formerly only half glimpsed, now beautifully clarified.

Readers will, we believe, discover here much about the forces that give energy and direction to a child's forward thrusts. They will also find many reminders of their own childhoods, their family relationships, their marriages, their responses to the challenge of parenthood. All play upon their children's lives. In several selections we see the reverse side of the coin: the very existence and appeal of children are potent forces in the lives of parents. In *The Door of Life, Wife Wooing, The Gift,* and others, the adults' own maturing is the pivotal point.

Literature about childhood is vast, and we make no claim to comprehensiveness. Readers may wonder at the omission of one or another of their personal favorites. For many reasons, including the limitations of space, we had to relinquish much that we would have liked to include.

We had also hoped to present more selections from writers of the past, but in the literature of yesterday there are surprisingly few portrayals of childhood that seem valid today. Indeed the child as *child* was scarcely perceived. Rousseau was one of the first to recognize the importance of children, and we are today the heirs of his beneficent influence. But basically he believed, as did Wordsworth later, that children come into the world trailing clouds of glory, and are wholly innocent and good until corrupted by civilization. Even the marvelously observant Dickens often descended to bathos, peopling his novels with defenseless children, victimized by cruel adults but ready at a moment's notice to respond wholeheartedly to love and kindness. Oliver Twist, for all his low-life, never lost his gentlemanly manners or command of the King's English. Not until Samuel Butler, who wrote in the middle of the nineteenth century but went almost unnoticed until much later, do we encounter a more astringent, clear-eyed view. We regret that we could not include a selection from *The Way of All Flesh,* a truly epochal book. It should be read as a whole.

The truth is that our view of children has undergone a radical change. We no longer regard them either as young limbs of Satan to be tamed and civilized by whatever drastic methods are required, or as angels of innocence. The shift has come as the result of a variety of broad social changes, including the continual widening of scientific boundaries and the accompanying habit of thinking scientifically. These changes, affecting artist and scholar alike, have ushered in wholly new approaches. Just as Newton is said to have asked "why" when he saw an apple fall to the ground, we are now beginning to ask "why" about human behavior, including child behavior. Freud's questions have surely been among the most searching. We can hardly fail to observe that the literature of today is shot through and through with Freudian insights, often so perfectly wedded to the genius of the artist that we are scarcely aware of the union. So fully have we accepted these insights that we even tend to judge the psychologic vision of earlier writers by the extent to which they anticipate Freud.

How hard it is now to understand our earlier failure to see that children even in the nursery can be jealous without reason, aggressive without provocation, libidinally interested in their own and other people's bodies —and that these impulses, the rule rather than the exception, normal not perverse, must be reckoned with in any philosophy of child-rearing. Perhaps our earlier blindness was in part the result of a *refusal* to see these things. When children act out our own least acceptable impulses in a form naked and unashamed, it is bound to be painful.

We have also rid ourselves of the myth that childhood is altogether happy and carefree. We can now admit that it also has times of loneliness and anguish, and that children may be haunted by anxieties that they cannot or will not reveal. Because their reality sense is immature, they live, in large measure, in a world where anything might happen. This threat of danger often accounts for some of the behavior in children that grownups find both trying and baffling. The perceptive writer today is keenly aware of this side of childhood; his awareness may in part account for some of the depressed tone which allegedly is characteristic of literature in general today, and some of this is included here. Yet the reader will also find in these selections high spirits and humor, tenderness and family love, the excitement of adventure, the thrill of new discoveries, including the discovery of oneself. These too are real; and herein lies the drama—a drama in which childhood loneliness is juxtaposed with fun and lightheartedness and experiences rich in the promise of personal fulfillment.

We also discern a persistent theme throughout these selections, reminding us that children and grownups in many ways inevitably inhabit separate worlds, even when parents try hard to enter the child's domain. We find this thought in the last part of the Orwell selection, in Thomas Mann, in Gwen Raverat, even in such a light bit as that from Cornelia Otis Skinner. The child, they seem to say, has his reasons that the reasonable adult knows not of. The child, being the wiser, grasps this truth better than the grownup, who is forever trying to invade the child's private fortress only to find himself outwitted and the child adept at defending it. Yet, while respecting the child's need, we may nevertheless ask whether the effort to understand, and the good-will that prompts it, does not in some way pay off.

Another characteristic of the finest in literature is the absence of pat solutions. This fact should warn us that the deeper we explore human behavior the less we are able to give answers or offer formulas to ensure results (to develop, say, the "rounded," "adjusted" individual—even assuming that this is our goal). Though children's growth does follow certain broad patterns, within these patterns is infinite variety. Though we know that certain kinds of experiences within the parent-child relationship seem to be strength-giving—or weakening, as the case may be—it is still impossible to make positive predictions. But despite these uncertainties, readers will, we believe, gain from these selections a deepened insight that may guide them, each according to his particular star.

Some of these stories are forthright in treatment, clear as to the author's intent. Others are so packed with meaning on so many different levels, so laden with overtones and minor themes of major interest, that for full understanding they must be lived with and pondered. We have, however, limited the note that accompanies each selection to a few words that may serve as a kind of alert, reserving somewhat fuller comments for the introductions to the various sections.

For who can speak better for a writer than the writer himself? Literature is by nature profoundly personal, destined to impart different messages to different people at different times. Meaning depends always on what particular chord in each of us at a particular moment of experience is tuned to respond. Not until we feel those answering vibrations within does a work of art become truly a part of ourselves.

Anna W. M. Wolf

PART ONE

In The Beginning

THE STORY of any childhood if told fully is almost equally the story of the child-parent bond. Between child and mother especially, the involvement at first may be all-enveloping. Long before an infant talks or understands the exact meaning of words, he and his mother have begun to send messages back and forth and sense what the other is saying.

"I've had enough to eat," says the baby quite plainly or, "How I love to splash in my bath!" And he knows that his mother is saying "Splash away—and *my*, I think you are beautiful!" He learns to understand too when she pulls down the shades and leaves his room. He knows when she *really* means it.

Inevitably too, there are days when mother and child fail to understand each other. Then both suffer from a feeling of emptiness until the interplay is resumed. In this earliest and most basic love relationship, the small child's need for his parents and their intense response to his need is so overwhelming that it is not surprising to find parents and adult children, years later, still struggling to be free of this mutual dependence that once, long ago, was entirely valid.

The experiences of pregnancy and birth seem to intensify this involvement. Enid Bagnold's portrayal of a woman in labor with her fifth child describes her in the grip of an all-absorbing solemn joy—self-sufficient, wholly in command of this elemental world. This is not always the way it is. A younger woman about to bear her first child will very likely be frightened when her time comes. Afterward, like so many, she may experience a vague, guilt-laden disappointment. Like the young woman in Shirley Jackson's story, she is silently wondering whether these daily doubts and frustrations inflicted on her by the newcomer are really the goal to which her whole life has been tending. Yet her ties to her child are no less binding for her than they are for the more mature mother.

Though parents and children must indeed someday accomplish a measure of liberation from each other, in the early months and years of life the mother's full acceptance of her child's total need of her is not only a condition of his physical survival; it is equally necessary for his emotional well-being. Without the certainty of a secure haven, he dare not venture forth into rougher waters. "Loving" his parents in a fiercely demanding way and learning gradually to trust them, the way is paved for him in later life to love others less demandingly. His future strength is rooted in this early experience. Children gain self-reliance not through parents' withholding themselves and presenting a cool, detached front to infant needs, but by generous whole-hearted giving followed by wise and gradual weaning as the child grows.

This, then, is the parents' two-pronged task—acceptance of the child's early dependence and later, as they sense his readiness, the encouragement of new steps toward maturity. But the way is not clear and simple. Parents have as much to contend with in themselves as in their children. Though both have everything to gain by moving steadily forward they are also prey to irresistible moments of pulling back to the old familiar ways where Mother both controls and gratifies. Surely by building into our very fiber this pattern of mutual dependence which must constantly be redesigned as the child grows older, nature has played us a scurvy trick. Yet the deepest satisfactions during the years ahead and throughout adult life depend almost wholly on how well parents and children together set aside the early bondage, and how well they work out a new pattern built upon the old.

The selection from Proust portrays such a struggle in a mother and son. The child here is no longer an infant; he is five years old. The parents are quite right to expect him to go to bed as a child should and relinquish demands for long-drawn-out ministrations from his mother—who should now be left in peace with her husband and guests. But abetted by a compliant husband and tempted beyond her strength by her son's blandishments, the mother succumbs. She goes to the boy, caters to his babyishness, and caps it all by spending the night in his room. We can guess that this passage between them was by no means unusual and that it was very likely a mere prelude to a whole sequence of small events by which this mother bound her son irrevocably.

In a wholly different manner Thomas Mann weaves a subtle story around a similar theme. In the crazy, chaotic Germany of the period following the first World War, a middle-aged professor, spiritually estranged from this disordered world, his nearly-grown children slipping from him, finds his one solace in love for his small five-year-old daughter. Yet even as he pours all his emotions into this child, he is aware that there is something

In The Beginning

"not quite right" in this intense involvement; it rests on his image of her as a wondrous bit of perfection rather than as a vital and changing human being. When the child turns away from him, a captive to the charms of a young guest who has taken her fancy, he suffers twinges of real jealousy. He tries to console her for the young man's neglect, but his logic makes no impression. In the end, it is a servant who finds the means to dry her tears, and this too is humiliating. But unlike the mother in Proust, the father does not try to bind his "little sweetheart" to him. Life is like this, he seems to realize; and as the years roll away, the child will surely find other new loves. He can accept the inevitable and let her go.

The young child's life is bounded by family. Though he yearns to be "big," and often plays at it, it is hard for him to believe that he ever will be. Feeling his helplessness, he both demands that his parents care for him and resents it when they do. His brothers and sisters are likely to be further storm centers—necessary and valued allies, but also dangerous rivals. The ensuing quarrels and conflicts lead to times of family friction that parents find hard to bear. How grateful we are when Ogden Nash in *Birdies* bids us find this state of affairs universal and so assures us that at least we aren't alone. It's the same *everywhere,* he says. The child as well as the parents bears the burden for these quarrels. He is quite aware that these fights are among the many things that make his parents angry. He expects retribution in some form or other. "What if my parents should leave me and never come back?" he wonders. "What if something awful comes and eats me up for wanting my brother to go away and stay away!" And so his world, especially alone in the dark, becomes peopled with threatening shapes.

We tell our child he isn't bad, that we love him and that the fearsome lions aren't real. Perhaps it helps for a while. But in the end, the child himself learns to cope with his fears in his own ways. Sometimes, as in *Strong Man,* he does this by declaring that it's not he but someone else who is afraid. Wisely, the father in this story does not unmask his young son's defensive gambit. It will serve well enough until the youngster discovers for himself that the frightening things that come at bedtime are merely shadows without substance.

This continued learning "to cope" is one of the truly lovely things to behold in children. We are forever surprised at their growing strength and how they draw it from unexpected sources. In Katherine Mansfield's *At The Bay,* Kezia, through her love for a wise grandma, is enabled to take one quick look at the fact of death. Although she averts her gaze quickly, at least she has made a beginning. Eleanor Roosevelt, shy, awkward, homely, and motherless feels secure and even beautiful in the presence of a father who drank too much and whom the world called weak. The strength she derived from his confidence in her made it possible for her finally to break out of her chrysalis.

This capacity to respond creatively to new events and requirements and to change direction flexibly when change means widened horizons, deeper experiences, is the safeguard against arrested growth. For those who possess it, living and learning ensure never-ending adventure.

GENEVIEVE TAGGARD

With Child

Now I am slow and placid, fond of sun,
Like a sleek beast, or a worn one,
No slim and languid girl—not glad
With the windy trip I once had,
But velvet-footed, musing of my own,
Torpid, mellow, stupid as a stone.

You cleft me with your beauty's pulse, and now
Your pulse has taken body. Care not how
The old grace goes, how heavy I am grown,
Big with this loneliness, how you alone
Ponder our love. Touch my feet and feel
How earth tingles, teeming at my heel!
Earth's urge, not mine—my little death, not hers;
And the pure beauty yearns and stirs.

It does not heed our ecstasies, it turns
With secrets of its own, its own concerns,
Toward a windy world of its own, toward stark
And solitary places. In the dark
Defiant even now, it tugs and moans
To be untangled from these mother's bones.

Joy in a new baby is sometimes overshadowed by self-doubt. Amid the humdrum jobs of domestic life, a new mother's pleasure in the coming of her baby may alternate with the gnawing question, "But am I really a good mother?"

SHIRLEY JACKSON

How to Perfect Maternal Feelings of Guilt

SOONER OR LATER you are going to be left alone with this baby. All alone, just you and Baby and an all-pervading panic.

You are reasonably sure by now that you are not going to sit down on him, or put the diaper on over his head, but by golly, that is just about all you *are* sure of. Here is the same old place you have been living in right along. There is the couch, and the table with the ash tray on it that your husband won playing golf in the Salesman's Tournament, and the curtains you made yourself, and the rug you still haven't paid for, and there is the kitchen with the dishes you have washed over and over again (standing by the sink, dreaming idly of what it would be like when Baby came, wondering if it would be a boy or a girl, standing there with the dishcloth in your hand and the soapsuds melting away) and the pots and pans and the little white enamel pan you bought for heating Baby's bottle. There is the bed you half-slept in all these months, longing to turn over and sleep on your stomach, promising yourself that once it was over and you could get a good night's sleep without the aching back, the aching ankles, the weary shoulders . . . oh, once it was over you would really *sleep* again. There are the clothes you have waited all this time to wear once more (do they fit? No) and the high-heeled shoes you haven't dared to put on yet.

There is the crib you set up so lovingly for Baby, you and his father, telling one another delightedly that Baby would lie *here,* and his little clothes would be put in *there,* and we can hear him if he makes the slightest noise at night. (Hear him? Get three blocks away and see if you

How to Perfect Maternal Feelings of Guilt

can hear him make the slightest noise at night) and *here* is where he'll have his bath, and *here* . . . well, here is Baby.

It's over. You can tie your shoes again. You can bend over to pick up a pin from the floor if you want to. You can sleep on your stomach again, except you've forgotten how to breathe sleeping on your stomach. The same dishes and pots and pans are there waiting to be washed, and waiting and waiting and waiting, while you try to find your way through the maze of the kitchen to get the little white enamel pot to heat up Baby's bottle. Baby is lying there, incredibly real and solid and pink, a real honest to goodness baby, with all his arms and legs and toes and altogether beautiful and wonderful, possessing such breathtaking instinctive knowledges as how to close those small eyes and how to yawn (how does a baby yawn? Is it real?) and carrying somewhere within him the potential ability to grow a tooth, or smile at his daddy, or reach out those small hands to his mother. And what is he doing, this baby, rich in infinite knowledge, full of beauty and wonder and delight, perfect and small and most incredible of all—alive and individual? You know what he is doing.

The little eyes are closed all right, screwed tight shut. The perfect little hands are clenched, the pink little face is red with fury and the little mouth which will so soon grow teeth is wide open. The legs are kicking wildly, muscles which will someday be carrying him down a football field are rigid and tight, and he is making a racket altogether out of proportion to his size and strength. The nurses in the hospital knew what to do when he yelled like that. In the hospital they could *always* do something. He never yelled like this before. There must be something they forgot to tell you, some vital fact they all assumed you would know, some perfectly natural thing to do when Baby cries; perhaps there is something which normal maternal instinct would tell you right off ought to be done and because you are—oh, face it—not a normal mother you don't know what it is . . . no one else's baby cries like this. There is something wrong with you; your baby is crying and you don't know what to do. Here everyone else knows what to do when a baby cries and there is something lacking in your makeup and you had no right to have children at all and the doctor should have told you instead of letting you go ahead and what will your mother say when she finds out you are some kind of a monster instead of a normal mother and maybe if you called the hospital and asked them nicely they would take him back because if that yelling doesn't stop for one minute so you can catch your breath and get hold of an aspirin . . . No, he won't stop. But go ahead and call your doctor anyway, if you want to. You won't be able to hear anything over the phone, of course, but you will have the reassuring feeling that there is some other human being in the world besides you and this noise machine.

Don't bother to call your husband. He will only tell you that gosh, maybe there's something wrong with the kid, and you better call the doctor. When you say you've just *called* the doctor he will say well, maybe you better call the doctor again. After you have talked to your husband you can always call your mother. If she is a sensible grandmother—and grandmothers are almost always eminently sensible in this respect—she will have to hang up because she is laughing her head off. This is no comfort. And if she is as sensible a grandmother as all that she will wait a good twenty-four hours before coming to see you and she will finally come and walk through the front door saying, "Well, did Baby ever stop crying?" Then she will laugh. If she has your mother-in-law with her they will look at each other and laugh.

Meanwhile you will have entered into the O-God-Am-I-Fit-To-Raise-A-Child guilt. This is different from the I-May-Not-Covet-My-Neighbor's-Curls guilt, but similar to the Perhaps-I-Do-Not-Love-Him-As-I-Ought guilt. Basic to all these guilty feelings, of course, is the secret, and accurate, conviction that this baby is asking more of you than any human being ought to ask of another, and the complementary feeling that a Mother ought to be prepared to Give All for her offspring. These two feelings are complementary, but not reconcilable. The mother who is damned if she is going to give all to her offspring, but wonders all the same if she should, is going to have to take up the slack somehow by kicking herself around a little, and there is absolutely no field which offers such opportunity for guilty self-criticism as bringing up a child.

Guilt about coveting one's neighbor's curls leads naturally to such self-punishing remarks as: "What perfectly magnificent curls little Abercrombie has! I do wish *my* baby had such lovely hair; tell me—have you checked with your doctor about that wicked squint in Abercrombie's left eye?" Or "My husband and I were remarking only yesterday on what lovely curly hair the little fellow has. What a pity he's not a girl!" Abercrombie's mother, ridden by her own doubts, will then thank you politely for your compliments upon the curls, point out that your baby seems so sallow these days—is he getting enough vitamins, do you think?—and you will wheel your carriages in different directions. In five or six years, when your little bruiser hits Abercrombie over the head with a rock, Abercrombie's mother will have more to say about you and your child-raising methods, but by then you will have had more practice in the tigress defending her cubs business, and will have little or no feeling of envy over Abercrombie, that crybaby.

Doubts about being fit to raise a child are best settled before the child is old enough to bring them up himself. Believe me, when he is around fifteen he will have refined this child-torture bit to such an extent that unless you are fully insulated against it you are going to find that you are being made to reproach yourself for not giving in weakmindedly to such indulgences as movies on school nights or—if your child-psychologist is a girl—wearing high-heeled shoes to school. The truly farsighted baby

How to Perfect Maternal Feelings of Guilt

is the one who learns in his cradle that his mother is going to wonder endlessly about her shortcomings as a parent, and who never allows her to stop wondering for a minute. Prepare your defense: assume from the very first minute that Mother *does* know best, that no week-old child can dictate to *you*, that your own solid common sense and proverbial intelligence are enough to carry you through, that from this very minute on, you are never going to reverse a decision once made, and whatever you say, agreeable or not, is going to be final.

Let me know how you come out. For my part, I find myself saying over and over again, "Tomorrow I will do better. Tomorrow I will be patient, no matter what happens. Tomorrow I will not be cross under any provocation. Tomorrow I will start trying to be a model mother." I'll let you know how *I* come out. Exactly nowhere, that's how I come out. "Tomorrow," I say, "tomorrow I will lay down the law absolutely. I will be reasonable, I will not raise my voice, but I will make it abundantly clear that movies on school nights are . . ."

The worst aspect of all the centuries of tradition and sentiment about mother love and the one hand always reaching out to help, the one face always smiling, the one heart that never loses faith . . . well, the *worst* of it is that it's so easy to think you're falling behind the rest. Certainly you will always leave a light in the window for your wandering boy, but right now someone's got to feed him his strained apricots. You will always be waiting for him, smiling through your tears, glorying in his triumphs, sharing in his defeats, but first you've got to get a dry sheet on his crib. Motherhood is glorious, but it's also one hell of a lot of work, and it's just too easy to get so bogged down in feedings and washings and changings and airings that sometimes days and days go by when you keep forgetting to lift your head and smile proudly through your tears.

There's one very good way to use up any extra guilt you've got left over after being a failure as a mother. Suppose your baby were menaced by a cobra; naturally you would leap in front of the baby and fight off the cobra with your bare hands. Wouldn't you? *Wouldn't* you? It is perfectly possible to reduce yourself to a tearful head-beating wreck over that cobra, because—well, *would* you? Do you love your child enough to rescue him from that cobra? Go on and worry about it. It will do to keep you awake the few nights that the baby sleeps through his two o'clock bottle. If your husband wakes up and asks what on earth are you doing sitting over there by the window wringing your hands you be sure and tell him you're wondering if you would have courage enough to save your baby from a cobra. Yes, you tell him that.

Worry, incidentally, is something else again. Worry is when you sit over there by the window all night wringing your hands and picturing *real* dangers, like the probability that Baby will fall out of his crib the minute you are asleep, or the good chance that he will grow up and marry and you will not get along with his wife, or the ever-present perils of mad dogs and those live cartridges that careless people are always leaving around, or smallpox.

Or, if you're still not sleepy, you can just sit there thinking what a miserable wretch you are, the way you treated Baby today when you were so cross. The little sweetheart didn't *mean* to make you unhappy and even though he kicked the cereal bowl out of your hand *he* didn't know he was doing wrong and even though no mother would ever punish a tiny baby there is no question but what you put him down more abruptly than you would have if you hadn't been angry. The poor little thing can't understand when all of a sudden he looks at his mother whom he trusts and adores above all other human beings and she is scowling and snarling at him and calling him a little beast and the little angel is bewildered and insecure and so he cries and then the mother he has learned to love so dearly almost . . . well, she doesn't actually *spank* him, and anyway those diapers are very thick. But she is very much annoyed. Poor little baby. And he thought his mother loved him. The shortsighted mother will now go tearfully through the darkness to the side of the crib and kiss Baby while he sleeps so exquisitely, and whisper, "Mommy didn't mean it, darling, Mommy's sorry." This almost always wakes the baby, who cries, and before long Mother has completely forgotten that he doesn't really *mean* it when he tries to drive her crazy.

An Englishwoman called "the Squire," her husband absent in India, is about to give birth to her fifth child. The following selections, from a short novel focused wholly on the birth and the hours just preceding it, portray this woman's heightened responsiveness to her children Boniface, Lucy, Henry, and Jay; to the midwife (in England, midwife is the name for a baby nurse); to the doctor—and especially to her own private and profound experience.

ENID BAGNOLD

from *The Door of Life*

SHE who had once been thirsty and gay, square-shouldered, fair and military, strutting about life for spoil, was thickened now, vigorous, leonine, occupied with her house, her nursery, her servants, her knot of human lives, antagonistic or loving. Twelve years married to a Bombay merchant and nearly five times a mother, she was accustomed to her husband's long absences, and to her own supreme command.

"But to leave you this time through a birth!" he had said. "I have never left you through a birth!"

"It's the one time to leave me," she had replied. "I shall be sunk in stupefied content. The edge will be gone from all my sharp sensations, good or bad. And you will come back and find a two months' child!" . . .

* * *

. . . The squire thought of her family and her children as an old actress thinks of the stage. The children drew her, fatigued, devoured, but drew her. One by one they rose like apparitions out of the witches' cauldron and addressed her as though she were another Macbeth interrogating the future. "Boniface . . ." What man's name had held her with such tenderness, such memory of effort and hope as his? (But this was unfair; she did not now remember the glamour of love.) Boniface, red of face, asking no help, intent upon some inner life which would not swim up into his difficult speech. Boniface, unhelpable, resolved to lead the life of a man before he was fit to leave babyhood for childhood. Inarticulate, eccentric, living like a mole in his world, putting into dangerous execution plans to which no one had the key. Stitches in his hand and forehead before he was four, half-gassed at the gas-ring, half-chloroformed at the medicine cupboard, and not because he was mischievous, but because of those projects of which no one knew beforehand. He was not daring, not vain-glorious, but alone with his thoughts, oblivious to the height of walls, the softness of his body, the liquid depths of water.

"If Boniface gets through," thought his mother. "If Boniface pulls it off!" And she gasped, sucking in her lip.

Behind Boniface, sheltered, overgrown by Boniface, came something smaller still, called by nicknames, endearments, diminutives. Could it be called Henry, the creature like a resolute angel that ran naked in the garden in the summer, with dirty feet that picked up leaves with the toes? It was called Henry; and would slowly draw on "Henry" like a cloak, carving its own coffee-coloured face into thought, brushing the silver tufts on its head with oil, wrapping its skin in the uniform of man so that only very privileged women would then see how Henry grew— from his feet to his knees, from his knees up his dappled and quilted legs, from his flat stomach to his swelling ribs, and over the shining shoulder to the face of Henry, adulterated with life. Henry grown wise. Henry reflecting.

The creature that ran now in the garden in summer was no more wise than kind. It was filled with desire from top to toe. It reached, stretched, felt, pulled, stole and demanded. And all the time that it desired and demanded and play-acted and was filled with a wild lust for possession it went cloaked in beauty, with a face and body of silk and satin.

This did not melt the squire, nor the brothers and sister, nor his nurse. They had had ten years of babies, some of them. They knew that this divine thing could slip its glory and become a nursery menace, and the sister and brothers watched with lynx-eyes for signs of weakness in the elders. When Henry desired and was refused, then his brow reddened, his face grew scarlet, and he flung himself backwards upon the ground, shooting his bolt. Then Lucy, the sister, would tweak her brother Jay's sleeve, whispering, "Come away. Don't look at him. He's showing off!" And Henry, watching them with his wild thrush's eye, and seeing their cold receding backs, would know his bolt was shot; and having failed, he dismissed his desire.

He matched his strength with theirs all day long. All day long he watched for openings, watched for matches, drawing-pins, scissors, butter, jugs of milk, substances, qualities, things that would crash, would tip, would pour, would squelch, would glitter. He put his finger into holes. Into the cane holes of the chair-seat, into empty knots in the wood floor, into channels where they stuck and would not come out. It was as though, his thought not perfectly and constantly clarified into speech, his mind flickered restlessly in his fingers. Like the blind and the dumb his hands spoke for him. His eyes saw and his hands asked. His own toys he threw away like a lesson learnt.

from *The Door of Life* [27]

He knew certain obediences. Not obedience to the unexpected, but obedience to the yoke of his routine. When he was laid down at night he never murmured, hardly troubled to watch the receding back. Food he ate. And if he refused it was not caprice but his beautifully ordered stomach which dictated his refusal. His delicate instincts, like those of a wild animal, though they were still his mentors, were dying away under the puzzles and rising voices of man.

Boniface, the lately-ousted, the last king to get from his throne, had strange thoughts about him. The squire could see, by murmurs and tangents, that Boniface had this in mind. So it was that each child in turn had watched the lap-enveloped baby, the bathing, the nursing, and with that queer inability to savour the present had felt the yearning for yesterday's evaporating past.

Thinking of them, sitting in dazzled silence, a little drugged, a little mystic, thoughts and pictures drifted slowly to the edge of the mother's mind, hung and returned, so slender was the breeze of impetus.

And from them all at last her eyes were lowered, the eyes of her mind lowered their lids, and she glanced with them at the embryo, impersonal, saying nothing to her, the companion. She had no tenderness for it, only the keenest expectation. It had no youth, it was old, filled with instinct. It acted like a god, as her master, directing her. She had no control over it. It had nothing to do with the born baby that was to fall with a crash from age to trembling youth, that, once born, would throw up its mastery and lie, shocked and naked, just within the gates of the world.

But now at the table behind the fall of the tablecloth, behind the sheath of skin, hanging head downwards between cliffs of bone, was the baby, its arms all but clasped about its neck, its face aslant upon its arms, hair painted upon its skull, closed, secret eyes, a diver poised in albumen, ancient and epic, shot with delicate spasms, as old as a Pharaoh in its tomb. . . .

* * *

. . . Downstairs she saw to her papers and bills and glanced at the weekly books for payment, standing up with one light burning over her desk in the long empty room, tapping the papers into place, signing her name, passing a bill. Every now and then she looked through the black glass into the night where she had drawn back the curtains, seeming to listen for the pain, staring straight ahead of her, but its touch was so tender she could not pin it down. A thrum of the harp cords came as she moved, and was gone when she stood still.

"What an extraordinary adventure!" she said aloud suddenly. She did not think of death for a moment, never so absent from the thought of death. The room seemed filled with her excitement, while she listened. So a horse in a loose box hears the hounds on the wind.

Two hours later she lay on the sofa with the midwife on her knees beside her, her long, thin hands spread over the naked belly of her patient. The midwife's eyes were shut. She was listening and divining with her hands; then she glanced up at the clock. The night was still; the fire died down. Now and then the midwife spoke, and the squire lay looking at the ceiling and smiling.

"It's very indefinite," said the midwife at last. "I shan't call yet."

"What's your rule of thumb?" said the squire.

"It's hard to say," said the midwife absently, and laid her hands on the mounded belly again.

"Surely this one's definite?" said the squire presently, her eyes on a fly walking over its shadow on the ceiling.

"Better," said the midwife, and she looked again at the clock.

"Well then?"

"One mustn't call too soon, one mustn't call too late."

. . . She lay down waiting on the vague pains, and presently slept.

When she woke the doctor was opening her door. The midwife was behind him.

"The monk and the nun!" thought the squire and, twisting, caught her breath. "Bad one coming!" she gasped, and pain surged up her back.

". . . that caps it," she murmured vaguely as another pain began.

. . . The doctor was drinking his coffee with gusto. The squire came back to life, sweating. "It must be near now!"

"Nonsense!" he said. "You women never learn. Got to walk miles before it's nearer."

He began a conversation with the midwife; the squire joined in when she could. She held the edges of the chair-seat with her hands and sweated, then back came life and comfort, and she ate her crisp sausage and nodded to them both. She looked at her doctor and was so filled with trust it was like love.

"Out onto the lawn!" he said, when they had finished their odd meal, "and find me the *Times!*"

"You are staying with me! You're not leaving me!"

"Get me the *Times*, and I'll have a morning off in a deck chair."

So he lay in a deck chair, his hat cocked over his nose and turned the big sheets of paper; and now and then he would look round at her and say, "Get on! Get on!" The midwife disappeared upstairs on her own errands.

The quiet morning wore on. . . . The squire walked. She trod slowly, thinking of nothing, swept alternately by beauty and by pain. When the beauty came it was unearthly, because threatened. Her eyes took in the

from *The Door of Life*

distances beyond the trees, the quantity of light allowed to fill the spaces. She was filled with sight. Then once more came the pain. . . . Was it pain, pressure, a swelling of the blood, that they saw so strangely and so newly-well? She wandered on, till—steady—steady—lean against the tree —for here it comes again! At eleven she made a run for the stairs, the doctor instantly at her side as she sank on the bottom step. "Can't you do another round?"

"No, I can't! I won't. I must get onto my bed."

"Very well."

She went up and once in her room and the bed near she could afford to walk again. She walked a little longer, anxious to please her doctor. Then, as she lay again on the pillow her face to one side, her hands holding the wooden bedhead she saw the midwife pass the open door of her room to the outer balcony where the cot was standing. Over her arms were blankets for the cot, and under one clenched elbow a hot water bottle pressed against her waist. Rest and glory filled the squire between the pains. She watched the preparations for the unborn; watched the things laid out with which to wash what WAS NOT THERE, to warm the feet of what DID NOT BREATHE, the settling of the pillows and the blankets for what COULD NOT BE TOUCHED. There she lay, beached for a moment, panting, quivering, aware. And now she spoke no more, only savouring her moments of release; waiting for the sea to heave her from her beach and drown her in its pressure of black violence.

The monk and the nun were about her bed, acutely directed on her, tuned to her every manifestation. With eyes fast shut she lent herself to their quiet directions, clinging to the memory of her resolve that when the river began to pull she would swim down with it, clutching at no banks. With a touch of anaesthetic from a gauze mask to help her she went forward. Her mind went down and lived in her body, ran out of her brain and lived in her flesh. She had eyes and nose and ears and senses in her body, in her backbone, living like a spiny woodlouse, doubled in a ball, having no beginning and no end. Now the first twisting spate of pain began. Swim then, swim with it for your life. If you resist, horror, and impediment! If you swim, not pain but sensation! Who knows the heart of pain, the silver, whistling hub of pain, the central bellows of childbirth which expels one being from another? None knows it who, in disbelief and dread has drawn back to the periphery, contradicting the will of pain, braking against inexorable movements. Keep abreast of it, rush together, you and the violence which is also you! Wild movements, hallucinated swimming! Other things exist than pain!

It is hard to gauge pain. By her movements, by her exclamations she would have struck horror into any one but her monk and her nun. She would have seemed tortured, tossing, crying, muttering, grunting. She was not unconscious but she had left external life. She was blind and deaf to world surface. Every sense she had was down in Earth to which she belonged, fighting to maintain a hold on the pain, to keep pace with it, not to take an ounce of will from her assent to its passage. It was as though the dark river rushed her to a glossy arch. A little more, a little more, a little longer. She was not in torture, she was in labour; she had been thus before and knew her way. The corkscrew swirl swept her shuddering, until she swam into a tunnel—the first seconds of anaesthesia.

The shocked and vigorous cry of the born rang through the room. From its atavistic dim cradle, from a passage like death, crying with rage, resenting birth, came the freed and furious cave-child, coated in mystery, the heavy-headed, vulnerable young, the triumph of the animal world, the triumph of life.

Now out of her river the mother was drawn upwards, she became the welcomed, the applauded, the humoured. Faces smiled over her. "What is it?" Nine months of wondering in one second solved.

"A boy, a beauty!"

"Doctors," said the mother, "say that! There are terrible things . . . that are not beauties."

In a moment she had the creature laid into her arm, clad already in a woollen jersey and woollen leggings, the strange habits of man which it would wear to its death, now put on for the first time. Folded, and filled with a tiny flutter, its arms stirred, its fingers remained pointed, spatulate, a hand of stars. It had lately breathed. It was like death, this terrific and gay moment; she was solemn and light, weak, mystical and excited.

"Is it lunch time?"

"Two o'clock."

"I'd like bread and milk and brown sugar."

Bread and milk and brown sugar were brought by magic. Idly she watched the gay activity in the room; the baby in his cot, warmed, overwarmed, like a child that has been fished out of the sea—the midwife folding garments. The doctor came in from the bathroom and pulled on his coat.

The squire tried to show her strength, to put herself back into life.

"Only two hours ago I was in the garden!"

"Keep quiet," said the doctor. "You look as though you were going to pop out of bed."

"She won't," said the midwife, tyranny in her eye.

"I'm frightfully excited, excited," complained the squire. "I want to talk, to brag. I'm twitching with excitement."

The doctor went to his bag and pulled out a hypodermic. "I'll give you a quarter of morphia," he said.

She held up her arm, and when the needle was withdrawn she waited, thinking of the baby. The curtains were pulled across the windows. Far

from *The Door of Life*

away a telephone rang, but she listened more intently to the sleep that was drifting into her knees, creeping down from her knees to her ankles, stealing to her thighs, from her thighs to her heavy arms, and so it stole, hushing her body, member by member, into peace. Now only her head floated, like a happy globe, staring at the pallor of the curtains. It was heaven to lie like this, she did not want to sleep, but sleep she did.

A father suffers a moment of panic during a familiar game of make-believe.

E. W. TEDLOCK, JR.

'Tis a Fond Ambush

IN THE BLIND TIME between sun-bright things and dream-dark shapes, the boy and the father would play in the shaded garden. Only the sounds and lights of the house played with them, calling toward bed and the good, warm time until dawn. From the older brother's phonograph, soft tunes enchanted them home. Where the sister sat close to the radio, hits strikes and outs muttered near victory. And where the mother made things to wear against winter, the whir of the sewing machine never stopped. Only Freckles the dog was quiet, contentedly curled like a white ball where water had cooled the great bush by the wall.

"Where is that boy? Where can he be?" the father would call after him, into the not quite dark night in the green-shaped yard.

The father would look under the cherry tree, where the birds had left seeds like fallen Christmas tree things. He would peer through the shadows of the big-fruited peach tree, where the leaves curled far down. He would search along the dim pattern of the walk, looking behind the slender curve of a chair or under the dark red wood of the picnic table.

"Where can that boy have gone now?" he could call, letting the worry climb in his voice, not knowing when the boy would jump laughing out to surprise him. For the words were magic, the "abracadabra," the "presto changeo," of their game. They could do anything.

The boy and the father played until bed time, over and over, without getting tired. They always began the same way. They started off, holding each other's hand, down the walk, away from the house and the light and the sounds, into the dark. The farther they went, the stranger it was. The walk was a road, and they were exploring the night-changed world.

"What a fine night it is," the father would say, as if nothing could

'Tis a Fond Ambush [33]

happen. "Look at this apple tree. See how it has grown. What a fine tree it makes."

But as he talked of fine nights and fine trees, the boy's hand slipped out of his and vanished soundlessly into the big darkness.

At first the father pretended not to notice. "What a fine tree it is," he said. "How it has grown. We should have apples next year."

Then he was surprised that the boy was no longer beside him, looking and listening. He could see nothing but the high leaves of the apple tree, the vacant curve of the walk, the shadows of things in the night. The radio still muttered its far off game. The music rushed in the hollow house. The hum of the sewing machine stopped, and started again. But the boy had vanished.

Freckles the dog was not worried. He stirred and sighed sleepily in his cool water nest. At home in his hutch in the playhouse, Cotton the rabbit thumped twice unconcernedly. The apple tree kept on growing, toward next year's fruit. But the father was worried. He had to search, up and down, back and forth, until he found the hidden, waiting boy.

He went fearfully along the dim pattern of the walk to the big-fruited peach tree, and parted the spaces between the curled leaves. He peered under the cherry tree, but only the bird-fallen seeds glinted back. And he called, "Where is that boy? Where can he be?"

He turned toward the house, where light shone dimly out among the chairs and onto the picnic table. And as he went, he began to sound very worried, calling "Where is he? I wonder where that boy has gone to now!"

He looked behind the slender, curving chairs, and of course there was no one there. Then he turned to the dark cave under the roof of the picnic table. And as he bent down, very worried, to look in, the darkness jumped. With a sudden loud "Here I am" the boy leaped up and threw his arms around his neck and caught him tight.

That night this was the last time they played the magic game. The father was glad, not because he was tired, but because once, in the middle of the game, just after the boy had vanished, he had felt, just for a moment, as if it had really happened. The way the boy did it was magic, and you did not want to forget the magic words.

Though this author treats a weighty theme with tongue-in-cheek cheerfulness, many a painful truth can hide behind a jest.

FRANK O'CONNOR

My Oedipus Complex

FATHER WAS in the army all through the war—the first war, I mean—so, up to the age of five, I never saw much of him, and what I saw did not worry me. Sometimes I woke and there was a big figure in khaki peering down at me in the candlelight. Sometimes in the early morning I heard the slamming of the front door and the clatter of nailed boots down the cobbles of the lane. These were Father's entrances and exits. Like Santa Claus he came and went mysteriously.

In fact, I rather liked his visits, though it was an uncomfortable squeeze between Mother and him when I got into the big bed in the early morning. He smoked, which gave him a pleasant musty smell, and shaved, an operation of astounding interest. Each time he left a trail of souvenirs—model tanks and Gurkha knives with handles made of bullet cases, and German helmets and cap badges and button-sticks, and all sorts of military equipment—carefully stowed away in a long box on top of the wardrobe, in case they ever came in handy. There was a bit of the magpie about Father; he expected everything to come in handy. When his back was turned, Mother let me get a chair and rummage through his treasures. She didn't seem to think so highly of them as he did.

The war was the most peaceful period of my life. The window of my attic faced southeast. My mother had curtained it, but that had small effect. I always woke with the first light and, with all the responsibilities of the previous day melted, feeling myself rather like the sun, ready to illumine and rejoice. Life never seemed so simple and clear and full of possibilities as then. I put my feet out from under the clothes—I called them Mrs. Left and Mrs. Right—and invented dramatic situations for them in which they discussed the problems of the day. At least Mrs. Right did; she was very demonstrative, but I hadn't the same control of Mrs. Left, so she

[34]

My Oedipus Complex

mostly contented herself with nodding agreement.

They discussed what Mother and I should do during the day, what Santa Claus should give a fellow for Christmas, and what steps should be taken to brighten the home. There was that little matter of the baby, for instance. Mother and I could never agree about that. Ours was the only house in the terrace without a new baby, and Mother said we couldn't afford one till Father came back from the war because they cost seventeen and six. That showed how simple she was. The Geneys up the road had a baby, and everyone knew they couldn't afford seventeen and six. It was probably a cheap baby, and Mother wanted something really good, but I felt she was too exclusive. The Geneys' baby would have done us fine.

Having settled my plans for the day, I got up, put a chair under the attic window, and lifted the frame high enough to stick out my head. The window overlooked the front gardens of the terrace behind ours, and beyond these it looked over a deep valley to the tall, red-brick houses terraced up the opposite hillside, which were all still in shadow, while those at our side of the valley were all lit up, though with long strange shadows that made them seem unfamiliar; rigid and painted.

After that I went into Mother's room and climbed into the big bed. She woke and I began to tell her of my schemes. By this time, though I never seem to have noticed it, I was petrified in my nightshirt, and I thawed as I talked until, the last frost melted, I fell asleep beside her and woke again only when I heard her below in the kitchen, making the breakfast.

After breakfast we went into town; heard Mass at St. Augustine's and said a prayer for Father, and did the shopping. If the afternoon was fine we either went for a walk in the country or a visit to Mother's great friend in the convent, Mother St. Dominic. Mother had them all praying for Father, and every night, going to bed, I asked God to send him back safe from the war to us. Little, indeed, did I know what I was praying for!

One morning, I got into the big bed, and there, sure enough, was Father in his usual Santa Claus manner, but later, instead of uniform, he put on his best blue suit, and Mother was as pleased as anything. I saw nothing to be pleased about, because, out of uniform, Father was altogether less interesting, but she only beamed, and explained that our prayers had been answered, and off we went to Mass to thank God for having brought Father safely home.

The irony of it! That very day when he came in to dinner he took off his boots and put on his slippers, donned the dirty old cap he wore about the house to save him from colds, crossed his legs, and began to talk gravely to Mother, who looked anxious. Naturally, I disliked her looking anxious, because it destroyed her good looks, so I interrupted him.

"Just a moment, Larry!" she said gently.

This was only what she said when we had boring visitors, so I attached no importance to it and went on talking.

"Do be quiet, Larry!" she said impatiently. "Don't you hear me talking to Daddy?"

This was the first time I had heard those ominous words, "talking to Daddy," and I couldn't help feeling that if this was how God answered prayers, he couldn't listen to them very attentively.

"Why are you talking to Daddy?" I asked with as great a show of indifference as I could muster.

"Because Daddy and I have business to discuss. Now, don't interrupt again!"

In the afternoon, at Mother's request, Father took me for a walk. This time we went into town instead of out the country, and I thought at first, in my usual optimistic way, that it might be an improvement. It was nothing of the sort. Father and I had quite different notions of a walk in town. He had no proper interest in trams, ships, and horses, and the only thing that seemed to divert him was talking to fellows as old as himself. When I wanted to stop he simply went on, dragging me behind him by the hand; when he wanted to stop I had no alternative but to do the same. I noticed that it seemed to be a sign that he wanted to stop for a long time whenever he leaned against a wall. The second time I saw him do it I got wild. He seemed to be settling himself forever. I pulled him by the coat and trousers, but, unlike Mother who, if you were too persistent, got into a wax and said: "Larry, if you don't behave yourself, I'll give you a good slap," Father had an extraordinary capacity for amiable inattention. I sized him up and wondered would I cry, but he seemed to be too remote to be annoyed even by that. Really, it was like going for a walk with a mountain! He either ignored the wrenching and pummeling entirely, or else glanced down with a grin of amusement from his peak. I had never met anyone so absorbed in himself as he seemed.

At teatime, "talking to Daddy" began again, complicated this time by the fact that he had an evening paper, and every few minutes he put it down and told Mother something new out of it. I felt this was foul play. Man for man, I was prepared to compete with him any time for Mother's attention, but when he had it all made up for him by other people it left me no chance. Several times I tried to change the subject without success.

"You must be quiet while Daddy is reading, Larry," Mother said impatiently.

It was clear that she either genuinely liked talking to Father better than talking to me, or else that he had some terrible hold on her which made her afraid to admit the truth.

"Mummy," I said that night when she was tucking me up, "do you think if I prayed hard God would send Daddy back to the war?"

She seemed to think about that for a moment.

My Oedipus Complex [37]

"No, dear," she said with a smile. "I don't think he would."

"Why wouldn't he, Mummy?"

"Because there isn't a war any longer, dear."

"But, Mummy, couldn't God make another war, if He liked?"

"He wouldn't like to, dear. It's not God who makes wars, but bad people."

"Oh!" I said.

I was disappointed about that. I began to think that God wasn't quite what he was cracked up to be.

Next morning I woke at my usual hour, feeling like a bottle of champagne. I put out my feet and invented a long conversation in which Mrs. Right talked of the trouble she had with her own father till she put him in the Home. I didn't quite know what the Home was but it sounded the right place for Father. Then I got my chair and stuck my head out of the attic window. Dawn was just breaking, with a guilty air that made me feel I had caught it in the act. My head bursting with stories and schemes, I stumbled in next door, and in the half-darkness scrambled into the big bed. There was no room at Mother's side so I had to get between her and Father. For the time being I had forgotten about him, and for several minutes I sat bolt upright, racking my brains to know what I could do with him. He was taking up more than his fair share of the bed, and I couldn't get comfortable, so I gave him several kicks that made him grunt and stretch. He made room all right, though. Mother waked and felt for me. I settled back comfortably in the warmth of the bed with my thumb in my mouth.

"Mummy!" I hummed, loudly and contentedly.

"Sssh! dear," she whispered. "Don't wake Daddy!"

This was a new development, which threatened to be even more serious than "talking to Daddy." Life without my early-morning conferences was unthinkable.

"Why?" I asked severely.

"Because poor Daddy is tired."

This seemed to me a quite inadequate reason, and I was sickened by the sentimentality of her "poor Daddy." I never liked that sort of gush; it always struck me as insincere.

"Oh!" I said lightly. Then in my most winning tone: "Do you know where I want to go with you today, Mummy?"

"No, dear," she sighed.

"I want to go down the Glen and fish for thornybacks with my new net, and then I want to go out to the Fox and Hounds, and—"

"Don't-wake-Daddy!" she hissed angrily, clapping her hand across my mouth.

But it was too late. He was awake, or nearly so. He grunted and reached for the matches. Then he stared incredulously at his watch.

"Like a cup of tea, dear?" asked Mother in a meek, hushed voice I had never heard her use before. It sounded almost as though she were afraid.

"Tea?" he exclaimed indignantly. "Do you know what the time is?"

"And after that I want to go up the Rathcooney Road," I said loudly, afraid I'd forget something in all those interruptions.

"Go to sleep at once, Larry!" she said sharply.

I began to snivel. I couldn't concentrate, the way that pair went on, and smothering my early-morning schemes was like burying a family from the cradle.

Father said nothing, but lit his pipe and sucked it, looking out into the shadows without minding Mother or me. I knew he was mad. Every time I made a remark Mother hushed me irritably. I was mortified. I felt it wasn't fair; there was even something sinister in it. Every time I had pointed out to her the waste of making two beds when we could both sleep in one, she had told me it was healthier like that, and now here was this man, this stranger, sleeping with her without the least regard for her health!

He got up early and made tea, but though he brought Mother a cup he brought none for me.

"Mummy," I shouted, "I want a cup of tea, too."

"Yes, dear," she said patiently. "You can drink from Mummy's saucer."

That settled it. Either Father or I would have to leave the house. I didn't want to drink from Mother's saucer; I wanted to be treated as an equal in my own home, so, just to spite her, I drank it all and left none for her. She took that quietly, too.

But that night when she was putting me to bed she said gently:

"Larry, I want you to promise me something."

"What is it?" I asked.

"Not to come in and disturb poor Daddy in the morning. Promise?"

"Poor Daddy" again! I was becoming suspicious of everything involving that quite impossible man.

"Why?" I asked.

"Because poor Daddy is worried and tired and he doesn't sleep well."

"Why doesn't he, Mummy?"

"Well, you know, don't you, that while he was at the war Mummy got the pennies from the Post Office?"

"From Miss MacCarthy?"

"That's right. But now, you see, Miss MacCarthy hasn't any more pennies, so Daddy must go out and find us some. You know what would happen if he couldn't?"

"No," I said, "tell us."

"Well, I think we might have to go out and beg for them like the poor old woman on Fridays. We wouldn't like that, would we?"

"No," I agreed. "We wouldn't."

My Oedipus Complex

"So you'll promise not to come in and wake him?"

"Promise."

Mind you, I meant that. I knew pennies were a serious matter, and I was all against having to go out and beg like the old woman on Fridays. Mother laid out all my toys in a complete ring round the bed so that, whatever way I got out, I was bound to fall over one of them.

When I woke I remembered my promise all right. I got up and sat on the floor and played—for hours, it seemed to me. Then I got my chair and looked out the attic window for more hours. I wished it was time for Father to wake; I wished someone would make me a cup of tea. I didn't feel in the least like the sun; instead, I was bored and so very, very cold! I simply longed for the warmth and depth of the big featherbed.

At last I could stand it no longer. I went into the next room. As there was still no room at Mother's side I climbed over her and she woke with a start.

"Larry," she whispered, gripping my arm very tightly, "what did you promise?"

"But I did, Mummy," I wailed, caught in the very act. "I was quiet for ever so long."

"Oh, dear, and you're perished!" she said sadly, feeling me all over. "Now, if I let you stay will you promise not to talk?"

"But I want to talk, Mummy," I wailed.

"That has nothing to do with it," she said with a firmness that was new to me. "Daddy wants to sleep. Now, do you understand that?"

I understood it only too well. I wanted to talk, he wanted to sleep—whose house was it, anyway?

"Mummy," I said with equal firmness, "I think it would be healthier for Daddy to sleep in his own bed."

That seemed to stagger her, because she said nothing for a while.

"Now, once for all," she went on, "you're to be perfectly quiet or go back to your own bed. Which is it to be?"

The injustice of it got me down. I had convicted her out of her own mouth of inconsistency and unreasonableness, and she hadn't even attempted to reply. Full of spite, I gave Father a kick, which she didn't notice but which made him grunt and open his eyes in alarm.

"What time is it?" he asked in a panic-stricken voice, not looking at Mother but at the door, as if he saw someone there.

"It's early yet," she replied soothingly. "It's only the child. Go to sleep again. . . . Now, Larry," she added, getting out of bed, "you've wakened Daddy and you must go back."

This time, for all her quiet air, I knew she meant it, and knew that my principal rights and privileges were as good as lost unless I asserted them at once. As she lifted me, I gave a screech, enough to wake the dead, not to mind Father. He groaned.

"That damn child! Doesn't he ever sleep?"

"It's only a habit, dear," she said quietly, though I could see she was vexed.

"Well, it's time he got out of it," shouted Father, beginning to heave in the bed. He suddenly gathered all the bedclothes about him, turned to the wall, and then looked back over his shoulder with nothing showing only two small, spiteful, dark eyes. The man looked very wicked.

To open the bedroom door, Mother had to let me down, and I broke free and dashed for the farthest corner, screeching. Father sat bolt upright in bed.

"Shut up, you little puppy!" he said in a choking voice.

I was so astonished that I stopped screeching. Never, never had anyone spoken to me in that tone before. I looked at him incredulously and saw his face convulsed with rage. It was only then that I fully realized how God had codded me, listening to my prayers for the safe return of this monster.

"Shut up, you!" I bawled, beside myself.

"What's that you said?" shouted Father, making a wild leap out of the bed.

"Mick, Mick!" cried Mother. "Don't you see the child isn't used to you?"

"I see he's better fed than taught," snarled Father, waving his arms wildly. "He wants his bottom smacked."

All his previous shouting was as nothing to these obscene words referring to my person. They really made my blood boil.

"Smack your own!" I screamed hysterically. "Smack your own! Shut up! Shut up!"

At this he lost his patience and let fly at me. He did it with the lack of conviction you'd expect of a man under Mother's horrified eyes, and it ended up as a mere tap, but the sheer indignity of being struck at all by a stranger, a total stranger who had cajoled his way back from the war into our big bed as a result of my innocent intercession, made me completely dotty. I shrieked and shrieked, and danced in my bare feet, and Father, looking awkward and hairy in nothing but a short grey army shirt, glared down at me like a mountain out for murder. I think it must have been then that I realized he was jealous too. And there stood Mother in her nightdress, looking as if her heart was broken between us. I hoped she felt as she looked. It seemed to me that she deserved it all.

From that morning out my life was a hell. Father and I were enemies, open and avowed. We conducted a series of skirmishes against one another, he trying to steal my time with Mother and I his. When she was sitting on my bed, telling me a story, he took to looking for some pair of old boots which he alleged he had left behind him at the beginning of the war. While he talked to Mother I played loudly with my toys to show my total lack of concern. He created a terrible scene one evening when he

My Oedipus Complex

came in from work and found me at his box, playing with his regimental badges, Gurkha knives and button-sticks. Mother got up and took the box from me.

"You mustn't play with Daddy's toys unless he lets you, Larry," she said severely. "Daddy doesn't play with yours."

For some reason Father looked at her as if she had struck him and then turned away with a scowl.

"Those are not toys," he growled, taking down the box again to see had I lifted anything. "Some of those curios are very rare and valuable."

But as time went on I saw more and more how he managed to alienate Mother and me. What made it worse was that I couldn't grasp his method or see what attraction he had for Mother. In every possible way he was less winning than I. He had a common accent and made noises at his tea. I thought for a while that it might be the newspapers she was interested in, so I made up bits of news of my own to read to her. Then I thought it might be the smoking, which I personally thought attractive, and took his pipes and went round the house dribbling into them till he caught me. I even made noises at my tea, but Mother only told me I was disgusting. It all seemed to hinge round that unhealthy habit of sleeping together, so I made a point of dropping into their bedroom and nosing round, talking to myself, so that they wouldn't know I was watching them, but they were never up to anything that I could see. In the end it beat me. It seemed to depend on being grown-up and giving people rings, and I realized I'd have to wait.

But at the same time I wanted him to see that I was only waiting, not giving up the fight. One evening when he was being particularly obnoxious, chattering away well above my head, I let him have it.

"Mummy," I said, "do you know what I'm going to do when I grow up?"

"No, dear," she replied. "What?"

"I'm going to marry you," I said quietly.

Father gave a great guffaw out of him, but he didn't take me in. I knew it must only be pretence. And Mother, in spite of everything, was pleased. I felt she was probably relieved to know that one day Father's hold on her would be broken.

"Won't that be nice?" she said with a smile.

"It'll be very nice," I said confidently. "Because we're going to have lots and lots of babies."

"That's right, dear," she said placidly. "I think we'll have one soon, and then you'll have plenty of company."

I was no end pleased about that because it showed that in spite of the way she gave in to Father she still considered my wishes. Besides, it would put the Geneys in their place.

It didn't turn out like that, though. To begin with, she was very preoccupied—I supposed about where she would get the seventeen and six—

and though Father took to staying out late in the evenings it did me no particular good. She stopped taking me for walks, became as touchy as blazes, and smacked me for nothing at all. Sometimes I wished I'd never mentioned the confounded baby—I seemed to have a genius for bringing calamity on myself.

And calamity it was! Sonny arrived in the most appalling hullabaloo—even that much he couldn't do without a fuss—and from the first moment I disliked him. He was a difficult child—so far as I was concerned he was always difficult—and demanded far too much attention. Mother was simply silly about him, and couldn't see when he was only showing off. As company he was worse than useless. He slept all day, and I had to go round the house on tiptoe to avoid waking him. It wasn't any longer a question of not waking Father. The slogan now was "Don't-wake-Sonny!" I couldn't understand why the child wouldn't sleep at the proper time, so whenever Mother's back was turned I woke him. Sometimes to keep him awake I pinched him as well. Mother caught me at it one day and gave me a most unmerciful flaking.

One evening, when Father was coming in from work, I was playing trains in the front garden. I let on not to notice him; instead, I pretended to be talking to myself, and said in a loud voice: "If another bloody baby comes into this house, I'm going out."

Father stopped dead and looked at me over his shoulder.

"What's that you said?" he asked sternly.

"I was only talking to myself," I replied, trying to conceal my panic. "It's private."

He turned and went in without a word. Mind you, I intended it as a solemn warning, but its effect was quite different. Father started being quite nice to me. I could understand that, of course. Mother was quite sickening about Sonny. Even at mealtimes she'd get up and gawk at him in the cradle with an idiotic smile, and tell Father to do the same. He was always polite about it, but he looked so puzzled you could see he didn't know what she was talking about. He complained of the way Sonny cried at night, but she only got cross and said that Sonny never cried except when there was something up with him—which was a flaming lie, because Sonny never had anything up with him, and only cried for attention. It was really painful to see how simple-minded she was. Father wasn't attractive, but he had a fine intelligence. He saw through Sonny, and now he knew that I saw through him as well.

One night I woke with a start. There was someone beside me in the bed. For one wild moment I felt sure it must be Mother, having come to her senses and left Father for good, but then I heard Sonny in convulsions in the next room, and Mother saying: "There! There! There!" and I knew it wasn't she. It was Father. He was lying beside me, wide awake, breathing hard and apparently as mad as hell.

My Oedipus Complex

After a while it came to me what he was mad about. It was his turn now. After turning me out of the big bed, he had been turned out himself. Mother had no consideration now for anyone but that poisonous pup, Sonny. I couldn't help feeling sorry for Father. I had been through it all myself, and even at that age I was magnanimous. I began to stroke him down and say: "There! There!" He wasn't exactly responsive.

"Aren't you asleep either?" he snarled.

"Ah, come on and put your arm around us, can't you?" I said, and he did, in a sort of way. Gingerly, I suppose, is how you'd describe it. He was very bony but better than nothing.

At Christmas he went out of his way to buy me a really nice model railway.

LEE HATFIELD

To Telemachus

If you must leave these shores, my son,
Go by other ways than we have gone,
That your ribs be not broken
On the shingled strand of Circe's island—
That on the Sirens' reef your blood
Shall not be mingled with the ancient corpses.

For between the whirlpool and the rock
The channel is a narrow one, and not without its
Fickle tides and doldrums; and we who
Once sailed too near the Scylla wonder often
In the night, in the calm between two dreams,
Whether we survived or perished there.

And so if you must leave these shores
Listen first to those warnings that the seas
Whisper hoarsely in the night,
And go by ways less treacherous than these.

For by whatever course you travel
You will learn that the way leads always
Back to Ithaca.

          And once returned, it is only
By a difference in the patterns of our wounds
That you will know
                Yourself
                      From myself.

A small boy attempts to cope with his night-time fears.

NICCOLÒ TUCCI

Strong Man

"Afraid? ... Who, me? ... No!" Of course Vieri is not afraid. It's Bimba who wants the bathroom light on, so that she will be able to see it from her bed. *He* wants darkness; he is, in fact, so courageous that he says, turning restlessly in his bed, "It's so boring, just pitch dark ... Daddy!"

"What is it?" I ask. "Do you want light, too?"

"Oh, no. It's boring because it isn't dangerous enough. If there only were lions in the room, or a man outside the window, pointing a pistol at me—"

Bimba begins to cry.

"Now, Vieri," I say, "stop that nonsense, please. You scare her so."

"But I was only *saying* these things. There are no lions here. I was saying *if* there were lions, or a man with a gun—"

"All right. Now stop it, and good night."

I try to say good night to Bimba, too, but she is somewhere under the blankets, where even the lions could not find her. I go back to my study, and from there I hear Vieri call, "Bimba, Bimba, listen!"

She gives no answer.

"Listen," he pleads. "This will not scare you."

She must be peeping out now, for I hear her voice whisper, "What?"

"Do you think I am strong?" he asks.

"Oh, yes," she says. "You are the strongest man of all lions and elephants."

"Silly. One cannot be the strongest man of all lions or elephants. You can only say that I am a strong man. Now, Bimba, say, do you believe that I am a strong man? Answer me, now, quick."

"But you are more than that."

"Quit it. You really believe I am strong?"

[45]

"Oh, yes, I—"

"Quit it. Let me talk. So listen, now. *If*—I say *if*—there were lions under your bed, or—"

Bimba must have disappeared again, because I hear Vieri jump out of his bed. When I get to their room, I find that he has thrown every one of her blankets onto the floor, and she is trying to hide under a pillow. He is scolded, threatened with punishment, and sent back to bed, and while I am doing Bimba's bed again, he protests. "All I said was *if*, and she is even scared of words. And you, too," he says.

"I am scared of words?"

"Yes. You believe in freedom of speech, and then you are afraid when I say *if* to Bimba."

"All right," I answer. "Say what you were going to say, and then go to sleep, both of you."

"Bimba," he calls, and Bimba, made courageous by my presence, sits up in bed and hears the words of the strong man.

"If there were lions," he begins, and she trembles a little while he thinks up the rest of his sentence. "If there were lions under your bed, or a murderer with a black mask on his face and a gun in his right hand, and—"

She clings to me, crying and begging me to stop him.

"All right," he shouts, at the height of his indignation. "I was just going to say that if they came, I would defend you, but now I won't. So if they come, they will eat you up or kill you, and I will say, 'Ha-ha.'"

I tell Bimba that she is a sissy and Vieri that he is a very courageous man, and finally I get them to stay quiet, because it is late. This whole procedure, with rare and slight variations, is standard in our family.

But the other night, things were different. I must explain that Vieri has been sleeping in our room lately—mine and my wife's—because we have a guest Bimba's age, a little girl just as much of a sissy as Bimba is. The children's room is now equipped with a number of phosphorescent toys, yet the girls still complain of the darkness. I must also explain that it was a very windy night and that Vieri had been ill in bed for over a week. So I was not surprised to hear him call me in from the living room quite late one evening. I went into the bedroom. "I don't want the lights on," he said, and his voice was quivering. "I don't."

This being a delicate matter, I could not call his attention to the fact that the lights were not on at all, either in the room or in the hall, and even less could I inquire whether he did want them on. So all I answered was "All right." On second thought, I took the liberty of turning on the hall light without saying a word to him.

"I am not like the girls," he said.

"I know. You would not be afraid of lions or anything."

"Oh, no," he said. "And even if three or even four or even five men looked at me from outside the window, and even if they grinned, I would not be afraid."

"That's fine," I said. "Good night, now."

"But listen."

"What?"

"At times—not always, only at times—it is darker than at other times."

"Yes," I said. "When the moon isn't there, for instance."

"But also at *other* times."

"When?"

"When there is wind, like tonight."

"Why?"

"Because the wind pushes the world into the night. And it is very dark there, in the center of the night, but the wind keeps pushing the world—"

"That is not true," I said. "If the wind could do that, it would first push the houses away from where they are. So don't be afraid for the world. You see, even the windows are not blown in."

"But the houses are tied to the world," he said, "while the world is alone, tied to nothing, and the wind keeps pushing it."

"Nonsense," I said. "The wind can't do that. Good night, now. Shall I leave the door open?"

"No," he said. "Close it tight and turn out the light in the hall."

I obeyed.

After a minute, he called again, in an anguished tone, "Daddy!"

"What is it?"

"I have a toothache." And he cried.

In a dialogue with a dearly-loved grandmother, a little girl has a sudden brief flash of the reality of aging and death.

KATHERINE MANSFIELD

from *At the Bay*

THE TIDE was out; the beach was deserted; lazily flopped the warm sea. The sun beat down, beat down hot and fiery on the fine sand, baking the grey and blue and black and white-veined pebbles. It sucked up the little drop of water that lay in the hollow of the curved shells; it bleached the pink convolvulus that threaded through and through the sand-hills. Nothing seemed to move but the small sand-hoppers. Pit-pit-pit! They were never still.

Over there on the weed-hung rocks that looked at low tide like shaggy beasts come down to the water to drink, the sunlight seemed to spin like a silver coin dropped into each of the small rock pools. They danced, they quivered, and minute ripples laved the porous shores. Looking down, bending over, each pool was like a lake with pink and blue houses clustered on the shores; and oh! the vast mountainous country behind those houses—the ravines, the passes, the dangerous creeks and fearful tracks that led to the water's edge. Underneath waved the sea-forest—pink thread-like trees, velvet anemones, and orange berry-spotted weeds. Now a stone on the bottom moved, rocked, and there was a glimpse of a black feeler; now a thread-like creature wavered by and was lost. Something was happening to the pink, waving trees; they were changing to a cold moonlight blue. And now there sounded the faintest "plop." Who made that sound? What was going on down there? And how strong, how damp the seaweed smelt in the hot sun. . . .

The green blinds were drawn in the bungalows of the summer colony. Over the verandahs, prone on the paddock, flung over the fences, there were exhausted-looking bathing-dresses and rough striped towels. Each back window seemed to have a pair of sand-shoes on the sill and some lumps of rock or a bucket or a collection of pawa shells. The bush quivered

from *At the Bay*

in a haze of heat; the sandy road was empty except for the Trouts' dog Snooker, who lay stretched in the very middle of it. His blue eye was turned up, his legs stuck out stiffly, and he gave an occasional desperate-sounding puff, as much as to say he had decided to make an end of it and was only waiting for some kind cart to come along.

"What are you looking at, my grandma? Why do you keep stopping and sort of staring at the wall?"

Kezia and her grandmother were taking their siesta together. The little girl, wearing only her short drawers and her underbodice, her arms and legs bare, lay on one of the puffed-up pillows of her grandma's bed, and the old woman, in a white ruffled dressing-gown, sat in a rocker at the window, with a long piece of pink knitting in her lap. This room that they shared, like the other rooms of the bungalow, was of light varnished wood and the floor was bare. The furniture was of the shabbiest, the simplest. The dressing table, for instance, was a packing-case in a sprigged muslin petticoat, and the mirror above was very strange; it was as though a little piece of forked lightning was imprisoned in it. On the table there stood a jar of sea-pinks, pressed so tightly together they looked more like a velvet pincushion, and a special shell which Kezia had given her grandma for a pin-tray, and another even more special which she had thought would make a very nice place for a watch to curl up in.

"Tell me, grandma," said Kezia.

The old woman sighed, whipped the wool twice round her thumb, and drew the bone needle through. She was casting on.

"I was thinking of your Uncle William, darling," she said quietly.

"My Australian Uncle William?" said Kezia. She had another.

"Yes, of course."

"The one I never saw?"

"That was the one."

"Well, what happened to him?" Kezia knew perfectly well, but she wanted to be told again.

"He went to the mines, and he got a sunstroke there and died," said old Mrs. Fairfield.

Kezia blinked and considered the picture again . . . a little man fallen over like a tin soldier by the side of a big black hole.

"Does it make you sad to think about him, grandma?" She hated her grandma to be sad.

It was the old woman's turn to consider. Did it make her sad? To look back, back. To stare down the years, as Kezia had seen her doing. To look after *them* as a woman does, long after *they* were out of sight. Did it make her sad? No, life was like that.

"No, Kezia."

"But why?" asked Kezia. She lifted one bare arm and began to draw things in the air. "Why did Uncle William have to die? He wasn't old."

Mrs. Fairfield began counting the stitches in threes. "It just happened," she said in an absorbed voice.

"Does everybody have to die?" asked Kezia.

"Everybody!"

"*Me?*" Kezia sounded fearfully incredulous.

"Some day, my darling."

"But, grandma." Kezia waved her left leg and waggled the toes. They felt sandy. "What if I just won't?"

The old woman sighed again and drew a long thread from the ball.

"We're not asked, Kezia," she said sadly. "It happens to all of us sooner or later."

Kezia lay still thinking this over. She didn't want to die. It meant she would have to leave here, leave everywhere, for ever, leave—leave her grandma. She rolled over quickly.

"Grandma," she said in a startled voice.

"What, my pet!"

"*You're* not to die." Kezia was very decided.

"Ah, Kezia"—her grandma looked up and smiled and shook her head—"don't let's talk about it."

"But you're not to. You couldn't leave me. You couldn't not be there." This was awful. "Promise me you won't ever do it, grandma," pleaded Kezia.

The old woman went on knitting.

"Promise me! Say never!"

But still her grandma was silent.

Kezia rolled off the bed; she couldn't bear it any longer, and lightly she leapt on to her grandma's knees, clasped her hands round the old woman's throat and began kissing her, under the chin, behind the ear, and blowing down her neck.

"Say never . . . say never . . . say never—" She gasped between the kisses. And then she began, very softly and lightly, to tickle her grandma.

"Kezia!" The old woman dropped her knitting. She swung back in the rocker. She began to tickle Kezia. "Say never, say never, say never," gurgled Kezia, while they lay there laughing in each other's arms. "Come, that's enough, my squirrel! That's enough, my wild pony!" said old Mrs. Fairfield, setting her cap straight. "Pick up my knitting."

Both of them had forgotten what the "never" was about.

In this selection from his many-volumed work, Remembrance of Things Past, *the author describes his feelings at age five, when his parents' friend, the elegant Mr. Swann, has come to dinner, and the child realizes that his mother's goodnights must therefore be curtailed.*

MARCEL PROUST

from *Remembrance of Things Past* (*Swann's Way*)

... I NEVER took my eyes off my mother. I knew that when they were at table I should not be permitted to stay there for the whole of dinner-time, and that Mamma, for fear of annoying my father, would not allow me to give her in public the series of kisses that she would have had in my room. And so I promised myself that in the dining-room, as they began to eat and drink and as I felt the hour approach, I would put beforehand into this kiss, which was bound to be so brief and stealthy in execution, everything that my own efforts could put into it: would look out very carefully first the exact spot on her cheek where I would imprint it, and would so prepare my thoughts that I might be able, thanks to these mental preliminaries, to consecrate the whole of the minute Mamma would allow me to the sensation of her cheek against my lips, as a painter who can have his subject for short sittings only prepares his palette, and from what he remembers and from rough notes does in advance everything which he possibly can do in the sitter's absence. But to-night, before the dinner-bell had sounded, my grandfather said with unconscious cruelty: "The little man looks tired; he'd better go up to bed. Besides, we are dining late to-night."

And my father, who was less scrupulous than my grandmother or mother in observing the letter of a treaty, went on: "Yes, run along; to bed with you."

I would have kissed Mamma then and there, but at that moment the dinner-bell rang.

"No, no, leave your mother alone. You've said good night quite enough. These exhibitions are absurd. Go on upstairs."

[51]

And so I must set forth without viaticum; must climb each step of the staircase 'against my heart,' as the saying is, climbing in opposition to my heart's desire, which was to return to my mother, since she had not, by her kiss, given my heart leave to accompany me forth. That hateful staircase, up which I always passed with such dismay, gave out a smell of varnish which had to some extent absorbed, made definite and fixed the special quality of sorrow that I felt each evening, and made it perhaps even more cruel to my sensibility because, when it assumed this olfactory guise, my intellect was powerless to resist it. When we have gone to sleep with a maddening toothache and are conscious of it only as a little girl whom we attempt, time after time, to pull out of the water, or as a line of Molière which we repeat incessantly to ourselves, it is a great relief to wake up, so that our intelligence can disentangle the idea of toothache from any artificial semblance of heroism or rhythmic cadence. It was the precise converse of this relief which I felt when my anguish at having to go up to my room invaded my consciousness in a manner infinitely more rapid, instantaneous almost, a manner at once insidious and brutal as I breathed in—a far more poisonous thing than any moral penetration—the peculiar smell of the varnish upon that staircase.

Once in my room I had to stop every loophole, to close the shutters, to dig my own grave as I turned down the bed-clothes, to wrap myself in the shroud of my nightshirt. But before burying myself in the iron bed which had been placed there because, on summer nights, I was too hot among the rep curtains of the four-poster, I was stirred to revolt, and attempted the desperate stratagem of a condemned prisoner. I wrote to my mother begging her to come upstairs for an important reason which I could not put in writing. My fear was that Françoise, my aunt's cook who used to be put in charge of me when I was at Combray, might refuse to take my note. I had a suspicion that, in her eyes, to carry a message to my mother when there was a stranger in the room would appear flatly inconceivable, just as it would be for the door-keeper of a theatre to hand a letter to an actor upon the stage. For things which might or might not be done she possessed a code at once imperious, abundant, subtle, and uncompromising on points themselves imperceptible or irrelevant, which gave it a resemblance to those ancient laws which combine such cruel ordinances as the massacre of infants at the breast with prohibitions, of exaggerated refinement, against "seething the kid in his mother's milk," or "eating of the sinew which is upon the hollow of the thigh." This code, if one could judge it by the sudden obstinacy which she would put into her refusal to carry out certain of our instructions, seemed to have foreseen such social complications and refinements of fashion as nothing in Françoise's surroundings or in her career as a servant in a village household could have put into her head; and we were obliged to assume that there was latent in her some past existence in the ancient history of France, noble and little understood, just as from *Remembrance of Things Past (Swann's Way)* [53]

there is in those manufacturing towns where old mansions still testify to their former courtly days, and chemical workers toil among delicately sculptured scenes of the Miracle of Theophilus or the Quatre Fils Aymon.

In this particular instance, the article of her code which made it highly improbable that—barring an outbreak of fire—Françoise would go down and disturb Mamma when M. Swann was there for so unimportant a person as myself was one embodying the respect she shewed not only for the family (as for the dead, for the clergy, or for royalty), but also for the stranger within our gates; a respect which I should perhaps have found touching in a book, but which never failed to irritate me on her lips, because of the solemn and gentle tones in which she would utter it, and which irritated me more than usual this evening when the sacred character in which she invested the dinner-party might have the effect of making her decline to disturb its ceremonial. But to give myself one chance of success I lied without hesitation, telling her that it was not in the least myself who had wanted to write to Mamma, but Mamma who, on saying good night to me, had begged me not to forget to send her an answer about something she had asked me to find, and that she would certainly be very angry if this note were not taken to her. I think that Françoise disbelieved me, for, like those primitive men whose senses were so much keener than our own, she could immediately detect, by signs imperceptible by the rest of us, the truth or falsehood of anything that we might wish to conceal from her. She studied the envelope for five minutes as though an examination of the paper itself and the look of my handwriting could enlighten her as to the nature of the contents, or tell her to which article of her code she ought to refer the matter. Then she went out with an air of resignation which seemed to imply: "What a dreadful thing for parents to have a child like this!"

A moment later she returned to say that they were still at the ice stage and that it was impossible for the butler to deliver the note at once, in front of everybody; but that when the finger-bowls were put round he would find a way of slipping it into Mamma's hand. At once my anxiety subsided; it was now no longer (as it had been a moment ago) until to-morrow that I had lost my mother, for my little line was going —to annoy her, no doubt, and doubly so because this contrivance would make me ridiculous in Swann's eyes—but was going all the same to admit me, invisibly and by stealth, into the same room as herself, was going to whisper from me into her ear; for that forbidden and unfriendly dining-room, where but a moment ago the ice itself—with burned nuts in it—and the finger-bowls seemed to me to be concealing pleasures that were mischievous and of a mortal sadness because Mamma was tasting of them and I was far away, had opened its doors to me and, like a ripe fruit which bursts through its skin, was going to pour out into my intoxicated heart the gushing sweetness of Mamma's attention while she was reading what I had written. Now I was no longer separated from her; the barriers were down; an exquisite thread was binding us. Besides, that was not all, for surely Mamma would come.

As for the agony through which I had just passed, I imagined that Swann would have laughed heartily at it if he had read my letter and had guessed its purpose; whereas, on the contrary, as I was to learn in due course, a similar anguish had been the bane of his life for many years, and no one perhaps could have understood my feelings at that moment so well as himself; to him, that anguish which lies in knowing that the creature one adores is in some place of enjoyment where oneself is not and cannot follow—to him that anguish came through Love, to which it is in a sense predestined, by which it must be equipped and adapted; but when, as had befallen me, such an anguish possesses one's soul before Love has yet entered into one's life, then it must drift, awaiting Love's coming, vague and free, without precise attachment, at the disposal of one sentiment to-day, of another to-morrow, of filial piety or affection for a comrade. And the joy with which I first bound myself apprentice, when Françoise returned to tell me that my letter would be delivered; Swann, too, had known well that false joy which a friend can give us, or some relative of the woman we love, when on his arrival at the house or theatre where she is to be found, for some ball or party or 'first-night' at which he is to meet her, he sees us wandering outside, desperately awaiting some opportunity of communicating with her. He recognises us, greets us familiarly, and asks what we are doing there. And when we invent a story of having some urgent message to give to his relative or friend, he assures us that nothing could be more simple, takes us in at the door, and promises to send her down to us in five minutes. How much we love him—as at that moment I loved Françoise —the good-natured intermediary who by a single word has made supportable, human, almost propitious the inconceivable, infernal scene of gaiety in the thick of which we had been imagining swarms of enemies, perverse and seductive, beguiling away from us, even making laugh at us, the woman whom we love. If we are to judge of them by him, this relative who has accosted us and who is himself an initiate in those cruel mysteries, then the other guests cannot be so very demoniacal. Those inaccessible and torturing hours into which she had gone to taste of unknown pleasures—behold, a breach in the wall, and we are through it. Behold, one of the moments whose series will go to make up their sum, a moment as genuine as the rest, if not actually more important to ourself because our mistress is more intensely a part of it; we picture it to ourselves, we possess it, we intervene upon it, almost we have created it: namely, the moment in which he goes to tell her that we are waiting there below. And very probably the other moments of the party will not be essentially different, will contain nothing else so exquisite or so well able to make us

from *Remembrance of Things Past* (*Swann's Way*) [55]

suffer, since this kind friend has assured us that "Of course, she will be delighted to come down! It will be far more amusing for her to talk to you than to be bored up there." Alas! Swann had learned by experience that the good intentions of a third party are powerless to control a woman who is annoyed to find herself pursued even into a ball-room by a man whom she does not love. Too often, the kind friend comes down again alone.

My mother did not appear, but with no attempt to safeguard my self-respect (which depended upon her keeping up the fiction that she had asked me to let her know the result of my search for something or other) made Françoise tell me, in so many words "There is no answer"—words I have so often, since then, heard the hall-porters in 'mansions' and the flunkeys in gambling-clubs and the like, repeat to some poor girl, who replies in bewilderment: "What! he's said nothing? It's not possible. You did give him my letter, didn't you? Very well, I shall wait a little longer." And just as she invariably protests that she does not need the extra gas which the porter offers to light for her, and sits on there, hearing nothing further, except an occasional remark on the weather which the porter exchanges with a messenger whom he will send off suddenly, when he notices the time, to put some customer's wine on the ice; so, having declined Françoise's offer to make me some tea or to stay beside me, I let her go off again to the servants' hall, and lay down and shut my eyes, and tried not to hear the voices of my family who were drinking their coffee in the garden.

But after a few seconds I realised that, by writing that line to Mamma, by approaching—at the risk of making her angry—so near to her that I felt I could reach out and grasp the moment in which I should see her again, I had cut myself off from the possibility of going to sleep until I actually had seen her, and my heart began to beat more and more painfully as I increased my agitation by ordering myself to keep calm and to acquiesce in my ill-fortune. Then, suddenly, my anxiety subsided, a feeling of intense happiness coursed through me, as when a strong medicine begins to take effect and one's pain vanishes: I had formed a resolution to abandon all attempts to go to sleep without seeing Mamma, and had decided to kiss her at all costs, even with the certainty of being in disgrace with her for long afterwards, when she herself came up to bed. The tranquillity which followed my anguish made me extremely alert, no less than my sense of expectation, my thirst for and my fear of danger.

Noiselessly I opened the window and sat down on the foot of my bed; hardly daring to move in case they should hear me from below. Things outside seemed also fixed in mute expectation, so as not to disturb the moonlight which, duplicating each of them and throwing it back by the extension, forwards, of a shadow denser and more concrete than its substance, had made the whole landscape seem at once thinner and longer, like a map which, after being folded up, is spread out upon the ground. What had to move—a leaf of the chestnut-tree, for instance—moved. But its minute shuddering, complete, finished to the least detail and with utmost delicacy of gesture, made no discord with the rest of the scene, and yet was not merged in it, remaining clearly outlined. Exposed upon this surface of silence, which absorbed nothing from them, the most distant sounds, those which must have come from gardens at the far end of the town, could be distinguished with such exact 'finish' that the impression they gave of coming from a distance seemed due only to their 'pianissimo' execution, like those movements on muted strings so well performed by the orchestra of the Conservatoire that, although one does not lose a single note, one thinks all the same that they are being played somewhere outside, a long way from the concert hall, so that all the old subscribers, and my grandmother's sisters too, when Swann had given them his seats, used to strain their ears as if they had caught the distant approach of an army on the march, which had not yet rounded the corner of the Rue de Trévise.

I was well aware that I had placed myself in a position than which none could be counted upon to involve me in graver consequences at my parents' hands; consequences far graver, indeed, than a stranger would have imagined, and such as (he would have thought) could follow only some really shameful fault. But in the system of education which they had given me faults were not classified in the same order as in that of other children, and I had been taught to place at the head of the list (doubtless because there was no other class of faults from which I needed to be more carefully protected) those in which I can now distinguish the common feature that one succumbs to them by yielding to a nervous impulse. But such words as these last had never been uttered in my hearing; no one had yet accounted for my temptations in a way which might have led me to believe that there was some excuse for my giving in to them, or that I was actually incapable of holding out against them. Yet I could easily recognise this class of transgressions by the anguish of mind which preceded, as well as by the rigour of the punishment which followed them; and I knew that what I had just done was in the same category as certain other sins for which I had been severely chastised, though infinitely more serious than they. When I went out to meet my mother as she herself came up to bed, and when she saw that I had remained up so as to say good night to her again in the passage, I should not be allowed to stay in the house a day longer, I should be packed off to school next morning; so much was certain. Very good: had I been obliged, the next moment, to hurl myself out of the window, I should still have preferred such a fate. For what I wanted now was Mamma, and to say good night to her. I had gone too far along the road which led to the realisation of this desire to be able to retrace my steps.

from *Remembrance of Things Past* (*Swann's Way*) [57]

I could hear my parents' footsteps as they went with Swann; and, when the rattle of the gate assured me that he had really gone, I crept to the window. Mamma was asking my father if he had thought the lobster good, and whether M. Swann had had some of the coffee-and-pistachio ice. "I thought it rather so-so," she was saying; "next time we shall have to try another flavour."

"I can't tell you," said my great-aunt, "what a change I find in Swann. He is quite antiquated!" She had grown so accustomed to seeing Swann always in the same stage of adolescence that it was a shock to her to find him suddenly less young than the age she still attributed to him. And the others too were beginning to remark in Swann that abnormal, excessive, scandalous senescence, meet only in a celibate, in one of that class for whom it seems that the great day which knows no morrow must be longer than for other men, since for such a one it is void of promise, and from its dawn the moments steadily accumulate without any subsequent partition among his offspring.

"I fancy he has a lot of trouble with that wretched wife of his, who 'lives' with a certain Monsieur de Charlus, as all Combray knows. It's the talk of the town."

My mother observed that, in spite of this, he had looked much less unhappy of late. "And he doesn't nearly so often do that trick of his, so like his father, of wiping his eyes and passing his hand across his forehead. I think myself that in his heart of hearts he doesn't love his wife any more."

"Why, of course he doesn't," answered my grandfather. "He wrote me a letter about it, ages ago, to which I took care to pay no attention, but it left no doubt as to his feelings, let alone his love for his wife. Hullo! you two; you never thanked him for the Asti!" he went on, turning to his sisters-in-law.

"What! we never thanked him? I think, between you and me, that I put it to him quite neatly," replied my aunt Flora.

"Yes, you managed it very well; I admired you for it," said my aunt Céline.

"But you did it very prettily, too."

"Yes; I liked my expression about 'nice neighbours.'"

"What! Do you call that thanking him?" shouted my grandfather. "I heard that all right, but devil take me if I guessed it was meant for Swann. You may be quite sure he never noticed it."

"Come, come; Swann is not a fool. I am positive he appreciated the compliment. You didn't expect me to tell him the number of bottles, or to guess what he paid for them."

My father and mother were left alone and sat down for a moment; then my father said: "Well, shall we go up to bed?"

"As you wish, dear, though I don't feel in the least like sleeping. I don't know why; it can't be the coffee-ice—it wasn't strong enough to keep me awake like this. But I see a light in the servants' hall: poor Françoise has been sitting up for me, so I will get her to unhook me while you go and undress."

My mother opened the latticed door which led from the hall to the staircase. Presently I heard her coming upstairs to close her window. I went quietly into the passage; my heart was beating so violently that I could hardly move, but at least it was throbbing no longer with anxiety, but with terror and with joy. I saw in the well of the stair a light coming upwards, from Mamma's candle. Then I saw Mamma herself: I threw myself upon her. For an instant she looked at me in astonishment, not realising what could have happened. Then her face assumed an expression of anger. She said not a single word to me; and, for that matter, I used to go for days on end without being spoken to, for far less offences than this. A single word from Mamma would have been an admission that further intercourse with me was within the bounds of possibility, and that might perhaps have appeared to me more terrible still, as indicating that, with such a punishment as was in store for me, mere silence, and even anger, were relatively puerile.

A word from her then would have implied the false calm in which one converses with a servant to whom one has just decided to give notice; the kiss one bestows on a son who is being packed off to enlist, which would have been denied him if it had merely been a matter of being angry with him for a few days. But she heard my father coming from the dressing-room, where he had gone to take off his clothes, and, to avoid the 'scene' which he would make if he saw me, she said, in a voice half-stifled by her anger: "Run away at once. Don't let your father see you standing there like a crazy jane!"

But I begged her again to "Come and say good night to me!" terrified as I saw the light from my father's candle already creeping up the wall, but also making use of his approach as a means of blackmail, in the hope that my mother, not wishing him to find me there, as find me he must if she continued to hold out, would give in to me, and say: "Go back to your room. I will come."

Too late: my father was upon us. Instinctively I murmured, though no one heard me, "I am done for!"

I was not, however. My father used constantly to refuse to let me do things which were quite clearly allowed by the more liberal charters granted me by my mother and grandmother, because he paid no heed to 'Principles,' and because in his sight there were no such things as 'Rights of Man.' For some quite irrelevant reason, or for no reason at all, he would at the last moment prevent me from taking some particular walk, one so regular and so consecrated to my use that to deprive me of it was a clear breach of faith; or again, as he had done this evening, long before the appointed hour he would snap out: "Run along up to bed now; no

from *Remembrance of Things Past (Swann's Way)* [59]

excuses!" But then again, simply because he was devoid of principles (in my grandmother's sense), so he could not, properly speaking, be called inexorable. He looked at me for a moment with an air of annoyance and surprise, and then when Mamma had told him, not without some embarrassment, what had happened, said to her: "Go along with him, then; you said just now that you didn't feel like sleep, so stay in his room for a little. I don't need anything."

"But dear," my mother answered timidly, "whether or not I feel like sleep is not the point; we must not make the child accustomed . . ."

"There's no question of making him accustomed," said my father, with a shrug of the shoulders; "you can see quite well that the child is unhappy. After all, we aren't gaolers. You'll end by making him ill, and a lot of good that will do. There are two beds in his room; tell Françoise to make up the big one for you, and stay beside him for the rest of the night. I'm off to bed, anyhow; I'm not nervous like you. Good night."

It was impossible for me to thank my father; what he called my sentimentality would have exasperated him. I stood there, not daring to move; he was still confronting us, an immense figure in his white nightshirt, crowned with the pink and violet scarf of Indian cashmere in which, since he had begun to suffer from neuralgia, he used to tie up his head, standing like Abraham in the engraving after Benozzo Gozzoli which M. Swann had given me, telling Sarah that she must tear herself away from Isaac. Many years have passed since that night. The wall of the staircase, up which I had watched the light of his candle gradually climb, was long ago demolished. And in myself, too, many things have perished which, I imagined, would last for ever, and new structures have arisen, giving birth to new sorrows and new joys which in those days I could not have foreseen, just as now the old are difficult of comprehension. It is a long time, too, since my father has been able to tell Mamma to "Go with the child." Never again will such hours be possible for me. But of late I have been increasingly able to catch, if I listen attentively, the sound of the sobs which I had the strength to control in my father's presence, and which broke out only when I found myself alone with Mamma. Actually, their echo has never ceased: it is only because life is now growing more and more quiet round about me that I hear them afresh, like those convent bells which are so effectively drowned during the day by the noises of the streets that one would suppose them to have been stopped for ever, until they sound out again through the silent evening air.

Mamma spent that night in my room: when I had just committed a sin so deadly that I was waiting to be banished from the household, my parents gave me a far greater concession than I should ever have won as the reward of a good action. Even at the moment when it manifested itself in this crowning mercy, my father's conduct towards me was still somewhat arbitrary, and regardless of my deserts, as was characteristic of him and due to the fact that his actions were generally dictated by chance expediencies rather than based on any formal plan. And perhaps even what I called his strictness, when he sent me off to bed, deserved that title less, really, than my mother's or grandmother's attitude, for his nature, which in some respects differed more than theirs from my own, had probably prevented him from guessing, until then, how wretched I was every evening, a thing which my mother and grandmother knew well; but they loved me enough to be unwilling to spare me that suffering, which they hoped to teach me to overcome, so as to reduce my nervous sensibility and to strengthen my will. As for my father, whose affection for me was of another kind, I doubt if he would have shewn so much courage, for as soon as he had grasped the fact that I was unhappy he had said to my mother: "Go and comfort him."

Mamma stayed all night in my room, and it seemed that she did not wish to mar by recrimination those hours, so different from anything that I had had a right to expect; for when Françoise (who guessed that something extraordinary must have happened when she saw Mamma sitting by my side, holding my hand and letting me cry unchecked) said to her: "But, Madame, what is little Master crying for?" she replied: "Why Françoise, he doesn't know himself: it is his nerves. Make up the big bed for me quickly and then go off to your own." And thus for the first time my unhappiness was regarded no longer as a fault for which I must be punished, but as an involuntary evil which had been officially recognised a nervous condition for which I was in no way responsible. . . .

My agony was soothed; I let myself be borne upon the current of this gentle night on which I had my mother by my side. I knew that such a night could not be repeated; that the strongest desire I had in the world, namely, to keep my mother in my room through the sad hours of darkness, ran too much counter to general requirements and to the wishes of others for such a concession as had been granted me this evening to be anything but a rare and casual exception. To-morrow night I should again be the victim of anguish and Mamma would not stay by my side. But when these storms of anguish grew calm I could no longer realise their existence; besides, tomorrow evening was still a long way off; I reminded myself that I should still have time to think about things, albeit that remission of time could bring me no access of power, albeit the coming event was in no way dependent upon the exercise of my will, and seemed not quite inevitable only because it was still separated from me by this short interval.

A beloved American recalls her childhood days, surrounded by starchy upper-crust relations—and also her father (not starchy), who "fired a child's imagination."

ELEANOR ROOSEVELT

from *This Is My Story*

MY MOTHER was one of the most beautiful women I have ever seen. The Halls were noted for their beauty and charm in the days when New York City was small enough to have a society spelled with a capital S! She had been largely brought up by her father, who died when she was seventeen. It must have been a curious household, for my Grandfather Hall never engaged in business. He lived on what his father and mother gave him.

He had a house in New York City at 11 West 37th Street, and he built a house on the Hudson River about five miles above the village of Tivoli, on land which was part of the old Chancellor Livingston estate. My grandmother's mother was a Miss Livingston, and so we were related to the Livingstons, the Clarksons, the DePeysters, who lived in the various houses up and down the River Road.

My Grandfather Hall's great interest was in the study of theology, and in his library were immense books dealing with religion. Most of them were of little interest to me as a child, but the Bible illustrated by Doré occupied many hours—and I think, probably gave me many nightmares!

A clergyman, Mr. W. C. P. Rhoades, lived with my grandfather in order that he might have some one with whom to talk on equal terms! My Grandmother Hall—who had been a Miss Ludlow—a beauty and a belle, was treated like a cherished but somewhat spoiled child. She was expected to bring children into the world and seven children were born, but she was not expected to bring them up. My grandfather bought her clothes and adornments of every kind, but he told her nothing about business, never even taught her to draw a check, and died without a

[61]

will, leaving her with six children under seventeen years of age, a responsibility for which she was totally unprepared. . . .

. . . My mother belonged to that New York City Society which thought itself all-important. Old Mr. Peter Marié, who gave choice parties and whose approval stamped young girls and young matrons a success, called my mother a queen, and bowed before her charm and beauty, and to her this was important.

In that Society you were kind to the poor, you did not neglect your philanthropic duties in whatever community you lived, you assisted the hospitals and did something for the needy. You accepted invitations to dine and to dance with the right people only, you lived where you would be in their midst. You thought seriously about your children's education, you read the books that everybody read, you were familiar with good literature. In short, you conformed to the conventional pattern.

My father, Elliott Roosevelt, charming, good looking, loved by all who came in contact with him, high or low, had a background and upbringing which were a bit alien to her pattern. He had a physical weakness which he himself probably never quite understood. As a boy of about fifteen he left St. Paul's School after one year because of illness, and went out with Dr. Metcalf, a friend of the family, to what was then the "wild and woolly west" of Texas. He made friends with the officers of Fort McKavit, a frontier fort, and stayed with them, hunting wild turkeys and game of every sort, and scouting in search of hostile Indians. He loved the life and was a natural sportsman, a good shot and a good rider. I think the life left an indelible impression on him. The illness left its mark on him, too, on those inner reserves of strength which we all have to call on at times in our lives. He returned to his family in New York apparently well and strong. . . .

. . . I was a shy, solemn child even at the age of two, and I am sure that even when I danced, which I did frequently, I never smiled.

My earliest recollections are of being dressed up and allowed to come down into what must have been a dining room and dance for a group of gentlemen who applauded and laughed as I pirouetted before them. Finally, my father would pick me up and hold me high in the air. All this is rather vague to me, but my father was never vague. He dominated my life as long as he lived, and was the love of my life for many years after he died.

With my father I was perfectly happy. He would take me into his dressing room in the mornings, or when he was dressing for dinner, and let me watch each thing he did. There is still a woodeny painting of a child with a straight bang across her forehead, very solemn, with an uplifted finger and an admonishing attitude, which he always enjoyed and from *This Is My Story* [63]

referred to as "Little Nell scolding Elliott."

We had a country house at Hempstead, Long Island, so that he could hunt and play polo. He loved horses and dogs, and we always had both. During this time he was in business, and with this, added to work and the sports, the gay and popular young couple lived a busy, social life. Some of the older members of my father's family have told me since that they thought the strain on his health was very great, but my mother and he himself probably never realized this. I knew only that he was the center of my world, and that all around him loved him. . . .

. . . A short time after must have come a serious accident. My father was riding in a society circus held, I believe, on Mr. James M. Waterbury's estate in Westchester County. His leg was broken, and later it had to be rebroken and reset. I remember the day well, for we were alone in his room when he told me about it. Little as I was, I sensed that this was a terrible ordeal, and when he went hobbling out on crutches to the waiting doctors, I was dissolved in tears and sobbed my heart out for hours. From this illness my father never quite recovered.

Whether it was some weakness from his early years which the strain of the life he was living accentuated, whether it was the pain he endured, I do not know, for of course at that time I had no realization that anything was wrong—he began, however, to drink, and for my mother and his brother Theodore, and his sisters began the period of harrowing anxiety which was to last until his death in 1894.

My father and mother, my little brother and I went to Italy for the winter of 1890 as the first step in the fight for his health and power of self-control. Of this trip I have only vague pictures in my mind. I remember my father acting as gondolier, taking me out on the Venice canals, singing with the other boatmen, to my intense joy. I think there never was a child who was less able to carry a tune and had less gift for music than I. I loved his voice, however, and, above all, I loved the way he treated me. He called me "Little Nell," after the Little Nell in Dickens' "Old Curiosity Shop." Later he made me read the book, but at that time I only knew it was a term of affection, and I never doubted that I stood first in his heart.

He could, however, be annoyed with me, particularly when I disappointed him in such things as physical courage—and this, unfortunately, I did quite often. We went to Sorrento and I was given a donkey and a donkey boy so I could ride over the beautiful roads. One day the others overtook me and offered to let me go with them, but at the first steep descent which they slid down I turned pale, and preferred to stay on the high road. I can remember still the tone of disapproval in his voice, though his words of reproof have long since faded away.

I was about five and a half and very sensitive to physical suffering, and quite overcome by the fact that my little donkey boy's feet were always cut and bleeding. On one occasion we returned with the boy on the donkey and I was running along beside him, my explanation being that his feet bled too much!

I remember my trip to Vesuvius with my father and one other person, and the throwing of pennies which were returned to us encased in lava, and then an endless trip down. I suppose there was some block in the traffic, but I can only remember my utter weariness and my effort to bear it without tears so that my father would not be displeased.

Two other experiences stand out in my mind. One was in Germany, where my father went to a sanitarium. Perhaps it illustrates how one's childhood marks one's future life!

We often went to the cafés, and the older people drank steins of beer with the delicious looking foam on top. I saw little German children drinking it, too. I begged my father to let me have one of the small mugs, as the other children. He refused for a while and then said: "Very well, but remember, if you have it, you have to drink the whole glass." I promised without a suspicion of the horror before me. When I took my first taste, instead of something sweet and delicious, I found I had something very bitter which I could hardly swallow. I was a disillusioned and disappointed child, but I had to finish the glass! Never since then have I cared for beer.

I remember, too, that we children were left to travel into Paris following the older members of the family. My father's man and our nurse looked after us. The nurse and I got out at one of the stations and managed to be left behind! Such excitement on the part of the nurse, for, of course, she had neither money nor tickets! Such terror for me and exasperation on the part of the station master! Finally, after much telegraphing, we were put on a train and met later that night by a worried but distinctly annoyed father and mother in Paris.

My mother took a house in Neuilly, outside of Paris, and settled down for several months, as another baby was expected the end of June. My father entered a sanitarium while his older sister, Anna, our Auntie Bye, came to stay with my mother.

The house was small, so it was decided to put me in a convent to learn French, and to have me out of the way when the baby arrived. In those days children were expected to believe that babies dropped from Heaven, or were brought in the doctor's satchel.

The convent experience was a very unhappy one. Of course, I was not yet six years old, and I must have been very sensitive, with an inordinate desire for affection and praise—perhaps brought on by the fact that I was fully conscious of my plain looks and lack of manners. My mother was always a little troubled by my lack of beauty, and I knew

from *This Is My Story*

it as a child senses those things. She tried very hard to bring me up well so my manners would in some way compensate for my looks, but her efforts only made me more keenly conscious of my shortcomings.

The little girls of my age in the convent could hardly be expected to take much interest in a child who did not speak their language and did not belong to their religion. They had a little shrine of their own and often worked hard for hours beautifying it. I longed to be allowed to join them, but was always kept on the outside and wandered by myself in the walled-in garden.

Finally, I fell a prey to temptation. One of the girls swallowed a penny. The excitement was great, every attention was given her, she was the center of everybody's interest. I longed to be in her place. One day I went to one of the sisters and told her that I had swallowed a penny. I think it must have been evident that my story was not true, but I could not be shaken, so they sent for my mother and told her that they did not believe me. She took me away in disgrace. Understanding as I do now my mother's character, I realize how terrible it must have seemed to her to have a child who would lie!

I finally confessed to my mother, but never could explain my motives. I suppose I did not really understand them then, and certainly my mother did not understand them.

I remember the drive home as one of utter misery, for I could bear swift punishment of any kind far better than long scoldings. I could cheerfully lie any time to escape a scolding, whereas if I had known that I would simply be put to bed or be spanked I probably would have told the truth.

My father had come home for the baby's arrival, and I am sorry to say he was causing my mother and his sister a great deal of anxiety—but he was the only person who did not treat me as a criminal! . . .

. . . I had my troubles, too. The doctors did not want me to have sugar, and I had a very sweet tooth. I loved candy and sugar, so when we had dinner parties and there were sweets to go on the table, I stole into the pantry, and if I could find a paper bag with any of the sweets, I not only ate them but once or twice, fearing I would not have a chance to eat them on the spot, I took the whole bag and decided the best hiding place was down the front of my dress. I remember sitting on the lap of my brother's nurse, who was very strict with me, and when she felt something crackle she demanded to know what it was. I evaded the question, and, of course, was discovered at once. She scolded me, and then I was taken in to my mother, who scolded me again and sent me to bed in disgrace.

This habit of lying stayed with me for a number of years. I now realize I was a great trial to my mother. She did not understand that a child may lie from fear; I myself never understood it until I reached the age when I suddenly realized that there was nothing to fear.

. . . All in all, however, life moved smoothly. Suddenly everything was changed!

* * *

My Mother's Death

We children were sent out of the house. I went to stay with my godmother, Mrs. Henry Parish, and the boys went to my mother's aunt, Mrs. Ludlow. My grandmother left her own house and family to nurse my mother, for she had diphtheria and there was then no antitoxin. Bob Ferguson sat on the stairs outside her room to do any errands that might be asked of him, both day and night. My father was sent for, but came too late from his exile in Virginia. Diphtheria went fast in those days.

I can remember standing by a window when Cousin Susie (Mrs. Parish) told me that my mother was dead. She was very sweet to me, and I must have known that something terrible had happened. Death meant nothing to me, and one fact wiped out everything else—my father was back and I would see him very soon.

This was on December 7th, 1892.

He did not come right away, and later I knew what a tragedy of utter defeat this meant for him. No hope now of ever wiping out the sorrowful years he had brought upon my mother—and she had left her mother as guardian for her children. My grandmother did not feel that she could trust my father to take care of us. He had no wife, no children, no hope!

Finally, he came to take me out driving, and as I climbed up beside him in the high dog cart, everything but the excitement of seeing him was forgotten.

He was driving his best hunter, Mohawk by name, and as we went up Madison Avenue, a street car frightened the horse, and we nearly had an accident. My father lost his hat, which a policeman restored to him. He looked down at me and said: "You weren't afraid, were you, Little Nell?"

When we reached the Park, with its long line of carriages and horses, he again looked at me and said: "If I were to say 'hoopla' to Mohawk he would try to jump them all." Inwardly I prayed that he would do nothing of the kind.

In spite of my abject terror, those drives were the high points of my existence.

Finally, it was arranged that we three children were to go and live with my Grandmother Hall. I realize now what that must have meant in dislocation of her household, and I marvel at the sweetness of my two uncles and the two aunts who were still at home, for never by word or deed did any of them make us feel that we were not in our own house.

After we were installed, my father came to see me, and I remember going down into the high ceilinged, dim library on the first floor of the house in West 37th Street. He sat in a big chair. He was dressed all in black, looking very sad. He held out his arms and gathered me to him. In a little while he began to talk, to explain to me that my mother was gone, that she had been all the world to him, and now he only had my brothers and myself, that my brothers were very young, and that he and I must keep close together. Some day I would make a home for him again, we would travel together and do many things which he painted as interesting and pleasant, to be looked forward to in the future together.

Somehow it was always he and I. I did not understand whether my brothers were to be our children or whether he felt that they would be at school and college and later independent.

There started that day a feeling which never left me—that he and I were very close together, and some day would have a life of our own together. He told me to write to him often, to be a good girl, not to give any trouble, to study hard, to grow up into a woman he could be proud of, and he would come to see me whenever it was possible.

When he left, I was all alone to keep our secret of mutual understanding and to adjust myself to my new existence. . . .

. . . Though he was so little with us, my father dominated all this period of my life. Subconsciously I must have been waiting always for his visits. They were irregular, and he rarely sent word before he arrived, but never was I in the house, even in my room two long flights of stairs above the entrance door, that I did not hear his voice the minute he entered the front door. Walking down stairs was far too slow. I slid down the banisters and usually catapulted into his arms before his hat was hung up.

. . . My father never missed an opportunity for giving us presents, so Christmas was, of course, a great day for us, and I still remember one memorable Christmas when I had two stockings, for my grandmother had filled one and my father was in New York and had one brought to me on Christmas morning.

I was still supposed to believe in Santa Claus, but I think my belief must have been shaken that year. However, I pretended for years that I believed in him, and used to try to stay awake and play 'possum in the hope that I would see someone come to fill my stocking hanging on the foot of my bed, but I always fell asleep and woke to find it mysteriously filled. . . .

* * *

My First Pony

It was on my birthday, however, that my father lavished the greatest thought. He was anxious that I should be a good horsewoman, and gave me a pony when I was still quite young. The pony arrived with a cart when we were in Newport one summer with my great-aunt, Mrs. Ludlow. Mrs. Parish took us out driving, and the pony ran away. He was returned! Later, at Tivoli, I had a pony of my own called Captain, and on my birthday came a saddle of my own. Captain was a fair-sized pony and quite spirited. . . .

. . . I remained quite fearless until one sad day, when I was fourteen, I rode a gray polo pony sent up by one of my aunt's friends. He ran away with me twice and from that day I've been full of fears and very grateful that my father never knew it.

He was always writing me about riding with all the little children down in Abingdon, Virginia, where he lived, and I was always longing to join the group and know some of the children who seemed to be so much a factor in his life. One child in particular I remember, Miriam Trigg, and I envied her very much because he was so very fond of her. She used to come in and sit in his sitting room and play with his fox terriers. He had a great many of these, and several horses which were taken care of by an excellent and very willing darky groom.

Only three years ago I met a number of the Trigg family when I went down to the music festival at White Top, which is near Abingdon. The old darky who had been my father's servant came to see me that day and brought me one of the teacups which he had cherished all these years and which I recognized at once as being part of the same service which belonged to my Grandmother Roosevelt, some of which I still have and use today.

One more sorrow came to my father the winter that my mother died. My little brother, Ellie, was simply too good for this world, and he never seemed to thrive after my mother's death. Both he and the baby, Josh, got scarlet fever, and I was returned to my Cousin Susie, and, of course, quarantined.

The baby got well without any complications, but Ellie developed diphtheria and died. My father came to take me out occasionally, but the anxiety over the little boys was too great for him to give me a great deal of his time.

I am deeply grateful to my cousin, Mrs. J. West Roosevelt, who lived not very far from Mrs. Parish, and who allowed me to come over and have supper and play with her children, Laura, Nicholas and Oliver, very frequently. They were much younger than I was, but I was accustomed to being with my own little brothers.

I think that, in all probability, having only lessons to do alone, as I could not go to school, and going for walks in the afternoons, there were occasions when time hung rather heavily on my hands.

Mrs. Parish has always been very closely connected with my life. She was kindness itself to me when I was small and I took it all for granted, though now I realize that my care must have been quite a problem. She kept house at that time with the same precision and care as her mother, Mrs. Ludlow. Meals were always at the same hour; no one was ever late. Unexpected guests were unheard of, and life was a pretty well regulated pattern into which a small child could hardly fit easily. Yet I never remember a time when I needed a home that it was not offered to me by Mr. and Mrs. Henry Parish. . . .

. . . On August 14th, 1894, just before I was ten years old, word came that my father had died. My aunts told me, but I simply refused to believe it, and while I wept long and went to bed still weeping, I finally went to sleep and began the next day living in my dream world as usual.

My grandmother decided that we children should not go to the funeral, and so I had no tangible thing to make death real to me. From that time on I knew in my mind that my father was dead, and yet I lived with him more closely, probably, than I had when he was alive.

OGDEN NASH

Birdies, Don't Make Me Laugh

Once there was a poem, and it was serious and not in jest,
And it said children ought to agree like little birdies in their nest.
Oh forsooth forsooth!
That poem was certainly more poetry than truth,

Because do you believe that little birdies in their nest agree
It doesn't sound very probable to me.
Ah no, but I can tell you what does sound probable,
And that is that life in a nest is just one long quarrel and squabbable.
Look at that young mother robin over in that elm, or is it a beech,
She has two little robins and she thinks she has solved her problem because she has learned not to bring home just one worm but a worm for each.
She is very pleased with her understanding of fledgling psychology, but in just about two minutes she is going to lose a year's growth,
Because she's going to find that one little robin gets no worms and the other little robin gets both,
And if one little robin gets out of the nest on the wrong side and nothing can please it,
Why the other little robin will choose that moment to tease it,
And if one little robin starts a game the other little robin will stop it,
And if one little robin builds a castle the other little robin will knock it down and if one little robin blows a bubble the other little robin will pop it.
Yes, I bet that if you walked up to any nest and got a good revealing glimpse,
Why, you would find that our little feathered friendlets disagree just like

Birdies, Don't Make Me Laugh

human imps,
And I also bet that their distracted feathered parents quote feathered poetry to them by whoever the most popular feathered poet may be,
All about why don't they like little children in their nurseries agree.
Well, to put the truth about youth in a very few words,
Why the truth is that little birds do agree like children and children do agree like little birds,
Because you take offspring, and I don't care whether a house or a tree is their abode,
They may love each other but they aren't going to agree with each other anywhere except in an ode.
It doesn't seem to have occurred to the poet,
That nobody agrees with anybody else anyhow, but adults conceal it and infants show it.

Though moral object lessons for children often—as in these stories—miscarry, the power of this father's tenderness and humor may one day give them meaning.

CARL EWALD

My Little Boy

MY LITTLE BOY and I have had an exceedingly interesting walk in the Frederiksberg Park.

There was a mouse, which was irresistible. There were two chaffinches, husband and wife, which built their nest right before our eyes, and a snail, which had no secrets for us. And there were flowers, yellow and white, and there were green leaves, which told us the oddest adventures: in fact, as much as we can find room for in our little head.

Now we are sitting on a bench and digesting our impressions.

Suddenly the air is shaken by a tremendous roar:

"What was that?" asks my little boy.

"That was the lion in the Zoological Gardens," I reply.

No sooner have I said this than I curse my own stupidity.

I might have said that it was a gunshot announcing the birth of a prince; or an earthquake; or a china dish falling from the sky and breaking into pieces: anything whatever, rather than the truth.

For now my little boy wants to know what sort of thing the Zoological Gardens is.

I tell him.

The Zoological Gardens is a horrid place, where they lock up wild beasts who have done no wrong and who are accustomed to walk about freely in the distant foreign countries where they come from. The lion is there, whom we have just heard roaring. He is so strong that he can kill a policeman with one blow of his paw; he has great, haughty eyes and awfully sharp teeth. He lives in Africa and, at night, when he roars, all the other beasts tremble in their holes for fear. He is called the king of beasts. They caught him one day in a cunning trap and bound him and dragged him here and locked him up in a cage with iron bars to it.

My Little Boy [73]

The cage is no more than half as big as Petrine's room. And there the king walks up and down, up and down, and gnashes his teeth with sorrow and rage and roars so that you can hear him ever so far away. Outside his cage stand cowardly people and laugh at him, because he can't get out and eat them up, and poke their sticks through the rails and tease him.

My little boy stands in front of me and looks at me with wide-open eyes:

"Would he eat them up, if he got out?" he asks.

"In a moment."

"But he can't get out, can he?"

"No. That's awfully sad. He can't get out."

"Father, let us go and look at the lion."

I pretend not to hear and go on to tell him of the strange birds there: great eagles, which used to fly over every church-steeple and over the highest trees and mountains and swoop down upon lambs and hares and carry them up to their young in the nest. Now they are sitting in cages, on a perch, like canaries, with clipped wings and blind eyes. I tell him of gulls, which used to fly all day long over the stormy sea: now they splash about in a puddle of water, screaming pitifully. I tell him of wonderful blue and red birds, which, in their youth, used to live among wonderful blue and red flowers, in balmy forests a thousand times bigger than the Frederiksberg Park, where it was as dark as night under the trees with the brightest sun shining down upon the tree-tops: now they sit there in very small cages and hang their beaks while they stare at tiresome boys in dark-blue suits and black stockings and waterproof boots and sailor-hats.

"Are those birds really blue?" asks my little boy.

"Sky-blue," I answer. "And utterly broken-hearted."

"Father, can't we go and look at the birds?"

I take my little boy's hands in mine:

"I don't think we will," I say. "Why should still more silly boys do so? You can't imagine how it goes to one's heart to look at those poor captive beasts."

"Father, I should so much like to go."

"Take my advice and don't. The animals there are not the real animals, you see. They are ill and ugly and angry because of their captivity and their longing and their pain."

"I should so much like to see them."

"Now let me tell you something. To go to the Zoological Gardens costs five cents for you and ten cents for me. That makes fifteen cents altogether, which is an awful lot of money. We won't go there now, but we'll buy the biggest money-box we can find: one of those money-boxes shaped like a pig. Then we'll put fifteen cents in it. And every Thursday we'll put fifteen cents in the pig. By-and-by, that will grow into quite a fortune: it will make such a lot of money that, when you are grown up, you can take a trip to Africa and go to the desert and hear the wild, the real lion roaring and tremble just like the people tremble down there. And you can go to the great, dark forests and see the real blue birds flying proud and free among the flowers. You can't think how glad you will be, how beautiful they will look and how they will sing to you. . . ."

"Father, I would rather go to the Zoological Gardens now."

My little boy does not understand a word of what I say. And I am at my wit's end.

"Shall we go and have some cakes at Josty's?" I ask.

"I would rather go to the Zoological Gardens."

I can read in his eyes that he is thinking of the captive lion. Ugly human instincts are waking up in his soul. The mouse is forgotten and the snail; and the chaffinches have built their nest to no purpose.

At last I get up and say, bluntly, without any further explanation:

"You are *not* going to the Zoological Gardens. Now we'll go home."

And home we go. But we are not in a good temper.

Of course, I get over it and I buy an enormous money-box pig. Also we put the money into it and he thinks that most interesting.

But, later in the afternoon, I find him in the bed-room engaged in a piteous game.

He has built a cage, in which he has imprisoned the pig. He is teasing it and hitting it with his whip, while he keeps shouting to it:

"You can't get out and bite me, you stupid pig! You can't get out!" . . .

. . . It has been decreed in the privy council that my little boy shall have a weekly income of one cent. Every Sunday morning, that sum shall be paid to him, free of income-tax, out of the treasury and he has leave to dispose of it entirely at his own pleasure.

He receives this announcement with composure and sits apart for a while and ponders on it.

"Every Sunday?" he asks.

"Every Sunday."

"All the time till the summer holidays?"

"All the time till the summer holidays."

In the summer holidays, he is to go to the country, to stay with his godmother, in whose house he was pleased to allow himself to be born. The summer holidays are, consequently, the limits of his calculation of time: beyond them lies, for the moment, his Nirvana.

And we employ this restricted horizon of ours to further our true happiness.

That is to say, we calculate, with the aid of the almanac, that, if everything goes as heretofore, there will be fifteen Sundays before the summer holidays. We arrange a drawer with fifteen compartments and in each compartment we put one cent. Thus we know exactly what we have and are able at any time to survey our financial status.

And, when he sees that great lot of cents lying there, my little boy's breast is filled with mad delight. He feels endlessly rich, safe for a long time. The courtyard rings with his bragging, with all that he is going to do with his money. His special favorites are invited to come up and view his treasure.

The first Sunday passes in a normal fashion, as was to be expected.

He takes his cent and turns it straightway into a stick of chocolate of the best sort, with almonds on it and sugar, in short, an ideal stick in every way. The whole performance is over in five minutes: by that time, the stick of chocolate is gone, with the sole exception of a remnant in the corners of our mouth, which our ruthless mother wipes away, and a stain on our collar, which annoys us.

He sits by me, with a vacant little face, and swings his legs. I open the drawer and look at the empty space and at the fourteen others:

"So *that's* gone," I say.

My accent betrays a certain melancholy, which finds an echo in his breast. But he does not deliver himself of it at once.

"Father . . . is it long till next Sunday?"

"Very long, my boy; ever so many days."

We sit a little, steeped in our own thoughts. Then I say, pensively:

"Now, if you had bought a top, you would perhaps have had more pleasure out of it. I know a place where there is a lovely top: red, with a green ring round it. It is just over the way, in the toyshop. I saw it yesterday. I should be greatly mistaken if the toyman was not willing to sell it for a cent. And you've got a whip, you know."

We go over the way and look at the top in the shop-window. It is really a splendid top.

"The shop's shut," says my little boy, despondently.

I look at him with surprise:

"Yes, but what does that matter to us? Anyway, we can't buy the top before next Sunday. You see, you've spent your cent on chocolate. Give me your handkerchief: there's still a bit on your cheek."

There is no more to be said. Crestfallen and pensively, we go home. We sit a long time at the dining-room window, from which we can see the window of the shop.

During the course of the week, we look at the top daily, for it does not do to let one's love grow cold. One might so easily forget it. And the top shines always more seductively. We go in and make sure that the price is really in keeping with our means. We make the shop-keeper take a solemn oath to keep the top for us till Sunday morning, even if boys should come and bid him much higher sums for it.

On Sunday morning, we are on the spot before nine o'clock and acquire our treasure with trembling hands. And we play with it all day and sleep with it at night, until, on Wednesday morning, it disappears without a trace, after the nasty manner which tops have.

When the turn comes of the next cent, something remarkable happens.

There is a boy in the courtyard who has a skipping-rope and my little boy, therefore, wants to have a skipping-rope too. But this is a difficult matter. Careful enquiries establish the fact that a skipping-rope of the sort used by the upper classes is nowhere to be obtained for less than five cents.

The business is discussed as early as Saturday:

"It's the simplest thing in the world," I say. "You must not spend your cent tomorrow. Next Sunday you must do the same and the next and the next. On the Sunday after that, you will have saved your five cents and can buy your skipping-rope at once."

"When shall I get my skipping-rope then?"

"In five Sundays from now."

He says nothing, but I can see that he does not think my idea very brilliant. In the course of the day, he derives, from sources unknown to me, an acquaintance with financial circumstances which he serves up to me on Sunday morning in the following words:

"Father, you must lend me five cents for the skipping-rope. If you will lend me five cents for the skipping-rope, I'll give you *forty* cents back . . ."

He stands close to me, very red in the face and quite confused. I perceive that he is ripe for falling into the claws of the usurers:

"I don't do that sort of business, my boy," I say. "It wouldn't do you any good either. And you're not even in a position to do it, for you have only thirteen cents, as you know."

He collapses like one whose last hope is gone.

"Let us just see," I say.

And we go to our drawer and stare at it long and deeply.

"We might perhaps manage it this way, that I give you five cents now. And then I should have your cent and the next four cents . . ."

He interrupts me with a loud shout. I take out my purse, give him five cents and take one cent out of the drawer:

"That won't be pleasant next Sunday," I say, "and the next and the next and the next . . ."

But the thoughtless youth is gone.

Of course, the instalments of his debt are paid off with great ceremony. He is always on the spot himself when the drawer is opened and sees how the requisite cent is removed and finds its way into my pocket instead of his.

The first time, all goes well. It is simply an amusing thing that I should have the cent; and the skipping-rope is still fresh in his memory, because of the pangs which he underwent before its purchase. Next Sunday, al-

My Little Boy

ready the thing is not *quite* so pleasant and, when the fourth instalment falls due, my little boy's face looks very gloomy:

"Is anything the matter?" I ask.

"I should so much like a stick of chocolate," he says, without looking at me.

"Is that all? You can get one in a fortnight. By that time, you will have paid for the skipping-rope and the cent will be your own again."

"I should so much like to have a stick of chocolate now."

Of course I am full of the sincerest compassion, but I can't help it. What's gone is gone. We saw it with our own eyes and we know exactly where it has gone to. And, that Sunday morning, we part in a dejected mood.

Later in the day, however, I find him standing over the drawer with raised eyebrows and a pursed-up mouth. I sit down quietly and wait. And I do not have to wait long before I learn that his development as an economist is taking quite its normal course.

"Father, suppose we moved the cent now from here into this Sunday's place and I took it and bought the chocolate-stick . . ."

"Why, then you won't have your cent for the other Sunday."

"I don't mind that, Father . . ."

We talk about it, and then we do it. And, with that, as a matter of course, we enter upon the most reckless peculations.

The very next Sunday, he is clever enough to take the furthest cent, which lies just before the summer holidays. He pursues the path of vice without a scruple, until, at last, the blow falls and five long Sundays come in a row without the least chance of a cent.

Where should they come from? They were there. We know that. They are gone. We have spent them ourselves.

But, during those drab days of poverty, we sit every morning over the empty drawer and talk long and profoundly about that painful phenomenon, which is so simple and so easy to understand and which one must needs make the best of.

And we hope and trust that our experience will do us good, when, after our trip, we start a new set of cents.

One of the world's great writers wonders at the selectivity of early memories, through which so much is lost.

LEO TOLSTOI

First Recollections

HERE ARE my first recollections (which I cannot reduce to order, not knowing what came first, what afterward, while of some I know not whether they were dreams or reality). But here they are.

I am tied down; I want to raise my arms, but I cannot do it, and I wail and weep and my cry is disagreeable to myself; but I cannot stop. It must be that some one stands bending over me, but I don't remember who. And all this takes place in a semi-darkness. But I remember that there are two. My crying has an effect on them, they are alarmed at my cry, but they do not unloose me as I wish, and I cry louder than ever. It seems to them necessary (that is, that I be tied down), while I know that it is not necessary, and I want to prove it to them, and I burst out into a cry disgusting to myself but unrestrainable.

I am conscious of the injustice and cruelty, not of people, because they pity me, but of fate, and feel pity for myself. I do not know and never shall learn what this was: whether they swaddled me when I was a suckling and I pulled out my hands; or whether they swaddled me when I was more than a year old so that I might not scratch the tetter; or whether I have gathered many impressions into one as happens in dreams, —but apparently this was my first and most powerful impression of life. And it was not my crying or my suffering that I retain in my recollection, but the complication, the contradiction, of the impression. I wanted freedom; it would not disturb any one, and I who needed the strength was weak while they were strong.

The second impression was pleasurable. I am sitting in a tub, and I am surrounded by a new and disagreeable odor of some object by which my small body is galled. Apparently this was bran, and apparently in the water and in the trough, but the novelty of the impression made by the

First Recollections

bran awakened me, and I for the first time noticed and observed my little body, with the ribs plainly outlined, and the smooth, dark tub, and the nurse with her arms tucked up, and the dark, warm, threatening water, and the swash of it, and especially the feeling of smoothness of the wet edges of the tub when I put my little hands on it. Strange and terrible to think that from my birth up to my third year, all the time while I was nursing, while I was weaned, when I was beginning to creep, to walk, to speak, however I rack my memory, I can find no impression except these two.

When did I begin? When did I begin to live? And why is it pleasant to imagine myself as I was then, but it used to be terrible to me, as now it is terrible to many, to imagine myself as I shall be when I again enter into that condition of death from which there will be no recollections expressible in words? Was I not alive when I was learning to look, to hear, to understand, to talk, when I slept, when I pressed my lips to my mother's breast, and laughed and rejoiced my mother? I was alive and blissfully alive. Did I not then get all that whereby I live now, and get in such abundance, and so rapidly, that in all the rest of my life I have not got a hundredth part so much?

From a five-year-old child to me is only a step. From the new-born baby to the five-year-old child there is a terrible gap. From the embryo to the new-born baby there is an abyss. And from non-existence to the embryo there is not an abyss, but incomprehensibility. Moreover space and time and cause are forms of thought and the existence of life outside of these forms, but all our life is a continually increasing subjection to these forms and then again emancipation from them.

The following recollections of mine refer to my fourth and fifth years, but even of these there are very few, and not one of these refers to life outside of the walls of my home.

Nature up to the age of five does not exist for me. All that I remember refers to bed and chamber. No grass, no leaves, no sky, no sun exist for me. It cannot be that they did not let me play with the flowers and leaves, or see the grass, that they did not protect me from the sun, but up to five years, up to six years, there is not one recollection of what we call Nature. Apparently it is necessary to go away from her in order to see her, and I was Nature!

The recollection that comes after that of the tub is that of *Yeremeyevna*. "Yeremeyevna" was a word with which they used to frighten us children. And apparently they began early to frighten us with it, but my recollection of it is as follows:—

I am in my little bed and feeling good and happy as always, and I should not remember this but suddenly my nurse, or some one of those that constituted my life, says something in a voice entirely new to me, and goes out, and I begin to feel a sensation of terror besides that of gaiety. And I remember that I am not alone, but some one is there with me very much the same as I.

This must have been my sister Mashenka, a year younger than I, for our beds stood in one room together.

And I remember that there is a canopy over my bed, and my sister and I used to share our pleasures and terrors—whatever unexpected thing happened to us—and I used to hide in the pillow, and I would hide and peek out to look at the door from which I expected anything new and gay. And we used to laugh and hide and be full of expectations. And here comes some one in a gown and head-dress such as I had never seen before, but I know that it is the person who is always with me—a nurse or auntie, I don't know which, and this some one speaks in a deep voice which I recognize, and says something terrible about naughty children, and about Yeremeyevna! I squeal with terror and delight, and I am terrified, and at the same time delighted because I am terrified, and I wish that the one who frightened me did not know that I know her! We become silent, but soon again we begin to whisper on purpose to bring back Yeremeyevna.

Similar to the recollection of Yeremeyevna is another, apparently later in time because it is more distinct, but it always remains incomprehensible to me. In this remembrance the chief rôle is played by a German, Feodor Ivanovitch, our teacher; but I know assuredly that I was not as yet under his supervision, consequently this must have taken place before I was five. And this is my first impression of Feodor Ivanovitch. And it happens so early that I do not remember any one—my brothers, nor my father, nor any one. If I have an idea of any person whatever besides, it is only of my sister, and solely because she and I were associated in terror of Yeremeyevna.

With this recollection is connected also my first conception that our house had an upper story. How I got there, whether I went there by myself or who took me there, I do not remember at all; I only remember that there were several of us, we all took hold of hands in a khorovod; among those holding one another by the hand were several strange women, —because I recollect that these were the laundry girls,—and we all began to turn and spring, and Feodor Ivanovitch capered about, lifting his legs very high and making a terrible noise and thumping, and I had a consciousness that this was not the right thing to do, that it was bad, and I noticed him and I seemed to burst out crying, and it all came to an end.

This is all I remember up to my fifth year. I remember nothing of my nurses, my aunties, my brothers, my sisters, or of my father, or my rooms, or my toys—nothing at all. My recollections grow more definite from the time when I was taken down to Feodor Ivanovitch and to the older boys.

When I was taken down to Feodor Ivanovitch and the other boys, I

First Recollections

experienced, for the first time, and therefore more strongly than ever again, the feeling called the sense of duty, called the sense of the cross, which every man is called upon to wear. I felt sorry to leave what I had grown accustomed to—accustomed to from eternity!—I felt melancholy, poetically melancholy to leave, not so much the people, my sister, my nurse, my aunt, as the bed, the canopy, the pillows; and the new life into which I had entered was terrible to me. I tried to find something cheerful in the new life which was before me; I tried to credit the flattering speeches with which Feodor Ivanovitch allured me to himself. I tried not to see the scorn with which the boys received me, their younger brother; I tried to think that it was disgraceful for a big boy to live with girls, and that there was nothing good in the up-stair life with the nurse; but in the depths of my soul I was terribly homesick, and I knew that I had irrevocably lost my innocence and joy, and only a feeling of personal dignity, a consciousness that I was doing my duty, sustained me.

Many times since in life it has been my fortune to undergo such moments at the dividing of the ways, where new paths opened out before me. I experienced a gentle grief at the irrevocableness of what was lost. And still I did not believe that it would be. Though they told me that I was to be taken down to the boys, I remember that my khalat with its belt, sewed to the back, which they put on me, seemed to separate me forever from the upper rooms, and I now, for the first time, noticed others besides those with whom I had lived upstairs, but the chief personage was the one at whose house I was living and whom I do not remember before. This was my Aunt T—— A——.[1] I remember her as short, stout, with black hair, kind, affectionate, gentle. She put on me my khalat, tightened the belt and fastened it, kissed me, and I saw that she was experiencing the same feelings as I was, that she was sorry, awfully sorry, but it had to be.

For the first time I realized that life is not play, but hard work. Not otherwise shall I feel when I come to die; I shall discover that death or the future life is not play, but hard work.

May 17, 1878

[1] Probably Tatyana Aleksandreyevna Eyelskaya.

In this small masterpiece, a quiet, scholarly family man oppressed by the disorders of a world he never made—the troubled Germany of the great inflation before World War II—finds his own nearly-grown children and their friends alien to all he has known. He turns for consolation to his small daughter, who at first responds joyously to her father's love, then "betrays" him for another.

THOMAS MANN

Disorder and Early Sorrow

THE PRINCIPAL DISH at dinner had been croquettes made of turnip greens. So there follows a trifle, concocted out of those dessert powders we use nowadays, that taste like almond soap. Xaver, the youthful manservant, in his outgrown striped jacket, white woollen gloves, and yellow sandals, hands it round, and the "big folk" take this opportunity to remind their father, tactfully, that company is coming today.

The "big folk" are two, Ingrid and Bert. Ingrid is brown-eyed, eighteen, and perfectly delightful. She is on the eve of her exams, and will probably pass them, if only because she knows how to wind masters, and even headmasters, round her finger. She does not, however, mean to use her certificate once she gets it; having leanings towards the stage, on the ground of her ingratiating smile, her equally ingratiating voice, and a marked and irresistible talent for burlesque. Bert is blond and seventeen. He intends to get done with school somehow, anyhow, and fling himself into the arms of life. He will be a dancer, or a cabaret actor, possibly even a waiter—but not a waiter anywhere else save at Cairo, the night-club, whither he has once already taken flight, at five in the morning, and been brought back crestfallen. Bert bears a strong resemblance to the youthful manservant, Xaver Kleinsgutl, of about the same age as himself; not because he looks common—in features he is strikingly like his father, Professor Cornelius—but by reason of an approximation of types, due in its turn to far-reaching compromises in matters of dress and bearing generally. Both lads wear their heavy hair very long on top, with a cursory parting in the middle, and give their heads the same characteristic toss to throw it off the forehead. When one of them leaves the house, by the garden gate, bareheaded in all weathers, in a blouse rakishly girt with a leather strap, and sheers off bent well over with his head on

[82]

one side; or else mounts his push-bike—Xaver makes free with his employers', of both sexes, or even, in acutely irresponsible mood, with the Professor's own—Dr. Cornelius from his bedroom window cannot, for the life of him, tell whether he is looking at his son or his servant. Both, he thinks, look like young moujiks. And both are impassioned cigarette-smokers, though Bert has not the means to compete with Xaver, who smokes as many as thirty a day, of a brand named after a popular cinema star. The big folk call their father and mother the "old folk"—not behind their backs, but as a form of address and in all affection: "Hullo, old folks," they will say; though Cornelius is only forty-seven years old and his wife eight years younger. And the Professor's parents, who lead in his household the humble and hesitant life of the really old, are on the big folk's lips the "ancients." As for the "little folk," Ellie and Snapper, who take their meals upstairs with blue-faced Ann—so-called because of her prevailing facial hue—Ellie and Snapper follow their mother's example and address their father by his first name, Abel. Unutterably comic it sounds, in its pert, confiding familiarity; particularly on the lips, in the sweet accents, of five-year-old Eleanor, who is the image of Frau Cornelius's baby pictures and whom the Professor loves above everything else in the world.

"Darling old thing," says Ingrid affably, laying her large but shapely hand on his, as he presides in proper middle-class style over the family table, with her on his left and the mother opposite: "Parent mine, may I ever so gently jog your memory, for you have probably forgotten: this is the afternoon we were to have our little jollification, our turkey-trot with eats to match. You haven't a thing to do but just bear up and not funk it; everything will be over by nine o'clock."

"Oh—ah!" says Cornelius, his face falling. "Good!" he goes on, and nods his head to show himself in harmony with the inevitable. "I only meant—is this really the day? Thursday, yes. How time flies! Well, what time are they coming?"

"Half past four they'll be dropping in, I should say," answers Ingrid, to whom her brother leaves the major rôle in all dealings with the father. Upstairs, while he is resting, he will hear scarcely anything, and from seven to eight he takes his walk. He can slip out by the terrace if he likes.

"Tut!" says Cornelius deprecatingly, as who should say: "You exaggerate." But Bert puts in: "It's the one evening in the week Wanja doesn't have to play. Any other night he'd have to leave by half past six, which would be painful for all concerned."

Wanja is Ivan Herzl, the celebrated young leading man at the Stadttheater. Bert and Ingrid are on intimate terms with him, they often visit him in his dressing-room and have tea. He is an artist of the modern school, who stands on the stage in strange and, to the Professor's mind, utterly affected dancing attitudes, and shrieks lamentably. To a professor of history, all highly repugnant; but Bert has entirely succumbed to Herzl's influence, blackens the lower rim of his eyelids—despite painful but fruitless scenes with the father—and with youthful carelessness of the ancestral anguish declares that not only will he take Herzl for his model if he becomes a dancer, but in case he turns out to be a waiter at the Cairo he means to walk precisely thus.

Cornelius slightly raises his brows and makes his son a little bow—indicative of the unassumingness and self-abnegation that befits his age. You could not call it a mocking bow or suggestive in any special sense. Bert may refer it to himself or equally to his so talented friend.

"Who else is coming?" next inquires the master of the house. They mention various people, names all more or less familiar, from the city, from the suburban colony, from Ingrid's school. They still have some telephoning to do, they say. They have to phone Max. This is Max Hergesell, an engineering student; Ingrid utters his name in the nasal drawl which according to her is the traditional intonation of all the Hergesells. She goes on to parody it in the most abandonedly funny and lifelike way, and the parents laugh until they nearly choke over the wretched trifle. For even in these times when something funny happens people have to laugh.

From time to time the telephone bell rings in the Professor's study, and the big folk run across, knowing it is their affair. Many people had to give up their telephones the last time the price rose, but so far the Corneliuses have been able to keep theirs, just as they have kept their villa, which was built before the war, by dint of the salary Cornelius draws as professor of history—a million marks, and more or less adequate to the chances and changes of postwar life. The house is comfortable, even elegant, though sadly in need of repairs that cannot be made for lack of materials, and at present disfigured by iron stoves with long pipes. Even so, it is still the proper setting of the upper middle class, though they themselves look odd enough in it, with their worn and turned clothing and altered way of life. The children, of course, know nothing else; to them it is normal and regular, they belong by birth to the "villa proletariat." The problem of clothing troubles them not at all. They and their like have evolved a costume to fit the time, by poverty out of taste for innovation: in summer it consists of scarcely more than a belted linen smock and sandals. The middle-class parents find things rather more difficult.

The big folk's table-napkins hang over their chair-backs, they talk with their friends over the telephone. These friends are the invited guests who have rung up to accept or decline or arrange; and the conversation is carried on in the jargon of the clan, full of slang and high spirits, of which the old folk understand hardly a word. These consult together meantime about the hospitality to be offered to the impending guests. The Professor displays a middle-class ambitiousness: he wants to serve a sweet—or something that looks like a sweet—after the Italian salad and brownbread sandwiches. But Frau Cornelius says that would be going too far. The guests would not expect it, she is sure—and the big folk, returning once more to their trifle, agree with her.

The mother of the family is of the same general type as Ingrid, though not so tall. She is languid; the fantastic difficulties of the housekeeping have broken and worn her. She really ought to go and take a cure, but feels incapable; the floor is always swaying under her feet, and everything seems upside down. She speaks of what is uppermost in her mind: the eggs, they simply must be bought today. Six thousand marks apiece they are, and just so many are to be had on this one day of the week at one single shop fifteen minutes' journey away. Whatever else they do, the big folk must go and fetch them immediately after luncheon, with Danny, their neighbour's son, who will soon be calling for them; and Xaver Kleinsgutl will don civilian garb and attend his young master and mistress. For no single household is allowed more than five eggs a week; therefore the young people will enter the shop singly, one after another, under assumed names, and thus wring twenty eggs from the shopkeeper for the Cornelius family. This enterprise is the sporting event of the week for all participants, not excepting the moujik Kleinsgutl, and most of all for Ingrid and Bert, who delight in misleading and mystifying their fellow-men and would revel in the performance even if it did not achieve one single egg. They adore impersonating fictitious characters; they love to sit in a bus and carry on long lifelike conversations in a dialect which they otherwise never speak, the most commonplace dialogue about politics and people and the price of food, while the whole bus listens open-mouthed to this incredibly ordinary prattle, though with a dark suspicion all the while that something is wrong somewhere. The conversation waxes ever more shameless, it enters into revolting detail about these people who do not exist. Ingrid can make her voice sound ever so common and twittering and shrill as she impersonates a shop-girl with an illegitimate child, said child being a son with sadistic tendencies, who lately out in the country treated a cow with such unnatural cruelty that no Christian could have borne to see it. Bert nearly explodes at her twittering, but restrains himself and displays a grisly sympathy; he and the unhappy shop-girl entering into a long, stupid, depraved, and shuddery conversation over the particular morbid cruelty involved; until an old gentleman opposite, sitting with his ticket folded between his index finger and his seal ring, can bear it no more and makes public protest against the nature of the themes these young folk are discussing with such particularity. He uses the Greek plural: "themata." Whereat Ingrid pretends to be dissolving in tears, and Bert behaves as though his wrath against the old gentleman was with difficulty being held in check and would probably burst out before long. He clenches his fists, he gnashes his teeth, he shakes from head to foot; and the unhappy old gentleman, whose intentions had been of the best, hastily leaves the bus at the next stop.

Such are the diversions of the big folk. The telephone plays a prominent part in them: they ring up any and everybody—members of government, opera singers, dignitaries of the Church—in the character of shop assistants, or perhaps as Lord or Lady Doolittle. They are only with difficulty persuaded that they have the wrong number. Once they emptied their parents' card-tray and distributed its contents among the neighbours' letter-boxes, wantonly, yet not without enough impish sense of the fitness of things to make it highly upsetting, God only knowing why certain people should have called where they did.

Xaver comes in to clear away, tossing the hair out of his eyes. Now that he has taken off his gloves you can see the yellow chain-ring on his left hand. And as the Professor finishes his watery eight-thousand-mark beer and lights a cigarette, the little folk can be heard scrambling down the stair, coming, by established custom, for their after-dinner call on Father and Mother. They storm the dining-room, after a struggle with the latch, clutched by both pairs of little hands at once; their clumsy small feet twinkle over the carpet, in red felt slippers with the socks falling down on them. With prattle and shoutings each makes for his own place: Snapper to Mother, to climb on her lap, boast of all he has eaten, and thump his fat little tum; Ellie to her Abel, so much hers because she is so very much his; because she consciously luxuriates in the deep tenderness—like all deep feeling, concealing a melancholy strain—with which he holds her small form embraced; in the love in his eyes as he kisses her little fairy hand or the sweet brow with its delicate tracery of tiny blue veins.

The little folk look like each other, with the strong undefined likeness of brother and sister. In clothing and haircut they are twins. Yet they are sharply distinguished after all, and quite on sex lines. It is a little Adam and a little Eve. Not only is Snapper the sturdier and more compact, he appears consciously to emphasize his four-year-old masculinity in speech, manner, and carriage, lifting his shoulders and letting the little arms hang down quite like a young American athlete, drawing down his mouth when he talks and seeking to give his voice a gruff and forthright ring. But all this masculinity is the result of effort rather than natively his. Born and brought up in these desolate, distracted times, he has been endowed by them with an unstable and hypersensitive nervous system and suffers greatly under life's disharmonies. He is prone to sudden anger and outbursts of bitter tears, stamping his feet at every trifle; for this reason he is his mother's special nursling and care. His round, round eyes are chestnut brown and already inclined to squint, so that he will need

Disorder and Early Sorrow

glasses in the near future. His little nose is long, the mouth small—the father's nose and mouth they are, more plainly than ever since the Professor shaved his pointed beard and goes smooth-faced. The pointed beard had become impossible—even professors must make some concession to the changing times.

But the little daughter sits on her father's knee, his Eleonorchen, his little Eve, so much more gracious a little being, so much sweeter-faced than her brother—and he holds his cigarette away from her while she fingers his glasses with her dainty wee hands. The lenses are divided for reading and distance, and each day they tease her curiosity afresh.

At bottom he suspects that his wife's partiality may have a firmer basis than his own: that Snapper's refractory masculinity perhaps is solider stuff than his own little girl's more explicit charm and grace. But the heart will not be commanded, that he knows; and once and for all his heart belongs to the little one, as it has since the day she came, since the first time he saw her. Almost always when he holds her in his arms he remembers that first time: remembers the sunny room in the Women's Hospital, where Ellie first saw the light, twelve years after Bert was born. He remembers how he drew near, the mother smiling the while, and cautiously put aside the canopy of the diminutive bed that stood beside the large one. There lay the little miracle among the pillows: so well formed, so encompassed, as it were, with the harmony of sweet proportions, with little hands that even then, though so much tinier, were beautiful as now; with wide-open eyes blue as the sky and brighter than the sunshine—and almost in that very second he felt himself captured and held fast. This was love at first sight, love everlasting: a feeling unknown, unhoped for, unexpected—in so far as it could be a matter of conscious awareness; it took entire possession of him, and he understood, with joyous amazement, that this was for life.

But he understood more. He knows, does Dr. Cornelius, that there is something not quite right about this feeling, so unaware, so undreamed of, so involuntary. He has a shrewd suspicion that it is not by accident it has so utterly mastered him and bound itself up with his existence; that he had—even subconsciously—been preparing for it, or, more precisely, been prepared for it. There is, in short, something in him which at a given moment was ready to issue in such a feeling; and this something, highly extraordinary to relate, is his essence and quality as a professor of history. Dr. Cornelius, however, does not actually say this, even to himself; he merely realizes it, at odd times, and smiles a private smile. He knows that history professors do not love history because it is something that comes to pass, but only because it is something that *has* come to pass; that they hate a revolution like the present one because they feel it is lawless, incoherent, irrelevant—in a word, unhistoric; that their hearts belong to the coherent, disciplined, historic past. For the temper of timelessness, the temper of eternity—thus the scholar communes with himself when he takes his walk by the river before supper—that temper broods over the past; and it is a temper much better suited to the nervous system of a history professor than are the excesses of the present. The past is immortalized; that is to say, it is dead; and death is the root of all godliness and all abiding significance. Dr. Cornelius, walking alone in the dark, has a profound insight into this truth. It is this conservative instinct of his, his sense of the eternal, that has found in his love for his little daughter a way to save itself from the wounding inflicted by the times. For father love, and a little child on its mother's breast—are not these timeless, and thus very, very holy and beautiful? Yet Cornelius, pondering there in the dark, descries something not perfectly right and good in his love. Theoretically, in the interests of science, he admits it to himself. There is something ulterior about it, in the nature of it; that something is hostility, hostility against the history of today, which is still in the making and thus not history at all, in behalf of the genuine history that has already happened—that is to say, death. Yes, passing strange though all this is, yet it is true; true in a sense, that is. His devotion to this priceless little morsel of life and new growth has something to do with death, it clings to death as against life; and that is neither right nor beautiful—in a sense. Though only the most fanatical asceticism could be capable, on no other ground than such casual scientific perception, of tearing this purest and most precious of feelings out of his heart.

He holds his darling on his lap and her slim rosy legs hang down. He raises his brows as he talks to her, tenderly, with a half-teasing note of respect, and listens enchanted to her high, sweet little voice calling him Abel. He exchanges a look with the mother, who is caressing her Snapper and reading him a gentle lecture. He must be more reasonable, he must learn self-control; today again, under the manifold exasperations of life, he has given way to rage and behaved like a howling dervish. Cornelius casts a mistrustful glance at the big folk now and then, too; he thinks it not unlikely they are not unaware of those scientific preoccupations of his evening walks. If such be the case they do not show it. They stand there leaning their arms on their chair-backs and with a benevolence not untinctured with irony look on at the parental happiness.

The children's frocks are of a heavy, brick-red stuff, embroidered in modern "arty" style. They once belonged to Ingrid and Bert and are precisely alike, save that little knickers come out beneath Snapper's smock. And both have their hair bobbed. Snapper's is a streaky blond, inclined to turn dark. It is bristly and sticky and looks for all the world like a droll, badly fitting wig. But Ellie's is chestnut brown, glossy and fine as silk, as pleasing as her whole little personality. It covers her ears —and these ears are not a pair, one of them being the right size, the other distinctly too large. Her father will sometimes uncover this little ab-

Disorder and Early Sorrow [89]

normality and exclaim over it as though he had never noticed it before, which both makes Ellie giggle and covers her with shame. Her eyes are now golden brown, set far apart and with sweet gleams in them—such a clear and lovely look! The brows above are blond; the nose still unformed, with thick nostrils and almost circular holes; the mouth large and expressive, with a beautifully arching and mobile upper lip. When she laughs, dimples come in her cheeks and she shows her teeth like loosely strung pearls. So far she has lost but one tooth, which her father gently twisted out with his handkerchief after it had grown very wobbling. During this small operation she had paled and trembled very much. Her cheeks have the softness proper to her years, but they are not chubby; indeed, they are rather concave, due to her facial structure, with its somewhat prominent jaw. On one, close to the soft fall of her hair, is a downy freckle.

Ellie is not too well pleased with her looks—a sign that already she troubles about such things. Sadly she thinks it is best to admit it once for all, her face is "homely"; though the rest of her, "on the other hand," is not bad at all. She loves expressions like "on the other hand"; they sound choice and grown-up to her, and she likes to string them together, one after the other: "very likely," "probably," "after all." Snapper is self-critical too, though more in the moral sphere: he suffers from remorse for his attacks of rage and considers himself a tremendous sinner. He is quite certain that heaven is not for such as he; he is sure to go to "the bad place" when he dies, and no persuasions will convince him to the contrary—as that God sees the heart and gladly makes allowances. Obstinately he shakes his head, with the comic, crooked little peruke, and vows there is no place for him in heaven. When he has a cold he is immediately quite choked with mucus; rattles and rumbles from top to toe if you even look at him; his temperature flies up at once and he simply puffs. Nursy is pessimistic on the score of his constitution: such fat-blooded children as he might get a stroke any minute. Once she even thought she saw the moment at hand: Snapper had been in one of his berserker rages, and in the ensuing fit of penitence stood himself in the corner with his back to the room. Suddenly Nursy noticed that his face had gone all blue, far bluer, even, than her own. She raised the alarm, crying out that the child's all too rich blood had at length brought him to his final hour; and Snapper, to his vast astonishment, found himself, so far from being rebuked for evil-doing, encompassed in tenderness and anxiety— until it turned out that his colour was not caused by apoplexy but by the distempering on the nursery wall, which had come off on his tear-wet face.

Nursy has come downstairs too, and stands by the door, sleek-haired, owl-eyed, with her hands folded over her white apron, and a severely dignified manner born of her limited intelligence. She is very proud of the care and training she gives her nurslings and declares that they are "enveloping wonderfully." She has had seventeen suppurated teeth lately removed from her jaws and been measured for a set of symmetrical yellow ones in dark rubber gums; these now embellish her peasant face. She is obsessed with the strange conviction that these teeth of hers are the subject of general conversation, that, as it were, the sparrows on the housetops chatter of them. "Everybody knows I've had a false set put in," she will say; "there has been a great deal of foolish talk about them." She is much given to dark hints and veiled innuendo: speaks, for instance, of a certain Dr. Bleifuss, whom every child knows, and "there are even some in the house who pretend to be him." All one can do with talk like this is charitably to pass it over in silence. But she teaches the children nursery rhymes: gems like:

>"Puff, puff, here comes the train!
>Puff, puff, toot, toot,
>Away it goes again."

Or that gastronomical jingle, so suited, in its sparseness, to the times, and yet seemingly with a blitheness of its own:

>"Monday we begin the week,
>Tuesday there's a bone to pick.
>Wednesday we're half way through,
>Thursday what a great to-do!
>Friday we eat what fish we're able,
>Saturday we dance round the table.
>Sunday brings us pork and greens—
>Here's a feast for kings and queens!"

Also a certain four-line stanza with a romantic appeal, unutterable and unuttered:

>"Open the gate, open the gate
>And let the carriage drive in.
>Who is it in the carriage sits?
>A lordly sir with golden hair."

Or, finally that ballad about golden-haired Marianne who sat on a, sat on a, sat on a stone, and combed out her, combed out her, combed out her hair; and about bloodthirsty Rudolph, who pulled out a, pulled out a, pulled out a knife—and his ensuing direful end. Ellie enunciates all these ballads charmingly, with her mobile little lips, and sings them in her sweet little voice—much better than Snapper. She does everything better than he does, and he pays her honest admiration and homage and obeys her in all things except when visited by one of his attacks. Sometimes she teaches him, instructs him upon the birds in the picture-book and tells him their proper names: "This is a chaffinch, Buddy, this is a bullfinch, this is a cowfinch." He has to repeat them after her. She gives him medical instruction too, teaches him the names of diseases, such as infammation of the lungs, infammation of the blood, infammation of the air. If he does not pay attention and cannot say the words after her, she stands him in the corner. Once she even boxed his ears, but was so ashamed that she stood herself in the corner for a long time. Yes, they are fast friends, two souls with but a single thought, and have all their adventures in common. They come home from a walk and relate as with one voice that they have seen two moolies and a teenty-weenty baby calf. They are on familiar terms with the kitchen, which consists of Xaver and the ladies Hinterhofer, two sisters once of the lower middle class who, in these evil days, are reduced to living *"au pair"* as the phrase goes and officiating as cook and housemaid for their board and keep. The little ones have a feeling that Xaver and the Hinterhofers are on much the same footing with their father and mother as they are themselves. At least sometimes, when they have been scolded, they go downstairs and announce that the master and mistress are cross. But playing with the servants lacks charm compared with the joys of playing upstairs. The kitchen could never rise to the height of the games their father can invent. For instance, there is "four gentlemen taking a walk." When they play it Abel will crook his knees until he is the same height with themselves and go walking with them, hand in hand. They never get enough of this sport; they could walk round and round the dining-room a whole day on end, five gentlemen in all, counting the diminished Abel.

Then there is the thrilling cushion game. One of the children, usually Ellie, seats herself, unbeknownst to Abel, in his seat at table. Still as a mouse she awaits his coming. He draws near with his head in the air, descanting in loud, clear tones upon the surpassing comfort of his chair; and sits down on top of Ellie. "What's this, what's this?" says he. And bounces about, deaf to the smothered giggles exploding behind him. "Why have they put a cushion in my chair? And what a queer, hard, awkward-shaped cushion it is!" he goes on. "Frightfully uncomfortable to sit on!" And keeps pushing and bouncing about more and more on the astonishing cushion and clutching behind him into the rapturous giggling and squeaking, until at last he turns round, and the game ends with a magnificent climax of discovery and recognition. They might go through all this a hundred times without diminishing by an iota its power to thrill.

Today is no time for such joys. The imminent festivity disturbs the atmosphere, and besides there is work to be done, and, above all, the eggs to be got. Ellie has just time to recite "Puff, puff," and Cornelius to discover that her ears are not mates, when they are interrupted by the arrival of Danny, come to fetch Bert and Ingrid. Xaver, meantime, has exchanged his striped livery for an ordinary coat, in which he looks rather rough-and-ready, though as brisk and attractive as ever. So then

Nursy and the children ascend to the upper regions, the Professor withdraws to his study to read, as always after dinner, and his wife bends her energies upon the sandwiches and salad that must be prepared. And she has another errand as well. Before the young people arrive she has to take her shopping-basket and dash into town on her bicycle, to turn into provisions a sum of money she has in hand, which she dares not keep lest it lose all value.

Cornelius reads, leaning back in his chair, with his cigar between his middle and index fingers. First he reads Macaulay on the origin of the English public debt at the end of the seventeenth century; then an article in a French periodical on the rapid increase in the Spanish debt towards the end of the sixteenth. Both these for his lecture on the morrow. He intends to compare the astonishing prosperity which accompanied the phenomenon in England with its fatal effects a hundred years earlier in Spain, and to analyse the ethical and psychological grounds of the difference in results. For that will give him a chance to refer back from the England of William III, which is the actual subject in hand, to the time of Philip II and the Counter-Reformation, which is his own special field. He has already written a valuable work on this period; it is much cited and got him his professorship. While his cigar burns down and gets strong, he excogitates a few pensive sentences in a key of gentle melancholy, to be delivered before his class next day: about the practically hopeless struggle carried on by the belated Philip against the whole trend of history: against the new, the kingdom-disrupting power of the Germanic ideal of freedom and individual liberty. And about the persistent, futile struggle of the aristocracy, condemned by God and rejected of man, against the forces of progress and change. He savours his sentences; keeps on polishing them while he puts back the books he has been using; then goes upstairs for the usual pause in his day's work, the hour with drawn blinds and closed eyes, which he so imperatively needs. But today, he recalls, he will rest under disturbed conditions, amid the bustle of preparations for the feast. He smiles to find his heart giving a mild flutter at the thought. Disjointed phrases on the theme of black-clad Philip and his times mingle with a confused consciousness that they will soon be dancing down below. For five minutes or so he falls asleep.

As he lies and rests he can hear the sound of the garden gate and the repeated ringing at the bell. Each time a little pang goes through him, of excitement and suspense, at the thought that the young people have begun to fill the floor below. And each time he smiles at himself again—though even his smile is slightly nervous, is tinged with the pleasurable anticipations people always feel before a party. At half past four—it is already dark—he gets up and washes at the wash-stand. The basin has been out of repair for two years. It is supposed to tip, but

Disorder and Early Sorrow [93]

has broken away from its socket on one side and cannot be mended because there is nobody to mend it; neither replaced because no shop can supply another. So it has to be hung up above the vent and emptied by lifting in both hands and pouring out the water. Cornelius shakes his head over this basin, as he does several times a day—whenever, in fact, he has occasion to use it. He finishes his toilet with care, standing under the ceiling light to polish his glasses till they shine. Then he goes downstairs.

On his way to the dining-room he hears the gramophone already going, and the sound of voices. He puts on a polite, society air; at his tongue's end is the phrase he means to utter: "Pray don't let me disturb you," as he passes directly into the dining-room for his tea. "Pray don't let me disturb you"—it seems to him precisely the *mot juste;* towards the guests cordial and considerate, for himself a very bulwark.

The lower floor is lighted up, all the bulbs in the chandelier are burning save one that has burned out. Cornelius pauses on a lower step and surveys the entrance hall. It looks pleasant and cosy in the bright light, with its copy of Marées over the brick chimney-piece, its wainscoted walls—wainscoted in soft wood—and red-carpeted floor, where the guests stand in groups, chatting, each with his tea-cup and slice of bread-and-butter spread with anchovy paste. There is a festal haze, faint scents of hair and clothing and human breath come to him across the room, it is all characteristic and familiar and highly evocative. The door into the dressing-room is open, guests are still arriving.

A large group of people is rather bewildering at first sight. The Professor takes in only the general scene. He does not see Ingrid, who is standing just at the foot of the steps, in a dark silk frock with a pleated collar falling softly over the shoulders, and bare arms. She smiles up at him, nodding and showing her lovely teeth.

"Rested?" she asks, for his private ear. With a quite unwarranted start he recognizes her, and she presents some of her friends.

"May I introduce Herr Zuber?" she says. "And this is Fräulein Plaichinger."

Herr Zuber is insignificant. But Fräulein Plaichinger is a perfect Germania, blond and voluptuous, arrayed in floating draperies. She has a snub nose, and answers the Professor's salutation in the high, shrill pipe so many stout women have.

"Delighted to meet you," he says. "How nice of you to come! A classmate of Ingrid's, I suppose?"

And Herr Zuber is a golfing partner of Ingrid's. He is in business; he works in his uncle's brewery. Cornelius makes a few jokes about the thinness of the beer and professes to believe that Herr Zuber could easily do something about the quality if he would. "But pray don't let me disturb you," he goes on, and turns towards the dining-room.

"There comes Max," says Ingrid. "Max, you sweep, what do you mean by rolling up at this time of day?" For such is the way they talk to each other, offensively to an older ear; of social forms, of hospitable warmth, there is no faintest trace. They all call each other by their first names.

A young man comes up to them out of the dressing-room and makes his bow; he has an expanse of white shirt-front and a little black string tie. He is as pretty as a picture, dark, with rosy cheeks, clean-shaven of course, but with just a sketch of side-whisker. Not a ridiculous or flashy beauty, not like a gypsy fiddler, but just charming to look at, in a winning, well-bred way, with kind dark eyes. He even wears his dinner-jacket a little awkwardly.

"Please don't scold me, Cornelia," he says; "it's the idiotic lectures." And Ingrid presents him to her father as Herr Hergesell.

Well, and so this is Herr Hergesell. He knows his manners, does Herr Hergesell, and thanks the master of the house quite ingratiatingly for his invitation as they shake hands. "I certainly seem to have missed the bus," says he jocosely. "Of course I have lectures today up to four o'clock; I would have; and after that I had to go home to change." Then he talks about his pumps, with which he has just been struggling in the dressing-room.

"I brought them with me in a bag," he goes on. "Mustn't tramp all over the carpet in our brogues—it's not done. Well, I was ass enough not to fetch along a shoe-horn, and I find I simply can't get in! What a sell! They are the tightest I've ever had, the numbers don't tell you a thing, and all the leather today is just cast iron. It's not leather at all. My poor finger"—he confidingly displays a reddened digit and once more characterizes the whole thing as a "sell," and a putrid sell into the bargain. He really does talk just as Ingrid said he did, with a peculiar nasal drawl, not affectedly in the least, but merely because that is the way of all the Hergesells.

Dr. Cornelius says it is very careless of them not to keep a shoe-horn in the cloak-room and displays proper sympathy with the mangled finger. "But now you *really* must not let me disturb you any longer," he goes on. "*Auf wiedersehen!*" And he crosses the hall into the dining-room.

There are guests there too, drinking tea; the family table is pulled out. But the Professor goes at once to his own little upholstered corner with the electric light bulb above it—the nook where he usually drinks his tea. His wife is sitting there talking with Bert and two other young men, one of them Herzl, whom Cornelius knows and greets; the other a typical "Wandervogel" named Möller, a youth who obviously neither owns nor cares to own the correct evening dress of the middle classes (in fact, there is no such thing any more), nor to ape the manners of a gentleman (and, in fact, there is no such thing any more either). He has a wilderness of hair, horn spectacles, and a long neck, and wears golf stockings and a belted blouse. His regular occupation, the Professor learns, is banking, but he is by way of being an amateur folk-lorist and collects folk-songs from all localities and in all languages. He sings them, too, and at Ingrid's command has brought his guitar; it is hanging in the dressing-room in an oilcloth case. Herzl, the actor, is small and slight, but he has a strong growth of black beard, as you can tell by the thick coat of powder on his cheeks. His eyes are larger than life, with a deep and melancholy glow. He has put on rouge besides the powder—those dull carmine high-lights on the cheeks can be nothing but a cosmetic. "Queer," thinks the Professor. "You would think a man would be one thing or the other—not melancholic and use face paint at the same time. It's a psychological contradiction. How can a melancholy man rouge? But here we have a perfect illustration of the abnormality of the artist soul-form. It can make possible a contradiction like this—perhaps it even consists in the contradiction. All very interesting—and no reason whatever for not being polite to him. Politeness is a primitive convention—and legitimate. . . . Do take some lemon, Herr Hofschauspieler!"

Court actors and court theatres—there are no such things any more, really. But Herzl relishes the sound of the title, notwithstanding he is a revolutionary artist. This must be another contradiction inherent in his soul-form; so, at least, the Professor assumes, and he is probably right. The flattery he is guilty of is a sort of atonement for his previous hard thoughts about the rouge.

"Thank you so much—it's really too good of you, sir," says Herzl, quite embarrassed. He is so overcome that he almost stammers; only his perfect enunciation saves him. His whole bearing towards his hostess and the master of the house is exaggeratedly polite. It is almost as though he had a bad conscience in respect of his rouge; as though an inward compulsion had driven him to put it on, but now, seeing it through the Professor's eyes, he disapproves of it himself, and thinks, by an air of humility towards the whole of unrouged society, to mitigate its effect.

They drink their tea and chat: about Möller's folk-songs, about Basque folk-songs and Spanish folk-songs; from which they pass to the new production of *Don Carlos* at the Stadttheater, in which Herzl plays the title-rôle. He talks about his own rendering of the part and says he hopes his conception of the character has unity. They go on to criticize the rest of the cast, the setting, and the production as a whole; and Cornelius is struck, rather painfully, to find the conversation trending towards his own special province, back to Spain and the Counter-Reformation. He has done nothing at all to give it this turn, he is perfectly innocent, and hopes it does not look as though he had sought an occasion to play the professor. He wonders, and falls silent, feeling relieved when the little folk come up to the table. Ellie and Snapper have on their blue velvet

Sunday frocks; they are permitted to partake in the festivities up to bedtime. They look shy and large-eyed as they say how-do-you-do to the strangers and, under pressure, repeat their names and ages. Herr Möller does nothing but gaze at them solemnly, but Herzl is simply ravished. He rolls his eyes up to heaven and puts his hands over his mouth; he positively blesses them. It all, no doubt, comes from his heart, but he is so addicted to theatrical methods of making an impression and getting an effect that both words and behaviour ring frightfully false. And even his enthusiasm for the little folk looks too much like part of his general craving to make up for the rouge on his cheeks.

The tea-table has meanwhile emptied of guests, and dancing is going on in the hall. The children run off, the Professor prepares to retire. "Go and enjoy yourselves," he says to Möller and Herzl, who have sprung from their chairs as he rises from his. They shake hands and he withdraws into his study, his peaceful kingdom, where he lets down the blinds, turns on the desk lamp, and sits down to his work.

It is work which can be done, if necessary, under disturbed conditions: nothing but a few letters and a few notes. Of course, Cornelius's mind wanders. Vague impressions float through it: Herr Hergesell's refractory pumps, the high pipe in that plump body of the Plaichinger female. As he writes, or leans back in his chair and stares into space, his thoughts go back to Herr Möller's collection of Basque folk-songs, to Herzl's posings and humility, to "his" Carlos and the court of Philip II. There is something strange, he thinks, about conversations. They are so ductile, they will flow of their own accord in the direction of one's dominating interest. Often and often he has seen this happen. And while he is thinking, he is listening to the sounds next door—rather subdued, he finds them. He hears only voices, no sound of footsteps. The dancers do not glide or circle round the room; they merely walk about over the carpet, which does not hamper their movements in the least. Their way of holding each other is quite different and strange, and they move to the strains of the gramophone, to the weird music of the new world. He concentrates on the music and makes out that it is a jazz-band record, with various percussion instruments and the clack and clatter of castanets, which, however, are not even faintly suggestive of Spain, but merely jazz like the rest. No, not Spain. . . . His thoughts are back at their old round.

Half an hour goes by. It occurs to him it would be no more than friendly to go and contribute a box of cigarettes to the festivities next door. Too bad to ask the young people to smoke their own—though they have probably never thought of it. He goes into the empty dining-room and takes a box from his supply in the cupboard: not the best ones, nor yet the brand he himself prefers, but a certain long, thin kind he is not averse to getting rid of—after all, they are nothing but youngsters. He

Disorder and Early Sorrow

takes the box into the hall, holds it up with a smile, and deposits it on the mantel-shelf. After which he gives a look round and returns to his own room.

There comes a lull in dance and music. The guests stand about the room in groups or round the table at the window or are seated in a circle by the fireplace. Even the built-in stairs, with their worn velvet carpet, are crowded with young folk as in an amphitheatre: Max Hergesell is there, leaning back with one elbow on the step above and gesticulating with his free hand as he talks to the shrill, voluptuous Plaichinger. The floor of the hall is nearly empty, save just in the centre: there, directly beneath the chandelier, the two little ones in their blue velvet frocks clutch each other in an awkward embrace and twirl silently round and round, oblivious of all else. Cornelius, as he passes, strokes their hair, with a friendly word; it does not distract them from their small solemn preoccupation. But at his own door he turns to glance round and sees young Hergesell push himself off the stair by his elbow—probably because he noticed the Professor. He comes down into the arena, takes Ellie out of her brother's arms, and dances with her himself. It looks very comic, without the music, and he crouches down just as Cornelius does when he goes walking with the four gentlemen, holding the fluttered Ellie as though she were grown up and taking little "shimmying" steps. Everybody watches with huge enjoyment, the gramophone is put on again, dancing becomes general. The Professor stands and looks, with his hand on the door-knob. He nods and laughs; when he finally shuts himself into his study the mechanical smile still lingers on his lips.

Again he turns over pages by his desk lamp, takes notes, attends to a few simple matters. After a while he notices that the guests have forsaken the entrance hall for his wife's drawing-room, into which there is a door from his own study as well. He hears their voices and the sounds of a guitar being tuned. Herr Möller, it seems, is to sing—and does so. He twangs the strings of his instrument and sings in a powerful bass a ballad in a strange tongue, possibly Swedish. The Professor does not succeed in identifying it, though he listens attentively to the end, after which there is great applause. The sound is deadened by the portière that hangs over the dividing door. The young bank-clerk begins another song. Cornelius goes softly in.

It is half-dark in the drawing-room; the only light is from the shaded standard lamp, beneath which Möller sits, on the divan, with his legs crossed, picking his strings. His audience is grouped easily about; as there are not enough seats, some stand, and more, among them many young ladies, are simply sitting on the floor with their hands clasped round their knees or even with their legs stretched out before them. Hergesell sits thus, in his dinner-jacket, next the piano, with Fräulein Plaichinger beside him. Frau Cornelius is holding both children on her lap as she sits in her easy-chair opposite the singer. Snapper, the Bœotian, begins to talk loud and clear in the middle of the song and has to be intimidated with hushings and finger-shakings. Never, never would Ellie allow herself to be guilty of such conduct. She sits there daintily erect and still on her mother's knee. The Professor tries to catch her eye and exchange a private signal with his little girl; but she does not see him. Neither does she seem to be looking at the singer. Her gaze is directed lower down.

Möller sings the "joli tambour":

> "Sire, mon roi, donnez-moi votre
> fille—"

They are all enchanted. "How good!" Hergesell is heard to say, in the odd, nasally condescending Hergesell tone. The next one is a beggar ballad, to a tune composed by young Möller himself; it elicits a storm of applause:

> "Gypsy lassie a-goin' to the fair,
> Huzza!
> Gypsy laddie a-goin' to be there—
> Huzza, diddlety umpty dido!"

Laughter and high spirits, sheer reckless hilarity, reigns after this jovial ballad. "Frightfully good!" Hergesell comments again, as before. Follows another popular song, this time a Hungarian one; Möller sings it in its own outlandish tongue, and most effectively. The Professor applauds with ostentation. It warms his heart and does him good, this outcropping of artistic, historic, and cultural elements all amongst the shimmying. He goes up to young Möller and congratulates him, talks about the songs and their sources, and Möller promises to lend him a certain annotated book of folk-songs. Cornelius is the more cordial because all the time, as fathers do, he has been comparing the parts and achievements of this young stranger with those of his own son, and being gnawed by envy and chagrin. This young Möller, he is thinking, is a capable bank-clerk (though about Möller's capacity he knows nothing whatever) and has this special gift besides, which must have taken talent and energy to cultivate. "And here is my poor Bert, who knows nothing and can do nothing and thinks of nothing except playing the clown, without even talent for that!" He tries to be just; he tells himself that, after all, Bert has innate refinement; that probably there is a good deal more to him than there is to the successful Möller; that perhaps he has even something of the poet in him, and his dancing and table-waiting are due to mere boyish folly and the distraught times. But paternal envy and pessimism win the upper hand; when Möller begins another song, Dr. Cornelius goes back to his room.

He works as before, with divided attention, at this and that, while it gets on for seven o'clock. Then he remembers a letter he may just as well write, a short letter and not very important, but letter-writing is wonderful for the way it takes up the time, and it is almost half past when he has finished. At half past eight the Italian salad will be served; so now is the prescribed moment for the Professor to go out into the wintry darkness to post his letters and take his daily quantum of fresh air and exercise. They are dancing again, and he will have to pass through the hall to get his hat and coat; but they are used to him now, he need not stop and beg them not to be disturbed. He lays away his papers, takes up the letters he has written, and goes out. But he sees his wife sitting near the door of his room and pauses a little by her easy-chair.

She is watching the dancing. Now and then the big folk or some of their guests stop to speak to her; the party is at its height, and there are more onlookers than these two: blue-faced Ann is standing at the bottom of the stairs, in all the dignity of her limitations. She is waiting for the children, who simply cannot get their fill of these unwonted festivities, and watching over Snapper, lest his all too rich blood be churned to the danger-point by too much twirling round. And not only the nursery but the kitchen takes an interest: Xaver and the two ladies Hinterhofer are standing by the pantry door looking on with relish. Fräulein Walburga, the elder of the two sunken sisters (the culinary section—she objects to being called a cook), is a whimsical, good-natured sort, brown-eyed, wearing glasses with thick circular lenses; the nose-piece is wound with a bit of rag to keep it from pressing on her nose. Fräulein Cecilia is younger, though not so precisely young either. Her bearing is as self-assertive as usual, this being her way of sustaining her dignity as a former member of the middle class. For Fräulein Cecilia feels acutely her descent into the ranks of domestic service. She positively declines to wear a cap or other badge of servitude, and her hardest trial is on the Wednesday evening when she has to serve the dinner while Xaver has his afternoon out. She hands the dishes with averted face and elevated nose—a fallen queen; and so distressing is it to behold her degradation that one evening when the little folk happened to be at table and saw her they both with one accord burst into tears. Such anguish is unknown to young Xaver. He enjoys serving and does it with an ease born of practice as well as talent, for he was once a "piccolo." But otherwise he is a thorough-paced good-for-nothing and windbag—with quite distinct traits of character of his own, as his long-suffering employers are always ready to concede, but perfectly impossible and a bag of wind for all that. One must just take him as he is, they think, and not expect figs from thistles. He is the child and product of the disrupted times, a perfect specimen of his generation, follower of the revolution, Bolshevist sympathizer. The Professor's name for him is the "minute-man," because he is always to be counted on in any sudden crisis, if only it address his sense of humour or love of novelty, and will display therein amazing readiness and resource. But he utterly lacks a sense of duty and can as little be trained to the performance of the daily round and common task as some kinds of dog can be taught to jump over a stick. It goes so plainly against the grain that criticism is disarmed. One becomes resigned. On grounds that appealed to him as unusual and amusing he would be ready to turn out of his bed at any hour of the night. But he simply cannot get up before eight in the morning, he cannot do it, he will not jump over the stick. Yet all day long the evidence of this free and untrammelled existence, the sound of his mouth-organ, his joyous whistle, or his raucous but expressive voice lifted in song, rises to the hearing of the world above-stairs; and the smoke of his cigarettes fills the pantry. While the Hinterhofer ladies work he stands and looks on. Of a morning while the Professor is breakfasting, he tears the leaf off the study calendar—but does not lift a finger to dust the room. Dr. Cornelius has often told him to leave the calendar alone, for he tends to tear off two leaves at a time and thus to add to the general confusion. But young Xaver appears to find joy in this activity, and will not be deprived of it.

Again, he is fond of children, a winning trait. He will throw himself into games with the little folk in the garden, make and mend their toys with great ingenuity, even read aloud from their books—and very droll it sounds in his thick-lipped pronunciation. With his whole soul he loves the cinema; after an evening spent there he inclines to melancholy and yearning and talking to himself. Vague hopes stir in him that some day he may make his fortune in that gay world and belong to it by rights—hopes based on his shock of hair and his physical agility and daring. He likes to climb the ash tree in the front garden, mounting branch by branch to the very top and frightening everybody to death who sees him. Once there he lights a cigarette and smokes it as he sways to and fro, keeping a look-out for a cinema director who might chance to come along and engage him.

If he changed his striped jacket for mufti, he might easily dance with the others and no one would notice the difference. For the big folk's friends are rather anomalous in their clothing: evening dress is worn by a few, but it is by no means the rule. There is quite a sprinkling of guests, both male and female, in the same general style as Möller the ballad-singer. The Professor is familiar with the circumstances of most of this young generation he is watching as he stands beside his wife's chair; he has heard them spoken of by name. They are students at the high school or at the School of Applied Art; they lead, at least the masculine portion, that precarious and scrambling existence which is purely the product of the time. There is a tall, pale, spindling youth, the son of a dentist, who lives by speculation. From all the Professor hears, he is a perfect Aladdin. He keeps a car, treats his friends to champagne suppers,

Disorder and Early Sorrow [101]

and showers presents upon them on every occasion, costly little trifles in mother-of-pearl and gold. So today he has brought gifts to the young givers of the feast: for Bert a gold lead-pencil, and for Ingrid a pair of earrings of barbaric size, great gold circlets that fortunately do not have to go through the little ear-lobe, but are fastened over it by means of a clip. The big folk come laughing to their parents to display these trophies; and the parents shake their heads even while they admire—Aladdin bowing over and over from afar.

The young people appear to be absorbed in their dancing—if the performance they are carrying out with so much still concentration can be called dancing. They stride across the carpet, slowly, according to some unfathomable prescript, strangely embraced; in the newest attitude, tummy advanced and shoulders high, waggling the hips. They do not get tired, because nobody could. There is no such thing as heightened colour or heaving bosoms. Two girls may dance together or two young men—it is all the same. They move to the exotic strains of the gramophone, played with the loudest needles to procure the maximum of sound: shimmies, foxtrots, one-steps, double foxes, African shimmies, Java dances, and Creole polkas, the wild musky melodies follow one another, now furious, now languishing, a monotonous Negro programme in unfamiliar rhythm, to a clacking, clashing, and strumming orchestral accompaniment.

"What is that record?" Cornelius inquires of Ingrid, as she passes him by in the arms of the pale young speculator, with reference to the piece then playing, whose alternate languors and furies he finds comparatively pleasing and showing a certain resourcefulness in detail.

"*Prince of Pappenheim:* 'Console thee, dearest child,' " she answers, and smiles pleasantly back at him with her white teeth.

The cigarette smoke wreathes beneath the chandelier. The air is blue with a festal haze compact of sweet and thrilling ingredients that stir the blood with memories of green-sick pains and are particularly poignant to those whose youth—like the Professor's own—has been oversensitive. . . . The little folk are still on the floor. They are allowed to stay up until eight, so great is their delight in the party. The guests have got used to their presence; in their own way, they have their place in the doings of the evening. They have separated, anyhow: Snapper revolves all alone in the middle of the carpet, in his little blue velvet smock, while Ellie is running after one of the dancing couples, trying to hold the man fast by his coat. It is Max Hergesell and Fräulein Plaichinger. They dance well, it is a pleasure to watch them. One has to admit that these mad modern dances, when the right people dance them, are not so bad after all—they have something quite taking. Young Hergesell is a capital leader, dances according to rule, yet with individuality. So it looks. With what aplomb can he walk backwards—when space permits! And he knows how to be graceful standing still in a crowd. And his partner supports him well, being unsuspectedly lithe and buoyant, as fat people often are. They look at each other, they are talking, paying no heed to Ellie, though others are smiling to see the child's persistence. Dr. Cornelius tries to catch up his little sweetheart as she passes and draw her to him. But Ellie eludes him, almost peevishly; her dear Abel is nothing to her now. She braces her little arms against his chest and turns her face away with a persecuted look. Then escapes to follow her fancy once more.

The Professor feels an involuntary twinge. Uppermost in his heart is hatred for this party, with its power to intoxicate and estrange his darling child. His love for her—that not quite disinterested, not quite unexceptionable love of his—is easily wounded. He wears a mechanical smile, but his eyes have clouded, and he stares fixedly at a point in the carpet, between the dancers' feet.

"The children ought to go to bed," he tells his wife. But she pleads for another quarter of an hour; she has promised already, and they do love it so! He smiles again and shakes his head, stands so a moment and then goes across to the cloak-room, which is full of coats and hats and scarves and overshoes. He has trouble in rummaging out his own coat, and Max Hergesell comes out of the hall, wiping his brow.

"Going out, sir?" he asks, in Hergesellian accents, dutifully helping the older man on with his coat. "Silly business this, with my pumps," he says. "They pinch like hell. The brutes are simply too tight for me, quite apart from the bad leather. They press just here on the ball of my great toe"—he stands on one foot and holds the other in his hand—"it's simply unbearable. There's nothing for it but to take them off; my brogues will have to do the business. . . . Oh, let me help you, sir."

"Thanks," says Cornelius. "Don't trouble. Get rid of your own tormentors. . . . Oh, thanks very much!" For Hergesell has gone on one knee to snap the fasteners of his snow-boots.

Once more the Professor expresses his gratitude; he is pleased and touched by so much sincere respect and youthful readiness to serve. "Go and enjoy yourself," he counsels. "Change your shoes and make up for what you have been suffering. Nobody can dance in shoes that pinch. Good-bye, I must be off to get a breath of fresh air."

"I'm going to dance with Ellie now," calls Hergesell after him. "She'll be a first-rate dancer when she grows up, and that I'll swear to."

"Think so?" Cornelius answers, already half out. "Well, you are a connoisseur, I'm sure. Don't get curvature of the spine with stooping."

He nods again and goes. "Fine lad," he thinks as he shuts the door. "Student of engineering. Knows what he's bound for, got a good clear head, and so well set up and pleasant too." And again paternal envy rises as he compares his poor Bert's status with this young man's, which he puts in the rosiest light that his son's may look the darker. Thus he sets out on his evening walk.

He goes up the avenue, crosses the bridge, and walks along the bank on the other side as far as the next bridge but one. The air is wet and cold, with a little snow now and then. He turns up his coat-collar and slips the crook of his cane over the arm behind his back. Now and then he ventilates his lungs with a long deep breath of the night air. As usual when he walks, his mind reverts to his professional preoccupations, he thinks about his lectures and the things he means to say tomorrow about Philip's struggle against the Germanic revolution, things steeped in melancholy and penetratingly just. Above all just, he thinks. For in one's dealings with the young it behoves one to display the scientific spirit, to exhibit the principles of enlightenment—not only for purposes of mental discipline, but on the human and individual side, in order not to wound them or indirectly offend their political sensibilities; particularly in these days, when there is so much tinder in the air, opinions are so frightfully split up and chaotic, and you may so easily incur attacks from one party or the other, or even give rise to scandal, by taking sides on a point of history. "And taking sides is unhistoric anyhow," so he muses. "Only justice, only impartiality is historic." And could not, properly considered, be otherwise. . . . For justice can have nothing of youthful fire and blithe, fresh, loyal conviction. It is by nature melancholy. And, being so, has secret affinity with the lost cause and the forlorn hope rather than with the fresh and blithe and loyal—perhaps this affinity is its very essence and without it it would not exist at all! . . . "And is there then no such thing as justice?" the Professor asks himself, and ponders the question so deeply that he absently posts his letters in the next box and turns round to go home. This thought of his is unsettling and disturbing to the scientific mind—but is it not after all itself scientific, psychological, conscientious, and therefore to be accepted without prejudice, no matter how upsetting? In the midst of which musings Dr. Cornelius finds himself back at his own door.

On the outer threshold stands Xaver, and seems to be looking for him.

"Herr Professor," says Xaver, tossing back his hair, "go upstairs to Ellie straight off. She's in a bad way."

"What's the matter?" asks Cornelius in alarm. "Is she ill?"

"No-o, not to say ill," answers Xaver. "She's just in a bad way and crying fit to bust her little heart. It's along o' that chap with the shirt-front that danced with her—Herr Hergesell. She couldn't be got to go upstairs peaceably, not at no price at all, and she's b'en crying bucketfuls."

"Nonsense," says the Professor, who has entered and is tossing off his things in the cloak-room. He says no more; opens the glass door and without a glance at the guests turns swiftly to the stairs. Takes them two at a time, crosses the upper hall and the small room leading into the nursery. Xaver follows at his heels, but stops at the nursery door.

A bright light still burns within, showing the gay frieze that runs all round the room, the large row of shelves heaped with a confusion of toys, the rocking-horse on his swaying platform, with red-varnished nostrils and raised hoofs. On the linoleum lie other toys—building blocks, railway trains, a little trumpet. The two white cribs stand not far apart, Ellie's in the window corner, Snapper's out in the room.

Snapper is asleep. He has said his prayers in loud, ringing tones, prompted by Nurse, and gone off at once into vehement, profound, and rosy slumber—from which a cannon-ball fired at close range could not rouse him. He lies with both fists flung back on the pillows on either side of the tousled head with its funny crooked little slumber-tossed wig.

A circle of females surrounds Ellie's bed: not only blue-faced Ann is there, but the Hinterhofer ladies too, talking to each other and to her. They make way as the Professor comes up and reveal the child sitting all pale among her pillows, sobbing and weeping more bitterly than he has ever seen her sob and weep in her life. Her lovely little hands lie on the coverlet in front of her, the nightgown with its narrow lace border has slipped down from her shoulder—such a thin, birdlike little shoulder —and the sweet head Cornelius loves so well, set on the neck like a flower on its stalk, her head is on one side, with the eyes rolled up to the corner between wall and ceiling above her head. For there she seems to envisage the anguish of her heart and even to nod to it—either on purpose or because her head wobbles as her body is shaken with the violence of her sobs. Her eyes rain down tears. The bow-shaped lips are parted, like a little *mater dolorosa's,* and from them issue long, low wails that in nothing resemble the unnecessary and exasperating shrieks of a naughty child, but rise from the deep extremity of her heart and wake in the Professor's own a sympathy that is well-nigh intolerable. He has never seen his darling so before. His feelings find immediate vent in an attack on the ladies Hinterhofer.

"What about the supper?" he asks sharply. "There must be a great deal to do. Is my wife being left to do it alone?"

For the acute sensibilities of the former middle class this is quite enough. The ladies withdraw in righteous indignation, and Xaver Kleingutl jeers at them as they pass out. Having been born to low life instead of achieving it, he never loses a chance to mock at their fallen state.

"Childie, childie," murmurs Cornelius, and sitting down by the crib enfolds the anguished Ellie in his arms. "What is the trouble with my darling?"

She bedews his face with her tears.

"Abel . . . Abel . . ." she stammers between sobs. "Why—isn't Max —my brother? Max ought to be—my brother!"

Alas, alas! What mischance is this? Is this what the party has wrought, with its fatal atmosphere? Cornelius glances helplessly up at blue-faced

Disorder and Early Sorrow

Ann standing there in all the dignity of her limitations with her hands before her on her apron. She purses up her mouth and makes a long face. "It's pretty young," she says, "for the female instincts to be showing up."

"Hold your tongue," snaps Cornelius, in his agony. He has this much to be thankful for, that Ellie does not turn from him now; she does not push him away as she did downstairs, but clings to him in her need, while she reiterates her absurd, bewildered prayer that Max might be her brother, or with a fresh burst of desire demands to be taken downstairs so that he can dance with her again. But Max, of course, is dancing with Fräulein Plaichinger, that behemoth who is his rightful partner and has every claim upon him; whereas Ellie—never, thinks the Professor, his heart torn with the violence of his pity, never has she looked so tiny and birdlike as now, when she nestles to him shaken with sobs and all unaware of what is happening in her little soul. No, she does not know. She does not comprehend that her suffering is on account of Fräulein Plaichinger, fat, overgrown, and utterly within her rights in dancing with Max Hergesell, whereas Ellie may only do it once, by way of a joke, although she is incomparably the more charming of the two. Yet it would be quite mad to reproach young Hergesell with the state of affairs or to make fantastic demands upon him. No, Ellie's suffering is without help or healing and must be covered up. Yet just as it is without understanding, so it is also without restraint—and that is what makes it so horribly painful. Xaver and blue-faced Ann do not feel this pain, it does not affect them—either because of native callousness or because they accept it as the way of nature. But the Professor's fatherly heart is quite torn by it, and by a distressful horror of this passion, so hopeless and so absurd.

Of no avail to hold forth to poor Ellie on the subject of the perfectly good little brother she already has. She only casts a distraught and scornful glance over at the other crib, where Snapper lies vehemently slumbering, and with fresh tears calls again for Max. Of no avail either the promise of a long, long walk tomorrow, all five gentlemen, round and round the dining-room table; or a dramatic description of the thrilling cushion games they will play. No, she will listen to none of all this, nor to lying down and going to sleep. She will not sleep, she will sit bolt upright and suffer. . . . But on a sudden they stop and listen, Abel and Ellie; listen to something miraculous that is coming to pass, that is approaching by strides, two strides, to the nursery door, that now overwhelmingly appears. . . .

It is Xaver's work, not a doubt of that. He has not remained by the door where he stood to gloat over the ejection of the Hinterhofers. No, he has bestirred himself, taken a notion; likewise steps to carry it out. Downstairs he has gone, twitched Herr Hergesell's sleeve, and made a thick-lipped request. So here they both are. Xaver, having done his part, remains by the door; but Max Hergesell comes up to Ellie's crib; in his dinner-jacket, with his sketchy side-whisker and charming black eyes; obviously quite pleased with his rôle of swan knight and fairy prince, as one who should say: "See, here am I, now all losses are restored and sorrows end!"

Cornelius is almost as much overcome as Ellie herself.

"Just look," he says feebly, "look who's here. This is uncommonly good of you, Herr Hergesell."

"Not a bit of it," says Hergesell. "Why shouldn't I come to say goodnight to my fair partner?"

And he approaches the bars of the crib, behind which Ellie sits struck mute. She smiles blissfully through her tears. A funny, high little note that is half a sigh of relief comes from her lips, then she looks dumbly up at her swan knight with her golden-brown eyes—tear-swollen though they are, so much more beautiful than the fat Plaichinger's. She does not put up her arms. Her joy, like her grief, is without understanding; but she does not do that. The lovely little hands lie quiet on the coverlet, and Max Hergesell stands with his arms leaning over the rail as on a balcony.

"And now," he says smartly, "she need not 'sit the livelong night and weep upon her bed'!" He looks at the Professor to make sure he is receiving due credit for the quotation. "Ha ha!" he laughs, "she's beginning young. 'Console thee, dearest child!' Never mind, you're all right! Just as you are you'll be wonderful! You've only got to grow up. . . . And you'll lie down and go to sleep like a good girl, now I've come to say good-night? And not cry any more, little Lorelei?"

Ellie looks up at him, transfigured. One birdlike shoulder is bare; the Professor draws the lace-trimmed nighty over it. There comes into his mind a sentimental story he once read about a dying child who longs to see a clown he had once, with unforgettable ecstasy, beheld in a circus. And they bring the clown to the bedside marvellously arrayed, embroidered before and behind with silver butterflies; and the child dies happy. Max Hergesell is not embroidered, and Ellie, thank God, is not going to die, she has only been "in a bad way." But, after all, the effect is the same. Young Hergesell leans over the bars of the crib and rattles on, more for the father's ear than the child's, but Ellie does not know that—and the father's feelings towards him are a most singular mixture of thankfulness, embarrassment, and hatred.

"Good night, little Lorelei," says Hergesell, and gives her his hand through the bars. Her pretty, soft, white little hand is swallowed up in the grasp of his big, strong, red one. "Sleep well," he says, "and sweet dreams! But don't dream about me—God forbid! Not at your age—ha ha!" And then the fairy clown's visit is at an end. Cornelius accompanies him

Disorder and Early Sorrow

to the door. "No, no, positively, no thanks called for, don't mention it," he large-heartedly protests; and Xaver goes downstairs with him, to help serve the Italian salad.

But Dr. Cornelius returns to Ellie, who is now lying down, with her cheek pressed into her flat little pillow.

"Well, wasn't that lovely?" he says as he smooths the covers. She nods, with one last little sob. For a quarter of an hour he sits beside her and watches while she falls asleep in her turn, beside the little brother who found the right way so much earlier than she. Her silky brown hair takes the enchanting fall it always does when she sleeps; deep, deep lie the lashes over the eyes that late so abundantly poured forth their sorrow; the angelic mouth with its bowed upper lip is peacefully relaxed and a little open. Only now and then comes a belated catch in her slow breathing.

And her small hands, like pink and white flowers, lie so quietly, one on the coverlet, the other on the pillow by her face—Dr. Cornelius, gazing, feels his heart melt with tenderness as with strong wine.

"How good," he thinks, "that she breathes in oblivion with every breath she draws! That in childhood each night is a deep wide gulf between one day and the next. Tomorrow, beyond all doubt, young Hergesell will be a pale shadow, powerless to darken her little heart. Tomorrow, forgetful of all but present joy, she will walk with Abel and Snapper, all five gentlemen, round and round the table, will play the ever-thrilling cushion game."

Heaven be praised for that!

PART TWO

The World Widens

WITH SOME DISMAY a mother wakes up one day to find that her son or daughter is absent from home hours at a time and only comes home when he has to. Growth is gradual, to be sure, and times come along when the school-age child is just as family-centered, just as dependent, confiding, and self-revealing as in the earlier years. For all his enchantment with the outside world, he still needs to know he can touch home base whenever he wants to. Yet his center of gravity is shifting. The "My-mommie, my-daddy" feeling of yesterday is giving way to "us kids."

Though usually not as stormy or demanding as he used to be, he now exasperates us by his silences, even secrecy. To his parents' hopeful questions about his doings, he may just shrug and refuse to give. He (or more likely she) is subject to prolonged giggling fits suggestive of guilty knowledge shared only with a friend. He sees no virtue in neatness, personal cleanliness, or punctuality. Mornings may be a recurrent struggle to get him to school on time. Even the austere and venerated Henry Adams, we note from the selection that follows, at age six had to be led to the schoolhouse and was already finding education discouraging. But though at this age the "nicest" children may look like tramps and violate every civilized standard of fitness and aesthetics, they can also do a right-about-face and amaze us by their maturity and their occasional touching awareness of the needs and feelings of other people.

Already girls and boys are beginning to develop differently, and though these early psychological differences in the sexes are not always sharp and clear, their interests in most cases tend to diverge. Secretly, we suspect, the girl admires the boy's greater bodily strength, the self-assertiveness he manifests through sheer noise and muscular energy. Especially she admires his greater daring. Feeling outclassed, she withdraws into her feminine world with her girl friends and quieter pursuits, glaring out at the boys with a feigned contempt that ill conceals her envy. Not until adolescence does she discover how the male can be brought to heel. Though there are some boy-girl friendships in these middle years, they are relatively rare. "Best friends," as we should all remember from our own youth, are important and precious at this time of life—the source of both joy and anguish. Simone de Beauvoir in describing her own experiences shows us vividly how a friendship with a girl quite different from herself, by virtue of this very difference, greatly enriched her life.

For both boys and girls, the widening world is at their doorstep and it offers two great attractions: One is the joy to be found in companionship with others their own age. In these stimulating contacts with their peers, children can be rid for a while of the irksome company of their parents whom they see as the representatives of conformity, and who seem to be forever pressuring them to adopt alien—that is, grown-up—standards. It's hard to live with people like parents, so discouragingly virtuous, forever right about everything. But with their own kind, children relax in the knowledge that their friends are no better than they are. From now on, for many years, what their friends say, think, do, and wear will be fiercely espoused. Yet withal and in their hearts, family standards continue to be far more important to the younger generation than appears. Covertly, these children are sensitive to how their parents are judging their friends. In the end, they usually discover that their own values are not so different after all from those of their home. Even if finally they branch out in wholly new directions, the parents' imprint in some form is likely to remain.

The second great discovery at this time of life is the deep satisfaction that comes through the mastery of skills and the broadening of knowledge. Not only does a child now learn to read, write and figure—he becomes fact-hungry and he loves to parade his learning. He is also acquiring mastery of his body. He learns athletic and manual skills, becomes agile and well-coordinated, gains the self-assurance to go about his neighborhood under his own steam. Physical prowess becomes immensely important and he tends—often too much—to judge himself and others by physical daring and athletic competence. But he is also learning the important lessons of good sportsmanship.

A child is fortunate if he is physically proficient and if at the same time intellectual learning goes ahead unimpeded. Growth, however, may lag in some ways and spurt ahead in others. Not everyone can be "rounded," and this may be just as well. The young Moss Hart, spiritually alienated from his parents, was clearly a dud at the games and pastimes so important in the life of the less-protected city child turned loose in streets, alleyways, and waterfronts. The child Moss (everyone thought the name itself odd) was timid, bookish, could not fit in. But stumbling one day on the discovery that he had a skill which could be made to fill the gap, he began to use it fully to give himself the longed-for status among his fellows. After that he could turn his back on them and go forth with self-confidence to win his way to another world of his own choosing.

It is hard to imagine more widely contrasting childhoods than Alfred Kazin's and Winston Churchill's. Kazin, the child of an immigrant Jewish family in a New York City slum, beset by a hateful speech defect, was never for a second able to forget that he had to learn everything from scratch. He must "be an American," think like one, talk and act like one, learn to feel like one. Even harder, he must learn to feel at home among those strangers called gentiles. Above all, he must excel in his studies—get ahead, get ahead—or he would be left behind completely. Vividly and painfully he recalls those school days.

Churchill, the upper-class Briton, born to the purple, also had troubles at school, also struggled to discover what it was he could do well so he might believe in his own competence. Both boys, from the extreme ends of the social scale, succeeded magnificently. To be sure, the price in emotional tension and suffering is great as revealed by Kazin, while Churchill seems relaxed, slyly humorous, even buoyant throughout it all. Yet we may ask whether this seeming ease is not merely the traditional screen with which the British hide personal hardship by understatement. In spite of his retrospective wisdom we should recall that for Churchill, too, the way to fulfillment was long.

For the young Lore Segal, the world indeed widened—beyond reach of her home, beyond the boundaries of her native Austria. Sent to England to escape the Nazi persecution she finds herself in a well-meaning but unimaginative family which, though Jewish like her own, could never make her feel she was one of them. Yet her loneliness never really overwhelmed her. The expectation of reunion with her own colorful, loyal, resourceful family is the firm faith that carries her through.

It is during this middle period of a child's life that parents first begin to fret, to doubt and sometimes grow desperate about whether their children are "developing a sense of responsibility." Will they ever learn the importance of *duty*—home duties, school requirements, decent consideration for the feelings of others? Will they ever get some of that iron into their souls that is so needed for getting along in a hard world? Back of these parental fears is perhaps another one—that the child is slipping away from them; somehow they can't seem to reach him.

Children do have their defenses up in these years and those parents are wise who sense they had better not hammer at them too persistently; their youngsters are likely to be less resistant to the counsel of people

The World Widens

outside the family—models and mentors who are *not* their parents. "Heroes" from fiction, history or real life can be true sources of inspiration. Growing boys and girls are fortunate if they can also find a mature friend in a teacher or older relative. The story here by Faulkner tells of a boy who finds such a hero in a much older brother and how he learned to accept from him a stern lesson.

But family life, while it has its points of conflict, also has long days of serenity, such as are so beautifully suggested in two brief stories by Colette from the volume, *My Mother's House*. It would seem—and we can believe it—that whatever rifts there may have been between this writer and her mother, they were always of the kind that could be healed. Throughout their whole long life these two women loved and accepted each other, each in her own orbit. The mother, strong, simple, and undemanding—possessed a wonderful, inescapable integrity, and this was the quality that kept her always articulately herself, but never badgering. Is this the secret? How to achieve it? What wouldn't we give to know?

A master of the English language describes his ups and downs as a pupil in Harrow and a candidate for the English Military Academy, Sandhurst.

WINSTON CHURCHILL

from *A Roving Commission*

I HAD SCARCELY passed my twelfth birthday when I entered the inhospitable regions of examinations, through which for the next seven years I was destined to journey. These examinations were a great trial to me. The subjects which were dearest to the examiners were almost invariably those I fancied least. I would have liked to have been examined in history, poetry and writing essays. The examiners, on the other hand, were partial to Latin and mathematics. And their will prevailed. Moreover, the questions which they asked on both these subjects were almost invariably those to which I was unable to suggest a satisfactory answer. I should have liked to be asked to say what I knew. They always tried to ask what I did not know. When I would have willingly displayed my knowledge, they sought to expose my ignorance. This sort of treatment had only one result: I did not do well in examinations.

This was especially true of my Entrance Examination to Harrow. The Headmaster, Dr. Welldon, however, took a broad-minded view of my Latin prose: he showed discernment in judging my general ability. This was the more remarkable, because I was found unable to answer a single question in the Latin paper. I wrote my name at the top of the page. I wrote down the number of the question 'I.' After much reflection I put a bracket round it thus '(I).' But thereafter I could not think of anything connected with it that was either relevant or true. Incidentally there arrived from nowhere in particular a blot and several smudges. I gazed for two whole hours at this sad spectacle: and then merciful ushers collected my piece of foolscap with all the others and carried it up to the Headmaster's table. It was from these slender indications of scholarship that Dr. Welldon drew the conclusion that I was worthy to pass into Harrow. It is very much to his credit. It showed that he

from *A Roving Commission*

was a man capable of looking beneath the surface of things: a man not dependent upon paper manifestations. I have always had the greatest regard for him.

In consequence of his decision, I was in due course placed in the third, or lowest, division of the Fourth, or bottom, Form. The names of the new boys were printed in the School List in alphabetical order; and as my correct name, Spencer-Churchill, began with an 'S,' I gained no more advantage from the alphabet than from the wider sphere of letters. I was in fact only two from the bottom of the whole school; and these two, I regret to say, disappeared almost immediately through illness or some other cause.

The Harrow custom of calling the roll is different from that of Eton. At Eton the boys stand in a cluster and lift their hats when their names are called. At Harrow they file past a Master in the school yard and answer one by one. My position was therefore revealed in its somewhat invidious humility. It was the year 1887. Lord Randolph Churchill had only just resigned his position as Leader of the House of Commons and Chancellor of the Exchequer, and he still towered in the forefront of politics. In consequence large numbers of visitors of both sexes used to wait on the school steps, in order to see me march by; and I frequently heard the irreverent comment, 'Why, he's last of all!'

I continued in this unpretentious situation for nearly a year. However, by being so long in the lowest form I gained an immense advantage over the cleverer boys. They all went on to learn Latin and Greek and splendid things like that. But I was taught English. We were considered such dunces that we could learn only English. Mr. Somervell—a most delightful man, to whom my debt is great—was charged with the duty of teaching the stupidest boys the most disregarded thing—namely, to write mere English. He knew how to do it. He taught it as no one else has ever taught it. Not only did we learn English parsing thoroughly, but we also practiced continually English analysis. Mr. Somervell had a system of his own. He took a fairly long sentence and broke it up into its components by means of black, red, blue and green inks. Subject, verb, object: Relative Clauses, Conditional Clauses, Conjunctive and Disjunctive Clauses! Each had its colour and its bracket. It was a kind of drill. We did it almost daily. As I remained in the Third Fourth (β) three times as long as anyone else, I had three times as much of it. I learned it thoroughly. Thus I got into my bones the essential structure of the ordinary British sentence —which is a noble thing. And when in after years my schoolfellows who had won prizes and distinction for writing such beautiful Latin poetry and pithy Greek epigrams had to come down again to common English, to earn their living or make their way, I did not feel myself at any disadvantage. Naturally I am biassed in favour of boys learning English. I would make them all learn English: and then I would let the clever ones learn Latin as an honour, and Greek as a treat. But the only thing I would whip them for would be for not knowing English. I would whip them hard for that.

I first went to Harrow in the summer term. The school possessed the biggest swimming-bath I had ever seen. It was more like the bend of a river than a bath, and it had two bridges across it. Thither we used to repair for hours at a time and bask between our dips eating enormous buns on the hot asphalt margin. Naturally it was a good joke to come up behind some naked friend, or even enemy, and push him in. I made quite a habit of this with boys of my own size or less. One day when I had been no more than a month in the school, I saw a boy standing in a meditative posture wrapped in a towel on the very brink. He was no bigger than I was, so I thought him fair game. Coming stealthily behind I pushed him in, holding on to his towel out of humanity, so that it should not get wet. I was startled to see a furious face emerge from the foam, and a being evidently of enormous strength making its way by fierce strokes to the shore. I fled, but in vain. Swift as the wind my pursuer overtook me, seized me in a ferocious grip and hurled me into the deepest part of the pool. I soon scrambled out on the other side, and found myself surrounded by an agitated crowd of younger boys. 'You're in for it,' they said. 'Do you know what you have done? It's Amery, he's in the Sixth Form. He is Head of his House; he is champion at Gym; he has got his football colours.' They continued to recount his many titles to fame and reverence and to dilate upon the awful retribution that would fall upon me. I was convulsed not only with terror, but with the guilt of sacrilege. How could I tell his rank when he was in a bath-towel and so small? I determined to apologise immediately. I approached the potentate in lively trepidation. 'I am very sorry,' I said. 'I mistook you for a Fourth Form boy. You are so small.' He did not seem at all placated by this; so I added in a most brilliant recovery, 'My father, who is a great man, is also small.' At this he laughed, and after some general remarks about my 'cheek' and how I had better be careful in the future, signified that the incident was closed.

I have been fortunate to see a good deal more of him, in times when three years' difference in age is not so important as it is at school. We were afterwards to be Cabinet colleagues for a good many years.

It was thought incongruous that while I apparently stagnated in the lowest form, I should gain a prize open to the whole school for reciting to the Headmaster twelve hundred lines of Macaulay's 'Lays of Ancient Rome' without making a single mistake. I also succeeded in passing the preliminary examination for the Army while still almost at the bottom of the school. This examination seemed to have called forth a very special effort on my part, for many boys far above me in the school failed in it. I also had a piece of good luck. We knew that among other questions we should be asked to draw from memory a map of some country or other.

from *A Roving Commission*

The night before by way of final preparation I put the names of all the maps in the atlas into a hat and drew out New Zealand. I applied my good memory to the geography of that Dominion. Sure enough the first question in the paper was: 'Draw a map of New Zealand.' This was what is called at Monte Carlo an *en plein,* and I ought to have been paid thirty-five times my stake. However, I certainly got paid very high marks for my paper.

I was now embarked on a military career. This orientation was entirely due to my collection of soldiers. I had ultimately nearly fifteen hundred. They were all of one size, all British, and organised as an infantry division with a cavalry brigade. My brother Jack commanded the hostile army. But by a Treaty for the Limitation of Armaments he was only allowed to have coloured troops, and they were not allowed to have artillery. Very important! I could muster myself only eighteen field-guns—besides fortress pieces. But all the other services were complete—except one. It is what every army is always short of—transport. My father's old friend, Sir Henry Drummond Wolff, admiring my array, noticed this deficiency and provided a fund from which it was to some extent supplied.

The day came when my father himself paid a formal visit of inspection. All the troops were arranged in the correct formation of attack. He spent twenty minutes studying the scene—which was really impressive—with a keen eye and captivating smile. At the end he asked me if I would like to go into the Army. I thought it would be splendid to command an Army, so I said 'Yes' at once: and immediately I was taken at my word. For years I thought my father with his experience and flair had discerned in me the qualities of military genius. But I was told later that he had only come to the conclusion that I was not clever enough to go to the Bar. However that may be, the toy soldiers turned the current of my life. Henceforward all my education was directed to passing into Sandhurst, and afterwards to the technical details of the profession of arms. Anything else I had to pick up for myself. . . .

* * *

. . . It took me three tries to pass into Sandhurst. There were five subjects, of which Mathematics, Latin and English were obligatory, and I chose in addition French and Chemistry. In this hand I held only a pair of Kings—English and Chemistry. Nothing less than three would open the jackpot. I had to find another useful card. Latin I could not learn. I had a rooted prejudice which seemed to close my mind against it. Two thousand marks were given for Latin. I might perhaps get 400! French was interesting but rather tricky, and difficult to learn in England. So there remained only Mathematics. After the first Examination was over, when one surveyed the battlefield, it was evident that the war could not be won without another army being brought into the line. Mathematics was the only resource available. I turned to them—I turned on them—in desperation. All my life from time to time, I have had to get up disagreeable subjects at short notice, but I consider my triumph, moral and technical, was in learning Mathematics in six months. At the first of these three ordeals I got no more than 500 marks out of 2,500 for Mathematics. At the second I got nearly 2,000. I owe this achievement not only to my own 'back-to-the-wall' resolution—for which no credit is too great; but to the very kindly interest taken in my case by a much respected Harrow master, Mr. C.H.P. Mayo. He convinced me that Mathematics was not a hopeless bog of nonsense, and that there were meanings and rhythms behind the comical hieroglyphics; and that I was not incapable of catching glimpses of some of these.

Of course what I call Mathematics is only what the Civil Service Commissioners expected you to know to pass a very rudimentary examination. I suppose that to those who enjoy this peculiar gift, Senior Wranglers and the like, the waters in which I swam must seem only a duck-puddle compared to the Atlantic Ocean. Nevertheless, when I plunged in, I was soon out of my depth. When I look back upon those care-laden months, their prominent features rise from the abyss of memory. Of course I had progressed far beyond Vulgar Fractions and the Decimal System. We were arrived in an 'Alice-in-Wonderland' world, at the portals of which stood 'A Quadratic Equation.' This with a strange grimace pointed the way to the Theory of Indices, which again handed on the intruder to the full rigours of the Binomial Theorem. Further dim chambers lighted by sullen, sulphurous fires were reputed to contain a dragon called the 'Differential Calculus.' But this monster was beyond the bounds appointed by the Civil Service Commissioners who regulated this stage of Pilgrim's heavy journey. We turned aside, not indeed to the uplands of the Delectable Mountains, but into a strange corridor of things like anagrams and acrostics called Sines, Cosines and Tangents. Apparently they were very important, especially when multiplied by each other, or by themselves! They had also this merit—you could learn many of their evolutions off by heart. There was a question in my third and last Examination about these Cosines and Tangents in a highly square-rooted condition which must have been decisive upon the whole of my after life. It was a problem. But luckily I had seen its ugly face only a few days before and recognized it at first sight.

I have never met any of these creatures since. With my third and successful examination they passed away like the phantasmagoria of a fevered dream. I am assured that they are most helpful in engineering, astronomy and things like that. It is very important to build bridges and canals and to comprehend all the stresses and potentialities of matter, to say nothing of counting all the stars and even universes and measuring how far off they are, and foretelling eclipses, the arrival of comets and

from *A Roving Commission*

such like. I am very glad there are quite a number of people born with a gift and a liking for all of this; like great chess-players who play sixteen games at once blindfold and die quite soon of epilepsy. Serve them right! I hope the Mathematicians, however, are well rewarded. I promise never to black-leg their profession nor take the bread out of their mouths.

I had a feeling once about Mathematics, that I saw it all—Depth beyond depth was revealed to me—the Byss and the Abyss. I saw, as one might see the transit of Venus—or even the Lord Mayor's Show, a quantity passing through infinity and changing its sign from plus to minus. I saw exactly how it happened and why the tergiversation was inevitable: and how the one step involved all the others. It was like politics. But it was after dinner and I let it go!

The author's reflections on his life in an English boarding school a mere thirty years ago.

GEORGE ORWELL

Such, Such Were the Joys . . .

SOON AFTER I arrived at Crossgates (not immediately, but after a week or two, just when I seemed to be settling into the routine of school life) I began wetting my bed. I was now aged eight, so that this was a reversion to a habit which I must have grown out of at least four years earlier.

Nowadays, I believe, bed-wetting in such circumstances is taken for granted. It is a normal reaction in children who have been removed from their homes to a strange place. In those days, however, it was looked on as a disgusting crime which the child committed on purpose and for which the proper cure was a beating. For my part I did not need to be told it was a crime. Night after night I prayed, with a fervour never previously attained in my prayers, "Please God, do not let me wet my bed! Oh, please God, do not let me wet my bed!" but it made remarkably little difference. Some nights the thing happened, others not. There was no volition about it, no consciousness. You did not properly speaking *do* the deed: you merely woke up in the morning and found that the sheets were wringing wet.

After the second or third offence I was warned that I should be beaten next time, but I received the warning in a curiously roundabout way. One afternoon, as we were filing out from tea, Mrs. Simpson, the headmaster's wife, was sitting at the head of one of the tables, chatting with a lady of whom I know nothing, except that she was on an afternoon's visit to the school. She was an intimidating, masculine-looking person wearing a riding habit, or something that I took to be a riding habit. I was just leaving the room when Mrs. Simpson called me back, as though to introduce me to the visitor.

Mrs. Simpson was nicknamed Bingo, and I shall call her by that name for I seldom think of her by any other. (Officially, however, she was addressed as Mum, probably a corruption of the "Ma'am" used by public school boys to their housemasters' wives.) She was a stocky square-built woman with hard red cheeks, a flat top to her head, prominent brows and deepset, suspicious eyes. Although a great deal of the time she was full of false heartiness, jollying one along with mannish slang ("*Buck* up, old chap!" and so forth), and even using one's Christian name, her eyes never lost their anxious, accusing look. It was very difficult to look her in the face without feeling guilty, even at moments when one was not guilty of anything in particular.

"Here is a little boy," said Bingo, indicating me to the strange lady, "who wets his bed every night. Do you know what I am going to do if you wet your bed again?" she added, turning to me. "I am going to get the Sixth Form to beat you."

The strange lady put on an air of being inexpressibly shocked, and exclaimed "I-should-think-so!" And here occurred one of those wild, almost lunatic misunderstandings which are part of the daily experience of childhood. The Sixth Form was a group of older boys who were selected as having "character" and were empowered to beat smaller boys. I had not yet learned of their existence, and I mis-heard the phrase "the Sixth Form" as "Mrs. Form." I took it as referring to the strange lady—I thought, that is, that her name was Mrs. Form. It was an improbable name, but a child has no judgement in such matters. I imagined, therefore, that it was *she* who was to be deputed to beat me. It did not strike me as strange that this job should be turned over to a casual visitor in no way connected with the school. I merely assumed that "Mrs. Form" was a stern disciplinarian who enjoyed beating people (somehow her appearance seemed to bear this out) and I had an immediate terrifying vision of her arriving for the occasion in full riding kit and armed with a hunting whip. To this day I can feel myself almost swooning with shame as I stood, a very small, round-faced boy in short corduroy knickers, before the two women. I could not speak. I felt that I should die if "Mrs. Form" were to beat me. But my dominant feeling was not fear or even resentment: it was simply shame because one more person, and that a woman, had been told of my disgusting offence.

A little later, I forget how, I learned that it was not after all "Mrs. Form" who would do the beating. I cannot remember whether it was that very night that I wetted my bed again, but at any rate I did wet it again quite soon. Oh, the despair, the feeling of cruel injustice, after all my prayers and resolutions, at once again waking between the clammy sheets! There was no chance of hiding what I had done. The grim statuesque matron, Daphne by name, arrived in the dormitory specially to inspect my bed. She pulled back the clothes, then drew herself up, and the dreaded words seemed to come rolling out of her like a peal of thunder:

"REPORT YOURSELF to the headmaster after breakfast!"

I do not know how many times I heard that phrase during my early years at Crossgates. It was only very rarely that it did not mean a beating. The words always had a portentous sound in my ears, like muffled drums or the words of the death sentence.

When I arrived to report myself, Bingo was doing something or other at the long shiny table in the anteroom to the study. Her uneasy eyes searched me as I went past. In the study Mr. Simpson, nicknamed Sim, was waiting. Sim was a round-shouldered curiously oafish-looking man, not large but shambling in gait, with a chubby face which was like that of an overgrown baby, and which was capable of good humour. He knew, of course, why I had been sent to him, and had already taken a bone-handled riding crop out of the cupboard, but it was part of the punishment of reporting yourself that you had to proclaim your offence with your own lips. When I had said my say, he read me a short but pompous lecture, then seized me by the scruff of the neck, twisted me over and began beating me with the riding crop. He had a habit of continuing his lecture while he flogged you, and I remember the words "you dir-ty little boy" keeping time with the blows. The beating did not hurt (perhaps as it was the first time, he was not hitting me very hard), and I walked out feeling very much better. The fact that the beating had not hurt was a sort of victory and partially wiped out the shame of the bed-wetting. I was even incautious enough to wear a grin on my face. Some small boys were hanging about in the passage outside the door of the ante-room.

"D'you get the cane?"

"It didn't hurt," I said proudly.

Bingo had heard everything. Instantly her voice came screaming after me:

"Come here! Come here this instant! What was that you said?"

"I said it didn't hurt," I faltered out.

"How dare you say a thing like that? Do you think that is a proper thing to say? Go in and REPORT YOURSELF AGAIN!"

This time Sim laid on in real earnest. He continued for a length of time that frightened and astonished me—about five minutes, it seemed—ending up by breaking the riding crop. The bone handle went flying across the room.

"Look what you've made me do!" he said furiously, holding up the broken crop.

I had fallen into a chair, weakly snivelling. I remember that this was the only time throughout my boyhood when a beating actually reduced me to tears, and curiously enough I was not even now crying because of the pain. The second beating had not hurt very much either. Fright

Such, Such Were the Joys . . .

and shame seemed to have anesthetised me. I was crying partly because I felt that this was expected of me, partly from genuine repentance, but partly also because of a deeper grief which is peculiar to childhood and not easy to convey: a sense of desolate loneliness and helplessness, of being locked up not only in a hostile world but in a world of good and evil where the rules were such that it was actually not possible for me to keep them.

I knew that bed-wetting was (a) wicked and (b) outside my control. The second fact I was personally aware of, and the first I did not question. It was possible, therefore, to commit a sin without knowing that you committed it, without wanting to commit it, and without being able to avoid it. Sin was not necessarily something that you did: it might be something that happened to you. I do not want to claim that this idea flashed into my mind as a complete novelty at this very moment, under the blows of Sim's cane: I must have had glimpses of it even before I left home, for my early childhood had not been altogether happy. But at any rate this was the great, abiding lesson of my boyhood: that I was in a world where it was *not possible* for me to be good. And the double beating was a turning-point, for it brought home to me for the first time the harshness of the environment into which I had been flung. Life was more terrible, and I was more wicked, than I had imagined. At any rate, as I sat on the edge of a chair in Sim's study, with not even the self-possession to stand up while he stormed at me, I had a conviction of sin and folly and weakness, such as I do not remember to have felt before.

In general, one's memories of any period must necessarily weaken as one moves away from it. One is constantly learning new facts, and old ones have to drop out to make way for them. At twenty I could have written the history of my schooldays with an accuracy which would be quite impossible now. But it can also happen that one's memories grow sharper after a long lapse of time, because one is looking at the past with fresh eyes and can isolate and, as it were, notice facts which previously existed undifferentiated among a mass of others. Here are two things which in a sense I remembered, but which did not strike me as strange or interesting until quite recently. One is that the second beating seemed to me a just and reasonable punishment. To get one beating, and then to get another and far fiercer one on top of it, for being so unwise as to show that the first had not hurt—that was quite natural. The gods are jealous, and when you have good fortune you should conceal it. The other is that I accepted the broken riding crop as my own crime. I can still recall my feeling as I saw the handle lying on the carpet—the feeling of having done an ill-bred clumsy thing, and ruined an expensive object. *I* had broken it: so Sim told me, and so I believed. This acceptance of guilt lay unnoticed in my memory for twenty or thirty years.

So much for the episode of the bed-wetting. But there is one more thing to be remarked. This is that I did not wet my bed again—at least, I did wet it once again, and received another beating, after which the trouble stopped. So perhaps this barbarous remedy does work, though at a heavy price, I have no doubt. . . .

* * *

All this was thirty years ago and more. The question is: Does a child at school go through the same kind of experiences nowadays?

The only honest answer, I believe, is that we do not with certainty know. Of course it is obvious that the present-day *attitude* towards education is enormously more humane and sensible than that of the past. The snobbishness that was an integral part of my own education would be almost unthinkable today, because the society that nourished it is dead. I recall a conversation that must have taken place about a year before I left Crossgates. A Russian boy, large and fair-haired, a year older than myself, was questioning me.

"How much a year has your father got?"

I told him what I thought it was, adding a few hundreds to make it sound better. The Russian boy, neat in his habits, produced a pencil and a small notebook and made a calculation.

"My father has over two hundred times as much money as yours," he announced with a sort of amused contempt.

That was in 1915. What happened to that money a couple of years later, I wonder? And still more I wonder, do conversations of that kind happen at preparatory schools now?

Clearly there has been a vast change of outlook, a general growth of "enlightenment," even among ordinary, unthinking middle-class people. Religious belief, for instance, has largely vanished, dragging other kinds of nonsense after it. I imagine that very few people nowadays would tell a child that if it masturbates it will end in the lunatic asylum. Beating, too, has become discredited, and has even been abandoned at many schools. Nor is the underfeeding of children looked on as a normal, almost meritorious act. No one now would openly set out to give his pupils as little food as they could do with, or tell them that it is healthy to get up from a meal as hungry as you sat down. The whole status of children has improved, partly because they have grown relatively less numerous. And the diffusion of even a little psychological knowledge has made it harder for parents and schoolteachers to indulge their aberrations in the name of discipline. Here is a case, not known to me personally, but known to someone I can vouch for, and happening within my own lifetime. A small girl, daughter of a clergyman, continued wetting her bed at an age when she should have grown out of it. In order to punish her for this dreadful deed, her father took her to a large garden party and there introduced her to the whole company as a little girl who wetted

Such, Such Were the Joys . . .

her bed; and to underline her wickedness he had previously painted her face black. I do not suggest that Bingo and Sim would actually have done a thing like this, but I doubt whether it would have much surprised them. After all, things do change. And yet—!

The question is not whether boys are still buckled into Eton collars on Sunday, or told that babies are dug up under gooseberry bushes. That kind of thing is at an end, admittedly. The real question is whether it is still normal for a school child to live for years amid irrational terrors and lunatic misunderstandings. And here one is up against the very great difficulty of knowing what a child really feels and thinks. A child which appears reasonably happy may actually be suffering horrors which it cannot or will not reveal. It lives in a sort of alien under-water world which we can only penetrate by memory or divination. Our chief clue is the fact that we were once children ourselves, and many people appear to forget the atmosphere of their own childhood almost entirely. Think for instance of the unnecessary torments that people will inflict by sending a child back to school with clothes of the wrong pattern, and refusing to see that this matters! Over things of this kind a child will sometimes utter a protest, but a great deal of the time its attitude is one of simple concealment. Not to expose your true feelings to an adult seems to be instinctive from the age of seven or eight onward. Even the affection that one feels for a child, the desire to protect and cherish it, is a cause of misunderstanding. One can love a child, perhaps, more deeply than one can love another adult, but is rash to assume that the child feels any love in return. Looking back on my own childhood, after the infant years were over, I do not believe that I ever felt love for any mature person, except my mother, and even her I did not trust, in the sense that shyness made me conceal most of my real feelings from her. Love, the spontaneous, unqualified emotion of love, was something I could only feel for people who were young. Towards people who were old—and remember that "old" to a child means over thirty, or even over twenty-five—I could feel reverence, respect, admiration or compunction, but I seemed cut off from them by a veil of fear and shyness mixed up with physical distaste. People are too ready to forget the child's *physical* shrinking from the adult. The enormous size of grownups, their ungainly, rigid bodies, their coarse wrinkled skins, their great relaxed eyelids, their yellow teeth, and the whiffs of musty clothes and beer and sweat and tobacco that disengage from them at every movement! Part of the reason for the ugliness of adults, in a child's eyes, is that the child is usually looking upwards, and few faces are at their best when seen from below. Besides, being fresh and unmarked itself, the child has impossibly high standards in the matter of skin and teeth and complexion. But the greatest barrier of all is the child's misconception about age. A child can hardly envisage life beyond thirty, and in judging people's ages it will make fantastic mistakes. It will think that a person of twenty-five is forty, that a person of forty is sixty-five, and so on. Thus, when I fell in love with Elsie I took her to be grown up. I met her again, when I was thirteen and she, I think, must have been twenty-three; she now seemed to me a middle-aged woman, somewhat past her best. And the child thinks of growing old as an almost obscene calamity, which for some mysterious reason will never happen to itself. All who have passed the age of thirty are joyless grotesques, endlessly fussing about things of no importance and staying alive without, so far as the child can see, having anything to live for. Only child life is real life. The schoolmaster who imagines he is loved and trusted by his boys is in fact mimicked and laughed at behind his back. An adult who does not seem dangerous nearly always seems ridiculous.

I base these generalisations on what I can recall of my own childhood outlook. Treacherous though memory is, it seems to me the chief means we have of discovering how a child's mind works. Only by resurrecting our own memories can we realise how incredibly distorted is the child's vision of the world. Consider this, for example. How would Crossgates appear to me now, if I could go back, at my present age, and see it as it was in 1915? What should I think of Bingo and Sim, those terrible, all-powerful monsters? I should see them as a couple of silly, shallow, ineffectual people, eagerly clambering up a social ladder which any thinking person could see to be on the point of collapse. I would be no more frightened of them than I would be frightened of a dormouse. Moreover, in those days they seemed to me fantastically old, whereas—though of this I am not certain—I imagine they must have been somewhat younger than I am now. And how would Johnny Hall appear, with his blacksmith's arms and his red, jeering face? Merely a scruffy little boy, barely distinguishable from hundreds of other scruffy little boys. The two sets of facts can lie side by side in my mind, because these happen to be my own memories. But it would be very difficult for me to see with the eyes of any other child, except by an effort of the imagination which might lead me completely astray. The child and the adult live in different worlds. If that is so, we cannot be certain that school, at any rate boarding school, is not still for many children as dreadful an experience as it used to be. Take away God, Latin, the cane, class distinctions and sexual taboos, and the fear, the hatred, the snobbery and the misunderstanding might still all be there. It will have been seen that my own main trouble was an utter lack of any sense of proportion or probability. This led me to accept outrages and believe absurdities, and to suffer torments over things which were in fact of no importance. It is not enough to say that I was "silly" and "ought to have known better." Look back into your own childhood and think of the nonsense you used to believe and the trivialities which could make you suffer. Of course

Such, Such Were the Joys . . .

my own case had its individual variations, but essentially it was that of countless other boys. The weakness of the child is that it starts with a blank sheet. It neither understands nor questions the society in which it lives, and because of its credulity other people can work upon it, infecting it with the sense of inferiority and the dread of offending against mysterious, terrible laws. It may be that everything that happened to me at Crossgates could happen in the most "enlightened" school, though perhaps in subtler forms. Of one thing, however, I do feel fairly sure, and that is that boarding schools are worse than day schools. A child has a better chance with the sanctuary of its home near at hand. And I think the characteristic faults of the English upper and middle classes may be partly due to the practice, general until recently, of sending children away from home as young as nine, eight or even seven.

I have never been back to Crossgates. In a way it is only within the last decade that I have really thought over my schooldays, vividly though their memory has haunted me. Nowadays, I believe, it would make very little impression on me to see the place again, if it still exists. And if I went inside and smelt again the inky, dusty smell of the big schoolroom, the rosiny smell of the chapel, the stagnant smell of the swimming bath and the cold reek of the lavatories, I think I should only feel what one invariably feels in revisiting any scene of childhood: How small everything has grown, and how terrible is the deterioration in myself!

A well-known actress and writer ponders youth's unaccountable need for secrecy and fortunately remembers her own girlhood.

CORNELIA OTIS SKINNER

Those Friends of His

HOW WELL most parents ever really know their children is a debatable question. How well they know their children's friends is another question and one that, speaking for myself, I should say is not even debatable, for my son's acquaintances have always been shrouded in a curious sort of mystery I long ago gave up attempting to solve. Let me hasten to say that there is nothing wrong with any of them. On the contrary, they all seem to be completely acceptable and often quite delightful young persons. But they apparently hail from a region beyond an Iron Curtain that recognizes no parental passport. To be sure, those who come to the house are always politely introduced to my husband and me, but except for the mere pronouncing of their names our son vouchsafes no information about them. We are never told how or when he met them, and we've learned that to ask him questions about their families or habitats is considered about as tactless as it would be to ask for their Wassermann reports. By this I do not wish to give the impression that my son is a secretive or even a particularly reticent type. His is an outgoing nature, and he is always most communicative with his parents, except when it comes to discussing his friends. I'm certain that he's not at all ashamed of them, and the horrid suspicion that he may perhaps be ashamed of his parents I put away rapidly as unworthy. I guess it just strikes him as too complicated to explain us to them and them to us.

This has been the state of affairs ever since our child started carving out his own social life—to be specific, since the day he toddled away from my bench in the park to grasp the immense hand of an Irish policeman, with whom he carried on a long, solemn conversation, and then toddled back to the bench and put a quietus on my maternal curiosity

Those Friends of His

with a terse "He's a friend of mine." When I asked how this friendship had ripened, his response was still terser: "I just know him." Then, waxing expansive, he added, "He's Officer McKenna." At that period, the boy's circle of friends was, with the spectacular exception of Officer McKenna, hardly of his own choosing, composed as it was of the children of my acquaintances and the small charges of his various nurses' co-tyrants— a traditionally unjust system of social forcible feeding that for generations all politely brought-up small fry must have resented.

The real influx of my son's unidentifiable companions began at about the time we went to live in the country. He was then ten years old, and it had been our idea to remove him from the little-gentleman atmosphere of one of those expensive Manhattan day schools whose scholars wear diminutive caps bearing heraldic insignia, refer to their instructors as "masters," and address them as "sir." We wanted to expose the boy to the more democratic, if perhaps less intellectually stimulating, way of life of a rural public school, where the scholars wear either no caps at all or else the sort that advertises Purina Chows, call their instructor "Teacher," and address her as "Hey!" The new school was an immediate success, and my son's friends began to arrive at our house. At first, when he announced that he was bringing home someone named Jimmy or Leroy (pronounced *Lee*-roy) to supper, I would make the maternal blunder of asking who Jimmy was or who Leroy was (even bravely echoing the pronunciation *Lee*-roy), but I soon learned to hope for no further elucidation than a cryptic "A friend of mine." The Jimmys and the *Lee*-roys were all very nice little boys. At least, they *appeared* to be nice, for my only chance to estimate their characters was during the brief period of supper, a repast to which our young visitors paid tribute with lively appetites and dead silence. No time was wasted on chitchat. As for drawing them out, any conversational ball-tossing on my part met with no response at all or was returned with monosyllabic finality. Occasionally, my son, in an access of Rotarian geniality, would make an opening for one of his pals' better anecdotes with some such introduction as "Hey, *Lee*-roy, tell about how your father got his hand caught in a tractor!" And the *Lee*-roy of the evening, after a pause that would have done credit to Maurice Evans, would, without looking up from his plate, come forth with the carefully thought-out "Well, you know my Dad? Well, he got his hand caught in a tractor." My son might then add encouragement with an enthusiastic "He had to have ten stitches taken, didn't he?," which expansion of theme our guest would cut short with a hollow "Ten," and, except for a feeble "How awful!" or "My!" from me, that would be that. If, after Jimmy (or *Lee*-roy) left, I asked where he lived, the answer was usually an impatient "Oh, Mom, if I *told* you, you wouldn't know."

I was to realize the truth of this last statement on the occasion when our boy was quarantined at home with mumps and prevailed on me to take his two pet hamsters to the unknown house of one of those unknown *Lee*-roys. The hamster is a highly unprepossessing species of rodent whose purpose in Nature's scheme I have yet to discover, and though my son's ostensible reason for wanting me to remove his pets was that he feared they might come down with mumps, I believe his real reason was a thorough cooling off of his affection for the miserable little creatures. After considerable difficulty, I located the home of the friend in question and deposited the hamsters with the boy's mother, who received them with amazement and suspicion. Her doubts were well justified, for the hamsters eventually came down not with mumps but with a great many more hamsters, in a Shmoo-like fruition that proved acutely unpopular with their new owner's mother. She appealed to me to help her dispose of the animals, and as I drove about the countryside in a car teeming with hamsters, trying to find the dwellings of other buddies who might be Bide-A-Wee-minded, I again realized the truth of my son's assertion that if he told me, I wouldn't know where his pals lived.

When our son was at this tender age, the friends could usually be counted upon to be of the masculine gender, but I do recall that our table was occasionally graced by the presence of one femme fatale, who must have been all of fifteen and who went by the iridescent name of Opal. Opal was a placid, amiable girl, and there seems to have been a special bond of affection between her and boys of fourth-grade age, for I learned that she had been a favorite of quite a succession of fourth grades. Actually, that was all I ever did learn about Opal.

If I had any notion that after our son was dispatched to boarding school I'd begin to know a little more about his acquaintances, I had another guess coming. During his first Christmas holiday, my hopeful inquiries about his new set of pals were parried with the same old noncommittal replies. He eventually risked exposing one of his new friends to the inspection of his family during the spring vacation. When he told us that "a guy" was coming down for the night, I, not unnaturally, asked "Who?," and he laconically replied "Struther." When I made bold to ask where Struther came from, he narrowed it down to "Somewhere out West." The guy named Struther turned out to be a pallid, rather doleful little boy, and "Somewhere out West" a large city in Ohio. During his brief visit, we didn't find out much more about him than that. My only intimate encounter with the child occurred at 2 A.M., when my husband and I awoke to hear curious scuffling sounds issuing from our bathroom. Fearfully, we opened the bathroom door, and discovered our son and Struther there in their pajamas. The former was ransacking the medicine closet while the latter stood apathetically behind him, looking like a character in a William Blake vision. Seeing my startled face, my son announced, in tones that were half sepulchral, half delighted, "Mom,

Struther's dying." And, indeed, it looked that way, for Struther's face was the color of green Chartreuse. I asked him where he felt worst, an expression of concern and interest that obviously struck my son as irrelevant, for he repeated his announcement of Struther's rapidly approaching demise. Trying to assume the manner of one who seeks to soothe a panic-stricken crowd, I managed to restrain my son from administering the last rites to Struther in the form of a mixture of Bromo-Seltzer, castor oil, and Stokes' Expectorant, which he had already stirred up in a tumbler, and practiced my own, less drastic therapy. This was to hold the boy's head while he dispensed with his latest meal and, it would seem, quite a few previous ones.

During the ensuing school years, many unidentifiable lads have stayed in our house, and our son has gone to stay in houses where I presume that he, in turn, is equally unidentifiable, for I believe that this fetish of keeping their friends and activities as hush-hush as the identity and wartime movements of battleships is characteristic of all boys in their early teens. At any rate, it consoles me to think so. During that trying period, our boy had a way of taking my most casual inquiry as if it were one of the F.B.I.'s trick screening questions. If I asked where he was going, the reply would, as likely as not, be "Out," and "Who with?" would be answered by the usual "A friend of mine." This air of mystery manifested itself particularly over the telephone, when unknowns would call up and, in the tones of an actor in a radio thriller, ask whether our offspring was at home. If he was not, they'd mutter "Oh," and there would follow an ominous pause. If I asked whether there was any message, a voice that was a dead ringer for the Shadow's would say it would call back later. (Sometimes the voice went into an adolescent crack, and then it seemed a lot less like the Shadow's.) If my son was home, he would dive for whatever telephone extension was farthest removed from the one I was on, and, coming on the wire, he'd say, in his own radio manner of speech, "O.K., Mother, you can hang up." As he reached his midteens, the feminine element started to raise its pretty head, but not its voice, which seldom rose above a whisper. The little girls who called up sounded as if they were speaking over a bad connection from Cape Town, or as if they were just coming out of ether. They were even less communicative than the boys, and, despite my efforts to sound cordial (even to a fatuous, potential-mother-in-law degree), it was all too clear that they regarded me much as they would have a menacing duenna or an agent from Moscow.

My child must have been about sixteen when he received his first long-distance call. It came just before dinner and was from Omaha, and although I answered the ring on an upstairs extension, I had, with admirable self-control, hung up before the connection came through, even though I was consumed with curiosity. Not that my curiosity was of a particularly prying nature; I just thought it unusual for anyone to be telephoning from Omaha to a sixteen-year-old in New York. I restrained myself until dinner was two-thirds over and then, with elaborate casualness, asked, "By the way, who was it who called long distance?," whereupon the boy and his father rose and shook hands, and the latter handed the former a quarter. It seems that they had had a bet as to whether my inevitable inquiry would come before the dessert course. I thought it quite vulgar of them.

Their attitude would have grieved my maternal heart more had I not just then begun to go over in my mind my Junior Misshood and, with a belated pang of remorse for my parents, remembered that I must have acted in a very similar fashion. I, too, kept my friends pretty much of a secret. (Some of them, as I recall, not without a slight shudder, were best kept secret, and a dark one at that—especially that girl named Clarisse, who came from Kansas City and was considered "fast" because she used rouge and wore three frat pins all at the same time.) I, too, was mysterious in regard to phone calls. In those mechanically unblessed days, there was only one telephone instrument to a home, and it was usually kept in the most inconvenient possible location. Ours was in a coat closet off a small vestibule. When one of my friends called me, I would close both the vestibule and the closet doors, and, smothering myself and my voice in a welter of raincoats, I would carry on long, muffled conversations, the gist of which was, nine times out of ten, that I would meet my friend at Glocker's for a banana split. If I heard the sound of approaching footsteps, I'd mutter hastily, "I'll have to hang up now, my mother's coming."

Perhaps they grow out of it. Our son is now eighteen, and his advancing years have mellowed him considerably. He no longer treats the telephone as if it were a Secret Service mechanism, and now carries on in our presence fairly intelligible conversations with his friends. He shows signs of becoming actually expansive about his acquaintances and quite often tells us who their parents are. And just last week he told me in detail where he was going for the evening. Not only that but he gave me the approximate hour I might expect him home. Things are looking up.

A boy who never "belonged" either in his family or to the world of children, accidentally discovers he has something to give and so begins to feel his strength.

MOSS HART

from *Act One*

A CITY CHILD'S summer is spent in the street in front of his home, and all through the long summer vacations I sat on the curb and watched the other boys on the block play baseball or prisoner's base or gutter hockey. I was never asked to take part even when one team had a member missing—not out of any special cruelty, but because they took it for granted I would be no good at it. They were right, of course. Yet much of the bitterness and envy and loneliness I suffered in those years could have been borne better if a single wise teacher or a knowledgeable parent had made me understand that there were compensations for the untough and the non-athletic; that the world would not always be bounded by the curbstone in front of the house.

One of those compensations I blundered into myself, and its effect was electric on both me and the tough world of the boys on the block. I have never forgotten the joy of that wonderful evening when it happened. There was no daylight-saving in those days, and the baseball and other games ended about eight or eight thirty, when it grew dark. Then it was the custom of the boys to retire to a little stoop that jutted out from the candy store on the corner and that somehow had become theirs through tribal right. No grownup ever sat there or attempted to. There the boys would sit, talking aimlessly for hours on end. There were the usual probings of sex and dirty jokes, not too well defined or clearly understood; but mostly the talk was of the games played during the day and of the game to be played tomorrow. Ultimately, long silences would fall and then the boys would wander off one by one. It was just after one of those long silences that my life as an outsider changed, and for one glorious summer I was accepted on my own terms as one of the tribe. I can no longer remember which boy it was that summer evening who broke the silence with a question; but whoever he was, I nod

[131]

to him in gratitude now. "What's in those books you're always reading?" he asked idly. "Stories," I answered. "What kind?" asked somebody else without much interest.

Nor do I know what impelled me to behave as I did, for usually I just sat there in silence, glad enough to be allowed to remain among them; but instead of answering his question, I launched full tilt into the book I was immersed in at the moment. The book was *Sister Carrie* and I told them the story of Sister Carrie for two full hours. They listened bug-eyed and breathless. I must have told it well, but I think there was another and deeper reason that made them so flattering an audience. Listening to a tale being told in the dark is one of the most ancient of man's entertainments, but I was offering them as well, without being aware of doing it, a new and exciting experience.

The books they themselves read were the *Rover Boys* or *Tom Swift* or G. A. Henty. I had read them too, but at thirteen I had long since left them behind. Since I was much alone I had become an omnivorous reader and I had gone through the books-for-boys-series in one vast gulp. In those days there was no intermediate reading material between children's and grownups' books, or I could find none, and since there was no one to say me nay, I had gone right from *Tom Swift and His Flying Machine* to Theodore Dreiser and *Sister Carrie*. Dreiser had hit my young mind and senses with the impact of a thunderbolt, and they listened to me tell the story with some of the wonder that I had had in reading it.

It was, in part, the excitement of discovery—the discovery that there could be another kind of story that gave them a deeper kind of pleasure than the *Rover Boys*—blunderingly, I was giving them a glimpse of the riches contained outside the world of *Tom Swift*. Not one of them left the stoop until I had finished, and I went upstairs that wonderful evening not only a member of the tribe but a figure in my own right among them.

The next night and many nights thereafter, a kind of unspoken ritual took place. As it grew dark, I would take my place in the center of the stoop and, like Scheherezade, begin the evening's tale. Some nights, in order to savor my triumph more completely, I cheated. I would stop at the most exciting part of a story of Jack London or Frank Norris or Bret Harte, and without warning tell them that that was as far as I had gone in the book and it would have to be continued the following evening. It was not true, of course; but I had to make certain of my new-found power and position, and with a sense of drama that I did not know I possessed, I spun out the long summer evenings until school began again in the fall. Other words of mine have been listened to by larger and more fashionable audiences, but for that tough and grimy one that huddled on the stoop outside the candy store, I have an unreasoning affection that will last forever. It was a memorable summer, and it was the last I was to spend with the boys on the block.

A gifted Frenchwoman describes some childhood disappointments, her relationship to her sister, and also a "best friend" who opens her eyes to a new world.

SIMONE DE BEAUVOIR

from *Memoirs of a Dutiful Daughter*

... I WAS GLAD, too, that I was not entirely at the mercy of grown-ups; I was not alone in my children's world; I had an equal: my sister, who began to play a considerable role in my life about my sixth birthday.

We called her Poupette; she was two and a half years younger than I. People said she took after Papa. She was fair-haired, and in the photographs taken during our childhood her blue eyes always appear to be filled with tears. Her birth had been a disappointment, because the whole family had been hoping for a boy; certainly no one ever held it against her for being a girl, but it is perhaps not altogether without significance that her cradle was the center of regretful comment. Great pains were taken to treat us both with scrupulous fairness; we wore identical clothes, we nearly always went out together; we shared a single existence, though as the elder sister I did in fact enjoy certain advantages. I had my own room, which I shared with Louise, and I slept in a big carved wooden bed, a copy of an antique, over which hung a reproduction of Murillo's *Assumption of the Blessed Virgin*. A cot was set up for my sister in a narrow corridor. While Papa was undergoing his army training, it was I who accompanied Mama when she went to see him. Relegated to a secondary position, the "little one" felt almost superfluous. I was a new experience for my parents: my sister found it much more difficult to surprise and astonish them; I had never been compared with anyone: she was always being compared with me. At the Cours Désir the ladies in charge made a habit of holding up the older children as examples to the younger ones; whatever Poupette might do, and however well she might do it, the passing of time and the sublimations of the legend all contributed to the idea that I had done everything much better. No amount of effort or achievement was sufficient to break through that impenetrable barrier. The victim of some obscure curse, she was hurt and perplexed, and often in the evening she would sit crying on her little chair. She was accused of having a sulky disposition; one more inferiority she had to put up with. She might have taken a thorough dislike to me, but paradoxically she only felt sure of herself when she was with me. Comfortably settled in my role of elder sister, I preened myself only on the superiority accorded to my greater age; I thought Poupette was remarkably bright for her years; I accepted her for what she was—someone like myself, only a little younger; she was grateful for my approval, and responded to it with an absolute devotion. She was my liegeman, my alter ego, my double; we could not do without each other.

I was sorry for children who had no brother or sister; solitary amusements seemed insipid to me: no better than a means of killing time. But when there were two, hopscotch or a game of ball were adventurous undertakings, and rolling hoops an exciting competition. Even when I was just doing decalcomanias or daubing the pictures in a book with water colors I felt the need of an associate. Collaborating and vying with one another, we each found a purpose in our work that saved it from being pointless. The games I was fondest of were those in which I assumed another character; and in these I had to have an accomplice. We hadn't many toys; our parents used to lock away the nicest ones—the leaping tiger and the elephant that could stand on his hind legs; they would occasionally bring them out to show to admiring guests. I didn't mind. I was flattered to possess objects which could amuse grown-ups; and I loved them because they were precious: familiarity would have bred contempt. In any case the rest of our playthings—grocer's shop, kitchen utensils, nurse's outfit—gave very little encouragement to the imagination. A partner was absolutely essential to me if I was to bring my imaginary stories to life.

A great number of the anecdotes and situations which we dramatized were, we realized, rather banal; the presence of the grown-ups did not disturb us when we were selling hats or defying the Boches' artillery fire. But other scenarios, the ones we liked best, required secret performances. They were, on the surface, perfectly innocent; but in sublimating the adventure of our childhood or anticipating the future, they drew upon something secret and intimate within us which would not bear the searching light of adult gazes. I shall speak later of those games which, from my point of view, were the most significant. In fact, I was always the one who expressed myself through them; I imposed them upon my sister, assigning her the minor roles which she accepted with complete docility. At that evening hour when the stillness, the dark weight, and the tedium of our middle-class domesticity began to invade the hall, I would unleash my phantasms; we would make them materialize with great gestures and

from *Memoirs of a Dutiful Daughter*

copious speeches, and sometimes, spellbound by our play, we succeeded in taking off from the earth and leaving it far behind until an imperious voice suddenly brought us back to reality. Next day we would start all over again. "We'll play *you know what*," we would whisper to each other as we prepared for bed. The day would come when a certain theme, worked over too long, would no longer have the power to inspire us; then we would choose another, to which we would remain faithful for a few hours or even for weeks.

I owe a great debt to my sister for helping me to externalize many of my dreams in play: she also helped me to rescue my daily life from silence; through her I got into the habit of wanting to communicate with people. When she was not there I hovered between two extremes: words were either insignificant noises which I made with my mouth, or, whenever I addressed my parents, they became deeds of the utmost gravity; but when Poupette and I talked together, words had a meaning yet did not weigh too heavily upon us. I never knew with her the pleasure of sharing or exchanging things, because we always held everything in common; but as we recounted to one another the day's incidents and emotions, they took on added interest and importance. There was nothing wrong in what we told each other; nevertheless, because of the importance we both attached to our conversations, they created a bond between us which isolated us from the grown-ups; when we were together, we had our own secret garden.

We found this arrangement very useful. The traditions of our family compelled us to take part in a large number of duty visits, especially around the new year; we had to attend interminable family dinners with aunts and first cousins removed to the hundredth degree, and pay visits to decrepit old ladies. We often found release from boredom by running into the hall and playing at *"you know what."* In summer, Papa was very keen on organizing expeditions to the woods at Chaville or Meudon; the only means we had of enlivening the boredom of these long walks was our private chatter; we would make plans and recall all the things that had happened to us in the past; Poupette would ask me questions; I would relate episodes from French or Roman history or stories which I made up myself.

What I appreciated most in our relationship was that I had a real hold over her. The grown-ups had me at their mercy. If I demanded praise from them, it was still up to them to decide whether to praise me or not. Certain aspects of my behavior seemed to have an immediate effect upon my mother, an effect which had not the slightest connection with what I had intended. But between my sister and myself things happened naturally. We would disagree, she would cry, I would become cross, and we would hurl the supreme insult at one another: "You're stupid!" and then we'd make up. Her tears were real, and if she laughed at one of my jokes,

I knew she wasn't trying to humor me. She alone endowed me with authority; adults sometimes gave in to me: she obeyed me.

One of the most durable bonds that bound us together was that which exists between master and pupil. I loved studying so much that I found teaching enthralling. Playing school with my dolls did not satisfy me at all: I didn't just want to go through the motions of teaching: I really wanted to pass on the knowledge I had acquired.

Teaching my sister to read, write, and count gave me, from the age of six onward, a sense of pride in my own efficiency. I liked scribbling phrases or pictures on sheets of paper: but then I knew only how to create imitation objects. When I started to change ignorance into knowledge, when I started to impress truths upon a virgin mind, I felt I was at last creating something real. I was not just imitating grown-ups: I was on their level, and my success had nothing to do with their indulgence. It satisfied in me an aspiration that was more than mere vanity. Until then, I had contented myself with responding dutifully to the care that was lavished upon me: but now, for the first time, I, too, was being of service to someone. I was breaking away from the passivity of childhood and entering the great human circle in which everyone is useful to everyone else. Since I had started working seriously time no longer flew by, but left its mark on me: by sharing my knowledge with another, I was fixing time on another's memory, making it doubly secure.

Thanks to my sister I was asserting my right to personal freedom; she was my accomplice, my subject, my creature. It is plain that I only thought of her as being "the same, but different," which is one way of claiming one's pre-eminence. Without ever formulating it in so many words, I assumed that my parents accepted this hierarchy, and that I was their favorite. My room gave on to the corridor where my sister slept and at the end of which was my father's study; from my bed I could hear my father talking to my mother in the evenings, and this peaceful murmur often lulled me to sleep. But one evening my heart almost stopped beating; in a calm voice which held barely a trace of curiosity, Mama asked: "Which of the two do you like best?" I waited for Papa to say my name, but he hesitated for a moment that seemed like an eternity: "Simone is more serious-minded, but Poupette is so affectionate . . ." They went on weighing the pros and the cons of our case, speaking their inmost thoughts quite freely; finally they agreed that they loved us both equally well: it was just like what you read in books about wise parents whose love is the same for all their children. Nevertheless I felt a certain resentment. I could not have borne it if one of them had preferred my sister to me; if I was resigned to enjoying an equal share of their affection, it was because I felt that it was to my advantage to do so. But I was older, wiser, and more experienced than my sister: if my parents felt an equal affection for us, then at least I was entitled to more consideration from them; they

from *Memoirs of a Dutiful Daughter*

ought to feel how much closer I was to their maturity than my sister was. . . .

❖ ❖ ❖

The day I entered the fourth-first form—I was then almost ten—the seat next to mine was occupied by a new girl: she was small, dark, thin-faced, with short hair. While we waited for Mademoiselle to come in, and when the class was over, we talked together. Her name was Elizabeth Mabille, and she was the same age as I. Her schooling, begun with a governess, had been interrupted by a serious accident: in the country, while roasting some potatoes out in the open, her dress had caught fire; third-degree burns on her thighs had made her scream with agony for night after night; she had had to remain lying down for a whole year; under her pleated skirt, her flesh was still swollen. Nothing as important as that had ever happened to me: she seemed to me at once to be somebody. The manner in which she spoke to the teachers astounded me; her natural inflections contrasted strongly with the stereotyped, expressionless voices of the rest of the pupils. Her conquest of me was complete when, a few days later, she mimicked Mademoiselle Bodet to perfection; everything she had to say was either interesting or amusing.

Despite certain gaps in her knowledge due to enforced inactivity, Elizabeth soon became one of the foremost in the class; I only just managed to beat her at composition. Our friendly rivalry pleased our teachers: they encouraged our association. At the musical and dramatic performance which was given every year at Christmas time, we played in a sketch. I, in a pink dress, my hair all in ringlets, impersonated Madame de Sévigné as a little girl; Elizabeth took the part of a high-spirited boy cousin; her young man's costume suited her, and she enchanted the audience with her vivacity and competence. The rehearsals, our repeated conversations in the glow of the footlights drew us closer and closer together; from then on we were called "the two inseparables."

My father and mother had long discussions about the different branches of various families they had heard of called Mabille; they decided that there was some vague connection between Elizabeth's parents and themselves. Her father was a railway engineer, and held a very high post; her mother, nee Larivière, belonged to a dynasty of militant Catholics; she had nine children and was an active charity worker. She sometimes put in an appearance at our school in the Rue Jacob. She was a handsome woman of about forty, dark-haired, with flashing eyes and a fixed smile, who wore a black velvet ribbon adorned with an old-fashioned piece of jewelry around her neck. She softened her regal bearing with a deliberate amiability of manner. She completely won Mama over by addressing her as "petite madame" (my dear lady) and by telling her that she could easily have mistaken her for my older sister. Elizabeth and I were allowed to go and play in each other's homes.

On my first visit to her home in the Rue de Varennes my sister went with me and we were both scared to death. Elizabeth—who was known in the family circle as Zaza—had an older sister, a grown-up brother, six brothers and sisters younger than herself, and a whole horde of cousins and friends. They would run and jump about, clamber on the tables, overturn the furniture, and shout all the time at the tops of their voices. At the end of the afternoon, Madame Mabille entered the drawing room, picked up a fallen chair, and smilingly wiped perspiring brows; I was astonished at her indifference to bumps and bruises, stained carpets and chair covers and smashed plates; she never got cross. I didn't care much for those wild games, and often Zaza too grew tired of them. We would take refuge in Monsieur Mabille's study, and, far away from the tumult, we would talk. This was a novel pleasure for me. My parents used to talk to me, and I used to talk to them, but we never chatted together; there was not sufficient distance between my sister and me to encourage discussion. But with Zaza I had real conversations, like the ones Papa had in the evenings with Mama. We would talk about our schoolwork, our reading, our classmates, our teachers, and about what we knew of the world: we never talked about ourselves. We never exchanged girlish confidences. We did not allow ourselves any kind of familiarity. We addressed each other formally as *"vous"* (never *"tu"*!), and, except at the ends of letters, we did not give each other kisses.

Zaza, like myself, liked books and studying; in addition, she was endowed with a host of talents to which I could lay no claim. Sometimes when I called at the Rue de Varennes I would find her busy making shortbread or caramels; or she would spike orange sections, a few dates, and some prunes on a knitting needle and immerse the lot in a saucepan full of a sirupy concoction smelling of warm vinegar: the results looked just as delicious as if they had been made by a real confectioner. Then she used to hectograph a dozen or so copies of a *Family Chronicle* which she edited and produced herself each week for the benefit of grandmothers, uncles, and aunts who lived outside Paris. I admired, as much as the liveliness of her tales, her skill in making a thing which very closely resembled a real newspaper. She took a few piano lessons with me, but very soon became much more proficient and moved up into a higher grade. Puny-armed and skinny-legged, she nevertheless was able to perform all sorts of feats; when the first fine days of spring came along, Madame Mabille would take us out to a suburb abloom with flowers—I believe it was Nanterre—and Zaza would run into a field and turn cartwheels and all kinds of somersaults; she would climb trees and hang down from branches by her heels. In everything she did, she displayed an easy mastery which always amazed me. At the age of ten she would walk about the streets on her own; at the Cours Désir she did not have the awkward from *Memoirs of a Dutiful Daughter* [139]

manners that I had; she would talk to the teachers in a polite but unself-conscious way, almost as if she were their equal. One year at a music recital she did something while she was playing the piano which was very nearly scandalous. The hall was packed. In the front rows were pupils in their best frocks, curled and ringleted and beribboned, who were awaiting their turn to show off their talents. Behind them sat the teachers and tutors in stiff black silk bodices, and wearing white gloves. At the back of the hall the parents and their guests were seated. Zaza, resplendent in blue taffeta, played a piece which her mother thought was too difficult for her; she always stumbled through a few of the bars: but this time she played it perfectly, and, casting a triumphant glance at Madame Mabille, put out her *tongue* at her! All the little girls' ringlets trembled with apprehension and the teachers' faces froze into disapproving masks. But when Zaza came down from the platform her mother gave her such a lighthearted kiss that no one dared to reprimand her. For me this exploit surrounded her with a halo of glory. Although I was subject to laws, to conventional behavior, to prejudice, I nevertheless liked anything novel, sincere, and spontaneous. I was completely won over by Zaza's vivacity and independence.

I did not immediately consider what place this friendship had in my life; I was still not much cleverer than I was as a baby at realizing what was going on inside me. I had been brought up to equate appearances with reality; I had not learned to examine what was concealed behind conventions of speech and action. It went without saying that I had the tenderest affection for all the members of my family, including even my most distant cousins. For my parents and sister I felt love, a word that covered everything. Nuances and fluctuations of feeling had no claim to existence in my world. Zaza was my best friend: and that was all. In a well-regulated human heart friendship occupies an honorable position, but it neither has the mysterious splendor of Love, nor the sacred dignity of filial devotion. And I never called this hierarchy of the emotions into question.

That year, as in all other years, the month of October brought with it the exciting prospect of the return to school. The new books cracked when I opened them, and smelled just as good; seated in the leather armchair, I gloated over what the future had in store for me.

None of my expectations were realized. In the Luxembourg Gardens there were the bonfire smells and the yellowing leaves of autumn: they failed to move me; the blue of heaven had been dimmed. The classes bored me; I learned my lessons and did my homework joylessly, and pushed my way sullenly through the front door of the Cours Désir. It was my own past coming to life again, and yet I did not recognize it: it had lost all its radiant colors; my life was dull and monotonous. I had everything, yet my hands were empty. I was walking along the Boulevard

Raspail with Mama and I suddenly asked myself the anguished question: "What is happening to me? Is this what my life is to be? Nothing more? And will it always be like this, always?" The idea of living through an infinity of days, weeks, months, and years that were lighted by neither hope nor promise completely took my breath away: it was as if, without any warning, the whole world had died. But I was unable to give a name to this distress either.

For ten to fifteen days I dragged myself somehow, on legs that seemed as weak as water, from hour to hour, from day to day. One afternoon I was taking off my things in the cloakroom at school when Zaza came up to me. We began to talk, to relate various things that had happened to us, and to comment on them; my tongue was suddenly loosened, and a thousand bright suns began blazing in my breast; radiant with happiness, I told myself: "That's what was wrong; I needed Zaza!" So complete had been my ignorance of the workings of the heart that I hadn't thought of telling myself: "I miss her." I needed her presence to realize how much I needed her. This was a blinding revelation. All at once, conventions, routines, and the careful categorizing of emotions were swept away and I was overwhelmed by a flood of feeling that had no place in any code. I found myself moved by a wave of joy which went on mounting inside me, as violent and fresh as a waterfall, as naked, beautiful, and bare as a granite cliff. A few days later, arriving early at school, I looked in stupefaction at Zaza's empty seat. "What if she were never to sit there again, what if she were to die, then what would happen to me?" It was rather frightening: she came and went unconcerned with my life, and all my happiness, my very existence, lay in her hands. I imagined Madame Gontran coming in, her long black skirts sweeping the floor, and saying, "Children, let us pray; your little companion, Elizabeth Mabille, was called away to the arms of God last night." Well, if that were to happen, I told myself, I should die on the spot. I would slide off my seat and fall lifeless to the ground. This rationalization gave me comfort. I didn't really believe that God in His divine wisdom would take my life; neither did I really believe that I was afraid of Zaza dying. I had gone as far as to admit the extent of the dependence which my attachment to her placed upon me: I did not dare envisage all its consequences.

I didn't require Zaza to have any such definite feelings about me: it was enough to be her best friend. The admiration I felt for her did not diminish me in my own eyes. Love is not envy. I could think of nothing better in the world than being myself, and loving Zaza.

A mother totally immersed in her son never wavers in her determination to make him a great man. He both adores and resents this exasperating yet in many ways admirable woman.

ROMAIN GARY

from *Promise at Dawn*

I STILL CONTINUED with my efforts to triumph on sea, on land and in the air and to become the champion of the world at something or other. I often had the feeling that I would die of smallness, helplessness and love. I went on with my swimming, running and high-jumping, but it was only at ping-pong that I could really give everything I had in me and return home crowned with laurel. It was the only victory I could offer my mother, and the silver medal, engraved with my name and housed in a violet velvet case, stood on her bedside table until the day of her death.

I also tried my hand at tennis, having been given a racquet by the parents of one of my friends, but to become a member of the Club du Parc Impérial meant paying, and the membership fee was far beyond our means. Seeing that lack of money made it impossible for me to enter the Parc Impérial, my mother became righteously indignant. The matter, she announced, would not rest at that. She stubbed out her cigarette in a saucer, grabbed her cloak and her cane, and ordered me to fetch my racquet and to follow her that very instant to the Club du Parc Impérial. There, the club secretary was summoned, and, since my mother had a very carrying voice, he lost no time in obeying, followed by the club president, who rejoiced in the admirable name of Garibaldi and who also answered the call at full speed. My mother, standing in the middle of the room, with her hat slightly askew, and brandishing her cane, let them know exactly what she thought of them. What! With a little practice I might become a champion of France and defend my country's flag against foreigners, but no, because of some trivial and vulgar matter of money, I was forbidden to go onto the courts! All she was prepared to say to these gentlemen at this time was that they had not the interests of their country at heart, and this she would proclaim at the top of her voice, as the mother of a Frenchman—I was not yet naturalized but that, obviously, was a minor matter—and she insisted on my being admitted to the Club courts, there and then. I had not held a tennis racquet in my hand more than three or four times in my life, and the thought that these gentlemen might suddenly ask me to go onto the court and show what I could do made me tremble. But the two distinguished officials were far too overcome with astonishment to give a thought to my possible talents as a tennis player. It was, I think, M. Garibaldi, who, in the hope of calming my mother, hit on the fatal idea which led to a scene the memory of which fills me with confusion even to this day.

"Madame," he said, "I must ask you to moderate your voice. His Majesty King Gustav of Sweden is sitting only a few steps from here, and I beg you not to make a scandal."

His words had on my mother an almost magical effect. A smile, at once naive and radiant with wonder, which I knew only too well, showed on her face and she rushed forward.

An old gentleman was taking tea on the lawn under a white parasol. He was wearing white flannel trousers, a blue and black blazer and a straw "boater" slightly tilted over one ear. King Gustav V was a frequent visitor to the Riviera and its tennis courts. His celebrated straw hat appeared regularly on the front page of the local papers.

My mother did not hesitate for a moment. She made a deep curtsy and then, pointing her stick at the president and secretary of the club, exclaimed: "I crave justice of Your Majesty! My young son, who will soon be fourteen, has a quite extraordinary gift for lawn tennis and these bad Frenchmen are making it impossible for him to practice here. The whole of our fortune has been seized by the Bolsheviks and we are unable to pay the subscription. I come to Your Majesty for help and protection."

This performance was conducted according to the best tradition of popular Russian legends in the time of Ivan the Terrible or Peter the Great. At its conclusion, my mother turned triumphant eyes upon the numerous and interested audience. Could I have melted into thin air or dissolved into the earth, my last conscious moment would have been one of tremendous relief. But I was not to be allowed to get off so lightly. I had to stand there under the amused gaze of beautiful women and handsome men and win the only world championship that seemed always to be open to me, that of shame and ridicule. But even there my true laurels were yet to come—I had merely qualified for the finals.

His Majesty Gustav V was, at that time, already a very old man and this, combined no doubt with Swedish phlegm, accounted for the fact that he seemed not in the least surprised. He took the cigar from his lips, gave my mother a solemn look and me a casual glance and, turning

from *Promise at Dawn* [143]

to his coach: "Hit a few up with him," he said, "and let's see how he does."

My mother's face brightened. The fact that I was completely inexperienced as a tennis player didn't worry her in the least. She had confidence in me. She knew who I was. She knew that I had it in me. The trivial day-to-day details of life, the little practical considerations didn't count for her. For a second I hesitated, then, at sight of that expression of utter confidence and love, I swallowed my shame and my fear, sighed deeply, lowered my head and went forth to my execution.

It was a quick business, but it sometimes seems to me that I am still on that court. Needless to say, I did my best. I jumped, dived, bounced, pirouetted, ran, fell, bounced up again, flew through the air, clanging and spinning like a disjointed marionette, but the most I can say is that I did, just once, touch the ball, and then only on the wood of my racquet—and all this under the imperturbable gaze of the King of Sweden, who watched me coldly from under his famous straw hat. Some will no doubt ask why I let myself be led to the slaughter, why I ever ventured onto the court at all. The truth of the matter is that I had not forgotten the lesson I had learned in Warsaw, the slap on the face I had received, nor the voice of my mother saying: "Next time I expect to see you brought back home on a stretcher, you understand?" There could be no question of my turning back. For her sake I was prepared to play the clown as well as the hero.

I must also confess that, in spite of my fourteen years, I still believed, just a little bit, in fairy tales. I believed in the magic wand and, when I risked myself on the court, I was not absolutely sure that some just and indulgent Power might not intervene in my favor, that some almighty and mysterious hand might not guide my racquet—and it was just possible that the balls themselves would suddenly come to my rescue. But it was not to be: the miracle was probably busy elsewhere. I am bound to admit that this failure of the wonderful to materialize has left so deep a mark on me that I sometimes wonder whether the story of Puss in Boots is not, perhaps, just an invention, and whether the mice really came in the night and sewed buttons on the coat of the Tailor of Gloucester. In short, at forty-four, I am beginning to ask myself certain questions. But my life as a champion of the world has taken a lot out of me, and too much attention should not be paid to my occasional and passing doubts.

When the coach at last took pity on me, and I went back to the lawn, my mother welcomed me as though I had not disgraced myself. She helped me on with my pullover, she wiped my face and neck with her handkerchief. Then she turned to the audience. How can I describe the silence, the very attentive and reflective manner in which she stared at them with just a trace of an almost inviting smile on her tightly pressed lips? The mockers seemed to be just a shade put out of countenance, and the beautiful ladies, picking up their straws, lowered their eyelashes and gave all their attention to their lemonade. Some vague, humble cliché about the female defending her young may have occurred to them. My mother, however, had no need to go into action. The King of Sweden saved us and the guests from a scene that would be too awful even to try to imagine. The old gentleman touched his straw hat and with infinite courtesy and kindliness—though it used to be reported that he was not an easy man to get on with—said: "I think that these gentlemen will agree with me: we have just witnessed something quite admirable . . . Monsieur Garibaldi"—and I remember that the word "Monsieur" had a more than usually sepulchral sound on his lips—"I will pay this young man's subscription: he has shown both courage and determination."

Ever since then I have loved Sweden. But I never again set foot in the Parc Impérial.

A child is sent from Austria to England during the Hitler terror and finds that even uncongenial surroundings, separation from a loved family, and inner tension can be borne.

LORE GROSZMANN SEGAL

Mrs. Levine's House

WE WERE twenty little girls. We had started out from the refugee camp on England's east coast so early in the morning that the rest of the five hundred children were still sleeping in the cottages and the camp was silent. It was snowing. We met in the great dining hall made of glass and iron. One trestle table had been set up for our breakfast and only one lamp was lit above it. We could see the blue-black air outside all around. It was the bitter cold December of 1938. We travelled north all day and arrived in Liverpool in the early evening, where people from the Committee were waiting with cars to take us to a house.

I had not seen a house with stairs and carpets since I left my parents, twenty days before, to come to England with the transport bringing Jewish children out of Hitler Vienna. I remember that this house seemed very big and that all the doors stood open. Lights were on in all the rooms and hallways, and many people were walking everywhere. Our rucksacks and suitcases stood on the landing. Some ladies took off our coats and caps and gloves and piled them on the beds. Someone asked me if I wanted to go to the bathroom, but I wondered how I was going to find my way back, and I didn't even know where it was. It seemed too complicated. I said I didn't need to go.

In a big room, a long table with a white cloth was laid for a party. On the far side of the room was a fire burning in a square hole in the wall. I went and stood in front of it. A tall gentleman stood looking at me. I told him I had never seen a fire in a wall before and that in Vienna we had stoves. He said how nicely I spoke English, and we chatted until a lady from the Committee came to lead me to my seat. It seemed it was the first day of Chanukah. Candles were lit. Everyone stood still and sang a song I did not know. Then all the children sat around the table. We had

[145]

cakes and little plates with colored jelly such as I had never seen before. If you poked it with a finger, it went on wobbling for a while.

A Committee lady going about with a list of names came to stand behind me with a lady whom I shall call Mrs. Levine. She said, "This is a nice little girl."

I turned, eager to charm. There was an enormous, prickly-looking fur coat rising sheer above me. An old woman looked at me with a sour expression from behind her glasses. She had a small, gray, untidy face with a lot of hat and hair and spectacle about it. She frightened me. I had imagined that the family who would choose me would be very special, very beautiful people. I signalled to the lady with the list that I wanted to go with somebody else, but she didn't see, because she was attending to the fur-coated woman, who said, "How old is she? See, we wanted to have one about ten years old—you know, old enough to do for herself but not too old to learn nice ways."

I watched them talking together over my head, and I kept thinking that if I listened harder I would know what they were saying, but always it seemed that my mind wandered, and when I tried to remember to listen I couldn't tell if I had to go with this person. After a bit, I wasn't even sure if they were still talking about me, so I said in desperation, out loud, "I'm not ten. I'm half past ten. I'm nearly eleven."

They looked surprised. The old woman in the fur coat grinned shyly at me and I felt better. She asked me where my things were and took my hand and we went and found my coat in the bedroom. There was a young man who carried my luggage out of the house to one of the cars in the snow in the street. He got into the driver's seat. The old woman made me get in behind with her. I remember that as the car started up I looked back through the rear window in a panic moment to see if I could see one of the Committee ladies. I wondered if they would let my parents know where I was. I wondered if they knew I was being taken away. But I could not frighten myself for long. My childhood had not prepared me to expect harm from people. I was an only child, an only grandchild, and an only niece of a doting family. I think I rather felt I had a way with grownups, and as soon as we were settled in the car I started to tell the old woman how I had studied English at school, and privately as well, and that I always got A's in my reports. In the half dark of the back seat, I could not tell if this stolid, fur-wrapped person beside me was properly impressed. I said, "And I can figure-skate and dance on my toes." She said something to the young man in front that I could not make out, I had become so sleepy. I was too tired to try and think up more English conversation; I decided to leave it all till later and closed my eyes and went to sleep.

I was set on my feet in the dark and shivering cold and I closed my eyes, wanting only to go back to sleep, but they walked me up the garden path

Mrs. Levine's House

toward the house. There were many lights and people, and in the background I saw a maid in a black dress and white cap and apron looking at me over their heads. Someone took off my coat again. An old man with glasses sat on the far side of another fireplace. He drew a little low footstool from under his chair for me to sit on, in front of the fire. A maid in uniform brought a cup of tea. It had milk in it and I hated the taste. I said it was too hot to drink and that I wanted to go to sleep, but they said I must have a bath first and called a maid whose name, they said, was Annie. They told me she would give me a bath, but I was ashamed—I said at home I always bathed myself. They took me upstairs into a bathroom and let the water run and went out and shut the door, and I was so sleepy I thought I would stand and pretend, but then it seemed easier to get in the hot water.

I think it was one of the several daughters of the house who took me up another flight of stairs to my room. I know there was a maid peering at me through the banisters, and when I was in bed, just before the lights went out, I thought I saw a white-capped head stuck around the door. This made five maids. I was impressed. My parents had only had one maid at a time. Then I went back to sleep.

There was a maid in the full daylight to which I awoke. She stood just inside the door, looking at me and saying, "Taimtarais." I looked back at her without raising my head from the pillow. She stood very straight, heels together, toes turned out, and her arms hung neatly by her sides. She wore a bright-blue linen dress, and over it a white apron so long that it hung below the hemline of her dress. She was a big, firmly fleshed girl, with black hair and bright round cheeks. Her nose was incredibly uptilted.

I said, "Pardon?," not having understood what she had said, and she said again, "It's taimtarais," and went out the door.

I wondered if I should get up. I lay there a bit, looking around the big, light, chilly room. Someone had brought up my suitcase and set it on the chest of drawers. It looked oddly familiar in its strange new surroundings. Presently I got out of bed and dressed. I wondered if I was supposed to go downstairs. I thought I might look silly just to turn up down there among all those people I didn't know, so I took my writing pad and pen with me. I would go in and I would say, "I have to write a letter to my mother," and they would say to each other, "See what a good child. She loves her parents."

When I came out onto the landing outside my room, my heart was pounding. There was a door opposite. It stood slightly ajar. I could see, reflected in its own mirror, the top of a neat dressing table. There were photographs stuck all round the mirror, and on the table were a brush-and-comb set, and a pincushion in the shape of a heart. I held my breath. I gave the door a little push. I saw the corner of a bed with a green satin counterpane and wanted to look further in, but got frightened and backed away. The house was very quiet. I wondered where all the people might be and peered over the banisters to the floor below. I saw a green carpet and a number of doors, but they were all shut. I think I got the notion then that the five maids in uniform were inside the rooms, cleaning. Slowly I made my way down to the floor with the green carpet and then down the next flight to the ground floor. I thought I heard voices behind a door and tried to look through its frosted-glass inset. I could make out nothing, but my silhouette must have appeared upon it, because a voice inside said, "Come along. Come along in."

I came into a warm, pleasant kitchen-living room with a big table in the middle and a fire burning briskly in the fireplace. A fat lady sat by the window, sewing. She said, "Come in. Sit down. Annie will bring your breakfast."

I said, "I have to write to my parents, to say where I am."

"Well, you can have your breakfast first."

The maid in the blue linen dress came in with a boiled egg for me, and tea and toast. She pushed in my chair and buttered my bread. Miserably, I watched her pour milk into my tea. I looked up at her. Her nose had such an upward sweep that from where I sat I could see way into the black caverns of her round little nostrils. It occurred to me that she was winking at me, but I wasn't sure and I kept my eyes on my food and ate it, peering around me now and then. I expected every moment that the doors upstairs would open and release all the people I had seen last night. Everything was quiet. The fire crackled. The fat lady sewed. The maid was clattering pans in the scullery, and when I was finished she came and fetched away my dishes.

I sat at the table happily writing a letter. I wrote how last night at the railway station there had been an ugly old woman who had chosen me and how I had not wanted to go with her. It had been like a slave market, I said, and this, I thought, was pretty clever. I wrote, "The people I am going to live with are very rich. They have five maids. There is a fat lady here sewing. She said I should call her Auntie Essie, but I'm not going to. She doesn't look like an auntie to me. She is very fat." It amused and excited me to be writing to my mother about this person who was sitting there within touching distance. I felt a rush of blood to my head; it had come to me in a flash that this was the identical old woman in the fur coat—and yet it wasn't, either. This lady had on a loose cotton dress. She was quite different. But she was elderly, too, and large, and she wore glasses. Perhaps it was the same one, and yet perhaps it was not. I kept looking surreptitiously across at her. She raised her head. Quickly and guiltily, I bent mine over my letter. I wrote that I had found the chocolate my mother had hidden for me in the bottom of my suitcase. Then I said I loved them, in block capitals, and that it was *very* important to write me what was the meaning of the word "Taimtarais."

When my letter was sealed and addressed, Mrs. Levine gave me a stamp to put on it and told me to find Annie and she would post it for me.

Annie was in the drawing room, in the front of the house, lighting the fire. The flames were rushing with a fierce hiss upward into the chimney. I sat down on the little footstool and watched. I wanted to cry. I cradled my head in my hands and planted my elbows on my knees and let homesickness overcome me as one might draw up a blanket to cover one's head. I never knew when the maid left the room or how the day passed. Once, I came to as if with the wearing off of a drug that left me sober and sorrowless in this strange room; I looked curiously about me.

There was an old man sitting on the far side of the fireplace. His little eyes blinked incessantly behind his thick glasses, and he was watching me across the quiet of the room. I recognized him immediately; he was the same old man who had pulled out this footstool for me last night. I had a notion that he had been sitting there ever since, watching me gently and patiently, with the fire crackling between us. He was curling his finger for me to come to him. I got up and stood beside him. I could see his little wrinkled left eye from the side, and a second time through the lens, magnified and yet as from a tremendous distance behind the sevenfold rings and more of the thick glass. He was tickling a silver sixpence out of his purse. When he gave it to me, he put his finger to his lips and winked at me to signify secrecy. I nodded conspiratorially. I had to laugh —and that frightened me. I sat down quickly, wanting to lose myself again in my grief.

In the course of that day, I developed a technique: I found that if I sat curled into myself on the low stool facing the fire, and stared into the heart of flame so that my eyes stung, and kept the stare fixed until my chest was full of a rich, dark ache, I could at will fill up my head with tears and bring them to the point of weeping but arrest them there so that they neither flowed nor receded. Though I know when, toward evening, the house filled up again with people and that they were in the room whispering about me, I would not turn around, lest I disturb the delicate balance of my tears.

I must have been a great trial to the Levines in that first week.

"Have some tea," Mrs. Levine would say. "Annie, go and bring her a nice hot cup of tea. It'll make you feel better."

I shook my head. I said I didn't like tea.

"She doesn't like tea," Mrs. Levine said. "Here, how about going for a walk. Eh? The fresh air will do you good." She smiled encouragingly in my face. "You want to go for a nice run in the park with Auntie Essie?"

I said I didn't feel like going for a walk. It was cold, I said, and I liked to watch the fire.

Mrs. Levine's smile froze. She straightened up so that her face looked at me from the distance of her full height. I think it frightened her that the refugee she had brought into her innermost house to protect from persecution was talking back to her and watching her out of melancholic and conscious eyes—I caught the look she looked over my head at Annie, with a turning outward of her hands and a turning down of the right corner of her mouth. I did not then take in the meaning of what she was saying (I quickly thought, She didn't mean me. She's probably thinking of something quite different), but my ears retained the sounds intact and when I was in my room that night, lying in bed, I remembered and understood that what she had said was "I'm telling you, Annie, I was saying to Mrs. Green from the Committee only today, I said, if she isn't going to be happy with us here, perhaps I'd better exchange her." I explained it to myself. Mrs. Levine could not have understood when I told her how I always got A's in my report; I must tell her that I was always first in my class. I would say to her the bit about the slave market. I would write the very next day to my father and ask him how to say it in English. I lay in bed thinking up clever things to say to Mrs. Levine and I imagined sentimental situations in which to say them, calling her Auntie Essie, and so excited myself that I couldn't go to sleep.

But when I came downstairs the next morning, Mrs. Levine was sitting with her head bent over her sewing. I found I could not say "Auntie Essie" then, because it sounded silly in daylight and face to face, nor could I call her "Mrs. Levine," because she had told me to say Auntie Essie. I watched and waited for her to raise her head from her work before I addressed her, and poor Mrs. Levine, happening to look up, meaning to poke the fire, was startled to find herself under this close scrutiny. "What are you staring at me for, for goodness' sake!" she cried out. Immediately she recollected herself, though flustered still. "Why don't you read a book or go for a walk? Take her for a run in the park," she said to Annie, who had a way of appearing on the scene whenever there was any excitement. "Come on, now," she said rather desperately to me. "You don't want to cry—I didn't mean to shout at you. Now, come on, will you?"

It occurred to me to say, "In Vienna, Jews aren't allowed to go in the park."

The effect was instantaneous and marvellous. Mrs. Levine bent down and took me in her arms, but not before I had seen her face flush and her eyes fill with tears, and I knew they were for me. I was immensely impressed. I held myself very stiff against her unfamiliar and solid bosom; I felt restless in that embrace and began politely to extricate myself. I said I had to go and write a letter to my parents.

But all day I was grieved because Mrs. Levine had taken me in her arms and I had not liked it. I kept trying to think up ways in English to avoid the direct address, so that I could have conversation with her, but I never could think of one when I needed it. And now I didn't dare look at her in case I caught her eye and she thought I was staring. My nervousness around her increased with the day, until by evening whenever Mrs. Levine came into a room I must get up and walk out of it. I am sure that I wounded her deeply.

As the weeks went by, I began to spend a good deal of my time in the sanctuary of Annie's kitchen. I thought Annie was beautiful. I liked to watch her trip busily about, like the good sister in the fairy tale my father had taken me to see in the children's theatre. She looked so tidy in her linen dress and long apron. Her eyes were lowered demurely, but her little round nostrils stared outrageously. There was a game I played: I would stalk her around the kitchen, trying to maneuver myself into positions from which I could get a good look into the inside of Annie's nose.

Annie never told me to cheer up, or to do something, and she never pulled me up when I used German words instead of the English ones I didn't know. Mostly, Annie was not particularly listening. It gave me a certain freedom in talking with her.

I would say, "Annie, do you like Mrs. Levine?"

And Annie would say, "Yes. Mrs. Levine is a very nice lady."

I said, "I like her. I didn't like her in the beginning, but now I do, except she always makes me drink up my tea with milk and it makes me sick. I like Sally. Do you like Sally, Annie?" And I would discuss with Annie my impressions of the daughters of the house and ask Annie which one she thought was the prettiest. I knew that there were six. But I was still trying to figure out which of them lived in which of the rooms on the second floor, and which of them were married and only came to visit. I did not dare to talk to any of them, because their names and faces were interchangeable. Then I would say, "And Uncle Reuben, he is nice," with surprise to come across him in my mind, just as I was always surprised to come into a room and find him in it. This household full of women was inclined to forget Uncle Reuben except at mealtimes, to feed, or at times when he was sick, to fuss over. But whenever I did recall his existence, I liked him awfully. "He is kind," I said. "He gives me sixpence every Sunday. I like him very much."

Annie said yes, Mr. Levine was a very nice gentleman.

I enjoyed talking things over with Annie. I liked Annie. Then one day I went into the kitchen to look for her (there were visitors in the drawing room and I didn't know if I was supposed to go in) and Annie was not in the kitchen. I went up to the floor with the green carpet, but she wasn't there. All the doors were shut and blind. I stood listening, and I wondered about those five maids in their caps and aprons. I never had seen any of them again or ever stopped expecting to. (I suppose it must have occurred to me at some point that there never had been any maid but my own Annie, but mystification had become a habit of mind. Only now, with this writing down, is it obvious how Annie's curiosity had taken five separate peeks at the little refugee that first night; only now does Auntie Essie merge absolutely with the ugly old woman in fur and do I understand the word "taimtarais," which Annie said every morning when she came to wake me and which my father never did find in any dictionary.)

Annie's dustpan and broom leaned outside my room on the top floor. Annie was inside, but she wasn't cleaning. She was standing at my dressing table eating my chocolate. I heard the small rustle of her finger poking choosily in the box of sweets my mother had hidden in my suitcase for me —saw with my own eyes how Annie lifted one out and popped it into her mouth. I dared not breathe in case Annie should turn around and know that I had seen her. With a beating heart, I backed away, wondering how I should ever face her again, or what I would say to her when we met. I crept down the stairs.

I didn't want to stay alone in the kitchen. From the drawing room came the happy squealing of a little child. I felt such a curiosity and desire to be in there, too, that I opened the door and went self-consciously in. One of the married daughters had brought her small son to visit. The baby was running around in circles. Mrs. Levine said, "This is little Lore. Look who's come to play with you, Lore. This is our Bobby," and she caught hold of the child and she squeezed him and hugged him and said that she would like to eat him up.

"Oh, Ma!" said the daughter. "You spoil him. Say hello to the little girl. Go and shake hands." But the child escaped from his grandmother's grasp and slipped past his mother and continued his crazy circling, making airplane noises the while, and wouldn't stop to look at me.

Little Bobby had a pair of those peculiar ghetto eyes—as if a whole history of huckstering and dreaming were gathered in the baby's deep eyes. His cheeks were soft and round. I thought he was the most beautiful child I had ever seen. I yearned toward him.

So did his grandfather. Uncle Reuben kept curling his beckoning finger and holding out a silver shilling, which the little boy caught from him like a relay runner snatching the baton, not staying to see his grandfather wink and put a conspiratorial finger to his lips. Bobby's mother said, "Now say thank you to your grandfather and come here at once. Come when I tell you. I'll put your shilling in my purse for you, or you'll lose it. Take his hand," she said to me, "and bring him here."

I put my hand out gladly, but the baby ducked and yelled and ran. I ran after him a little way, but I felt foolish and stopped. I thought, He's only little. I don't run around like that any more. I meant to stand there watching him smilingly, the way grownups watch children, but I did not know how. I rubbed the back of my hand against my temple in an agony of self-consciousness. I wished I had my little footstool to curl up on, but

Mrs. Levine's House

it was on the other side of the fireplace and it was impossible to think of walking so far with them watching me.

Now they had begun to talk about me. "That's all she ever does," Mrs. Levine was saying to her married daughter. "Write letters home or she just sits. I tell her she should occupy herself. She's got to try and be happy with us here. But she doesn't even try."

"But I am," I said. "I am happy." I thought I was, for after the first few days I lost the trick of crying whenever I felt like it, and after the first week I stopped feeling like it. I wondered and thought myself heartless. I said, "I'm not even unhappy any more."

"So why do you sit here all day long just moping," Mrs. Levine said, looking at me through her spectacles.

Little Bobby, who could not brook divided attention, crept between his grandmother's knees and pushed his shilling into her chin, saying, "Look what I got, Grandma! Grand-maaa!"

"I'm not moping," I said. "I just like sitting by the fire."

"Always an answer," Mrs. Levine said. "I never saw such a child for arguing. And you think I can get her to go out for some fresh air?"

"Look, Grandma!" little Bobby said. "Look what I can do!" And he tipped his head back and laid the shilling on his forehead.

"My little Bubele!" cried Mrs. Levine. She squeezed his face between her hands and kissed him on the mouth.

"I will go," I said very loud. "I will go for a walk."

"You want to go now?" Mrs. Levine said. "Will you go with Annie?"

I blushed furiously, thinking of Annie and the chocolate, but I was committed to saying yes. I was almost glad I was going for a walk with Annie. I wanted to be angry with her.

I decided not to talk to Annie. We walked through the park gates. I knew that Annie was bad. I removed my hand from hers in a gesture of disassociation. I looked up from time to time with horror and awe at this Annie who had stolen my chocolate, but she was walking very straight, her nose pointing upward. I started kicking little stones; Annie let me. My freed hand kept getting in the way. I put it in my pocket, but it felt as if it didn't belong there and I took it out again. Presently I held it up for Annie, and she took it and swung it as we walked. I helped her swing it higher.

"You know," I said and looked up expectantly, "where I come from Jews aren't allowed to go into the parks?"

"Aren't they, now," Annie said. We walked on.

"You know what! You know what I'm going to do with my money? I'm saving it for when my parents come here."

Annie said, "How much you got?"

"Three shillings. Uncle Reuben gives me sixpence every Sunday. He gives Bobby a whole shilling, and he doesn't even say thank you," I said in a mean voice. "He's spoiled," I said, for the anger that was working in my chest and had bounced off Annie now found its mark. "All he can do is run around and make noises. He's just a baby, isn't he, Annie! I bet he doesn't even know what to do with all that money."

"Oh, well," said Annie comfortably, "there's always something you can do with money."

That very night, Annie knocked at my bedroom door. She was all dressed up in a navy-blue uniform with a red collar and red-ribboned bonnet, and she looked very smart and strange, almost like somebody I didn't know at all. She said could she come in, and did, and stood just inside my door.

I was proud to have her in my room in her uniform. "Where are you going in that?" I asked, making conversation.

"It's my Salvation Army day. We got a meeting," Annie said. "We have a band and hymn singing. We sing hymns and sacred songs and we have this collection to give food to the poor people and bring them the Word of the Lord."

I listened intelligently. Annie had never spoken such a long sentence to me before. I was flattered. She was even coming over and sitting down on the edge of my bed.

"Today I don't know if I'm going, because I don't have any money to put in the collection. So I don't know if I'm going." Annie looked down at her immaculate black shoes and gave them a dusting with her black-gloved hand.

I noticed absently that her stockings were black, too. There was a brand-new thought working in my mind. It was so tremendous it made me dizzy. I blushed. I said, "If you like, I can lend you some money."

"Oh, no," Annie said. "No, that I never would. I wouldn't borrow money from you, though you are a darling child, that you are, and I'll pay you back every penny come payday—half a crown if you can spare it."

I was shocked at the largeness of the sum, for though I valued friendship above money, I had an attachment to the silver coins that had accumulated over the weeks. I counted five of the six into Annie's upturned palm and watched her take out her black purse and drop them in and clap it shut.

Then Annie asked me if I would like to come into her room. I blushed again, because Annie was taking so much account of me, and because I wanted so very badly to go into her room I said no, and immediately regretted it, especially after Annie had gone and her footsteps sounded away down the stairs.

It was, I think, on the following afternoon that something happened. I came downstairs. Mrs. Levine was sitting by the window just where she had sat the first morning, and she was sewing a blue dress for me. I remembered with a shock of remorse how I had not liked her and how I had written about her to my mother. I suddenly liked her enormously. I was glad that she was old and ugly and I thought that I would love her forever, even if nobody else did, and was casting about in my mind for something to say to her so that I could call her "Auntie Essie" saying it, but she spoke first.

"Is that you, Lore? Come here. I want you." She had not raised her head and I could tell by her voice that there was something the matter. I looked around and I was glad that Annie was there, busying herself in the far corner of the dusky room. "I have to speak with you," Mrs. Levine said. "I hear that you are going around telling people we don't give you enough pocket money. I was very upset. I think that's very ungrateful of you."

"I didn't," I said, but without conviction; I was trying to recall to whom I had said such a thing. "I never," I said.

Mrs. Levine said, "I was quite upset. We do everything for you, and when I hear you are saying Uncle Reuben gives Bobby more money than he gives you I get very upset. And criticizing everybody—how my grandson is spoiled, and this one you like, and that one you don't like. You don't do that when you live in other people's houses."

I felt the blood pounding in my head—confused because she was accusing me of thoughts I did not recognize, and not accusing me of thoughts for which I had long felt guilty. I wanted to go away and think this out, but I knew I must stand and let Mrs. Levine scold me as long as she felt like it.

Her hands were trembling. Her needle rushed in and out of her seam. "It's not that I expect gratitude," she said. "But you might at least say 'thank you, Auntie Essie' when you see me sitting here sewing a dress for you, but you never notice what people do for you."

"I do," I said. "I do notice," but there was a small sulky voice inside me that said, "If she doesn't know I love her, I'm not going to tell her."

Mrs. Levine had not done with me yet. She was thoroughly worked up and she said excitedly, "And how often have I asked you to call me 'Auntie Essie,' but you never even remember—though you always say 'Uncle Reuben' to him, and then you go around telling people he doesn't give you enough pocket money and I'm sure he gives you as much as he can afford." Mrs. Levine was silent, sewing agitatedly on my dress.

I stood trembling. I looked toward Annie. I thought that any moment she would speak up and tell Mrs. Levine that there had been a mistake, and everything would be all right again, but Annie seemed still to be dusting the same shelf, and her back was to me.

I ran out and up to my room and threw myself on the bed meaning to cry and cry, but I managed only a few dry sobs. I was thinking how that little Bobby really did get twice as much money as I. It surprised me that I had not thought of it before. It made me angry. I decided that I would not go downstairs for supper, nor to breakfast the next day, nor ever again. I would stay in my room and starve. I tried to cry some more, but

I did not particularly feel like crying. I wondered if there was something the matter with me. I began to dream a dream—I imagined that I was weeping bitterly and that Mrs. Levine came into my room and saw me so and softly begged me to tell her why, and I could not speak because of the tears in my throat. My heart ached deliciously, imagining how Mrs. Levine wept for me.

I lifted my head from the pillow, listening to footsteps coming upstairs. Perhaps Mrs. Levine was coming. I held my breath, but they had stopped on the floor below. A door opened and shut. I heard the bathroom chain pulled and then somebody went back down. That was the front doorbell now—Uncle Reuben coming from his shop. Soon the girls would be home. They would all go into the dining room without me.

I was getting bored. I thought of writing a letter to my mother, but I didn't move from the bed. There was too much now that I could not tell her; it had shocked me profoundly to realize that everybody did not love me, and I knew if my mother were to find out that there were people who did not think me perfectly good and charming she could not bear it. The room had become dark and it was chilly. I thought how Annie would have to come up to my floor when she went to bed. Maybe I would call her. Maybe she would come in. I thought, If she invites me again to come into her room, I will go. I wondered how long it would be before Annie came upstairs.

After a bit, I walked out onto the landing and sat on the top step. Presently I went down to the floor with the green carpet and hung around there, and then I went all the way down to the ground floor. Everybody would be home by now. I could hear them talking in the living room, but I didn't know if I should go in. I wondered if Mrs. Levine was telling them all those things about me. I stood outside the door trying to hear what they were saying, but my figure limned itself on the frosted glass and Mrs. Levine called out, "All right, then, so come in. You don't have to listen behind the door."

I came in with my head on fire. Mrs. Levine was biting off her basting thread. She asked Annie if we had time to try on before supper, and though I kept waiting all that evening and for days afterward for the catastrophe to follow, it seemed as if Mrs. Levine had forgotten the things she had said to me.

Annie, too, seemed to have forgotten about the half crown I had lent her. I studied Annie. From the free and easy way that she talked and laughed with me, I could tell she had forgotten that she owed me two shillings and sixpence. I was too shy to remind her, but I never quit thinking that sometime she would remember and give me back my money. This expectation became attached to Annie like an attribute—like the playful angle of her nose and the warm grip with which she swung my

Mrs. Levine's House

hand when we two walked together. I always liked Annie.

Mrs. Levine I went on loving when she wasn't looking. There was now no hope of our coming together, for the accumulated mutual frustration and misapprehension had set a pattern for us; the phrases that she spoke to me and the tone in which I answered had become ritual. Now, seeing me sit idly by the fire, she would often say, "Don't you even want to go and write a letter to your parents?" And I would say, "No, I don't feel like writing."

Mrs. Levine said, "My goodness, I never saw such a child for sitting around and moping."

I said, "I'm not moping."

"Yes, you are," Mrs. Levine said.

"No, I'm not."

And if Annie was around, Mrs. Levine would turn her hands outward and her mouth down and say, "Listen to that! I've never seen such a child for arguing."

The truth was that I never exactly understood the word "moping," because I could not determine what Mrs. Levine saw in me when she used it. Often when I giggled in the kitchen with Annie, I stopped myself in horror—I had been enjoying myself; it was hours since I had remembered my parents.

My parents arrived in England in March, when I had been with the Levines four months. They stayed for three days and then went on south to fulfill the terms of the "domestic-service" visa, which had allowed them to immigrate. Their employer invited me to spend two weeks of the summer holidays with them. On my arrival, my mother made me write the Levines a very grateful letter. They answered immediately and most affectionately. They said how happy it made them to think how happy I must be near my beloved parents, and wouldn't I be happier staying there for good. Besides, a cousin had fallen ill and Mrs. Levine was nursing her and Mrs. Levine herself was feeling poorly.

The refugee committee in town found a new foster family for me to live with. After a while, an aunt of theirs fell ill, too, and then I lived with another family, and when they moved out of town I lived with another family. I had a serial story running through those years that I continued in bed every night, about a pale, tragic-eyed girl. Her hair was long and sad and she wept much. She suffered. She kept herself to herself. I regretted my daytime self, which was always wanting to be where everyone else was, though I never did learn to come into a room without stopping outside to hear if they were talking about me, to gather myself together, invent some little local excuse, or think up some bright thing to say, as if it might look foolish for me to just open a door and walk in.

A scion of an almost unbearably distinguished family tells how it feels to be disciplined—ever so wisely and gently, it appears—by a grandfather, who is also an ex-president of the United States.

HENRY ADAMS

from *The Education of Henry Adams*

BOYS ARE WILD ANIMALS, rich in the treasures of sense, but the New England boy had a wider range of emotions than boys of more equable climates. He felt his nature crudely, as it was meant. To the boy Henry Adams, summer was drunken. Among senses, smell was the strongest—smell of hot pine-woods and sweet-fern in the scorching summer noon; of new-mown hay; of ploughed earth; of box hedges; of peaches, lilacs, syringas; of stables, barns, cow-yards; of salt water and low tide on the marshes; nothing came amiss. Next to smell came taste, and the children knew the taste of everything they saw or touched, from pennyroyal and flagroot to the shell of a pignut and the letters of a spelling-book—the taste of A-B, AB, suddenly revived on the boy's tongue sixty years afterwards. Light, line, and color as sensual pleasures, came later and were as crude as the rest. The New England light is glare, and the atmosphere harshens color. The boy was a full man before he ever knew what was meant by atmosphere; his idea of pleasure in light was the blaze of a New England sun. His idea of color was a peony, with the dew of early morning on its petals. The intense blue of the sea, as he saw it a mile or two away, from the Quincy hills; the cumuli in a June afternoon sky; the strong reds and greens and purples of colored prints and children's picture-books, as the American colors then ran; these were ideals. The opposites or antipathies, were the cold grays of November evenings, and the thick, muddy thaws of Boston winter. With such standards, the Bostonian could not but develop a double nature. Life was a double thing. After a January blizzard, the boy who could look with pleasure into the violent snow-glare of the cold white sunshine, with its intense light and shade, scarcely knew what was meant by tone. He could reach it only by education.

from *The Education of Henry Adams*

Winter and summer, then, were two hostile lives, and bred two separate natures. Winter was always the effort to live; summer was tropical license. Whether the children rolled in the grass, or waded in the brook, or swam in the salt ocean, or sailed in the bay, or fished for smelts in the creeks, or netted minnows in the salt-marshes, or took to the pine-woods and the granite quarries, or chased muskrats and hunted snapping-turtles in the swamps, or mushrooms or nuts on the autumn hills, summer and country were always sensual living, while winter was always compulsory learning. Summer was the multiplicity of nature; winter was school. . . .

The attachment to Quincy was not altogether sentimental or wholly sympathetic. Quincy was not a bed of thornless roses. Even there the curse of Cain set its mark. There as elsewhere a cruel universe combined to crush a child. As though three or four vigorous brothers and sisters, with the best will, were not enough to crush any child, every one else conspired towards an education which he hated. From cradle to grave this problem of running order through chaos, direction through space, discipline through freedom, unity through multiplicity, has always been, and must always be, the task of education, as it is the moral of religion, philosophy, science, art, politics, and economy; but a boy's will is his life, and he dies when it is broken, as the colt dies in harness, taking a new nature in becoming tame. Rarely has the boy felt kindly towards his tamers. Between him and his master has always been war. Henry Adams never knew a boy of his generation to like a master, and the task of remaining on friendly terms with one's own family, in such a relation, was never easy.

All the more singular it seemed afterwards to him that his first serious contact with the President should have been a struggle of will, in which the old man almost necessarily defeated the boy, but instead of leaving, as usual in such defeats, a lifelong sting, left rather an impression of as fair treatment as could be expected from a natural enemy. The boy met seldom with such restraint. He could not have been much more than six years old at the time—seven at the utmost—and his mother had taken him to Quincy for a long stay with the President during the summer. What became of the rest of the family he quite forgot; but he distinctly remembered standing at the house door one summer morning in a passionate outburst of rebellion against going to school. Naturally his mother was the immediate victim of his rage; that is what mothers are for, and boys also; but in this case the boy had his mother at unfair disadvantage, for she was a guest, and had no means of enforcing obedience. Henry showed a certain tactical ability by refusing to start, and he met all efforts at compulsion by successful, though too vehement protest. He was in fair way to win, and was holding his own, with sufficient energy, at the bottom of the long staircase which led up to the door of the President's library, when the door opened, and the old man slowly came down. Putting on his hat, he took the boy's hand without a word, and walked with him, paralyzed by awe, up the road to the town. After the first moments of consternation at this interference in a domestic dispute, the boy reflected that an old gentleman close on eighty would never trouble himself to walk near a mile on a hot summer morning over a shadeless road to take a boy to school, and that it would be strange if a lad imbued with the passion of freedom could not find a corner to dodge around, somewhere before reaching the school door. Then and always, the boy insisted that this reasoning justified his apparent submission; but the old man did not stop, and the boy saw all his strategical points turned, one after another, until he found himself seated inside the school, and obviously the centre of curious if not malevolent criticism. Not till then did the President release his hand and depart.

The point was that this act, contrary to the inalienable rights of boys, and nullifying the social compact, ought to have made him dislike his grandfather for life. He could not recall that it had this effect even for a moment. With a certain maturity of mind, the child must have recognized that the President, though a tool of tyranny, had done his disreputable work with a certain intelligence. He had shown no temper, no irritation, no personal feeling, and had made no display of force. Above all, he had held his tongue. During their long walk he had said nothing; he had uttered no syllable of revolting cant about the duty of obedience and the wickedness of resistance to law; he had shown no concern in the matter; hardly even a consciousness of the boy's existence. Probably his mind at that moment was actually troubling itself little about his grandson's iniquities, and much about the iniquities of President Polk, but the boy could scarcely at that age feel the whole satisfaction of thinking that President Polk was to be the vicarious victim of his own sins, and he gave his grandfather credit for intelligent silence. For this forbearance he felt instinctive respect. He admitted force as a form of right; he admitted even temper, under protest; but the seeds of a moral education would at that moment have fallen on the stoniest soil in Quincy, which is, as every one knows, the stoniest glacial and tidal drift known in any Puritan land. . . .

"*I was not like the others.*"

In the slums of New York a Jewish boy from an immigrant family responds to the challenge to succeed and to become American.

ALFRED KAZIN

from *A Walker in the City*

ALL MY EARLY LIFE lies open to my eye within five city blocks. When I passed the school, I went sick with all my old fear of it. With its standard New York public-school brown brick courtyard shut in on three sides of the square and the pretentious battlements overlooking that cockpit in which I can still smell the fiery sheen of the rubber ball, it looks like a factory over which has been imposed the façade of a castle. It gave me the shivers to stand up in that courtyard again; I felt as if I had been mustered back into the service of those Friday morning "tests" that were the terror of my childhood.

It was never learning I associated with that school: only the necessity to succeed, to get ahead of the others in the daily struggle to "make a good impression" on our teachers, who grimly, wearily, and often with ill-concealed distaste watched against our relapsing into the natural savagery they expected of Brownsville boys. The white, cool, thinly ruled record book sat over us from their desks all day long, and had remorselessly entered into it each day—in blue ink if we had passed, in red ink if we had not—our attendance, our conduct, our "effort," our merits and demerits; and to the last possible decimal point in calculation, our standing in an unending series of "tests"—surprise tests, daily tests, weekly tests, formal midterm tests, final tests. They never stopped trying to dig out of us whatever small morsel of fact we had managed to get down the night before. We had to prove that we were really alert, ready for anything, always in the race. That white thinly ruled record book figured in my mind as the judgment seat; the very thinness and remote blue lightness of its lines instantly showed its cold authority over me; so much space had been left on each page, columns and columns in which to note down everything about us, implacably and forever. As it lay there on a teacher's desk, I stared at it all day long with such fear and anxious propriety that I had no trouble believing that God, too, did nothing but keep such record books, and that on the final day He would face me with an account in Hebrew letters whose phonetic dots and dashes looked strangely like decimal points counting up my every sinful thought on earth.

All teachers were to be respected like gods, and God Himself was the greatest of all school superintendents. Long after I had ceased to believe that our teachers could see with the back of their heads, it was still understood, by me, that they knew everything. They were the delegates of all visible and invisible power on earth—of the mothers who waited on the stoops every day after three for us to bring home tales of our daily triumphs; of the glacially remote Anglo-Saxon principal, whose very name was King; of the incalculably important Superintendent of Schools who would someday rubberstamp his name to the bottom of our diplomas in grim acknowledgment that we had, at last, given satisfaction to him, to the Board of Superintendents, and to our benefactor the City of New York—and so up and up, to the government of the United States and to the great Lord Jehovah Himself. My belief in teachers' unlimited wisdom and power rested not so much on what I saw in them—how impatient most of them looked, how wary—but on our abysmal humility, at least in those of us who were "good" boys, who proved by our ready compliance and "manners" that we wanted to get on. The road to a professional future would be shown us only as we pleased *them. Make a good impression the first day of the term, and they'll help you out. Make a bad impression, and you might as well cut your throat.* This was the first article of school folklore, whispered around the classroom the opening day of each term. You made the "good impression" by sitting firmly at your wooden desk, hands clasped; by silence for the greatest part of the live-long day; by standing up obsequiously when it was so expected of you; by sitting down noiselessly when you had answered a question; by "speaking nicely," which meant reproducing their painfully exact enunciation; by "showing manners," or an ecstatic submissiveness in all things; by outrageous flattery; by bringing little gifts at Christmas, on their birthdays, and at the end of the term—the well-known significance of these gifts being that they came not from us, but from our parents, whose eagerness in this matter showed a high level of social consideration, and thus raised our standing in turn.

It was not just our quickness and memory that were always being tested. Above all, in that word I could never hear without automatically seeing it raised before me in gold-plated letters, it was our *character*. I always felt anxious when I heard the word pronounced. Satisfactory as my "character" was, on the whole, except when I stayed too long in the playground reading; outrageously satisfactory, as I can see now, the very

from *A Walker in the City*

sound of the word as our teachers coldly gave it out from the end of their teeth, with a solemn weight on each dark syllable, immediately struck my heart cold with fear—they could not believe I really had it. Character was never something you had; it had to be trained in you, like a technique. I was never very clear about it. On our side *character* meant demonstrative obedience; but teachers already had it—how else could they have become teachers? They had it; the aloof Anglo-Saxon principal whom we remotely saw only on ceremonial occasions in the assembly was positively encased in it; it glittered off his bald head in spokes of triumphant light; the President of the United States had the greatest conceivable amount of it. Character belonged to great adults. Yet we were constantly being driven onto it; it was the great threshold we had to cross. *Alfred Kazin, having shown proficiency in his course of studies and having displayed satisfactory marks of character* . . . Thus someday the hallowed diploma, passport to my further advancement in high school. But there—I could already feel it in my bones—they would put me through even more doubting tests of character; and after that, if I should be good enough and bright enough, there would be still more. *Character* was a bitter thing, racked with my endless striving to please. The school—from every last stone in the courtyard to the battlements frowning down at me from the walls—was only the stage for a trial. I felt that the very atmosphere of learning that surrounded us was fake—that every lesson, every book, every approving smile was only a pretext for the constant probing and watching of me, that there was not a secret in me that would not be decimally measured into that white record book. All week long I lived for the blessed sound of the dismissal gong at three o'clock on Friday afternoon.

I was awed by this system, I believed in it, I respected its force. The alternative was "going bad." The school was notoriously the toughest in our tough neighborhood, and the dangers of "going bad" were constantly impressed upon me at home and in school in dark whispers of the "reform school" and in examples of boys who had been picked up for petty thievery, rape, or flinging a heavy inkwell straight into a teacher's face. Behind any failure in school yawned the great abyss of a criminal career. Every refractory attitude doomed you with the sound "Sing Sing." Anything less than absolute perfection in school always suggested to my mind that I might fall out of the daily race, be kept back in the working class forever, or—dared I think of it?—fall into the criminal class itself.

I worked on a hairline between triumph and catastrophe. Why the odds should always have felt so narrow I understood only when I realized how little my parents thought of their own lives. It was not for myself alone that I was expected to shine, but for them—to redeem the constant anxiety of their existence. I was the first American child, their offering to the strange new God; I was to be the monument of their liberation from the shame of being—what they were. And that there was shame in this was a fact that everyone seemed to believe as a matter of course. It was in the gleeful discounting of themselves—what do we know?—with which our parents greeted every fresh victory in our savage competition for "high averages," for prizes, for a few condescending words of official praise from the principal at assembly. It was in the sickening invocation of "Americanism"—the word itself accusing us of everything we apparently were not. Our families and teachers seemed tacitly agreed that we were somehow to be a little ashamed of what we were. Yet it was always hard to say why this should be so. It was certainly not—in Brownsville!—because we were Jews, or simply because we spoke another language at home, or were absent on our holy days. It was rather that a "refined," "correct," "nice" English was required of us at school that we did not naturally speak, and that our teachers could never be quite sure we would keep. This English was peculiarly the ladder of advancement. Every future young lawyer was known by it. Even the Communists and Socialists on Pitkin Avenue spoke it. It was bright and clean and polished. We were expected to show it off like a new pair of shoes. When the teacher sharply called a question out, then your name, you were expected to leap up, face the class, and eject those new words fluently off the tongue.

There was my secret ordeal: I could never say anything except in the most roundabout way; I was a stammerer. Although I knew all those new words from my private reading—I read walking in the street, to and from the Children's Library on Stone Avenue; on the fire escape and the roof; at every meal when they would let me; read even when I dressed in the morning, propping my book up against the drawers of the bureau as I pulled on my long black stockings—I could never seem to get the easiest words out with the right dispatch, and would often miserably signal from my desk that I did not know the answer rather than get up to stumble and fall and crash on every word. If, angry at always being put down as lazy or stupid, I did get up to speak, the black wooden floor would roll away under my feet, the teacher would frown at me in amazement, and in unbearable loneliness I would hear behind me the groans and laughter: tuh-tuh-tuh-tuh.

The word was my agony. The word that for others was so effortless and so neutral, so unburdened, so simple, so exact, I had first to meditate in advance, to see if I could make it, like a plumber fitting together odd lengths and shapes of pipe. I was always preparing words I could speak, storing them away, choosing between them. And often, when the word did come from my mouth in its great and terrible birth, quailing and bleeding as if forced through a thornbush, I would not be able to look the others in the face, and would walk out in the silence, the infinitely echoing silence behind my back, to say it all cleanly back to myself as I walked

from *A Walker in the City*

in the streets. Only when I was alone in the open air, pacing the roof with pebbles in my mouth, as I had read Demosthenes had done to cure himself of stammering; or in the street, where all words seemed to flow from the length of my stride and the color of the houses as I remembered the perfect tranquillity of a phrase in Beethoven's *Romance in F* I could sing back to myself as I walked—only then was it possible for me to speak without the infinite premeditations and strangled silences I toiled through whenever I got up at school to respond with the expected, the exact answer.

It troubled me that I could speak in the fullness of my own voice only when I was alone on the streets, walking about. There was something unnatural about it; unbearably isolated. I was not like the others! I was not like the others! At midday, every freshly shocking Monday noon, they sent me away to a speech clinic in a school in East New York, where I sat in a circle of lispers and cleft palates and foreign accents holding a mirror before my lips and rolling difficult sounds over and over. To be sent there in the full light of the opening week, when everyone else was at school or going about his business, made me feel as if I had been expelled from the great normal body of humanity. I would gobble down my lunch on my way to the speech clinic and rush back to the school in time to make up for the classes I had lost. One day, one unforgettable dread day, I stopped to catch my breath on a corner of Sutter Avenue, near the wholesale fruit markets, where an old drugstore rose up over a great flight of steps. In the window were dusty urns of colored water floating off iron chains; cardboard placards advertising hairnets, Ex-Lax; a great illustrated medical chart headed THE HUMAN FACTORY, which showed the exact course a mouthful of food follows as it falls from chamber to chamber of the body. I hadn't meant to stop there at all, only to catch my breath; but I so hated the speech clinic that I thought I would delay my arrival for a few minutes by eating my lunch on the steps. When I took the sandwich out of my bag, two bitterly hard pieces of hard salami slipped out of my hand and fell through a grate onto a hill of dust below the steps. I remember how sickeningly vivid an odd thread of hair looked on the salami, as if my lunch were turning stiff with death. The factory whistles called their short, sharp blasts stark through the middle of noon, beating at me where I sat outside the city's magnetic circle. I had never known, I knew instantly I would never in my heart again submit to, such wild passive despair as I felt at that moment, sitting on the steps before THE HUMAN FACTORY, where little robots gathered and shoveled the food from chamber to chamber of the body. They had put me out into the streets, I thought to myself; with their mirrors and their everlasting pulling at me to imitate their effortless bright speech and their stupefaction that a boy could stammer and stumble on every other English word he carried in his head, they had put me out into the streets, had left me high and dry on the steps of that drugstore staring at the remains of my lunch turning black and grimy in the dust.

In the great cool assembly hall, dominated by the gold sign above the stage KNOWLEDGE IS POWER, the windowsills were lined with Dutch bulbs, each wedged into a mound of pebbles massed in a stone dish. Above them hung a giant photograph of Theodore Roosevelt. Whenever I walked in to see the empty assembly hall for myself, the shiny waxed floor of the stage dangled in the middle of the air like a crescent. On one side was a great silk American flag, the staff crowned by a gilt eagle. Across the dry rattling of varnish-smelling empty seats bowing to the American flag, I saw in the play of the sun on those pebbles wildly sudden images of peace. *There* was the other land, crowned by the severe and questioning face of Theodore Roosevelt, his eyes above the curiously endearing straw-dry mustache, behind the pince-nez glittering with light, staring and staring me through as if he were uncertain whether he fully approved of me.

The light pouring through window after window in that great empty varnished assembly hall seemed to me the most wonderful thing I had ever seen. It was that thorough varnished cleanness that was of the new land, that light dancing off the glasses of Theodore Roosevelt, those green and white roots of the still raw onion-brown bulbs delicately flaring up from the hill of pebbles into which they were wedged. The pebbles moved me in themselves, there were so many of them. They rose up around the bulbs in delicately strong masses of colored stone, and as the sun fell between them, each pebble shone in its own light. Looking across the great rows of empty seats to those pebbles lining the windowsills, I could still smell summer from some long veranda surrounded by trees. On that veranda sat the family and friends of Theodore Roosevelt. I knew the name: Oyster Bay. Because of that picture, I had read *The Boy's Life of Theodore Roosevelt;* knew he had walked New York streets night after night as Police Commissioner, unafraid of the Tenderloin gangsters; had looked into *Theodore Roosevelt's Letters to His Children,* pretending that those hilarious drawings on almost every page were for me. *There* was America, I thought, the real America, *his* America, where from behind the glass on the wall of our assembly hall he watched over us to make sure we did right, thought right, lived right.

"Up, boys! Up San Juan Hill!" I still hear our roguish old civics teacher, a little white-haired Irishman who was supposed to have been with Teddy in Cuba, driving us through our Friday morning tests with these shouts and cries. He called them "Army Navy" tests, to make us feel big, and dividing the class between Army and Navy, got us to compete with each other for a coveted blue star. Civics was city government, state government, federal government; each government had functions; you had to get them out fast in order to win for the Army or the Navy. Sometimes this required filling in three or four words, line by line, down one side of the grimly official yellow foolscap that was brought out for tests. (In the tense silence just before the test began, he looked at us sharply, the watch in his hand ticking as violently as the sound of my heart, and on command, fifty boys simultaneously folded their yellow test paper and evened the fold with their thumbnails in a single dry sigh down the middle of the paper.) At other times it meant true-or-false tests; then he stood behind us to make sure we did not signal the right answers to each other in the usual way—for true, nodding your head; for false, holding your nose. You could hear his voice barking from the rear. "*Come on now, you Army boys! On your toes like West Point cadets! All ready now? Get set! Go! Three powers of the legislative branch? The judiciary? The executive? The subject of the fifteenth amendment? The capital of Wyoming? Come on, Navy! Shoot those landlubbers down! Give 'em a blast from your big guns right through the middle! The third article of the Bill of Rights? The thirteenth amendment? The sixteenth? True or false, Philadelphia is the capital of Pennsylvania. Up and at 'em, Navy! Mow them down! COME ON!!!*" Our "average" was calculated each week, and the boys who scored 90 per cent or over were rewarded by seeing *their own names* lettered on the great blue chart over the blackboard. Each time I entered that room for a test, I looked for my name on the blue chart as if the sight of it would decide my happiness for all time.

Down we go, down the school corridors of the past smelling of chalk, lysol out of the open toilets, and girl sweat. The staircases were a gray stone I saw nowhere else in the school, and they were shut in on both sides by some thick unreflecting glass on which were pasted travel posters inviting us to spend the summer in the Black Forest. Those staircases created a spell in me that I had found my way to some distant, cool, neutral passageway deep in the body of the school. There, enclosed within the thick, green boughs of a classic summer in Germany, I could still smell the tense probing chalk smells from every classroom, the tickling high surgical odor of lysol from the open toilets, could still hear that continuous babble, babble of water dripping into the bowls. Sex was instantly connected in my mind with the cruel openness of those toilets, and in the never-ending sound of the bowls being flushed I could detect, as I did in the maddeningly elusive fragrance of cologne brought into the classroom by Mrs. B., the imminence of something severe, frightening, obscene. Sex, as they said in the "Coney Island" dives outside the school, was like going to the toilet; there was a great contempt in this that made me think of the wet rings left by our sneakers as we ran down the gray stone steps after school.

Outside the women teachers' washroom on the third floor, the tough guys would wait for the possible appearance of Mrs. B., whose large goiterous eyes seemed to bulge wearily with mischief, who always looked tired and cynical, and who wore thin chiffon dresses that affected us much more than she seemed to realize. Mrs. B. often went about the corridors in the company of a trim little teacher of mathematics who was a head shorter than she and had a mustache. Her chiffon dresses billowed around him like a sail; she seemed to have him in tow. It was understood by us as a matter of course that she wore those dresses to inflame us; that she *was* tired and cynical, from much practice in obscene lovemaking; that she was a "bad one" like the young Polish blondes from East New York I occasionally saw in the "Coney Island" dives sitting on someone's lap and smoking a cigarette. How wonderful and unbelievable it was to find this in a teacher; to realize that the two of them, after we had left the school, probably met to rub up against each other in the faculty toilet. Sex was a grim test where sooner or later you would have to prove yourself doing things to women. In the smell of chalk and sweat and the unending smirky babble of the water as it came to me on the staircase through my summer's dream of old Germany, I could feel myself being called to still another duty—to conquer Mrs. B., to rise to the challenge she had whispered to us in her slyness. I had seen pictures of it on the block—they were always passing them around between handball games —the man's face furious, ecstatic with lewdness as he proudly looked down at himself; the woman sniggering as she teased him with droplets from the contraceptive someone had just shown me in the gutter—its crushed, filmy slyness the very sign of the forbidden.

They had never said anything about this at home, and I thought I knew why. Sex was the opposite of books, of pictures, of music, of the open air, even of kindness. They would not let you have both. Something always lingered to the sound of those toilets to test you. In and out of the classroom they were always testing you. *Come on, Army! Come on, Navy!* As I stood up in that school courtyard and smelled again the familiar sweat, heard again the unending babble from the open toilets, I suddenly remembered how sure I had always been that even my failures in there would be entered in a white, thinly ruled, official record book.

An English family on a remote island decides to do something about the education of its youngest member, who, since the age of two, has been interested only in animals and wild-life. The author, now fully literate, still loves animals and writes hilariously about them.

GERALD DURRELL

from *My Family and Other Animals*

SCARCELY had we settled into the strawberry-pink villa before Mother decided that I was running wild, and that it was necessary for me to have some sort of education. But where to find this on a remote Greek island? As usual when a problem arose the entire family flung itself with enthusiasm into the task of solving it. Each member had his or her own idea of what was best for me, and each argued with such fervour that any discussion about my future generally resulted in an uproar.

"Plenty of time for him to learn," said Leslie; "after all, he can read, can't he? I can teach him to shoot, and if we bought a boat I could teach him to sail."

"But, dear, that wouldn't *really* be much use to him later on," Mother pointed out, adding vaguely, "unless he was going into the Merchant Navy or something."

"I think it's essential that he learns to dance," said Margo, "or else he'll grow up into one of these awful tongue-tied hobbledehoys."

"Yes, dear; but that sort of thing can come *later*. He should be getting some sort of grounding in things like mathematics and French . . . and his spelling's appalling."

"Literature," said Larry, with conviction, "that's what he wants, a good solid grounding in literature. The rest will follow naturally. I've been encouraging him to read some good stuff."

"But don't you think Rabelais is a little *old* for him?" asked Mother doubtfully.

"Good, clean fun," said Larry airily; "it's important that he gets sex in its right perspective now."

"You've got a mania about sex," said Margo primly; "it doesn't matter what we're discussing, you always have to drag it in."

"What he wants is a healthy, outdoor life; if he learned to shoot and sail—" began Leslie.

"Oh, stop talking like a bishop. You'll be advocating cold baths next."

"The trouble with you is you get in one of these damned supercilious moods where you think you know best, and you won't even listen to anyone else's point of view."

"With a point of view as limited as yours, you can hardly expect me to listen to it."

"Now, now, there's no sense in fighting," said Mother.

"Well, Larry's so bloody unreasonable."

"I like that!" said Larry indignantly; "I'm far and away the most reasonable member of the family."

"Yes, dear, but fighting doesn't solve the problem. What we want is someone who can teach Gerry and who'll encourage him in his interests."

"He appears to have only one interest," said Larry bitterly, "and that's this awful urge to fill things with animal life. I don't think he ought to be encouraged in *that*. Life is fraught with danger as it is. I went to light a cigarette only this morning and a damn' great bumble-bee flew out of the box."

"It was a grasshopper with me," said Leslie gloomily.

"Yes, I think that sort of thing ought to be stopped," said Margo. "I found the *most revolting* jar of wriggling things on the dressing-table, of all places."

"He doesn't mean any harm, poor little chap," said Mother pacifically; "he's so interested in all these things."

"I wouldn't mind being attacked by bumble-bees, if it *led* anywhere," Larry pointed out. "But it's just a phase . . . he'll grow out of it by the time he's fourteen."

"He's been in this phase from the age of two," said Mother, "and he's showing no signs of growing out of it."

"Well, if you insist on stuffing him full of useless information, I suppose George would have a shot at teaching him," said Larry.

"*That's* a brain-wave," said Mother delightedly. "Will you go over and see him? I think the sooner he starts the better."

Sitting under the open window in the twilight, with my arm round Roger's shaggy neck, I had listened with interest, not unmixed with indignation, to the family discussion on my fate. Now that it was settled, I wondered vaguely who George was, and why it was so necessary for me to have lessons. But the dusk was thick with flower scents, and the olive groves were dark, mysterious, and fascinating. I forgot about the imminent danger of being educated, and went off with Roger to hunt for glow-worms in the sprawling brambles.

I discovered that George was an old friend of Larry's, who had come to Corfu to write. There was nothing very unusual about this, for all

from *My Family and Other Animals*

Larry's acquaintances in those days were either authors, poets, or painters. It was George, moreover, who was really responsible for our presence in Corfu, for he had written such eulogistic letters about the place that Larry had become convinced we could live nowhere else. Now George was to pay the penalty for his rashness. He came over to the villa to discuss my education with Mother, and we were introduced. We regarded each other with suspicion. George was a very tall and extremely thin man who moved with the odd disjointed grace of a puppet. His lean, skull-like face was partially concealed by a finely pointed brown beard and a pair of large tortoise-shell spectacles. He had a deep, melancholy voice, a dry and sarcastic sense of humour. Having made a joke, he would smile in his beard with a sort of vulpine pleasure which was quite unaffected by anyone else's reactions.

Gravely George set about the task of teaching me. He was undeterred by the fact that there were no school-books available on the island; he simply ransacked his own library and appeared on the appointed day armed with a most unorthodox selection of tomes. Sombrely and patiently he taught me the rudiments of geography from the maps in the back of an ancient copy of *Pears Cyclopædia,* English from books that ranged from Wilde to Gibbon, French from a fat and exciting book called *Le Petit Larousse,* and mathematics from memory. From my point of view, however, the most important thing was that we devoted some of our time to natural history, and George meticulously and carefully taught me how to observe and how to note down observations in a diary. At once my enthusiastic but haphazard interest in nature became focused, for I found that by writing things down I could learn and remember much more. The only mornings that I was ever on time for my lessons were those which were given up to natural history.

Every morning at nine George would come stalking through the olive trees, clad in shorts, sandals, and an enormous straw hat with a frayed brim, clutching a wedge of books under one arm, swinging a walking-stick vigorously.

"Good morning. The disciple awaits the master agog with anticipation, I trust?" he would greet me, with a saturnine smile.

In the little dining-room of the villa the shutters would be closed against the sun, and in the green twilight George would loom over the table, methodically arranging the books. Flies, heat-drugged, would crawl slowly on the walls or fly drunkenly about the room, buzzing sleepily. Outside the cicadas were greeting the new day with shrill enthusiasm.

"Let me see, let me see," George would murmur, running a long fore-finger down our carefully prepared time-table; "yes, yes, mathematics. If I remember rightly, we were involved in the Herculean task of discovering how long it would take six men to build a wall if three of them took a week. I seem to recall that we have spent almost as much time on this problem as the men spent on the wall. Ah, well, let us gird our loins and do battle once again. Perhaps it's the *shape* of the problem that worries you, eh? Let us see if we can make it more exciting."

He would droop over the exercise book pensively, pulling at his beard. Then in his large, clear writing he would set the problem out in a fresh way.

"If it took two caterpillars a week to eat eight leaves, how long would four caterpillars take to eat the same number? Now, apply yourself to that."

While I struggled with the apparently insoluble problem of the caterpillars' appetites, George would be otherwise occupied. He was an expert fencer, and was at that time engaged in learning some of the local peasant dances, for which he had a passion. So, while waiting for me to finish the sum, he would drift about in the gloom of the room, practising fencing stances or complicated dancing steps, a habit that I found disconcerting, to say the least, and to which I shall always attribute my inability to do mathematics. Place any simple sum before me, even now, and it immediately conjures up a vision of George's lanky body swaying and jerking round the dimly lit dining-room. He would accompany the dancing sequences with a deep and tuneless humming, like a hive of distraught bees.

"Tum-ti-tum-ti-tum . . . tiddle tiddle tumty *dee* . . . left leg over . . . three steps right . . . tum-ti-tum-ti-tum-ti-*dum* . . . back, round, down, and up . . . tiddle iddle umpty *dee* . . . ," he would drone, as he paced and pirouetted like a dismal crane. Then, suddenly, the humming would stop, a steely look would creep into his eyes, and he would throw himself into an attitude of defence, pointing an imaginary foil at an imaginary enemy. His eyes narrowed, his spectacles a-glitter, he would drive his adversary back across the room, skilfully avoiding the furniture. When his enemy was backed into the corner, George would dodge and twist round him with the agility of a wasp, stabbing, thrusting, guarding. I could almost see the gleam of steel. Then came the final moment, the upward and outward flick that would catch his opponent's weapon and twist it harmlessly to one side, the swift withdrawal, followed by the long, straight lunge that drove the point of his foil right through the adversary's heart. Through all this I would be watching him, fascinated, the exercise book lying forgotten in front of me. Mathematics was not one of our more successful subjects.

In geography we made better progress, for George was able to give a more zoological tinge to the lesson. We would draw giant maps, wrinkled with mountains, and then fill in the various places of interest, together with drawings of the more exciting fauna to be found there. Thus for me the chief products of Ceylon were tapirs and tea, of India tigers and rice, of Australia kangaroos and sheep, while the blue curves of currents we

from My Family and Other Animals

drew across the oceans carried whales, albatross, penguins, and walrus, as well as hurricanes, trade winds, fair weather and foul. Our maps were works of art. The principal volcanoes belched such flames and sparks one feared they would set the paper continents alight; the mountain ranges of the world were so blue and white with ice and snow that it made one chilly to look at them. Our brown, sun-drenched deserts were lumpy with camel humps and pyramids, and our tropical forests so tangled and luxuriant that it was only with difficulty that the slouching jaguars, lithe snakes, and morose gorillas managed to get through them, while on their outskirts emaciated natives hacked wearily at the painted trees, forming little clearings apparently for the purpose of writing "coffee" or perhaps "cereals" across them in unsteady capitals. Our rivers were wide, and blue as forget-me-nots, freckled with canoes and crocodiles. Our oceans were anything but empty, for where they had not frothed themselves into a fury of storms or drawn themselves up into an awe-inspiring tidal wave that hung over some remote, palm-shaggy island, they were full of life. Good-natured whales allowed unseaworthy galleons, armed with a forest of harpoons, to pursue them relentlessly; bland and innocent-looking octopi tenderly engulfed small boats in their arms; Chinese junks, with jaundiced crews, were followed by shoals of well-dentured sharks, while fur-clad Eskimos pursued obese herds of walrus through ice fields thickly populated by polar bears and penguins. They were maps that lived, maps that one could study, frown over, and add to; maps, in short, that really *meant* something.

Our attempts at history were not, at first, conspicuously successful, until George discovered that by seasoning a series of unpalatable facts with a sprig of zoology and a sprinkle of completely irrelevant detail, he could get me interested. Thus I became conversant with some historical data, which, to the best of my knowledge, have never been recorded before. Breathlessly, history lesson by history lesson, I followed Hannibal's progress over the Alps. His reason for attempting such a feat and what he intended to do on the other side were details that scarcely worried me. No, my interest in what I considered to be a very badly planned expedition lay in the fact that *I knew the name of each and every elephant*. I also knew that Hannibal had appointed a special man not only to feed and look after the elephants, *but to give them hot-water bottles when the weather got cold*. This interesting fact seems to have escaped most serious historians. Another thing that most history books never seem to mention is that Columbus's first words on setting foot ashore in America were, "Great heavens, look . . . a jaguar!" With such an introduction, how could one fail to take an interest in the continent's subsequent history? So George, hampered by inadequate books and a reluctant pupil, would strive to make his teaching interesting, so that the lessons did not drag. . . .

... It was hard to concentrate, for the sun would pour through the shutters, tiger-striping the table and floor, reminding me of all the things I might be doing.

There around me were the vast, empty olive groves echoing with cicadas; the moss-grown stone walls that made the vineyards into steps where the painted lizards ran; the thickets of myrtle alive with insects, and the rough headland where the flocks of garish goldfinches fluttered with excited pipings from thistle-head to thistle-head.

Realizing this, George wisely instituted the novel system of outdoor lessons. Some mornings he arrived, carrying a large furry towel, and together we would make our way down through the olive groves and along the road that was like a carpet of white velvet under its layer of dust. Then we branched off onto a goat track that ran along the top of miniature cliffs, until it led us to a bay, secluded and small, with a crescent-shaped fringe of white sand running round it. A grove of stunted olives grew there, providing a pleasant shade. From the top of the little cliff the water in the bay looked so still and transparent that it was hard to believe there was any at all. Fishes seemed to drift over the wave-wrinkled sand as though suspended in mid-air, while through six feet of clear water you could see rocks on which anemones lifted frail, coloured arms, and hermit crabs moved, dragging their top-shaped homes.

We would strip beneath the olives and walk out into the warm, bright water, to drift, face down, over the rocks and clumps of seaweed, occasionally diving to bring up something that caught our eye: a shell more brightly coloured than the rest; or a hermit crab of massive proportions, wearing an anemone on his shell, like a bonnet with a pink flower on it. . . .

... We would hunt for new shells for my collection, or hold long discussions on the other fauna we had found; George would suddenly realize that all this, though most enjoyable, could hardly be described as education in the strictest sense of the word, so we would drift back to the shallows and lie there. The lesson then proceeded, while the shoals of little fish would gather about us and nibble gently at our legs.

"So the French and British Fleets were slowly drawing together for what was to be the decisive sea battle of the war. When the enemy was sighted, Nelson was on the bridge bird-watching through his telescope. . . . He had already been warned of the Frenchmen's approach by a friendly gull . . . eh? . . . oh, a greater black-backed gull I think it was. Well, the ships manoeuvred round each other . . . of course they couldn't move so fast in those days, for they did everything by sail . . . no engines . . . no, not even outboard engines . . . The British sailors were a bit worried because the French seemed so strong, but when they saw that Nelson was so little affected by the whole thing that he was sitting on the

from *My Family and Other Animals*

bridge labelling his birds'-egg collection, they decided that there was really nothing to be scared about. . . ."

The sea was like a warm, silky coverlet that moved my body gently to and fro. There were no waves, only this gentle underwater movement, the pulse of the sea, rocking me softly. Around my legs the coloured fish flicked and trembled, and stood on their heads while they mumbled at me with toothless gums. In the drooping clusters of olives a cicada whispered gently to itself.

". . . and so they carried Nelson down below as quickly as possible, so that none of the crew would know he had been hit. . . . He was mortally wounded, and lying below decks with the battle still raging above, he murmured his last words, 'Kiss me, Hardy,' and then he died. . . . What? Oh, yes. Well, he had already told Hardy that if anything happened to him he could have his birds' eggs . . . so, though England had lost her finest seaman, the battle had been won, and it had far-reaching effects in Europe . . ."

Across the mouth of the bay a sun-bleached boat would pass, rowed by a brown fisherman in tattered trousers, standing in the stern and twisting an oar in the water like a fish's tail. He would raise one hand in lazy salute, and across the still, blue water you could hear the plaintive squeak of the oar as it twisted, and the soft clop as it dug into the sea.

The profound love between two brothers in the Mississippi back-country leads the younger far from home—and back again.

WILLIAM FAULKNER

Two Soldiers

ME AND PETE would go down to Old Man Killegrew's and listen to his radio. We would wait until after supper, after dark, and we would stand outside Old Man Killegrew's parlor window, and we could hear it because Old Man Killegrew's wife was deaf, and so he run the radio as loud as it would run, and so me and Pete could hear it plain as Old Man Killegrew's wife could, I reckon, even standing outside with the window closed.

And that night I said, "What? Japanese? What's a pearl harbor?" and Pete said, "Hush."

And so we stood there, it was cold, listening to the fellow in the radio talking, only I couldn't make no heads nor tails neither out of it. Then the fellow said that would be all for a while, and me and Pete walked back up the road to home, and Pete told me what it was. Because he was nigh twenty and he had done finished the Consolidated last June and he knowed a heap: about them Japanese dropping bombs on Pearl Harbor and that Pearl Harbor was across the water.

"Across what water?" I said. "Across that Government reservoy up at Oxford?"

"Naw," Pete said. "Across the big water. The Pacific Ocean."

We went home. Maw and pap was already asleep, and me and Pete laid in the bed, and I still couldn't understand where it was, and Pete told me again—the Pacific Ocean.

"What's the matter with you?" Pete said. "You're going on nine years old. You been in school now ever since September. Ain't you learned nothing yet?"

"I reckon we ain't got as fer as the Pacific Ocean yet," I said.

We was still sowing the vetch then that ought to been all finished by the fifteenth of November, because pap was still behind, just like he had been ever since me and Pete had knowed him. And we had firewood to git in, too, but every night me and Pete would go down to Old Man Killegrew's and stand outside his parlor window in the cold and listen to his radio; then we would come back home and lay in the bed and Pete would tell me what it was. That is, he would tell me for a while. Then he wouldn't tell me. It was like he didn't want to talk about it no more. He would tell me to shut up because he wanted to go to sleep, but he never wanted to go to sleep.

He would lay there, a heap stiller than if he was asleep, and it would be something, I could feel it coming out of him, like he was mad at me even, only I knowed he wasn't thinking about me, or like he was worried about something, and it wasn't that neither, because he never had nothing to worry about. He never got behind like pap, let alone stayed behind. Pap give him ten acres when he graduated from the Consolidated, and me and Pete both reckoned pap was durn glad to get shut of at least ten acres, less to have to worry with himself; and Pete had them ten acres all sowed to vetch and busted out and bedded for the winter, and so it wasn't that. But it was something. And still we would go down to Old Man Killegrew's every night and listen to his radio, and they was at it in the Philippines now, but General MacArthur was holding um. Then we would come back home and lay in the bed, and Pete wouldn't tell me nothing or talk at all. He would just lay there still as a ambush and when I would touch him, his side or his leg would feel hard and still as iron, until after a while I would go to sleep.

Then one night—it was the first time he had said nothing to me except to jump on me about not chopping enough wood at the wood tree where we was cutting—he said, "I got to go."

"Go where?" I said.

"To that war," Pete said.

"Before we even finish gettin' in the firewood?"

"Firewood, hell," Pete said.

"All right," I said. "When we going to start?"

But he wasn't even listening. He laid there, hard and still as iron in the dark. "I got to go," he said. "I jest ain't going to put up with no folks treating the Unity States that way."

"Yes," I said. "Firewood or no firewood, I reckon we got to go."

This time he heard me. He laid still again, but it was a different kind of still.

"You?" he said. "To a war?"

"You'll whup the big uns and I'll whup the little uns," I said.

Then he told me I couldn't go. At first I thought he just never wanted me tagging after him, like he wouldn't leave me go with him when he went sparking them girls of Tull's. Then he told me the Army wouldn't leave me go because I was too little, and then I knowed he really meant it and that I couldn't go nohow noways. And somehow I hadn't believed until then that he was going himself, but now I knowed he was and that he wasn't going to leave me go with him a-tall.

"I'll chop the wood and tote the water for you-all then!" I said. "You got to have wood and water!"

Anyway, he was listening to me now. He wasn't like iron now.

He turned onto his side and put his hand on my chest because it was me that was laying straight and hard on my back now.

"No," he said. "You got to stay here and help pap."

"Help him what?" I said. "He ain't never caught up nohow. He can't get no further behind. He can sholy take care of this little shirttail of a farm while me and you are whupping them Japanese. I got to go too. If you got to go, then so have I."

"No," Pete said. "Hush now. Hush." And he meant it, and I knowed he did. Only I made sho from his own mouth. I quit.

"So I just can't go then," I said.

"No," Pete said. "You just can't go. You're too little, in the first place, and in the second place—"

"All right," I said. "Then shut up and leave me go to sleep."

So he hushed then and laid back. And I laid there like I was already asleep, and pretty soon he was asleep and I knowed it was the wanting to go to the war that had worried him and kept him awake, and now that he had decided to go, he wasn't worried any more.

The next morning he told maw and pap. Maw was all right. She cried.

"No," she said, crying. "I don't want him to go. I would rather go myself in his place, if I could. I don't want to save the country. Them Japanese could take it and keep it, so long as they left me and my family and my children alone. But I remember my brother Marsh in that other war. He had to go to that one when he wasn't but nineteen, and our mother couldn't understand it then any more than I can now. But she told Marsh if he had to go, he had to go. And so, if Pete's got to go to this one, he's got to go to it. Jest don't ask me to understand why."

But pap was the one. He was the feller. "To the war?" he said. "Why, I just don't see a bit of use in that. You ain't old enough for the draft, and the country ain't being invaded. Our President in Washington, D.C., is watching the conditions and he will notify us. Besides, in that other war your ma just mentioned, I was drafted and sent clean to Texas and was held there nigh eight months until they finally quit fighting. It seems to me that that, along with your Uncle Marsh who received a actual wound on the battlefields of France, is enough for me and mine to have to do to protect the country, at least in my lifetime. Besides, what'll I do for help on the farm with you gone? It seems to me I'll get mighty far behind."

"You been behind as long as I can remember," Pete said. "Anyway, I'm going. I got to."

"Of course he's got to go," I said. "Them Japanese—"

"You hush your mouth!" maw said, crying. "Nobody's talking to you! Go and get me a armful of wood! That's what you can do!"

So I got the wood. And all the next day, while me and Pete and pap was getting in as much wood as we could in that time because Pete said how pap's idea of plenty of wood was one more stick laying against the wall that maw ain't put on the fire yet, maw was getting Pete ready to go. She washed and mended his clothes and cooked him a shoe box of vittles. And that night me and Pete laid in the bed and listened to her packing his grip and crying, until after a while Pete got up in his nightshirt and went back there, and I could hear them talking, until at last maw said, "You got to go, and so I want you to go. But I don't understand it, and I won't never, and so don't expect me to." And Pete come back and got into the bed again and laid again still and hard as iron on his back, and then he said, and he wasn't talking to me, he wasn't talking to nobody: "I got to go. I just got to."

"Sho you got to," I said. "Them Japanese—" He turned over hard, he kind of surged over onto his side, looking at me in the dark.

"Anyway, you're all right," he said. "I expected to have more trouble with you than with all the rest of them put together."

"I reckon I can't help it neither," I said. "But maybe it will run a few years longer and I can get there. Maybe someday I will jest walk in on you."

"I hope not," Pete said. "Folks don't go to wars for fun. A man don't leave his maw crying just for fun."

"Then why are you going?" I said.

"I got to," he said. "I just got to. Now you go on to sleep. I got to ketch that early bus in the morning."

"All right," I said. "I hear tell Memphis is a big place. How will you find where the Army's at?"

"I'll ask somebody where to go to join it," Pete said. "Go on to sleep now."

"Is that what you'll ask for? Where to join the Army?" I said.

"Yes," Pete said. He turned onto his back again. "Shut up and go to sleep."

We went to sleep. The next morning we et breakfast by lamplight because the bus would pass at six o'clock. Maw wasn't crying now. She jest looked grim and busy, putting breakfast on the table while we et it. Then she finished packing Pete's grip, except he never wanted to take no grip to the war, but maw said decent folks never went nowhere, not even to a war, without a change of clothes and something to tote them in. She put in the shoe box of fried chicken and biscuits and she put the Bible in, too, and then it was time to go. We didn't know until then that maw wasn't going to the bus. She jest brought Pete's cap and overcoat, and still she didn't cry no more, she jest stood with her hands on Pete's shoulders and she didn't move, but somehow, and just holding Pete's shoulders, she looked as hard and fierce as when Pete had turned toward me in the bed last night and tole me that anyway I was all right.

"They could take the country and keep the country, so long as they never bothered me and mine," she said. Then she said, "Don't never forget who you are. You ain't rich and the rest of the world outside of Frenchman's Bend never heard of you. But your blood is good as any blood anywhere, and don't you never forget it."

Then she kissed him, and then we was out of the house, with pap toting Pete's grip whether Pete wanted him to or not. There wasn't no dawn even yet, not even after we had stood on the highway by the mailbox, a while. Then we seen the lights of the bus coming and I was watching the bus until it come up and Pete flagged it, and then, sho enough, there was daylight—it had started while I wasn't watching. And now me and Pete expected pap to say something else foolish, like he done before, about how Uncle Marsh getting wounded in France and that trip to Texas pap taken in 1918 ought to be enough to save the Unity States in 1942, but he never. He done all right too. He jest said, "Good-by, son. Always remember what your ma told you and write her whenever you find the time." Then he shaken Pete's hand, and Pete looked at me a minute and put his hand on my head and rubbed my head durn nigh hard enough to wring my neck off and jumped into the bus, and the feller wound the door shut and the bus began to hum; then it was moving, humming and grinding and whining louder and louder; it was going fast, with two little red lights behind it that never seemed to get no littler, but just seemed to be running together until pretty soon they would touch and jest be one light. But they never did, and then the bus was gone, and even like it was, I could have pretty nigh busted out crying, nigh to nine years old and all.

Me and pap went back to the house. All that day we worked at the wood tree, and so I never had no good chance until about middle of the afternoon. Then I taken my slingshot and I would have liked to took all my bird eggs, too, because Pete had give me his collection and he holp me with mine, and he would like to git the box out and look at them as good as I would, even if he was nigh twenty years old. But the box was too big to tote a long ways and have to worry with, so I just taken the shikepoke egg, because it was the best un, and wropped it up good into a matchbox and hid it and the slingshot under the corner of the barn. Then we et supper and went to bed, and I thought then how if I would 'a' had to stayed in that room and that bed like that even for one more night, I jest couldn't 'a' stood it. Then I could hear pap snoring, but I never heard

Two Soldiers [181]

no sound from maw, whether she was asleep or not, and I don't reckon she was. So I taken my shoes and drapped them out the window, and then I clumb out like I used to watch Pete do when he was still jest seventeen and pap held that he was too young yet to be tomcatting around at night, and wouldn't leave him out, and I put on my shoes and went to the barn and got the slingshot and the shikepoke egg and went to the highway.

It wasn't cold, it was jest durn confounded dark, and that highway stretched on in front of me like, without nobody using it, it had stretched out half again as fer just like a man does when he lays down, so that for a time it looked like full sun was going to ketch me before I had finished them twenty-two miles to Jefferson. But it didn't. Daybreak was jest starting when I walked up the hill into town. I could smell breakfast cooking in the cabins and I wished I had thought to brought me a cold biscuit, but that was too late now. And Pete had told me Memphis was a piece beyond Jefferson, but I never knowed it was no eighty miles. So I stood there on that empty square, with daylight coming and coming and the street lights still burning and that Law looking down at me, and me still eighty miles from Memphis, and it had took me all night to walk jest twenty-two miles, and so, by the time I got to Memphis at that rate, Pete would 'a' done already started for Pearl Harbor.

"Where do you come from?" the Law said.

And I told him again. "I got to get to Memphis. My brother's there."

"You mean you ain't got any folks around here?" the Law said. "Nobody but that brother? What are you doing way off down here and your brother in Memphis?"

And I told him again, "I got to get to Memphis. I ain't got no time to waste talking about it and I ain't got time to walk it. I got to git there today."

"Come on here," the Law said.

We went down another street. And there was the bus, jest like when Pete got into it yestiddy morning, except there wasn't no lights on it now and it was empty. There was a regular bus dee-po like a railroad dee-po, with a ticket counter and a feller behind it, and the Law said, "Set down over there," and I set down on the bench, and the Law said, "I want to use your telephone," and he talked in the telephone a minute and put it down and said to the feller behind the ticket counter, "Keep your eye on him. I'll be back as soon as Mrs. Habersham can arrange to get herself up and dressed." He went out. I got up and went to the ticket counter.

"I want to go to Memphis," I said.

"You bet," the feller said. "You set down on the bench now. Mr. Foote will be back in a minute."

"I don't know no Mr. Foote," I said. "I want to ride that bus to Memphis."

"You got some money?" he said. "It'll cost you seventy-two cents."

I taken out the matchbox and unwropped the shikepoke egg. "I'll swap you this for a ticket to Memphis," I said.

"What's that?" he said.

"It's a shikepoke egg," I said. "You never seen one before. It's worth a dollar. I'll take seventy-two cents fer it."

"No," he said, "the fellers that own that bus insist on a cash basis. If I started swapping tickets for bird eggs and livestock and such, they would fire me. You go and set down on the bench now, like Mr. Foote—"

I started for the door, but he caught me, he put one hand on the ticket counter and jumped over it and caught up with me and reached his hand out to ketch my shirt. I whupped out my pocketknife and snapped it open.

"You put a hand on me and I'll cut it off," I said.

I tried to dodge him and run at the door, but he could move quicker than any grown man I ever see, quick as Pete almost. He cut me off and stood with his back against the door and one foot raised a little, and there wasn't no other way to get out. "Get back on that bench and stay there," he said.

And there wasn't no other way out. And he stood there with his back against the door. So I went back to the bench. And then it seemed like to me that dee-po was full of folks. There was that Law again, and there was two ladies in fur coats and their faces already painted. But they still looked like they had got up in a hurry and they still never liked it, a old one and a young one, looking down at me.

"He hasn't got a overcoat!" the old one said. "How in the world did he ever get down here by himself?"

"I ask you," the Law said. "I couldn't get nothing out of him except his brother is in Memphis and he wants to get back up there."

"That's right," I said. "I got to git to Memphis today."

"Of course you must," the old one said. "Are you sure you can find your brother when you get to Memphis?"

"I reckon I can," I said. "I ain't got but one and I have knowed him all my life. I reckon I will know him again when I see him."

The old one looked at me. "Somehow he doesn't look like he lives in Memphis," she said.

"He probably don't," the Law said. "You can't tell though. He might live anywhere, overhalls or not. This day and time they get scattered overnight from he—hope to breakfast; boys and girls, too, almost before they can walk good. He might have been in Missouri or Texas either yestiddy, for all we know. But he don't seem to have any doubt his brother is in Memphis. All I know to do is send him up there and leave him look."

"Yes," the old one said.

The young one set down on the bench by me and opened a hand satchel and taken out a artermatic writing pen and some papers.

Two Soldiers

"Now, honey," the old one said, "we're going to see that you find your brother, but we must have a case history for our files first. We want to know your name and your brother's name and where you were born and when your parents died."

"I don't need no case history neither," I said. "All I want is to get to Memphis. I got to get there today."

"You see?" the Law said. He said it almost like he enjoyed it. "That's what I told you."

"You're lucky, at that, Mrs. Habersham," the bus feller said. "I don't think he's got a gun on him, but he can open that knife da— I mean, fast enough to suit any man."

But the old one just stood there looking at me.

"Well," she said. "Well. I really don't know what to do."

"I do," the bus feller said. "I'm going to give him a ticket out of my own pocket, as a measure of protecting the company against riot and bloodshed. And when Mr. Foote tells the city board about it, it will be a civic matter and they will not only reimburse me, they will give me a medal too. Hey, Mr. Foote?"

But never nobody paid him no mind. The old one still stood looking down at me. She said "Well," again. Then she taken a dollar from her purse and give it to the bus feller. "I suppose he will travel on a child's ticket, won't he?"

"Wellum," the bus feller said, "I just don't know what the regulations would be. Likely I will be fired for not crating him and marking the crate Poison. But I'll risk it."

Then they were gone. Then the Law come back with a sandwich and give it to me.

"You're sure you can find that brother?" he said.

"I ain't yet convinced why not," I said. "If I don't see Pete first, he'll see me. He knows me too."

Then the Law went out for good, too, and I et the sandwich. Then more folks come in and bought tickets, and then the bus feller said it was time to go, and I got into the bus just like Pete done, and we was gone.

I seen all the towns. I seen all of them. When the bus got to going good, I found out I was jest about wore out for sleep. But there was too much I hadn't never saw before. We run out of Jefferson and run past fields and woods, then we would run into another town and out of that un and past fields and woods again, and then into another town with stores and gins and water tanks, and we run along by the railroad for a spell and I seen the signal arm move, and then I seen the train and then some more towns, and I was jest about plumb wore out for sleep, but I couldn't resk it. Then Memphis begun. It seemed like, to me, it went on for miles. We would pass a patch of stores and I would think that was sholy it and the bus would even stop. But it wouldn't be Memphis yet and we would go on again past water tanks and smokestacks on top of the mills, and if they was gins and sawmills, I never knowed there was that many and I never seen any that big, and where they got enough cotton and logs to run um I don't know.

Then I seen Memphis. I knowed I was right this time. It was standing up into the air. It looked like about a dozen whole towns bigger than Jefferson was set up on one edge in a field, standing up into the air higher than ara hill in all Yoknapatawpha County. Then we was in it, with the bus stopping ever' few feet, it seemed like to me, and cars rushing past on both sides of it and the street crowded with folks from ever' where in town that day, until I didn't see how there could 'a' been nobody left in Mis'sippi a-tall to even sell me a bus ticket, let alone write out no case histories. Then the bus stopped. It was another bus dee-po, a heap bigger than the one in Jefferson. And I said, "All right. Where do folks join the Army?"

"What?" the bus feller said.

And I said it again, "Where do folks join the Army?"

"Oh," he said. Then he told me how to get there. I was afraid at first I wouldn't ketch on how to do in a town big as Memphis. But I caught on all right. I never had to ask but twice more. Then I was there, and I was durn glad to git out of all them rushing cars and shoving folks and all that racket fer a spell, and I thought, It won't be long now, and I thought how if there was any kind of a crowd there that had done already joined the Army, too, Pete would likely see me before I seen him. And so I walked into the room. And Pete wasn't there.

He wasn't even there. There was a soldier with a big arrer-head on his sleeve, writing, and two fellers standing in front of him, and there was some more folks there, I reckon. It seems to me I remember some more folks there.

I went to the table where the soldier was writing, and I said, "Where's Pete?" and he looked up and I said, "My brother. Pete Grier. Where is he?"

"What?" the soldier said. "Who?"

And I told him again. "He joined the Army yestiddy. He's going to Pearl Harbor. So am I. I want to ketch him. Where you all got him?" Now they were all looking at me, but I never paid them no mind. "Come on," I said. "Where is he?"

The soldier had quit writing. He had both hands spraddled out on the table. "Oh," he said. "You're going, too, hah?"

"Yes," I said. "They got to have wood and water. I can chop it and tote it. Come on. Where's Pete?"

The soldier stood up. "Who let you in here?" he said. "Go on. Beat it."

"Durn that," I said. "You tell me where Pete—"

I be dog if he couldn't move faster than the bus feller even. He never come over the table, he come around it, he was on me almost before I knowed it, so that I jest had time to jump back and whup out my pocket-knife and snap it open and hit one lick, and he hollered and jumped back and grabbed one hand with the other and stood there cussing and hollering.

One of the other fellers grabbed me from behind, and I hit at him with the knife, but I couldn't reach him.

Then both of the fellers had me from behind, and then another soldier come out of a door at the back. He had on a belt with a britching strop over one shoulder.

"What the hell is this?" he said.

"That little son cut me with a knife!" the first soldier hollered. When he said that I tried to get at him again, but both them fellers was holding me, two against one, and the soldier with the backing strop said, "Here, here. Put your knife up, feller. None of us are armed. A man don't knife-fight folks that are barehanded." I could begin to hear him then. He sounded jest like Pete talked to me. "Let him go," he said. They let me go. "Now what's all the trouble about?" And I told him. "I see," he said. "And you come up to see if he was all right before he left."

"No," I said. "I came to—"

But he had already turned to where the first soldier was wropping a handkerchief around his hand.

"Have you got him?" he said. The first soldier went back to the table and looked at some papers.

"Here he is," he said. "He enlisted yestiddy. He's in a detachment leaving this morning for Little Rock." He had a watch stropped on his arm. He looked at it. "The train leaves in about fifty minutes. If I know country boys, they're probably all down there at the station right now."

"Get him up here," the one with the backing strop said. "Phone the station. Tell the porter to get him a cab. And you come with me," he said.

It was another office behind that un, with jest a table and some chairs. We set there while the soldier smoked, and it wasn't long; I knowed Pete's feet soon as I heard them. Then the first soldier opened the door and Pete come in. He never had no soldier clothes on. He looked jest like he did when he got on the bus yestiddy morning, except it seemed to me like it was at least a week, so much had happened, and I had done had to do so much traveling. He come in and there he was, looking at me like he hadn't never left home, except that here we was in Memphis, on the way to Pearl Harbor.

"What in durnation are you doing here?" he said.

And I told him, "You got to have wood and water to cook with. I can chop it and tote it for you-all."

"No," Pete said. "You're going back home."

"No, Pete," I said. "I got to go too. I got to. It hurts my heart, Pete."

"No," Pete said. He looked at the soldier. "I jest don't know what could have happened to him, lootenant," he said. "He never drawed a knife on anybody before in his life." He looked at me. "What did you do it for?"

"I don't know," I said. "I jest had to. I jest had to git here. I jest had to find you."

"Well, don't you never do it again, you hear?" Pete said. "You put that knife in your pocket and you keep it there. If I ever again hear of you drawing it on anybody, I'm coming back from wherever I am at and whup the fire out of you. You hear me?"

"I would pure cut a throat if it would bring you back to stay," I said. "Pete," I said. "Pete."

"No," Pete said. Now his voice wasn't hard and quick no more, it was almost quiet, and I knowed now I wouldn't never change him. "You must go home. You must look after maw, and I am depending on you to look after my ten acres. I want you to go back home. Today. Do you hear?"

"I hear," I said.

"Can he get back home by himself?" the soldier said.

"He come up here by himself," Pete said.

"I can get back, I reckon," I said. "I don't live in but one place. I don't reckon it's moved."

Pete taken a dollar out of his pocket and give it to me. "That'll buy your bus ticket right to our mailbox," he said. "I want you to mind the lootenant. He'll send you to the bus. And you go back home and you take care of maw and look after my ten acres and keep that durn knife in your pocket. You hear me?"

"Yes, Pete," I said.

"All right," Pete said. "Now I got to go." He put his hand on my head again. But this time he never wrung my neck. He just laid his hand on my head a minute. And then I be dog if he didn't lean down and kiss me, and I heard his feet and then the door, and I never looked up and that was all, me setting there, rubbing the place where Pete kissed me and the soldier throwed back in his chair, looking out the window and coughing. He reached into his pocket and handed something to me without looking around. It was a piece of chewing gum.

"Much obliged," I said. "Well, I reckon I might as well start back. I got a right fer piece to go."

"Wait," the soldier said. Then he telephoned again and I said again I better start back, and he said again, "Wait. Remember what Pete told you."

So we waited, and then another lady come in, old, too, in a fur coat, too, but she smelled all right, she never had no artermatic writing pen nor no case history neither. She come in and the soldier got up, and she looked around quick until she saw me, and come and put her hand on my shoulder light and quick and easy as maw herself might 'a' done it.

Two Soldiers

"Come on," she said. "Let's go home to dinner."

"Nome," I said. "I got to ketch the bus to Jefferson."

"I know. There's plenty of time. We'll go home and eat dinner first."

She had a car. And now we was right down in the middle of all them other cars. We was almost under the busses, and all them crowds of people on the street close enough to where I could have talked to them if I had knowed who they was. After a while she stopped the car. "Here we are," she said, and I looked at it, and if all that was her house, she sho had a big family. But all of it wasn't. We crossed a hall with trees growing in it and went into a little room without nothing in it but a nigger dressed up in a uniform a heap shinier than them soldiers had, and the nigger shut the door, and then I hollered, "Look out!" and grabbed, but it was all right; that whole little room jest went right on up and stopped and the door opened and we was in another hall, and the lady unlocked a door and we went in, and there was another soldier, a old feller, with a britching strop, too, and a silver-colored bird on each shoulder.

"Here we are," the lady said. "This is Colonel McKellogg. Now, what would you like for dinner?"

"I reckon I'll jest have some ham and eggs and coffee," I said.

She had done started to pick up the telephone. She stopped. "Coffee?" she said. "When did you start drinking coffee?"

"I don't know," I said. "I reckon it was before I could remember."

"You're about eight, aren't you?" she said.

"Nome," I said. "I'm eight and ten months. Going on eleven months."

She telephoned then. Then we set there and I told them how Pete had jest left that morning for Pearl Harbor and I had aimed to go with him, but I would have to go back home to take care of maw and look after Pete's ten acres, and she said how they had a little boy about my size, too, in a school in the East. Then a nigger, another one, in a short kind of shirttail coat, rolled a kind of wheelbarrer in. It had my ham and eggs and a glass of milk and a piece of pie, too, and I thought I was hungry. But when I taken the first bite I found out I couldn't swallow it, and I got up quick.

"I got to go," I said.

"Wait," she said.

"I got to go," I said.

"Just a minute," she said. "I've already telephoned for the car. It won't be but a minute now. Can't you drink the milk even? Or maybe some of your coffee?"

"Nome," I said. "I ain't hungry. I'll eat when I git home." Then the telephone rung. She never even answered it.

"There," she said. "There's the car." And we went back down in that 'ere little moving room with the dressed-up nigger. This time it was a big car with a soldier driving it. I got into the front with him. She give the soldier a dollar. "He might get hungry," she said. "Try to find a decent place for him."

"O.K., Mrs. McKellogg," the soldier said.

Then we was gone again. And now I could see Memphis good, bright in the sunshine, while we was swinging around it. And first thing I knowed, we was back on the same highway the bus run on this morning —the patches of stores and them big gins and sawmills, and Memphis running on for miles, it seemed like to me, before it begun to give out. Then we was running again between the fields and woods, running fast now, and except for that soldier, it was like I hadn't never been to Memphis a-tall. We was going fast now. At this rate, before I knowed it we would be home again, and I thought about me riding up to Frenchman's Bend in this big car with a soldier running it, and all of a sudden I begun to cry. I never knowed I was fixing to, and I couldn't stop it. I set there by that soldier, crying. We was going fast.

PART THREE

Fun, Fantasy and Adventure

SO MANY solemn things are written about children nowadays that we are glad when we can remember also the times when their spirits soar and they set forth in search of fun. Childhood is the time for adventuring. Out of the wild imaginings of youth grow mankind's great achievements. Boys, as we know, are usually more daring than girls, often displaying a positive lust for risking their lives and keeping their mothers on tenterhooks. Girls, in these middle years between the nursery and adolescence, go adventuring too but—with some exceptions—in a milder, quieter way. On the whole, they are preparing to keep the home-fires burning. It seems improbable that a woman will win the race to the moon.

Stories of boyhood adventure will always enjoy a very special place in literature. Here the young reign supreme. The appeal of *Huckleberry Finn* lies in its being altogether about boys in an all-boy world. Grownups are just so much background. How wonderful to go floating down the Mississippi on a raft, gazing up at the stars at night with just one other youthful companion, meeting each new hazard unaided, solving every problem with one's own wits! How thrilling, in the first place, to belong to a gang that swears allegiance *in blood* and pledges itself to kill any unfaithful member! Bloodshed and killing—lawlessness too—quite evidently have an unholy fascination for the young, but most youngsters resolve it harmlessly. In Saroyan's story, read "car" for "horse," transport this boy from his folksy, settled community into an unneighborly slum or mushrooming suburb, then it will probably not be an old-time family friend but the police-court that will settle his fate. Suppose the small boy in *His Oceanic Majesty's Goldfish* had been a few years older and the object that seemed to him so deeply necessary for acceptance by his peers had been really costly—what then?

So it is that the so-called "innocent" play of children often provides us with uncomfortable reminders of less innocent impulses. Watching our youngsters transfixed before *that screen* with its ever-ready diet of crime and violence, besieged by their demands to possess as-real-as-possible firearms and knives, we can hardly escape the knowledge that though children may shudder, they also find dreams of bloodshed irresistible. We are not the first to notice this. The philosopher Fourier, writing near the turn of the eighteenth century, takes account of the bloodthirstiness of children and offers his own solution for turning it to good use. In the idyllic society of his imagination where everyone lives in peaceful cooperation, who among the gentled citizenry, he asks, should be assigned the dirty work? Who should slaughter the animals for food? Why, the children, of course! The majority of them would do it and love it.

As our open spaces shrink and crowding increases, fewer youngsters can translate their natural yearning for action and romance into real-life doings. Children can, however, try to satisfy this need in daydreams where they become the heroic and glamorous persons they long to be. In this private world of the imagination even the timid stay-at-home achieves power; every wish is fulfilled. Charlie Chaplin the younger tells us how in a midnight excursion among some forbidden objects in a vast, dark house he became powerful and fearless. No longer was he merely the small son of a great man.

The girl in "The Centaur," pretending she is riding and mastering a powerful animal, goes even further in her imaginings—she also possesses and very nearly *becomes* the animal. Such imaginings, typical of the horse-crazy girl, assuage for the time being her grievance in being outclassed by the boy in sheer strength. A passion for horses is surprisingly frequent in girls this age. Though she herself is far from understanding the underlying meaning of her preoccupation with horses, they nevertheless often dominate her dream-life until, as she matures, she discovers the greater satisfactions in her special powers as a girl and woman.

But there are discomforts as well as pleasures in floating passively with these wish-fulfilling dreams. For one thing, children become increasingly aware that such fantasies do not actually prove satisfactory; they do not, in fact, assure them the coveted place in the real world. There is, besides, the vague awareness that unknown dangers lurk in the very fulfillment of such desires. The girl whose walls are covered with pictures of theatrical stars and who in her dreams achieves glamour and sex appeal, is also exposed to her unacknowledged fears about the adult sex relationship now near at hand. The boy who, in imagination, becomes the powerful leader and strong man senses the dangers that reside in his own aggressive drives. As anxiety increases it may show itself in many ways. Gwen Raverat in her reminiscences tells of the imagined thief in the night, the sense of personal threat that even as late as eighteen she felt in witnessing street scenes of violence or imagined violence. Many such preposterous imaginings and wholly irrational fears continue into adult life; scarcely one of us is without them. Even Oliver Wendell Holmes, who records a quiet, seemingly innocuous dream-life, notes the persistence and irrationality of his obsessions.

The best antidote to the less healthy side of daydreaming is to be found in a life solidly grounded in reality and in having grownups around who neither coddle children nor leave them to struggle alone. Children may still have their bad dreams and their personal troubles. But the process of self-testing which comes of learning to cope with real problems gives them at least a fair chance to gain strength. In the finest literature of today, there is a paucity of such tales; the contemporary writer is inclined to remember his childhood as a time of loneliness and bewilderment.

Adventure spells danger, and—for those who dare to live life fully—there will always be dangers both from without and within. Not even the most watchful parent can be sure of averting them. In *A Game of Catch* we have the not unfamiliar spectacle of a lad under an inner compulsion to assert power and win social acceptance even at real risk to life and limb. Girls too are sometimes prey to such compulsions. But for them the dangers are apt to be subtler, less likely to reside in physical risks than in the pitfalls along the arduous road to finding themselves both as woman and as person.

In their need for real-life adventuring, both boys and girls are fortunate if there is elbowroom and space where they may roam at will in comparative safety; and where there are also opportunities for testing mind and character as well as brawn. Children, all of them, are hungry for the kind of work they can see some sense to and which school does not always provide. When they can measure themselves and discover their actual strengths and limitations, preposterous fantasies of heroism will fade; true self-knowledge can then begin.

When two boys take possession of a neighbor's horse in a friendly community, the result apparently is just an engaging boyish prank.

WILLIAM SAROYAN

The Summer of the Beautiful White Horse

ONE DAY back there in the good old days when I was nine and the world was full of every imaginable kind of magnificence, and life was still a delightful and mysterious dream, my cousin Mourad, who was considered crazy by everybody who knew him except me, came to my house at four in the morning and woke me up by tapping on the window of my room.

Aram, he said.

I jumped out of bed and looked out the window.

I couldn't believe what I saw.

It wasn't morning yet, but it was summer and with daybreak not many minutes around the corner of the world it was light enough for me to know I wasn't dreaming.

My cousin Mourad was sitting on a beautiful white horse.

I stuck my head out of the window and rubbed my eyes.

Yes, he said in Armenian. It's a horse. You're not dreaming. Make it quick if you want a ride.

I knew my cousin Mourad enjoyed being alive more than anybody else who had ever fallen into the world by mistake, but this was more than even I could believe.

In the first place, my earliest memories had been memories of horses and my first longings had been longings to ride.

This was the wonderful part.

In the second place, we were poor.

This was the part that wouldn't permit me to believe what I saw.

We were poor. We had no money. Our whole tribe was poverty-stricken.

The Summer of the Beautiful White Horse

Every branch of the Garoghlanian family was living in the most amazing and comical poverty in the world. Nobody could understand where we ever got money enough to keep us with food in our bellies, not even the old men of the family. Most important of all, though, we were famous for our honesty. We had been famous for our honesty for something like eleven centuries, even when we had been the wealthiest family in what we liked to think was the world. We were proud first, honest next, and after that we believed in right and wrong. None of us would take advantage of anybody in the world, let alone steal.

Consequently, even though I could *see* the horse, so magnificent; even though I could *smell* it, so lovely; even though I could *hear* it breathing, so exciting; I couldn't *believe* the horse had anything to do with my cousin Mourad or with me or with any of the other members of our family, asleep or awake, because I *knew* my cousin Mourad couldn't have *bought* the horse, and if he couldn't have bought it he must have *stolen* it, and I refused to believe he had stolen it.

No member of the Garoghlanian family could be a thief.

I stared first at my cousin and then at the horse. There was a pious stillness and humor in each of them which on the one hand delighted me and on the other frightened me.

Mourad, I said, where did you steal this horse?

Leap out of the window, he said, if you want to ride.

It was true, then. He *had* stolen the horse. There was no question about it. He had come to invite me to ride or not, as I chose.

Well, it seemed to me stealing a horse for a ride was not the same thing as stealing something else, such as money. For all I knew, maybe it wasn't stealing at all. If you were crazy about horses the way my cousin Mourad and I were, it wasn't stealing. It wouldn't become stealing until we offered to sell the horse, which of course I knew we would never do.

Let me put on some clothes, I said.

All right, he said, but hurry.

I leaped into my clothes.

I jumped down to the yard from the window and leaped up onto the horse behind my cousin Mourad.

That year we lived at the edge of town, on Walnut Avenue. Behind our house was the country: vineyards, orchards, irrigation ditches, and country roads. In less than three minutes we were on Olive Avenue, and then the horse began to trot. The air was new and lovely to breathe. The feel of the horse running was wonderful. My cousin Mourad who was considered one of the craziest members of our family began to sing. I mean, he began to roar.

Every family has a crazy streak in it somewhere, and my cousin Mourad was considered the natural descendant of the crazy streak in our tribe. Before him was our uncle Khosrove, an enormous man with a powerful head of black hair and the largest mustache in the San Joaquin Valley, a man so furious in temper, so irritable, so impatient that he stopped anyone from talking by roaring, *It is no harm; pay no attention to it.*

That was all, no matter what anybody happened to be talking about. Once it was his own son Arak running eight blocks to the barber shop where his father was having his mustache trimmed to tell him their house was on fire. The man Khosrove sat up in the chair and roared, It is no harm; pay no attention to it. The barber said, But the boy says your house is on fire. So Khosrove roared, Enough, it is no harm, I say.

My cousin Mourad was considered the natural descendant of this man, although Mourad's father was Zorab, who was practical and nothing else. That's how it was in our tribe. A man could be the father of his son's flesh, but that did not mean that he was also the father of his spirit. The distribution of the various kinds of spirit of our tribe had been from the beginning capricious and vagrant.

We rode and my cousin Mourad sang. For all anybody knew we were still in the old country where, at least according to our neighbors, we belonged. We let the horse run as long as it felt like running.

At last my cousin Mourad said, Get down. I want to ride alone.

Will you let me ride alone? I said.

That is up to the horse, my cousin said. Get down.

The *horse* will let me ride, I said.

We shall see, he said. Don't forget that I have a way with a horse.

Well, I said, any way you have with a horse, I have also.

For the sake of your safety, he said, let us hope so. Get down.

All right, I said, but remember you've got to let me try to ride alone.

I got down and my cousin Mourad kicked his heels into the horse and shouted, *Vazire,* run. The horse stood on its hind legs, snorted, and burst into a fury of speed that was the loveliest thing I had ever seen. My cousin Mourad raced the horse across a field of dry grass to an irrigation ditch, crossed the ditch on the horse, and five minutes later returned, dripping wet.

The sun was coming up.

Now it's my turn to ride, I said.

My cousin Mourad got off the horse.

Ride, he said.

I leaped to the back of the horse and for a moment knew the awfulest fear imaginable. The horse did not move.

Kick into his muscles, my cousin Mourad said. What are you waiting for? We've got to take him back before everybody in the world is up and about.

I kicked into the muscles of the horse. Once again it reared and snorted. Then it began to run. I didn't know what to do. Instead of running across the field to the irrigation ditch the horse ran down the road to the vine-

The Summer of the Beautiful White Horse

yard of Dikran Halabian where it began to leap over vines. The horse leaped over seven vines before I fell. Then it continued running.

My cousin Mourad came running down the road.

I'm not worried about you, he shouted. We've got to get that horse. You go this way and I'll go this way. If you come upon him, be kindly. I'll be near.

I continued down the road and my cousin Mourad went across the field toward the irrigation ditch.

It took him half an hour to find the horse and bring him back.

All right, he said, jump on. The whole world is awake now.

What will we do? I said.

Well, he said, we'll either take him back or hide him until tomorrow morning.

He didn't sound worried and I knew he'd hide him and not take him back. Not for a while, at any rate.

Where will you hide him? I said.

I know a place, he said.

How long ago did you steal this horse? I said.

It suddenly dawned on me that he had been taking these early morning rides for some time and had come for me this morning only because he knew how much I longed to ride.

Who said anything about stealing a horse? he said.

Anyhow, I said, how long ago did you begin riding every morning?

Not until this morning, he said.

Are you telling the truth? I said.

Of course not, he said, but if we are found out, that's what you're to say. I don't want both of us to be liars. All you know is that we started riding this morning.

All right, I said.

He walked the horse quietly to the barn of a deserted vineyard which at one time had been the pride of a farmer named Fetvajian. There were some oats and dry alfalfa in the barn.

We began walking home.

It wasn't easy, he said, to get the horse to behave so nicely. At first it wanted to run wild, but as I've told you, I have a way with a horse. I can get it to want to do anything *I* want it to do. Horses understand me.

How do you do it? I said.

I have an understanding with a horse, he said.

Yes, but what sort of an understanding? I said.

A simple and honest one, he said.

Well, I said, I wish I knew how to reach an understanding like that with a horse.

You're still a small boy, he said. When you get to be thirteen you'll know how to do it.

I went home and ate a hearty breakfast.

That afternoon my uncle Khosrove came to our house for coffee and cigarettes. He sat in the parlor, sipping and smoking and remembering the old country. Then another visitor arrived, a farmer named John Byro, an Assyrian who, out of loneliness, had learned to speak Armenian. My mother brought the lonely visitor coffee and tobacco and he rolled a cigarette and sipped and smoked, and then at last, sighing sadly, he said, My white horse which was stolen last month is still gone. I cannot understand it.

My uncle Khosrove became very irritated and shouted, It's no harm. What is the loss of a horse? Haven't we all lost the homeland? What is this crying over a horse?

That may be all right for you, a city dweller, to say, John Byro said, but what of my surrey? What good is a surrey without a horse?

Pay no attention to it, my uncle Khosrove roared.

I walked ten miles to get here, John Byro said.

You have legs, my uncle Khosrove shouted.

My left leg pains me, the farmer said.

Pay no attention to it, my uncle Khosrove roared.

That horse cost me sixty dollars, the farmer said.

I spit on money, my uncle Khosrove said.

He got up and stalked out of the house, slamming the screen door.

My mother explained.

He has a gentle heart, she said. It is simply that he is homesick and such a large man.

The farmer went away and I ran over to my cousin Mourad's house.

He was sitting under a peach tree, trying to repair the hurt wing of a young robin which could not fly. He was talking to the bird.

What is it? he said.

The farmer, John Byro, I said. He visited our house. He wants his horse. You've had it a month. I want you to promise not to take it back until I learn to ride.

It will take you a *year* to learn to ride, my cousin Mourad said.

We could keep the horse a year, I said.

My cousin Mourad leaped to his feet.

What? he roared. Are you inviting a member of the Garoghlanian family to steal? The horse must go back to its true owner.

When? I said.

In six months at the latest, he said.

He threw the bird into the air. The bird tried hard, almost fell twice, but at last flew away, high and straight.

Early every morning for two weeks my cousin Mourad and I took the horse out of the barn of the deserted vineyard where we were hiding it and rode it, and every morning the horse, when it was my turn to ride alone, leaped over grape vines and small trees and threw me and ran away. Nevertheless, I hoped in time to learn to ride the way my cousin Mourad rode.

One morning on the way to Fetvajian's deserted vineyard we ran into the farmer John Byro who was on his way to town.

Let me do the talking, my cousin Mourad said. I have a way with farmers.

Good morning, John Byro, my cousin Mourad said to the farmer.

The farmer studied the horse eagerly.

Good morning, sons of my friends, he said. What is the name of your horse?

My Heart, my cousin Mourad said in Armenian.

A lovely name, John Byro said, for a lovely horse. I could swear it is the horse that was stolen from me many weeks ago. May I look into its mouth?

Of course, Mourad said.

The farmer looked into the mouth of the horse.

Tooth for tooth, he said. I would swear it *is* my horse if I didn't know your parents. The fame of your family for honesty is well known to me. Yet the horse *is* the twin of my horse. A suspicious man would believe his eyes instead of his heart. Good day, my young friends.

Good day, John Byro, my cousin Mourad said.

Early the following morning we took the horse to John Byro's vineyard and put it in the barn. The dogs followed us around without making a sound.

The dogs, I whispered to my cousin Mourad. I thought they would bark.

They would at somebody else, he said. I have a way with dogs.

My cousin Mourad put his arms around the horse, pressed his nose into the horse's nose, patted it, and then we went away.

That afternoon John Byro came to our house in his surrey and showed my mother the horse that had been stolen and returned.

I do not know what to think, he said. The horse is stronger than ever. Better-tempered, too. I thank God.

My uncle Khosrove, who was in the parlor, became irritated and shouted, Quiet, man, quiet. Your horse has been returned. Pay no attention to it.

Dreams of bloodshed and violence, secrecy and killing, are perennially relished by the young—were so even in the rural America of yesterday.

SAMUEL CLEMENS

from *Adventures of Huckleberry Finn*

... WHEN TOM AND ME got to the edge of the hilltop we looked away down into the village and could see three or four lights twinkling, where there was sick folks, maybe; and the stars over us was sparkling ever so fine; and down by the village was the river, a whole mile broad, and awful still and grand. We went down the hill and found Joe Harper and Ben Rogers, and two or three more of the boys, hid in the old tanyard. So we unhitched a skiff and pulled down the river two mile and a half, to the big scar on the hillside, and went ashore.

We went to a clump of bushes, and Tom made everybody swear to keep the secret, and then showed them a hole in the hill, right in the thickest part of the bushes. Then we lit the candles, and crawled in on our hands and knees. We went about two hundred yards, and then the cave opened up. Tom poked about amongst the passages, and pretty soon ducked under a wall where you wouldn't 'a' noticed that there was a hole. We went along a narrow place and got into a kind of room, all damp and sweaty and cold, and there we stopped. Tom says:

"Now, we'll start this band of robbers and call it Tom Sawyer's Gang. Everybody that wants to join has got to take an oath, and write his name in blood."

Everybody was willing. So Tom got out a sheet of paper that he had wrote the oath on, and read it. It swore every boy to stick to the band, and never tell any of the secrets; and if anybody done anything to any boy in the band, whichever boy was ordered to kill that person and his family must do it, and he mustn't eat and he mustn't sleep till he had killed them and hacked a cross in their breasts, which was the sign of the band. And nobody that didn't belong to the band could use that mark, and if he did he must be sued; and if he done it again he must be killed.

[198]

from Adventures of Huckleberry Finn

And if anybody that belonged to the band told the secrets, he must have his throat cut, and then have his carcass burnt up and the ashes scattered all around, and his name blotted off the list with blood and never mentioned again by the gang, but have a curse put on it and be forgot forever.

Everybody said it was a real beautiful oath, and asked Tom if he got it out of his own head. He said some of it, but the rest was out of pirate-books and robber-books, and every gang that was high-toned had it.

Some thought it would be good to kill the *families* of boys that told the secrets. Tom said it was a good idea, so he took a pencil and wrote it in. Then Ben Rogers says:

"Here's Huck Finn, he hain't got no family; what you going to do 'bout him?"

"Well, hain't he got a father?" says Tom Sawyer.

"Yes, he's got a father, but you can't never find him these days. He used to lay drunk with the hogs in the tanyard, but he hain't been seen in these parts for a year or more."

They talked it over, and they was going to rule me out, because they said every boy must have a family or somebody to kill, or else it wouldn't be fair and square for the others. Well, nobody could think of anything to do—everybody was stumped, and set still. I was most ready to cry; but all at once I thought of a way, and so I offered them Miss Watson—they could kill her. Everybody said:

"Oh, she'll do. That's all right. Huck can come in."

Then they all stuck a pin in their fingers to get blood to sign with, and I made my mark on the paper.

"Now," says Ben Rogers, "what's the line of business of this Gang?"

"Nothing only robbery and murder," Tom said.

"But who are we going to rob?—houses, or cattle, or—"

"Stuff! stealing cattle and such things ain't robbery; it's burglary," says Tom Sawyer. "We ain't burglars. That ain't no sort of style. We are highwaymen. We stop stages and carriages on the road, with masks on, and kill the people and take their watches and money."

"Must we always kill the people?"

"Oh, certainly. It's best. Some authorities think different, but mostly it's considered best to kill them—except some that you bring to the cave here, and keep them till they're ransomed."

"Ransomed? What's that?"

"I don't know. But that's what they do. I've seen it in books; and so of course that's what we've got to do."

"But how can we do it if we don't know what it is?"

"Why, blame it all, we've *got* to do it. Don't I tell you it's in the books? Do you want to go to doing different from what's in the books, and get things all muddled up?"

"Oh, that's all very fine to *say,* Tom Sawyer, but how in the nation are these fellows going to be ransomed if we don't know how to do it to them?—that's the thing *I* want to get at. Now, what do you *reckon* it is?"

"Well, I don' know. But per'aps if we keep them till they're ransomed, it means that we keep them till they're dead."

"Now, that's something *like.* That'll answer. Why couldn't you said that before? We'll keep them till they're ransomed to death; and a bothersome lot they'll be, too—eating up everything, and always trying to get loose."

"How you talk, Ben Rogers. How can they get loose when there's a guard over them, ready to shoot them down if they move a peg?"

"A guard! Well, that *is* good. So somebody's got to set up all night and never get any sleep, just so as to watch them. I think that's foolishness. Why can't a body take a club and ransom them as soon as they get here?"

"Because it ain't in the books so—that's why. Now, Ben Rogers, do you want to do things regular, or don't you?—that's the idea. Don't you reckon that the people that made the books knows what's the correct thing to do? Do you reckon *you* can learn 'em anything? Not by a good deal. No, sir, we'll just go on and ransom them in the regular way."

"All right. I don't mind; but I say it's a fool way, anyhow. Say, do we kill the women, too?"

"Well, Ben Rogers, if I was as ignorant as you I wouldn't let on. Kill the women? No; nobody ever saw anything in the books like that. You fetch them to the cave, and you're always as polite as pie to them; and by and by they fall in love with you, and never want to go home any more."

"Well, if that's the way I'm agreed, but I don't take no stock in it. Mighty soon we'll have the cave so cluttered up with women, and fellows waiting to be ransomed, that there won't be no place for the robbers. But go ahead, I ain't got nothing to say."

Little Tommy Barnes was asleep now, and when they waked him up he was scared, and cried, and said he wanted to go home to his ma, and didn't want to be a robber any more.

So they all made fun of him, and called him crybaby, and that made him mad, and he said he would go straight and tell all the secrets. But Tom give him five cents to keep quiet, and said we would all go home and meet next week, and rob somebody and kill some people.

Ben Rogers said he couldn't get out much, only Sundays, and so he wanted to begin next Sunday; but all the boys said it would be wicked to do it on Sunday, and that settled the thing. They agreed to get together and fix a day as soon as they could, and then we elected Tom Sawyer first captain and Joe Harper second captain of the Gang, and so started home.

I clumb up the shed and crept into my window just before day was breaking. My new clothes was all greased up and clayey, and I was dog-tired.

Charles Darwin's granddaughter records her secret fears and fantasies, first as a child then as a young girl. She sounds the keynote when she says "I could not have endured the touch of their stupid kind sympathetic fingers on my private soul."

GWEN RAVERAT

from *Period Piece*

THE ONLY GHOST I ever saw was at Down, and it was a rabbit. All the best beds at Down were great four-posters, with ceilings and curtains of stiff shiny chintz hanging all round them. One night, when I was sleeping in a little bed beside my mother's big one, I saw, I most certainly saw, a rabbit come out on the top of the canopy and run all along it and disappear at the far end. They never would believe me about this, which was unkind of them, for the tops of beds were always dangerous places.

In our own house at Cambridge, there were no four-posters—my mother did not approve of them—and bed-curtains were becoming vestigial; but still, all proper grown-up beds had muslin curtains hanging from small round canopies, which were fixed to hooks in the ceilings. That was where the tigers lived. I never actually saw one myself, but that only made it the more frightening. This was one of the reasons why I never liked sleeping in my mother's room. Fortunately, ordinary beds for children no longer had any curtains at all, so that the night-nursery was quite safe. The tigers can't have been very comfortable on the canopies, which were only about a yard across, but that was their own business. One really must not start being sentimental about tigers.

Anyhow, I had very little sense of relative size in those days. I remember a fierce argument with Charles, in which I maintained that Dobbin, our rocking horse, was as big as a real cart-horse. Dobbin was about three foot high. And I was always afraid of being sucked down the bath-hole when the water ran away with that dreadful scrautching noise.

One of the chief advantages of going to boarding school was that there I slept in a room with other girls; and surely neither tigers, ghosts, night-

[201]

mares nor burglars would dare to come into a room stuffed so full of people? Whereas my lonely bedroom at home was often quite stiff with horrors. Once, when I was about fifteen, I spent a whole night of panic lying awake listening to a strange muffled knocking on the wall. It was not till the next day that it occurred to me that it might have been the beating of my own heart. Another time, when my parents were away, I am ashamed to say that the footsteps and whispering in the garden under my window grew so alarming that I actually telephoned to the Police. Who came and said it was Cats. Cats! It would be cats; they knew I didn't like them, the devils.

My room was always full of dreams. The worst one was Joan of Arc. She came one windy night in full armour, and galloped up and down the passage outside my bedroom, stopping sometimes to shake and bang at my door and vow that she would kill me when she got in. Fortunately the door held and I woke before she broke it down; but the clanking of her armour and the fury of her feet have given me a permanent dislike to her. If you once dream about a person, the taste of your dream, bad or good, will cling to him or her for the rest of your life.

I suppose it was because one so often saw fallen and ill-used horses in those days, that I came to identify myself with them. It is still a great relief to me that one so seldom sees them now; even though this is only because there are so few horses to see. And that is really a sad business, for surely horses, like men, would rather exist than not exist at all, in spite of all the drawbacks of living.

At any rate, I often dreamt I was a horse, and I know exactly what it feels like to be one. I even know what it feels like to be able to twitch the skin on my shoulder, and shudder away a fly. Once I dreamt that I was a young yellow mare, and I was trying to hide behind a gorse bush from a very wicked bull. My yellow legs were so long that it was difficult to keep them folded up, and I was afraid that spots of my hide would shine out through the holes in the bush; but I woke before the bull got me. . . .

. . . My dreams were always rather melodramatic, though mostly in a more agreeable way. I was generally a boy, swimming rivers with a dagger in my mouth, or riding for my life with a message, or shooting my way out of a fray; in fact, I led at night a sort of Henty existence of most pleasurably exciting adventures. And so I still do, thank God.

But by day I was not nearly so brave as I was at night . . .

. . . Even when we went with Nana and the pram we were sometimes stoned; and we saw unpleasant things: a drunken man, or a child being beaten. The sight I remember with most horror was a little group of dreadful boys near the pump and horse trough at the corner of Shelly from *Period Piece*

Row. They were wringing the neck of a white hen; and a smaller boy stood apart, sobbing pitifully. I suppose it was his hen. Nana hurried us by. As we grew older, the danger from the boys grew less, and gradually ceased altogether. I suppose there may still be such gangs about, terrifying to the children, but imperceptible to the grown-up people; but I hope I am right in thinking that their activities are not quite so public as they used to be then.

The Poor always frightened me very much. There was a most evil Blind Man, with a beard, who sat in a little hole in the railings, which seemed to be specially made for beggars, opposite the Bull Hotel of those days. Beggars sometimes sit there still. He always had a dog, but it was never the same dog for long. We thought perhaps he murdered his dogs? I have only now realized that the reason why Blind Pew in *Treasure Island* frightened me so extremely, was that I gave him the face of our own Blind Man. The lame crossing-sweeper at the corner of the Backs had a terrible mutilated face. I tried never to see him, though his crossing was so near our house that it was difficult to avoid doing so sometimes. . . .

. . . One evening, in Cambridge, I saw something really frightening, and I never told anyone anything about it. When I was about eighteen I used to play second flute in the little C.U.M.S. orchestra of those days. I did not play well and was always afraid of coming in on the wrong beat after counting 153 empty bars. However, Mr. Dent and Clive Carey, who were the conductors, were very kind to me, and I dare say I did not do very much harm. One evening the friend, who generally went with me, did not turn up. I was not supposed to go out alone after dinner, but I thought that silly, and anyhow if they didn't know, they wouldn't mind. So I went off alone, rather nervously. Well, I was coming quietly home again by myself just about ten o'clock, and there was nobody at all to be seen, as I turned into the narrow darkness of Silver Street. I was just abreast of the little public-house, the Anchor, which stands at the town end of the bridge, when suddenly a small gang of rather disreputable undergraduates came running quickly towards me from the other side of the river.

They were carrying, flat out, the body of a woman who seemed to be dead.

Drowned in the river? That was my first thought. And then at once all kinds of possibilities rushed into my mind. Murdered? Or captured for some nameless purpose? Something horrible and vague and improper? It did not occur to me that she might be drunk. Men got drunk; women didn't. Anyhow, the men were in desperate haste and looked frightened and guilty, in their smashed-in caps and tattered gowns. They took no notice of me, but dashed across the Bridge and huddled quickly into the safety of the Anchor. Two or three more men, who were behind, came running up—one was carrying the girl's hat—and followed the others into the public-house and banged the door behind them. And then everything was quite quiet and ordinary again; as if death and melodrama had never been there at all.

I went slowly on, wondering what on earth I ought to do. Surely someone ought to find out what had been happening? There was something so evil about the whole affair. Ought I to tell my father? But I could hardly endure the thought of speaking to him about it. Perhaps it was something improper as well as wicked? And that would make him even more uncomfortable than it would make me—intolerably embarrassing to us both, to know that the other knew of it. Of course, in those days it would have been inconceivable to me that any respectable woman should go into a public-house on any occasion whatever; far less a young girl like me. A public-house was a mysterious sinister haunt, full of Bad Women, where decent working men might occasionally go for a glass of beer (though it would be better if they didn't); but where a Gentleman would only go (a) if he were Fast, or (b) if he were showing off and pretending to be Fast, or (c) if he were on a walking tour. I had never been into the bar of any public-house till some time in the 'twenties, and then I felt very shy and out of place. But naturally my father could have gone there on an errand of inquiry.

Undecided I went on home and went into the study. It was the usual domestic scene. My father was working with his shoes off as always, and his feet in their dark red socks in the fender. He looked up at my entrance and waited, in his kind patient way, for things to settle down again, before going on with his long neat rows of little figures and symbols. My mother was sitting there, too, surrounded by heaps of papers: advertisements, old bills, letters, newspapers, flotsam and jetsam, most of which would have been better in the waste-paper basket. It was all very quiet and humdrum, and I burst into the familiar room, feeling like a bomb so highly charged with horror and emotion that I should blow the whole house up if I exploded.

My mother said: 'Gwenny dear, just add up the milkman's book, will you, please? I can't make it come right.' They had noticed nothing at all. These old people! They never did notice anything, so blind and deaf and insensitive as they were. The most appalling, the most shattering things, could happen under their very noses, and they would know nothing about them. It was perfectly easy to hide anything from them, from Love to a bad cold and cough. In fact, if you wanted them to know something, you absolutely had to shout it at them, and even then they probably would not grasp it. When I wanted to tell my father that I was engaged to be married, I had to follow him up and down the meadow for nearly an hour—he was absorbed in shooting with a bow on the Lammas Land—

from *Period Piece* [205]

before I could bring myself to interrupt him. He had never noticed that I was trying to attract his attention, till I spoke; and then he reproached me for not having done so sooner!

So I quite coldly decided to mind my own business and to say nothing about what I had seen. I knew I was being cowardly, and that this was wrong, but I did not regret my decision. Though I would still like to know what had really been happening that night?

But anyhow, that was one great comfort: that it was perfectly easy to hide one's feelings from the old people. They never knew about any of the things I have written in this chapter. I simply could not have endured the touch of their stupid, kind sympathetic fingers on my private soul.

Yes, it was a great comfort, how easy it was to be secret.

A grass-roots American describes boyish high jinks in a neighborly country town of yesteryear, and the culprits' rounding up by the police.

CARL SANDBURG

from *Always the Young Strangers*

ON THE WOODEN SIDEWALKS of Berrien Street we played one kind of mumble-peg and in the grass of the front yard or the grass between sidewalk and gutter ditch we played the more complicated and interesting one with jump-the-fence, thread-the-needle, plow-forty-acres, and plow-eighty-acres. The loser saw us trim a peg the length of the knife blade we played with. Then each of us took a whack at the top of the peg with the knife top, holding the blade, aiming to drive the peg as deep as we could. It was up to the loser to *mumble* his mouth and teeth around that peg and bring it out of the ground. On the wooden sidewalks we spun tops, flipped jackstones, chalked tit-tat-toe.

On the street, however, we played baseball, two-old-cat, choose-up, knocking-up flies. Shinny was worth the time. For knocking a tin can or a block of wood toward a goal any kind of club would do, though the fellow with a plow handle had the best of it. Duck-on-a-rock has its points. The duck is a small rock that sits on a large rock. When you knock the duck off the rock, you have to run and pick up your own rock and get back to taw without being tagged. Or you can refuse to touch your rock and stand by it till another player knocks the duck off the rock and take a chance on picking up your rock and running for taw. If you get caught you're "it" and your rock becomes the duck. It sounds simple but it can be as scientific and complicated as some of the more famous games.

After we had been to see the commencement Field Day on the Knox or Lombard campus, we put on our own little field day, barefoot in the summer dust of Berrien Street. Some boy usually had a two-dollar-and-a-half Waterbury watch and timed us as we ran fifty yards, one hundred yards, a few seconds slower than the college runners, and five or six seconds under the world's record. We knew how near we came to the

from *Always the Young Strangers*

college records in the standing broad jump, the running broad jump, the hop-skip-and-a-step, the standing high jump and the running high jump. Whoever could throw a crowbar the farthest was counted put-and-shot "champeen." We did about everything the college athletes did except the pole vault. How can you have a pole vault setup on a public street where it would scare the living daylights out of all but the gentlest and weariest horses? The mile run we did of afternoons, breaking no records except some of our own, yet satisfying ourselves that there is such a thing as "second wind" and if you can get it you can finish your mile.

I haven't seen a field day since those days in the late '80's and early '90's. Yet because of the way we went in for those sports events in our own crude way on a dusty street, I can follow news reports and photographs of the Olympic games a little as though I had trained for some of the events. If as a boy you have put all you've got into a few hundred-yard dashes or running broad jumps you know better what is going on in the hearts, lungs, and minds of those who train, struggle, and hope for Olympic championships. Once in the cubicle of a magazine office I met in a near-by cubicle a fellow who had broken a world's mile-run record. He was a worn man, older than his years. He had trained too hard and run more miles than was good for him.

Of those days of play and sport in the street in front of our house one tender and curious memory stands out. The house next east to ours straight across the street was an average two-story frame affair, with a porch perhaps fifteen feet long. In the street in front of this house was our home base when playing ball. Often we saw on that porch in a rocking chair a little old woman, her hair snow-white with the years. She had a past, a rather bright though not dazzling past, you might say. She could lay claim to fame, if she chose. Millions of children reading the McGuffey and other school readers had met her name and memorized lines she had written. For there was in the course of her years no short poem in the English language more widely published, known, and recited than her lines about "Little Things":

Little drops of water,
Little grains of sand,
Make the mighty ocean
And the pleasant land. . . .

Little deeds of kindness
Little words of love,
Help to make earth happy
Like the heaven above.

She was Julia Carney, her sons Fletcher and James being Universalists and Lombard graduates, Fletcher serving three or four terms as mayor of Galesburg. There she sat in the quiet of her backward-gazing thoughts, sometimes gently rocking, while we hooted and yelled over hits, runs, putouts. There she sat, an image of silence and rest, while the air rang with boy screams, "Hit it bang on the nose now!" "Aw, he couldn't hit a balloon!" "Down went McGinty to the bottom of the sea!" Rarely she turned her head to see what we were doing. She made no request "for the benefit of those who have retired." To us at that time she was just one more nice old woman who wouldn't bother boys at play. We didn't know that her writings were in books and newspaper reprints that reached millions of readers. The Carneys were good neighbors and she was one of them—that was all we knew.

We should have heard about her in school. We should have read little pieces about her in the papers. She has a tiny quaint niche in the history of American literature under which one line could be written: "She loved children and wrote poems she hoped children would love." As late as the year 1952 Mrs. Dwight D. Eisenhower in a magazine article quoted the poem "Little Things" as one of her childhood delights.

It wasn't long before the fathers and mothers along Berrien Street had new troubles with their boys. Under that electric light at Day and Berrien the boys had a new playground. They could turn night into day. There was night baseball, night shinny, night duck-on-a-rock, night tug-of-war. There were winners yelling because they had won. There were losers yelling that next time they would make the winners eat dirt. Both winners and losers might be hooting each other at the same time. "Yah, yah, yuh hayseeds you, you couldn't tell your hind end from a hole in the ground!" Vehement remarks like that floated in through windows into rooms where honest Q. shopmen and worthy railroad firemen and brakemen were trying for a little sleep because they had worked today and hoped to work tomorrow.

One of the sleepers who couldn't sleep had a voice like a big-league umpire and it was like shooting had started when one night he clamored from his bedroom window, "You boys shut up with your goddam noise and go home with you. If you don't I'll get the police on you." The noise stopped—no more hoots and yells. We sat cross-legged on a patch of grass next to a sidewalk and talked in whispers: "Do you s'pose he means it?" "Aw, what the hell, we got a right to holler, this is a free country." "Yeah, but what if he means it? We'll get run in." "Yeah, I don't want no patrol-wagon ride." About then came a woman who wanted her sonnyboy and she took him by one ear and led him away and his face had a sheepish look. Then came two men. They were fathers. They spotted their boys, collared them and led them away like two sheep for slaughter. Mart and I went home. If we didn't get into the house by nine o'clock after our street play we would get scoldings or worse. We knew too what we would get if we didn't wash our dirty dusty feet. Into a wash basin they went—or we put them under the pump spout before coming into the house.

On a later night the boys forgot themselves and the hullabaloo they made could be heard a block away. Then as promised, the patrol wagon came. Before it could stop, five or six boys skedaddled to their homes. That left five or six of us who weren't going to run. If we ran it would

from *Always the Young Strangers*

show we were scared. We stood in a huddle waiting. Out of the patrol wagon under the electric light came two policemen in blue uniforms with a row of brass buttons shining, their nickel-plated stars shining too on their coats. One of them, Frank Peterson, weighed about two hundred and twenty pounds, and looked like a battleship coming toward us. We expected some hard words from Policeman Peterson. He spoke in a soft voice like what he was saying was confidential. "Don't you boys know you're makin a hell of a noise here and it disturbs people who are tryin to sleep?" What could we say to a nice quiet intelligent question like that? One boy said, "Yes," another, "Well, you know we was just tryin to have some fun." "Yes," said Peterson, again quiet and confidential like, "but ain't there some way you can have your fun without keepin people awake that's tryin to sleep?" We had come to like Policeman Peterson. We saw he wasn't mad at us and it didn't look like we were going to be put in the wagon and hauled to the calaboose. We said yes, we would try to have our fun without making so much noise. Before walking away to the wagon Peterson said, "Now that's a promise, boys, and I expect you to keep it. If you don't stop your noise, we'll have to run you in." And his voice got a little hard as he said, "Remember that. We don't like to arrest young fellows like you but sometimes we have to do it." That word "arrest" stuck in our ears. They could have arrested us. When you're arrested that means you're a criminal. And if you're a criminal, where are you?

The patrol wagon drove away. When the rumble of its wheels had died away we sat on the grass and talked in low tones near a whisper. All of us agreed that from now on we had better try to have our fun without hollering and yelling all the time like there was bloody murder or a house on fire. All agreed except the boy who had on another night said, "Aw, what the hell, we got a right to holler, this is a free country." This boy was saying, "Aw, that stinkin cop Peterson, I'd like to tie a bunch of firecrackers to his tail." He guessed he'd rather stay away and have some other kind of fun than come around and be a nice good boy like the police told him. And he did stay away and later he took to the poolrooms and the saloons and still later put in a year in the Pontiac reformatory for petty larceny.

We went on playing under the electric light and trying to keep quiet but it was a strain on us. What is duck-on-a-rock if you can't holler? I had got a job where I had to report at six-thirty in the morning and had gone home early one night, leaving the boys in a hot game of shinny, back in their old hooting and yelling. They told me the next day that a railroad fireman had come out in his night shirt with a club and a revolver. He shot in the air twice to show the gun was loaded. He sent a bullet into a sidewalk plank and had them look at the bullet. He was wild-eyed, cursed them, slapped one of them in the face, kicked another, then took out a watch and said if every last one of them wasn't gone in two minutes he would shoot to kill. Half the boys ran and the rest went away on a fast walk. From then on there were not as many boys came to that corner for night ball, night shinny, night duck-on-a-rock. The corner became reasonably quiet, and decent people could sleep. There was hate for the shooting-iron fireman and when boys passed him on the street and he was out of hearing they called him the dirtiest names they could think of. And Policeman Frank Peterson they would point out with, "He ain't a bad fellow, do you know?"

One Halloween night we paid a debt to a man who had lectured and gabbed us for smoking cornsilk cigarettes we had made. He said we would go from cornsilk to tobacco and tobacco was bad. We strung a dozen tin cans on a rope, made another like it. We passed his house when it was lighted, came back later when it was dark. We threw our two strings of tin cans one after the other against his front door. Then we ran and hid behind a fence across the street. We saw the door open. We saw him come out and stand there looking suspiciously at the crazy tin cans on the porch floor. They might be bombs and they might explode, we guessed he was thinking. They might be a kind of dynamite can made by the Chicago anarchists we were reading about then. He kicked the cans around a little as though ready to run if any can exploded. He went to the front gate, looked up and down the street, muttering words we couldn't hear. He went back to the cans, picked up one string of them, and took it into the house, came out again and took the other string of cans in. Then we saw the door close. We waited a while, came out from behind the fence and ran lickety-split up the street. We had had our revenge and it was sweet. We talked about what smart devilish things we could think up when we hated somebody. Our next trick wasn't so good.

A quiet elderly couple had their home on the south side of Berrien west of Pearl. They had been there a year or two and we hadn't heard their name or what they lived on. When they sat on their front porch they might look at each other once in a while but they didn't speak to each other. When us kids passed by they didn't look at us. They just went on looking straight ahead at nothing in particular. They seemed to be living in a quiet world of their own. They looked quiet and acted quiet. They were so still and peaceable that we got to talking about how still and peaceable they were and we ought to do something about it. One boy said, "Let's give 'em the tin cans." It wasn't a case of hate. We didn't hate them. We were just curious about them and we thought maybe something funny would happen. Again we strung together a dozen cans on each of two ropes. We saw their light on, waited and saw their kerosene lamp go out, waited a while longer and then sent the two strings of cans slam-bang against the front door. We skipped across the street, three

from *Always the Young Strangers*

of us and each behind his own tree. We waited. Nothing happened. The door didn't open. Nobody came out. We waited a while wondering whether the man had gone out the back door and was circling around to surprise us. We picked up our feet and ran.

It was several months later that one of the boys went into a Main Street grocery and saw this couple. For how many bars of soap they wanted or how many pounds of butter, they held up their fingers, two fingers for two bars of soap and so on. They didn't say a word. They were deaf and dumb. When the three of us heard this we were honest with each other. We asked why we had done such a fool thing. "What the hell," said one boy as he turned his back to me and stooped, "kick me." I gave him a swift kick in the hind end, then stooped for him to kick me. Each of the three of us gave the other two a swift kick. Once later when I passed the house and saw the couple sitting quiet and peaceable on their front porch I looked straight at them and touched my hat. They didn't nod nor smile. They just went on looking ahead at nothing in particular. . . .

The author relates a boyhood adventure in which he obtained (by theft) the object of his desires and tells how everything worked out better than he had a right to expect.

AUSTIN STRONG

His Oceanic Majesty's Goldfish

THE LARGE MUSTACHE was my father, the beautiful dark eyes my mother. I was aware of tears, champagne glasses, laughing speeches, and farewell shouts as we stood at the ship's rail looking back at Meiggs Wharf and the receding city of San Francisco.

Our heavy sails turned to iron as the northeast wind struck them with a howl, sending the tiny schooner scudding through the Golden Gate to breast the angry Pacific waiting outside to pounce on us. Suddenly everything went mad; screaming sea gulls were blown high; the vessel leaped into the air and fell on her side, half capsized by a knock-down flaw, her lee rail disappearing under a wash of green water and foaming suds.

The young couple fell to the deck clutching their small son. They laughingly held me between them as we all three slid down the careening deck to be rescued in the nick of time by grinning brown sailors smelling of tar, coconut oil, and chewing tobacco. One of them, at the request of my mother, tied a double bowline around my waist, making the end fast to a ring bolt on the white deck.

Here I was tethered, a none too safe prisoner, every day for fourteen terrifying days. Tied to that slanting, heaving floor, which was half under water the whole length of the ship, I was buffeted, jerked off my feet, stung by flying spray, deafened by the never ending roar of the wind and sea.

Green waters full of iridescent bubbles snatched at my feet when they swept by, leaving long damp stains on the deck. The winds blew up my sleeves, whipping my hair in all directions. Everywhere there was wild excitement—banging of blocks, angry shouts, sudden rushings of the crew to take in or let out the main and jib sheets. No one had to tell me that our lives were in the four hands of the two struggling men at the wheel and that the angel with the dark wings was hovering over our masts.

The large mustache would prick my cheek as my father brought his reassuring face close to mine, while my mother held me safe, and together they would sing to keep fear away from me. I would look into the eyes of my mother, searching for any sign of anxiety in the clear, quiet depths, and finding none I would breathe again, feeling the iron band about my heart relax. I caught the infection of their happiness and we would all laugh together for no reason at all.

They were filled with high hope, for riches and honors lay ahead of us. No wonder they were gay, for had not our good rich friend commissioned my father to go to Honolulu to paint a picture of the volcano Mauna Loa in full eruption? And hadn't they an important letter of introduction to a real king who sat on a real throne, wore a real crown, and lived in a real palace, His Oceanic Majesty, King Kalakaua of the Hawaiian Archipelago?

Since we were too poor to afford tickets on a Pacific liner, our benefactor had given us free passage on one of his trading schooners, the *Consuelo*, and these two babes in the wood, with their solemn offspring, were blown at last around Diamond Head under the lee of Punchbowl into the breathless heat of Honolulu Harbor, dangerous seas now far behind, fame and fortune beckoning us from the shores.

A long, graceful boat manned by singing natives in uniform shot out from the king's boathouse. She was dazzling white, with a canvas awning the length of her and a gilded crown on either side of her bow. This was the royal barge coming alongside with tossed oars to row us ashore in state.

We went to live in a wooden cottage that might have been taken from a child's picture book. It was set back from Fort Street, almost lost in a fragrant garden of big leaves and strange-looking flowers. Young attachés and their wives from all the legations annexed my parents with joy, and our wide veranda fairly glistened with naval gold lace from the British, French, Russian, and Chilean men-of-war. My gay parents must have been a godsend to those exiles of every nationality.

I lived to the tune of their laughter and endless parties, but in spite of belonging to the king's set, in spite of my father's success as an artist, I was not happy. The children who lived on our street looked down their noses at me.

It was the fashion in those days to have at the entrances of one's driveway half a tub constantly filled by a pipe with fresh water for the horses. The rich people had handsome tubs painted with bright colors at their gates and, to add to their prestige, their tubs were alive with goldfish. Our was old and unpainted, a shabby affair with rusty hoops, and, alas, contained no fish. The neighboring children made faces at me and with an ancient malice insisted that we were too poor to have goldfish in our disreputable tub. It troubled me that my hilarious parents had no idea that we were losing face with our neighbors' children, but boylike I kept my suffering to myself.

One day the Japanese attachés from the legation across the way came over for lunch. They were dressed like dark butterflies in their national costume. I stood on the outer edge of the veranda and overheard them telling about the beautiful double-tailed goldfish the Emperor of Japan had just sent to King Kalakaua and how they had emptied them officially that morning into the lily pond of the royal Kapiolani Park. They told my mother these sacred fish were very rare and belonged to the royal family of Japan.

My heart skipped a beat; I was stabbed by a sudden overwhelming desire. In one moment I had become a thief. From then on I saw nothing but an imperial fish swimming in our battered tub, giving face to my carefree parents and despair to my enemies.

Kapiolani Park was out of town near Waikiki, and it cost five cents to go there in the mule-car. Finding I had ten cents in my tin-can bank, I dashed up to the friendly old Chinese groceryman at the head of our street and for five cents bought a ball of red, white, and blue string. I then took two bright new pins from my Portuguese nurse's sewing basket and plunged into action.

This was my first adventure alone into the great out-of-doors away from the safe and protected area under my nurse's eye. With a pounding heart I hailed the mule-car, a wide open-air affair with a cool covering of white canvas and bobbing tassels. It was driven by a barefoot Kanaka with a sleepy face. I held up a timid finger and to my astonishment I was obeyed—the car stopped at my command. I felt important and apologetic at the same time when I found I was the only passenger, for it was the hot, buzzy time of the afternoon when everyone retires for a siesta.

With one wheel flat and squeaking, we swayed and bumped along through the deserted city, down freshly watered avenues kept in perpetual twilight by the shade of flowering trees overhead. The air was filled with the stinging scent of roasting coffee and burnt sugar, while over all hung the redoubtable smell of distant Chinatown, that potent mixture of teeming humanity, rotting fish, sandalwood, and incense.

I heard a warning voice within as I paid my carfare with my last remaining nickel. It whispered, "How are you going to come back with no money?" But I shut my ears tight, and going forward with a pounding heart, I sat close to the driver as we came out of the city into the blinding white road which ran along the shore.

"Want to drive?" he asked, smiling through an enormous yawn as he held out the reins. I clutched the stiff hot leather while the driver disappeared inside, curled up on the bench, and promptly fell asleep. This was my first meeting with responsibility. Though my bare feet were being burned alive by the heat of the sun on the platform, I stood motionless.

The mule, with his large ears encased in netted fly-bags, feeling the hand of inexperience, promptly relaxed and reduced his speed to a crawl. He dragged us at a snail's pace along the edge of the beach and I could see the lines on lines of charging surf running white over the hidden reefs. To the left I could see half-naked Chinese, with their big coneshaped hats, working like animated mushrooms, thigh-deep in mud, planting rice in the flat watery fields against a background of green mountains.

We crept along until at last the mule stopped of himself, poked his head around his stern, whisked a fly away with his tail, and looked at me with distaste. The driver woke with a start, shouting automatically as if I were a full carload of passengers: "All out for Kapiolani Park!"

I thanked him politely as he lifted me down in front of the entrance to the Park and I asked him to read me a freshly painted sign at the side of the gates. He slowly read the words: "Fishing in the Park is strictly prohibited and will be punished with the full severity of the law.—KALAKAUA, REX."

I stood rooted to the ground as the driver, with a sleepy grin drove the bobbing mule-car around a curve and out of sight, leaving me with my ball of twine, my pins, and my pockets empty of money. I stood for a time stunned. "Full severity of the law" meant only one thing when a king caught you. Your head was chopped off on a block of wood in the Tower of London and popped into a basket. Slowly I drew half circles in the dust with my big toe, waiting for my heart to quiet down.

By fine degrees courage returned to me. It came first in the shape of curiosity. I edged my way slowly through the gates, tiptoeing out of the blinding heat into the chill cathedral gloom of the Park. I saw two Chinese gardeners sweeping the driveway. Again I stood still for a long time. Finding they paid no attention to me, I took a few cautious steps farther in and once more became rooted to the ground, for there, quite near me, squatting on his haunches, was a half-naked Chinese with the face of a joss-house mask. He was cutting the grass with an evil-looking scimitar. Standing still until he had worked himself out of sight round a tree, I dashed off the roadway across the lawn into a beautiful Chinese garden with gray stone lanterns, pagodas, and frog-faced lions goggle-eyed with ferocity.

I came to a pond filled with water lilies, the edges of their enormous pads neatly turned up, like little fences. A moonbridge arched over the still water and I climbed the slippery incline, which is very steep until the circle flattens out on top; here I lay on my stomach, quaking. Guilt had laid a cold hand on me. I was a robber in a royal domain.

Placing my straw hat beside me and slowly raising my head, I looked carefully about for sign of a human being, but apparently this garden was a place apart. It was empty of life save for one pink flamingo who stared at me suspiciously. I peered down into the pool below and saw a small white object which stared up at me with frightened eyes. It was my own face reflected among the lilies.

Then I saw them! I couldn't believe my good luck. I had found them at last, the noble goldfish of the Emperor of Japan. Prodigious fellows, obviously aristocrats of high degree, wearing feathery fins and tails like court trains, trailing clouds of glory.

Quickly I bent a pin, and fastening it to the end of my red, white, and blue string I lowered it, hand over hand, into the liquid crystal below. The leisurely fish, as bright as porcelain, glided haughtily past my pin, not deigning to notice it. Why I thought a fish would swallow my baitless hook I do not know. It was a triumph of hope over experience, however, for after I had lain patiently on my stomach for a long time the miracle happened!

A large, dignified grand duke of a goldfish, attracted by the brightness of my pin, made the stupid mistake of thinking it was something good to eat. He slowly opened his bored face and swallowed it. A hard tug nearly toppled me off the bridge. I hauled up the sacred fish and soon had him indignantly flopping beside me, where he spat out the hook with disdain and would have flopped off the bridge had I not covered him with my straw hat. Again I peered around, now guilty in fact, for the deed was done.

The flamingo was still there, standing motionless on one leg, staring at me with an unblinking, accusing eye. In panic I hastily stuffed the fish into the crown of my hat, and jamming it on my head, with the victim struggling inside, I flew with the heels of terror out into the open road.

To my dismay I found the day almost spent as I ran before a following wind; the whole sky was afire with a red sunset which threw my gigantic shadow like a dancing hobgoblin far ahead of me on the wide road.

The awful voice spoke to me again. "There, what did I tell you? You have no money, so now you have an all-night walk in the dark."

But my only thought was how to keep my fish alive until I got him in our tub. I saw a wide irrigation ditch, which fed the paddy fields with water, running by the side of the road. Slipping down the bank, I removed my hat, and holding the fish by his golden tail, I plunged him into the water, arguing that to a fish this was like a breath of air to a suffocated man.

I held him under until he grew lively again and then I went on my interminable journey, running fast along the road, slipping down to the side of the ditch to souse my imperial highness until he revived enough for the next lap. I don't know how many times I did this, or how many hundred feet I had advanced along the way, but my legs began to ache and my head swam with weariness and wet fish. Then suddenly I was in

His Oceanic Majesty's Goldfish [217]

the midst of warning shouts, angry men's voices, stamping horses, jingling harness, military commands—a carriage had nearly run over me.

I was too young to know about palace revolutions and the necessity for armed escorts. I only knew I was terrified to find myself surrounded by grave men on horseback. An officer leaped from his saddle and stood before me.

I had the presence of mind to jam my prize under my hat as I was led to a shining C-spring victoria which smelled of elegance, varnish, polished leather, and well-groomed horses.

In it rode a fine figure of a man, calm and immaculate in white ducks and pipe-clayed shoes. He sat in noble repose, his strong face, his hands, and his clothes dyed crimson by the tropical sunset. My heart began to jump about, for I recognized the face which was stamped on all the silver coins of his island realm. He wore his famous hat made of woven peacock quills as fine as straw, with its broad band of tiny sea shells. He eyed me gravely as I stood in the road before him, wet to the skin, with muddy hands and feet, my fish violently protesting under my hat. Would he order his soldiers to execute me on the spot?

"Why, it's Mrs. Strong's little boy!" the deep voice was saying. "What are you doing so far away from home?"

I was speechless.

"Your mother must be very anxious. Come, get in and I'll take you home."

The officer deposited me, dirty and damp, on the spotless cushion beside the king. An order rang out and away we dashed, a fine cavalcade with outriders galloping ahead and men on horseback thundering behind.

His Majesty began to question me tactfully, trying, as is the way with kings, to put his guest at ease, but the fish was too much on my mind and head. I realized it would soon die if I held my tongue, but if I told, what would be my punishment? Try as I might, I couldn't hold back unmanly tears. The king removed his cigar in concern.

"Are you in pain, Austin?" he asked. I began to shake all over in an agony of indecision. "Won't you tell me what's the matter?"

I heard another and a craven voice blurting out of me.

"Oh, please don't cut off my head!" it cried.

The king replied gravely, "I have no intention of cutting off your head."

Removing my hat, I showed him his gift from the Emperor of Japan. The king raised a hand, the cavalcade came to a halt, again the officer was alongside. The king cried, "Stop at the nearest horse trough. Be quick!"

Away we flew, the king with his arm about me, trying vainly to comfort me as I saw my fish growing weaker and weaker. At last we drew up in front of a native hut. I jumped out and plunged my fish into an overflowing horse trough while the king and his men looked on with polite interest. A native was sent running for a large calabash, and the fish was put in it, his sacred life spared, his dignity restored.

I was rolled home in triumph, fast asleep against His Majesty's protecting shoulder, to be roused by shouts of laughter from my relieved parents, who were astounded by my royal return. They watched me with puzzled faces as, struggling with sleep, I staggered away from them to empty my golden prize into our tub.

No one ever knew why I stole that fish; wild horses couldn't drag an explanation from me. I woke very early the next day and crept out through the cool shadows of the morning across the wet lawn in my bare feet and peered anxiously into our tub. There, sure enough, was the grand duke swimming proudly in our shabby barrel, restoring face to my parents and raising their social standing in the society of my enemies.

There is no moral to this story—in fact it is a most unmoral one, for later that morning a smart equerry on horseback, dressed in a glistening uniform, dismounted before our gate. He came bearing a large gilt-bordered envelope on which was stamped the crown of Hawaii.

It was a royal grant to one Master Austin Strong, giving him permission to fish in Kapiolani Park for the rest of his days. It was signed "KALAKAUA, REX."

*A boy gets lost in London and almost relishes his adventure—
until evening and darkness find him still far from home.*

CHARLES DICKENS

Gone Astray

WHEN I WAS a very small boy, indeed, both in years and stature, I got lost one day in the City of London. I was taken out by Somebody (shade of Somebody forgive me for remembering no more of thy identity!), as an immense treat, to be shown the outside of Saint Giles's Church. I had romantic ideas in connection with that religious edifice; firmly believing that all the beggars who pretended through the week to be blind, lame, one-armed, deaf and dumb, and otherwise physically afflicted, laid aside their pretences every Sunday, dressed themselves in holiday clothes, and attended divine service in the temple of their patron saint. . . .

. . . It was in the spring-time when these tender notions of mine, bursting forth into new shoots under the influence of the season, became sufficiently troublesome to my parents and guardians to occasion Somebody to volunteer to take me to see the outside of Saint Giles's Church, which was considered likely (I suppose) to quench my romantic fire, and bring me to a practical state. We set off after breakfast. I have an impression that Somebody was got up in a striking manner—in cord breeches of fine texture and milky hue, in long jean gaiters, in a green coat with bright buttons, in a blue neckerchief, and a monstrous shirt-collar. I think he must have newly come (as I had myself) out of the hopgrounds of Kent. I considered him the glass of fashion and the mould of form: a very Hamlet without the burden of his difficult family affairs.

We were conversational together, and saw the outside of Saint Giles's Church with sentiments of satisfaction, much enhanced by a flag flying from the steeple. I infer that we then went down to Northumberland House in the Strand to view the celebrated lion over the gateway. At all events, I know that in the act of looking up with mingled awe and

[219]

admiration at that famous animal I lost Somebody.

The child's unreasoning terror of being lost, comes as freshly on me now as it did then. I verily believe that if I had found myself astray at the North Pole instead of in the narrow, crowded, inconvenient street over which the lion in those days presided, I could not have been more horrified. But, this first fright expended itself in a little crying and tearing up and down; and then I walked, with a feeling of dismal dignity upon me, into a court, and sat down on a step to consider how to get through life.

To the best of my belief, the idea of asking my way home never came into my head. It is possible that I may, for the time, have preferred the dismal dignity of being lost; but I have a serious conviction that in the wide scope of my arrangements for the future, I had no eyes for the nearest and most obvious course. I was but very juvenile; from eight to nine years old, I fancy.

I had one and fourpence in my pocket, and a pewter ring with a bit of red glass in it on my little finger. This jewel had been presented to me by the object of my affections, on my birthday, when we had sworn to marry, but had foreseen family obstacles to our union, in her being (she was six years old) of the Wesleyan persuasion, while I was devotedly attached to the Church of England. The one and fourpence were the remains of half-a-crown presented on the same anniversary by my god-father—a man who knew his duty and did it.

Armed with these amulets, I made up my little mind to seek my fortune. When I had found it, I thought I would drive home in a coach and six, and claim my bride. I cried a little more at the idea of such a triumph, but soon dried my eyes and came out of the court to pursue my plans. These were, first to go (as a species of investment) and see the Giants in Guildhall, out of whom I felt it not improbable that some prosperous adventure would arise; failing that contingency, to try about the City for any opening of a Whittington nature; baffled in that too, to go into the army as a drummer.

So, I began to ask my way to Guildhall; which I thought meant, somehow, Gold or Golden Hall; I was too knowing to ask my way to the Giants, for I felt it would make people laugh. I remember how immensely broad the streets seemed now I was alone, how high the houses, how grand and mysterious everything. When I came to Temple Bar, it took me half an hour to stare at it, and I left it unfinished even then. I had read about heads being exposed on the top of Temple Bar, and it seemed a wicked old place, albeit a noble monument of architecture and a paragon of utility. When at last I got away from it, behold I came, the next minute, on the figures at St. Dunstan's! Who could see those obliging monsters strike upon the bells and go? Between the quarters there was the toy-shop to look at—still there, at this present writing, in a new form—and even when that enchanted spot was escaped from, after an hour and more, then Saint Paul's arose, and how was I to get beyond its dome, or take my eyes from its cross of gold? I found it a long journey to the Giants, and a slow one.

I came into their presence at last, and gazed up at them with dread and veneration. They looked better-tempered, and were altogether more shiny-faced, than I had expected; but they were very big, and, as I judged their pedestals to be about forty feet high, I considered that they would be very big indeed if they were walking on the stone pavement. I was in a state of mind as to these and all such figures, which I suppose holds equally with most children. While I knew them to be images made of something that was not flesh and blood, I still invested them with attributes of life—with consciousness of my being there, for example, and the power of keeping a sly eye upon me. Being very tired I got into the corner under Magog, to be out of the way of his eye, and fell asleep.

When I started up after a long nap, I thought the giants were roaring, but it was only the City. The place was just the same as when I fell asleep: no beanstalk, no fairy, no princess, no dragon, no opening in life of any kind. So, being hungry, I thought I would buy something to eat, and bring it in there and eat it, before going forth to seek my fortune on the Whittington plan.

I was not ashamed of buying a penny roll in a baker's shop, but I looked into a number of cooks' shops before I could muster courage to go into one. At last I saw a pile of cooked sausages in a window with the label, 'Small Germans, A Penny.' Emboldened by knowing what to ask for, I went in and said, 'If you please will you sell me a small German?' which they did, and I took it, wrapped in paper in my pocket, to Guildhall.

The giants were still lying by, in their sly way, pretending to take no notice, so I sat down in another corner, when what should I see before me but a dog with his ears cocked. He was a black dog, with a bit of white over one eye, and bits of white and tan in his paws, and he wanted to play—frisking about me, rubbing his nose against me, dodging at me sideways, shaking his head and pretending to run away backwards, and making himself good-naturedly ridiculous, as if he had no consideration for himself, but wanted to raise my spirits. Now, when I saw this dog I thought of Whittington, and felt that things were coming right; I encouraged him by saying, 'Hi, boy!' 'Poor fellow!' 'Good dog!' and was satisfied that he was to be my dog for ever afterwards, and that he would help me to seek my fortune.

Very much comforted by this (I had cried a little at odd times ever since I was lost), I took the small German out of my pocket, and began my dinner by biting off a bit and throwing it to the dog, who immediately swallowed it with a one-sided jerk, like a pill. While I took a bit myself, and he looked me in the face for a second piece, I considered by what name I should call him. I thought Merrychance would be an expressive name, under the circumstances; and I was elated, I recollect, by inventing such a good one, when Merrychance began to growl at me in a most ferocious manner.

I wondered he was not ashamed of himself, but he didn't care for that; on the contrary he growled a good deal more. With his mouth watering, and his eyes glistening, and his nose in a very damp state, and his head very much on one side, he sidled about on the pavement in a threatening manner and growled at me, until he suddenly made a snap at the small German, tore it out of my hand, and went off with it. He never came back to help me seek my fortune. From that hour to the present, when I am forty years of age, I have never seen my faithful Merrychance again.

I felt very lonely. Not so much for the loss of the small German, though it was delicious, (I knew nothing about highly peppered horse at that time), as on account of Merrychance's disappointing me so cruelly; for I had hoped he would do every friendly thing but speak, and perhaps even come to that. I cried a little more, and began to wish that the object of my affections had been lost with me, for company's sake. But, then I remembered that *she* could not go into the army as a drummer; and I dried my eyes and ate my loaf. Coming out, I met a milkwoman, of whom I bought a pennyworth of milk; quite set up again by my repast, I began to roam about the City, and to seek my fortune in the Whittington direction. . . .

. . . Thus I wandered about the City, like a child in a dream, staring at the British merchants, and inspired by a mighty faith in the marvellousness of everything. Up courts and down courts—in and out of yards and little squares—peeping into countinghouse passages and running away—poorly feeding the echoes in the court of the South Sea House with my timid steps—roaming down into Austin Friars, and wondering how the Friars used to like it—ever staring at the British merchants, and never tired of the shops—I rambled on, all through the day. In such stories as I made, to account for the different places, I believed as devoutly as in the City itself. I particularly remember that when I found myself on 'Change, and saw the shabby people sitting under the placards about ships, I settled that they were Misers, who had embarked all their wealth to go and buy gold-dust or something of that sort, and were waiting for their respective captains to come and tell them that they were ready to set sail. I observed that they all munched dry biscuits, and I thought it was to keep off sea-sickness.

This was very delightful; but it still produced no result according to the Whittington precedent. There was a dinner preparing at the Mansion House, and when I peeped in at a grated kitchen window, and saw the

Gone Astray

men cooks at work in their white caps, my heart began to beat with hope that the Lord Mayor, or the Lady Mayoress, or one of the young Princesses their daughters, would look out of an upper apartment and direct me to be taken in. But nothing of the kind occurred. It was not until I had been peeping in some time that one of the cooks called to me (the window was open) 'Cut away, you sir!' which frightened me so, on account of his black whiskers, that I instantly obeyed. . . .

. . . I suffered very much, all day, from boys; they chased me down turnings, brought me to bay in doorways, and treated me quite savagely, though I am sure I gave them no offence. One boy, who had a stump of black-lead pencil in his pocket, wrote his mother's name and address (as he said) on my white hat, outside the crown. MRS. BLORES, WOODEN LEG WALK TOBACCO-STOPPER ROW, WAPPING. And I couldn't rub it out.

I recollect resting in a little churchyard after this persecution, disposed to think upon the whole, that if I and the object of my affections could be buried there together, at once, it would be comfortable. But, another nap, and a pump, and a bun, and above all a picture that I saw, brought me round again.

I must have strayed by that time, as I recall my course, into Goodman's Fields, or somewhere thereabouts. The picture represented a scene in a play then performing at a theatre in that neighbourhood which is no longer in existence. It stimulated me to go to that theatre and see that play. . . .

I found out the theatre—of its external appearance I only remember the loyal initials G.R. untidily painted in yellow ochre on the front—and waited, with a pretty large crowd, for the opening of the gallery doors. The greater part of the sailors and others composing the crowd, were of the lowest description, and their conversation was not improving; but I understood little or nothing of what was bad in it then, and it had no depraving influence on me. I have wondered since, how long it would take, by means of such association, to corrupt a child nurtured as I had been, and innocent as I was. . . .

I was no sooner comfortably settled, than a weight fell upon my mind, which tormented it most dreadfully, and which I must explain. It was a benefit night—the benefit of the comic actor—a little fat man with a very large face and, as I thought then, the smallest and most diverting hat that ever was seen. This comedian, for the gratification of his friends and patrons, had undertaken to sing a comic song on a donkey's back, and afterwards to give away the donkey so distinguished, by lottery. In this lottery, every person admitted to the pit and gallery had a chance. On paying my sixpence, I had received the number, forty-seven; and I now thought, in a perspiration of terror, what should I ever do if that number was to come up the prize, and I was to win the donkey!

It made me tremble all over to think of the possibility of my good fortune. I knew I never could conceal the fact of my holding forty-seven, in case that number came up, because, not to speak of my confusion, which would immediately condemn me, I had shown my number to the baker. Then, I pictured to myself the being called upon to come down on the stage and receive the donkey. I thought how all the people would shriek when they saw it had fallen to a little fellow like me. How should I lead him out—for of course he wouldn't go? If he began to bray, what should I do? If he kicked, what would become of me? Suppose he backed into the stage-door, and stuck there, with me upon him? For I felt that if I won him, the comic actor would have me on his back, the moment he could touch me. Then if I got him out of the theatre, what was I to do with him? How was I to feed him? Where was I to stable him? It was bad enough to have gone astray by myself, but to go astray with a donkey, too, was a calamity more tremendous than I could bear to contemplate.

These apprehensions took away all my pleasure in the first piece. When the ship came on—a real man-of-war she was called in the bills—and rolled prodigiously in a very heavy sea, I couldn't, even in the terrors of the storm, forget the donkey. It was awful to see the sailors pitching about, with telescopes and speaking trumpets (they looked very tall indeed aboard the man-of-war), and it was awful to suspect the pilot of treachery, though impossible to avoid it, for when he cried—'We are lost! To the raft, to the raft! A thunderbolt has struck the mainmast!'— I myself saw him take the mainmast out of its socket and drop it overboard; but even these impressive circumstances paled before my dread of the donkey. Even, when the good sailor (and he was very good) came to good fortune, and the bad sailor (and he was very bad) threw himself into the ocean from the summit of a curious rock, presenting something of the appearance of a pair of steps, I saw the dreadful donkey through my tears.

At last the time came when the fiddler struck up the comic song, and the dreaded animal, with new shoes on, as I inferred from the noise they made, came clattering in with the comic actor on his back. He was dressed out with ribbons (I mean the donkey was) and as he persisted in turning his tail to the audience, the comedian got off him, turned about, and sitting with his face that way, sang the song three times, amid thunders of applause. All this time I was fearfully agitated; and when two pale people, a good deal splashed with the mud of the streets, were invited out of the pit to superintend the drawing of the lottery, and were received with a round of laughter from everybody else, I could have begged and prayed them to have mercy on me, and not draw number forty-seven.

Gone Astray [225]

But I was soon put out of my pain now, for a gentleman behind me, in a flannel jacket and a yellow neck-kerchief, who had eaten two fried soles and all his pockets-full of nuts before the storm began to rage, answered to the winning number, and went down to take possession of the prize. This gentleman had appeared to know the donkey, rather, from the moment of his entrance, and had taken a great interest in his proceedings; driving him to himself, if I use an intelligible phrase, and saying, almost in my ear, when he made any mistake, 'Kum up, you precious Moke. Kum up!' He was thrown by the donkey on first mounting him, to the great delight of the audience (including myself), but rode him off with great skill afterwards, and soon returned to his seat quite calm. Calmed myself by the immense relief I had sustained, I enjoyed the rest of the performance very much indeed. I remember there were a good many dances, some in fetters and some in roses, and one by a most divine little creature, who made the object of my affections look but commonplace. In the concluding drama, she re-appeared as a boy (in arms, mostly), and was fought for, several times. I rather think a Baron wanted to drown her, and was on various occasions prevented by the comedian, a ghost, a Newfoundland dog, and a church bell. I only remember beyond this, that I wondered where the Baron expected to go to, and that he went there in a shower of sparks. The lights were turned out while the sparks died out, and it appeared to me as if the whole play—ship, donkey, men and women, divine little creature, and all—were a wonderful firework that had gone off, and left nothing but dust and darkness behind it.

It was late when I got out into the streets, and there was no moon, and there were no stars, and the rain fell heavily. When I emerged from the dispersing crowd, the ghost and the baron had an ugly look in my remembrance; I felt unspeakably forlorn; and now, for the first time, my little bed and the dear familiar faces came before me, and touched my heart. By daylight, I had never thought of the grief at home. I had never thought of my mother. I had never thought of anything but adapting myself to the circumstances in which I found myself, and going to seek my fortune.

For a boy who could do nothing but cry, and run about, saying, 'O I am lost!' to think of going into the army was, I felt sensible, out of the question. I abandoned the idea of asking my way to the barracks—or rather the idea abandoned me—and ran about, until I found a watchman in his box. It is amazing to me, now, that he should have been sober; but I am inclined to think he was too feeble to get drunk.

This venerable man took me to the nearest watch-house;—I say he took me, but in fact I took him, for when I think of us in the rain, I recollect that we must have made a composition, like a vignette of Infancy leading Age. He had a dreadful cough, and was obliged to lean against a wall, whenever it came on. We got at last to the watch-house, a warm and drowsy sort of place embellished with great-coats and rattles hanging up. When a paralytic messenger had been sent to make inquiries about me, I fell asleep by the fire, and awoke no more until my eyes opened on my father's face. This is literally and exactly how I went astray. They used to say I was an odd child, and I suppose I was. I am an odd man perhaps.

Shade of Somebody, forgive me for the disquiet I must have caused thee! When I stand beneath the Lion, even now, I see thee rushing up and down, refusing to be comforted. I have gone astray since, many times, and farther afield. May I therein have given less disquiet to others, than herein I gave to thee!

Sons of great men rarely find growing up easy. Young Charles, his brother gone off to boarding school, his father and wife sleeping "behind their locked doors," is wakeful and frightened. He roams the great house in the dark seeking out these potent and forbidden objects which give him the illusion of strength.

CHARLES CHAPLIN, JR.
AND N. & M. RAU

from *My Father, Charlie Chaplin*

I MISSED SYD most at bedtime, alone in my bedroom with only my vivid imagination to keep me company.

I remember the first night the idea came to me. It was an especially lonely night, with a gusty California wind blowing outside. You could hear the intermittent scraping of the tree branches against the windows. I thought of Syd there in his bed at Black-Foxe. I thought of Paulette and Dad behind their locked doors, and the servants in their quarters in the basement. I felt completely shut off from everyone.

Then I remembered Dad's pistol in the night stand by his bed, and the wonderful samurai swords in the cabinet in the living room. I thought of them lying there side by side, curved and sharp in their lacquered sheaths.

"Don't touch them, don't ever play with them," Dad had told us so often. "Why, you might cut off your hand."

I thought of his order and how he disliked disobedience; I thought again of the samurai swords. Cautiously I went to my door and opened it and looked down the hall. Everything was quiet. I hurried down the hall and the stairs. I was alone on the ground floor of the dark, mysterious house. I found the light switch and turned it on. There was light now in the lower hall. I flew down it barefoot to the living room, past the gaping mouth of the dining-room door—the dark room where Dr. Reynolds' fanciful cadaver had lain, perhaps was lying still, a ghost to rise up and stop me.

I reached the living room, turned on a light and ran to the cabinet. I was terrified. My breath was coming in gasps. I flung open the cabinet door. In the hands of a giant samurai the big sword might prove very serviceable for executions, but it was too unwieldy for me. My fingers closed on the handle of the smaller one. I took it out of its sheath and left that in its customary place on the cabinet shelf, so no one would notice the sword was gone.

I shut the cabinet door and gingerly tested the razor-sharp edge with my finger. Then I flashed the sword over my head several times. Suddenly I felt safe. Who could overpower me with a weapon like this? I turned off the living-room light, and my heart sank a little with the sudden darkness. I waved my sword in the direction of the dining room, at the ghost of the cadaver lurking there, and then sped down the hall for the stairway. How shocked Dad would have been to see me flying along with that naked sword in my hand!

I turned off the lower-hall light and crept upstairs and down the upper hall to my own room. I shut my door and locked it. I climbed into my bed, laying the sword on the night table beside me, and almost at once I fell into a deep, dreamless sleep.

I woke with the dawn and got the sword back in its cabinet before anyone discovered it was gone. No one ever found out about it, though it wasn't the last night by far that it kept me company.

Looking back on his father's practical joke, this boy wonders whether the final joy in the Christmas gift was perhaps the greater for the agony of disappointment that came before.

LINCOLN STEFFENS

A Miserable, Merry Christmas

MY FATHER'S BUSINESS seems to have been one of slow but steady growth. He and his local partner, Llewelen Tozer, had no vices. They were devoted to their families and to "the store," which grew with the town, which, in turn, grew and changed with the State from a gambling, mining, and ranching community to one of farming, fruit-raising, and building. Immigration poured in, not gold-seekers now, but farmers, business men and home-builders, who settled, planted, reaped and traded in the natural riches of the State, which prospered greatly, "making" the people who will tell you that they "made the State."

As the store made money and I was getting through the primary school, my father bought a lot uptown, at Sixteenth and K Streets, and built us a "big" house. It was off the line of the city's growth, but it was near a new grammar school for me and my sisters, who were coming along fast after me. This interested the family, not me. They were always talking about school; they had not had much of it themselves, and they thought they had missed something. My father used to write speeches, my mother verses, and their theory seems to have been that they had talents which a school would have brought to flower. They agreed, therefore, that their children's gifts should have all the schooling there was. My view, then, was that I had had a good deal of it already, and I was not interested at all. It interfered with my own business, with my own education.

And indeed I remember very little of the primary school. I learned to read, write, spell, and count, and reading was all right. I had a practical use for books, which I searched for ideas and parts to play with, characters to be, lives to live. The primary school was probably a good one, but I cannot remember learning anything except to read aloud "perfectly" from a teacher whom I adored and who was fond of me. She used to embrace

[229]

me before the whole class and she favored me openly to the scandal of the other pupils, who called me "teacher's pet." Their scorn did not trouble me; I saw and I said that they envied me. I paid for her favor, however. When she married I had queer, unhappy feelings of resentment; I didn't want to meet her husband, and when I had to I wouldn't speak to him. He laughed, and she kissed me—happily for her, to me offensively. I never would see her again. Through with her, I fell in love immediately with Miss Kay, another grown young woman who wore glasses and had a fine, clear skin. I did not know her, I only saw her in the street, but once I followed her, found out where she lived, and used to pass her house, hoping to see her, and yet choking with embarrassment if I did. This fascination lasted for years; it was still a sort of super-romance to me when later I was "going with" another girl nearer my own age.

What interested me in our new neighborhood was not the school, nor the room I was to have in the house all to myself, but the stable which was built back of the house. My father let me direct the making of a stall, a little smaller than the other stalls, for my pony, and I prayed and hoped and my sister Lou believed that that meant that I would get the pony, perhaps for Christmas. I pointed out to her that there were three other stalls and no horses at all. This I said in order that she should answer it. She could not. My father, sounded, said that some day we might have horses and a cow; meanwhile a stable added to the value of a house. "Some day" is a pain to a boy who lives in and knows only "now." My good little sisters, to comfort me, remarked that Christmas was coming, but Christmas was always coming and grown-ups were always talking about it, asking you what you wanted and then giving you what they wanted you to have. Though everybody knew what I wanted, I told them all again. My mother knew that I told God, too, every night. I wanted a pony, and to make sure that they understood, I declared that I wanted nothing else.

"Nothing but a pony?" my father asked.

"Nothing," I said.

"Not even a pair of high boots?"

That was hard. I did want boots, but I stuck to the pony. "No, not even boots."

"Nor candy? There ought to be something to fill your stocking with, and Santa Claus can't put a pony into a stocking."

That was true, and he couldn't lead a pony down the chimney either. But no. "All I want is a pony," I said. "If I can't have a pony, give me nothing, nothing."

Now I had been looking myself for the pony I wanted, going to sales stables, inquiring of horsemen, and I had seen several that would do. My father let me "try" them. I tried so many ponies that I was learning

A Miserable, Merry Christmas

fast to sit a horse. I chose several, but my father always found some fault with them. I was in despair. When Christmas was at hand I had given up all hope of a pony, and on Christmas Eve I hung up my stocking along with my sisters', of whom, by the way, I now had three. I haven't mentioned them or their coming because, you understand, they were girls, and girls, young girls, counted for nothing in my manly life. They did not mind me either; they were so happy that Christmas Eve that I caught some of their merriment. I speculated on what I'd get; I hung up the biggest stocking I had, and we all went reluctantly to bed to wait till morning. Not to sleep; not right away. We were told that we must not only sleep promptly, we must not wake up till seven-thirty the next morning —or if we did, we must not go to the fireplace for our Christmas. Impossible.

We did sleep that night, but we woke up at six A.M. We lay in our beds and debated through the open doors whether to obey till, say, half-past six. Then we bolted. I don't know who started it, but there was a rush. We all disobeyed; we raced to disobey and get first to the fireplace in the front room downstairs. And there they were, the gifts, all sorts of wonderful things, mixed-up piles of presents; only, as I disentangled the mess, I saw that my stocking was empty; it hung limp; not a thing in it; and under and around it—nothing. My sisters had knelt down, each by her pile of gifts; they were squealing with delight, till they looked up and saw me standing there in my nightgown with nothing. They left their piles to come to me and look with me at my empty place. Nothing. They felt my stocking: nothing.

I don't remember whether I cried at that moment, but my sisters did. They ran with me back to my bed, and there we all cried till I became indignant. That helped some. I got up, dressed, and driving my sisters away, I went alone out into the yard, down to the stable, and there, all by myself, I wept. My mother came out to me by and by; she found me in my pony stall, sobbing on the floor, and she tried to comfort me. But I heard my father outside; he had come part way with her, and she was having some sort of angry quarrel with him. She tried to comfort me; besought me to come to breakfast. I could not; I wanted no comfort and no breakfast. She left me and went on into the house with sharp words for my father.

I don't know what kind of a breakfast the family had. My sisters said it was "awful." They were ashamed to enjoy their own toys. They came to me, and I was rude. I ran away from them. I went around to the front of the house, sat down on the steps, and, the crying over, I ached. I was wronged, I was hurt—I can feel now what I felt then, and I am sure that if one could see the wounds upon our hearts, there would be found still upon mine a scar from that terrible Christmas morning. And my father, the practical joker, he must have been hurt, too, a little. I saw him looking out of the window. He was watching me or something for an hour or two, drawing back the curtain ever so little lest I catch him, but I saw his face, and I think I can see now the anxiety upon it, the worried impatience.

After—I don't know how long—surely an hour or two—I was brought to the climax of my agony by the sight of a man riding a pony down the street, a pony and a brand-new saddle; the most beautiful saddle I ever saw, and it was a boy's saddle; the man's feet were not in the stirrups; his legs were too long. The outfit was perfect; it was the realization of all my dreams, the answer to all my prayers. A fine new bridle, with a light curb bit. And the pony! As he drew near, I saw that the pony was really a small horse, what we called an Indian pony, a bay, with black mane and tail, and one white foot and a white star on his forehead. For such a horse as that I would have given, I could have forgiven, anything.

But the man, a disheveled fellow with a blackened eye and a fresh-cut face, came along, reading the numbers on the houses, and, as my hopes —my impossible hopes—rose, he looked at our door and passed by, he and the pony, and the saddle and the bridle. Too much. I fell upon the steps, and having wept before, I broke now into such a flood of tears that I was a floating wreck when I heard a voice.

"Say, kid," it said, "do you know a boy named Lennie Steffens?"

I looked up. It was the man on the pony, back again, at our horse block.

"Yes," I spluttered through my tears. "That's me."

"Well," he said, "then this is your horse. I've been looking all over for you and your house. Why don't you put your number where it can be seen?"

"Get down," I said, running out to him.

He went on saying something about "ought to have got here at seven o'clock; told me to bring the nag here and tie him to your post and leave him for you. But, hell, I got into a drunk—and a fight—and a hospital, and—"

"Get down," I said.

He got down, and he boosted me up to the saddle. He offered to fit the stirrups to me, but I didn't want him to. I wanted to ride.

"What's the matter with you?" he said, angrily. "What you crying for? Don't you like the horse? He's a dandy, this horse. I know him of old. He's fine at cattle; he'll drive 'em alone."

I hardly heard, I could scarcely wait, but he persisted. He adjusted the stirrups, and then, finally, off I rode, slowly, at a walk, so happy, so thrilled, that I did not know what I was doing. I did not look back at the house or the man, I rode off up the street, taking note of everything— of the reins, of the pony's long mane, of the carved leather saddle. I had never seen anything so beautiful. And mine! I was going to ride up past Miss Kay's house. But I noticed on the horn of the saddle some stains

A Miserable, Merry Christmas

like rain-drops, so I turned and trotted home, not to the house but to the stable. There was the family, father, mother, sisters, all working for me, all happy. They had been putting in place the tools of my new business: blankets, currycomb, brush, pitchfork—everything, and there was hay in the loft.

"What did you come back so soon for?" somebody asked. "Why didn't you go on riding?"

I pointed to the stains. "I wasn't going to get my new saddle rained on," I said. And my father laughed. "It isn't raining," he said. "Those are not rain-drops."

"They are tears," my mother gasped, and she gave my father a look which sent him off to the house. Worse still, my mother offered to wipe away the tears still running out of my eyes. I gave her such a look as she had given him, and she went off after my father, drying her own tears. My sisters remained and we all unsaddled the pony, put on his halter, led him to his stall, tied and fed him. It began really to rain; so all the rest of that memorable day we curried and combed that pony. The girls plaited his mane, forelock, and tail, while I pitchforked hay to him and curried and brushed, curried and brushed. For a change we brought him out to drink; we led him up and down, blanketed like a race-horse; we took turns at that. But the best, the most inexhaustible fun, was to clean him. When we went reluctantly to our midday Christmas dinner, we all smelt of horse, and my sisters had to wash their faces and hands. I was asked to, but I wouldn't, till my mother bade me look in the mirror. Then I washed up—quick. My face was caked with the muddy lines of tears that had coursed over my cheeks to my mouth. Having washed away that shame, I ate my dinner, and as I ate I grew hungrier and hungrier. It was my first meal that day, and as I filled up on the turkey and the stuffing, the cranberries and the pies, the fruit and the nuts—as I swelled, I could laugh. My mother said I still choked and sobbed now and then, but I laughed, too; I saw and enjoyed my sisters' presents till—I had to go out and attend to my pony, who was there, really and truly there, the promise, the beginning, of a happy double life. And—I went and looked to make sure—there was the saddle, too, and the bridle.

But that Christmas, which my father had planned so carefully, was it the best or the worst I ever knew? He often asked me that; I never could answer as a boy. I think now that it was both. It covered the whole distance from broken-hearted misery to bursting happiness—too fast. A grown-up could hardly have stood it.

A boy gets himself out on a limb, and almost comes to grief.

RICHARD WILBUR

A Game of Catch

MONK AND GLENNIE were playing catch on the side lawn of the firehouse when Scho caught sight of them. They were good at it, for seventh-graders, as anyone could see right away. Monk, wearing a catcher's mitt, would lean easily sidewise and back, with one leg lifted and his throwing hand almost down to the grass, and then lob the white ball straight up into the sunlight. Glennie would shield his eyes with his left hand and, just as the ball fell past him, snag it with a little dart of his glove. Then he would burn the ball straight toward Monk, and it would spank into the round mitt and sit, like a still-life apple on a plate, until Monk flipped it over into his right hand and, with a negligent flick of his hanging arm, gave Glennie a fast grounder.

They were going on and on like that, in a kind of slow, mannered luxurious dance in the sun, their faces perfectly blank and entranced, when Glennie noticed Scho dawdling along the other side of the street and called hello to him. Scho crossed over and stood at the front edge of the lawn, near an apple tree, watching.

"Got your glove?" asked Glennie after a time. Scho obviously hadn't.

"You could give me some easy grounders," said Scho. "But don't burn 'em."

"All right," Glennie said. He moved off a little, so the three of them formed a triangle, and they passed the ball around for about five minutes, Monk tossing easy grounders to Scho, Scho throwing to Glennie, and Glennie burning them in to Monk. After a while, Monk began to throw them back to Glennie once or twice before he let Scho have his grounder, and finally Monk gave Scho a fast, bumpy grounder that hopped over his shoulder and went into the brake on the other side of the street.

"Not so hard," called Scho as he ran across to get it.

[234]

A *Game of Catch* [235]

"You should've had it," Monk shouted.

It took Scho a little while to find the ball among the ferns and dead leaves, and when he saw it, he grabbed it up and threw it toward Glennie. It struck the trunk of the apple tree, bounced back at an angle, and rolled steadily and stupidly onto the cement apron in front of the firehouse, where one of the trucks was parked. Scho ran hard and stopped it just before it rolled under the truck, and this time he carried it back to his former position on the lawn and threw it carefully to Glennie.

"I got an idea," said Glennie. "Why don't Monk and I catch for five minutes more, and then you can borrow one of our gloves?"

"That's all right with me," said Monk. He socked his fist into his mitt, and Glennie burned one in.

"All right," Scho said, and went over and sat under the tree. There in the shade he watched them resume their skillful play. They threw lazily fast or lazily slow—high, low, or wide—and always handsomely, their expressions serene, changeless, and forgetful. When Monk missed a low backhand catch, he walked indolently after the ball and, hardly even looking, flung it sidearm for an imaginary put-out. After a good while of this, Scho said, "Isn't it five minutes yet?"

"One minute to go," said Monk, with a fraction of a grin.

Scho stood up and watched the ball slap back and forth for several minutes more, and then he turned and pulled himself up into the crotch of the tree.

"Where are you going?" Monk asked.

"Just up the tree," Scho said.

"I guess he doesn't want to catch," said Monk.

Scho went up and up through the fat light-gray branches until they grew slender and bright and gave under him. He found a place where several supple branches were knit to make a dangerous chair, and sat there with his head coming out of the leaves into the sunlight. He could see the two other boys down below, the ball going back and forth between them as if they were bowling on the grass, and Glennie's crew-cut head looking like a sea urchin.

"I found a wonderful seat up here," Scho said loudly. "If I don't fall out." Monk and Glennie didn't look up or comment, and so he began jouncing gently in his chair of branches and singing "Yo-ho, heave ho" in an exaggerated way.

"Do you know what, Monk?" he announced in a few moments. "I can make you two guys do anything I want. Catch that ball, Monk! Now you catch it, Glennie!"

"I was going to catch it anyway," Monk suddenly said. "You're not making anybody do anything when they're already going to do it anyway."

"I made you say what you just said," Scho replied joyfully.

"No, you didn't," said Monk, still throwing and catching but now less serenely absorbed in the game.

"That's what I wanted you to say," Scho said.

The ball bounded off the rim of Monk's mitt and plowed into a gladiolus bed beside the firehouse, and Monk ran to get it while Scho jounced in his treetop and sang, "I wanted you to miss that. Anything you do is what I wanted you to do."

"Let's quit for a minute," Glennie suggested.

"We might as well, until the peanut gallery shuts up," Monk said.

They went over and sat cross-legged in the shade of the tree. Scho looked down between his legs and saw them on the dim, spotty ground, saying nothing to one another. Glennie soon began abstractedly spinning his glove between his palms; Monk pulled his nose and stared out across the lawn.

"I want you to mess around with your nose, Monk," said Scho, giggling. Monk withdrew his hand from his face.

"Do that with your glove, Glennie," Scho persisted. "Monk, I want you to pull up hunks of grass and chew on it."

Glennie looked up and saw a self-delighted, intense face staring down at him through the leaves. "Stop being a dope and come down and we'll catch for a few minutes," he said.

Scho hesitated, and then said, in a tentatively mocking voice, "That's what I wanted you to say."

"All right, then, nuts to you," said Glennie.

"Why don't you keep quiet and stop bothering people?" Monk asked.

"I made you say that," Scho replied, softly.

"Shut up," Monk said.

"I made you say that, and I want you to be standing down there looking sore. And I want you to climb up the tree. I'm making you do it!"

Monk was scrambling up through the branches, awkward in his haste, and getting snagged on twigs. His face was furious and foolish, and he kept telling Scho to shut up, shut up, shut up, while the other's exuberant and panicky voice poured down upon his head.

"*Now* you shut up or you'll be sorry," Monk said, breathing hard as he reached up and threatened to shake the cradle of slight branches in which Scho was sitting.

"I *want*—" Scho screamed as he fell. Two lower branches broke his rustling, crackling fall, but he landed on his back with a deep thud and lay still, with a strangled look on his face and his eyes clenched. Glennie knelt down and asked breathlessly, "Are you okay, Scho? Are you okay?" while Monk swung down through the leaves crying that honestly he hadn't even touched him, the crazy guy just let go. Scho doubled up and turned over on his right side, and now both the other boys knelt beside him, pawing at his shoulder and begging to know how he was.

A Game of Catch

Then Scho rolled away from them and sat partly up, still struggling to get his wind but forcing a species of smile onto his face.

"I'm sorry, Scho," Monk said. "I didn't mean to make you fall."

Scho's voice came out weak and gravelly, in gasps. "I meant—you to do it. You—had to. You can't do—anything—unless I want—you to."

Glennie and Monk looked helplessly at him as he sat there, breathing a bit more easily and smiling fixedly, with tears in his eyes. Then they picked up their gloves and the ball, walked over to the street, and went slowly away down the sidewalk, Monk punching his fist into the mitt, Glennie juggling the ball between glove and hand.

From under the apple tree, Scho, still bent over a little for lack of breath, croaked after them in triumph and misery, "I want you to do whatever you're going to do for the whole rest of your life!"

MAY SWENSON

The Centaur

The summer that I was ten—
Can it be there was only one
summer that I was ten? It must

have been a long one then—
each day I'd go out to choose
a fresh horse from my stable

which was a willow grove
down by the old canal.
I'd go on my two bare feet.

But when, with my brother's jack-knife,
I had cut me a long limber horse
with a good thick knob for a head,

and peeled him slick and clean
except a few leaves for the tail,
and cinched my brother's belt

around his head for a rein,
I'd straddle and canter him fast
up the grass bank to the path,

trot along in the lovely dust
that talcumed over his hoofs,
hiding my toes, and turning

The Centaur

his feet to swift half-moons.
The willow knob with the strap
jouncing between my thighs

was the pommel and yet the poll
of my nickering pony's head.
My head and my neck were mine,

yet they were shaped like a horse.
My hair flopped to the side
like the mane of a horse in the wind.

My forelock swung in my eyes,
my neck arched and I snorted.
I shied and skittered and reared,

stopped and raised my knees,
pawed at the ground and quivered.
My teeth bared as we wheeled

and swished through the dust again.
I was the horse and the rider,
and the leather I slapped to his rump

spanked my own behind.
Doubled, my two hoofs beat
a gallop along the bank,

the wind twanged in my mane,
my mouth squared to the bit.
And yet I sat on my steed

quiet, negligent riding,
my toes standing the stirrups,
my thighs hugging his ribs.

At a walk we drew up to the porch.
I tethered him to a paling.
Dismounting, I smoothed my skirt

and entered the dusky hall.
My feet on the clean linoleum
left ghostly toes in the hall.

Where have you been? said my mother.
Been riding, I said from the sink,
and filled me a glass of water.

What's that in your pocket? she said.
Just my knife. It weighted my pocket
and stretched my dress awry.

Go tie back your hair, said my mother,
and *Why is your mouth all green?*
*Rob Roy, he pulled some clover
as we crossed the field,* I told her.

Remembrances of growing up in a small Welsh town, where, though politics (violent), religion (primitive), school (deadly dull) are the daily lot, kids have fun and find their own ways around it all.

DEREK MORGAN

A Bit of Hiraeth

SOUTH WALES, for those who came by road, lay at the bottom of a steep hill and over a small stream where the knights of nearby Camelot may once have paused to drink but which, as I remember it, flowed by the gasworks and chimneys of the Cardiff suburb of Rhumney. There was nothing to mark the border. People who came to the coalfield presumably did not need to be told where they were, and if you had strayed here by accident the best thing to do was stop at once and get clear instructions about how to get safely back to Cheltenham Spa for the night. There were good hotels there. And no one in his senses ever came among the Welsh by choice.

They are a mean-spirited people, deeply distrusted by the English, who rarely invite them to dinner. They are tolerated in London as milkmen or schoolteachers, and of course their countrymen send some of them to Parliament, where they sit, close-eyed and treacherous, upon the Opposition benches, watching malevolently the business of Empire and ridden with pangs of *hiraeth*—a sort of maudlin longing to be home. Unfortunately, they never do go home but stay on, inflicting their sentimental maunderings on their hosts—out of place everywhere.

Every three years or so we would have a few days of summer. But summer or no, on August Bank Holiday everyone in the valleys would come to Barry Island, where there was sand and ice cream, which the children ate in equal parts—along with chocolate and pickled eels, licorice and shrimps, aniseed balls and damson jam and Barry Island Rock.

If the sun was out, we sat, a quarter million strong, with jam sandwiches and thermoses of tea, upon the beach—a tide of toddlers with our best-dressed mums and sweating dads (the legs of their trousers and long

[241]

underwear rolled up in abandoned adoration of the sun, and their waistcoats unbuttoned to display the reddening throats that would keep them awake and groaning through the night and come out in blisters tomorrow, when they would rub themselves with Vaseline and go off to the pits, a greasy-necked throng, to curse softly in the cool coal dark).

But usually there was no danger from the sun, and as the rain poured down we huddled (a quarter million strong, with jam sandwiches and thermoses of tea) in the doorways of the ice-cream shops or, for convenience, near the conveniences, whose walls were covered with imprecations upon Stanley Baldwin: children with their spades and buckets and sopping little Welsh flags; mums militant, struggling with wet jam sandwiches, tempers tightening as the hours went by and the wailing of ten thousand toddlers rose above the baleful sibilance of the rain, with now and then a shriller yell as a shining wet balloon floated free at last above the scene. The dads stared thoughtfully ahead, saying nothing.

But life was not all holidays and we had some good times too. The road to school was full of friends to meet and stones to throw and horses to smell, the chatter of the pitwheels and Mrs. Solva Thomas singing *Traviata* as she picked radishes in her yard, the night shift coming through the streets, fed up and filthy, slabs of laver bread and whelks and pigs' feet, a clang and a clash from the blacksmith's shop ("Festering hell, watch my bloody fingers!"), mums on their hands and knees scrubbing at their stoops, shining brass doorknobs—a whistling and a singing and shirts on the line. And through it all, carbolic-clean and full of porridge, we made our nose-picking way.

"School bell's stopped—we'll have to run like drains!" And we ducked through the cemetery, dodging gravestones, leaping merrily over the dull departed, scrambling into the schoolroom just in time to be marked present, and then marched breathlessly into the hall to sing, pure and pink and puffing, "*Coronwch! Coronwch!*"—"Crown Him Lord of All!"

School was all to do with the "scholarship" examination, which was in English and arithmetic, and which we all sat when we were eleven years old. Those who came out in the top quarter could go on to the grammar school and perhaps later to the university at Cardiff to become schoolteachers themselves; for the rest, it was hanging around doing odd jobs for the teachers or playing truant until they were fourteen, and then the pits.

Mr. Rotten Hopkins, our teacher, was at pains to impress us with the gravity of it all. "Wales and the Labour Party," said Rotten Hopkins, who was not a man to prevaricate, "need educated men. Stanley Baldwin won't live forever, praise God, and when the time comes we must be ready to replace him and his kind with decent men of our own." Time and its trickeries were a favorite theme with Rotten Hopkins. "Time and tide wait for no man," he would inform us at intervals during the day as he passed among us slapping his thigh with his cane, and although our ten years' experience was to the contrary, we began to think he may be right. Certainly our eleventh birthdays did seem to be getting closer. And so we worked patriotically away at sums and grammar, with growing trepidation as the slapping of the cane became more and more impatient and the day approached when, choc-a-bloc with parts of speech and stiff with fright, we would stumble blindly through the five hours of examination that would decide our lives, while the mums paced outside the schoolroom, their faces as stark as if they had been at the pithead with the disaster hooter blowing.

School lasted until four o'clock, and then there were two hours before tea and they were all our own! On a hill outside the village there was a ring of cromlech stones and we would climb up there to play. One of the stones had Stanley Baldwin's face drawn on it in chalk and we used that one instead of cricket stumps to bowl at, or threw rocks at it for bets of marbles and toffee. When we were tired of that, we riffled our innocent hours away chalking dirty words among the intertwined hearts that were carved on the stones' undersides, each with its ancient date of plighted love: "Gryffyth Evans loves Sian Lewis, 1919"—and he did too, and Four-Eyes Evans was here to prove it.

The stones were also used for dares—climb the headstone, jump off the capstone, and sometimes someone would take a dare to go up there at night alone. It was the loneliest walk a boy ever took. Along Dyfed Street, its brass doorknobs alight with reflected night flames, past the Bump Hotel, that stood in a beery haze of song and laughter, and Tynewydd Chapel, with the sound of the men's choir practicing for the amateur operatics; and then to climb out of the village, past the Band of Hope Rugby field, through the cemetery—up to the stones.

And as he climbed, the human sounds of the village were lost in the gigantic clamor of the night. Hooters blew and steel shrieked until it seemed that there was nothing left of the world but flame and smoke and the brainless grunting of machines. He climbed in simple terror past howling caves where once the witches lived and boulders that had been thrown where they lay, men said, by demons in the armies of the warring princes.

And then he came to the stones. Suddenly the terror was gone and the world was Wales again. For here were Stanley Baldwin and the dent in the mud where Four-Eyes Evans hit his head jumping off the capstone with his hands tied. And here were the vows of lovers made long ago, before we were even born. And of course the stones themselves, for they were old friends. Old, old stones, that knew my people's ways and talk three thousand years ago. Old stones that stand mute and measureless to strangers but know me well. Here my people came to pray and here the hectic trumpets sang with dreams of kindred stars. And here I prayed too, and dreamt amid the Pleiades. Time moved among the houses far below, the hooters screamed on Dowlais Top.

Even God must have been bored with Wales on Sunday. Regularly at ten on Saturday night, when the revels in the Bump Hotel had ended, the village settled into a seige of glum righteousness that lasted until we dared to breathe again on Monday. It was the dads' day off, and we went to chapel in the morning, ate our Sunday dinner, and then shut up.

Chapel, in fact, was the bright spot of the day. The Reverend William Williams was a good Socialist, and in his sermons devoted himself as much to Wales and Whitehall as to heaven and hell. He lived in the next valley and Sunday officially began when he came striding down the mountain with his copy of the *Sunday Pictorial* under his arm. And he sang as he came:

> "Though cowards flinch and traitors sneer
> We'll keep the Red Flag flying here . . ."

(He had the worst voice in Wales but his heart was in the right place.) You could hear him coming half a mile away. He'd interrupt the song to greet his flock:

"Morning, Mrs. Bronwen Rees, how's your husband's bunions? . . . Hello, Dai Price—did you read about Duff Cooper? Ought to be hung by his cloven hoofs from Admiralty Arch. . . .

> *Then raise the scarlet standard high,*
> *Within its shade we'll live or—*

Owen Owens! First time I've seen you sober since Ash Wednesday."

The children would all stick their heads through the windows to say "Good morning, Reverend Williams" (first time we'd been allowed to speak today so far) and to receive pats on the head (he didn't interrupt the song for us).

And so he made his unmelodious way through the Sunday morning streets, and as the scarlet standard faded in the distance, he left behind a wake of hatpin adjusting and gulping of second cups of tea and children being yelled for through toilet doors as we hurried to follow in our spiritual leader's footsteps to Tynewydd Baptist Chapel on the hill.

He would be waiting for us there with his Bible and his *Sunday Pictorial*, and as the service proceeded he would read impartially from both. The Bible seethed with scorn for Downing Street, and it was difficult not to cheer as he rang through the roll call of our enemies, documenting his derision with boiling gospels and hot-blooded hymns. Growls of enthusiasm and encouragement would echo through the dark rafters and wobble the chalices on the altar.

Then we went home to lamb and dumplings, and after that stared moodily at pictures in the fire as dads and mums and dogs and cats slept loudly through the silent afternoon.

Two boys suffer disappointment—each in his separate way. They quarrel but their feud is soon forgotten in plotting revenge against the enemy adult.

KENNETH GRAHAME

from *Dream Days*

GROWN-UP PEOPLE really ought to be more careful. Among themselves it may seem but a small thing to give their word and take back their word. For them there are so many compensations. Life lies at their feet, a parti-coloured india-rubber ball; they may kick it this way or kick it that, it turns up blue, yellow or green, but always coloured and glistening. Thus, one sees it happen almost every day, and, with a jest and a laugh, the thing is over, and the disappointed one turns to fresh pleasure, lying ready to his hand. But with those who are below them, whose little globe is swayed by them, who rush to build star-pointing alhambras on their most casual word, they really ought to be more careful.

In this case of the circus, for instance, it was not as if we had led up to the subject. It was they who began it entirely—prompted thereto by the local newspaper. "What, a circus!" said they in their irritating, casual way: "that would be nice to take the children to. Wednesday would be a good day. Suppose we go on Wednesday. Oh, and pleats are being worn again, with rows of deep braid," etc.

What the others thought I know not; what they said, if they said anything, I did not comprehend. For me the house was bursting, walls seemed to cramp and stifle, the roof was jumping and lifting. Escape was the imperative thing—to escape into the open air, to shake off bricks and mortar, and to wander in the unfrequented places of the earth, the more properly to take in the passion and the promise of the giddy situation.

Nature seemed prim and staid that day, and the globe gave no hint that it was flying round a circus ring of its own. Could they really be true, I wondered, all those bewildering things I had heard tell of circuses? Did long-tailed ponies really walk on their hind-legs and fire off pistols? Was it humanly possible for clowns to perform one-half of the bewitching drol-

from *Dream Days*

leries recorded in history? And how, oh, how dare I venture to believe that, from off the backs of creamy Arab steeds, ladies of more than earthly beauty discharged themselves through paper hoops? No, it was not altogether possible, there must have been some exaggeration. Still, I would be content with very little, I would take a low percentage—a very small proportion of the circus myth would more than satisfy me. But again, even supposing that history were, once in a way, no liar, could it be that I myself was really fated to look upon this thing in the flesh and to live through it, to survive the rapture? No, it was altogether too much. Something was bound to happen, one of us would develop measles, the world would blow up with a loud explosion. I must not dare, I must not presume, to entertain the smallest hope. I must endeavour sternly to think of something else.

Needless to say, I thought, I dreamed of nothing else, day or night. Waking, I walked arm-in-arm with a clown, and cracked a portentous whip to the brave music of a band. Sleeping, I pursued—perched astride of a coalblack horse—a princess all gauze and spangles, who always managed to keep just one unattainable length ahead. In the early morning Harold and I, once fully awake, cross-examined each other as to the possibilities of this or that circus tradition, and exhausted the lore long ere the first housemaid was stirring. In this state of exaltation we slipped onward to what promised to be a day of all white days—which brings me right back to my text, that grown-up people really ought to be more careful.

I had known it could never really be; I had said so to myself a dozen times. The vision was too sweetly ethereal for embodiment. Yet the pang of the disillusionment was none the less keen and sickening, and the pain was as that of a corporeal wound. It seemed strange and foreboding, when we entered the breakfast-room, not to find everybody cracking whips, jumping over chairs, and whooping in ecstatic rehearsal of the wild reality to come. The situation became grim and pallid indeed when I caught the expressions "garden-party" and "my mauve tulle," and realized that they both referred to that very afternoon. And every minute, as I sat silent and listened, my heart sank lower and lower, descending relentlessly like a clock-weight into my boot soles.

Throughout my agony I never dreamed of resorting to a direct question, much less a reproach. Even during the period of joyful anticipation some fear of breaking the spell had kept me from any bald circus talk in the presence of them. But Harold, who was built in quite another way, so soon as he discerned the drift of their conversation and heard the knell of all his hopes, filled the room with wail and clamour of bereavement. The grinning welkin rang with "Circus!" "Circus!" shook the window-panes; the mocking walls re-echoed "Circus!" Circus he would have, and the whole circus, and nothing but the circus. No compromise for him, no evasions, no fallacious, unsecured promises to pay. He had drawn his cheque on the Bank of Expectation, and it had got to be cashed then and there;

else he would yell, and yell himself into a fit, and come out of it and yell again. Yelling should be his profession, his art, his mission, his career. He was qualified, he was resolute, and he was in no hurry to retire from the business.

The noisy ones of the world, if they do not always shout themselves into the imperial purple, are sure at least of receiving attention. If they cannot sell everything at their own price, one thing—silence—must, at any cost, be purchased of them. Harold accordingly had to be consoled by the employment of every specious fallacy and base-born trick known to those whose doom it is to handle children. For me their hollow cajolery had no interest, I could pluck no consolation out of their bankrupt though prodigal pledges. I only waited till that hateful, well-known "Some other time, dear!" told me that hope was finally dead. Then I left the room without any remark. It made it worse—if anything could—to hear that stale, worn-out old phrase, still supposed by those dullards to have some efficacy.

To nature, as usual, I drifted by instinct, and there, out of the track of humanity, under a friendly hedge-row had my black hour unseen. The world was a globe no longer, space was no more filled with whirling circuses of spheres. That day the old beliefs rose up and asserted themselves, and the earth was flat again—ditch-riddled, stagnant, and deadly flat. The undeviating roads crawled straight and white, elms dressed themselves stiffly along inflexible hedges, all nature, centrifugal no longer, sprawled flatly in lines out to its farthest edge, and I felt just like walking out to that terminus, and dropping quietly off. Then, as I sat there, morosely chewing bits of stick, the recollection came back to me of certain fascinating advertisements I had spelled out in the papers—advertisements of great and happy men, owning big ships of tonnage running into four figures, who yet craved, to the extent of public supplication, for the sympathetic co-operation of youths as apprentices. I did not rightly know what apprentices might be, nor whether I was yet big enough to be styled a youth; but one thing seemed clear, that, by some such means as this, whatever the intervening hardships, I could eventually visit all the circuses of the world—the circuses of merry France and gaudy Spain, of Holland and Bohemia, of China and Peru. Here was a plan worth thinking out in all its bearings; for something had presently to be done to end this intolerable state of things.

Midday, and even feeding-time, passed by gloomily enough, till a small disturbance occurred which had the effect of releasing some of the electricity with which the air was charged. Harold, it should be explained, was of a very different mental mould, and never brooded, moped, nor ate his heart out over any disappointment. One wild outburst—one dissolution of a minute into his original elements of air and water, and tears and outcry—so much insulted nature claimed. Then he would pull himself to-from *Dream Days*

gether, iron out his countenance with a smile, and adjust himself to the new condition of things.

If the gods are ever grateful to man for anything, it is when he is so good as to display a short memory. The Olympians were never slow to recognize this quality of Harold's, in which, indeed, their salvation lay, and on this occasion their gratitude had taken the practical form of a fine fat orange, tough-rinded as oranges of those days were wont to be. This he had eviscerated in the good old-fashioned manner, by biting out a hole in the shoulder, inserting a lump of sugar therein, and then working it cannily till the whole soul and body of the orange passed glorified through the sugar into his being. Thereupon, filled full of orange-juice and iniquity, he conceived a deadly snare. Having deftly patted and squeezed the orange-skin till it resumed its original shape, he filled it up with water, inserted a fresh lump of sugar in the orifice, and, issuing forth, blandly proffered it to me as I sat moodily in the doorway dreaming of strange wild circuses under tropic skies.

Such a stale old dodge as this would hardly have taken me in at ordinary moments. But Harold had reckoned rightly upon the disturbing effect of ill-humour, and had guessed, perhaps, that I thirsted for comfort and consolation, and would not criticize too closely the source from which they came. Unthinkingly I grasped the golden fraud, which collapsed at my touch, and squirted its contents into my eyes and over my collar, till the nethermost parts of me were damp with the water that had run down my neck. In an instant I had Harold down, and, with all the energy of which I was capable, devoted myself to grinding his head into the gravel; while he, realizing that the closure was applied, and that the time for discussion or argument was past, sternly concentrated his powers on kicking me in the stomach.

Some people can never allow events to work themselves out quietly. At this juncture one of Them swooped down on the scene, pouring shrill, misplaced abuse on both of us: on me for ill-treating my younger brother, whereas it was distinctly I who was the injured and the deceived; on him for the high offence of assault and battery on a clean collar—a collar which I had myself deflowered and defaced, shortly before, in sheer desperate ill-temper. Disgusted and defiant we fled in different directions, rejoining each other later in the kitchen-garden; and as we strolled along together, our short feud forgotten, Harold observed gloomily: "I should like to be a cave-man, like Uncle George was tellin' us about: with a flint hatchet and no clothes, and live in a cave and not know anybody!"

"And if any one came to see us we didn't like," I joined in, catching on to the points of the idea, "we'd hit him on the head with the hatchet till he dropped down dead."

"And then," said Harold, warming up, "we'd drag him into the cave and *skin him!*"

For a space we gloated silently over the fair scene our imaginations had conjured up. It was *blood* we felt the need of just then. We wanted no luxuries, nothing dear-bought nor far-fetched. Just plain blood, and nothing else, and plenty of it. . . .

The first bearer of this famous name remembers the fears, fantasies, and superstitions of his childhood, noting how long they last.

OLIVER WENDELL HOLMES

from *The Autocrat of the Breakfast-Table*

I WAS BORN and bred, as I have told you twenty times, among books and those who knew what was in books. I was carefully instructed in things temporal and spiritual. But up to a considerable maturity of childhood I believed Raphael and Michael Angelo to have been superhuman beings. The central doctrine of the prevalent religious faith of Christendom was utterly confused and neutralized in my mind for years by one of those too common stories of actual life, which I overheard repeated in a whisper.—Why did I not ask? you will say.—You don't remember the rosy pudency of sensitive children. The first instinctive movement of the little creatures is to make a *cache*, and bury it in beliefs, doubts, dreams, hopes, and terrors. I am uncovering one of these *caches*. Do you think I was necessarily a greater fool and coward than another?

I was afraid of ships. Why, I could never tell. The masts looked frightfully tall,—but they were not so tall as the steeple of our old yellow meeting-house. At any rate I used to hide my eyes from the sloops and schooners that were wont to lie at the end of the bridge, and I confess that traces of this undefined terror lasted very long.—One other source of alarm had a still more fearful significance. There was a great wooden HAND,—a glove-maker's sign, which used to swing and creak in the blast, as it hung from a pillar before a certain shop a mile or two outside of the city. Oh, the dreadful hand! Always hanging there ready to catch up a little boy, who would come home to supper no more, nor yet to bed,—whose porringer would be laid away empty thenceforth, and his half-worn shoes wait until his small brother grew to fit them.

As for all manner of superstitious observances, I used once to think

[251]

I must have been peculiar in having such a list of them, but I now believe that half the children of the same age go through the same experiences. No Roman soothsayer ever had such a catalogue of *omens* as I found in the Sibylline leaves of my childhood. That trick of throwing a stone at a tree and attaching some mighty issue to hitting or missing, which you will find mentioned in one or more biographies, I well remember. Stepping on or over certain particular things or spots,—Dr. Johnson's especial weakness,—I got the habit of at a very early age.—I won't swear that I have not some tendency to these not wise practices even at this present date. [How many of you that read these notes can say the same thing!]

With these follies mingled sweet delusions, which I loved so well I would not outgrow them, even when it required a voluntary effort to put a momentary trust in them. Here is one which I cannot help telling you.

The firing of the great guns at the Navy-yard is easily heard at the place where I was born and lived. "There is a ship of war come in," they used to say, when they heard them. Of course, I supposed that such vessels came in unexpectedly, after indefinite years of absence,—suddenly as falling stones; and that the great guns roared in their astonishment and delight at the sight of the old war-ship splitting the bay with her cut-water. Now, the sloop-of-war the *Wasp*, Captain Blakely, after gloriously capturing the *Reindeer* and the *Avon*, had disappeared from the face of the ocean, and was supposed to be lost. But there was no proof of it, and, of course, for a time, hopes were entertained that she might be heard from. Long after the last real chance had utterly vanished, I pleased myself with the fond illusion that somewhere on the waste of waters she was still floating, and there were *years* during which I never heard the sound of the great gun booming inland from the Navy-yard without saying to myself, "The *Wasp* has come!" and almost thinking I could see her, as she rolled in, crumpling the water before her, weather-beaten, barnacled, with shattered spars and threadbare canvas, welcomed by the shouts and tears of thousands. This was one of those dreams that I nursed and never told. Let me make a clean breast of it now, and say, that, so late as to have outgrown childhood, perhaps to have got far on towards manhood, when the roar of the cannon has struck suddenly on my ear, I have started with a thrill of vague expectation and tremulous delight, and the long-unspoken words have articulated themselves in the mind's dumb whisper, *The Wasp has come!*

—Yes, children believe plenty of queer things. I suppose all of you have had the pocket-book fever when you were little?—What do I mean? Why, ripping up old pocket-books in the firm belief that bank-bills to an immense amount were hidden in them.—So, too, you must all remember some splendid unfulfilled promise of somebody or other, which fed you with hopes perhaps for years, and which left a blank in your life which nothing has ever filled up.—O.T. quitted our household carrying with

from *The Autocrat of the Breakfast-Table*

him the passionate regrets of the more youthful members. He was an ingenious youngster; wrote wonderful copies, and carved the two initials given above with great skill on all available surfaces. I thought, by the way, they were all gone; but the other day I found them on a certain door which I will show you some time. How it surprised me to find them so near the ground! I had thought the boy of no trivial dimensions. Well, O.T., when he went, made a solemn promise to two of us. I was to have a ship, and the other a martin-house (last syllable pronounced as in the word tin). Neither ever came; but, oh, how many and many a time I have stolen to the corner—the cars pass close by it at this time,—and looked up that long avenue, thinking that he must be coming now, almost sure, as I turned to look northward, that there he would be trudging toward me, the ship in one hand and the mar*tin*-house in the other! . . .

PART FOUR

Growing Up

"WHERE ARE THE CHILDREN?" asks Phyllis McGinley, and so almost overnight do thousands of other parents.

In the years just before puberty we cannot forget that our sons and daughters are still children. Why else their uncouth manners, their baffling mental absences and those other moments when they suddenly turn to us for help and protection? Now, in adolescence, all this new blossoming and burgeoning, working transformations before our eyes, leaves us breathless. Even the awkwardness of this age takes on special charm, for it is full of promise. Instead of children, it is a young man and young woman who will be here tomorrow.

Emotionally, these adolescent youngsters are intense and volatile. Intellectually, they may go branching off in all directions, displaying the wildest contradictions. At one moment they seem responsibly grown up, at another, unbelievably childish. They are given to bull-sessions, theorizing, introspection, and hifalutin notions of acceptable behavior, yet often they are unable to perform the necessary tasks under their very noses. For all their moments of startling perceptiveness they may be flagrantly oblivious to other people's feelings. Even when they and their friends seem wholly light-minded, taken up with dates, clothes, gossip and the quest for popularity, they are actually far from sure of themselves. Their surface cockiness conceals their continuous struggle with the questions: Who am I? What will I be good for in the unprotected adult world? Finding no clear answers, they are frightened.

Emily, an actual captive aboard a pirate ship on her "innocent voyage" can ask these questions in a comfortable, ruminative way. She is only eleven and the world is far away. Right now, while she lives in the irresponsible present, she can cherish her illusions and entertain marvelous possibilities. All the horrifying events of the past months have been successfully sealed off from memory and feeling. They never happened. Her day of reckoning will come, but it is not yet.

For Anne Frank, a bit older, more intelligent, gifted and articulate, there is no exit from the stark realities other than through writing the diary she has left us and her tentative explorations of sex and love as she tries to make them real through the boy Peter. Her life is full of grubby work and uncongenial company suffered at close quarters. Inescapable always are the threatening present, the uncertain future. The wonder for the reader is in the spectacle of life and growth going on just the same even in these dire straits. Anne herself is aware of the forces stirring within her. "I feel so strong," she writes, "as if I can bear a great deal. I feel so free and young." She gives us pages of self-analysis. Was her insight true? In part. Was her self-reproach sincere or mere posturing? A little of both. Reading between the lines, we can believe that this talkative, precocious, egocentric child who noisily challenged everything and everybody must have been hard to live with. Why wasn't she peeling potatoes instead of spending hours writing, or talking about goodness knows what with Peter in the attic? Was her father really the perfect friend she describes? (In the manner of lovers' quarrels she is angry at him periodically.) Was her mother really unable to "understand"? We will never know the full answers. At this age the young see their parents not as they are, but as they need to see them.

Adolescents are right to be frightened; their world is out of joint. Sexually mature at fourteen, they are forbidden sex relations until marriage, for which in our society they are emotionally unready until much later. Vocationally they are all at sea. Education exacts long servitude, and it will be years before they can support a family. Wholly untested, they do not know what they are good for or who they really are. For all their thrashing about and declarations of independence, they will be dependents for a long time to come, and the knowledge bites deep.

In *First Love and Other Sorrows*, we find a young boy struggling in just this morass. Sixteen and fully grown, for him, sex is an ever-present problem. A friend titillates his imagination with tales of easy-to-come-by sexual exploits, and though he finds some respite from loneliness in the affections of a troubled girl, he is always aware that his own fulfillment must be long postponed. His older sister's romance is a further reminder of personal frustrations, and his widowed mother, all aflutter at the prospects of a good match for her daughter that would lighten the burden of the family's poverty, has thoughts for nothing else. To this youth, as to so many, it is all too clear that he himself is a burden on the family and will be for many years; the compromises that life is forcing on his sister seem to him the dismal foreshadowing of his own future.

At the same time that young people are understandably frightened about their ability to play their part creditably in the years ahead, the older generation is frightened by youth. Overwhelmed by those loud demands to be "let alone" and "to live as I please," they tend to capitulate, confining themselves largely to standing on the sidelines, setting the stage for the fancied requirements of youth in whatever ways convention dictates and praying that calamity may be averted. Unmindful that in any sane society the mature members have always assumed responsibility for counseling and providing leadership for the young, they bow out all too easily.

The course which the father in *The Legacy* attempts to follow on the advice of a busybody neighbor is bound to miscarry and go wide of the mark. The advice is a shallow cliché prescription which takes no account of this girl's deeper needs or the recent loss of her mother. Though nagged by inner misgivings, the father tries nevertheless to conform to advice and play his part; and his daughter, equally gallantly, tries to go along. They fail. But in their failure they find each other and together uncover some far more durable values to live by. This story, surely a parable for today, exposes the superficiality of one of our most entrenched notions—the mad pursuit of social success which, beginning early in youth, characterizes so much of middle-class life in America.

A Night Visitor is another story that lays bare the confusion of well-meaning parents who rate their children's surface happiness above all else and so seek to protect them as far as possible from contact with whatever in life is sad or sordid. Here, the appearance of an unwelcome relative squarely confronts this family with a crisis of conscience. The easygoing mother, too eager to please everyone, succumbs to her eldest son's plan for getting rid of a poor derelict, so that the family may maintain a smooth front to the world. Instead of enlisting her children in the search for a humane solution to a thorny dilemma, or helping them face up to the skeleton in the family closet, she surrenders to the easier course by which they can once again cover it up, forget it all, and without pity dispose of a human being whose presence in their home threatens to be socially embarrassing.

Young people today, whether aware of it or not, are hungry for leadership, readier than they appear to be to respond to a call to effort and sacrifice. On those occasions when they have spoken out, they have made clear that what they miss in their elders is moral conviction, seasoned thought, and—along with a listening ear to rebel voices—an ability to hew to their own lines, knowing why they have chosen a certain course and making clear the reasons for their choice. Then, at least, young people would not feel mired down in a bog of adult uncertainties. With firm foundations, if they still decide to reject their parents' choices, they will at least find something firm and hard and worthy of their mettle to fight against.

Growing Up

Because growing up is not just for children, we have included at the end of this section a story highlighting one of those forward leaps in adult growth that at times are so clear and dramatic. In *The Gift,* a young father, still bound by old childhood resentments toward his parents, given to fits of adolescent pettishness, is suddenly awakened by a lesson simply and unconsciously taught by his small daughter. For the first time he sees his own unkindnesses for what they are. With this new vision, all that is best and most generous in him quickens into life and now at last can take over.

PHYLLIS MCGINLEY

Ballade of Lost Objects

Where are the ribbons I tie my hair with?
  Where is my lipstick? Where are my hose—
The sheer ones hoarded these weeks to wear with
  Frocks the closets do not disclose?
Perfumes, petticoats, sports chapeaux,
  The blouse Parisian, the earring Spanish—
Everything suddenly ups and goes.
  And where in the world did the children vanish?

This is the house I used to share with
  Girls in pinafores, shier than does.
I can recall how they climbed my stair with
  Gales of giggles, on their tiptoes.
Last seen wearing both braids and bows
  (But looking rather Raggedy-Annish),
When they departed nobody knows—
  Where in the world did the children vanish?

Two tall strangers, now I must bear with,
  Decked in my personal furbelows,
Raiding the larder, rending the air with
  Gossip and terrible radios.
Neither my friends nor quite my foes,
  Alien, beautiful, stern, and clannish,
Here they dwell, while the wonder grows:
  Where in the world did the children vanish?

Prince, I warn you, under the rose,
   Time is the thief you cannot banish.
These are my daughters, I suppose.
   But where in the world did the children vanish?

Even when their external world is highly unusual, children go right on being children. Emily, a captive aboard a pirate ship, after her Jamaican home has been wrecked by a hurricane, makes the great discovery that she is she, just as many another child has done in more humdrum circumstances.

RICHARD HUGHES

from *A High Wind in Jamaica*

AND THEN an event did occur, to Emily, of considerable importance. She suddenly realized who she was.

There is little reason that one can see why it should not have happened to her five years earlier, or even five later; and none, why it should have come that particular afternoon.

She had been playing houses in a nook right in the bows, behind the windlass (on which she had hung a devil's-claw as a door-knocker); and tiring of it was walking rather aimlessly aft, thinking vaguely about some bees and a fairy queen, when it suddenly flashed into her mind that she was she.

She stopped dead, and began looking over all of her person which came within the range of her eyes. She could not see much, except a foreshortened view of the front of her frock, and her hands when she lifted them for inspection; but it was enough for her to form a rough idea of the little body she suddenly realised to be hers.

She began to laugh, rather mockingly. "Well!" she thought, in effect: "Fancy you, of all people, going and getting caught like this!—You can't get out of it now, not for a very long time: you'll have to go through with being a child, and growing up, and getting old, before you'll be quit of this mad prank!"

Determined to avoid any interruption of this highly important occasion, she began to climb the ratlines, on her way to her favourite perch at the masthead. Each time she moved an arm or a leg in this simple action, however, it struck her with fresh amazement to find them obeying her so readily. Memory told her, of course, that they had always done so before: but before, she had never realised how surprising this was.

Once settled on her perch, she began examining the skin of her hands

from *A High Wind in Jamaica*

with the utmost care: for it was hers. She slipped a shoulder out of the top of her frock; and having peeped in to make sure she really was continuous under her clothes, she shrugged it up to touch her cheek. The contact of her face and the warm bare hollow of her shoulder gave her a comfortable thrill, as if it was the caress of some kind friend. But whether the feeling came to her through her cheek or her shoulder, which was the caresser and which the caressed, that no analysis could tell her.

Once fully convinced of this astonishing fact, that she was now Emily Bas-Thornton (why she inserted the "now" she did not know, for she certainly imagined no transmigrational nonsense of having been anyone else before), she began seriously to reckon its implications.

First, what agency had so ordered it that out of all the people in the world who she might have been, she was this particular one, this Emily; born in such-and-such a year out of all the years in Time, and encased in this particular rather pleasing little casket of flesh? Had she chosen herself, or had God done it?

At this, another consideration: who was God? She had heard a terrible lot about Him, always: but the question of His identity had been left vague, as much taken for granted as her own. Wasn't she perhaps God, herself? Was it that she was trying to remember? However, the more she tried, the more it eluded her. (How absurd, to disremember such an important point as whether one was God or not!) So she let it slide: perhaps it would come back to her later.

Secondly, why had all this not occurred to her before? She had been alive for over ten years, now, and it had never once entered her head. She felt like a man who suddenly remembers at eleven o'clock at night, sitting in his own arm-chair, that he had accepted an invitation to go out to dinner that night. There is no reason for him to remember it now: but there seems equally little why he should not have remembered it in time to keep his engagement. How could he have sat there all the evening, without being disturbed by the slightest misgiving? How could Emily have gone on being Emily for ten years, without once noticing this apparently obvious fact?

It must not be supposed that she argued it all out in this ordered, but rather long-winded fashion. Each consideration came to her in a momentary flash, quite innocent of words; and in between her mind lazed along, either thinking of nothing or returning to her bees and the fairy queen. If one added up the total of her periods of conscious thought, it would probably reach something between four and five seconds; nearer five, perhaps; but it was spread out over the best part of an hour.

Well then, granted she was Emily, what were the consequences, besides enclosure in that particular little body (which now began on its own account to be aware of a sort of unlocated itch, most probably somewhere on the right thigh), and lodgement behind a particular pair of eyes?

It implied a whole series of circumstances. In the first place, there was her family, a number of brothers and sisters from whom, before, she had never entirely dissociated herself; but now she got such a sudden feeling of being a discrete person that they seemed as separate from her as the ship itself. However, willy-nilly she was almost as tied to them as she was to her body. And then there was this voyage, this ship, this mast round which she had wound her legs. She began to examine it with almost as vivid an illumination as she had studied the skin of her hands. And when she came down from the mast, what would she find at the bottom? There would be Jonsen, and Otto, and the crew: the whole fabric of a daily life which up to now she had accepted as it came, but which now seemed vaguely disquieting. What was going to happen? Were there disasters running about loose, disasters which her rash marriage to the body of Emily Thornton made her vulnerable to?

A sudden terror struck her: did anyone know? (Know, I mean, that she was someone in particular, Emily—perhaps even God—not just any little girl.) She could not tell why, but the idea terrified her. It would be bad enough if they should discover she was a particular person—but if they should discover she was God! At all costs she must hide that from them. —But suppose they knew already, had simply been hiding it from her (as guardians might from an infant king)? In that case, as in the other, the only thing to do was to continue to behave as if she did not know, and so outwit them.

But if she was God, why not turn all the sailors into white mice, or strike Margaret blind, or cure somebody, or do some other Godlike act of the kind? Why should she hide it? She never really asked herself why: but instinct prompted her strongly of the necessity. Of course, there was the element of doubt (suppose she had made a mistake, and the miracle missed fire): but more largely it was the feeling that she would be able to deal with the situation so much better when she was a little older. Once she had declared herself there would be no turning back; it was much better to keep her godhead up her sleeve, for the present.

Grown-ups embark on a life of deception with considerable misgiving, and generally fail. But not so children. A child can hide the most appalling secret without the least effort, and is practically secure against detection. Parents, finding that they see through their child in so many places the child does not know of, seldom realise that, if there is some point the child really gives his mind to hiding, their chances are nil.

So Emily had no misgivings when she determined to preserve her secret, and needed have none.

A lad growing up in a simple country town in the English Cotswolds indiscriminately devours books—later making "an explosive discovery" that guides him to literature.

LAURIE LEE

True Adventures of the Boy Reader

ONE OF MY earliest memories is that of a small boy sitting in our village street surrounded by a group of grey-whiskered old men. Bored and fidgety, his mind clearly elsewhere, he is reading aloud in fluent sing-song the war news from a tattered newspaper.

This boy and I were of one generation and we shared the same trick of enlightenment: we were both the inheritors, after centuries of darkness, of our country's first literate peasantry. My mother and father, the children of a coachman and a sailor, read well and were largely self-taught. But their parents could do little more than spell out their names—which they were not often called on to do—and if given a book were likely to turn it over in their hands, cough loudly, and put it away.

Not that there were many books available at that time; our elders had little more to contend with, in the way of printed script, than their almanacs and their Sunday psalmbooks, which, of course, they knew mostly by heart. About the only other bound reading material available to greet the new gift of literacy were the widely-sold "Penny Readers," which offered irreproachable love stories of an unearthly gentility, tales of martyrs and foreign missionaries, collected church sermons and strictures on drink, and certain moral epics devoted to the loyalty and devotion owed by the serving classes to the gentry.

Even so, the existence of these "Penny Readers" created a revolution in home entertainment, and the gossip of grannies in chimney-corners began to be silenced by family-readings-aloud. It was through this practice that I first knew the printed word, its power and its glory, its persuasive magic and ready gift of hallucination.

Many a winter's night we would settle round the lamp-lit kitchen, after supper had been cleared, while our mother took down one of her "Penny" volumes and read to us by the hour. Through mother's voice, and the awful tales she read, we saw the world through crystal casements, never doubting that this was the way it looked or that its people were less than the noblest. Alas, I can remember but two volumes now (perhaps they were all we had). One was "J. Cole," the life-story of a footman who became a butler through thrift and prayer; and the other, called simply "Although He Was Black," a posthumous tribute to a young Negro houseboy who, in spite of his color, made good as a servant by sacrificing his life to his mistress in a fire. These tales, in spite of their frequent readings, never failed to bathe us in tears.

Perhaps through over-indulgence in mother's fireside entertainments I was myself a tardy reader. When I was lent my first book, by a rich old neighbor, I thought she was off her head. It was called "Aikman's Scotland" and was bound in red leather and was just a three-dimensional object to me. Then one day the old lady stopped me in the street and asked me how I was enjoying the book, adding that she only lent it to me because she knew I loved reading and that I would treat it with special care. I was astonished; it had never occurred to me to read it; I had used it as a tunnel for my clockwork train.

At that time, in those Cotswold villages of the Twenties, we may have been literate, but by no means literary. We had no regular newspapers and of course no radio or television, and were as yet unracked by their tortuous linguistics. We were the inheritors still of an oral tradition of language, and the stream, though thin, was pure. Outside our own class, which was that of farms and cloth mills, hardly anyone spoke to us save from the pulpit. Our vocabulary was small, though naturally virile; our words ancient, round, warm from the tongue. If we were affected by any literary influence at all, it was from the King James Bible.

Such was my background, and in some ways it still rules me. I am made uneasy by any form of writing which cannot readily be spoken aloud. From my earliest years, as soon as I could read, I was at home only with those particular classics which approached in style our country speech and the Bible. The three books that continue to stand out like megaliths in the empty reaches of my early reading are "Pilgrim's Progress," "Robinson Crusoe" and "Gulliver's Travels." As I read them then, so I read them now—with instant recognition. There are old folk still living in the village today who continue to address each other with the austere formalities of Christian addressing the demons. Robinson Crusoe's is the voice of a local bachelor-farmer boasting how he got through the year single-handed. The satirical fantasies and crudities of Gulliver are still much the mood of our village inn.

I was at the village school when I read these books (having bought the three of them at a rummage sale for a penny). At the school itself there were few books, except things about cats and mats, or terse little pam-

True Adventures of the Boy Reader

phlets stating that Jill was ill and Jack had Broken his Back. Those were innocent, crisp, monosyllabic days, of which I was the last to complain.

Then at the age of twelve I was sent to the school in the town, and my reading changed abruptly. Here were dog-eared books for every pupil, mostly the works of Sir Walter Scott. After the fat-bacon language of my earlier reading I hated Scott's dry, latinized prose, finding its false medievalism and over-wrought fretwork merely a grating for dust and boredom.

I was made to read Scott for over two years—and have managed to avoid him since. But instead of being put off books forever I developed a passion for out-of-school reading. This marked the beginning of an indiscriminate gorging that was to continue throughout my teens. There was no one to tell me what to read; there was no one I knew who knew. As it is for most adolescents it was a matter of prodigious intake, mountains of chaff for a grain of wheat.

On my way home from school I developed a special technique: At several pages a day, while loitering at the bookstall in Woolworth's, I found I could read most of their stock in a year. Behind the manager's back, in the town's other bookshop, I slyly repeated the performance. Zane Grey, Jack London, Nat Gould, Edgar Wallace—such was the good, plain fare of that time, presenting a picture of both the Old World and the New which has never been equaled for innocent violence.

Then suddenly, by chance, I stumbled on Dickens, finding his Collected Works on a bonfire. Some old neighbor had thrown them out, and the rain had saved them from burning. Though scorched and mildewed I stole them home, cleaned them up, and read through the lot. After tea, with a volume propped up on an oil-lamp, the damp pages steaming gently, I was borne straightway into the stews of old London, until I could no longer remember my own name.

Reading at home, with a family of seven in the room, required a special brand of abstraction. But one had it then; it was no trouble at all, a concentration both intense and happy, which brothers or sisters, with all their fighting and singing, could never hope to break through. (True, in summertime I could go and read up a tree, or hide tiger-like out in the grass. But this was less through the fear of distracted attention than of being given odd jobs to do.)

Up till now my reading had been in a large sense Victorian, and quite a lot of it even more dated. Then with a bang something happened that really shook my foundations—I discovered the public library. I think it had been in the town some years, but no one had thought to tell me. But late or soon, it was an explosive discovery, coming at my most inflammable time.

As I gazed at its great shelves of books—none chained to the walls, all free—the world of "J. Cole" slowly folded up and died, wrapped in its sheets of old maid's lavender. But reading by stealth had become a habit and a free library took a moment to get used to. I started by working straight through the poetry shelf, beginning with the books nearest the door. Yeats, D. H. Lawrence, James Joyce, T. S. Eliot—I'd never heard of any of them before. My mother, of course, had introduced me to poetry, but she knew of no one later than Tennyson. Now vibrant new voices assailed and alarmed me, cracked in my ears like whips, so that for weeks I moved only to their urgent drivings and tossed at night to their echoes. This sharp, hard language, with its attractive bitterness, seemed to cut me to the very bone, purging my heart of its romantic dews and generally stiffening up the blood.

Amazed, to begin with, at finding such books in the town, I also fancied I was the first to discover them. They led me to a door marked "Heresy and Schism," which till then I had sworn to fly from. I began to feel personally responsible for these authors' views, as though I had originally thought of them myself, and when the poems of Joyce and Lawrence took me to their prose the fat was truly then in the fire.

From that moment I never glanced at another Western or thriller; my happy apprenticeship as a reader was over. Before my books had been the playthings of the village; now they were my private and loaded bombs. Through the once-open fields of my Christian valley I wandered secretively, proud and alone.

My decline was now rapid, and damnation near. It was finally completed at age fifteen. I had started work as an officeboy in the town, and one day a traveling salesman came in and offered me my own library for a shilling a week. I ordered Lawrence, Shaw, Huxley's "Brave New World," Gogol, Engels and Marx. I knocked up a bookcase from a rabbit's hutch and nailed the library to my bedroom wall.

Things were never quite the same again; the snug days had gone for good. Then the vicar discovered me reading "Brave New World" and took it away and burnt it. It was the end, in a way, of my country childhood and of its carefree acquiescence.

A sixteen-year-old boy is caught in the agony of adolescent self-doubt about himself and his whole future.

HAROLD BRODKEY

First Love and Other Sorrows

TOWARD THE END of March, in St. Louis, slush fills the gutters, and dirty snow lies heaped alongside porch steps, and everything seems to be suffocating in the embrace of a season that lasts too long. Radiators hiss mournfully, no one manages to be patient, the wind draws tears from your eyes, the clouds are filled with sadness. Women with scarves around their heads and their feet encased in fur-lined boots pick their way carefully over patches of melting ice. It seems that winter will last forever, that this is the decision of nature and nothing can be done about it.

At the age when I was always being warned by my mother not to get overheated, spring began on that evening when I was first allowed to go outside after dinner and play kick-the-can. The ground would be moist, I'd manage to get muddy in spite of what seemed to me extreme precautions, my mother would call me home in the darkness, and when she saw me she would ask, "What *have* you done to yourself?" "Nothing," I'd say hopefully. But by the time I was sixteen, the moment when the year passed into spring, like so many other things, was less clear. In March and early April, track began, but indoors; mid-term exams came and went; the buds appeared on the maples, staining all their branches red; but it was still winter, and I found myself having feelings in class that were like long petitions for spring and all its works. And then one evening I was sitting at my desk doing my trigonometry and I heard my sister coming home from her office; I heard her high heels tapping on the sidewalk, and realized that, for the first time since fall, all the windows in the house were open. My sister was coming up the front walk. I looked down through a web of budding tree branches and called out to her that it was spring, by God. She shrugged—she was very handsome and she

[267]

didn't approve of me—and then she started up the front steps and vanished under the roof of the porch.

I ran downstairs. "The bus was crowded tonight," my sister said, hanging up her coat. "I could hardly breathe. This is such a warm dress."

"You need a new spring dress," my mother said, her face lighting up. She was sitting in the living room with the evening paper on her lap.

She and my sister spread the newspaper on the dining-room table to look at the ads.

"We'll just have to settle for sandwiches tonight," my mother said to me. My father was dead, and my mother pretended that now all the cooking was done for my masculine benefit. "Look! That suit's awfully smart!" she cried, peering at the paper. "Montaldo's always has such nice suits." She sighed and went out to the kitchen, leaving the swinging door open so she could talk to my sister. "Ninety dollars isn't too much for a good suit, do you think?"

"No," my sister said. "I don't think it's too much. But I don't really want a suit this spring. I'd much rather have a sort of sky-blue dress—with a round neck that shows my shoulders a little bit. I don't look good in suits. I'm not old enough." She was twenty-two. "My face is too round," she added, in a low voice.

My mother said, "You're not too young for a suit." She also meant my sister was not too young to get married.

My sister looked at me and said, "Mother, do you think he shaves often enough? How often *do* you shave?"

"Every three days," I said, flushing up my neck and cheeks.

"Well, try it every other day."

"Yes, try to be neater," my mother said. "I'm sure girls don't like boys with fuzz on their chin."

"I think he's too proud of his beard to shave it," my sister said, and giggled.

"I feel sorry for the man who marries you," I said. "Because everybody thinks you're sweet and you're not."

She smiled pityingly at me, and then she looked down over the newspaper again.

Until I was four, we lived in a large white frame house overlooking the Mississippi River, south of St. Louis. This house had, among other riches, a porte-cochere, an iron deer on the lawn, and a pond with goldfish swimming in it. Once, I asked my mother why we had left that earlier house, and she said, "We lost our money—that's why. Your father was a very trusting man," she said. "He was always getting swindled."

She was not a mercenary woman, nor was she mean about money—except in spells that didn't come often—but she believed that what we lost with the money was much of our dignity and much of our happiness.

First Love and Other Sorrows [269]

She did not want to see life in a grain of sand; she wanted to see it from the shores of the Riviera, wearing a white sharkskin dress.

I will never forget her astonishment when she took us—she was dressed in her best furs, as a gesture, I suppose—to see the house that was to be our home from then on and I told her I liked it. It had nine rooms, a stained-glass window in the hall, and neighbors all up and down the block. She detested that house.

As she grew older, she changed, she grew less imperious. She put her hair into a roll, wore dark-colored clothes, said often, "I'm not a young woman any more," and began to take pride in being practical. But she remained determined; she had seen a world we didn't remember too clearly, and she wanted us to make our way back to it. "I had it all," she said once to my sister. "I was good-looking. We were rich. You have no idea what it was like. If I had died when I was thirty, I would have died completely happy. . . ."

But being practical did not come easy to her. She was not practical in her bones, and every spring brings back the memory of my mother peering nearsightedly, with surprise, at the tulip shoots in her flower border. And it brings back her look of distraught efficiency during spring housecleaning. "You'd better clear your closet shelves tonight," she would warn me, "because tomorrow Tillie and I are going in there with a vacuum cleaner, and we'll throw out everything we find." Year after year, I would run upstairs to save my treasures—even when I was sixteen and on the verge of a great embarkation, the nature of which I could not even begin to guess. My treasures consisted of my postcard collection—twenty-five hundred cards in all, arranged alphabetically by states of the Union and countries of the world (the wonder was that *I* lived in St. Louis)—an old baseball glove, my leaf collection, two obscene comic books I had won in a poker game at a Boy Scout jamboree, my marble collection, and thirty-five pages of secret thoughts written out in longhand. All these had to be taken out to the garage and hidden among the tools until the frenzy of cleaning was over and I could smuggle them back upstairs.

After supper, as the season grew warmer, my mother and sister and I would sit on the screened porch in the rear of the house, marooned among the shadows and the new leaves and the odor of insect spray, the light from our lamps sticking to the trees like bits of yellow paper. Usually the radio was on, and my mother, a book on her lap, her face abstracted (she was usually bored; her life was moved mainly by the burning urge to rise once more along the thin edge of social distinction), would listen to the comedians and laugh. When the phone rang, she would get up and go into the house with long strides, and if the call was for my sister, my mother would call her to the phone in a voice mottled with triumph.

Sometimes in the evening my mother would wash my sister's hair.

My sister would sit in front of the basin in Mother's bathroom, a towel around her shoulders, smiling. From my room across the hall I would hear my sister chattering about the men she knew—the ones she dated, the ones she wanted to date, the ones she wouldn't touch with a ten-foot pole. My mother would interrupt with accounts of her own cleverness, her sorties and successes when young, sometimes laughingly, but sometimes gloomily, because she regretted a lot of things. Then she and my sister would label my sister's suitors: one or two had family, one had money, one—a poor boy—had a brilliant future, and there were a few docile, sweet ones who were simply fillers, who represented the additional number of dates that raised my sister to the rank of a very popular girl.

In these conversations, my mother would often bring up matters of propriety. Late dates were improper, flirting with boys other than one's date, breaking dates. Then, too, she would try to instruct my sister in other matters, which had to do with keeping passion in its place and so preventing embarrassment for the boy and disaster for the girl. My sister would grow irritated. "I don't know why you talk like that—I behave very well," she would tell my mother. "Better than the other girls I know." Her irritation would please my mother, who would smile and say that only good-looking girls could afford to be good, and then they would both laugh.

I used to wonder why my mother didn't take my sister's success for granted. My sister was lovely, she had plenty of dates, the phone rang incessantly. Where was the danger? Why did she always lecture my sister?

Once, my mother said my sister ought not to dance with too many boys or she would frighten off the more serious ones. My sister was getting dressed for the spring dance at the country club. Arrogant and slender, she glistened like a water nymph, among her froth of bottles and jars and filmy clothes. She became furious; she screamed that she *liked* to dance. I closed the door to my room, but I could still hear the two of them. "Don't be so foolish," my mother kept saying, over and over again. "Please don't be foolish. . . ." Then my sister, on the verge of tears, said she just wanted to have a good time. My sister's date arrived, and I went downstairs to let him in, and by the time I came back upstairs, the two of them were laughing. My mother said she was just trying to be helpful; after all, my sister was impractical and her looks wouldn't last forever. My sister, as she opened the door of her room, said, under her breath, "They'll last a lot longer yet."

I'll never forget the wild rustling of her voluminous white skirt as she came down the hallway toward me. Her face was strangely still, as if seen by moonlight. Her hair was smooth and shining, her hands bent outward at the wrist, as if they were flowers. "How beautiful you look!" I cried. My sister smiled and then solemnly turned all the way around, and her huge skirt rose and fell like a splash of surf. She was so beautiful I could hardly bear it. I hugged her, and she laughed.

Later that night I asked my mother why she got so distraught. Wasn't my sister popular enough? My mother was sitting in the kitchen, in an old, faded yellow housecoat, drinking a glass of warm milk. "You don't know anything about it," she said, with such sadness that I rose from the table and fled to my room.

"I know what I'm saying!" my mother would cry when she argued with my sister. "You must listen to me. People talk. . . . You don't know who you'll meet on a date; it's good to accept even if you don't like the boy. . . . Girls have to be very careful. You're thoughtless. Don't you think in fifty years I've learned what makes the world go around? Now, listen to me. I know what I'm saying. . . ." But my sister's face was so radiant, her charm was so intense, she pushed her blond hair back from her face with a gesture so quick, so certain, so arrogant and filled with vanity, that no one, I thought, could doubt that whatever she did would be right.

I wanted to be arrogant, too. I didn't want to wear glasses and be one of the humorless, heavy-handed boys my sister despised. I was on her side as much as she'd let me be. She was the elder, and she often grew impatient with me. I didn't seem to understand all the things involved in being on her side.

Night after night I saw her come home from work tired—she had a secretarial job in a hospital and she hated it—and two hours later she would descend the stairs, to greet her date, her face alight with seriousness or with a large, bright smile, depending on her mood or on where her escort was taking her that evening. A concert or an art movie made her serious; one of the hotel supper clubs brought the smile to her face. She would trip down the stairs in her high heels, a light, flimsy coat thrown over one arm, one hand clutching a purse and gloves, her other hand on the banister. In the queer yellow light of the hall chandelier, her necklace or her earrings would shine dully, and sometimes, especially if she was all dressed up, in a black dress, say, with a low neck, because they were going out to a supper club, there would be an air, in spite of her gaiety, of the captive about her. It was part of her intense charm. In her voluminous white skirt, she went to the spring dance at the country club and brought back to my mother the news that she had captured the interest of Sonny Bruster, the oldest son of M. F. Bruster, a banker and a very rich man—more than interest, it turned out, because he started calling my sister up almost every day at work and taking her out almost every night. My mother was on the phone much of the afternoon explaining to her friends that my sister wasn't engaged. It was criminal the way some people gossiped, she said. My sister had only gone out with the boy ten or twelve times. They were just getting to know each other. Then my mother began to *receive* calls; someone had heard from a friend of Mrs. Bruster's that Mrs. Bruster had said her son was very serious about my sister, who was a very charming, very pretty girl, of good family. . . . My mother rubbed her hands with glee. She borrowed money from her brothers, and every week my sister had new clothes.

My sister would come home from work and run upstairs to change. Sonny would be due at seven, to take her out to dinner. My sister would kick her shoes off, struggle out of her dress, and dash around the upstairs in her slip.

"Mother, I can't find my earrings."

"Which earrings, dear?"

"The little pearls—the little tiny pearl ones that I got two Easters ago, to go with my black . . ."

My sister was delighted with herself. She loved being talked about, being envied.

"Mother, do you know what Ceil Johnson said to me today? She said that Beryl Feringhaus—you know, the real-estate people—was heartbroken because she thought Sonny Bruster was going to get engaged to her." My sister giggled. Her long hair was tangled, and my mother yanked a comb through it.

"Maybe you ought to cut your hair," my mother said, trying to hide her own excitement and to stay practical. During this period, my mother was living in the imminence of wealth. Whenever she stopped what she was doing and looked up, her face would be bright with visions.

That spring when I was sixteen, more than anything else in the world I wanted to be a success when I grew up. I did not know there was any other way of being lovable. My best friend was a boy named Preston, who already had a heavy beard. He was shy, and unfortunate in his dealings with other people, and he wanted to be a physicist. He had very little imagination, and he pitied anyone who did have it. "You and the word 'beautiful'!" he would say disdainfully, holding his nose and imitating my voice. "Tell me—what does 'beautiful' mean?"

"It's something you want," I would say.

"You're an aesthete," Preston would say. "I'm a scientist. That's the difference."

He and I used to call each other almost every night and have long, profound talks on the telephone.

On a date, Preston would sit beside his girl and stolidly eye her. Occasionally, toward the end of the evening, he would begin to breathe heavily, and he would make a few labored, daring jokes. He might catch the girl's hand and stare at her with inflamed and wistful eyes, or he might mutter incoherent compliments. Girls liked him, and escaped easily from his clumsy longing. They slipped their hands from his grasp and asked him to call them up again, but after a few dates with a girl Preston would say disgustedly, "All she does is talk. She's frigid or something. . . ." But the truth was, he was afraid of hurting them, of doing something wrong to them, and he never really courted them at all.

At school, Preston and I had afternoon study hall together. Study hall was in the library, which was filled with the breathing of a hundred and fifty students, and with the dim, half-fainting breezes of high spring, and with books: it was the crossroads of the world. Preston and I would sign out separately, and meet in the lavatory. There we would lean up against the stalls and talk. Preston was full of thoughts; he was tormented by all his ideas. "Do you know what relativity means?" he would ask me. "Do you realize how it affects every little detail of everyday life?" Or it might be Spinoza that moved him: "Eighteenth-century, but by God *there* was a rational man." I would pace up and down, half listening, half daydreaming, wishing *my* name would appear on Preston's list of people who had elements of greatness.

Or we talked about our problems. "I'm not popular," I would say. "I'm too gloomy."

"Why is that, do you think?" Preston would ask.

"I don't know," I would say. "I'm a virgin. That has a lot to do with everything."

"Listen," Preston said one day, "you may not be popular but you're likable. Your trouble is you're a snob." He walked up and down the white-tiled floor, mimicking me. He slouched, and cast his eyes down, and jutted his chin out, and pulled a foolish, serious look over his face.

"Is that me?" I cried, heartbroken.

"Well, almost," Preston said.

Or, leaning on the window sill, sticking our heads out into the golden afternoon air and watching a girl's gym class doing archery under the trees, we talked about sex.

"It starts in the infant," Preston said. "And it lasts forever."

"Saints escape it," I said mournfully.

"The hell they do," Preston said. The girls beneath us on the hillside drew their bows. Their thin green gym suits fluttered against their bodies. "Aren't they nice?" Preston asked longingly. "Aren't they wonderful?"

After school, Preston and I went out for track. The outdoor track was a cinder oval surrounding the football field. A steep, grassy hill led up to the entrance of the school locker room. "Run up that hill every night, boys," the coach pleaded—Old Mackyz, with his paunch and his iron-gray wavy hair—at the end of the practice period. "Run, boys, because when you're abso-lootly exhausted, that's when you got to give *more*. It's the *more*, boys, that makes champions." And then he'd stand there, humble, and touched by his own speech.

During our warmup sessions, we used to jogtrot the length of the field and back again, keeping our knees high. The grand inutility of this movement filled me with something like exaltation; and on every side of me, in irregular lines, my fellow-males jogged, keeping their knees high. What happiness!

"The turf's too springy," Preston would mumble. "Bad for the muscles." Preston was a miler. He was thickset and without natural grace; Mackyz said he had no talent, but he ran doggedly, and he became a good miler. I ran the 440. I was tall and thin, and even Mackyz said I ought to be good at it, but I wasn't. Mackyz said I didn't have the spirit. "All you smart boys are alike," he said. "You haven't got the *heart* for it. You always hold back. You're all a bunch of goldbricks." I tried to cure my maimed enthusiasm. As I ran, Mackyz would bawl desperately, "Hit the ground harder. Hit with your toes! Spring, boy! SPRING! Don't coddle yourself, for Christ's sake. . . ." After a race, I'd throw myself down on a knoll near the finish line, under a sycamore tree, where the track manager dug a new hole every day for us to puke in. Three or four others would join me, and we'd lie there wearily, our chests burning, too weak to move.

Among my other problems was that I was reduced nearly to a state of tears over my own looks whenever I looked at a boy named Joel Bush. Joel was so incredibly good-looking that none of the boys could quite bear the fact of his existence; his looks weren't particularly masculine or clean-cut, and he wasn't a fine figure of a boy—he was merely beautiful. He looked like a statue that had been rubbed with honey and warm wax, to get a golden tone, and he carried at all times, in the neatness of his features and the secret proportions of his face and body that made him so handsome in that particular way, the threat of seduction. Displease me, he seemed to say, and I'll get you. I'll make you fall in love with me and I'll turn you into a donkey. Everyone either avoided him or gave in to him; teachers refused to catch him cheating, boys never teased him, and no one ever told him off. One day I saw him saying goodbye to a girl after school, and as he left her to join me, walking toward the locker room, he said to her, "Meet you here at five-thirty." Track wasn't over until six, and I could tell that he had no intention of meeting her, and yet, when he asked me about some experiments we had done in physics, instead of treating him like someone who had just behaved like a heel, I told him everything I knew.

He never joined us under the sycamore tree, and he ran effortlessly. He would pass the finish line, his chest heaving under his sweat-stained track shirt, and climb into the stands and sit in the sunlight. I was watching him, one afternoon, as he sat there wiping his face and turning his head from side to side. At one moment it was all silver except for the charred hollows of his eyes, and the next it was young and perfect, the head we all recognized as his.

Mackyz saw him and called out to him to put his sweatshirt on before he caught a cold. As he slipped the sweatshirt on, Joel shouted, "Aw, go fry your head!" Mackyz laughed good-naturedly.

Sprinkled here and there on the football field were boys lifting their arms high and then sweeping them down to touch their toes, or lying on their backs and bicycling their legs in the air. I got up and walked toward them, to do a little jogtrotting and high-knee prancing. I looked at Joel. "I'm cooling off," he said to me. I walked on, and just then a flock of crows wheeled up behind the oak tree on the hill and filled the sky with their vibrant motion. Everyone—even Preston—paused and looked up. The birds rose in a half circle and then glided, scythelike, with wings outspread, on a down current of air until they were only twenty feet or so above the ground; then they flapped their wings with a noise like sheets being shaken out, and soared aloft, dragging their shadows up the stepped concrete geometry of the stands, past Joel's handsome, rigid figure, off into the sky.

"Whaddya know about that?" Mackyz said. "Biggest flock of crows I ever saw."

"Why didn't you get your gun and shoot a couple?" Joel called out. Everyone turned. "Then you'd have some crow handy whenever you had to eat some," Joel said.

"Take a lap," Mackyz bawled, his leathery face turning red up to the roots of his iron-gray hair.

"He was only kidding," I said, appalled at Mackyz's hurt.

Mackyz looked at me and scowled, "You can take a lap too, and don't talk so much."

I took off my sweatshirt and dropped it on the grass and set off around the track. As soon as I started running, the world changed. The bodies sprawled out across the green of the football field were parts of a scene remembered, not one real at this moment. The whole secret of effort is to keep on, I told myself. Not for the world would I have stopped then, and yet nothing—not even if I had been turned handsome as a reward for finishing—could have made up for the curious pain of the effort.

About halfway around the track, Joel caught up to me, and then he slowed down and ran alongside. "Mackyz isn't watching," he said. "Let's sneak up the hill." I looked and saw that Mackyz was lining up the team for high-jump practice. Joel sailed up over the crest of the hill, and I followed him.

"He's getting senile," Joel said, dropping to a sitting position, sighting over the crest of the hill at Mackyz, and then lying down. "Come on, jerk, lie down. You want Mackyz to see you?"

I was uneasy; this sort of fooling was all right for Joel, because he "made the effort," but if Mackyz caught me, he'd kick me off the team. I pointed this out to Joel.

"Aw, Mackyz takes everything too seriously. That's his problem," Joel said. "He's always up in the air about something. I don't see why he makes so much fuss. You ever notice how old men make a big fuss over everything?"

"Mackyz' not so old."

"All right, you ever notice how *middle-aged* men make a big fuss over everything?" A few seconds later, he said casually, his gaze resting on the underside of the leaves of the oak tree, "I got laid last night."

"No kidding?" I said.

He spread his fingers over his face, no doubt to see them turn orange in the sunlight, as children do. "Yeah," he said.

From the football field came the sounds of high-jump practice starting. Mackyz was shouting, "Now, start with your left foot—one, two, three —take off! TAKE OFF, GODDAMN IT! Spread your Goddamned legs, spread 'em. You won't get ruptured. There's sand to catch you, for Christ's sake." The jumper's footsteps made a series of thuds, there was a pause, and then the sound of the landing in the sand. Lifting my head, I could see the line of boys waiting to jump, the lead boy breaking into a run, leaping from the ground, and spreading his arms in athletic entreaty.

"It was disappointing," Joel said.

"How?" I asked.

"It's nothing very special."

I was aroused by this exposé. "You mean the books—"

"It's not like that at all." He turned sullenly and scrabbled with his fingers in the dirt. "It's like masturbation, kind of with bells."

"Maybe the girl didn't know how to do it."

"She was a grown woman!"

"Yeah, but—"

"She was a fully grown woman! She knew what she was doing!"

"Oh," I said. Then, after a minute, "Look, would you mind telling me what you said to her? If I ever had a chance, I wouldn't know what to say. I . . ."

"I don't remember," Joel said. "We just looked at each other, and then she got all tearful, and she told me to take my clothes off."

We lay there a moment, in the late afternoon sunshine, and then I said we'd better be getting back. We walked around behind the hill, and waited until Mackyz wasn't looking before we sprinted out onto the track.

The jumping went on for fifteen or twenty minutes more; then Mackyz raised his arms in a gesture of benediction. "All right, you squirts—all out on the track for a fast lap. And that includes you, goldbrick," he said to me, wagging his finger.

All the boys straightened up and started toward the track. The sun's light poured in long low rays over the roof of the school. Jostling and joking, we started to run. "Faster!" Mackyz yelled. "Faster! Whatsa matter —you all a bunch of girls! Faster! For Christ's sake, faster!"

Since Preston, in his dogged effort to become a good miler, ran three laps to everyone else's one, he was usually the last in the locker room. He would come in, worn out and breathing heavily; sometimes he even had to hold himself up with one hand on his locker while he undressed. Everyone else would long since have showered and would be almost ready to leave. They might make one or two remarks about Preston's running his legs down to stumps or trying to kill himself for Mackyz's sake. Preston would smile numbly while he tried to get his breath back, and somehow, I was always surprised by how little attention was paid to Preston, how cut off and how alone he was.

More often than not, Joel would be showing off in the locker room— walking around on his hands, singing dirty songs, or engaged in some argument or other. Preston would go into the shower. I would talk to Joel, dressing slowly, because I usually waited for Preston. By the time I was all dressed, the locker room would be empty and Preston would still be towelling himself off. Then, instead of hurrying to put his clothes on, he would run his hand over his chest, to curl the few limp hairs. "Oh come on!" I would say, disgustedly.

"Hold your horses," he would say, with his maddening physicist's serenity. "Just you hold your horses."

It took him half an hour to get dressed. He'd stand in front of the mirror and flex his muscles endlessly and admire the line his pectorals made across his broad rib cage, and he always left his shirt until last, even until after he had combed his hair. I found his vanity confusing; he was far from handsome, with his heavy mouth and bushy eyebrows and thick, sloping shoulders, but he loved his reflection and he'd turn and gaze at himself in the mirror from all sorts of angles while he buttoned his shirt. He hated Joel. "There's a guy who'll never amount to much," Preston would say. "He's chicken. And he's not very smart. I don't see why you want him to like you—except that you're a sucker. You let your eyes run away with your judgment." I put up with all this because I wanted Preston to walk me part way home. It seemed shameful somehow to have to walk home alone.

Finally, he would finish, and we would emerge from the now deserted school into the dying afternoon. As we walked, Preston harangued me about my lack of standards and judgment. The hunger I had for holding school office and for being well thought of he dismissed as a streak of lousy bourgeois cowardice. I agreed with him (I didn't like myself anyway); but what was to be done about it? "We might run away," Preston said, squinting up at the sky. "Hitchhike. Work in factories. Go to a whorehouse. . . ." I leaned against a tree trunk, and Preston stood with one foot on the curb and one foot in the street, and we lobbed pebbles back and forth. "We're doomed," Preston said. "Doom" was one of his favorite words, along with "culture," "kinetic," and "the Absolute." "We come from a dying culture," he said.

"I suppose you're right," I said. "It certainly looks that way." But then I cheered up. "After all, it's not as if we were insane or anything."

"It wouldn't show yet," Preston said gloomily. "It's still in the latent stage. It'll come out later. You'll see. After all, you're still living at home, and you've got your half-assed charm—"

I broke in; I'd never had a compliment from him before.

"I didn't say you were charming," he said. "I said you have a half-assed charm. You behave well in public. That's all I meant."

At the corner where we separated, Preston stood a moment or two. "It's hopeless," he said.

"God, do you really think so?" I asked.

"That's my honest opinion," he said.

He turned toward his house. I jogged a block or two, and then felt my stomach muscles. When I came to a maple with a low, straight branch, I ran and jumped up and swung from the branch, while a big green diesel bus rolled ponderously past, all its windows filled with tired faces that looked out at the street going by and at me hanging from the branch and smiling. I was doomed, but I was very likely charming.

I ran in the front door of my house and called out, "Mother! Mother!"

"What is it?" she answered. She was sitting on the screened porch, and I could see a little plume of cigarette smoke in the doorway. There was the faint mutter of a radio news program turned on low.

"Nothing," I said. "I'm home, that's all."

At the dinner table, I would try to disguise myself by slouching in my chair and thinking about my homework, but my mother and my sister always recognized me. "How was track today?" my sister would ask in a slightly amused way.

"Fine," I would say in a low voice.

My mother and my sister would exchange glances. I must have seemed comic to them, stilted, and slightly absurd, like all males.

Almost every evening, Sonny Bruster used to drive up to our house in his yellow convertible. The large car would glide to a stop at the curb, and Sonny would glance quickly at himself in the rear-view mirror, running his hand over his hair. Then he'd climb out and brush his pants off, too occupied with his own shyness to notice the children playing on the block. But they would stop what they were doing and watch him.

I would wait for him at the front door and let him in and lead him into the living room. I walked ahead of Sonny because I had noticed that he could not keep himself from looking up the stairs as we passed through the hallway, as if to conjure up my sister then and there with the intensity of his longing, and I hated to see him do this. I would sit in the high-backed yellow chair, and Sonny would settle himself on the couch and ask me about track, or if I'd picked a college yet. "You ought to think carefully about college," he would say. "I think Princeton is more civilized than Yale." His gentle, well-bred voice was carefully inexpressive. In his manner there was a touch of stiffness to remind you, and himself, that he was rich and if some disrespect was intended for him he wouldn't necessarily put up with it. But I liked him. He treated me with great politeness, and I liked the idea of his being my brother-in-law, and I sometimes thought of the benefits that would fall to me if my sister married him.

Then my sister would appear at the head of the stairs, dressed to go out, and Sonny would leap to his feet. "Are you ready?" he'd cry, as if he had never dared hope she would be. My sister would hand him her coat, and with elaborate care he'd hold it for her. It would be perhaps eight o'clock or a little after. The street lamps would be on, but looking pallid because it wasn't quite dark. Usually, Sonny would open the car door for my sister, but sometimes, with a quick maneuver, she would forestall him; she would hurry the last few steps, open the door, and slip inside before he could lift his hand.

Sonny was not the first rich boy who had loved my sister; he was the fourth or fifth. And in the other cases there had been scenes between my mother and sister in which my mother extolled the boy's eligibility and my sister argued that she was too young to marry and didn't want to stop having a good time yet. Each time she had won, and each time the boy had been sent packing, while my mother looked heartbroken and said my sister was throwing her chances away.

With Sonny, the same thing seemed about to happen. My sister missed going out with a lot of boys instead of with just one. She complained once or twice that Sonny was jealous and spoiled. There were times when she seemed to like him very much, but there were other times when she would greet him blankly in the evening when she came downstairs, and he would be apologetic and fearful, and I could see that her disapproval was the thing he feared most in the world.

My mother didn't seem to notice, or if she did, she hid her feelings. Then one night I was sitting in my room doing my homework and I heard my mother and sister come upstairs. They went into my sister's room.

"I think Sonny's becoming very serious," my mother said.

"Sonny's so short," I heard my sister say. "He's not really interesting, either, Mother."

"He seems to be very fond of you," my mother said.

"He's no fun," my sister said. "Mother, be careful! You're brushing too hard! You're hurting me!"

I stopped trying to work, and listened.

"Sonny's a very intelligent boy," my mother said. "He comes from a good family."

"I don't care," my sister said. "I don't want to waste myself on him."

"Waste yourself?" My mother laughed derisively. I got up and went to the door of my sister's room. My sister was sitting at her dressing table, her hair shining like glass and her eyes closed. My mother was walking back and forth, gesturing with the hairbrush. "He's the one who's throwing himself away," she said. "Who do you think we are, anyway? We're nobodies."

"I'm pretty!" my sister objected angrily.

My mother shrugged. "The woods are full of pretty girls. What's more, they're full of pretty, rich girls. Now, Sonny's a very *nice* boy—"

"Leave me alone!" My sister pulled her hair up from her shoulders and held it in a soft mop on the top of her head. "Sonny's a jerk! A jerk!"

"He's nice-looking!" my mother cried.

"Oh, what do *you* know about it?" my sister cried. "You're old, for God's sake!"

The air vibrated. My sister rose and looked at my mother, horrified at what she had said. She took her hands from her hair, and it fell tumbling to her shoulders, dry and pale and soft. "I don't care," she said suddenly, and brushed past me, and fled into the bathroom and locked the door. There was no further sound from her. The only trace of her in the house at that moment was the faint odor in her room of the flowery perfume she used that spring.

"Oh, she's so foolish," my mother said, and I saw that she was crying. "She doesn't know what she's doing. . . . Why is she so foolish?" Then she put the hairbrush down and raised her hands to her cheeks and began to pinch them.

I went back to my room and closed the door.

When I came out again, an hour later, my mother was in bed reading a magazine; she looked as if she had been wounded in a dozen places. My sister sat in her room, in front of the mirror. Her hair streamed down the back of her neck and lay in touching, defenseless little curls on the towel she had over her shoulders. She was studying her reflection thoughtfully. (Are flowers vain? Are trees? Are they consumed with vanity during those days when they are in bloom?) She raised her finger and pressed it against her lower lip to see, I think, if she would be prettier if her lip, instead of being so smooth, had a slight break in the center as some girls' did.

Shortly after this, my mother, who was neither stupid nor cruel, suggested that my sister stop seeing Sonny for a while. "Until you make up

First Love and Other Sorrows [281]

your mind," she said. "Otherwise you might break his heart, you know. Tell him you need some time to think. He'll understand. He'll think you're grown-up and responsible."

Sonny vanished from our house. In the evenings now, after dinner, the three of us would sit on the screened porch. My sister would look up eagerly when the phone rang, but the calls were never for her. None of her old boy friends knew she had stopped dating Sonny, and after a while, when the phone rang, she would compose her face and pretend she wasn't interested, or she would say irritably, "Who can that be?" She began to answer the phone herself (she never had before, because it wasn't good for a girl to seem too eager) and she would look sadly at herself in the hall mirror while she said, "Yes, Preston, he's here." She tried to read. She'd skim a few pages and then put the book down and gaze out through the screens at the night and the patches of light on the trees. She would listen with my mother to the comedians on the radio and laugh vaguely when my mother laughed. She picked on me. "Your posture's no good," she'd say. Or "Where do you learn your manners? Mother, he behaves like a zoot-suiter or something." Another time, she said, "If I don't make a good marriage, you'll be in trouble. You're too lazy to do anything on your own." She grew more and more restless. Toying with her necklace, she broke the string, and the beads rolled all over the floor, and there was something frantic in the way she went about retrieving the small rolling bits of glitter. It occurred to me that she didn't know what she was doing; she was not really as sure of everything as she seemed. It was a painfully difficult thought to arrive at, and it clung to me. Why hadn't I realized it before? Also, she sort of hated me, it seemed to me. I had never noticed that before, either. How could I have been so wrong, I wondered. Knowing how wrong I had been about this, I felt that no idea I had ever held was safe. For instance, we were not necessarily a happy family, with the most wonderful destinies waiting for my sister and me. We might make mistakes and choose wrong. Unhappiness was real. It was even likely. . . . How tired I became of studying my sister's face. I got so I would do anything to keep from joining the two women on the porch.

After three weeks of this, Sonny returned. I was never told whether he came of his own accord or whether he was summoned; but one night the yellow convertible drove up in front of our house and he was back. Now when my mother would watch my sister and Sonny getting into Sonny's car in the evenings, she would turn away from the window smiling. "I think your sister has found a boy she can respect," she would say, or "They'll be very happy together," or some such hopeful observation, which I could see no basis for, but which my mother believed with all the years and memories at her disposal, with all the weight of her past and her love for my sister. And I would go and call Preston.

I used to lie under the dining-room table, sheltered and private like that, looking up at the way the pieces of mahogany were joined together, while we talked. I would cup the telephone to my ear with my shoulder and hold my textbook up in the air, over my head, as we went over physics, which was a hard subject for me. "Preston," I asked one night, "what in God's name makes a siphon work?" They did work—everyone knew that—and I groaned as I asked it. Preston explained the theory to me, and I frowned, breathed heavily through my nose, squinted at the incomprehensible diagrams in the book, and thought of sex, of the dignity of man, of the wonders of the mind, as he talked. Every few minutes, he asked "Do you see" and I would sigh. It was spring, and there was meaning all around me, if only I were free—free of school, free of my mother, free of duties and inhibitions—if only I were mounted on a horse. . . . Where was the world? Not here, not near me, not under the dining room table. . . . "Not quite," I'd say, untruthfully, afraid that I might discourage him. "But I almost get it. Just tell me once more." And on and on he went, while I frowned, breathed hard, and squinted. And then it happened! "I see!" I cried. "I see! I see!" It was air pressure! How in the world had I failed to visualize air pressure? I could see it now. I would never again not see it; it was there in my mind, solid and indestructible, a whitish column sitting on the water. "God damn but science is wonderful!" I said, and heaved my physics book into the living room. "Really wonderful!"

"It's natural law," Preston said reprovingly. "Don't get emotion mixed up with it."

One evening when my sister and Sonny didn't have a date to go out, my mother tapped lightly on my foot, which protruded from under the dining-room table. "I have a feeling Sonny may call," she whispered. I told Preston I had to hang up, and crawled out from beneath the table. "I have a feeling that they're getting to the point," my mother said. "Your sister's nervous."

I put the phone back on the telephone table. "But, Mother—" I said, and the phone rang.

"Sh-h-h," she said.

The phone rang three times. My sister, on the extension upstairs, said, "Hello. . . . Oh, Sonny. . . ."

My mother looked at me and smiled. Then she pulled at my sleeve until I bent my head down, and she whispered in my ear, "They'll be so happy. . . ." She went into the hall, to the foot of the stairs. "Tell him he can come over," she whispered passionately.

"Sure," my sister was saying on the phone. "I'd like that. . . . If you want. . . . Sure. . . ."

My mother went on listening, her head tilted to one side, the light

First Love and Other Sorrows

falling on her aging face, and then she began to pantomime the answers my sister ought to be making—sweet yesses, dignified noes, and little bursts of alluring laughter.

I plunged down the hall and out the screen door. The street lamps were on, and there was a moon. I could hear the children: "I see Digger. One-two-three, you're caught, Digger. . . ." Two blocks away, the clock on the Presbyterian church was striking the hour. Just then a little girl left her hiding place in our hedge and ran shrieking for the tree trunk that was home-free base: "I'm home safe! I'm home safe! Everybody free!" All the prisoners, who had been sitting disconsolately on the bumpers of Mr. Karmgut's Oldsmobile, jumped up with joyful cries and scattered abruptly in the darkness.

I lifted my face—that exasperating factor, my face—and stared entranced at the night, at the waving tops of the trees, and the branches blowing back and forth, and the round moon embedded in the night sky, turning the nearby streamers of cloud into mother-of-pearl. It was all very rare and eternal-seeming. What a dreadful unhappiness I felt.

I walked along the curb, balancing with my arms outspread. Leaves hung over the sidewalk. The air was filled with their rustling, and they caught the light of the street lamps. I looked into the lighted houses. There was Mrs. Kearns, tucked girlishly into a corner of the living-room couch, reading a book. Next door, through the leaves of a tall plant, I saw the Lewises all standing in the middle of the floor. When I reached the corner, I put one arm around the post that held the street sign, and leaned there, above the sewer grating, where my friends and I had lost perhaps a hundred tennis balls, over the years. In numberless dusks, we had abandoned our games of catch and handball and gathered around the grating and stared into it at our ball, floating down in the darkness.

The Cullens' porch light was on, in the next block, and I saw Mr. and Mrs. Cullen getting into their car. Eleanor Cullen was in my class at school, and she had been dating Joel. Her parents were going out, and that meant she'd be home alone—if she was home. She might have gone to the library, I thought as the car started up; or to a sorority meeting. While I stood there looking at the Cullens' house, the porch light went off. A minute later, out of breath from running, I stood on the dark porch and rang the doorbell. There was no light on in the front hall, but the front door was open, and I could hear someone coming. It was Eleanor. "Who is it?" she asked.

"Me," I said. "Are you busy? Would you like to come out for a little while and talk?"

She drifted closer to the screen door and pressed her nose against it. She looked pale without make-up.

"Sure," she said. "I'll have to go put my shoes on. I'm not in a good mood or anything."

"That's all right," I said. "Neither am I. I just want to talk to somebody."

While I waited for Eleanor to come out, Mattie Seaton appeared, striding along the sidewalk. He was on the track team. "Hey, Mattie," I called out to him.

"Hi," he said.

"What's new?"

"Nothing much," he said. "You got your trig done?"

"No, not yet."

"You going with *her?*" he asked, pointing to the house.

"Naw," I said.

"Well, I got to get my homework done," he said.

"See you later," I called after him. I knew where he was going: Nancy Ellis's house, two blocks down.

"Who was that?" Eleanor asked. She stepped out on the porch. She had combed her hair and put on lipstick.

"Mattie Seaton," I said.

"He's pinned to Nancy," Eleanor said. "He likes her a lot. . . ." She sat down in a white metal chair. I sat on the porch railing, facing her. She fumbled in her pocket and pulled out a pack of cigarettes. "You want a cigarette?" she asked.

"No. I'm in training."

We looked at each other, and then she looked away, and I looked down at my shoes. I sat there liking her more and more.

"How come you're in a bad mood?" I asked her.

"Me? Oh, I don't know. How did you know I was in a bad mood?"

"You told me." I could barely make out her face and the dull color of her hands in the darkness.

"You know, I think I'm not basically a happy person," Eleanor said suddenly. "I always thought I was. . . . People expect you to be, especially if you're a girl."

"It doesn't surprise *me,*" I said.

A breeze set all the leaves in motion again. "It's going to rain," I said.

Eleanor stood up, smoothing her yellow skirt, and threw her cigarette off the porch; the glowing tip landed on the grass. She realized I was staring at her. She lifted her hand and pressed it against her hair. "You may have noticed I look unusually plain tonight," she said. She leaned over the porch railing beside me, supporting herself on her hands. "I was trying to do my geometry," she said in a low voice. "I couldn't do it. I felt stupid," she said. "So I cried. That's why I look so awful."

"I think you look all right," I said. "I think you look fine." I leaned forward and laid my cheek on her shoulder. Then I sat up quickly, flushing. "I don't like to hear you being so dissatisfied with yourself," I mum-

First Love and Other Sorrows [285]

bled. "You could undermine your self-confidence that way."

Eleanor straightened and faced me, in the moonlight. "You're beautiful," I burst out longingly. "I never noticed before. But you are."

"Wait," Eleanor said. Tears gathered in her eyes. "Don't like me yet. I have to tell you something first. It's about Joel."

"You don't have to tell me," I said. "I know you're going with him. I understand."

"Listen to me!" she said impatiently, stamping her foot. "I'm *not* going with him. He—" She suddenly pressed her hands against her eyes. "Oh, it's awful!" she cried.

A little shudder of interest passed through me. "O.K.," I said. "But I don't care if you don't tell me."

"I want to!" she cried. "I'm just a little embarrassed. I'll be all right in a minute—

"We went out Sunday night . . ." she began after a few seconds. They had gone to Medart's, in Clayton, for a hamburger. Joel had talked her into drinking a bottle of beer, and it had made her so drowsy that she had put her head on the back of the seat and closed her eyes. "What kind of car does Joel have?" I asked.

"A Buick," Eleanor said, surprised at my question.

"I see," I said. I pictured the dashboard of a Buick, and Joel's handsome face, and then, daringly, I added Eleanor's hand, with its bitten fingernails, holding Joel's hand. I was only half listening, because I felt the preliminary stirrings of an envy so deep it would make me miserable for weeks. I looked up at the sky over my shoulder; clouds had blotted out the moon, and everything had got darker. From the next block, in the sudden stillness, I heard the children shouting, uttering their Babylonian cries as they played kick-the-can. Their voices were growing tired and fretful.

"And then I felt his hand on my—" Eleanor, half-drowned in shadow was showing me, on her breast, where Joel had touched her.

"Is that all?" I said, suddenly smiling. Now I would not have to die of envy. "That's nothing!"

"I—I slapped his face!" She exclaimed. Her lip trembled. "Oh, I didn't mean—I sort of wanted— Oh, it's all so terrible!" she burst out. She ran down the front steps and onto the lawn, and leaned against the trunk of an oak tree. I followed her. The pre-storm stillness filled the sky, the air between the trees, the dark spaces among the shrubbery. "Oh, God!" Eleanor cried. "How I hate everything!"

My heart was pounding, and I didn't know why. I hadn't known I could feel like this—that I could pause on the edge of such feeling, which lay stretched like an enormous meadow all in shadow inside me. It seemed to me a miracle that human beings could be so elaborate. "Listen, Eleanor," I said, "you're all right! I've *always* liked you." I swallowed and moved closer to her; there were two moist streaks running down her face. I raised my arm and, with the sleeve of my shirt, I wiped away her tears. "I think you're wonderful! I think you're really something!"

"You look down on me," she said. "I know you do. I can tell."

"How can I, Eleanor. How *can* I?" I cried. "I'm nobody. I've been damaged by my heredity."

"You, too!" she exclaimed happily. "Oh, that's what's wrong with me!"

A sudden hiss swept through the air and then the first raindrops struck the street. "Quick!" Eleanor cried, and we ran up on her porch. Two bursts of lightning lit up the dark sky, and the rain streamed down. I held Eleanor's hand, and we stood watching the rain. "It's a real thundershower," she said.

"Do you feel bad because we only started being friends tonight? I mean, do you feel you're on the rebound and settling on the second-best?" I asked. There was a long silence and all around it was the sound of the rain.

"I don't think so," Eleanor said at last. "How about you?"

I raised my eyebrows and said, "Oh, no, it doesn't bother me at all."

"That's good," she said.

We were standing very close to one another. We talked industriously. "I don't like geometry," Eleanor said. "I don't see what use it is. It's supposed to train your mind, but I don't believe it. . . ."

I took my glasses off. "Eleanor—" I said. I kissed her, passionately, and then I turned away, pounding my fists on top of each other. "Excuse me," I whispered hoarsely. That kiss had lasted a long time, and I thought I would die.

Eleanor was watching the long, slanting lines of rain falling just outside the porch, gray in the darkness; she was breathing very rapidly. "You know what?" she said. "I could make you scrambled eggs. I'm a good cook." I leaned my head against the brick wall of the house and said I'd like some.

In the kitchen, she put on an apron and bustled about, rattling pans and silverware, and talking in spurts. "I think a girl should know how to cook, don't you?" she let me break the eggs into a bowl—three eggs, which I cracked with a flourish. "Oh, you're good at it," she said, and began to beat them with a fork while I sat on the kitchen table and watched her. "Did you know most eggs *aren't* baby chickens?" she asked me. She passed so close to me on her way to the stove that, because her cheeks were flushed and her eyes bright, I couldn't help leaning forward and kissing her. She turned pink and hurried to the stove. I sat on the kitchen table, swinging my legs and smiling to myself. Suddenly we heard a noise just outside the back door. I leaped off the table and took up a polite position by the sink. Eleanor froze. But no one opened the door; no one appeared.

"Maybe it was a branch falling," I said.

Eleanor nodded. Then she made a face and looked down at her hands. "I don't know why we got so nervous. We aren't doing anything wrong."

"It's the way they look at you," I said.

"Yes, that's it," she said. "You know, I think my parents are ashamed of me. But someday I'll show them. I'll do something wonderful, and they'll be amazed." She went back to the stove.

"When are your parents coming home?" I asked.

"They went to a double feature. They can't possibly be out before eleven."

"They might walk out on it," I said.

"Oh no!" Eleanor said. "Not if they pay for it . . ."

We ate our scrambled eggs and washed the dishes, and watched the rain from the dining-room windows without turning the light on. We kissed for a while, and then we both grew restless and uncomfortable. Her lips were swollen, and she went into the kitchen, and I heard her running the water; when she returned, her hair was combed and she had put on fresh lipstick. "I don't like being in the house," she said, and led me out on the porch. We stood with our arms around each other. The rain was slackening. "Good-bye, rain," Eleanor said sadly. It was as if we were watching a curtain slowly being lifted from around the house. The trees gleamed wetly near the street lamps.

When I started home, the rain had stopped. Water dripped on the leaves of the trees. Little plumes of mist hung over the wet macadam of the street. I walked very gently in order not to disturb anything.

I didn't want to run into anybody, and so I went home the back way, through the alley. At the entrance to the alley there was a tall cast-iron pseudo-Victorian lamppost, with an urn-shaped head and panes of frosted glass; the milky light it shed trickled part way down the alley, illuminating a few curiously still garage fronts and, here and there, the wet leaves of the bushes and vines that bordered the back yards and spilled in such profusion over the fences, hiding the ashpits and making the alley so pretty a place in spring. When I was younger, I had climbed on those ashpits, those brick squares nearly smothered under the intricacies of growing things, and I had searched in the debris for old, broken mirrors, discarded scarves with fringes, bits of torn decorated wrapping paper, and such treasures. But now I drifted down the alley, walking absently on the wet asphalt. I was having a sort of daydream where I was lying with my head on Eleanor's shoulder—which was bare—and I could hear the slow, even sound of her breathing as I began to fall asleep. I was now in the darkest part of the alley, the very center where no light reached, and in my daydream I turned over and kissed Eleanor's hands, her throat—and then I broke into a sprint down the alley, slipping and sliding on the puddles and wet places. I came out the other end of the alley and stood underneath the lamppost. I was breathing with difficulty.

Across the street from me, two women stood, one on the sidewalk, the other on the front steps of a house, hugging her arms. "It's not a bad pain," the woman on the sidewalk said, "but it persists."

"My dear, my dear," said the other. "Don't take any chances—not at our age . . ."

And a couple, a boy and a girl, were walking up the street, coming home from the Tivoli Theatre. The girl was slouching in order not to seem taller than the boy, who was very short and who sprang up and down on the balls of his feet as he walked.

I picked a spray of lilac and smelled it, but then I didn't know what to do with it—I didn't want to throw it away—and finally I put it in my pants pocket.

I vaulted our back fence and landed in our back yard, frightening a cat, who leaped out of the hedge and ran in zigzags across the dark lawn. It startled me so much I felt weak. I tucked my shirt in carefully and smoothed my hair. Suddenly, I looked down at my fingertips; they were blurred in the darkness and moist from the lilac, and I swept them to my mouth and kissed them.

The kitchen was dark. There was no sound in the house, no sound at all, and a tremor passed through me. I turned the kitchen light on and hurriedly examined myself for marks of what had happened to me. I peered at my shirt, my pants. I rubbed my face with both hands. Then I turned the light off and slipped into the dining room, which was dark, too, and so was the hallway. The porch light was on. I ran up the front stairs and stopped short at the top; there was a light on in my mother's room. She was sitting up in bed, with pillows at her back, a magazine across her lap, and a pad of paper on the magazine.

"Hello," I said.

I expected her to bawl me out for being late, but she just looked at me solemnly for a moment, and then she said, "Sonny proposed to your sister."

Because I hadn't had a chance to wash my face, I raised one hand and held it over my cheek and chin, to hide whatever traces of lipstick there might be.

She said, "They're going to be married in June. They went over to the Brusters' to get the ring. He proposed practically the first thing when he came. They were both so—they were *both* so *happy!*" she said. "They make such a lovely couple. . . . Oh, if you could have seen them."

She was in a very emotional state.

I started to back out the door.

"Where are you going?" my mother asked.

"To bed," I said, surprised. "I'm in training—"
"Oh, you ought to wait up for your sister."
"I'll leave her a note," I said.

I went to my room and took the white lilac out of my pocket and put it on my desk. I wrote, "I heard the news and think it's swell. Congratulations. Wake me up when you come in." I stuck the note in the mirror of her dressing table. Then I went back to my room and got undressed. Usually I slept raw, but I decided I'd better wear pajamas if my sister was going to come in and wake me up. I don't know how much later it was that I heard a noise and sat bolt upright in bed. I had been asleep. My sister was standing in the door of my room. She was wearing a blue dress that had little white buttons all the way down the front and she had white gloves on. "Are you awake?" she whispered.

"Yes," I said. "Where's Mother?"

"Downstairs," my sister said, coming into the room. "Sending telegrams. Do you want to see my ring?" She took her gloves off.

I turned the bedside-table lamp on, and she held her hand out. The ring was gold, and there was an emerald and four diamonds around it.

"It was his grandmother's," my sister said. I nodded. "It's not what I—" she said, and sat down on the edge of the bed, and forgot to finish her sentence. "Tell me," she said, "do you think he's really rich?" Then she turned a sad gaze on me, through her lashes. "Do you want to know something awful? I don't like my ring. . . ."

"Are you unhappy?" I asked.

"No, just upset. It's scary getting married. You have no idea. I kept getting chills all evening. I may get pneumonia. Do you have a cigarette?"

I said I'd get her one downstairs.

"No, there's some in my room," she said. "I'll get them. You know, Sonny and I talked about you. We're going to send you to college and everything. We planned it all out tonight." She played with her gloves for a while, and then she said, looking at the toes of her shoes, "I'm scared. What if Sonny's not good at business?" She turned to me. "You know what I mean? He's so young. . . ."

"You don't have to marry him," I said. "After all, you're—"

"You don't understand," my sister said hurriedly, warding off advice she didn't want. "You're too young yet." She laughed. "You know what he said to me?"

Just then, my mother called out from the bottom of the stairs, "Listen, how does this sound to you? 'Dear Greta—' It's a night letter, and we get a lot of words, and I thought Greta would like it better if I started that way. Greta's so touchy, you know. Can you hear me?"

"I have to go," my sister whispered. She looked at me, and then suddenly she leaned over and kissed me on the forehead. "Go to sleep," she said. "Have nice dreams." She got up and went out into the hall.

"'—Dodie got engaged tonight,'" my mother read. "Is 'got engaged' the right way to say it?"

"Became engaged," my sister said, in a distant voice.

I put on my bathrobe and slippers and went out into the hall. My sister was leaning over the banister, talking to my mother at the bottom of the stairs about the night letter. I slipped past her and down the back stairs and into the kitchen. I found a cold chicken in the icebox, put the platter on the kitchen table, and tore off a leg and began to eat.

The door to the back stairs swung open, and my sister appeared. "I'm hungry, too," she said. "I don't know why." She drifted over to the table, and bent over the chicken. "I guess emotion makes people hungry."

My mother pushed open the swinging door, from the dining-room side. "There you are," she said. She looked flustered. "I'll have to think some more, and then I'll write the whole thing over," she said to my sister. To me she said, "Are you *eating* at this time of night?"

My sister said that she was hungry, too.

"There's some soup," my mother said. "Why don't I heat it up." And suddenly her eyes filled with tears, and all at once we fell to kissing one another—to embracing and smiling and making cheerful predictions about one another—there in the white, brightly lighted kitchen. We had known each other for so long, and there were so many things that we all three remembered. . . . Our smiles, our approving glances, wandered from face to face. There was a feeling of politeness in the air. We were behaving the way we would in railway stations, at my sister's wedding, at the birth of her first child, at my graduation from college. This was the first of our reunions.

It is a hard moment for fourteen-year-old Juliet when the nurse she counts on deserts to the enemy, siding with her parents, who are pressuring her into a distasteful marriage. Today such pressures are perhaps a shade subtler, as we saw in the preceding story, First Love and Other Sorrows.

WILLIAM SHAKESPEARE

from *Romeo and Juliet*

Act three, Scene five

LADY CAPULET   But now I'll tell thee joyful tidings girl.
JULIET   And joy comes well in such a needy time.
  What are they, beseech your ladyship?
LADY CAPULET   Well, well, thou hast a careful father child,
  One who to put thee from thy heaviness
  Hath sorted out a sudden day of joy,
  That thou expects not, nor I looked not for.
JULIET   Madam, in happy time, what day is that?
LADY CAPULET   Marry my child, early next Thursday morn,
  The gallant, young, and noble gentleman,
  The County Paris, at Saint Peter's Church,
  Shall happily make thee there a joyful bride.
JULIET   Now by Saint Peter's Church, and Peter too,
  He shall not make me there a joyful bride.
  I wonder at this haste, that I must wed
  Ere he that should be husband comes to woo.
  I pray you tell my lord and father, madam,
  I will not marry yet, and when I do, I swear
  It shall be Romeo, whom you know I hate,
  Rather than Paris. These are news indeed.
LADY CAPULET   Here comes your father, tell him so yourself;
  And see how he will take it at your hands.
    Enter Capulet and Nurse.
CAPULET   When the sun sets, the earth doth drizzle dew;
  But for the sunset of my brother's son

It rains downright.
How now, a conduit, girl? What, still in tears?
Evermore showering? In one little body
Thou counterfeits a bark, a sea, a wind.
For still thy eyes, which I may call the sea,
Do ebb and flow with tears; the bark thy body is,
Sailing in this salt flood; the winds, thy sighs,
Who, raging with thy tears, and they with them,
Without a sudden calm, will overset
Thy tempest-tossed body. How now wife,
Have you delivered to her our decree?

LADY CAPULET   Ay sir, but she will none, she gives you thanks.
I would the fool were married to her grave.

CAPULET   Soft, take me with you, take me with you wife.
How will she none? Doth she not give us thanks?
Is she not proud? Doth she not count her blessed,
Unworthy as she is, that we have wrought
So worthy a gentleman to be her bridegroom?

JULIET   Not proud you have, but thankful that you have.
Proud can I never be of what I hate,
But thankful even for hate, that is meant love.

CAPULET   How, how, how, how, chop-logic, what is this?
Proud, and, I thank you, and, I thank you not;
And yet, not proud—mistress minion you,
Thank me no thankings, nor proud me no prouds,
But fettle your fine joints 'gainst Thursday next,
To go with Paris to Saint Peter's Church,
Or I will drag thee on a hurdle thither.
Out you green-sickness carrion, out you baggage,
You tallow-face!

LADY CAPULET   Fie, fie, what, are you mad?

JULIET   Good father, I beseech you on my knees,
Hear me with patience, but to speak a word.

CAPULET   Hang thee young baggage, disobedient wretch!
I tell thee what, get thee to church a Thursday,
Or never after look me in the face.
Speak not, reply not, do not answer me.
My fingers itch. Wife, we scarce thought us blessed,
That God had lent us but this only child;
But now I see this one is one too much,
And that we have a curse in having her.
Out on her, hilding!

NURSE   God in heaven bless her.
You are to blame my lord to rate her so.

from *Romeo and Juliet*

CAPULET   And why, my lady wisdom? Hold your tongue.
  Good Prudence, smatter with your gossips, go.
NURSE   I speak no treason.
CAPULET   O God ye god-den.
NURSE   May not one speak?
CAPULET   Peace you mumbling fool.
  Utter your gravity o'er a gossip's bowl,
  For here we need it not.
LADY CAPULET   You are too hot.
CAPULET   God's bread, it makes me mad.
  Day, night, hour; tide, time; work, play;
  Alone, in company; still my care hath been
  To have her matched; and having now provided
  A gentleman of princely parentage,
  Of fair demesnes, youthful and nobly trained,
  Stuffed as they say with honourable parts,
  Proportioned as one's thought would wish a man—
  And then to have a wretched puling fool,
  A whining mammet, in her fortune's tender,
  To answer, I'll not wed, I cannot love,
  I am too young, I pray you pardon me—
  But an you will not wed, I'll pardon you.
  Graze where you will, you shall not house with me.
  Look to't, I do not use to jest.
  Thursday is near, lay hand on heart, advise.
  An you be mine, I'll give you to my friend;
  An you be not, hang, beg, starve, die in the streets,
  For by my soul, I'll ne'er acknowledge thee,
  Nor what is mine shall never do thee good.
  Trust to't, bethink you. I'll not be forsworn.
  Exit.
JULIET   Is there no pity sitting in the clouds,
  That sees into the bottom of my grief?
  O sweet my mother cast me not away.
  Delay this marriage for a month, a week,
  Or if you do not, make the bridal bed
  In that dim monument where Tybalt lies.
LADY CAPULET   Talk not to me, for I'll not speak a word.
  Do as thou wilt, for I have done with thee.   (*Exit.*
JULIET   O God! O nurse, how shall this be prevented?
  My husband is on earth, my faith in heaven;
  How shall that faith return again to earth,
  Unless that husband send it me from heaven,
  By leaving earth? Comfort me, counsel me.

Alack, alack, that heaven should practise stratagems
Upon so soft a subject as myself.
What sayst thou, hast thou not a word of joy?
Some comfort, nurse.
NURSE Faith here it is. Romeo
Is banished; and all the world to nothing,
That he dares ne'er come back to challenge you;
Or if he do, it needs must be by stealth.
Then since the case so stands as now it doth,
I think it best you married with the County.
O he's a lovely gentleman.
Romeo's a dishclout to him; an eagle, madam,
Hath not so green, so quick, so fair an eye
As Paris hath. Beshrew my very heart,
I think you are happy in this second match,
For it excels your first; or if it did not,
Your first is dead, or 'twere as good he were,
As living here, and you no use of him.
JULIET Speak'st thou from thy heart?
NURSE And from my soul too, else beshrew them both.
JULIET Amen.
NURSE What?
JULIET Well thou hast comforted me marvellous much.
Go in, and tell my lady I am gone,
Having displeased my father, to Laurence' cell,
To make confession, and to be absolved.
NURSE Marry I will, and this is wisely done. (*Exit.*
JULIET Ancient damnation, o most wicked fiend!
Is it more sin to wish me thus forsworn,
Or to dispraise my lord with that same tongue
Which she hath praised him with above compare
So many thousand times? Go counsellor;
Thou and my bosom henceforth shall be twain.
I'll to the friar to know his remedy.
If all else fail, myself have power to die. (*Exit.*

Spurred by the well-meant advice of a female friend, a widower struggles manfully to set the stage for his daughter's social success.

B. J. CHUTE

The Legacy

IRENE SAID, "You're not being fair to the child, George. You're only thinking of yourself."

George Ashe looked up to meet his sister's hard kindly stare and shook his head. "I don't think I'm that single-minded," he said, "I don't mean to be."

"Of course you don't mean to be," she told him. "Nobody ever *means* to be anything. But a man your age can't be expected to understand anything at all about a fourteen-year-old girl. It's a woman's job."

He didn't say anything. Marjorie's mother had died when Marjorie was eight, leaving him their small intrepid child as a reason for living. He had needed a reason very badly. In a moment Irene would say that it had been six years ago. After six years you were entitled to scars, but not to pain. He waited and she said it. "It's been six years, George."

He said shortly, "I know that."

Irene went on. "It's chiefly Marjorie I'm thinking of. The child has no real social life at all."

"Depends on what you call a social life," George said. "Marjorie has plenty of friends."

"You know very well what I mean by a social life." She shifted in her chair and replanted her feet. She was not so much stout as of a geometric persuasion, with solid cubed corners. "When other girls are going to proms, Marjorie's home with her nose in a book. She reads too much. She's a lot worse than you ever were."

"I survived it. Marjorie likes books."

"That's not the point. Really, George, you're much too detached about things. I suppose it's being a professor but when Eleanor was alive you were a lot more human."

[295]

His mind warned her silently, talk about anyone else.

Luckily she did. "You say Marjorie has plenty of friends and I don't doubt it at all. She's a nice child. But that's not what I'm talking about, George. I'm talking about the kind of thing any normal girl wants—you know, going to dances and having boys cut in all the time." She gave him a sharp look. "Marjorie doesn't even have a dance frock, does she?"

He shook his head. "She doesn't care for dances."

"You mean she never gets asked," his sister said. "She's shy, George, she always has been. That's why she needs help right now."

George frowned. This picture of his daughter gave him a sudden inward wrench for which he was not prepared and against which he had no defenses. It was true that Marjorie was a shy, solemn child but she had always been shy and solemn, even when her mother was alive, although she had been subject to abrupt personal fits of delight when she would stalk the house from basement to attic, filling it with her hoarse triumphant chants. He had assumed that now, at fourteen, she was as contented and well adjusted as she seemed to be. He preferred not to believe that her admirable and selective young mind was really bemused by a picture of herself in a frilly dress, stampeding the stag line.

He sighed. Perhaps he was too much the detached professor, impatient of all these meaningless social patterns. Perhaps, to Marjorie, they were not meaningless at all but very wonderful.

Irene went on, her voice suddenly more gentle. "If Eleanor were alive, George, I wouldn't say anything. Eleanor could give the child what she needs. It's hard for a man to see it."

She had caught him on his most vulnerable point and it was out of a sense of his own inadequacy that he said, "What do you suggest, Irene?"

She told him promptly. "Have a talk with Anita Marshall. That pretty little daughter of hers is a tremendous hit. The boys are crazy about Lee."

George stirred uneasily. He liked Anita very much and her husband was a good friend of his, but the idea of Lee as a butterfly example for his daughter irritated him. He hedged. "I don't think I ought to impose on Anita—"

"Nonsense. She'd be delighted. After all, Lee's about the same age as Marjorie and that makes everything so much simpler. She must have at least one extra boy on her string that she wouldn't mind lending."

It sounded like a friendly exchange of polo ponies and he almost choked on it.

"I could speak to Anita, I suppose," he said reluctantly.

Irene rose. "I already have. She'll be expecting to hear from you." She looked at him with approval. "I'm glad to see you getting some sense, George."

It seemed unanswerable.

After she had gone, he went out into the kitchen. Mrs. Dolan, his small sparrowlike housekeeper, was peeling apples at the sink, the waxy green spirals falling back from her knife. She glanced at him and went on with her work.

"Marjorie not home yet?" he asked.

"Any time now, Mr. Ashe."

"Apple cobbler?"

She nodded. He watched her hands moving deftly and wished he could ask her what she thought about Marjorie but of course he couldn't. At that moment the back door opened and Marjorie came in.

He looked at her with what he told himself was implacable objectivity, as if she were anybody's child. It was the first time that he had realized she wasn't pretty. She had a square pale face, given a Celtic look by the heavy black eyebrows drawn straight over gray eyes. Her dark hair was pulled back by a ribbon and wind-tangled so that the uncompromising bangs looked like a Shetland pony's. She had a rather stocky figure and her hands were exceedingly capable. He could not, for the life of him, imagine those hands patting a masculine coat sleeve.

Her sweater and skirt outfit seemed all right. He said, "Hello, darling."

Economical of words, she smiled at him and put her pile of books on the table. He picked up the top one and glanced at the title. *Madame Bovary*. Flaubert seemed an odd choice at fourteen. "Is this required reading?"

Marjorie shook her head.

"Isn't it rather heavy going for you?"

"No." The Shetland shake of the head again. "She was a stupid woman, wasn't she? It's awful the way he knows everything about her."

He agreed, rather pleased. A lot of adults encountered Emma Bovary's pitiful vacancy without the faintest recognition of the awful brilliance (*awful* was exactly the word) that had created her.

Mrs. Dolan, speaking to the apples, said, "You read too much."

"I suppose." Marjorie accepted this as an apparently inescapable fact and picked up her books. George followed her out of the kitchen and she asked him over her shoulder about the plans for his lecture course.

"I finished the outline this morning."

"Daddy! That's the hardest part."

He would have liked nothing better than to tell her all about it but there was his promise to Irene. He sat down on the sofa and pulled Marjorie down beside him. "I want to talk to you, honey," he said. "Your aunt was here a little while ago." He waited a moment, got no assistance and went on. "She's worried about you, Margie."

"Me?" She seemed surprised.

"Yes. She doesn't feel you're getting any social life."

She traced the pattern of a rose on the carpet with a scuffed toe. "You mean dances—and things?" she said carefully.

He nodded. "Dances and things."

There was quite a long silence and she did the rose counter-clockwise. She was, perhaps, too used to being honest with him so that he was very afraid of forcing her. When she finally got the words shaped up in her mind, they came out sounding as if they had been pushed. She said, "I don't get asked, Daddy."

He had not wanted this admission at all, since it confirmed what Irene told him. He had wanted to be assured that dances and things didn't interest his daughter, that she was independent. Now he had to admit, with a pang of real discomfort that Irene was entirely right, that Marjorie was missing something she really wanted. He waited unhappily for her to go on.

She made a funny little movement with her shoulders. "I never seem to know what to talk about, for one thing."

"Just what interests you, honey."

"Oh, no." She looked at him then. "I know that much about it, Daddy. You're supposed to talk about what interests *them* but that's part of the trouble. I don't know what does. And if they do want to talk about what I want to talk about, that means they're what the other girls call drips and it's really better not to go to a dance at all than to go with a drip."

This was a long speech for Marjorie and it opened up vistas that confounded him. He remembered Irene's dictum that this was a woman's job and, with a real effort, he committed himself. "Marjorie, your aunt suggested I have a talk with Mrs. Marshall."

"About me?"

He nodded and then, because this seemed a little crude, he added a stumbling statement about Aunt Irene's thinking Mrs. Marshall could help with, well, clothes and things.

There was no need for his earnest tact. Marjorie viewed the prospect with unexpected eagerness. "Do you really think she would, Daddy? She's awfully nice." She stared past him at the wall, her lips parted. "There's a big school dance next week. Maybe—"

He wanted her to be happy. He said, "Do you want me to—to talk with Mrs. Marshall, dear?"

For a moment he thought she was going to say no, that she was contented with things the way they were. Then she turned suddenly and buried her nose against the lapel of his coat, a small child trick of hers from years ago. "Would you, Daddy?" she said, muffled. "Dresses and things?"

And things.

He said yes, he would.

He wanted nothing less the next day than to call Anita, but he had no morning lecture and consequently no excuse for putting off the inevitable. Prepared for his call, she had already made her plans and said she would drop in on him that afternoon. "That way I can see Marjorie at the same time," she said, "and we can fix everything up."

He was a little alarmed because she sounded so executive but she was being extremely kind and he made the suitable sounds of gratitude. When Anita came, everything went very smoothly. She talked to him before Marjorie came home and she stamped on the anxious retina of his mind an extremely clear picture of herself as a helpful and wise woman. She told him how necessary a real social life was to a young girl and she made it very plain how satisfyingly well her own daughter had done in this respect. "Of course, it's no credit to me," said Anita disarmingly.

"Lee has a better example than Marjorie, I'm afraid."

She smiled at him forgivingly. "You *are* rather a hermit, George, but after all you can't be expected to know what the child needs. She ought to be taking it for granted that she'll go to dances."

"She doesn't seem to get invited," he said with difficulty, feeling disloyal. "And I don't think she'd ever get around to just asking someone to take her. I suppose that wouldn't be protocol anyhow."

"Oh dear no!" She was amused by his innocence. "It's really just a matter of getting started. Men are such sheep about things like that and boys are even worse. If one asks a girl, the others will ask her."

"Well?" said George, not knowing how to set this desirable chain reaction going but anxious to be helpful.

Anita clasped her long-fingered hands together lightly. "I've arranged everything," she said reassuringly. "Lee has a cousin who will be in town just in time for the dance. He's a charming boy and there's no reason on earth why Marjorie shouldn't have him. Lee will tell him she's fixed up a blind date and there you are." She smiled. "Mind you, George, it's very good of Lee. She had a picture of herself with two escorts, but we talked it over and I've promised her a new dress instead." The barter-and-trade quality of this transaction must have eluded her, because she went on serenely. "Marjorie will need a new dress too, of course. That's all right, isn't it?"

He said hastily that, of course, it was all right. And when Marjorie came in at last, everything was settled and all Anita had to do was tell her the plans.

He had thought his nice-mannered daughter would be suitably grateful but he had not expected her to glow. He was glad for her and he was also distressed. The occasion seemed too slight.

But the day Marjorie came home with her new dress, he knew that he was wrong and that a piece of happiness is a piece of happiness, whether for large cosmic reasons or small social ones. She came flying into the living room, clutching a shiny white box and chanting. "We bought it! We bought my dress." Her neat square hands wrestled with the string and she finally had to break it before she could lift the dress reverently out of its tissue-paper nest. "Lee's coming over tonight to see it. Daddy, isn't it lovely?"

It was a charming shade of blue and in obvious good taste. "It's beautiful," he said.

She sighed deeply. "I hope Lee likes it."

He was annoyed. If she liked it herself, what did Lee's opinion matter? But then he remembered that Lee's social success was assured and her judgment counted.

Fortunately, Lee did approve. She came over after dinner, melting with delicious charm for the benefit of Marjorie's quaint old daddy and making him feel every century of his forty-five years. "It's just sweet," she told Marjorie, stroking the delicate folds of blue, "and it's definitely your type. Can you manage the long skirt, honey?"

Marjorie said, too humbly, that she hoped she could. He looked at them, standing together. Lee graceful and cuddly and pretty as a kitten, Marjorie with her hands hanging at her sides, simply because her skirt had no pockets, and her face flushed with rather childish enthusiasm. He knew if he were a boy which one he would want to take to the dance, and he damned the whole race of males.

"Bob's a senior in high school, you know, Margie," Lee went on. "He's really sweet."

Marjorie said, "He sounds nice," and George saw she was stiff with foreknowledge of uncertainty and clumsiness and the agony of going out with a senior. But Bob was hers, for that night he was hers, and who knew what wonders might follow the first real dance, the first genuine escort?

He said heartily, "You'll have a fine time."

"I hope he'll like me," said Marjorie.

She spent so much of the next week taking her new dress out of its cover that George became concerned for its health, but she only laid it most tenderly on her bed or held it up to yearn over her mirrored reflection. She had new shoes too, with heels much higher than they should be, but twice he heard her talking to them on such a note of love that he never mentioned his conviction that they were unsuitable for a little girl.

Unused to prayer, he merely relayed a request to God to make it a happy evening for his daughter.

But the tragedy came anyway and it was a real tragedy, small only because it had no dignity. It was ignoble from the beginning, starting as a severe cold in the head of Lee's escort, Johnny Dayton. The Dayton doctor ordered the Dayton pride and joy to bed and Mrs. Dayton phoned Anita Marshall. Anita phoned George immediately.

She was terribly distressed, telling him about Johnny, much more distressed than the occasion seemed to warrant. There seemed to be no

The Legacy

doubt of the young man's survival. "Lee's so upset," Anita said.

George said he was sorry and added, "Marjorie will be sorry too, but I'm sure she'll get along all right. Maybe it's better for her to be on her own."

There was a short silence. Then Anita's voice came over the wire again, and it had a curious, placating sound. "George, dear," she began, "I'm afraid—"

He waited, faintly uneasy.

He could almost hear her draw the long necessary breath. "I don't think we can ask Lee to be the one to stay home," she said.

He looked at the telephone in his hand. It was an excellent instrument, suitable for perfect communication. He had not heard wrongly. "But, Anita—"

"I know. It's a dreadful shame." He could imagine her smiling, expecting him to understand. "Your dear child's been looking forward to it so, the new dress and everything. But Lee's on the dance committee and of course Bob's counted on having her there and—George, there'll be plenty of other times for Marjorie. I'll see that there are. It's just that—"

He said that he understood. He reassured her automatically because she was talking so fast, almost distractedly. It was embarrassing for her, he understood that too. When he finally hung up she was still saying that she was so distressed, so really distressed . . .

Ahead of him was the task of telling Marjorie. All that morning his papers lay on his desk untouched.

In the end he didn't even try to explain. He just told her. Johnny Dayton was sick, Lee was going with Bob, there would be other dances. He looked at her anxiously, hoping that she wouldn't cry.

She didn't. She just stood quietly, accepting his words. After a while she said, "Well, I guess it's just one of those things. It's too bad about Johnny."

He looked at her helplessly, thinking that tears would almost have been a relief. After a moment, he thought he had better leave her alone.

It was just as he turned to go that he had his idea. It was the thought of the blue dress and the foolish little shoes that gave it to him. All she needed, surely, was an escort to take her to the dance. Once there, she could rely on Lee and the stag line and all the youngsters she must know.

Marjorie needed an escort and Marjorie's father had a perfectly good dinner jacket. He would take her himself. He turned back. "Darling, I've got an idea. How would it be if *I* took you to the dance?"

She looked startled. "Oh, Daddy, I don't think—I mean, nobody ever—" She stopped.

He tried not to show his disappointment. It had seemed such a good idea. A little stiffly, he said, "Well, I just thought—"

She flung herself suddenly into his arms and hugged him tight. "It would be wonderful," she said. "Would you really take me?"

He kissed the top of her head, feeling delightfully expansive. It was all going to work out fine in spite of everything. . . .

George looked down at his daughter. The blue dress was certainly very charming and suitable but they had been standing there glued to the wall for ten minutes now, watching the dancers move past in their intricate routines, faces smooth and absorbed. No one in the stag line had given Marjorie so much as a second glance. The bored young eyes rested on her father in faint surprise, then passed on.

It was ridiculous for a middle-aged man to feel so lost and awkward. In this small jungle he should be an amused explorer, and instead he felt like a rather backward monkey. This bit of self-criticism cheered him considerably. He told himself they were only children after all and pressed Marjorie's cold hand.

"Want to dance?"

She nodded dumbly and he took her in his arms. She was such a square little thing, he thought, so compact and somehow so nice. They moved out onto the floor.

He had never been a good dancer but he had always managed to get by without actual damage to his partners. This music, however, with its nervous beat was new to him, and it never seemed to be doing quite what he was doing. Marjorie was stiff in his arms and he couldn't say that he blamed her. What she needed was one of those tall young men with their relaxed and casual steps, half dance, half walk. He noticed the way the other girls, dancing past the stag line, smiled at the boys in it. He looked down at Marjorie and found she was staring at his lapel with dreadful earnestness.

"You know any of the boys in the stag line?" he said.

She gave them a quick sideways look and shook her head. "Just by sight," she said. "One or two. I don't know many of these boys."

He gave her a small playful hug and missed a step. "They might remember you—by sight—if you'd smile at them, sweetheart. They don't bite."

"No," said Marjorie.

He felt a mild prick of impatience. The stag line was only there to be danced with but he could see they would at least have to feel that a girl was willing. He could also see what Anita meant when she said Marjorie had a lot to learn. Poor kitten. He pulled her close to him and looked out over her head. "There's Lee," he said suddenly.

"Where?"

"Over there by the orchestra." Lee was radiant and, although the palm of his hand itched to smack her for her annexation of Marjorie's partner, he was still very glad to see someone who knew all the ropes. If that was Bob dancing with her, he was a good-looking youngster.

The Legacy

Marjorie said, "I guess that's Bob."

"I guess it is," said George and steered their way toward the orchestra. He knew a few ropes himself, he thought indignantly. When they bumped into Lee and Bob it was not unintentional.

"Why, Mr. Ashe! Marjorie!" The Marshall poise seemed to have forsaken Lee for a moment but its passing was brief and, almost at once, her voice was exactly like her mother's. "Of all people!" she drawled enchantedly. "Mr. Ashe, this is my cousin, Bob Wheeler. And Marjorie Ashe, Bobby—" Her hand made the correct social wave.

"Sir," said Bob and nodded to Marjorie. She gave him a small uncertain smile and her father felt again that dim annoyance. Surely, with her quick mind, she could think of something to say to the boy.

George sighed inwardly. He had brought her to the dance but apparently that wasn't going to be enough. He turned to Lee, said heartily, "How about finishing this dance with me, young lady?" and took her hand. She was surprised but most embraceable. There was nothing for Bob to do but turn to Marjorie, and George felt intensely relieved. Entranced by his own finesse, he moved away with Lee in his arms and found that he was dancing much better. He couldn't understand why she was so deliciously light and Marjorie so unmaneuverable; they had gone to the same dancing class as children.

He looked around for Marjorie and Bob and saw them, moving grim and wooden, unspeaking, glued together. A wave of honest anger swept over him with the knowledge that Bob was frankly sulking. Whatever they taught the exalted seniors in that young man's school, it was certainly not manners.

On the other hand, it was no use pretending that Marjorie had Lee's light touch. He wondered if it could be learned.

Lee said, with just the right blending of deference and admiration, "It was really sweet of you to bring Marjorie, Mr. Ashe. I know you think I was awfully bad but I couldn't have been more upset. I just *couldn't*."

"I'm afraid Marjorie isn't really socially minded," George said unhappily.

"Well, you were *sweet* to bring her," Lee said firmly. Someone tapped George's shoulder, and a tall boy said, "Sorry, sir."

George went back to the wall. He wasn't going to cut in on his own daughter. She had an official escort now and, whether she was happy or not, it looked all right from the sidelines.

Lee already had another change of partners. For the first time he understood the slight smugness in Anita's voice when she talked of her daughter. It would have been somehow so satisfying to see Marjorie whirl from one pair of arms to another. He only wanted it for her sake. If her mother were still alive, she would have known the things to tell Marjorie, the things a girl had to know for her own success and happiness. He sighed. Perhaps Anita—

The music ended in a crash. Marjorie and Bob stood in the middle of the floor, clapping. The orchestra leader lifted his baton for the next dance and, as the trumpet gave its first mewling wail, Bob took Marjorie by the elbow and steered her toward her father. Safe, stowing her within this paternal harbor, he murmured, "Lee'll be looking for me," and left them.

Marjorie said, "Thank you for the dance," to empty air. After a moment she said uncertainly, "I guess I was supposed to say that I enjoyed the dance, not thank him for it. The man is supposed to say thank you." She turned to her father. "I looked that up in an etiquette book at the library but then I forgot which way it went."

She had been reading etiquette books these days, then, not *Madame Bovary*. "It doesn't matter," George said.

Side by side, they waited for something to happen, someone to come. Finally, George held out his arms, "Dance, dear?" She nodded and they started out again. He was troubled because she was so quiet and her hands were still so cold, and then he began to be exasperated again. If she would only make some effort to attract the boys! Everyone was staring at them, father and daughter dancing interminably together, or at least it felt as if everyone was staring. When he looked around no one seemed even interested. Eyes were following the girls like Lee, casual and lovable, pressed against one faultless tuxedo after another. It wasn't a jungle really; it was more like an exclusive club and he couldn't get his daughter into it.

"Margie," said George.

She looked up at him and they both missed a step. He felt infernally clumsy. "Sweetheart," he said hopefully, "if you dance with Bob again, try to find out what he likes to talk about. He probably plays fullback or shortstop or something."

"He plays center on the basketball team and he's captain of the baseball team," said Marjorie, "and he's president of the dramatic society."

This was cheering news. "He told you all that?"

"I found out from Lee."

"Oh," said George.

They passed Lee at that moment, arm in arm with her current escort in a strolling dance-step. Her dress frothed out around her, and she smiled when George caught her eye. On an impulse, he spun Marjorie around so they were shoulder to shoulder. "Having fun, Lee?" he said casually.

She looked at him in surprise. "Wonderful," she said.

Deliberately, weighing the words so she would be sure to get the point, he said, "I must remember to give your mother a report on you, my dear."

A very pretty archness overlaid a slight uneasiness. "I hope it's a good report, Mr. Ashe," said Anita's daughter.

The Legacy

"I hope so," said Marjorie's father and moved away. When the dance ended, Lee turned up, admirably prompt, with a boy in tow. George beamed upon her, gently congratulating himself on the success of his social blackmail.

"Margie," said Lee, with something of the efficient kindliness of a very worldly aunt, "this is Dick Peterson. He's on the refreshment committee so he hasn't danced a step tonight, but he's just dying to." She smiled at the pink-cheeked representative of refreshments, then looked to George for approval. See? her look said. Tell Mother how good I've been, bringing boys around.

She left them and Dick gazed after her with the melting eyes of a cocker spaniel, then turned to Marjorie. "I didn't plan to dance tonight," he said. "I'm not much good at it but if you'd like to—"

George's heart warmed toward him. The youngster was half a head shorter than Marjorie and looked as if he belonged in grade school but any partner was better than none.

Marjorie smiled anxiously and the two moved off together. George lost some of his good cheer. Dick had understated the case against his dancing. Their feet, moving, collided. They tried again but the music was sharp and exact and unsympathetic. An earnest dew appeared on Dick's forehead, and Marjorie's smile was starched.

Her father felt suddenly irritated with the child. Everyone was doing everything they could for her. He had brought her to the dance himself, Lee had found her a partner, poor young Dick was struggling along as best he could. If she got mixed up with the dance steps, the least she could do was to make an effort and be charming to the boy, say something gay and amusing.

The dance stumbled to a close. The couples stood, politely clapping, waiting for the music to start again. The orchestra leader lifted his baton and Dick turned to Marjorie with a dreadful virtue. George's heart ached for him, martyr to his own good manners.

But unexpectedly, Marjorie was backing out of the reluctant grasp. "I have to powder my nose," she said fiercely, loud enough for George and nearly everyone else to hear and, picking up her long blue skirt, she fled across the floor.

Dick watched her go, relief and distress almost equal on his pink face.

George stayed where he was. He stayed there during the playing of two dances and he had just begun to be really worried when Marjorie reappeared. She looked very tidy and completely controlled, unlike the little girl who had run off the floor. She smiled at him and he drew her hand through the crook of his arm. "Want to go home, honey?"

"No, thank you," said Marjorie.

"Want to dance with me some more?"

"Please," said Marjorie.

They stayed on to the end and then Marjorie went and got her coat. Lee and Bob were on the steps outside and for a moment George thought of offering them a lift home, but reconsidered. He wasn't sure how Marjorie was feeling although she had seemed quite happy during the last dances with him. Maybe it hadn't been such a bad evening for her. After all, she had no previous standards to measure the dance by.

They drove home in silence. He wanted to ask her straight out, for his own reassurance, but all he could do was hope. When they got into the house he took off his coat and hat, laid them over a chair and then turned uncertainly to look at his daughter.

She was smiling, a really happy smile. It lit up her eyes. "Thank you for taking me," she said and suddenly she put her arms up and gave him a swift tight hug. "Oh, Daddy, I had the most *beautiful* time." She turned and ran up the stairs.

"Well!" said George. The whole dreadful weight of the evening rolled off him.

And that was the moment when the phone rang.

He almost didn't answer it because it was far too late to talk to anyone and then he hurried to it, realizing the call might be urgent.

"George?" said Anita's voice.

Good Lord, he thought, but he said, "Hello there," very cheerfully because here was someone who could share his relief and pleasure.

Anita said, "George, Lee just got home. She told me all about it—about you taking Marjorie." She sounded terribly wrought up. "George, how *could* you?"

"How could I what?"

"Take that child to a dance that way!" It was a moment before he realized she was accusing him. "Oh, I know you meant well but, good heavens—! Why didn't you phone first and ask me? I could have told you."

"But, Anita, I don't see what—"

"Lee said that everyone was laughing at her. Marjorie's not a fool, George, she must have known. A girl doesn't go to a dance like that. With her *father*. Like a baby. You might at least have considered her feelings." She must have realized that she sounded too sharp. Her voice smoothed out. "It's not that I'm blaming you, George. It's—"

"But, Anita—Marjorie said she had a beautiful time. She said—"

Suddenly his voice trailed off. He stood there, staring at the telephone in his hand. Dismay and a sense of shock held him for a moment, and then he did something he had never done to anyone before in his life. He hung up, without apology, without explanation.

He turned and walked upstairs and he was barely halfway up before the phone started ringing again. He let it ring.

He walked to Marjorie's room, and the door was closed. He leaned

The Legacy

against it, listening, and he heard what he had known he would hear from the moment he hung up the telephone.

He heard his daughter crying.

She wasn't noisy. They were long deep slow sobs, muffled against the pillow. They had a controlled quality about them. If he knocked on the door, they would stop at once.

He turned very slowly and walked downstairs. The phone had stopped ringing. He went into the living room and stood, hands in pockets, staring at the furniture. He and Eleanor had planned the room together, a long time ago now, and he hadn't changed anything.

It was Eleanor's daughter who was crying upstairs on her bed.

George knew what he wanted to do. He wanted to turn and go back to Marjorie. He wanted to take her in his arms and stroke her hair and comfort her. He wanted to tell his daughter that none of this mattered, that the flimsy world of social successes wasn't what counted, that there were other values, infinitely more important—

He stopped himself.

Marjorie already knew what was important, knew it better than he did. It was Eleanor's daughter who was crying upstairs on her bed, but it was also Eleanor's daughter who had put her arms around his neck and said, "Oh, Daddy, I had the most beautiful time."

The evening had hurt her. She would not let it hurt her father too.

Dismayed, he realized how completely he had failed her. He had wanted to see his daughter shine, he had been impatient with her inability to attract partners. He had wanted Marjorie to be successful as Lee was successful. He had admired Lee with her pretty ways, and he had been humiliatingly willing for Marjorie to learn from them.

He was ashamed of himself.

His daughter was crying upstairs now because she had been a failure in the world where Lee did everything so well. Eventually, he knew, she would stop her tears. She would blow her nose and go sensibly to bed. Tonight's world had been Lee's, not hers. Her enchanted hopes for it were all gone, and she would accept that now, this grown-up child of his, and let them go. There were other worlds. In the end, she would possess something that Lee could never hope for.

Meantime, she was crying, and he would be very careful never to let her know that he had stood outside her door and listened.

He walked upstairs to his bedroom. It was a lonely place, but tonight it was not quite so lonely as usual. Eleanor was less far away than she had ever been, and George Ashe was thinking of the very lucky man who would, some day, marry Eleanor's daughter.

A mother tries to help her three sons find some way around an unexpected family crisis.

CHARLES JACKSON

A Night Visitor

MOTHER SAID LATER, and smiled when she said it (but she could only say this, and smile, years after), that it couldn't have happened on a worse night. The Bartles were over, and Mother never had the Bartles over. They lived across the street; and though we had always known them as neighbors—with a bowing acquaintance—they were different from us and from most of the other people of the street: aloof, haughty, and (as I would have put it when I was old enough to know the expression) holier-than-thou. How they happened to be there this one night, I don't remember. If only it had been the Clarks, Mother said afterward, or the Kellers, or the Farrells, or indeed almost anybody else, she wouldn't have minded so much. Not that she did mind, really, any more than she minded the whole difficult ordeal; but it just gave the Bartles one more opportunity to be patronizing of the neighbors, and smile superiorly, and retire to their correct unhuman household where such an irregular and upsetting thing could never have happened.

Mr. Bartle was known as a nature-lover, a bird-lover, and a music-lover. He wore glasses with a black ribbon attached, and we never saw him without his coat on, even when he was walking around his extensive back yard with his hands clasped pompously behind him, inspecting the peonies and the hydrangeas and the birdbaths. It was said that Mr. Bartle knew every flower and plant and every bird by its name in the book; and it was always Mr. Bartle, each spring, who of all the residents in Arcadia was inevitably the one who saw the first robin. On summer nights his player piano resounded throughout the neighborhood, treating us all to "The Erl-King" and "Poet and Peasant" and "William Tell"; and on Saturday evenings when the band concerts were given in the village park, three streets away, he sat on his front porch nodding his head to the music

[308]

and waving an imaginary baton—for the benefit, of course, of the neighbors whose idea of music was "The Stars and Stripes Forever." Mrs. Bartle was a frail small woman who never ventured an opinion when her husband was present and whose infrequent remarks were interspersed with phrases like "It appears" and "It would seem" and "As a matter of fact." To our way of thinking, the Bartles were cultivated and well-educated people and we kids were always a little in awe of them. Consequently, the night they were over, we were only too glad to stay in our own rooms upstairs. Mother was just as well pleased too, as she knew that Mr. and Mrs. Bartle didn't like noisy children and it was hard not to raise our voices occasionally when we three boys were together.

I was in my bedroom reading *The Skeleton in Armour* and at the same time trying to listen to what was going on downstairs. The doors to the living room and parlor were closed but I could hear the conversation once in a while and the Galli-Curci records that Mother was playing to entertain the Bartles. About nine-thirty they were to have cake and ice cream, and Mother said she would send some up to us when it was ready. It was a warm night in early June, the front door was open, and there was no sound from the street except maybe once in a while during the evening when an automobile went by and when the schoolhouse clock chimed eight o'clock and then again, later, nine o'clock. A few minutes after that, there was a sudden knocking on the screen door.

I was surprised because nobody ever knocked at our house—they just opened the door and came in; and also because I hadn't heard anybody come up on the porch. There was a long pause—I guess Mother didn't hear it right away—and then the knock came again: a loud rapping on the wood of the screen.

The parlor door opened, then, and I heard Mother come out into the hall and switch on the porch light. "Hello—who is it?" she said. I heard a voice mumble something, and Mother asked again, "Who?" Then, "Oh," she said in a funny way, and again "Oh," as if she were trying to think of something to say. The voice mumbled once more for a second or two and then Mother called out, "Gerald! Don! Will one of you come down here a minute?"

I didn't move. After all, she had said Gerald first; and besides, Gerald was supposed to be the man of the family now that he was fifteen and Father had gone. I heard Gerald get up from a chair in his room and come out into the hall, and at the same time my little brother Warwick ran out into the hall, too. "What is it, Mother?" Gerald said.

"Come downstairs a moment, will you, son?" Mother said. "And Warwick, you go into Don's room, like a good boy. Don," Mother called to me, "keep Warwick with you. I'll be up in a few minutes."

All these directions were given without fuss or excitement, but just the same the Bartles had stopped talking in the parlor and were listening to what was going on in the hall—and I listened too. Then my older brother started down the stairs; and just as he reached the bottom, I heard Mother ask whoever it was to come in.

There was whispering in the hall, then, and after about a minute my brother Gerald started upstairs again, followed by heavy slow footsteps. Mother waited until they had reached the top and then she returned to the parlor. I heard her say, "I'm terribly sorry, Mrs. Bartle, but I'll have to ask you to excuse me for this evening. We have a visitor"; and just then Gerald came into my room with this man.

I had never seen anybody like him before, not even among the five or six tramps who turned up at our back door during the summer, which is what he reminded me of first. I wasn't scared because Mother had always said there was nothing to be scared of in tramps and we must always be nice to them; but I was uneasy and uncomfortable, I think mostly because he smelled so bad. The minute he came through the door I smelled him, and it got worse the longer he stood there. He smelled like the ashes down by the furnace after we kids had peed in them, especially the day afterward, after the heat of the furnace had made them smell worse. He stood in the doorway twisting his cap in his hands. He was tall and thin, with a broad high forehead but a very thin face. His mouth hung open in an embarrassed grin, he seemed to have no cheeks at all, and his teeth were long, crooked, and yellow-looking. He was dressed in a heavy gray sweater fastened at the front with a safety pin, blue denim pants, and heavy worn shoes. Warwick and I sat there staring at him; and then Gerald said, very coldly, "These are my two brothers."

The man grinned and nodded and fumbled with his cap. "How de-doo." His voice was deep, but not deep in a good way or manly way—just hollow, like a clown pretending to be an idiot.

"What do you want here?" Gerald said sharply. "Who are you, anyway?"

The man turned, looked at Gerald for a moment, and then giggled. He shifted uncomfortably, as if he was suspicious of us, and looked down at the floor. "Where's Gerald?" he said, and it was as if his voice came through a funnel or something.

"I'm Gerald," my brother said, "but if you mean my father, he isn't here any more."

The man was evidently very surprised at this. He stood up straight and peered at Gerald as if he didn't believe him. "*You* aren't married to Ellen —I know that much," he said stupidly. "I'm no fool!"

Mother was in the hall now, saying good night to the Bartles and apologizing for dismissing them so early. The man heard her, and immediately he turned and went out to the top of the stairs and looked down. "What's the matter, Ellen?" he said. "You ashamed of me?" There was a terrible pause. "Don't worry," he said over the banister, "your fine friends can stay. I ain't going to come down."

He said all this as gentle as a child, but I was scared now. Then I heard Mr. Bartle speak up. "Ellen, who is this man!"

"Come down, Henry, if you want to," Mother said.

The man went down a couple of steps to the landing, then stood there, hesitating.

Mrs. Bartle gave a little muffled cry and pushed open the screen door. "Ned," she whimpered, "don't you think we'd better—"

"It's all right," Mother said. "Mrs. Bartle, this is my brother Henry. . . . Henry, this is Mr. and Mrs. Bartle, who live across the street."

From the landing, he nodded and said in his sepulchral voice, "Pleased to meet you."

"And now," I heard Mother say, "maybe you'd better go. I'll try to come over and see you in the morning, Mrs. Bartle."

They were gone—shocked by the fact (no less than we were) that this terrible man was a relative of ours. Mother stood there a moment more, then switched off the porch light, hooked the screen door, and came upstairs.

"Boys," Mother said, "this is your Uncle Henry. You didn't know you had an Uncle Henry, did you?" She put her hand on his shoulder. "They've never seen you before, Henry—that's why they looked so surprised."

"Mother!" protested Gerald.

But Mother paid no attention to Gerald's anger, even though I'm sure, now, that her sympathies were with him at the time. "It's been so long since I've seen you too," Mother went on. "I'd almost forgotten how— Tell me, Henry, how are you? Have you seen Mama and Papa lately?"

At that moment he looked as though he was going to cry. "I was there last week," he said, and then he did begin to blubber. He took out a big blue handkerchief and wiped his nose.

"Oh, yes? How are they?"

"Good," he said.

"That's fine, Henry. And did Mama and Papa tell you where we live?"

Suddenly he became very secretive and sly. "I found out," he said.

"I'm very glad you did." Then Mother turned to us. "Boys," she said, "Uncle Henry is going to spend the night with us. We must find a place for him to sleep, mustn't we."

"I don't want to put you out," he said. He was really crying now.

"Why, what an idea—you won't put us out! We've got plenty of room, haven't we, boys?" We didn't say a thing. My brother Gerald gave Mother a look and walked out of the room. Mother pretended not to notice this. "You're tired," she went on. "A nice bath and a good bed—" She bit her lip and looked at us frowningly, as if thinking. Suddenly she seemed to brighten. "I've got an idea! Warwick, you sleep with Don tonight, and we'll give Uncle Henry your bed—how will that be? Then Gerald can sleep downstairs in my room and I'll sleep upstairs in his. That way I'll be up here with you in case Uncle Henry—well, wants anything. Isn't that all right?"

So it was arranged. I was sent down to the kitchen to light the gas heater so my mother's brother (like the others, I couldn't bring myself to call him Uncle Henry) could take a bath. Gerald stayed in his room with the door closed and refused to come out till Mother went in and asked him to take his night things and go down and sleep in her room; which he did, and we didn't see him again till morning. Then Mother went up into the attic to look for an old nightshirt of my father's. When she came down she also had with her one of my father's suits, some shoes, underwear, and several clean shirts that were still good. These she laid out on Warwick's bed, which for tonight was Henry's. She handed him the nightshirt, and took him down the hall to show him where the bathroom was. She started the water for him and then came back to us.

"Now you boys get to bed just as quickly and quietly as you can," she said. "I'll be upstairs here with you so you needn't be frightened. There's nothing to be frightened of, anyway, is there? Warwick, have you got your pajamas?"

Warwick ran into his room while Henry was in the bathroom and got his pajamas and ran back. He undressed quickly and got into bed. I began to undress too, and Mother went downstairs to get her own things and turn off the gas heater. I was in bed by the time she came back. Our room still smelled something awful, and Mother walked in and said, "You must be sure to open your windows wide. After all, there are two of you in here tonight and you'll need all the fresh air you can get." She pushed the windows up as far as they would go and turned out our light. She leaned over and kissed us both good night. "I'll come back in a few minutes and see you after Uncle Henry's had his bath," she said, "if you're still awake. But do try to go to sleep, won't you?" Then she left and tiptoed down the hall, to listen outside the bathroom door. Finally she called through the door. "You all right, Henry?" He said something I couldn't hear, and Mother answered, "All right, then; get to bed as soon as you can—it's getting late."

After a while he came down the hall in his bare feet and looked in at Warwick and me. He stood there in the doorway, looking very big in the nightshirt that was too small for him, and then he snickered. At the same moment, Mother came into the hall and stood beside him.

"I tell you, Ellen," he said, giggling, "why don't I just sleep in here with the little fellows? Be kind of fun and not so lonely like."

"Why, Henry," Mother said, "that's a silly idea. There's a perfectly good bed in Warwick's room, all for you. Now you just come on and have a good night's sleep, all by yourself." She took his arm. "Besides, I want to have a good visit with you first, and we mustn't keep the boys up any longer." Whereupon she led him into Warwick's room and closed the door—I suppose so we couldn't hear.

Warwick and I lay in bed talking in whispers of the visitor.

"Do you suppose he really is our uncle?" Warwick said.

"I don't know," I said. "Mother says so, and she ought to know."

"Just the same, he can't be our *uncle*," Warwick said. "Our uncle" meant Uncle Fred, that busy, noisy man who was a doctor in the city; and when you thought of him you couldn't imagine, then, that Henry was our uncle, too. Uncle Fred was always very clean and very business-like; he spoke in a rapid, loud voice, did things quickly, and smelled as clean as he looked. If what Mother said was true, this man was Uncle Fred's brother—which was almost harder to believe than that he was Mother's.

I hadn't gone to the bathroom before going to bed, so I got up now and went down the hall. On my way back, coming along in the half-dark in my bare feet, I stopped outside Warwick's room and listened. I heard Mother say, "But of course you understand that you can't stay here, don't you, Henry? There are the boys. You do understand that, don't you—and why?" There was no answer. "They come first," Mother said, "and I have to think of them. This is their home—you saw yourself how Gerald acted tonight. Henry, I'm glad you're here, and we'll take care of you for the night, but tomorrow—" He muttered something, and then suddenly Mother said, "Oh, dear! If only Papa had been the kind of father he should have been!"

I crept back to bed, and Warwick whispered, "What are they talking about?"

"I don't know," I said, "how should I know!"

"You were listening," he whispered, "I know you were. What did they say?"

"They didn't say anything. Shut up and go to sleep."

"No," Warwick said. "I'm going to get up and listen too." But at this moment we heard Mother open the door and come out. She closed the door behind her and came into our room.

"Asleep yet?" We kept still, making believe we were, but Mother said, "I know you're only fooling." She sat down on the edge of the bed. "Listen, boys." She took Warwick's hand, who was nearest her. "There are a lot of things in this world that you boys don't know. The way it is with you, and with us here, isn't the way it is with everybody. We're lucky enough to be a family, but lots of people are alone, with nobody to care for them or love them." She was sitting there beside us on the bed, out of the light that came in from the hall; and though I couldn't see her eyes, I knew she wasn't looking at us as she talked, but straight at the wall.

"I think I should tell you something about Henry so that you will understand, and not act the way Gerald did tonight, though heaven knows, poor boy, he isn't to blame," she said. "My mother died when I was seven years old. That was your grandmother, the real one. There were three of us children and I was the oldest of the three. Then came your Uncle Fred, and then Henry. He was only a little baby when my mother died—just a few months old. Papa had a hard time with three little children on his hands and no mother for them; and so, in about a year, he married Mamma, my stepmother, the grandmother you know. She was a German woman whose husband had died. Mamma was very hard on us in those days, though it was not entirely her fault; she couldn't be expected to take an interest in children who were not her own. She was often very cruel to us, but I never said anything to Papa about it because he wouldn't believe it. Then, a little over a year after they were married, Papa and Mamma had a child of their own, your Uncle Otto whom you've never met."

"Mother," Warwick whispered tensely in the dark, "what was the matter with Gerald tonight?"

"Listen, Warwick, and please don't interrupt. Uncle Henry is my little brother, just as you are Don's and Gerald's little brother. But different—oh, a lot different, though I didn't realize it for a long time, or how serious it was. On account of Mamma, I only stayed home till I was fourteen. By that time it was too hard for me. I couldn't get along with Mamma no matter how hard I tried, and I did try—for Papa's sake as much as for my own. So I left and went to Buffalo and got a job as—well, just a plain hired girl, taking care of other people's children. You never knew that, did you, that your mother was a hired girl? Well, I was. Then only a couple of years later I met your father and we got married almost at once. That's probably one of the reasons why I married so young: I was anxious to have a home of my own and belong somewhere. But here was the terrible thing. As your Uncle Henry grew up, we began to notice that he wasn't like other children—that he wasn't quite right at all. He couldn't learn properly, he couldn't take care of himself in any way, not even in the smallest things, like dressing or going to the bathroom; and it was this that always made your grandfather furious, all the more so because his and Mamma's own son Otto, even though he was younger than Henry, was so much brighter. Grandpa was—he was ashamed of Henry, and shouted at him for not being able to do the simplest things. But no matter how much he was shouted at, or punished, poor Henry couldn't understand and couldn't have corrected his habits if he had understood. Otto, of course, made fun of Henry all the time, and so did Uncle Fred in a way—it was only natural, they were just children, and maybe I'd have done the same thing if I hadn't been older."

"Mother," Warwick said, "is Gerald mad at something?"

"Warwick," Mother said, "I'm trying to tell you something about your

Uncle Henry. People like that— What I'm trying to say is that punishment does them no good and ridicule is even worse. He may have been hurt when he was born, but we didn't know anything was wrong till he was about four or five. What he needed was a good mother to love him and take time and patience with him, but of course Mamma couldn't be expected to do that when she had a son of her own, even younger. Henry used to cry, I remember, when Mamma would take Otto up in her lap and rock him—he cried, then, more than when he was punished, and would run out into the back yard and hide in the shed. I'm only telling you this because I want you to know how, from the very beginning, some people never have a chance. Almost every family has somebody that they'd rather not have around, and it's too bad that you boys had to find out about it in this way. On the other hand, there's really no reason why you shouldn't know, either."

At this point Mother stopped and lifted her head and I saw that she was listening. "Just a minute," she said, and she got up and went out into the hall. I knew that she was listening at the door to Warwick's room where Uncle Henry was sleeping, but in a few minutes she was back and sat on the bed again.

"You're still awake, aren't you, Don?" Mother said.

"Yes, Mother," I said, and Warwick said, "Yes, Mother," too.

"When I left home," Mother said, "Henry was about seven or eight. I didn't see much of him then for a long time because I was working in Buffalo, but Papa had promised he would take care of Henry after I left. After your father and I were married, I saw them even less, till you children began to come and then Papa would visit us once in a while. He didn't talk about Henry much. I understood why he didn't, and I felt sorry for him. He was always so ashamed, poor man, though he had no reason to be. It wasn't his fault or anyone's, but I knew he hated having a son like that. His shame made him try to ignore Henry and Henry's trouble, he paid attention to him less and less, and instead of trying to find a good place for Henry to stay, in some special kind of school or even some good home, he shirked his responsibilities more and more and just let Henry get worse. Papa didn't speak of these things when he visited us, but I knew Henry hadn't gotten any better and was still a little boy—worse than a little boy, in some ways. Then, when he was about fifteen, he disappeared. Exactly where he went nobody knows, but we learned later that he bummed around the country like a tramp, turning up at Papa's house about once a year, but only for a day or two, and then he'd be off again. How he got along I can't imagine, because he isn't as bright as other people and I don't know how he could manage to live by his wits. I guess somebody always looked out for him; at least I used to pray that they would. I only saw him once after he left, and that was at Papa's house about ten years ago. Your father and I were there for the day, and Henry had shown up the night before. I didn't know him at first and had to be told who he was—imagine, my own brother."

"Where did he come from tonight?" I asked. "How did he happen to come here?"

"He told me he was at Mamma's this week and she must have told him how to get here," Mother said. "I asked him about his life and how he got along, and he said he just goes around, riding the trains all over the country, and every year he usually spends the winter in jail somewhere. Then, when spring comes, he's out again and travels around some more. Your Uncle Fred tells me he comes there sometimes, because your Uncle always gives him money and buys him a railroad ticket to some place. He loves to ride in the passenger coaches."

"Mother," Warwick said, "why does he smell so bad?"

"Why, Warwick," Mother said, "he hasn't any other clothes! He's probably slept in the same clothes for a long time—he doesn't have the opportunities to bathe and change the way we do. You'll see, he won't be like that in the morning. He'll be all bathed and dressed in clean clothes, and be just like you and me, or Uncle Fred."

"Mother," Warwick said again, "what was the matter with Gerald tonight? Why wasn't he nice?"

"Gerald doesn't understand, that's all," Mother said, "but he will. I know what he was thinking. He's afraid of what people around town will say, our neighbors and his friends at school, if they should find out. He feels ashamed and doesn't want anyone to know. I know how it is; my own father was the same. They can't help it. We mustn't blame Gerald, Warwick—but still, we mustn't blame Henry, either."

Mother got up from the bed. "You boys must get some sleep now. Everything will be all right in the morning, and maybe Gerald will understand by then, too. We'll get Uncle Henry a ticket on the train and let him go where he wants to." Mother sighed deeply, then spoke as if thinking aloud. "Heaven only knows what the Bartles are thinking." Then she added, "But we don't care, do we?" She leaned over and kissed Warwick and then me. "Good night, Warwick. Good night, Don. Sleep well."

"Good night, Mother," we said; and she was gone. She put the light out in the hall, stood by the door to Warwick's room for a moment, and then I heard her quietly turn the key in the lock.

I did not fall asleep for a long time, partly because through the hall I could see that Mother still had the light on in Gerald's room, and partly because of the things she had told us. I knew, now, why Mother always fed tramps who came to the back door, and gave them clothes and sometimes a little money. Ours was the only house on the whole street where they ever stopped, and the neighbors used to remark about this. Maybe there was some truth to the popular notion that tramps always marked the places where they had been treated well, so that other tramps would know; but always, after a tramp had been at our house and had had a meal at the back door, Warwick and I used to go over every inch of the back porch and steps and every inch of the sidewalk, looking for some mark or sign that the tramp had left. We never found any, but we did not doubt that it was so. In fact, our failure to find the mysterious mark only added to the glamour of the idea: the tramps had a way of communicating with each other that we ordinary people wouldn't understand.

I fell asleep then, but after a while woke in what seemed the middle of the night, though it may have been only an hour or a half hour later. I didn't know what it was that had awakened me at first until I realized it was the light shining into the hall from Gerald's bedroom. After a moment I remembered that Mother was in there, and I wondered if she had fallen asleep with the light on. I got out of bed quietly so as not to wake Warwick, and tiptoed into the hall. But I did not go into Gerald's room. From the door I saw Mother lying in bed. She had a handkerchief over her face and was pressing it against her eyes with the fingers of both hands. She breathed deeply, and I could see—I could even hear—that she was crying softly, and trying not to cry out loud.

In the morning, when we came down, Gerald was already at breakfast and Mother was talking to him. I guess Uncle Henry was still asleep because his door was closed as we came through the hall. Gerald was quiet at breakfast; he didn't talk at all. He wouldn't look at Mother or even at us.

When we had finished eating, Mother said, "Don, you and Warwick run along to school now. You needn't wait for Gerald. He's going to stay home for a while and then take Uncle Henry to the station after everybody else is in school. Aren't you, Gerald? And then this noon, when you come home for dinner, it'll be just the same as it's always been. Your Uncle Henry will be gone, the Bartles will be the only ones who'll know anything, and we'll all try to forget about it. I mean by that," she said, "that it's been—well, a little unpleasant perhaps, for some of us, and I'm sure your Uncle Henry is the last person in the world who would want to cause any difficulty for Gerald or anybody else. Isn't that so, Gerald?"

Gerald didn't say a word.

"I'm sorry to have to ask you to do this," Mother said, "but you're the man of the house now, Gerald, and the only one to do it. . . . Go on, Don. You and Warwick run along now. Gerald won't be in school until later."

At noon, as Warwick and I came down the street and turned in at our house, we saw a strange sight on the back porch: the mattress from Warwick's bed where Uncle Henry had slept was spread over the railing, showing a big dark stain; and on the clothesline in the back yard were hanging the sheets from the bed and even the blankets.

Gerald came home a few minutes later and we sat down to dinner, all of us acutely embarrassed. After a while Mother said, "Well, are you going to tell me about it, Gerald? I'd like to know, if you feel like telling me."

"Why, yes," Gerald said evasively, "why not? We just walked over to the station, the back way, and I bought him a ticket to Chicago as you told me to. That's all."

"Did you wait for the train to come in," Mother asked, "and put him on?"

"Yes, I did," Gerald said, without looking at any of us. "He piled on and I handed him up that old suitcase you gave him, and then he waved and I waved and that's all there was to it. . . . I didn't meet anyone we know," he added sarcastically, "if that's what you mean."

"Never mind, Gerald," Mother said, "you know very well that isn't what I meant."

The meal went on in silence, then, until the telephone rang. Gerald got up to answer it. In a moment he came back and said, "Mother, it's for you. It's Father Dillon."

"Why, of all things," Mother said, getting up, "what would the Catholic priest be calling *me* for?"

"How should I know?" Gerald said. "He said he wanted you."

Mother went into the living-room to the telephone. We heard her say, "Yes, Father Dillon? . . . Yes . . . Oh! . . . Oh, I'm terribly sorry . . . Yes, he is . . . That's right, he is, Father Dillon . . . Well—please let me call you back, may I? I'll have to think first . . . Thank you, Father Dillon. I'll telephone you within a few minutes."

Mother came back into the dining room. She leaned on the table with both hands, looked at Gerald, and said, "Gerald, you lied to me! Why did you lie to me!"

"What do you mean," Gerald cried, "what's the matter?"

"Why didn't you do what I told you with your Uncle Henry?"

"I took him to the station!"

"You said that you waited and saw him on the train! Oh, Gerald, you fool," Mother said, and sat down in her chair. "Oh, you should have waited! You should have put him on the train!"

"Mother!" Gerald was almost shouting now. "I couldn't! I hated it there, I couldn't stand it! I didn't know *who* we might run into! And Mr. Jenner looking out at us from the ticket window and wondering who this awful bum— Mother, I'm sorry, but I couldn't wait! After I bought the ticket I left him—you would have, too, or Don, or anyone! How did I know he wouldn't go?"

Warwick began to cry. "Shut up, Wick," Gerald snapped. "Where is he now?"

"Father Dillon said that a man, a very strange man, turned up at the Parish house a half hour ago and said he was my brother. Father Dillon didn't believe it at first but the man kept insisting and so he phoned to ask me if it was true. Now he wants to know what I'd like him to do about it. He said he'd keep him there until I called back. What can I tell him?" Mother got up from the table and walked back and forth. "Oh, Gerald, don't you see? It would all have been so easy if you had only— For you and for everybody, even for poor Henry! Now—now you've only got it all to do over again."

Gerald suddenly thumped the table a terrific whack. "Damn it to hell, I *won't* do it again! The *cops* are going to take care of him *this* time, not me!" He sprang up from the table and ran into the hall. "That filthy bum's going to be out of this town in another hour or I'll never set foot in this house again!"

"Gerald!" Mother ran into the hall. "Don't be a fool, Gerald—you're only making things worse!"

"I know what I'm doing!" he shouted.

"Don't you *see*, Gerald," Mother cried, "you're only doing the very thing you wanted to prevent! You'll have everybody in town— Gerald! Gerald!"

The screen door slammed and we heard Gerald run down the steps and on up the street.

Warwick and I stared at each other across the table. We were too frightened to move. We listened, but Mother didn't make a sound. After a long time she came back into the dining room and sat down at her place at the table. She was crying now, but she noticed us sitting there not eating, and said, "Please eat your dinner, boys, it's almost time to go back to school." Even as we were eating, then, the school bell began to ring and Mother started to cry again. "Poor Gerald," she sobbed, leaning over her plate, "oh, poor Gerald . . ."

The annoying habits of this father, and their persistence through the years, might have been unbearably irritating to a growing son. But the son survived, and records the habits in a work reflecting humor and affection in a family where people took each other's oddities in their stride.

CLARENCE DAY

Father Opens My Mail

THERE WAS A TIME in my boyhood when I felt that Father had handicapped me severely in life by naming me after him, "Clarence." All literature, so far as I could see, was thronged with objectionable persons named Clarence. Percy was bad enough, but there had been some good fighters named Percy. The only Clarence in history was a duke who did something dirty at Tewkesbury, and who died a ridiculous death afterwards in a barrel of malmsey.

As for the Clarences in the fiction I read, they were horrible. In one story, for instance, there were two brothers, Clarence and Frank. Clarence was a "vain, disagreeable little fellow," who was proud of his curly hair and fine clothes, while Frank was a "rollicking boy who was ready to play games with anybody." Clarence didn't like to play games, of course. He just minced around looking on.

One day when the mother of these boys had gone out, this story went on, Clarence "tempted" Frank to disobey her and fly their kite on the roof. Frank didn't want to, but Clarence kept taunting him and daring him until Frank was stung into doing it. After the two boys went up to the roof, Frank got good and dirty, running up and down and stumbling over scuttles, while Clarence sat there, giving him orders, and kept his natty clothes tidy. To my horror, he even spread out his handkerchief on the trapdoor to sit on. And to crown all, this sneak told on Frank as soon as their mother came in.

This wasn't an exceptionally mean Clarence, either. He was just run-of-the-mill. Some were worse.

So far as I could ever learn, however, Father had never heard of these stories, and had never dreamed of there being anything objectionable in his name. Quite the contrary. And yet as a boy he had lived a good rough-and-tumble boy's life. He had played and fought on the city streets, and kept a dog in Grandpa's stable, and stolen rides to Greenpoint Ferry on the high, lurching bus. In the summer he had gone to West Springfield and had run down Shad Lane through the trees to the house where Grandpa was born, and had gone barefoot and driven the cows home just as though he had been named Tom or Bill.

He had the same character as a boy, I suppose, that he had as a man, and he was too independent to care if people thought his name fancy. He paid no attention to the prejudices of others, except to disapprove of them. He had plenty of prejudices himself, of course, but they were his own. He was humorous and confident and level-headed, and I imagine that if any boy had tried to make fun of him for being named Clarence, Father would simply have laughed and told him he didn't know what he was talking about.

I asked Mother how this name had ever happened to spring up in our family. She explained that my great-great-grandfather was Benjamin Day, and my great-grandfather was Henry, and consequently my grandfather had been named Benjamin Henry. He in turn had named his eldest son Henry and his second son Benjamin. The result was that when Father was born there was no family name left. The privilege of choosing a name for Father had thereupon been given to Grandma, and unluckily for the Day family she had been reading a novel, the hero of which was named Clarence.

I knew that Grandma, though very like Grandpa in some respects, had a dreamy side which he hadn't, a side that she usually kept to herself, in her serene, quiet way. Her romantic choice of this name probably made Grandpa smile, but he was a detached sort of man who didn't take small matters seriously, and who drew a good deal of private amusement from the happenings of everyday life. Besides, he was partly to blame in this case, because that novel was one he had published himself in his magazine.

I asked Mother, when she had finished, why I had been named Clarence too.

It hadn't been her choice, Mother said. She had suggested all sorts of names to Father, but there seemed to be something wrong with each one. When she had at last spoken of naming me after him, however, he had said at once that that was the best suggestion yet—he said it sounded just right.

Father and I would have had plenty of friction in any case. This identity of names made things worse. Every time that I had been more of a fool than he liked, Father would try to impress on me my responsibilities as his eldest son, and above all as the son to whom he had given his name, as he put it. A great deal was expected, it seemed to me, of a boy who was named after his father. I used to envy my brothers, who didn't have anything expected of them on this score at all.

I envied them still more after I was old enough to begin getting letters. I then discovered that when Father "gave" me his name he had also, not unnaturally, I had to admit, retained it himself, and when anything came for Clarence S. Day he opened it, though it was sometimes for me.

He also opened everything that came addressed to Clarence S. Day, Jr. He didn't do this intentionally, but unless the "Jr." was clearly written, it looked like "Esq.," and anyhow Father was too accustomed to open all Clarence Day letters to remember about looking carefully every time for a "Jr." So far as mail and express went, I had no name at all of my own.

For the most part nobody wrote to me when I was a small boy except firms whose advertisements I had read in the *Youth's Companion* and to whom I had written requesting them to send me their circulars. These circulars described remarkable bargains in magicians' card outfits, stamps and coins, pocket knives, trick spiders, and imitation fried eggs, and they seemed interesting and valuable to me when I got them. The trouble was that Father usually got them and at once tore them up. I then had to write for such circulars again, and if Father got the second one too, he would sometimes explode with annoyance. He became particularly indignant one year, I remember, when he was repeatedly urged to take advantage of a special bargain sale of false whiskers. He said that he couldn't understand why these offerings kept pouring in. I knew why, in this case, but at other times I was often surprised myself at the number he got, not realizing that as a result of my postcard request my or our name had been automatically put on several large general mailing lists.

During this period I got more of my mail out of Father's wastebasket than I did from the postman.

At the age of twelve or thirteen, I stopped writing for these childish things and turned to a new field. Father and I, whichever of us got at the mail first, then began to receive not merely circulars but personal letters beginning:

DEAR FRIEND DAY:

In reply to your valued request for one of our Mammoth Agents' Outfits, kindly forward postoffice order for $1.49 to cover cost of postage and packing, and we will put you in a position to earn a large income in your spare time with absolutely no labor on your part, by taking subscriptions for *The Secret Handbook of Mesmerism,* and our *Tales of Blood* series.

And one spring, I remember, as the result of what I had intended to be a secret application on my part, Father was assigned "the exclusive rights for Staten Island and Hoboken of selling the Gem Home Popper for Pop Corn. Housewives buy it at sight."

After Father had stormily endured these afflictions for a while, he and I began to get letters from girls. Fortunately for our feelings, these were rare, but they were ordeals for both of us. Father had forgotten, if he

Father Opens My Mail

ever knew, how silly young girls can sound, and I got my first lesson in how unsystematic they were. No matter how private and playful they meant their letters to be, they forgot to put "Jr." on the envelope every once in so often. When Father opened these letters, he read them all the way through, sometimes twice, muttering to himself over and over: "This is very peculiar. I don't understand this at all. Here's a letter to me from some person I never heard of. I can't see what it's about." By the time it had occurred to him that possibly the letter might be for me, I was red and embarrassed and even angrier at the girl than at Father. And on days when he had read some of the phrases aloud to the family, it nearly killed me to claim it.

Lots of fellows whom I knew had been named after their fathers without having such troubles. But although Father couldn't have been kinder-hearted or had any better intentions, when he saw his name on a package or envelope it never dawned on him that it might not be for him. He was too active in his habits to wait until I had a chance to get at it. And as he was also single-minded and prompt to attend to unfinished business, he opened everything automatically and then did his best to dispose of it.

This went on even after I grew up, until I had a home of my own. Father was always perfectly decent about it, but he never changed. When he saw I felt sulky, he was genuinely sorry and said so, but he couldn't see why all this should annoy me, and he was surprised and amused that it did. I used to get angry once in a while when something came for me which I particularly hadn't wished him to see and which I would find lying, opened, on the hall table marked "For Jr.?" when I came in; but nobody could stay angry with Father—he was too utterly guiltless of having meant to offend.

He often got angry himself, but it was mostly at things, not at persons, and he didn't mind a bit (as a rule) when persons got angry at him. He even declared, when I got back from college, feeling dignified, and told him that I wished he'd be more careful, that he suffered from these mistakes more than I did. It wasn't *his* fault, he pointed out, if my stupid correspondents couldn't remember my name, and it wasn't any pleasure to him to be upset at his breakfast by finding that a damned lunatic company in Battle Creek had sent him a box of dry bread crumbs, with a letter asserting that this rubbish would be good for his stomach. "I admit I threw it into the fireplace, Clarence, but what else could I do? If you valued this preposterous concoction, my dear boy, I'm sorry. I'll buy another box for you today, if you'll tell me where I can get it. Don't feel badly! I'll buy you a barrel. Only I hope you won't eat it."

In the days when Mrs. Pankhurst and her friends were chaining themselves to lamp-posts in London, in their campaign for the vote, a letter came from Frances Hand trustfully asking "Dear Clarence" to do something to help Woman Suffrage—speak at a meeting, I think. Father got red in the face. "Speak at one of their meetings!" he roared at Mother. "I'd like nothing better! You can tell Mrs. Hand that it would give me great pleasure to inform all those crackpots in petticoats exactly what I think of their antics."

"Now, Clare," Mother said, "you mustn't talk that way. I like that nice Mrs. Hand, and anyhow this letter must be for Clarence."

One time I asked Father for his opinion of a low-priced stock I'd been watching. His opinion was that it was not worth a damn. I thought this over, but I still wished to buy it, so I placed a scale order with another firm instead of with Father's office, and said nothing about it. At the end of the month this other firm sent me a statement, setting forth each of my little transactions in full, and of course they forgot to put the "Jr." at the end of my name. When Father opened the envelope, he thought at first in his excitement that this firm had actually opened an account for him without being asked. I found him telling Mother that he'd like to wring their damned necks.

"That must be for me, Father," I said, when I took in what had happened.

We looked at each other.

"You bought this stuff?" he said incredulously. "After all I said about it?"

"Yes, Father."

He handed over the statement and walked out of the room.

Both he and I felt offended and angry. We stayed so for several days, too, but we then made it up.

Once in a while when I got a letter that I had no time to answer I used to address an envelope to the sender and then put anything in it that happened to be lying around on my desk—a circular about books, a piece of newspaper, an old laundry bill—anything at all, just to be amiable, and yet at the same time to save myself the trouble of writing. I happened to tell several people about this private habit of mine at a dinner one night—a dinner at which Alice Duer Miller and one or two other writers were present. A little later she wrote me a criticism of Henry James and ended by saying that I needn't send her any of my old laundry bills because she wouldn't stand it. And she forgot to put on the "Jr."

"In the name of God," Father said bleakly, "this is the worst yet. Here's a woman who says I'd better not read *The Golden Bowl*, which I have no intention whatever of doing, and she also warns me for some unknown reason not to send her my laundry bills."

The good part of all these experiences, as I realize now, was that in the end they drew Father and me closer together. My brothers had only chance battles with him. I had a war. Neither he nor I relished its clashes, but they made us surprisingly intimate.

A woman learns gradually to understand her own part in a frightening sexual encounter when she was a girl of fifteen. Her increasing insight into this one small event prepares her to meet some hard experiences of later life.

DOROTHY CANFIELD FISHER

Sex Education

IT WAS three times—but at intervals of many years—that I heard my Aunt Minnie tell about an experience of her girlhood that had made a never-to-be-forgotten impression on her. The first time she was in her thirties, still young. But she had been married for ten years, so that to my group of friends, all in the early teens, she seemed quite of another generation.

The day she told us the story we had been idling on one end of her porch as we made casual plans for a picnic supper in the woods. Darning stockings at the other end, she paid no attention to us until one of the girls said, "Let's take blankets and sleep out there. It'd be fun."

"No," Aunt Minnie broke in sharply, "you mustn't do that."

"Oh, for goodness sake, why not!" said one of the younger girls, rebelliously. "The boys are always doing it. Why can't we, just once?"

Aunt Minnie laid down her sewing. "Come here, girls," she said, "I want you should hear something that happened to me when I was your age."

Her voice had a special quality which, perhaps, young people of today would not recognize. But we did. We knew from experience that it was the dark voice grown-ups used when they were going to say something about sex.

Yet at first what she had to say was like any dull family anecdote. She had been ill when she was fifteen; and afterwards she was run down, thin, with no appetite. Her folks thought a change of air would do her good, and sent her from Vermont out to Ohio—or was it Illinois? I don't remember. Anyway, one of those places where the corn grows high. Her mother's Cousin Ella lived there, keeping house for her son-in-law.

The son-in-law was the minister of the village church. His wife had died some years before, leaving him a young widower with two little girls

[325]

and a baby boy. He had been a normally personable man then, but the next summer, on the Fourth of July, when he was trying to set off some fireworks to amuse his children, an imperfectly manufactured rocket had burst in his face. The explosion had left one side of his face badly scarred. Aunt Minnie made us see it, as she still saw it, in horrid detail—the stiffened, scarlet scar-tissue distorting one cheek, the lower lip turned so far out at one corner that the moist red mucous membrane lining always showed, one lower eyelid hanging loose, and watering.

After the accident, his face had been a long time healing. It was then that his wife's elderly mother had gone to keep house and take care of the children. When he was well enough to be about again, he found his position as pastor of the little church waiting for him. The farmers and village people in his congregation, moved by his misfortune, by his faithful service and by his unblemished character, said they would rather have Mr. Fairchild, even with his scarred face, than any other minister. He was a good preacher, Aunt Minnie told us, "and the way he prayed was kind of exciting. I'd never known a preacher, not to live in the same house with him, before. And when he was in the pulpit, with everybody looking up at him, I felt the way his children did, kind of proud to think we had just eaten breakfast at the same table. I liked to call him 'Cousin Malcolm' before folks. One side of his face was all right, anyhow. You could see from that that he *had* been a good-looking man. In fact, probably one of those ministers that all the women—" Aunt Minnie paused, drew her lips together, and looked at us uncertainly.

Then she went back to the story as it happened—as it happened that first time I heard her tell it. "I thought he was a saint. Everybody out there did. That was all *they* knew. Of course, it made a person sick to look at that awful scar—the drooling corner of his mouth was the worst. He tried to keep that side of his face turned away from folks. But you always knew it was there. That was what kept him from marrying again, so Cousin Ella said. I heard her say lots of times that he knew no woman would touch any man who looked the way he did, not with a ten-foot pole.

"Well, the change of air did do me good. I got my appetite back, and ate a lot and played outdoors a lot with my cousins. They were younger than I (I had my sixteenth birthday there) but I still liked to play games. I got taller and laid on some weight. Cousin Ella used to say I grew as fast as the corn did. Their house stood at the edge of the village. Beyond it was one of those big cornfields they have out West. At the time when I first got there, the stalks were only up to a person's knee. You could see over their tops. But it grew like lightning, and before long, it was the way thick woods are here, way over your head, the stalks growing so close together it was dark under them.

"Cousin Ella told us youngsters that it was lots worse for getting lost in than woods, because there weren't any landmarks in it. One spot in a cornfield looked just like any other. 'You children keep out of it,' she used to tell us almost every day, *especially you girls.* It's no place for a decent girl. You could easy get so far from the house nobody could hear you if you hollered. There are plenty of men in this town that wouldn't like anything better than—' she never said what.

"In spite of what she said, my little cousins and I had figured out that if we went across one corner of the field, it would be a short-cut to the village, and sometimes, without letting on to Cousin Ella, we'd go that way. After the corn got really tall, the farmer stopped cultivating, and we soon beat a path in the loose dirt. The minute you were inside the field it was dark. You felt as if you were miles from anywhere. It sort of scared you. But in no time the path turned and brought you out on the far end of Main Street. Your breath was coming fast, maybe, but that was what made you like to do it.

"One day I missed the turn. Maybe I didn't keep my mind on it. Maybe it had rained and blurred the tramped-down look of the path. I don't know what. All of a sudden, I knew I was lost. And the minute I knew that, I began to run, just as hard as I could run. I couldn't help it, any more than you can help snatching your hand off a hot stove. I didn't even know I *was* running, till my heart was pounding so hard I had to stop.

"The minute I stood still, I could hear Cousin Ella saying, 'There are plenty of men in this town that wouldn't like anything better than—' I didn't know, not really, what she meant. But I knew she meant something horrible. I opened my mouth to scream. But I put both hands over my mouth to keep the scream in. If I made any noise, one of those men would hear me. I thought I heard one just behind me, and whirled around. And then I thought another one had tiptoed up behind me, the other way, and I spun around so fast I almost fell over. I stuffed my hands hard up against my mouth. And then—I couldn't help it—I ran again—but my legs were shaking so I soon had to stop. There I stood, scared to move for fear of rustling the corn and letting the men know where I was. My hair had come down, all over my face. I kept pushing it back and looking around, quick, to make sure one of the men hadn't found out where I was. Then I thought I saw a man coming toward me, and I ran away from him—and fell down, and burst some of the buttons off my dress, and was sick to my stomach—and thought I heard a man close to me and got up and staggered around, knocking into the corn because I couldn't even see where I was going.

"And then, off to one side, I saw Cousin Malcolm. Not a man— The minister. He was standing still, one hand up to his face, thinking. He hadn't heard me.

"I was so *terrible* glad to see him, instead of one of those men, I ran as fast as I could and just flung myself on him, to make myself feel how safe I was."

Aunt Minnie had become strangely agitated. Her hands were shaking, her face was crimson. She frightened us. We could not look away from her. As we waited for her to go on, I felt little spasms twitch at the muscles inside my body. "And what do you think that *saint*, that holy minister of the Gospel, did to an innocent child who clung to him for safety? The most terrible look came into his eyes—you girls are too young to know what he looked like. But once you're married, you'll find out. He grabbed hold of me—that dreadful face of his was *right on mine*—and began clawing the clothes off my back."

She stopped for a moment, panting. We were too frightened to speak. She went on: "He had torn my dress right down to the waist before I—then I *did* scream—all I could—and pulled away from him so hard I almost fell down, and ran and all of a sudden I came out of the corn, right in the backyard of the Fairchild house. The children were staring at the corn, and Cousin Ella ran out of the kitchen door. They had heard the screaming. Cousin Ella shrieked out, 'What is it? What happened? Did a man scare you?' And I said, 'Yes, yes, yes, a man—I ran—!' And then I fainted away. I must have. The next thing I knew I was on the sofa in the living-room and Cousin Ella was slapping my face with a wet towel."

She had to wet her lips with her tongue before she could go on. Her face was gray now. "There! That's the kind of thing girls' folks ought to tell them about—so they'll know what men are like."

She finished her story as if she were dismissing us. We wanted to go away, but we were too horrified to stir. Finally, one of the youngest girls asked in a low trembling voice, "Aunt Minnie, did you tell on him?"

"No, I was ashamed to," she said briefly. "They sent me home the next day, anyhow. Nobody ever said a word to me about it. And I never did either. Till now."

By what gets printed in some of the modern child psychology books, you would think that girls to whom such a story had been told would never develop normally. Yet, as far as I can remember what happened to the girls in that group, we all grew up about like anybody. Most of us married, some happily, some not so well. We kept house. We learned—more or less—how to live with our husbands; we had children and struggled to bring them up right—we went forward into life just as if we had never been warned not to.

Perhaps, young as we were that day, we had already had enough experience of life so that we were not quite blank paper for Aunt Minnie's frightening story. Whether we thought of it then or not, we couldn't have failed to see that at this very time Aunt Minnie had been married for ten years or more, comfortably and well married, too. Against what she tried by that story to brand into our minds, stood the cheerful homelife in

Sex Education [329]

that house, the good-natured, kind, hard-working husband, and the children—the three rough-and-tumble, nice little boys, so adored by their parents, and the sweet girl baby who died, of whom they could never speak without tears. It was such actual contact with adult life that probably kept generation after generation of girls from being scared by tales like Aunt Minnie's into a neurotic horror of living. . . .

Of course, since Aunt Minnie was so much older than we were, her boys grew up to be adolescents and young men while our children were still little enough so that our worries over them were nothing more serious than whooping cough and trying to get them to make their own beds. Two of our aunt's three boys followed, without losing their footing, the narrow path which leads across adolescence into normal adult life. But the middle one, Jake, repeatedly fell off into the morass. "Girl trouble," as the succinct family phrase put it. He was one of those boys who have "charm," whatever we mean by that, and he was always being snatched at by girls who would be "all wrong" for him to marry. And once, at nineteen, he ran away from home, whether with one of these girls or not we never heard, for through all her ups and downs with this son, Aunt Minnie tried fiercely to protect him from scandal that might cloud his later life.

Her husband had to stay on his job to earn the family living. She was the one who went to find Jake. When it was gossiped around that Jake was "in bad company" his mother drew some money from the family savings-bank account, and silent, white-cheeked, took the train to the city where rumor said he had gone.

Some weeks later he came back with her. With no girl. She had cleared him of that entanglement. As of others, which followed later. Her troubles seemed over when, at a "suitable" age, he fell in love with a "suitable" girl, married her and took her to live in our shire town, sixteen miles away, where he had a good position. Jake was always bright enough.

Sometimes, idly, people speculated as to what Aunt Minnie had seen that time she went after her runaway son, wondering where her search for him had taken her—very queer places for Aunt Minnie to be in, we imagined. And how could such an ignorant home-keeping woman ever have known what to say to an errant wilful boy to set him straight?

Well, of course, we reflected, watching her later struggles with Jake's erratic ways, she certainly could not have remained ignorant, after seeing over and over what she probably had; after talking with Jake about the things which, a good many times, must have come up with desperate openness between them.

She kept her own counsel. We never knew anything definite about the facts of those experiences of hers. But one day she told a group of us—all then married women—something which gave us a notion about what she had learned from them. . . .

We were hastily making a layette for a not especially welcome baby in a poor family. In those days, our town had no such thing as a district-nursing service. Aunt Minnie, a vigorous woman of fifty-five, had come in to help. As we sewed, we talked, of course; and because our daughters were near or in their teens, we were comparing notes about the bewildering responsibility of bringing up girls.

After a while, Aunt Minnie remarked: "Well, I hope you teach your girls some *sense*. From what I read, I know you're great on telling them 'the facts,' facts we never heard of when we were girls. Like as not, some facts I don't know, now. But knowing the facts isn't going to do them any more good than *not* knowing the facts ever did, unless they have some sense taught them too."

"What do you mean, Aunt Minnie?" one of us asked her uncertainly.

She reflected, threading a needle: "Well, I don't know but what the best way to tell you what I mean, is to tell you about something that happened to me, forty years ago. I've never said anything about it before. But I've thought about it a good deal. Maybe—"

She had hardly begun when I recognized the story—her visit to her Cousin Ella's midwestern home, the widower with his scarred face and saintly reputation and, very vividly, her getting lost in the great cornfield. I knew every word she was going to say—to the very end, I thought.

But no, I did not. Not at all.

She broke off, suddenly, to exclaim with impatience: "Wasn't I the big ninny? But not so big a ninny as that old cousin of mine. I could wring her neck for getting me in such a state. Only she didn't know any better, herself. That was the way they brought young people up in those days, scaring them out of their wits about the awfulness of getting lost, but not telling them a thing about how *not* to get lost. Or how to act, if they did.

"If I had had the sense I was born with, I'd have known that running my legs off in a zigzag was the worst thing I could do. I couldn't have been more than a few feet from the path when I noticed I wasn't on it. My tracks in the loose ploughed dirt must have been perfectly plain. If I'd h' stood still, and collected my wits, I could have looked down to see which way my footsteps went and just walked back over them to the path and gone on about my business.

"Now I ask you, if I'd been told how to do that, wouldn't it have been a lot better protection for me—if protection was what my cousin thought she wanted to give me—than to scare me so at the idea of being lost that I turned deef-dumb-and-blind when I thought I was?

"And anyhow that patch of corn wasn't as big as she let on. And she knew it wasn't. It was no more than a big field in a farming country. I was a well-grown girl of sixteen, as tall as I am now. If I couldn't have found the path, I could have just walked along one line of cornstalks—

straight—and I'd have come out somewhere in ten minutes. Fifteen at the most. Maybe not just where I wanted to go. But all right, safe, where decent folks were living."

She paused, as if she had finished. But at the inquiring blankness in our faces, she went on: "Well now, why isn't teaching girls—and boys, too, for the Lord's sake don't forget they need it as much as the girls—about this man-and-woman business, something like that? If you give them the idea—no matter whether it's *as* you tell them the facts, or as you *don't* tell them the facts, that it is such a terribly scary thing that if they take a step into it, something's likely to happen to them so awful that you're ashamed to tell them what—well, they'll lose their heads and run around like crazy things, first time they take one step away from the path.

"For they'll be trying out the paths, all right. You can't keep them from it. And a good thing, too. How else are they going to find out what it's like. Boys' and girls' going together is a path across one corner of growing up. And when they go together they're likely to get off the path some. Seems to me it's up to their folks to bring them up so, when they do, they don't start screaming and running in circles, but stand still, right where they are, and get their breath and figure out how to get back.

"And, anyhow, you don't tell 'em the truth about sex" (I was astonished to hear her use the actual word, tabu to women of her generation) "if they get the idea from you that it's all there is to living. It's not. If you don't get to where you want to go in it, well, there's a lot of landscape all around it a person can have a good time in.

"D'you know, I believe one thing that gives girls and boys the wrong idea is the way folks *look!* My old cousin's face, I can see her now, it was as red as a rooster's comb when she was telling me about men in that cornfield. I believe now she kind of *liked* to talk about it."

(Oh, Aunt Minnie—and yours! I thought.)

Someone asked, "But how *did* you get out, Aunt Minnie?"

She shook her head, laid down her sewing. "More foolishness. That minister my mother's cousin was keeping house for—her son-in-law—I caught sight of him, down along one of the aisles of cornstalks, looking down at the ground, thinking, the way he often did. And I was so glad to see him I rushed right up to him, and flung my arms around his neck and hugged him. He hadn't heard me coming. He gave a great start, put one arm around me and turned his face full toward me—I suppose for just a second he had forgotten how awful one side of it was. His expression, his eyes—well, you're all married women, you know how he looked, the way any able-bodied man thirty-six or seven, who'd been married and begotten children, would look—for a minute, anyhow, if a full-blooded girl of sixteen, who ought to have known better, flung herself at him without any warning, her hair tumbling down, her dress half-unbuttoned, and hugged him with all her might.

"I was what they called innocent in those days. That is, I knew just as little about what men are like as my folks could manage I should. But I was old enough to know all right what that look meant. And it gave me a start. But, of course, the real thing of it was that dreadful scar of his, so close to my face—that wet corner of his mouth, his eye drawn down with the red inside of the lower eyelid showing—

"It turned me so sick, I pulled away with all my might, so fast that I ripped one sleeve nearly loose, and let out a screech like a wildcat. And ran. Did I run! And in a minute, I was through the corn and had come out in the backyard of the house. I hadn't been more than a few feet from it, probably, any of the time. And then I fainted away. Girls were always fainting away; it was the way our corset-strings were pulled tight, I suppose, and then—oh, a lot of fuss."

"But, anyhow," she finished, picking up her work and going on, setting neat, firm stitches with steady hands, "there's one thing; I never told anybody it was Cousin Malcolm I had met in the cornfield. I told my old cousin that 'a man had scared me.' And nobody said anything more about it to me, not ever. That was the way they did in those days. They thought if they didn't let on about something, maybe it wouldn't have happened. I was sent back to Vermont right away and Cousin Malcolm went on being minister of the church."

"I've always been," said Aunt Minnie moderately, "kind of proud that I didn't go and ruin a man's life for just one second's slip-up. If you could have called it that. For it *would* have ruined him. You know how hard as stone people are about other folks' let-downs. If I'd have told, not one person in that town would have had any charity. Not one would have tried to understand. One slip, once, and they'd have pushed him down in the mud. If I had told, I'd have felt pretty bad about it, later—when I came to have more sense. But I declare, I can't see how I came to have the decency, dumb as I was then, to know that it wouldn't be fair. . . ."

It was not long after this talk that Aunt Minnie's elderly husband died, mourned by her, by all of us. She lived alone then. It was peaceful October weather for her, in which she kept a firm roundness of face and figure, as quiet-living countrywomen often do, on into her late sixties.

But then Jake, the boy who had girl trouble, had wife trouble. We heard he had taken to running after a young girl, or was it that she was running after him? It was something serious. For his nice wife had left him and come back with the children to live with her mother in our town. Poor Aunt Minnie used to go to see her for long talks which made them both cry. And she went to keep house for Jake, for months at a time.

She grew old, during those years. When finally she (or something) managed to get the marriage mended so that Jake's wife relented and went back to live with him, there was no trace left of her pleasant brisk freshness. She was stooped and slow-footed and shrunken. We, her kinspeople, although we would have given our lives for any one of our own children, wondered whether Jake was worth what it had cost his mother to—well, steady him, or reform him. Or perhaps just understand him. Whatever it took.

She came of a long-lived family and was able to go on keeping house for herself well into her eighties. Of course, we and the other neighbors stepped in often to make sure she was all right. Mostly, during those brief calls, the talk turned on nothing more vital than her geraniums. But one midwinter afternoon, sitting with her in front of her cozy stove, I chanced to speak in rather hasty blame of someone who had, I thought, acted badly. To my surprise this brought from her the story about the cornfield which she had evidently quite forgotten telling me, twice before.

This time she told it almost dreamily, swaying to and fro in her rocking-chair, her eyes fixed on the long slope of snow outside her window. When she came to the encounter with the minister she said, looking away from the distance and back into my eyes: "I know that I had been, all along, kind of *interested* in him, the way any girl as old as I was would be in any youngish man living in the same house with her. And a minister, too. They have to have the gift of gab so much more than most men, women get to thinking they are more alive than men who can't talk so well. I *thought* the reason I threw my arms around him was because I had been so scared. And I certainly had been scared by my old cousin's horrible talk about the cornfield being full of men waiting to grab girls. But that wasn't all the reason I flung myself at Malcolm Fairchild and hugged him. I know that now. Why in the world shouldn't I have been taught *some* notion of it then? 'Twould do girls good to know that they are just like everybody else—human nature *and* sex, all mixed up together. I didn't have to hug him. I wouldn't have, if he'd been dirty or fat and old, or chewed tobacco."

I stirred in my chair, ready to say, "But it's not so simple as all that to tell girls—" and she hastily answered my unspoken protest. "I know, I know, most of it can't be put into words. There just aren't any words to say something that's so both-ways-at-once all the time as this man-and-woman business. But look here, you know as well as I do that there are lots more ways than in words to teach young folks what you want 'em to know."

The old woman stopped her swaying rocker to peer far back into the past with honest eyes. "What was in my mind back there in the cornfield—partly, anyhow—was what had been there all the time I was living in the same house with Cousin Malcolm—that he had long straight legs, and broad shoulders, and lots of curly brown hair, and was nice and flat in front, and that one side of his face was good-looking. But most of all, that he and I were really alone, for the first time, without anybody to see us.

"I suppose, if it hadn't been for that dreadful scar, he'd have drawn me up, tight, and—most any man would—kissed me. I know how I must have looked, all red and hot and my hair down and my dress torn open. And, used as he was to big cornfields, he probably never dreamed that the reason I looked that way was because I was scared to be by myself in one. He may have thought—you know what he may have thought.

"Well—if his face had been like anybody's, when he looked at me the way he did, the way a man does look at a woman he wants to have, it would have scared me—some. I'd have cried, maybe. And probably he'd have kissed me again. You know how such things go. I might have come out of the cornfield halfway engaged to marry him. Why not? I was old enough, as people thought then. That would have been Nature. That was probably what he thought of, in that first instant.

"But what did I do? I had one look at his poor horrible face, and started back as though I'd stepped on a snake. And screamed and ran.

"What do you suppose *he* felt, left there in the corn? He must have been sure that I would tell everybody he had attacked me. He probably thought that when he came out and went back to the village he'd already be in disgrace and put out of the pulpit.

"But the worst must have been to find out, so rough, so plain from the way I acted—as if somebody had hit him with an ax—the way he would look to any woman he might try to get close to."

"That must have been," she drew a long breath, "well, pretty hard on him."

After a silence, she murmured pityingly, "Poor man!"

A girl's yearning for romance is heightened by the marriage of an older sister, and she can scarcely wait to leave the nest. Her mother frantically guards her remaining chick. In both these reminiscences of her childhood, but particularly in the second, a great woman writer pays tribute to her mother's strength, integrity, and "innate innocence."

COLETTE

The Abduction

"I CAN'T go on living like this!" exclaimed my mother. "Last night I dreamed again that you were being kidnapped. Three times I climbed the stairs to your door, and I got no sleep at all."

I looked at her with compassion, for she seemed both tired and anxious. I said nothing, however, as I knew of no cure for her anxiety.

"And is that all you care about it, little monstress?"

"Well, hang it all, mother! What do you want me to say? You look as though you blamed me for its being only a dream."

She raised her arms to heaven, and ran to the door. As she went she caught the cord of her pince-nez round the key of a drawer, then the ribbon of her lorgnette in the latch of the door, and entangled her knitted shawl in the gothic intricacies of a Second Empire chair. Repressing half an oath, she disappeared with an indignant glance at me, murmuring: "Nine years old! . . . And that's how she answers me when I speak of serious matters!"

My half-sister's marriage had recently left me in possession of her bedroom, the room on the first floor, starred with cornflowers upon a pearl-grey background.

Deserting my childhood's lair—formerly a porter's den, with huge beams and a tiled floor, perched over the carriage entrance and communicating with my mother's bedroom—I had been sleeping for four weeks in the bed that I had never even dared to covet, the bed whose white lace curtains lined with pitiless blue were held back by rosettes of burnished lead. The little cupboard-dressing room belonged to me too, and I could lean out of each of the windows with simulated melancholy and disdain at the hour when the small Blancvillains and the Trinitets passed by, gnawing their tea-time slices of bread liberally piled with red beans pickled in wine sauce.

At every opportunity I would say, "I'm going up to my room . . . Céline has left the shutters in my room open."

But my happiness was threatened: my mother was anxious and ever on the watch. Since my sister's marriage she was one child short, and at that time the front pages of the newspapers carried the picture of some young girl or other who had been abducted and kept in hiding. A tramp, refused admittance by our cook as night was falling, had refused to go away and stuck his stick in the jamb of the door until my father arrived on the scene. Finally some gipsies, encountered on the road, had offered with flashing smiles and looks of ill-concealed hatred to buy my hair; and M. Demange, an old gentleman who never spoke to anyone, had unbent so far as to offer me comfits from his snuffbox.

"None of which is really very serious," my father assured my mother.

"Oh, you! So long as no one interferes with your after-luncheon cigarette and your game of dominoes, you don't even stop to think that nowadays the Little One sleeps upstairs, and that a staircase, the dining-room, a passage and the sitting-room lie between her and my bedroom. I've had enough of this perpetual anxiety over my daughters. Already the eldest has gone off with that man. . . ."

"How, gone off?"

"Oh, well, married him if you prefer it. Married or not married, she has none the less gone away with a man whom she hardly knows."

She gave my father a look of loving suspicion.

"And after all, you, what have you to do with me? You aren't even a relation!"

During mealtimes I revelled in the veiled allusions, couched in the language so dear to parents, wherein an enigmatic term replaces the word in common use, and in which pursed lips and dramatic throat-clearings attract and rivet the attention of children.

"At Ghent, when I was young," my mother would relate, "one of our friends who was only sixteen was abducted—she was indeed! And, what's more, in a carriage and pair! The next day . . . Well . . . hum . . . naturally! There could be no question of returning her to her family. There are some—how shall I put it?—some breaches. . . . In the end they got married. There was no other way out."

"There was no other way out."

Imprudent words! A small old-fashioned engraving, hanging in a dark passage, suddenly interested me. It represented a post-chaise, harnessed to two queer horses with necks like fabulous beasts. In front of the gaping coach door a young man, dressed in taffeta, was carrying on one arm with the greatest of ease a fainting young woman. Her little mouth forming an O, and the ruffled petticoats framing her charming legs, strove to express extreme terror. *"The Abduction!"* My innocent imagination was

The Abduction

pleasantly stirred by the word and the picture.

One windy night, when the loose-fitting doors in the farmyard were banging and the loft was groaning over my head in the gusts that rushed in under the edges of the badly joined slates, sweeping it from west to east and playing tunes like a wheezy mouth-organ, I was sleeping soundly, worn out by a Thursday spent in the fields shaking down chestnuts and celebrating the brewing of the new cider. Did I dream that my door creaked on its hinges? So many hinges, so many weather-cocks were creaking around me. Two arms, singularly adept at lifting a sleeping form, encircled my waist and my neck, at the same time gathering the blankets and the sheet about me. My cheek felt the colder air of the stairs, a muffled heavy step descended slowly, rocking me at each pace with a gentle motion. Did I really wake? I doubt it. Only a dream could waft a little girl right out of her childhood and place her, neither surprised nor unwilling, in the very midst of a hypocritical and adventurous adolescence. Only a dream could thus turn a loving child into the ungrateful creature that she will become to-morrow, the crafty accomplice of the stranger, the forgetful one who will leave her mother's house without a backward glance. In such wise was I departing for the land where a post-chaise, amid the jangling of bells, stops before a church to deposit a young man dressed in taffeta and a young woman whose ruffled skirts suggest the rifled petals of a rose. I did not cry out. The two arms were so gentle, so careful to hold me close enough to protect my dangling feet at every doorway. A familiar rhythm actually seemed to lull me to sleep in the abducting arms.

When day broke, I failed to recognise my old garret, encumbered now with ladders and broken furniture, whither my anxious mother had borne me in the night, like a mother cat who secretly changes the hiding place of her little one. Tired out, she slept, and awoke only when the walls of my forgotten cell rang with my piercing cry:

"Mother! Come quick! I've been abducted!"

COLETTE

Laughter

SHE WAS EASILY MOVED to laughter, a youthful, rather shrill laughter that brought tears to her eyes, and which she would afterwards deplore as inconsistent with the dignity of a mother burdened with the care of four children and financial worries. She would master her paroxysms of mirth, scolding herself severely, "Come, now, come! . . ." and then fall to laughing again till her pince-nez trembled on her nose.

We would jealously compete in our efforts to evoke her laughter, especially as we grew old enough to observe in her face, as the years succeeded each other, the ever-increasing shadow of anxiety for the morrow, a kind of distress which sobered her whenever she thought of the fate of her penniless children, of her precarious health, of old age that was slowing the steps—a single leg and two crutches—of her beloved companion. When she was silent, my mother resembled all mothers who are scared at the thought of poverty and death. But speech brought back to her features an invincible youthfulness. Though she might grow thin with sorrow, she never spoke sadly. She would escape, as it were in one bound, from a painful reverie, and pointing her knitting needle at her husband would exclaim:

"What? Just you try to die first, and you'll see!"

"I shall do my best, dear heart," he would answer.

She would glare at him as savagely as if he had carelessly trodden on a pelargonium cutting or broken the little gold-enamelled Chinese teapot.

"Isn't that just like you! You've got all the selfishness of the Funels and the Colettes combined! Oh, why did I ever marry you?"

"Because, my beloved, I threatened to blow out your brains if you didn't."

"True enough. Even in those days, you see, you thought only of your-

[338]

self! And now here you are talking of nothing less than of dying before me. All I say is, only let me see you try!"

He did try, and succeeded at the first attempt. He died in his seventy-fourth year, holding the hands of his beloved, and fixing on her weeping eyes a gaze that gradually lost its colour, turned milky blue and faded like a sky veiled in mist. He was given the handsomest of village funerals, a coffin of yellow wood covered only by an old tunic riddled with wounds—the tunic he had worn as a captain in the 1st Zouaves—and my mother accompanied him steadily to the grave's edge, very small and resolute beneath her widow's veil, and murmuring under her breath words of love that only he must hear.

We brought her back to the house, and there she promptly lost her temper with her new mourning, the cumbersome crape that caught on the keys of doors and presses, the cashmere dress that stifled her. She sat resting in the drawing-room, near the big green chair in which my father would never sit again and which the dog had already joyfully invaded. She was dry-eyed, flushed and feverish and kept on repeating:

"Oh, how hot it is! Heavens! The heat of this black stuff! Don't you think I might change now, into my blue sateen?"

"Well . . ."

"Why not? Because of my mourning? But I simply loathe black! For one thing, it's melancholy. Why should I present a sad and unpleasant sight to everyone I meet? What connection is there between this cashmere and crape and my feelings? Don't let me ever see you in mourning for me! You know well enough that I only like you to wear pink, and some shades of blue."

She got up hastily, took several steps towards an empty room and stopped abruptly:

"Ah! . . . Of course. . . ."

She came back and sat down again, admitting with a simple and humble gesture that she had, for the first time that day, forgotten that *he* was dead.

"Shall I get you something to drink, mother? Wouldn't you like to go to bed?"

"Of course not. Why should I? I'm not ill!"

She sat there and began to learn patience, staring at the floor, where a dusty track from the door of the sitting-room to the door of the empty bedroom had been marked by rough, heavy shoes.

A kitten came in, circumspect and trustful, a common and irresistible little kitten four or five months old. He was acting a dignified part for his own edification, pacing grandly, his tail erect as a candle, in imitation of lordly males. But a sudden and unexpected somersault landed him head over heels at our feet, where he took fright at his own temerity, rolled himself into a ball, stood up on his hind legs, danced sideways, arched his back, and then spun round like a top.

"Look at him, oh, do look at him, Minet-Chéri! Goodness! Isn't he funny!"

And she laughed, sitting there in her mourning, laughed her shrill, young girl's laugh, clapping her hands with delight at the kitten. Then, of a sudden, searing memory stemmed that brilliant cascade and dried the tears of laughter in my mother's eyes. Yet she offered no excuse for having laughed, either on that day, or on the days that followed; for though she had lost the man she passionately loved, in her kindness for us she remained among us just as she always had been, accepting her sorrow as she would have accepted the advent of a long and dreary season, but welcoming from every source the fleeting benediction of joy. So she lived on, swept by shadow and sunshine, bowed by bodily torments, resigned, unpredictable and generous, rich in children, flowers and animals like a fruitful domain.

"I want to go on living even after my death."

During the Nazi terror, a gifted Jewish girl on the brink of womanhood bares her soul in a diary addressed to the imaginary "Kitty." Despite the grim setting, she tells a universal story of healthy adolescence.

ANNE FRANK

from *The Diary of a Young Girl*

Saturday, 7 November, 1942

Dear Kitty,

Mummy is frightfully irritable and that always seems to herald unpleasantness for me. Is it just chance that Daddy and Mummy never rebuke Margot and that they always drop on me for everything? Yesterday evening, for instance: Margot was reading a book with lovely drawings in it; she got up and went upstairs, put the book down ready to go on with it later. I wasn't doing anything, so picked up the book and started looking at the pictures. Margot came back, saw "her" book in my hands, wrinkled her forehead and asked for the book back. Just because I wanted to look a little further on, Margot got more and more angry. Then Mummy joined in: "Give the book to Margot; she was reading it," she said. Daddy came into the room. He didn't even know what it was all about, but saw the injured look on Margot's face and promptly dropped on me: "I'd like to see what you'd say if Margot ever started looking at one of your books!" I gave way at once, laid the book down, and left the room—offended, as they thought. It so happened I was neither offended nor cross, just miserable. It wasn't right of Daddy to judge without knowing what the squabble was about. I would have given Margot the book myself, and much more quickly, if Mummy and Daddy hadn't interfered. They took Margot's part at once, as though she were the victim of some great injustice.

It's obvious that Mummy would stick up for Margot; she and Margot always do back each other up. I'm so used to that that I'm utterly indifferent to both Mummy's jawing and Margot's moods.

I love them; but only because they are Mummy and Margot. With Daddy it's different. If he holds Margot up as an example, approves of what she does, praises and caresses her, then something gnaws at me inside, because I adore Daddy. He is the one I look up to. I don't love anyone in the world but him. He doesn't notice that he treats Margot differently from me. Now Margot is just the prettiest, sweetest, most beautiful girl in the world. But all the same I feel I have some right to be taken seriously too. I have always been the dunce, the ne'er-do-well of the family, I've always had to pay double for my deeds, first with the scolding and then again because of the way my feelings are hurt. Now I'm not satisfied with this apparent favoritism any more. I want something from Daddy that he is not able to give me.

I'm not jealous of Margot, never have been. I don't envy her good looks or her beauty. It is only that I long for Daddy's real love: not only as his child, but for me—Anne, myself.

I cling to Daddy because it is only through him that I am able to retain the remnant of family feeling. Daddy doesn't understand that I need to give vent to my feelings over Mummy sometimes. He doesn't want to talk about it; he simply avoids anything which might lead to remarks about Mummy's failings. Just the same, Mummy and her failings are something I find harder to bear than anything else. I don't know how to keep it all to myself. I can't always be drawing attention to her untidiness, her sarcasm, and her lack of sweetness, neither can I believe that I'm always in the wrong.

We are exact opposites in everything; so naturally we are bound to run up against each other. I don't pronounce judgment on Mummy's character, for that is something I can't judge. I only look at her as a mother, and she just doesn't succeed in being that to me; I have to be my own mother. I've drawn myself apart from them all; I am my own skipper and later on I shall see where I come to land. All this comes about particularly because I have in my mind's eye an image of what a perfect mother and wife should be; and in her whom I must call "Mother" I find no trace of that image.

I am always making resolutions not to notice Mummy's bad example. I want to see only the good side of her and to seek in myself what I cannot find in her. But it doesn't work; and the worst of it is that neither Daddy nor Mummy understands this gap in my life, and I blame them for it. I wonder if anyone can ever succeed in making their children absolutely content.

Sometimes I believe that God wants to try me, both now and later on; I must become good through my own efforts, without examples and without good advice. Then later on I shall be all the stronger. Who besides me will ever read these letters? From whom but myself shall I get comfort? As I need comforting often, I frequently feel weak, and dissatisfied with myself; my shortcomings are too great. I know this, and every day I try to improve myself, again and again.

from *The Diary of a Young Girl*

My treatment varies so much. One day Anne is so sensible and is allowed to know everything; and the next day I hear that Anne is just a silly little goat who doesn't know anything at all and imagines that she's learned a wonderful lot from books. I'm not a baby or a spoiled darling any more, to be laughed at, whatever she does. I have my own views, plans, and ideas, though I can't put them into words yet. Oh, so many things bubble up inside me as I lie in bed, having to put up with people I'm fed up with, who always misinterpret my intentions. That's why in the end I always come back to my diary. That is where I start and finish, because Kitty is always patient. I'll promise her that I shall persevere, in spite of everything, and find my own way through it all, and swallow my tears. I only wish I could see the results already or occasionally receive encouragement from someone who loves me.

Don't condemn me; remember rather that sometimes I too can reach the bursting point.

Yours, Anne

Saturday, 30 January, 1943

Dear Kitty,

I'm boiling with rage, and yet I mustn't show it. I'd like to stamp my feet, scream, give Mummy a good shaking, cry, and I don't know what else, because of the horrible words, mocking looks, and accusations which are leveled at me repeatedly every day, and find their mark, like shafts from a tightly strung bow, and which are just as hard to draw from my body.

I would like to shout to Margot, Van Daan, Dussel—and Daddy too—"Leave me in peace, let me sleep one night at least without my pillow being wet with tears, my eyes burning and my head throbbing. Let me get away from it all, preferably away from the world!" But I can't do that, they mustn't know my despair, I can't let them see the wounds which they have caused, I couldn't bear their sympathy and their kindhearted jokes, it would only make me want to scream all the more. If I talk, everyone thinks I'm showing off; when I'm silent they think I'm ridiculous; rude if I answer, sly if I get a good idea, lazy if I'm tired, selfish if I eat a mouthful more than I should, stupid, cowardly, crafty, etc., etc. The whole day long I hear nothing else but that I am an insufferable baby, and although I laugh about it and pretend not to take any notice, I *do* mind. I would like to ask God to give me a different nature, so that I didn't put everyone's back up. But that can't be done. I've got the nature that has been given to me and I'm sure it can't be bad. I do my very best to please everybody, far more than they'd ever guess. I try to laugh it all off, because I don't want to let them see my trouble. More than once, after a whole string of undeserved rebukes, I have flared up at Mummy: "I don't care what you say anyhow. Leave me alone: I'm a hopeless case anyway." Naturally, I was then told I was rude and was virtually ignored for two days; and then, all at once, it was quite forgotten, and I was treated like everyone else again. It is impossible for me to be all sugar one day and spit venom the next. I'd rather choose the golden mean (which is not so golden), keep my thoughts to myself, and try for *once* to be just as disdainful to them as they are to me. Oh, if only I could!

Yours, Anne

Friday, 2 April, 1943

Dear Kitty,

Oh dear: I've got another terrible black mark against my name. I was lying in bed yesterday evening waiting for Daddy to come and say my prayers with me, and wish me good night, when Mummy came into my room, sat on my bed, and asked very nicely, "Anne, Daddy can't come yet, shall I say your prayers with you tonight?" "No, Mummy," I answered.

Mummy got up, paused by my bed for a moment, and walked slowly towards the door. Suddenly she turned around, and with a distorted look on her face said, "I don't want to be cross, love cannot be forced." There were tears in her eyes as she left the room.

I lay still in bed, feeling at once that I had been horrible to push her away so rudely. But I knew too that I couldn't have answered differently. It simply wouldn't work. I felt sorry for Mummy; very, very sorry, because I had seen for the first time in my life that she minds my coldness. I saw the look of sorrow on her face when she spoke of love not being forced. It is hard to speak the truth, and yet it is the truth: she herself has pushed me away, her tactless remarks and her crude jokes, which I don't find at all funny, have now made me insensitive to any love from her side. Just as I shrink at her hard words, so did her heart when she realized that the love between us was gone. She cried half the night and hardly slept at all. Daddy doesn't look at me and if he does for a second, then I read in his eyes the words: "How can you be so unkind, how can you bring yourself to cause your mother such sorrow?"

They expect me to apologize; but this is something I can't apologize for because I spoke the truth and Mummy will have to know it sooner or later anyway. I seem, and indeed am, indifferent both to Mummy's tears and Daddy's looks, because for the first time they are both aware of something which I have always felt. I can only feel sorry for Mummy, who has now had to discover that I have adopted her own attitude. For myself, I remain silent and aloof; and I shall not shrink from the truth any longer, because the longer it is put off, the more difficult it will be for them when they do hear it.

Yours, Anne

from *The Diary of a Young Girl*

Wednesday, 5 January, 1944

Dear Kitty,

 . . . Yesterday I read an article about blushing by Sis Heyster. This article might have been addressed to me personally. Although I don't blush very easily, the other things in it certainly all fit me. She writes roughly something like this—that a girl in the years of puberty becomes quiet within and begins to think about the wonders that are happening to her body.

I experience that, too, and that is why I get the feeling lately of being embarrassed about Margot, Mummy, and Daddy. Funnily enough, Margot, who is much more shy than I am, isn't at all embarrassed.

I think what is happening to me is so wonderful, and not only what can be seen on my body, but all that is taking place inside. I never discuss myself or any of these things with anybody; that is why I have to talk to myself about them.

Each time I have a period—and that has only been three times—I have the feeling that in spite of all the pain, unpleasantness, and nastiness, I have a sweet secret, and that is why, although it is nothing but a nuisance to me in a way, I always long for the time that I shall feel that secret within me again.

Sis Heyster also writes that girls of this age don't feel quite certain of themselves, and discover that they themselves are individuals with ideas, thoughts, and habits. After I came here, when I was just fourteen, I began to think about myself sooner than most girls, and to know that I am a "person." Sometimes, when I lie in bed at night, I have a terrible desire to feel my breasts and to listen to the quiet rhythmic beat of my heart.

I already had these kinds of feelings subconsciously before I came here, because I remember that once when I slept with a girl friend I had a strong desire to kiss her, and that I did do so. I could not help being terribly inquisitive over her body, for she had always kept it hidden from me. I asked her whether, as a proof of our friendship, we should feel one another's breasts, but she refused. I go into ecstasies every time I see the naked figure of a woman, such as Venus, for example. It strikes me as so wonderful and exquisite that I have difficulty in stopping the tears rolling down my cheeks.

If only I had a girl friend!

Yours, Anne

Thursday, 6 January, 1944

Dear Kitty,

My longing to talk to someone became so intense that somehow or other I took it into my head to choose Peter.

Sometimes if I've been upstairs into Peter's room during the day, it always struck me as very snug, but because Peter is so retiring and would never turn anyone out who became a nuisance, I never dared stay long, because I was afraid he might think me a bore. I tried to think of an excuse to stay in his room and get him talking, without it being too noticeable, and my chance came yesterday. Peter has a mania for crossword puzzles at the moment and hardly does anything else. I helped him with them and we soon sat opposite each other at his little table, he on the chair and me on the divan.

It gave me a queer feeling each time I looked into his deep blue eyes, and he sat there with that mysterious laugh playing round his lips. I was able to read his inward thoughts. I could see on his face that look of helplessness and uncertainty as to how to behave, and, at the same time, a trace of his sense of manhood. I noticed his shy manner and it made me feel very gentle; I couldn't refrain from meeting those dark eyes again and again, and with my whole heart I almost beseeched him: oh, tell me, what is going on inside you, oh, can't you look beyond this ridiculous chatter?

But the evening passed and nothing happened, except that I told him about blushing—naturally not what I have written, but just so that he would become more sure of himself as he grew older.

When I lay in bed and thought over the whole situation, I found it far from encouraging, and the idea that I should beg for Peter's patronage was simply repellent. One can do a lot to satisfy one's longings, which certainly sticks out in my case, for I have made up my mind to go and sit with Peter more often and to get him talking somehow or other.

Whatever you do, don't think I'm in love with Peter—not a bit of it! If the Van Daans had had a daughter instead of a son, I should have tried to make friends with her too. . . .

Monday, 24 January, 1944

Dear Kitty,

Something has happened to me; or rather, I can hardly describe it as an event, except that I think it is pretty crazy. Whenever anyone used to speak of sexual problems at home or at school, it was something either mysterious or revolting. Words which had any bearing on the subject were whispered, and often if someone didn't understand he was laughed at. It struck me as very odd and I thought, "Why are people so secretive and tiresome when they talk about these things?" But as I didn't think that I could change things, I kept my mouth shut as much as possible, or sometimes asked girl friends for information. When I had learned quite a lot and had also spoken about it with my parents, Mummy said one day, "Anne, let me give you some good advice; never speak about this subject to boys and don't reply if they begin about it." I remember exactly what my answer was: I said, "No, of course not! The very idea!"

from *The Diary of a Young Girl* [347]

And there it remained.

When we first came here, Daddy often told me about things that I would really have preferred to hear from Mummy, and I found out the rest from books and things I picked up from conversations. Peter Van Daan was never as tiresome over this as the boys at school—once or twice at first perhaps—but he never tried to get me talking.

Mrs. Van Daan told us that she had never talked about these things to Peter, and for all she knew neither had her husband. Apparently she didn't even know how much he knew.

Yesterday, when Margot, Peter, and I were peeling potatoes, somehow the conversation turned to Boche. "We still don't know what sex Boche is, do we?" I asked.

"Yes, certainly," Peter answered. "He's a tom."

I began to laugh. "A tomcat that's expecting, that's marvelous!"

Peter and Margot laughed too over this silly mistake. You see, two months ago, Peter had stated that Boche would soon be having a family, her tummy was growing visibly. However, the fatness appeared to come from the many stolen bones, because the children didn't seem to grow fast, let alone make their appearance!

Peter just had to defend himself. "No," he said, "you can go with me yourself to look at him. Once when I was playing around with him, I noticed quite clearly that he's a tom."

I couldn't control my curiosity, and went with him to the warehouse. Boche, however, was not receiving visitors, and was nowhere to be seen. We waited for a while, began to get cold, and went upstairs again. Later in the afternoon I heard Peter go downstairs for the second time. I mustered up all my courage to walk through the silent house alone, and reached the warehouse. Boche stood on the packing table playing with Peter, who had just put him on the scales to weigh him.

"Hello, do you want to see him?" He didn't make any lengthy preparations, but picked up the animal, turned him over on to his back, deftly held his head and paws together, and the lesson began. "These are the male organs, these are just a few stray hairs, and that is his bottom." The cat did another half turn and was standing on his white socks once more.

If any other boy had shown me "the male organs," I would never have looked at him again. But Peter went on talking quite normally on what is otherwise such a painful subject, without meaning anything unpleasant, and finally put me sufficiently at my ease for me to be normal too. We played with Boche, amused ourselves, chattered together, and then sauntered through the large warehouse towards the door.

"Usually, when I want to know something, I find it in some book or other, don't you?" I asked.

"Why on earth? I just ask upstairs. My father knows more than me and has had more experience in such things."

We were already on the stair, so I kept my mouth shut after that.

"Things may alter," as Brer Rabbit said. Yes. Really I shouldn't have discussed these things in such a normal way with a girl. I know too definitely that Mummy didn't mean it that way when she warned me not to discuss the subject with boys. I wasn't quite my usual self for the rest of the day though, in spite of everything. When I thought over our talk, it still seemed rather odd. But at least I'm wiser about one thing, that there really are young people—and of the opposite sex too—who can discuss these things naturally without making fun of them.

I wonder if Peter really does ask his parents much. Would he honestly behave with them as he did with me yesterday? Ah, what would I know about it!

Yours, Anne

Sunday, 13 February, 1944

Dear Kitty,

Since Saturday a lot has changed for me. It came about like this. I longed—and am still longing—but . . . now something has happened, which has made it a little, just a little, less.

To my great joy—I will be quite honest about it—already this morning I noticed that Peter kept looking at me all the time. Not in the ordinary way, I don't know how, I just can't explain.

I used to think that Peter was in love with Margot, but yesterday I suddenly had the feeling that it is not so. I made a special effort not to look at him too much, because whenever I did, he kept on looking too and then—yes, then—it gave me a lovely feeling inside, but which I mustn't feel too often.

I desperately want to be alone. Daddy has noticed that I'm not quite my usual self, but I really can't tell him everything. "Leave me in peace, leave me alone," that's what I'd like to keep crying out all the time. Who knows, the day may come when I'm left alone more than I would wish!

Yours, Anne

Tuesday, 28 March, 1944

Dearest Kitty,

I could write a lot more about politics, but I have heaps of other things to tell you today. First, Mummy has more or less forbidden me to go upstairs so often, because, according to her, Mrs. Van Daan is jealous. Secondly, Peter has invited Margot to join us upstairs; I don't know whether it's just out of politeness or whether he really means it. Thirdly, I went and asked Daddy if he thought I need pay any regard to Mrs. Van Daan's jealousy, and he didn't think so. What next? Mummy is cross, perhaps jealous too. Daddy doesn't grudge us these times together, and thinks it's nice that we get on so well. Margot is fond of Peter too,

from *The Diary of a Young Girl*

but feels that two's company and three's a crowd.

Mummy thinks that Peter is in love with me; quite frankly, I only wish he were, then we'd be quits and really be able to get to know each other. She also says that he keeps on looking at me. Now, I suppose that's true, but still I can't help it if he looks at my dimples and we wink at each other occasionally, can I?

I'm in a very difficult position. Mummy is against me and I'm against her, Daddy closes his eyes and tries not to see the silent battle between us. Mummy is sad, because she does really love me, while I'm not in the least bit sad, because I don't think she understands. And Peter—I don't want to give Peter up, he's such a darling. I admire him so; it can grow into something beautiful between us; why do the "old 'uns" have to poke their noses in all the time? Luckily I'm quite used to hiding my feelings and I manage extremely well not to let them see how mad I am about him. Will he ever say anything? Will I ever feel his cheek against mine.

. . . When he lies with his head on his arm with his eyes closed, then he is still a child; when he plays with Boche, he is loving; when he carries potatoes or anything heavy, then he is strong; when he goes and watches the shooting, or looks for burglars in the darkness, then he is brave; and when he is so awkward and clumsy, then he is just a pet.

I like it much better if he explains something to me than when I have to teach him; I would really adore him to be my superior in almost everything.

What do we care about the two mothers? Oh, but if only he would speak!

Yours, Anne

Monday, 17 April, 1944

Dear Kitty,

Do you think that Daddy and Mummy would approve of my sitting and kissing a boy on a divan—a boy of seventeen and a half and a girl of just under fifteen? I don't really think they would, but I must rely on myself over this. . . .

Tuesday, 2 May, 1944

Dear Kitty,

On Saturday evening I asked Peter whether he thought that I ought to tell Daddy a bit about us; when we'd discussed it a little, he came to the conclusion that I should. I was glad, for it shows that he's an honest boy. As soon as I got downstairs I went off with Daddy to get some water; and while we were on the stairs I said, "Daddy, I expect you've gathered that when we're together Peter and I don't sit miles apart. Do you think it's wrong?" Daddy didn't reply immediately, then said, "No, I don't think it's wrong, but you must be careful, Anne; you're in such a confined space here." When we went upstairs, he said something else on the same lines. On Sunday morning he called me to him and said, "Anne, I have thought more about what you said." I felt scared already. "It's not really very right—here in this house, I thought that you were just pals. Is Peter in love?"

"Oh, of course not," I replied.

"You know that I understand both of you, but you must be the one to hold back. Don't go upstairs so often, don't encourage him more than you can help. It is the man who is always the active one in these things; the woman can hold him back. It is quite different under normal circumstances, when you are free, you see other boys and girls, you can get away sometimes, play games and do all kinds of other things; but here, if you're together a lot, and you want to get away, you can't; you see each other every hour of the day—in fact, all the time. Be careful, Anne, and don't take it too seriously!"

"I don't, Daddy, but Peter is a decent boy, really a nice boy!"

"Yes, but he is not a strong character; he can be easily influenced, for good, but also for bad; I hope for his sake that his good side will remain uppermost, because, by nature, that is how he is."

We talked on for a bit and agreed that Daddy should talk to him too.

On Sunday morning in the attic he asked, "And have you talked to your father, Anne?"

"Yes," I replied, "I'll tell you about it. Daddy doesn't think it's bad, but he says that here, where we're so close together all the time, clashes may easily arise."

"But we agreed, didn't we, never to quarrel; and I'm determined to stick to it!"

"So will I, Peter, but Daddy didn't think that it was like this, he just thought we were pals; do you think that we still can be?"

"I can—what about you?"

"Me too, I told Daddy that I trusted you. I do trust you, Peter, just as much as I trust Daddy, and I believe you to be worthy of it. You are, aren't you, Peter?"

"I hope so." (He was very shy and rather red in the face.)

"I believe in you, Peter," I went on, "I believe that you have good qualities, and that you'll get on in the world."

After that, we talked about other things. Later I said, "If we come out of here, I know quite well that you won't bother about me any more!"

He flared right up. "That's not true, Anne, oh no, I won't let you think that of me!"

Then I was called away.

Daddy has talked to him; he told me about it today. "Your father thought that the friendship might develop into love sooner or later,"

from *The Diary of a Young Girl*

he said. But I replied that we would keep a check on ourselves.

Daddy doesn't want me to go upstairs so much in the evenings now, but I don't want that. Not only because I like being with Peter; I have told him that I trust him. I do trust him and I want to show him that I do, which can't happen if I stay downstairs through lack of trust.

No, I'm going! . . .

Friday, 5 May, 1944

Dear Kitty,

Daddy is not pleased with me; he thought that after our talk on Sunday I automatically wouldn't go upstairs every evening. He doesn't want any "necking," a word I can't bear. It was bad enough talking about it, why must he make it so unpleasant now? I shall talk to him today. Margot has given me some good advice, so listen; this is roughly what I want to say:

"I believe, Daddy, that you expect a declaration from me, so I will give it you. You are disappointed in me, as you had expected more reserve from me, and I suppose you want me to be just as a fourteen-year-old should be. But that's where you're mistaken!

"Since we've been here, from July 1942 until a few weeks ago, I can assure you that I haven't had an easy time. If you only knew how I cried in the evenings, how unhappy I was, how lonely I felt, then you would understand that I want to go upstairs!

"I have now reached the stage that I can live entirely on my own, without Mummy's support or anyone else's for that matter. But it hasn't just happened in a night; it's been a bitter, hard struggle and I've shed many a tear, before I became as independent as I am now. You can laugh at me and not believe me, but that can't harm me. I know that I'm a separate individual and I don't feel in the least bit responsible to any of you. I am only telling you this because I thought that otherwise you might think that I was underhand, but I don't have to give an account of my deeds to anyone but myself.

"When I was in difficulties you all closed your eyes and stopped up your ears and didn't help me; on the contrary, I received nothing but warnings not to be so boisterous. I was only boisterous so as not to be miserable all the time. I was reckless so as not to hear that persistent voice within me continually. I played a comedy for a year and a half, day in, day out, I never grumbled, never lost my cue, nothing like that—and now, now the battle is over. I have won! I am independent both in mind and body. I don't need a mother any more, for all this conflict has made me strong.

"And now, now that I'm on top of it, now that I know that I've fought the battle, now I want to be able to go on in my own way too, the way that I think is right. You can't and mustn't regard me as fourteen, for all these troubles have made me older; I shall not be sorry for what I have done, but shall act as I think I can. You can't coax me into not going upstairs; *either* you forbid it, *or* you trust me through thick and thin, but then leave me in peace as well!"

Yours, Anne

Saturday, 6 May, 1944

Dear Kitty,

I put a letter, in which I wrote what I explained to you yesterday, in Daddy's pocket before supper yesterday. After reading it, he was, according to Margot, very upset for the rest of the evening. . . .

Sunday morning, 7 May, 1944

Dear Kitty,

Daddy and I had a long talk yesterday afternoon, I cried terribly and he joined in. Do you know what he said to me, Kitty? "I have received many letters in my life, but this is certainly the most unpleasant! You, Anne, who have received such love from your parents, you, who have parents who are always ready to help you, who have always defended you whatever it might be, can you talk of feeling no responsibility towards us? You feel wronged and deserted; no, Anne, you have done us a great injustice!

"Perhaps you didn't mean it like that, but it is what you wrote; no, Anne, we haven't deserved such a reproach as this!"

Oh, I have failed miserably; this is certainly the worst thing I've ever done in my life. I was only trying to show off with my crying and my tears, just trying to appear big, so that he would respect me. Certainly, I have had a lot of unhappiness, but to accuse the good Pim, who has done and still does do everything for me—no, that was too low for words.

It's right that for once I've been taken down from my inaccessible pedestal, that my pride has been shaken a bit, for I was becoming much too taken up with myself again. What Miss Anne does is by no means always right! Anyone who can cause such unhappiness to someone else, someone he professes to love, and on purpose, too, is low, very low!

And the way Daddy has forgiven me makes me feel more than ever ashamed of myself, he is going to throw the letter in the fire and is so sweet to me now, just as if he had done something wrong. No, Anne, you still have a tremendous lot to learn, begin by doing that first, instead of looking down on others and accusing them!

I have had a lot of sorrow, but who hasn't at my age? I have played the clown a lot too, but I was hardly conscious of it; I felt lonely, but hardly ever in despair! I ought to be deeply ashamed of myself, and indeed I am.

What is done cannot be undone, but one can prevent it happening again. I want to start from the beginning again and it can't be difficult, now that I have Peter. With him to support me, I can and will!

I'm not alone any more; he loves me. I love him, I have my books, my storybook and my diary. I'm not so frightfully ugly, not utterly stupid, have a cheerful temperament and want to have a good character!

Yes, Anne, you've felt deeply that your letter was too hard and that it was untrue. To think that you were even proud of it! I will take Daddy as my example, and I *will* improve.

Yours, Anne

Saturday, 15 July, 1944

Dear Kitty,

. . . I have one outstanding trait in my character, which must strike anyone who knows me for any length of time, and that is my knowledge of myself. I can watch myself and my actions, just like an outsider. The Anne of every day I can face entirely without prejudice, without making excuses for her, and watch what's good and what's bad about her. This "self-consciousness" haunts me, and every time I open my mouth I know as soon as I've spoken whether "that ought to have been different" or "that was right as it was." There are so many things about myself that I condemn; I couldn't begin to name them all. I understand more and more how true Daddy's words were when he said: "All children must look after their own upbringing." Parents can only give good advice or put them on the right paths, but the final forming of a person's character lies in their own hands.

In addition to this, I have lots of courage, I always feel so strong and as if I can bear a great deal, I feel so free and so young! I was glad when I first realized it, because I don't think I shall easily bow down before the blows that inevitably come to everyone.

But I've talked about these things so often before. . . . Why is it that Pim annoys me? So much so that I can hardly bear him teaching me, that his affectionate ways strike me as being put on, that I want to be left in peace and would really prefer it if he dropped me a bit, until I felt more certain in my attitude towards him. Because I still have a gnawing feeling of guilt over that horrible letter that I dared to write him when I was so wound up. Oh, how hard it is to be really strong and brave in every way!

. . . "For in its innermost depths youth is lonelier than old age." I read this saying in some book and I've always remembered it, and found it to be true. Is it true then that grownups have a more difficult time here than we do? No. I know it isn't. Older people have formed their opinions about everything, and don't waver before they act. It's twice as hard for us young ones to hold our ground, and maintain our opinions, in a time when all ideals are being shattered and destroyed, when people are showing their worst side, and do not know whether to believe in truth and right and God.

Anyone who claims that the older ones have a more difficult time here certainly doesn't realize to what extent our problems weigh down on us, problems for which we are probably much too young, but which thrust themselves upon us continually, until, after a long time, we think we've found a solution, but the solution doesn't seem able to resist the facts which reduce it to nothing again. That's the difficulty in these times: ideals, dreams, and cherished hopes rise within us, only to meet the horrible truth and be shattered.

It's really a wonder that I haven't dropped all my ideals, because they seem so absurd and impossible to carry out. Yet I keep them, because in spite of everything I still believe that people are really good at heart. I simply can't build up my hopes on a foundation consisting of confusion, misery, and death. I see the world gradually being turned into a wilderness, I hear the ever approaching thunder, which will destroy us too, I can feel the sufferings of millions and yet, if I look up into the heavens, I think that it will all come right, that this cruelty too will end, and that peace and tranquillity will return again.

In the meantime, I must uphold my ideals, for perhaps the time will come when I shall be able to carry them out.

Yours, Anne

A young father all too close to his own adolescence finds that an incident with his little girl releases his own dormant generosity and enables him to take a real stride toward maturity.

PETER SHRUBB

The Gift

WHAT YOU GET for nothing is exactly nothing, in Australia as much as anywhere else, and Bill Fry knew it as well as anyone in Sydney. That was why, on the autumn Sunday when Frannie, his wife, asked him if they were going to tell his parents that afternoon that she was happily p-r-e-g-n-a-n-t again—spelling it out because Clarissa, their daughter, five years old and all ears, was in the room with them—he quite cheerfully answered, "I don't see that we have to; I don't see what's in it for us, except publicity." It rolled off his tongue like gospel.

He was sitting on the window seat in the living room, with the sun on his back. Clarissa faced him from the center of the gray carpet, where she was having her ponytail tied. She looked solemn—and vacant, as if her whole mind pointed backward, to the ponytail. Behind her, Frannie said, "Oh, Bill."

" 'Oh, Bill' nothing," Bill said. "Tell Mum and you tell the world. It's our own private business. . . . Our child and nobody else's." Clarissa, touching her hair with her fingertips, walked away to the door.

Frannie said, "I really don't see the harm in it."

"What Mum doesn't know, she won't miss." But just as he said it, he imagined how his mother would smile and smile if she did know. "*At least* two children—everyone should have *at least* two!" she would say, and his father would make up some joke about the expense. His mother would say she didn't care what it was as long as it was healthy.

Bill saw clearly how important a vessel he was, to contain so great a gift, and, feeling generous already—admired, beloved, made much of—as he went toward the door after Clarissa, he said, "I'll tell you what; if it comes up in a natural way, I don't mind."

Frannie smiled. "We can't leave it till they can see for themselves, you

[355]

know."

"Anyone interested enough to look could see it now."

He tickled Clarissa all the way out to the car, and while they were waiting for Frannie to find her bag he chased her around the lawn. She shrieked, he cackled, and when Frannie came out at last she said they sounded like a zoo. "Whose zoo?" Bill tried to say, and got so tangled up in the two words that Clarissa nearly fell over with laughing.

Then off they set in the little blue Vauxhall, and for some minutes no one said anything. Bill drove carefully, and Frannie and Clarissa watched the Sunday-afternoon houses go past. On weekdays these houses were nothing; they were all red brick, with green and brown lawns in front of them, hedges in front of the lawns, and a few gray and brown trees, and people hid inside them for days at a time. But on Sunday afternoons, hey presto! Children flew over the lawns and around the trees, and even adults, like weights the children had dragged out after them, lay slumped here and there in corners, folded over flower beds and hedges, laboring minutely. There was plenty for people in cars to see.

A bulbous stone fence guarded the hedge that hid Mr. Fry's house, but the little Vauxhall found its way through the gate, past the rhododendrons lining the drive, and pulled up in the thin shade of a bottlebrush tree. Against the fence in the small back yard, between the lilac and the frangipani, in the sun but not the wind, Mr. and Mrs. Fry sat reading the Sunday paper. They waved, and from the car Bill and Clarissa waved back. Bill saw his mother laugh and say something that had no chance of reaching them over the loud death rattle of the engine, and all at once he felt so overwhelmed with love for her simpleness, which his secret would soon beatify, that he feared his face might already have given both him and his secret away. "You look like a couple of old porpoises sunning yourselves," he called.

"Porpoise yourself," his mother replied, coming over to open the door for Clarissa.

"Whozoo!" Clarissa hooted, laughing again. "That's what Daddy said!"

"Darling," Mrs. Fry said, lifting her out.

"Porpoises are in fact the gayest and most graceful creatures in the kingdom of the sea," Bill said.

His mother waved her hand in his face. "You," she said. She looked for Frannie and, finding her, smiled.

"It's lovely to have a spot like this out of the wind," Frannie said as she came round the front of the car. She gave Mrs. Fry a quick kiss and then stood back a pace. "I do like your hair."

Bill knew immediately from her voice that she had not told the whole truth, and silently condemned her for it. But his mother's ear was not so experienced, or perhaps was dulled a little by wishfulness, or age. "They have another man. Do you really?" Embarrassed at looking so new, and at showing her pleasure, she held her hands up and minced around like a mannequin so that they should see her head back, front, and sides.

"Exactly like a porpoise," Bill said, climbing out of the car. His father snorted, and Bill turned to him. "And there's the other one surfacing! Avast!"

Mrs. Fry turned to Frannie again. "What on earth has got into *him?*"

Frannie laughed, and Bill took off his father's green-brimmed canvas hat and put it on his own head. "Keep it under your little bonnet, *I* always say."

"Has he been in the sun, Frannie?"

"Come inside, all of you," said Mr. Fry in his deep voice.

Clarissa led, stretching her legs up the green steps to the back veranda and standing at the top to see if the others could manage them so comfortably. They all did, Frannie smoothing her skirt, Mrs. Fry watching Clarissa, Mr. Fry rubbing his gray stubble of hair, Bill watching his father's strong square back.

In the kitchen dimness it was cooler. Frannie sank into one of the chairs round the big table with a sigh. "Ooh, I get tired in the afternoons these days."

A dead giveaway, it seemed to Bill. He started to smile, but from shyness covered his smile with his hand and made it go.

Mrs. Fry tickled the soft back of Clarissa's neck and said, "One day you'll have to let us take this little bundle off your hands for a week."

One day sooner than you imagine, Bill thought. But he stood there with his hand on his mouth like a monkey and said nothing; after all, no one had said anything to him.

Clarissa pulled out the chair next to her mother's and climbed up on it. Mr. Fry bent over her. "Would you like to stay with Grandma and Grandpa in their house, Clarissa?" Mrs. Fry smiled and folded her arms on her waist. She was not a large woman, and her face was lined and her hair thinning, but to Bill she gave an impression of strength still.

Clarissa rested her chin on the edge of the table and put her hands over her ears. "Mmm," she said softly, a little doubtfully. Bill smiled at her.

"And sleep in the big spare bed at night, *all* by yourself?" Mr. Fry went on. "And let Mummy and Daddy have a nice holiday somewhere on the coast or in the mountains for a week, *all* by *them*selves?"

Clarissa put her hands over her eyes and said nothing.

"I think she likes her own little bed at home best," Mr. Fry said, patting her head. And sententiously added, "And so do I."

Clarissa slapped her hands on the table, and her ponytail flew out. "You'd be too big for my bed!"

Everyone laughed but Bill. Clarissa, swinging on her grandfather's arm, smiled at him. Mrs. Fry went over to the stove.

Bill sat down, and Mr. Fry sat opposite him with his hands on the table. To Bill, his broad, deep, flat fingernails—perfectly self-sufficient, eternal—looked like bright, clean stones.

"How's life treating you?" his father asked.

Bill made a face at the tabletop, grunted, looked up, and saw that no one had been watching for his reply. Frannie was listening to his mother, and his father had eyes only for Clarissa, who now stood with one foot on the bottom rung of her mother's chair and one on the bottom rung of her grandfather's. "Don't do that, Clarissa," Bill said quickly. "They're not made to stand on." He remembered how angry his father had always been when things got broken, and for just long enough to be recognized there stood in his mind the possibility that Clarissa might not be a welcome visitor in his father's house.

"On these old chairs it doesn't matter," said his mother from the stove. "You're only young once."

Heartened by this open declaration, Bill looked up at his father again. "I hear Surtex are putting out a par issue one for four," he said.

"Take them," Mr. Fry said quietly.

Without thinking to the end of what he was saying, Bill said, "That'll bring you up to the five-hundred mark, won't it?"

Mr. Fry smiled. "You'll find out about all that when I'm dead."

Frannie said, "It's lovely getting a letter about a par issue. Bill's explained it all to me, and when this one came I opened it and looked up what Surtex were selling for; and, really, we could get rid of the new shares tomorrow for half as much *again* as we're giving!"

"I wouldn't call it giving," Mr. Fry said.

Mrs. Fry came to the table with the teapot. "If I opened his mail, this monster here would bite my head off."

"Oh, it's only if I know it's just business stuff," Frannie said.

"That's all we seem to get."

"How awful!" Frannie exclaimed.

Her voice carried such a charge of life that Bill had for an instant a clear vision of his father's dry days, so unlike his own, and instead of being angry he almost felt sorry for him.

Frannie said, "My day's ruined if there's no mail."

Bill laughed. "That says a great deal for marriage, doesn't it?"

Mr. Fry now had Clarissa on his lap. "This says a lot," he replied, nuzzling her head with his chin. Clarissa wriggled under him and reached for a slice of buttered date loaf.

"Eat the date as well as the butter," Bill said, and could not help smiling at the eye-rolling, insincere nods with which she answered him. Like a conspirator, Clarissa smiled back.

For a minute or two, no one spoke. Bill watched Frannie and thought that one look at her beautifully pure skin and eyes should be all anyone needed, to know she was pregnant. Why his mother failed to remark on it with joy he could not imagine.

His father, giving Clarissa a sip of tea, said, "And how's life treating you, Bill?"

After a second, Bill said, "Not often." His mother attended to him this time, and nodded; but then he saw her glance slide off toward Clarissa and her face absolutely fill with light as she asked, "Not too hot for your little tongue?"

Clarissa shook her head. "Give me some more, Grandpa—more, more, more, more!" She acted, because now they were all watching her, and with play desperation she pressed her hands over Mr. Fry's mouth so that he could not drink anything.

"Poor Grandpa!" Frannie said. "Aren't you going to let him have any of his tea at all?"

Mrs. Fry put her hand over Frannie's wrist and said in a kindly voice, "How are you feeling now, dear?"

Bill began to wonder, but all Frannie said was, "Like a new woman."

Still warmly holding Frannie's hand, his mother went on, "Bill always liked his tea, too. I could always get round Bill, when he was a boy, with a cup of tea. He was like an old lady with his cup of tea."

"Get round him?" Frannie laughed. "When did you have to get round him, for goodness' sake?"

Mrs. Fry threw her hands in the air. "When did I not!"

"What's all this?" Bill asked.

His mother only smiled. "We survived it all," she said, and began telling Frannie about a Mrs. Jukes, who had not.

"Ha! Old Jukey!" Mr. Fry exclaimed in an unkind way, and returned to Clarissa.

Bill tried to listen to his mother, but Mrs. Jukes was nothing to him. Survived all what? Who? He began to feel left out of things, and inside him the secret seemed to have grown smaller; he imagined it now as being the size of the baby itself—too small, probably, to be seen. Suddenly he remembered what it was that they had all survived. It was his being the only child—and more a repository for hope than a child, he had often felt; more a well, from which pride and comfort were regularly to be drawn. He remembered the arguments this very kitchen had been noisy with when he had begun not to provide them.

Clarissa, the last to finish, gulped down the dregs of her grandfather's tea, jumped off his lap, and ran out to find something to do in the back yard. While Mrs. Fry and Frannie started washing up, Bill and his father went through to the living room. "The record club sent a Mozart piano concerto this month," Mr. Fry said.

Bill said, "Let's hear it, then."

Halfway through the first movement, Mrs. Fry tiptoed in. Bill sat up with a start when he saw her—she came in so softly—and then immediately and with delight guessed she had come to say that she knew. He felt his ears begin to redden and heat. He pressed his hands over them, gave his shoes a wry grin, and waited. But his mother merely stole over to the magazine rack, took up the top *House & Garden,* turned, and began her silent journey back to the door. Bill looked up in complete astonishment. His mother smiled at him and put her finger to her lips. It was the reverse of what he wanted, and angrily he said the reverse of what he would have liked to say. "If you think you're interrupting, you're perfectly right!" he snapped. His mother did not answer; on her face came a strained, set look in which he read that she had not even heard what he said, but only the irritation in which he had said it.

The door closed behind her, and for a moment Bill felt utterly locked in. He looked up, and saw the orange curtains that had silently strangled and suffocated light for as long as he could remember. From the curtain his eye fled to the familiar brown-stained picture rail, and followed it over two imitation-bronze plaques, to the van Gogh above the mantelpiece, to the Toulouse-Lautrec he himself had given them two years before, to the Paul Nash prints neat in a row. He felt sure, today, that the plaques and pictures were there to hide something. Perhaps his father had a safe behind each one, each safe hiding its contents from the other safes. Everything hidden, everything buttressed. A bullet, even if it penetrated the dark front of the house, could never burrow through the stuffing in the back of the settee.

The first side of the record ended, and his father turned it over in silence. Without looking up again, Bill heard the music through

Frannie and Mrs. Fry were in the back yard when Bill and his father went to join them. Behind the bulk of the house, the lilac and the frangipani were already sinking into an early dusk, and the ladies with them, in the chairs Mr. and Mrs. Fry had filled when the Vauxhall arrived. "We'll have to be getting along pretty soon," Bill announced.

"Oh, no, Daddy!" Clarissa cried. "I want to stay!"

Her exaggerated despair jangled a little in Bill's ears. More to Frannie and his mother than to Clarissa, he said, "It gets cool as soon as the sun starts going down. And if she plays inside, it always ends up with something broken." The words blew from his mouth, and in every one of them he heard his father's voice.

"I'll be good," Clarissa said.

"It isn't so easy," Bill said.

For another few minutes, Bill followed his father round the miniature vegetable garden behind the garage, listening; and then, by the time they came back to the lawn, it really was evening, with smoke in the air and a thin dark veil between earth and the blue zenith. Clarissa, pink-cheeked,

The Gift

stopped jumping when she saw them.

"Is it time, dear?" Frannie asked, pleasantly.

Bill nodded. Mrs. Fry hurried inside to get another *House & Garden* she wanted to lend Frannie, and in three minutes the Vauxhall was backing down the dim driveway. Bill, turning the car in a narrow street, left the waving goodbye to Frannie and Clarissa. "Come back soon!" Clarissa called.

For the first few minutes, no one spoke. Bill was glad, in his black mood, that autumn was a season of the year and early evening a time of day to which silence is sympathetic. On the footpaths, men in cardigans and pipes raked up the leaves of liquidambars and poplars slowly, as if they feared heart attacks. There were lights behind curtains. Soon everyone would be indoors, out of the dark and the cold.

They waited to turn onto the highway. Frannie said, "Your mother didn't actually say anything, but I wouldn't be surprised if she guessed."

Bill felt as if he were in a film and a great inevitable truck had just roared at him out of the dusk. "Why?" he asked quietly.

Frannie tried to see his face, but it was turned to the window. "Oh, just things she said, things she asked me. I think we should ring them up soon."

Bill jerked the car away in first. "Why wouldn't she say anything, if she thinks it?"

"Well, heavens, I don't know, Bill. I didn't think I was supposed to ask her."

"What the hell does she think she's doing, guessing things and not saying so! Is she the keeper of the keys, or some damn thing? Why wouldn't she come out and say it?"

"Don't shout at me, Bill," Frannie said, her own voice rising a little. "She probably didn't say anything because you didn't. You're being quite unreasonable."

Bill was so angry that he took his eyes from the road. "I suppose the truth is that you as good as told her! I suppose that's it, is it?"

Frannie turned away abruptly and looked out her window. No one said a word more. Under the Vauxhall's little shell of a roof, by the time they reached home, they could hardly even see one another.

Clarissa hurried over the dark lawn after Frannie, and without having to be asked sat herself at the kitchen table for supper. She wanted bacon, but Frannie said quietly that there was no time for bacon. So she settled for a glass of milk, a piece of toast with peanut butter on it, and a tiny cold lamb chop left over from lunch. Bill sat in the living room in front of the gas fire, reading the Sunday paper. Clarissa finished her toast in silence, and then said to her mother, who was moving around the kitchen, "There's a boy at school called Billy, and if he's not good I'll come up to him and say, 'Billy Davis, if you're not a good boy you'll have to go home this minute, do you hear? This minute!' "

"Just eat up, dear, and not too much talking," Frannie said.

" 'This minute!' " Clarissa went on, staring at a bad boy who lived in her head, raising her eyebrows at him, waving one finger. " ' Just exactly at this very very minute! No sooter, no laner!' " She burst into laughter. "Mummy, do you know what I just said? I was going to say—"

From the living room, Bill shouted, "Clarissa!"

Frannie said, quite calmly, "Just eat up, dear. It's school tomorrow, and you must have a big long sleep." She turned the gas down under the potatoes, said, "You be finished by the time I get back," and went into the living room to the fire. Bill did not look up as she sat in the other chair, with the comics, and Frannie did not speak to him.

When she had finished them, she called out, "Are you ready now, Clarissa?" There was no answer. "Clarissa, are you ready for your bath now?" No answer. Frannie waited, and then said, in a voice clear but not loud, "I'm in no mood for games now—are you ready? Tell me." There was still no answer. Bill lowered his paper, and Frannie, seeing him do it, got up quickly and went back to the kitchen. He heard her make a discontented sound and go through the kitchen into the hall that led to the bedrooms, switching on lights there and in the bathroom, softly calling Clarissa's name.

But in another minute or two she came back into the kitchen; she turned on the outside light and stood at the back door, calling. She went down the steps onto the back lawn, and then right around the house. When she reappeared at the back door, she was still alone.

"Haven't you found her yet, for God's sake!" Bill demanded, made more angry still by the sight of her white, frightened face. Without waiting for a reply, he stood up. "I'll find her," he said. Frannie said nothing, leaning on the corner of the sink, her face turned away.

As he crossed the room, however, his mind surrendered itself, like a thin wall falling, to all that could have happened. She might have gone for a walk, and be lost, or kidnapped, or run over; she might be in a place she could not get out of. She might already be dying. With every light in the house on, he swiftly searched each bright, empty room.

Then there was nothing else for it. He switched on the outside light again and went down the back steps, as Frannie had done before. His knee gave a sort of twitch, and he felt breathless. Frannie stood at the door, watching him. "I'll go and turn the front light on," she said.

Bill looked up at her and, doing so, saw—cuddled in the corner between the steps and the back terrace, smiling brightly through the branches of a small oleander—Clarissa.

His heart shuddered as the world righted itself again. When he had breath, he said, curtly, "Come out here at once."

"I found a good place, Daddy," Clarissa said; and, holding her chop bone in one hand, she bent down to creep out under the branches.

The Gift

As soon as she reached the edge of the lawn, Bill hit her on the shoulder. "What do you think you're doing?" he shouted. "Hiding! Playing games! When you were told to hurry up because it was nearly time for bed! What do you think you're doing?" He had knocked the bone out of her hand, and as she bent down to pick it up she burst into tears. He hit her again. She slipped over on the grass. "You're a naughty girl!" he shouted, and with one hand in her armpit he pulled her to her feet. "A very naughty girl!"

In the light, then, he saw her pale shocked face for the first time. He pushed her away from him, up the steps toward Frannie. "Go in with your mother and stay with her," he said.

He followed them inside and stood in the kitchen while Clarissa was led into the bathroom. "I just wanted him to come and find me!" she wailed. He went back to the fire and picked up his paper again.

His pounding heart worked to repair the damage rage and shame had done. He couldn't read; he could hardly even focus clearly. He sat back, closing his eyes against the light. But after a moment the lonely echoing darkness was more than he could bear, and he opened them again. There was peace in neither light nor dark. He heard Frannie come into the room and sit in the other chair, but he did not look at her. She didn't speak.

In a minute he stood and went back through the kitchen into the hall. He thought Clarissa could probably hear him, but to make sure she knew who it was, he coughed at her door as he pushed it open. There was no sound from the bed. He stepped over next to it and sat down on the edge. "Are you still awake, Clarissa?" he whispered.

She didn't answer.

He stroked her hair. With the tip of his finger he slowly and lightly outlined her ear, and slid from the lobe to the corner of her jaw, down to her chin, and to the hollow under her bottom lip. There he let his finger rest a minute. He knew from her breathing that she was still awake. He leaned forward and put his forehead on the pillow next to her. "I'm sorry I was angry, Clarissa," he whispered. There was no sound. "Mummy and I were frightened, little bird. We didn't know *where* you were." Saying it, he was so flooded with love that he began to lose the sense of his own location, of the conjunction of parts of his body. "I know it was just a sort of trick—but you're our only lovely little bird, and if anything happened to you I don't know what we would do." With a quick grateful movement he put his arm around her and squeezed her. "I don't know what we would do," he whispered again.

For a minute he lay there next to her in the darkness, imagining her small roundness, all her miniature perfections. Then he kissed her soft cheek and whispered good night.

He waited at the door of her silent room to gather himself for the journey back. He tried to lift his head as he entered the living room and sat down again, but it made only a passable show, and he didn't feel ready yet to look at Frannie. He shut his eyes.

Clarissa called out, "Can I get up?"

Frannie looked at Bill.

Clarissa called out again, "Can I get up, just for a minute?"

Bill nodded. Frannie went over and switched on the hall light. "Yes, come on—just for a minute. Daddy says you can get up for just a minute."

Clarissa came into the room with her hands behind her back, squinting against the light. "Come over near the fire," Bill said. "You mustn't get cold."

Frannie sat down again and Clarissa stood facing them both. "Hold out your hands," she said. "And shut your eyes."

They did as they were told. Bill smiled as something was pressed into his hand and small fingers closed his fingers down over it.

"Open your eyes," she said.

They opened their eyes. Bill wanted just to look at her, but obediently he looked at what was in his hand. It was a tiny red-and-white plastic charm that had broken from a bracelet a girl at school had given her on her fifth birthday. Frannie had a pencil sharpener.

"What are these for?" Bill asked.

"They're prizes."

Bill looked with wonder at her serene face. "Thank you very much. What are they prizes for?"

"For you and Mummy," Clarissa said. "I'm going to give you prizes often now."

Light came from behind her, fuzzing the edges of her nightgown and her hair, and from above, falling evenly on her even face. And from her face, it seemed to Bill, light fell—as if the charm were a magic one, after all—into his very soul. There was nothing hidden in her.

Bill fixed the little charm onto his key chain straightaway, to Clarissa's great delight; and after she was safely tucked back into bed again, all the way driving down to his parents he thought he could see it hanging there in the dim light of the dash, and even hear the new, soft sound it made when it touched the metal. And it ran through his mind that every child is a chance, a new hope, a new possibility for goodness. For everything else, too, of course. But what else matters? Goodness is our treasure.

He knocked on the kitchen door, went in without waiting for their reply, and said to his mother, who was sitting there sewing, with a very surprised look on her face, "I didn't tell you this afternoon that we're going to have another baby. We haven't even told Clarissa yet."

His mother said "Bless you!" and came round and hugged him. His father said that if they were triplets Bill might be able to sell them to a cereal firm for advertising purposes. But he wasn't serious.

PART FIVE

The Discovery of Ambiguity

HOW STRONG in all of us is the impulse to persuade children that the world is a just and orderly place where right and wrong can be clearly distinguished. How quickly we rush to shield our young from the sorrows and complications all around them, pushing away the evidence children give us daily that they are constantly busy uncovering the truth in their own way. Is it not ourselves we are protecting? The child's direct and simple confrontations with the hard, inescapable facts of the human condition catch us off guard, and we make haste to invent simple explanations where none such are possible. We shrink from admitting that the pain is real, that very much in life is unclear, and that we must struggle to find our way.

We deceive ourselves—but not the children. Very early they notice that even a good mother gets cross sometimes and is then a "bad" mother; a cherished toy is broken and can't be mended. (We instantly promise to replace it, thus saying in effect, "everything turns out well in the end.") Young people can get sick and die—not just very old ones, as they have been told. Someone might throw a bomb and burn up the whole world.

We notice that children are almost clairvoyant about the feelings and cross-currents between their parents and that they find especially troubling those under-cover tensions that tempt them to take sides and divide their loyalties. Most marriages weather out such tensions and the children accommodate themselves somehow. John Updike's *Wife Wooing* describes a small significant incident from that time in a marriage when disenchantment has set in and the humdrum round of domesticity takes over. But the story's unfolding suggests possibilities in this familiar impasse more heartening than mere resignation. This young father suddenly experiences a burst of insight into the surprising twists and turns of the way to sexual fulfillment with a loved and child-worn wife. There is joy and tenderness in his discoveries. Not only he and his wife but their children too will be the beneficiaries.

Most children tuck away for future use whatever bits of knowledge they glean and live pretty comfortably in the present. After all, there's lots of fun to be found here and now—birthday presents, a dog of one's own perhaps, a part in a school play, swimming in the ocean. Usually it's all right about the bad things because mostly they don't come too near. But sometimes they do, and then one gets awfully mixed up.

Incidents where a child uncovers some of life's ambiguities are to be found throughout this book; it is impossible to isolate them in one section. The young Orwell comes to the disturbing conclusion that it is impossible to be good. Can he be held responsible for wetting his bed when he doesn't even know when he is doing it? Colette makes a happier discovery: grief isn't always accompanied by tears and widows' weeds as convention has it. Her mother can laugh and wear a gay dress even while she mourns her husband. Both Orwell and the nearly grown Colette are moving another step toward realizing that questioning must go on, surfaces must be probed, things are more complicated than they seem at first.

But the way to such learning is in itself complicated—a two-steps-forward-one-step-back process. The child, like the grownup, hesitates to let himself know all in one simple illuminating flash those things that are bound to be hard. David Copperfield senses but does not wholly comprehend that the handsome man who is so kind and flattering and who takes him places is in reality an enemy in disguise; and that even his loving mother is about to bestow her love elsewhere. Peggotty, David's nurse, a great prop during all this hard time, was ever ready to listen when he talked; an attentive ear is in itself reassuring. Besides, she made possible all sorts of exciting discoveries in the brand new world she later opened up to him and which proved so healing.

In the brief selection from the story *Love and Like* we find a young father trying to make a verbal distinction clear to his two children. If they know that he and their mother *like* but no longer *love* each other, will not the pending divorce become more palatable? The children are bored with his efforts. They don't really see this difference (indeed, is it so clear?). All they know is that it will be awful to have the home they have known and depended on so unreasonably altered. They will learn, of course, in their own time and way how such things happen. So will the girl in the other story of divorce—*Shoe the Horse, Shoe the Mare*. Meanwhile it is hard, terribly hard at her time of life, to find that a wonderful father whom she yearns for has in truth drifted away from her, forgotten that her dog died, failed to see her beautiful new coat. Her problem is infinitely complicated because in spite of all she

The Discovery of Ambiguity

cannot help but find her father wonderfully glamorous and her staunch workaday mother whom she also needs distressingly drab. She is bound to be torn between them.

These are hard lessons but they can be learned, and learned without lifelong bitterness. Much more blighting are the experiences described in Richard Wright's *Black Boy*. Physical striking force and agility, hard fists and the will to defend one's own—these in some measure are values shared by the young male everywhere. Young Wright, growing up in a Negro slum, always one step from hunger and disaster, early discovers the even greater necessity for raw courage. Those who read the whole of this heartbreaking book will learn how illness, poverty, family breakdown and, above all, the necessity to come to some sort of terms with the cruelties and injustices of the white man plunge this boy into an abyss of confusion and bitterness. "The meaning of living," he tells us, "came only when one was struggling to win a meaning out of meaningless suffering." For the rest of his life he will carry "scars, visible and invisible."

Death as a fact of life poses the hardest problem of all. In earlier days, death was usual, something that happened all around. Today illness and death are relegated to the hospital, children are often sent to a neighbor's house when the end comes, excluded from funerals and mourning. Some of this may be inevitable, or desirable. Yet many of us grow to adulthood without knowing a loss greater than an animal pet or a remote relative or ever having actual contact with death and dying. Do we pay a price in keeping death so remote? Are we impoverishing our children when we exclude them from this primitive experience?

The children in Agee's book, *A Death in the Family*, from which a short excerpt is given, came closer to a direct contact with death than many. What did this father's sudden death mean to these children? Did they feel grief? Fear? When the boy Rufus goes outdoors announcing, almost boasting about the event to neighbors, is he really "callous," as is so often said of children? What is going on in him? Though we do not know precisely, the story rings true; we do not doubt that a great deal *is* going on. A little later we are shown how Rufus registers the minutest detail of this experience from first to last, and with a furious intensity. Perhaps this is not exactly grief, for it has a kind of detachment. But neither is it conceivably callousness. So the way may be paved for grief. At the end, we find Rufus close to being consoled by an uncle who almost makes him feel that there is after all something "nearly all right" about his father's death. Then everything changes again when his uncle unexpectedly reveals a depth of hatred for the things his mother deeply venerates. This discovery plunges Rufus once again into utter bleakness.

In Agee's story, we surmise that all this pain and confusion were more than this child could bear. We scarcely expect that he will come through unscathed. He had lived all his life in a veritable jungle of ambiguities and family strains. His father's death was the final blow, and there was no way to soften it.

The story of Rufus may perhaps warn us that when we can choose—and often we cannot—we need not heedlessly plunge children into knowledge that is wholly beyond their understanding or that may come at a time when they are struggling with other problems. Always we must ask: "Is this too great a load to place on this individual child at this particular time?" We must be prepared, when it seems wise, to shield certain children a little longer if it is in our power to do so or at least to give the truth little by little and gently. But equally we should be ready to ask a child to face hard experiences when we have taken his measure and decided he is strong enough. On the whole, we tend to underestimate youth's amazing strength.

The struggle to find meaning in life never ceases, and so there is something universal in the solution that the aging woman in the last story of this volume stumbles upon. There is no end to this personal quest, she seems to tell us. Always we must press forward, steadfastly refusing to cut ourselves off from what is vivid and alive even though it may also be painful. Having made her peace with contradictions and shadows, her children grown and steering their own courses far away, this wise woman continues to make new and hazardous commitments and so, to the very end, will continue to be fully alive.

Against a background strictly unromantic, the father of three small children courts his wife and discovers some unexpected turns in the path to fulfillment.

JOHN UPDIKE

Wife-Wooing

OH MY LOVE. Yes. Here we sit, on warm broad floor boards, before a fire, the children between us, in a crescent, eating. The girl and I share one half-pint of French-fried potatoes; you and the boy share another; and in the center, sharing nothing, making simple reflections within himself like a jewel, the baby, mounted in an Easy-baby, sucks at his bottle with frowning mastery, his selfish, contemplative eyes stealing glitter from the center of the flames. And you. You. You allow your skirt, the same black skirt in which this morning you with woman's soft bravery mounted a bicycle and sallied forth to play hymns in difficult keys on the Sunday school's old piano—you allow this black skirt to slide off your raised knees down your thighs, slide *up* your thighs in your body's absolute geography, so the parallel whiteness of their undersides is exposed to the fire's warmth and to my sight. Oh. There is a line of Joyce. I try to recover it from the legendary, imperfectly explored grottoes of "Ulysses": a garter snapped, to please Blazes Boylan, in a deep Dublin den. What? Smackwarm. That was the crucial word. Smacked smackwarm on her smackable warm woman's thigh. Something like that. A splendid man, to feel that. Smackwarm woman's. Splendid also to feel the curious and potent, inexplicable and irrefutably magical life language leads within itself. What soul took thought and knew that adding "wo" to man would make a woman? The difference exactly. The wide w, the receptive o. Womb. In our crescent the children for all their size seem to come out of you toward me, wet fingers and eyes, tinted bronze. Three children, five persons, seven years. Seven years since I wed wide warm woman, white-thighed. Wooed and wed. Wife. A knife of a word that for all its final bite did not end the wooing. To my wonderment.

We eat meat, meat I wrested warm from the raw hands of the hamburger girl in the diner a mile away, a ferocious place, slick with savagery, wild with chrome; young predators snarling dirty jokes menaced me, old men reached for me with coffee-warmed paws; I wielded my wallet, and won my way back. The fat brown bag of buns was warm beside me in the cold car; the smaller bag holding the two tiny cartons of French-fries emitted an even more urgent heat. Back through the black winter air to the fire, the intimate cave, where halloos and hurrahs greeted me, the deer, mouth agape and its cotton throat gushing, stretched dead across my shoulders. And now you, beside the white O of the plate upon which the children discarded with squeals of disgust the rings of translucent onion that came squeezed in the hamburgers—you push your toes an inch closer to the blaze, and the ashy white of the inside of your deep thigh is lazily laid bare, and the eternally elastic garter snaps smack-warm against my hidden heart.

Who would have thought, wide wife, back there in the white tremble of the ceremony (in the corner of my eye I held, despite the distracting hail of ominous vows, the vibration of the cluster of stephanotis clutched against your waist), that seven years would bring us no distance, through all those warm beds, to the same trembling point, of beginning? The cells change every seven years, and down in the atom, apparently, there is a strange discontinuity; as if God wills the universe anew every instant. (Ah God, dear God, tall friend of my childhood, I will never forget you, though they say dreadful things. They say rose windows in cathedrals are vaginal symbols.) Your legs, exposed as fully as by a bathing suit, yearn deeper into the amber wash of heat. Well: begin. A green jet of flame spits out sideways from a pocket of resin in a log, crying, and the orange shadows on the ceiling sway with fresh life. Begin.

"Remember, on our honeymoon, how the top of the kerosene heater made a great big rose window on the ceiling?"

"Vnn." Your chin goes to your knees, your shins draw in, all is retracted. Not much to remember, perhaps, for you; blood badly spilled, clumsiness of all sorts. "It was cold for June."

"Mommy, what was cold? What did you say?" the girl asks, enunciating angrily, determined not to let language slip on her tongue and tumble her so that we laugh.

"A house where Daddy and I stayed one time."

"I don't like dat," the boy says, and throws a half bun painted with chartreuse mustard onto the floor.

You pick it up and with beautiful sombre musing ask, "Isn't that funny? Did any of the others have mustard on them?"

"I *hate* dat," the boy insists; he is two. Language is to him thick vague handles swirling by; he grabs what he can.

"Here. He can have mine. Give me his." I pass my hamburger over, you

Wife-Wooing

take it, he takes it from you, there is nowhere a ripple of gratitude. There is no more praise of my heroism in fetching Sunday supper. Cunning, you sense, and sense that I sense your knowledge, that I had hoped to hoard your energy toward a later spending. We sense everything between us, every ripple, existent and nonexistent; it is tiring. Courting a wife takes tenfold the strength of winning an ignorant girl. The fire shifts, shattering fragments of newspaper that carry in lighter gray the ghost of the ink of their message. You huddle your legs and bring the skirt back over them. With a sizzling noise like the sighs of the exhausted logs, the baby sucks the last from his bottle, drops it to the floor with its distasteful hoax of vacant suds, and begins to cry. His egotist's mouth opens; the delicate membrane of his satisfaction tears. You pick him up and stand. You love the baby more than me.

Who would have thought, blood once spilled, that no barrier would be broken, that you would be each time healed into a virgin again? Tall, fair, obscure, remote, and courteous.

We put the children to bed, one by one, in reverse order of birth. I am limitlessly patient, paternal, good. Yet you know. We watch the paper bags and cartons ignite on the breathing pillow of embers, read, watch television, eat crackers, it does not matter. Eleven comes. For a tingling moment you stand on the bedroom rug in your underpants, untangling your nightie; oh, fat white sweet fat fatness. In bed you read. About Richard Nixon. He fascinates you; you hate him. You know how he defeated Jerry Voorhis, martyred Mrs. Douglas, how he played poker in the Navy despite being a Quaker, every trick, every adaptation. Oh my Lord. Let's let the poor man go to bed. We're none of us perfect. "Hey let's turn out the light."

"Wait. He's just about to get Hiss convicted. It's very strange. It says he acted honorably."

"I'm sure he did." I reach for the switch.

"No. Wait. Just till I finish this chapter. I'm sure there'll be something at the end."

"Honey, Hiss was guilty. We're all guilty. Conceived in concupiscence, we die unrepentant." Once my ornate words wooed you.

I lie against your filmy convex back. You read sideways, a sleepy trick. I see the page through the fringe of your hair, sharp and white as a wedge of crystal. Suddenly it slips. The book has slipped from your hand. You are asleep. Oh cunning trick, cunning. In the darkness I consider. Cunning. The headlights of cars accidentally slide fanning slits of light around our walls and ceiling. The great rose window was projected upward through the petal-shaped perforations in the top of the black kerosene stove, which we stood in the center of the floor. As the flame on the circular wick flickered, the wide soft star of interlocked penumbrae moved and waved as if it were printed on a silk cloth being gently tugged or slowly blown. Its color soft blurred blood. We pay dear in blood for our peaceful homes.

In the morning, to my relief, you are ugly. Monday's wan breakfast light bleaches you blotchily, drains the goodness from your thickness, makes the bathrobe a limp stained tube flapping disconsolately, exposing sallow décolletage. The skin between your breasts a sad yellow. I feast with the coffee on your drabness. Every wrinkle and sickly tint a relief and a revenge. The children yammer. The toaster sticks. Seven years have worn this woman.

The man, he arrows off to work, jousting for right of way, veering on the thin hard edge of the legal speed limit. Out of domestic muddle, softness, pallor, flaccidity: into the city. Stone is his province. The winning of coin. The maneuvering of abstractions. Making heartless things run. Oh the inanimate, adamant joys of job!

I return with my head enmeshed in a machine. A technicality it would take weeks to explain to you snags my brain; I fiddle with phrases and numbers all the blind evening. You serve me supper as a waitress—as less than a waitress, for I have known you. The children touch me timidly, as they would a steep girder bolted into a framework whose height they don't understand. They drift into sleep securely. We survive their passing in calm parallelity. My thoughts rework in chronic right angles the same snagging circuits on the same professional grid. You rustle the book about Nixon; vanish upstairs into the plumbing; the bathtub pipes cry. In my head I seem to have found the stuck switch at last: I push at it; it jams; I push; it is jammed. I grow dizzy, churning with cigarettes. I circle the room aimlessly.

So I am taken by surprise at a turning when at the meaningful hour of ten you come with a kiss of toothpaste to me moist and girlish and quick; the momentous moral of this story being, An expected gift is not worth giving.

David plies the immortal Peggotty with questions about marriage, half-knowing, half-refusing to know that a certain gentleman is courting his mother.

CHARLES DICKENS

from *David Copperfield*

... PEGGOTTY AND I were sitting one night by the parlour fire, alone. I had been reading to Peggotty about crocodiles. I must have read very perspicuously, or the poor soul must have been deeply interested, for I remember she had a cloudy impression, after I had done, that they were a sort of vegetable. I was tired of reading, and dead sleepy; but having leave, as a high treat, to sit up until my mother came home from spending the evening at a neighbour's, I would rather have died upon my post (of course) than have gone to bed. I had reached that stage of sleepiness when Peggotty seemed to swell and grow immensely large. I propped my eyelids open with my two forefingers, and looked perseveringly at her as she sat at work; at the little bit of wax candle she kept for her thread—how old it looked, being so wrinkled in all directions!—at the little house with a thatched roof where the yard measure lived; at her workbox with a sliding lid, with a view of St. Paul's Cathedral (with a pink dome) painted on the top; at the brass thimble on her finger; at herself, whom I thought lovely. I felt so sleepy, that I knew if I lost sight of anything, for a moment, I was gone.

"Peggotty," says I suddenly, "were you ever married?"

"Lord, Master Davy," replied Peggotty. "What's put marriage in your head?"

She answered with such a start that it quite awoke me. And then she stopped in her work, and looked at me, with her needle drawn out to its thread's length.

"But *were* you ever married, Peggotty?" says I. "You are a very handsome woman, an't you?"

I thought her in a different style from my mother, certainly; but of another school of beauty, I considered her a perfect example. There was

[373]

a red velvet footstool in the best parlour, on which my mother had painted a nosegay. The groundwork of that stool and Peggotty's complexion appeared to me to be one and the same thing. The stool was smooth, and Peggotty was rough, but that made no difference.

"Me handsome, Davy!" said Peggotty. "Lawk, no, my dear! But what put marriage in your head?"

"I don't know! You mustn't marry more than one person at a time, may you, Peggotty?"

"Certainly not," says Peggotty, with the promptest decision.

"But if you marry a person, and the person dies, why then you may marry another person, mayn't you, Peggotty?"

"You MAY," says Peggotty, "if you choose, my dear. That's a matter of opinion."

"But what is your opinion, Peggotty?" said I.

I asked her, and looked curiously at her, because she looked so curiously at me.

"My opinion is," said Peggotty, taking her eyes from me, after a little indecision, and going on with her work, "that I never was married myself, Master Davy, and that I don't expect to be. That's all I know about the subject."

"You an't cross, I suppose, Peggotty, are you?" said I, after sitting quiet for a minute.

I really thought she was, she had been so short with me. But I was quite mistaken; for she laid aside her work (which was a stocking of her own), and opening her arms wide, took my curly head within them, and gave it a good squeeze. I know it was a good squeeze, because, being very plump, whenever she made any little exertion after she was dressed, some of the buttons on the back of her gown flew off. And I recollect two bursting to the opposite side of the parlour while she was hugging me.

"Now let me hear some more about the crorkindills," said Peggotty, who was not quite right in the name yet, "for I an't heard half enough."

I couldn't quite understand why Peggotty looked so queer, or why she was so ready to go back to the crocodiles. However, we returned to those monsters, with fresh wakefulness on my part, and we left their eggs in the sand for the sun to hatch; and we ran away from them, and baffled them by constantly turning, which they were unable to do quickly, on account of their unwieldy make; and we went into the water after them, as natives, and put sharp pieces of timber down their throats; and, in short, we ran the whole crocodile gauntlet. *I* did, at least; but I had my doubts of Peggotty, who was thoughtfully sticking her needle into various parts of her face and arms all the time.

We had exhausted the crocodiles, and begun with the alligators, when the garden bell rang. We went out to the door, and there was my mother,

from *David Copperfield*

looking unusually pretty, I thought, and with her a gentleman with beautiful black hair and whiskers, who had walked home with us from church last Sunday.

As my mother stooped down on the threshold to take me in her arms and kiss me, the gentleman said I was a more highly privileged little fellow than a monarch—or something like that; for my later understanding comes, I am sensible, to my aid here.

"What does that mean?" I asked him, over her shoulder.

He patted me on the head; but somehow, I didn't like him or his deep voice, and I was jealous that his hand should touch my mother's in touching me—which it did. I put it away as well as I could.

"Oh, Davy!" remonstrated my mother.

"Dear boy!" said the gentleman. "I cannot wonder at his devotion!"

I never saw such a beautiful colour on my mother's face before. She gently chid me for being rude; and, keeping me close to her shawl, turned to thank the gentleman for taking so much trouble as to bring her home. She put out her hand to him as she spoke, and, as he met it with his own, she glanced, I thought, at me.

"Let us say 'good night,' my fine boy," said the gentleman, when he had bent his head—*I* saw him!—over my mother's little glove.

"Good night!" said I.

"Come! let us be the best friends in the world!" said the gentleman, laughing. "Shake hands!"

My right hand was in my mother's left, so I gave him the other.

"Why, that's the wrong hand, Davy!" laughed the gentleman.

My mother drew my right hand forward; but I was resolved, for my former reason, not to give it him, and I did not. I gave him the other, and he shook it heartily, and said I was a brave fellow, and went away.

At this minute I see him turn round in the garden, and give us a last look with his ill-omened black eyes, before the door was shut.

Peggotty, who had not said a word or moved a finger, secured the fastenings instantly, and we all went into the parlour. My mother, contrary to her usual habit, instead of coming to the elbow-chair by the fire, remained at the other end of the room, and sat singing to herself.

"Hope you have had a pleasant evening, ma'am," said Peggotty, standing as stiff as a barrel in the centre of the room, with a candlestick in her hand.

"Much obliged to you, Peggotty," returned my mother in a cheerful voice; "I have had a *very* pleasant evening."

"A stranger or so makes an agreeable change," suggested Peggotty.

"A very agreeable change, indeed," returned my mother.

Peggotty continuing to stand motionless in the middle of the room, and my mother resuming her singing, I fell asleep, though I was not so sound asleep but that I could hear voices, without hearing what they said. When I half awoke from this uncomfortable doze, I found Peggotty and my mother both in tears, and both talking.

"Not such a one as this, Mr. Copperfield wouldn't have liked," said Peggotty. "That I say, and that I swear!"

"Good heavens!" cried my mother, "you'll drive me mad! Was ever any poor girl so ill-used by her servants as I am? Why do I do myself the injustice of calling myself a girl? Have I never been married, Peggotty?"

"God knows you have, ma'am," returned Peggotty.

"Then, how can you dare," said my mother—"you know I don't mean how can you dare, Peggotty, but how can you have the heart—to make me so uncomfortable and say such bitter things to me, when you are well aware that I haven't, out of this place, a single friend to turn to?"

"The more's the reason," returned Peggotty, "for saying that it won't do. No! That it won't do. No! No price could make it do. No!"—I thought Peggotty would have thrown the candlestick away, she was so emphatic with it.

"How can you be so aggravating," said my mother, shedding more tears than before, "as to talk in such an unjust manner? How can you go on as if it was all settled and arranged, Peggotty, when I tell you over and over again, you cruel thing, that beyond the commonest civilities nothing has passed? You talk of admiration. What am I to do? If people are so silly as to indulge the sentiment, is it my fault? What am I to do, I ask you? Would you wish me to shave my head and black my face, or disfigure myself with a burn, or a scald, or something of that sort? I dare say you would, Peggotty. I dare say you'd quite enjoy it."

Peggotty seemed to take this aspersion very much to heart, I thought.

"And my dear boy," cried my mother, coming to the elbow-chair in which I was, and caressing me—"my own little Davy! Is it to be hinted to me that I am wanting in affection for my precious treasure, the dearest little fellow that ever was?"

"Nobody never went and hinted no such a thing," said Peggotty.

"You did, Peggotty!" returned my mother. "You know you did. What else was it possible to infer from what you said, you unkind creature, when you know as well as I do, that on his account only last quarter I wouldn't buy myself a new parasol, though that old green one is frayed the whole way up, and the fringe is perfectly mangy? You know it is, Peggotty; you can't deny it." Then, turning affectionately to me, with her cheek against mine, "Am I a naughty mamma to you, Davy? Am I a nasty, cruel, selfish, bad mamma? Say I am, my child—say 'yes,' dear boy, and Peggotty will love you; and Peggotty's love is a great deal better than mine, Davy. *I* don't love you at all, do I?"

At this we all fell a-crying together. I think I was the loudest of the party, but I am sure we were all sincere about it. I was quite heartbroken

from *David Copperfield*

myself, and am afraid that in the first transports of wounded tenderness I called Peggotty a "Beast." That honest creature was in deep affliction, I remember, and must have become quite buttonless on the occasion; for a little volley of those explosives went off, when, after having made it up with my mother, she kneeled down by the elbow-chair and made it up with me.

We went to bed greatly dejected. My sobs kept waking me, for a long time; and when one very strong sob quite hoisted me up in bed, I found my mother sitting on the coverlet, and leaning over me. I fell asleep in her arms, after that, and slept soundly.

Whether it was the following Sunday when I saw the gentleman again, or whether there was any greater lapse of time before he reappeared, I cannot recall. I don't profess to be clear about dates. But there he was, in church, and he walked home with us afterwards. He came in, too, to look at a famous geranium we had, in the parlour-window. It did not appear to me that he took much notice of it, but before he went he asked my mother to give him a bit of the blossom. She begged him to choose it for himself, but he refused to do that—I could not understand why—so she plucked it for him, and gave it into his hand. He said he would never, never part with it any more; and I thought he must be quite a fool not to know that it would fall to pieces in a day or two.

Peggotty began to be less with us, of an evening, than she had always been. My mother deferred to her very much—more than usual, it occurred to me—and we were all three excellent friends; still we were different from what we used to be, and were not so comfortable among ourselves. Sometimes I fancied that Peggotty perhaps objected to my mother's wearing all the pretty dresses she had in her drawers, or to her going so often to visit at that neighbour's; but I couldn't, to my satisfaction, make out how it was.

Gradually, I became used to seeing the gentleman with the black whiskers. I liked him no better than at first, and had the same uneasy jealousy of him; but if I had any reason for it beyond a child's instinctive dislike, and a general idea that Peggotty and I could make much of my mother without any help, it certainly was not *the* reason that I might have found if I had been older. No such thing came into my mind, or near it. I could observe, in little pieces, as it were; but as to making a net of a number of these pieces, and catching anybody in it, that was, as yet, beyond me.

One autumn morning I was with my mother in the front garden, when Mr. Murdstone—I knew him by that name now—came by, on horseback. He reined up his horse to salute my mother, and said he was going to Lowestoft to see some friends who were there with a yacht, and merrily proposed to take me on the saddle before him if I would like the ride.

The air was so clear and pleasant, and the horse seemed to like the idea of the ride so much himself, as he stood snorting and pawing at the garden-gate, that I had a great desire to go. So I was sent upstairs to Peggotty to be made spruce; and, in the meantime, Mr. Murdstone dismounted, and, with his horse's bridle drawn over his arm, walked slowly up and down on the outer side of the sweetbrier fence, while my mother walked slowly up and down on the inner, to keep him company. I recollect Peggotty and I peeping out at them from my little window. I recollect how closely they appeared to be examining the sweetbrier between them, as they strolled along; and how, from being in a perfectly angelic temper, Peggotty turned cross in a moment, and brushed my hair the wrong way, excessively hard.

Mr. Murdstone and I were soon off, and trotting along on the green turf by the side of the road. He held me quite easily with one arm, and I don't think I was restless usually; but I could not make up my mind to sit in front of him without turning my head sometimes, and looking up in his face. He had that kind of shallow black eye—I want a better word to express an eye that has no depth in it to be looked into—which, when it is abstracted, seems, from some peculiarity of light, to be disfigured, for a moment at a time, by a cast. Several times when I glanced at him I observed that appearance with a sort of awe, and wondered what he was thinking about so closely. His hair and whiskers were blacker and thicker, looked at so near, than even I had given them credit for being. A squareness about the lower part of his face, and the dotted indication of the strong black beard he shaved close every day, reminded me of the wax-work that had travelled into our neighbourhood some half a year before. This, his regular eyebrows, and the rich white, and black, and brown of his complexion—confound his complexion, and his memory!—made me think him, in spite of my misgivings, a very handsome man. I have no doubt that my poor dear mother thought him so too.

We went to an hotel by the sea, where two gentlemen were smoking cigars in a room by themselves. Each of them was lying on at least four chairs, and had a large rough jacket on. In a corner was a heap of coats and boat-cloaks, and a flag, all bundled up together.

They both rolled on to their feet, in an untidy sort of manner, when we came in, and said, "Halloa, Murdstone! We thought you were dead!"

"Not yet," said Mr. Murdstone.

"And who's this shaver?" said one of the gentlemen, taking hold of me.

"That's Davy," returned Mr. Murdstone.

"Davy who?" said the gentleman. "Jones?"

"Copperfield," said Mr. Murdstone.

"What! Bewitching Mrs. Copperfield's encumbrance?" cried the gentleman. "The pretty little widow?"

"Quinion," said Mr. Murdstone, "take care, if you please. Somebody's sharp."

from *David Copperfield*

"Who is?" asked the gentleman, laughing.

I looked up quickly, being curious to know.

"Only Brooks of Sheffield," said Mr. Murdstone.

I was quite relieved to find it was only Brooks of Sheffield, for at first I really thought it was I.

There seemed to be something very comical in the reputation of Mr. Brooks of Sheffield, for both the gentlemen laughed heartily when he was mentioned, and Mr. Murdstone was a good deal amused also. After some laughing, the gentleman whom he had called Quinion said:

"And what is the opinion of Brooks of Sheffield, in reference to the projected business?"

"Why, I don't know that Brooks understands much about it at present," replied Mr. Murdstone, "but he is not generally favourable, I believe."

There was more laughter at this, and Mr. Quinion said he would ring the bell for some sherry in which to drink to Brooks. This he did; and when the wine came, he made me have a little, with a biscuit, and, before I drank it, stand up and say, "Confusion to Brooks of Sheffield!" The toast was received with great applause, and such hearty laughter that it made me laugh too; at which they laughed the more. In short, we quite enjoyed ourselves.

We walked about on the cliff after that, and sat on the grass, and looked at things through a telescope—I could make out nothing myself when it was put to my eye, but I pretended I could—and then we came back to the hotel to an early dinner. All the time we were out the two gentlemen smoked incessantly—which, I thought, if I might judge from the smell of their rough coats, they must have been doing ever since the coats had first come home from the tailor's. I must not forget that we went on board the yacht, where they all three descended into the cabin, and were busy with some papers. I saw them quite hard at work when I looked down through the open skylight. They left me, during this time, with a very nice man, with a very large head of red hair and a very small shiny hat upon it, who had got a cross-barred shirt or waistcoat on, with "Skylark" in capital letters across the chest. I thought it was his name, and that as he lived on board ship and hadn't a street door to put his name on, he put it there instead; but when I called him Mr. Skylark, he said it meant the vessel.

I observed all day that Mr. Murdstone was graver and steadier than the two gentlemen. They were very gay and careless. They joked freely with one another, but seldom with him. It appeared to me that he was more clever and cold than they were, and that they regarded him with something of my own feeling. I remarked that, once or twice, when Mr. Quinion was talking, he looked at Mr. Murdstone sideways, as if to make sure of his not being displeased; and that once when Mr. Passnidge (the other gentleman) was in high spirits, he trod upon his foot, and gave him a secret caution with his eyes, to observe Mr. Murdstone, who was sitting stern and silent. Nor do I recollect that Mr. Murdstone laughed at all that day, except at the Sheffield joke—and that, by-the-by, was his own.

We went home early in the evening. It was a very fine evening, and my mother and he had another stroll by the sweetbrier, while I was sent in to get my tea. When he was gone, my mother asked me all about the day I had had, and what they had said and done. I mentioned what they had said about her, and she laughed, and told me they were impudent fellows who talked nonsense; but I knew it pleased her. I knew it quite as well as I know it now. I took the opportunity of asking if she was at all acquainted with Mr. Brooks of Sheffield; but she answered No, only she supposed he must be a manufacturer in the knife and fork way.

Can I say of her face—altered as I have reason to remember it, perished as I know it is—that it is gone, when here it comes before me at this instant, as distinct as any face that I may choose to look on in a crowded street? Can I say of her innocent and girlish beauty, that it faded, and was no more, when its breath falls on my cheek now, as it fell that night? Can I say she ever changed, when my remembrance brings her back to life, thus only, and, truer to its loving youth than I have been, or man ever is, still holds fast what it cherished then?

I write of her just as she was when I had gone to bed after this talk, and she came to bid me good-night. She kneeled down playfully by the side of the bed, and laying her chin upon her hands, and laughing, said, "What was it they said, Davy? Tell me again. I can't believe it."

"'Bewitching—'" I began.

My mother put her hands upon my lips to stop me.

"It was never bewitching," she said, laughing. "It never could have been bewitching, Davy. Now I know it wasn't!"

"Yes, it was. 'Bewitching Mrs. Copperfield,'" I repeated stoutly. "And 'pretty.'"

"No, no, it was never pretty. Not pretty," interposed my mother, laying her fingers on my lips again.

"Yes, it was. 'Pretty little widow.'"

"What foolish, impudent creatures!" cried my mother, laughing and covering her face. "What ridiculous men! An't they? Davy dear—"

"Well, ma."

"Don't tell Peggotty; she might be angry with them. I am dreadfully angry with them myself; but I would rather Peggotty didn't know."

I promised, of course; and we kissed one another over and over again, and I soon fell fast asleep.

It seems to me, at this distance of time, as if it were the next day when Peggotty broached the striking and adventurous proposition I am about to mention; but it was probably about two months afterwards.

from *David Copperfield*

We were sitting as before, one evening (when my mother was out as before), in company with the stocking and the yard-measure, and the bit of wax, and the box with St. Paul's on the lid, and the crocodile book, when Peggotty, after looking at me several times, and opening her mouth as if she were going to speak, without doing it—which I thought was merely gaping, or I should have been rather alarmed—said coaxingly:

"Master Davy, how should you like to go along with me and spend a fortnight at my brother's at Yarmouth? Wouldn't *that* be a treat?"

"Is your brother an agreeable man, Peggotty?" I inquired provisionally.

"Oh, what an agreeable man he is!" cried Peggotty, holding up her hands. "Then there's the sea; and the boats and ships; and the fishermen; and the beach; and Am to play with—"

Peggotty meant her nephew Ham, mentioned in my first chapter; but she spoke of him as a morsel of English Grammar.

I was flushed by her summary of delights, and replied that it would indeed be a treat, but what would my mother say?

"Why, then, I'll as good as bet a guinea," said Peggotty, intent upon my face, "that she'll let us go. I'll ask her, if you like, as soon as ever she comes home. There now!"

"But what's she to do while we are away?" said I, putting my small elbows on the table to argue the point. "She can't live by herself."

If Peggotty were looking for a hole, all of a sudden, in the heel of that stocking, it must have been a very little one indeed, and not worth darning.

"I say, Peggotty! She can't live by herself, you know."

"Oh, bless you!" said Peggotty, looking at me again at last. "Don't you know? She's going to stay for a fortnight with Mrs. Grayper. Mrs. Grayper's going to have a lot of company."

Oh! if that was it, I was quite ready to go. I waited, in the utmost impatience, until my mother came home from Mrs. Grayper's (for it was that identical neighbour), to ascertain if we could get leave to carry out this great idea. Without being nearly so much surprised as I had expected, my mother entered into it readily; and it was all arranged that night, and my board and lodging during the visit were to be paid for.

The day soon came for our going. It was such an early day that it came soon, even to me, who was in a fever of expectation, and half afraid that an earthquake, or a fiery mountain, or some other great convulsion of nature, might interpose to stop the expedition. We were to go in a carrier's cart, which departed in the morning after breakfast. I would have given any money to have been allowed to wrap myself up overnight, and sleep in my hat and boots.

It touches me nearly now, although I tell it lightly, to recollect how eager I was to leave my happy home; to think how little I suspected what I did leave for ever.

I am glad to recollect that when the carrier's cart was at the gate, and my mother stood there kissing me, a grateful fondness for her and for the old place I had never turned my back upon before, made me cry. I am glad to know that my mother cried too, and that I felt her heart beat against mine.

I am glad to recollect that when the carrier began to move, my mother ran out at the gate, and called to him to stop, that she might kiss me once more. I am glad to dwell upon the earnestness and love with which she lifted up her face to mine, and did so.

As we left her standing in the road, Mr. Murdstone came up to where she was, and seemed to expostulate with her for being so moved. I was looking back round the awning of the cart, and wondered what business it was of his. Peggotty, who was also looking back on the other side, seemed anything but satisfied, as the face she brought back into the cart denoted.

I sat looking at Peggotty for some time, in a reverie on this supposititious case: whether, if she were employed to lose me like the boy in the fairy tale, I should be able to track my way home again by the buttons she would shed. . . .

Now, all the time I had been on my visit, I had been ungrateful to my home again, and had thought little or nothing about it. But I was no sooner turned towards it than my reproachful young conscience seemed to point that way with a steady finger; and I felt, all the more for the sinking of my spirits, that it was my nest, and that my mother was my comforter and friend.

This gained upon me as we went along, so that the nearer we drew, and the more familiar the objects became that we passed, the more excited I was to get there, and to run into her arms. But Peggotty, instead of sharing in these transports, tried to check them (though very kindly), and looked confused and out of sorts.

Blunderstone Rookery would come, however, in spite of her, when the carrier's horse pleased—and did. How well I recollect it, on a cold grey afternoon, with a dull sky, threatening rain!

The door opened, and I looked, half laughing and half crying in my pleasant agitation, for my mother. It was not she, but a strange servant.

"Why, Peggotty!" I said ruefully, "isn't she come home?"

"Yes, yes, Master Davy," said Peggotty. "She's come home. Wait a bit, Master Davy, and I'll—I'll tell you something."

Between her agitation, and her natural awkwardness in getting out of the cart, Peggotty was making a most extraordinary festoon of herself, but I felt too blank and strange to tell her so. When she had got down, she took me by the hand; led me, wondering, into the kitchen; and shut the door.

from *David Copperfield* [383]

"Peggotty!" said I, quite frightened, "what's the matter?"

"Nothing's the matter, bless you, Master Davy dear!" she answered, assuming an air of sprightliness.

"Something's the matter, I'm sure. Where's mamma?"

"Where's mamma, Master Davy?" repeated Peggotty.

"Yes. Why hasn't she come out to the gate, and what have we come in here for? Oh, Peggotty!" My eyes were full, and I felt as if I were going to tumble down.

"Bless the precious boy!" cried Peggotty, taking hold of me. "What is it? Speak, my pet!"

"Not dead, too! Oh, she's not dead, Peggotty?"

Peggotty cried out No! with an astonishing volume of voice; and then sat down, and began to pant, and said I had given her a turn.

I gave her a hug to take away the turn, or to give her another turn in the right direction, and then stood before her, looking at her in anxious inquiry.

"You see, dear, I should have told you before now," said Peggotty, "but I hadn't an opportunity. I ought to have made it, perhaps, but I couldn't azackly"—that was always the substitute for exactly, in Peggotty's militia of words—"bring my mind to it."

"Go on, Peggotty," said I, more frightened than before.

"Master Davy," said Peggotty, untying her bonnet with a shaking hand, and speaking in a breathless sort of way, "what do you think? You have got a pa!"

I trembled, and turned white. Something—I don't know what, or how—connected with the grave in the churchyard, and the rising of the dead, seemed to strike me like an unwholesome wind.

"A new one," said Peggotty.

"A new one?" I repeated.

Peggotty gave a gasp, as if she were swallowing something that was very hard, and, putting out her hand, said, "Come and see him."

"I don't want to see him."

"And your mamma," said Peggotty.

I ceased to draw back, and we went straight to the best parlour, where she left me. On one side of the fire sat my mother; on the other, Mr. Murdstone. My mother dropped her work, and arose hurriedly, but timidly I thought.

"Now, Clara my dear," said Mr. Murdstone, "recollect! control yourself, always control yourself!—Davy boy, how do you do?"

I gave him my hand. After a moment of suspense, I went and kissed my mother. She kissed me, patted me gently on the shoulder, and sat down again to her work. I could not look at her, I could not look at him—I knew quite well that he was looking at us both—and I turned to the window and looked out there at some shrubs that were drooping their heads in the cold.

As soon as I could creep away, I crept upstairs. My old dear bedroom was changed, and I was to lie a long way off. I rambled downstairs to find anything that was like itself, so altered it all seemed, and roamed into the yard. I very soon started back from there, for the empty dog-kennel was filled up with a great dog—deep-mouthed and black-haired like Him—and he was very angry at the sight of me, and sprang out to get at me.

Two school boys, out for a carefree day in the country, recognize the shadow of evil as it falls unexpectedly across their path and sense their danger.

JAMES JOYCE

An Encounter

IT WAS JOE DILLON who introduced the Wild West to us. He had a little library made up of old numbers of *The Union Jack, Pluck* and *The Halfpenny Marvel*. Every evening after school we met in his back garden and arranged Indian battles. He and his fat young brother Leo, the idler, held the loft of the stable while we tried to carry it by storm; or we fought a pitched battle on the grass. But, however well we fought, we never won siege or battle and all our bouts ended with Joe Dillon's war dance of victory. His parents went to eight-o'clock mass every morning in Gardiner Street and the peaceful odour of Mrs. Dillon was prevalent in the hall of the house. But he played too fiercely for us who were younger and more timid. He looked like some kind of an Indian when he capered round the garden, an old tea-cosy on his head, beating a tin with his fist and yelling:

"Ya! yaka, yaka, yaka!"

Everyone was incredulous when it was reported that he had a vocation for the priesthood. Nevertheless it was true.

A spirit of unruliness diffused itself among us and, under its influence, differences of culture and constitution were waived. We banded ourselves together, some boldly, some in jest and some almost in fear: and of the number of these latter, the reluctant Indians who were afraid to seem studious or lacking in robustness, I was one. The adventures related in the literature of the Wild West were remote from my nature but, at least, they opened doors of escape. I liked better some American detective stories which were traversed from time to time by unkempt fierce and beautiful girls. Though there was nothing wrong in these stories and though their intention was sometimes literary they were circulated secretly at school. One day when Father Butler was hearing the four pages of Roman History clumsy Leo Dillon was discovered with a copy of *The Halfpenny Marvel.*

"This page or this page? This page? Now, Dillon, up! *'Hardly had the day'* . . . Go on! What day? *'Hardly had the day dawned'* . . . Have you studied it? What have you there in your pocket?"

Everyone's heart palpitated as Leo Dillon handed up the paper and everyone assumed an innocent face. Father Butler turned over the pages, frowning.

"What is this rubbish?" he said. *"The Apache Chief!* Is this what you read instead of studying your Roman History? Let me not find any more of this wretched stuff in this college. The man who wrote it, I suppose, was some wretched fellow who writes these things for a drink. I'm surprised at boys like you, educated, reading such stuff. I could understand it if you were . . . National School boys. Now, Dillon, I advise you strongly, get at your work or . . ."

This rebuke during the sober hours of school paled much of the glory of the Wild West for me and the confused puffy face of Leo Dillon awakened one of my consciences. But when the restraining influence of the school was at a distance I began to hunger again for wild sensations, for the escape which those chronicles of disorder alone seemed to offer me. The mimic warfare of the evening became at last as wearisome to me as the routine of school in the morning because I wanted real adventures to happen to myself. But real adventures, I reflected, do not happen to people who remain at home: they must be sought abroad.

The summer holidays were near at hand when I made up my mind to break out of the weariness of school-life for one day at least. With Leo Dillon and a boy named Mahony I planned a day's miching. Each of us saved up sixpence. We were to meet at ten in the morning on the Canal Bridge. Mahony's big sister was to write an excuse for him and Leo Dillon was to tell his brother to say he was sick. We arranged to go along the Wharf Road until we came to the ships, then to cross in the ferryboat and walk out to see the Pigeon House. Leo Dillon was afraid we might meet Father Butler or someone out of the college; but Mahony asked, very sensibly, what would Father Butler be doing out at the Pigeon House. We were reassured: and I brought the first stage of the plot to an end by collecting sixpence from the other two, at the same time showing them my own sixpence. When we were making the last arrangements on the eve we were all vaguely excited. We shook hands, laughing, and Mahony said:

"Till to-morrow, mates!"

That night I slept badly. In the morning I was first-comer to the bridge as I lived nearest. I hid my books in the long grass near the ashpit at the end of the garden where nobody ever came and hurried along the canal bank. It was a mild sunny morning in the first week of June. I

An Encounter

sat up on the coping of the bridge admiring my frail canvas shoes which I had diligently pipeclayed overnight and watching the docile horses pulling a tramload of business people up the hill. All the branches of the tall trees which lined the mall were gay with little light green leaves and the sunlight slanted through them on to the water. The granite stone of the bridge was beginning to be warm and I began to pat it with my hands in time to an air in my head. I was very happy.

When I had been sitting there for five or ten minutes I saw Mahony's grey suit approaching. He came up the hill, smiling, and clambered up beside me on the bridge. While we were waiting he brought out the catapult which bulged from his inner pocket and explained some improvements which he had made in it. I asked him why he had brought it and he told me he had brought it to have some gas with the birds. Mahony used slang freely, and spoke of Father Butler as Old Bunser. We waited on for a quarter of an hour more but still there was no sign of Leo Dillon. Mahony, at last, jumped down and said:

"Come along. I knew Fatty'd funk it."

"And his sixpence . . . ?" I said.

"That's forfeit," said Mahony. "And so much the better for us—a bob and a tanner instead of a bob."

We walked along the North Strand Road till we came to the Vitriol Works and then turned to the right along the Wharf Road. Mahony began to play the Indian as soon as we were out of public sight. He chased a crowd of ragged girls, brandishing his unloaded catapult and, when two ragged boys began, out of chivalry, to fling stones at us, he proposed that we should charge them. I objected that the boys were too small, and so we walked on, the ragged troop screaming after us: "*Swaddlers! Swaddlers!*" thinking that we were Protestants because Mahony, who was dark-complexioned, wore the silver badge of a cricket club in his cap. When we came to the Smoothing Iron we arranged a siege; but it was a failure because you must have at least three. We revenged ourselves on Leo Dillon by saying what a funk he was and guessing how many he would get at three o-clock from Mr. Ryan.

We came then near the river. We spent a long time walking about the noisy streets flanked by high stone walls, watching the working of cranes and engines and often being shouted at for our immobility by the drivers of groaning carts. It was noon when we reached the quays and, as all the labourers seemed to be eating their lunches, we bought two big currant buns and sat down to eat them on some metal piping beside the river. We pleased ourselves with the spectacle of Dublin's commerce—the barges signalled from far away by their curls of woolly smoke, the brown fishing fleet beyond Ringsend, the big white sailing-vessel which was being discharged on the opposite quay. Mahony said it would be right skit to run away to sea on one of those big ships and even I, looking at the high masts, saw, or imagined, the geography which had been scantily dosed to me at school gradually taking substance under my eyes. School and home seemed to recede from us and their influences upon us seemed to wane.

We crossed the Liffey in the ferryboat, paying our toll to be transported in the company of two labourers and a little Jew with a bag. We were serious to the point of solemnity, but once during the short voyage our eyes met and we laughed. When we landed we watched the discharging of the graceful three-master which we had observed from the other quay. Some bystander said that she was a Norwegian vessel. I went to the stern and tried to decipher the legend upon it but, failing to do so, I came back and examined the foreign sailors to see had any of them green eyes for I had some confused notion. . . . The sailors' eyes were blue and grey and even black. The only sailor whose eyes could have been called green was a tall man who amused the crowd on the quay by calling out cheerfully every time the planks fell:

"All right! All right!"

When we were tired of this sight we wandered slowly into Ringsend. The day had grown sultry, and in the windows of the grocers' shops musty biscuits lay bleaching. We bought some biscuits and chocolate which we ate sedulously as we wandered through the squalid streets where the families of the fishermen live. We could find no dairy and so we went into a huckster's shop and bought a bottle of raspberry lemonade each. Refreshed by this, Mahony chased a cat down a lane, but the cat escaped into a wide field. We both felt rather tired and when we reached the field we made at once for a sloping bank over the ridge of which we could see the Dodder.

It was too late and we were too tired to carry out our project of visiting the Pigeon House. We had to be home before four o'clock lest our adventure should be discovered. Mahony looked regretfully at his catapult and I had to suggest going home by train before he regained any cheerfulness. The sun went in behind some clouds and left us to our jaded thoughts and the crumbs of our provisions.

There was nobody but ourselves in the field. When we had lain on the bank for some time without speaking I saw a man approaching from the far end of the field. I watched him lazily as I chewed one of those green stems on which girls tell fortunes. He came along by the bank slowly. He walked with one hand upon his hip and in the other hand he held a stick with which he tapped the turf lightly. He was shabbily dressed in a suit of greenish-black and wore what we used to call a jerry hat with a high crown. He seemed to be fairly old for his moustache was ashen-grey. When he passed at our feet he glanced up at us quickly and then continued his way. We followed him with our eyes and saw that when he had gone on for perhaps fifty paces he turned about and

An Encounter

began to retrace his steps. He walked towards us very slowly, always tapping the ground with his stick, so slowly that I thought he was looking for something in the grass.

He stopped when he came level with us and bade us good-day. We answered him and he sat down beside us on the slope slowly and with great care. He began to talk of the weather, saying that it would be a very hot summer and adding that the seasons had changed greatly since he was a boy—a long time ago. He said that the happiest time of one's life was undoubtedly one's schoolboy days and that he would give anything to be young again. While he expressed these sentiments which bored us a little we kept silent. Then he began to talk of school and of books. He asked us whether we had read the poetry of Thomas Moore or the works of Sir Walter Scott and Lord Lytton. I pretended that I had read every book he mentioned so that in the end he said:

"Ah, I can see you are a bookworm like myself. Now," he added, pointing to Mahony who was regarding us with open eyes, "he is different; he goes in for games."

He said he had all Sir Walter Scott's works and all Lord Lytton's works at home and never tired of reading them. "Of course," he said, "there were some of Lord Lytton's works which boys couldn't read." Mahony asked why couldn't boys read them—a question which agitated and pained me because I was afraid the man would think I was as stupid as Mahony. The man, however, only smiled. I saw that he had great gaps in his mouth between his yellow teeth. Then he asked us which of us had the most sweethearts. Mahony mentioned lightly that he had three totties. The man asked me how many I had. I answered that I had none. He did not believe me and said he was sure I must have one. I was silent.

"Tell us," said Mahony pertly to the man, "how many have you yourself?"

The man smiled as before and said that when he was our age he had lots of sweethearts.

"Every boy," he said, "has a little sweetheart."

His attitude on this point struck me as strangely liberal in a man of his age. In my heart I thought that what he said about boys and sweethearts was reasonable. But I disliked the words in his mouth and I wondered why he shivered once or twice as if he feared something or felt a sudden chill. As he proceeded I noticed that his accent was good. He began to speak to us about girls, saying what nice soft hair they had and how soft their hands were and how all girls were not so good as they seemed to be if one only knew. There was nothing he liked, he said, so much as looking at a nice young girl, at her nice white hands and her beautiful soft hair. He gave me the impression that he was repeating something which he had learned by heart or that, magnetised by some words of his own speech, his mind was slowly circling round and round in the same orbit. At times he spoke as if he were simply alluding to some fact that everybody knew, and at times he lowered his voice and spoke mysteriously as if he were telling us something secret which he did not wish others to overhear. He repeated his phrases over and over again, varying them and surrounding them with his monotonous voice. I continued to gaze towards the foot of the slope, listening to him.

After a long while his monologue paused. He stood up slowly, saying that he had to leave us for a minute or so, a few minutes, and, without changing the direction of my gaze, I saw him walking slowly away from us towards the near end of the field. We remained silent when he had gone. After a silence of a few minutes I heard Mahony exclaim:

"I say! Look what he's doing!"

As I neither answered nor raised my eyes Mahony exclaimed again:

"I say . . . He's a queer old josser!"

"In case he asks us for our names," I said, "let you be Murphy and I'll be Smith."

We said nothing further to each other. I was still considering whether I would go away or not when the man came back and sat down beside us again. Hardly had he sat down when Mahony, catching sight of the cat which had escaped him, sprang up and pursued her across the field. The man and I watched the chase. The cat escaped once more and Mahony began to throw stones at the wall she had escaladed. Desisting from this, he began to wander about the far end of the field, aimlessly.

After an interval the man spoke to me. He said that my friend was a very rough boy and asked did he get whipped often at school. I was going to reply indignantly that we were not National School boys to be whipped, as he called it; but I remained silent. He began to speak on the subject of chastising boys. His mind, as if magnetised again by his speech, seemed to circle slowly round and round its new centre. He said that when boys were that kind they ought to be whipped and well whipped. When a boy was rough and unruly there was nothing would do him any good but a good sound whipping. A slap on the hand or a box on the ear was no good: what he wanted was to get a nice warm whipping. I was surprised at this sentiment and involuntarily glanced up at his face. As I did so I met the gaze of a pair of bottle-green eyes peering at me from under a twitching forehead. I turned my eyes away again.

The man continued his monologue. He seemed to have forgotten his recent liberalism. He said that if ever he found a boy talking to girls or having a girl for a sweetheart he would whip him and whip him; and that would teach him not to be talking to girls. And if a boy had a girl for a sweetheart and told lies about it then he would give him such a whipping as no boy ever got in this world. He said that there was nothing

An Encounter

in this world he would like so well as that. He described to me how he would whip such a boy as if he were unfolding some elaborate mystery. He would love that, he said, better than anything in this world; and his voice, as he led me monotonously through the mystery, grew almost affectionate and seemed to plead with me that I should understand him.

I waited till his monologue paused again. Then I stood up abruptly. Lest I should betray my agitation I delayed a few moments pretending to fix my shoe properly and then, saying that I was obliged to go, I bade him good-day. I went up the slope calmly but my heart was beating quickly with fear that he would seize me by the ankles. When I reached the top of the slope I turned round and, without looking at him, called loudly across the field:

"Murphy!"

My voice had an accent of forced bravery in it and I was ashamed of my paltry stratagem. I had to call the name again before Mahony saw me and hallooed in answer. How my heart beat as he came running across the field to me! He ran as if to bring me aid. And I was penitent; for in my heart I had always despised him a little.

A small child entangled in the web of a hate-riddled family is aware of the bitter hostilities between the grownups. Do such experiences inevitably establish a pattern of hate in a child? The story leaves us wondering.

KATHERINE ANNE PORTER

The Downward Path to Wisdom

IN THE SQUARE BEDROOM with the big window Mama and Papa were lolling back on their pillows handing each other things from the wide black tray on the small table with crossed legs. They were smiling and they smiled even more when the little boy, with the feeling of sleep still in his skin and hair, came in and walked up to the bed. Leaning against it, his bare toes wriggling in the white fur rug, he went on eating peanuts which he took from his pajama pocket. He was four years old.

"Here's my baby," said Mama. "Lift him up, will you?"

He went limp as a rag for Papa to take him under the arms and swing him up over a broad, tough chest. He sank between his parents like a bear cub in a warm litter, and lay there comfortably. He took another peanut between his teeth, cracked the shell, picked out the nut whole and ate it.

"Running around without his slippers again," said Mama. "His feet are like icicles."

"He crunches like a horse," said Papa. "Eating peanuts before breakfast will ruin his stomach. Where did he get them?"

"You brought them yesterday," said Mama, with exact memory, "in a grisly little cellophane sack. I have asked you dozens of times not to bring him things to eat. Put him out, will you? He's spilling shells all over me."

Almost at once the little boy found himself on the floor again. He moved around to Mama's side of the bed and leaned confidingly near her and began another peanut. As he chewed he gazed solemnly in her eyes.

"Bright-looking specimen, isn't he?" asked Papa, stretching his long legs and reaching for his bathrobe. "I suppose you'll say it's my fault

[392]

he's dumb as an ox."

"He's my little baby, my only baby," said Mama richly, hugging him, "and he's a dear lamb." His neck and shoulders were quite boneless in her firm embrace. He stopped chewing long enough to receive a kiss on his crumby chin. "He's sweet as clover," said Mama. The baby went on chewing.

"Look at him staring like an owl," said Papa.

Mama said, "He's an angel and I'll never get used to having him."

"We'd be better off if we never *had* had him," said Papa. He was walking about the room and his back was turned when he said that. There was silence for a moment. The little boy stopped eating, and stared deeply at his Mama. She was looking at the back of Papa's head, and her eyes were almost black. "You're going to say that just once too often," she told him in a low voice. "I hate you when you say that."

Papa said, "You spoil him to death. You never correct him for anything. And you don't take care of him. You let him run around eating peanuts before breakfast."

"You gave him the peanuts, remember that," said Mama. She sat up and hugged her only baby once more. He nuzzled softly in the pit of her arm. "Run along, my darling," she told him in her gentlest voice, smiling at him straight in the eyes. "Run along," she said, her arms falling away from him. "Get your breakfast."

The little boy had to pass his father on the way to the door. He shrank into himself when he saw the big hand raised above him. "Yes, get out of here and stay out," said Papa, giving him a little shove toward the door. It was not a hard shove, but it hurt the little boy. He slunk out, and trotted down the hall trying not to look back. He was afraid something was coming after him, he could not imagine what. Something hurt him all over, he did not know why.

He did not want his breakfast; he would not have it. He sat and stirred it round in the yellow bowl, letting it stream off the spoon and spill on the table, on his front, on the chair. He liked seeing it spill. It was hateful stuff, but it looked funny running in white rivulets down his pajamas.

"Now look what you're doing, dirty boy," said Marjory. "You dirty little old boy."

The little boy opened his mouth to speak for the first time. "You're dirty yourself," he told her.

"That's right," said Marjory, leaning over him and speaking so her voice would not carry. "That's right, just like your papa. Mean," she whispered, "mean."

The little boy took up his yellow bowl full of cream and oatmeal and sugar with both hands and brought it down with a crash on the table. It burst and some of the wreck lay in chunks and some of it ran all over everything. He felt better.

"You see?" said Marjory, dragging him out of the chair and scrubbing him with a napkin. She scrubbed him as roughly as she dared until he cried out. "That's just what I said. That's exactly it." Through his tears he saw her face terribly near, red and frowning under a stiff white band, looking like the face of somebody who came at night and stood over him and scolded him when he could not move or get away. "Just like your papa, *mean*."

The little boy went out into the garden and sat on a green bench dangling his legs. He was clean. His hair was wet and his blue woolly pull-over made his nose itch. His face felt stiff from the soap. He saw Marjory going past a window with the black tray. The curtains were still closed at the window he knew opened into Mama's room. Papa's room. Mommanpoppasroom, the word was pleasant, it made a mumbling snapping noise between his lips; it ran in his mind while his eyes wandered about looking for something to do, something to play with.

Mommanpoppas' voices kept attracting his attention. Mama was being cross with Papa again. He could tell by the sound. That was what Marjory always said when their voices rose and fell and shot up to a point and crashed and rolled like the two tomcats who fought at night. Papa was being cross, too, much crosser than Mama this time. He grew cold and disturbed and sat very still, wanting to go to the bathroom, but it was just next to Mommanpoppasroom; he didn't dare think of it. As the voices grew louder he could hardly hear them any more, he wanted so badly to go to the bathroom. The kitchen door opened suddenly and Marjory ran out, making the motion with her hand that meant he was to come to her. He didn't move. She came to him, her face still red and frowning, but she was not angry; she was scared just as he was. She said, "Come on, honey, we've got to go to your gran'ma's again." She took his hand and pulled him. "Come on quick, your gran'ma is waiting for you." He slid off the bench. His mother's voice rose in a terrible scream, screaming something he could not understand, but she was furious; he had seen her clenching her fists and stamping in one spot, screaming with her eyes shut; he knew how she looked. She was screaming in a tantrum, just as he remembered having heard himself. He stood still, doubled over, and all his body seemed to dissolve, sickly, from the pit of his stomach.

"Oh, my God," said Marjory. "Oh, my God. Now look at you. Oh, my God. I can't stop to clean you up."

He did not know how he got to his grandma's house, but he was there at last, wet and soiled, being handled with disgust in the big bathtub. His grandma was there in long black skirts saying, "Maybe he's sick; maybe we should send for the doctor."

"I don't think so, m'am," said Marjory. "He hasn't et anything; he's just scared."

The Downward Path to Wisdom [395]

The little boy couldn't raise his eyes, he was so heavy with shame. "Take this note to his mother," said Grandma.

She sat in a wide chair and ran her hands over his head, combing his hair with her fingers; she lifted his chin and kissed him. "Poor little fellow," she said. "Never you mind. You always have a good time at your grandma's, don't you? You're going to have a nice little visit, just like the last time."

The little boy leaned against the stiff, dry-smelling clothes and felt horribly grieved about something. He began to whimper and said, "I'm hungry. I want something to eat." This reminded him. He began to bellow at the top of his voice; he threw himself upon the carpet and rubbed his nose in a dusty woolly bouquet of roses. "I want my peanuts," he howled. "Somebody took my peanuts."

His grandma knelt beside him and gathered him up so tightly he could hardly move. She called in a calm voice above his howls to Old Janet in the doorway, "Bring me some bread and butter with strawberry jam."

"I want peanuts," yelled the little boy desperately.

"No, you don't, darling," said his grandma. "You don't want horrid old peanuts to make you sick. You're going to have some of grandma's nice fresh bread with good strawberries on it. That's what you're going to have." He sat afterward very quietly and ate and ate. His grandma sat near him and Old Janet stood by, near a tray with a loaf and a glass bowl of jam upon the table at the window. Outside there was a trellis with tube-shaped red flowers clinging all over it, and brown bees singing.

"I hardly know what to do," said Grandma, "it's very . . ."

"Yes, m'am," said Old Janet, "it certainly is . . ."

Grandma said, "I can't possibly see the end of it. It's a terrible . . ."

"It certainly is bad," said Old Janet, "all this upset all the time and him such a baby."

Their voices ran on soothingly. The little boy ate and forgot to listen. He did not know these women, except by name. He could not understand what they were talking about; their hands and their clothes and their voices were dry and far away; they examined him with crinkled eyes without any expression that he could see. He sat there waiting for whatever they would do next with him. He hoped they would let him go out and play in the yard. The room was full of flowers and dark red curtains and big soft chairs, and the windows were open, but it was still dark in there somehow; dark, and a place he did not know, or trust.

"Now drink your milk," said Old Janet, holding out a silver cup.

"I don't want any milk," he said, turning his head away.

"Very well, Janet, he doesn't have to drink it," said Grandma quickly. "Now run out in the garden and play, darling. Janet, get his hoop."

A big strange man came home in the evenings who treated the little boy very confusingly. "Say 'please,' and 'thank you,' young man," he would roar, terrifyingly, when he gave any smallest object to the little boy. "Well, fellow, are you ready for a fight?" he would say, again, doubling up huge, hairy fists and making passes at him. "Come on now, you must learn to box." After the first few times this was fun.

"Don't teach him to be rough," said Grandma. "Time enough for all that."

"Now, Mother, we don't want him to be a sissy," said the big man. "He's got to toughen up early. Come on now, fellow, put up your mitts." The little boy liked this new word for hands. He learned to throw himself upon the strange big man, whose name was Uncle David, and hit him on the chest as hard as he could; the big man would laugh and hit him back with his huge, loose fists. Sometimes, but not often, Uncle David came home in the middle of the day. The little boy missed him on the other days, and would hang on the gate looking down the street for him. One evening he brought a large square package under his arm.

"Come over here, fellow, and see what I've got," he said, pulling off quantities of green paper and string from the box which was full of flat, folded colors. He put something in the little boy's hand. It was limp and silky and bright green with a tube on the end. "Thank you," said the little boy nicely, but not knowing what to do with it.

"Balloons," said Uncle David in triumph. "Now just put your mouth here and blow hard." The little boy blew hard and the green thing began to grow round and thin and silvery.

"Good for your chest," said Uncle David. "Blow some more." The little boy went on blowing and the balloon swelled steadily.

"Stop," said Uncle David, "that's enough." He twisted the tube to keep the air in. "That's the way," he said. "Now I'll blow one, and you blow one, and let's see who can blow up a big balloon the fastest."

They blew and blew, especially Uncle David. He puffed and panted and blew with all his might, but the little boy won. His balloon was perfectly round before Uncle David could even get started. The little boy was so proud he began to dance and shout, "I beat, I beat," and blew in his balloon again. It burst in his face and frightened him so he felt sick. "Ha ha, ho ho ho," whooped Uncle David. "That's the boy. I bet I can't do that. Now let's see." He blew until the beautiful bubble grew and wavered and burst into thin air, and there was only a small colored rag in his hand. This was a fine game. They went on with it until Grandma came in and said, "Time for supper now. No, you can't blow balloons at the table. Tomorrow maybe." And it was all over.

The next day, instead of being given balloons, he was hustled out of bed early, bathed in warm soapy water and given a big breakfast of soft-boiled eggs with toast and jam and milk. His grandma came in to kiss him good morning. "And I hope you'll be a good boy and obey your teacher," she told him.

"What's teacher?" asked the little boy.

"Teacher is at school," said Grandma. "She'll tell you all sorts of things and you must do as she says."

Mama and Papa had talked a great deal about School, and how they must send him there. They had told him it was a fine place with all kinds of toys and other children to play with. He felt he knew about School. "I didn't know it was time, Grandma," he said. "Is it today?"

"It's this very minute," said Grandma. "I told you a week ago."

Old Janet came in with her bonnet on. It was a prickly looking bundle held with a black rubber band under her back hair. "Come on," she said. "This is my busy day." She wore a dead cat slung around her neck, its sharp ears bent over under her baggy chin.

The little boy was excited and wanted to run ahead. "Hold to my hand like I told you," said old Janet. "Don't go running off like that and get yourself killed."

"I'm going to get killed, I'm going to get killed," sang the little boy, making a tune of his own.

"Don't say that, you give me the creeps," said old Janet. "Hold to my hand now." She bent over and looked at him, not at his face but at something on his clothes. His eyes followed hers.

"I declare," said Old Janet, "I did forget. I was going to sew it up. I might have known. I *told* your grandma it would be that way from now on."

"What?" asked the little boy.

"Just look at yourself," said Old Janet crossly. He looked at himself. There was a little end of him showing through the slit in his short blue flannel trousers. The trousers came halfway to his knees above, and his socks came halfway to his knees below, and all winter long his knees were cold. He remembered now how cold his knees were in cold weather. And how sometimes he would have to put the part of him that came through the slit back again, because he was cold there too. He saw at once what was wrong, and tried to arrange himself, but his mittens got in the way. Janet said, "Stop that, you bad boy," and with a firm thumb she set him in order, at the same time reaching under his belt to pull down and fold his knit undershirt over his front.

"There now," she said, "try not to disgrace yourself today." He felt guilty and red all over, because he had something that showed when he was dressed that was not supposed to show then. The different women who bathed him always wrapped him quickly in towels and hurried him into his clothes, because they saw something about him he could not see for himself. They hurried him so he never had a chance to see whatever it was they saw, and though he looked at himself when his clothes were off, he could not find out what was wrong with him. Outside, in his clothes, he knew he looked like everybody else, but inside his clothes there was something bad the matter with him. It worried him and confused him and he wondered about it. The only people who never seemed to notice there was something wrong with him were Mommanpoppa. They never called him a bad boy, and all summer long they had taken all his clothes off and let him run in the sand beside a big ocean.

"Look at him, isn't he a love?" Mamma would say and Papa would look, and say, "He's got a back like a prize fighter." Uncle David was a prize fighter when he doubled up his mitts and said, "Come on, fellow."

Old Janet held him firmly and took long steps under her big rustling skirts. He did not like Old Janet's smell. It made him a little quivery in the stomach; it was just like wet chicken feathers.

School was easy. Teacher was a square-shaped woman with square short hair and short skirts. She got in the way sometimes, but not often. The people around him were his size; he didn't have always to be stretching his neck up to faces bent over him, and he could sit on the chairs without having to climb. All the children had names, like Frances and Evelyn and Agatha and Edward and Martin, and his own name was Stephen. He was not Mama's "Baby," nor Papa's "Old Man"; he was not Uncle David's "Fellow" or Grandma's "Darling," or even Old Janet's "Bad Boy." He was Stephen. He was learning to read, and to sing a tune to some strange-looking letters or marks written in chalk on a blackboard. You talked one kind of lettering, and you sang another. All the children talked and sang in turn, and then all together. Stephen thought it a fine game. He felt awake and happy. They had soft clay and paper and wires and squares of colors in tin boxes to play with, colored blocks to build houses with. Afterward they all danced in a big ring, and then they danced in pairs, boys with girls. Stephen danced with Frances, and Frances kept saying, "Now you just follow me." She was a little taller than he was, and her hair stood up in short, shiny curls, the color of an ash tray on Papa's desk. She would say, "You can't dance." "I can dance too," said Stephen, jumping around holding her hands, "I can, too, dance." He was certain of it. "*You* can't dance," he told Frances, "you can't dance at all."

Then they had to change partners, and when they came round again, Frances said, "I don't *like* the way you dance." This was different. He felt uneasy about it. He didn't jump quite so high when the phonograph record started going dumdiddy dumdiddy again. "Go ahead, Stephen, you're doing fine," said Teacher, waving her hands together very fast. The dance ended, and they all played "relaxing" for five minutes. They relaxed by swinging their arms back and forth, then rolling their heads round and round.

When Old Janet came for him he didn't want to go home. At lunch his grandma told him twice to keep his face out of his plate. "Is that what they teach you at school?" she asked. Uncle David was at home. "Here you are, fellow," he said and gave Stephen two balloons. "Thank you," said Stephen. He put the balloons in his pocket and forgot about them. "I told you that boy could learn something," said Uncle David to Grandma. "Hear him say 'thank you'?"

In the afternoon at school Teacher handed out big wads of clay and told the children to make something out of it. Anything they liked. Stephen decided to make a cat, like Mama's Meeow at home. He did not like Meeow, but he thought it would be easy to make a cat. He could not get the clay to work at all. It simply fell into one lump after another. So he stopped, wiped his hands on his pull-over, remembered his balloons and began blowing one.

"Look at Stephen's horse," said Frances. "Just look at it."

"It's not a horse, it's a cat," said Stephen. The other children gathered around. "It looks like a horse, a little," said Martin.

"It is a cat," said Stephen, stamping his foot, feeling his face turning hot. The other children all laughed and exclaimed over Stephen's cat that looked like a horse. Teacher came down among them. She sat usually at the top of the room before a big table covered with papers and playthings. She picked up Stephen's lump of clay and turned it round and examined it with her kind eyes. "Now, children," she said, "everybody has the right to make anything the way he pleases. If Stephen says this is a cat, it *is* a cat. Maybe you were thinking about a horse, Stephen?"

"It's a *cat*," said Stephen. He was aching all over. He knew then he should have said at first, "Yes, it's a horse." Then they would have let him alone. They would never have known he was trying to make a cat. "It's Meeow," he said in a trembling voice, "but I forgot how she looks."

His balloon was perfectly flat. He started blowing it up again, trying not to cry. Then it was time to go home, and Old Janet came looking for him. While Teacher was talking to other grown-up people who came to take other children home, Frances said, "Give me your balloon; I haven't got a balloon." Stephen handed it to her. He was happy to give it. He reached in his pocket and took out the other. Happily, he gave her that one too. Frances took it, then handed it back. "Now you blow up one and I'll blow up the other, and let's have a race," she said. When their balloons were only half filled Old Janet took Stephen by the arm and said, "Come on here, this is my busy day."

Frances ran after them, calling, "Stephen, you give me back my balloon," and snatched it away. Stephen did not know whether he was surprised to find himself going away with Frances' balloon, or whether he was surprised to see her snatching it as if it really belonged to her. He was badly mixed up in his mind, and Old Janet was hauling him along. One thing he knew, he liked Frances, he was going to see her again tomorrow, and he was going to bring her more balloons.

That evening Stephen boxed awhile with his uncle David, and Uncle David gave him a beautiful orange. "Eat that," he said, "it's good for your health."

"Uncle David, may I have some more balloons?" asked Stephen.

"Well, what do you say first?" asked Uncle David, reaching for the box on the top bookshelf.

"Please," said Stephen.

"That's the word," said Uncle David. He brought out two balloons, a red and a yellow one. Stephen noticed for the first time they had letters on them, very small letters that grew taller and wider as the balloon grew rounder. "Now that's all, fellow," said Uncle David. "Don't ask for any more because that's all." He put the box back on the bookshelf, but not before Stephen had seen that the box was almost full of balloons. He didn't say a word, but went on blowing, and Uncle David blew also. Stephen thought it was the nicest game he had ever known.

He had only one left, the next day, but he took it to school and gave it to Frances. "There are a lot," he said, feeling very proud and warm; "I'll bring you a lot of them."

Frances blew it up until it made a beautiful bubble, and said, "Look, I want to show you something." She took a sharp-pointed stick they used in working the clay; she poked the balloon, and it exploded. "Look at that," she said.

"That's nothing," said Stephen, "I'll bring you some more."

After school, before Uncle David came home, while Grandma was resting, when Old Janet had given him his milk and told him to run away and not bother her, Stephen dragged a chair to the bookshelf, stood upon it and reached into the box. He did not take three or four as he believed he intended; once his hands were upon them he seized what they could hold and jumped off the chair, hugging them to him. He stuffed them into his reefer pocket where they folded down and hardly made a lump.

He gave them all to Frances. There were so many, Frances gave most of them away to the other children. Stephen, flushed with his new joy, the lavish pleasure of giving presents, found almost at once still another happiness. Suddenly he was popular among the children; they invited him specially to join whatever games were up; they fell in at once with his own notions for play, and asked him what he would like to do next. They had festivals of blowing up the beautiful globes, fuller and rounder and thinner, changing as they went from deep color to lighter, paler tones, growing glassy thin, bubbly thin, then bursting with a thrilling loud noise like a toy pistol.

For the first time in his life Stephen had almost too much of something he wanted, and his head was so turned he forgot how this fullness came about, and no longer thought of it as a secret. The next day was

The Downward Path to Wisdom [401]

Saturday, and Frances came to visit him with her nurse. The nurse and Old Janet sat in Old Janet's room drinking coffee and gossiping, and the children sat on the side porch blowing balloons. Stephen chose an apple-colored one and Frances a pale green one. Between them on the bench lay a tumbled heap of delights still to come.

"I once had a silver balloon," said Frances, "a beyootiful silver one, not round like these; it was a long one. But these are even nicer, I think," she added quickly, for she did want to be polite.

"When you get through with that one," said Stephen, gazing at her with the pure bliss of giving added to loving, "you can blow up a blue one and then a pink one and a yellow one and a purple one." He pushed the heap of limp objects toward her. Her clear-looking eyes, with fine little rays of brown in them like the spokes of a wheel, were full of approval for Stephen. "I wouldn't want to be greedy, though, and blow up all your balloons."

"There'll be plenty more left," said Stephen, and his heart rose under his thin ribs. He felt his ribs with his fingers and discovered with some surprise that they stopped somewhere in front, while Frances sat blowing balloons rather halfheartedly. The truth was, she was tired of balloons. After you blow six or seven your chest gets hollow and your lips feel puckery. She had been blowing balloons steadily for three days now. She had begun to hope they were giving out. "There's boxes and boxes more of them, Frances," said Stephen happily. "Millions more. I guess they'd last and last if we didn't blow too many every day."

Frances said somewhat timidly, "I tell you what. Let's rest awhile and fix some liquish water. Do you like liquish?"

"Yes, I do," said Stephen, "but I haven't got any."

"Couldn't we buy some?" asked Frances. "It's only a cent a stick, the nice rubbery, twisty kind. We can put it in a bottle with some water, and shake it and shake it, and it makes foam on top like soda pop and we can drink it. I'm kind of thirsty," she said in a small, weak voice. "Blowing balloons all the time makes you thirsty, I think."

Stephen, in silence, realized a dreadful truth and a numb feeling crept over him. He did not have a cent to buy licorice for Frances and she was tired of his balloons. This was the first real dismay of his whole life, and he aged at least a year in the next minute, huddled, with his deep, serious blue eyes focused down his nose in intense speculation. What could he do to please Frances that would not cost money? Only yesterday Uncle David had given him a nickel, and he had thrown it away on gumdrops. He regretted that nickel so bitterly his neck and forehead were damp. He was thirsty too.

"I tell you what," he said, brightening with a splendid idea, lamely trailing off on second thought, "I know something we can do, I'll—I . . ."

"I *am* thirsty," said Frances with gentle persistence. "I think I'm so thirsty maybe I'll have to go home." She did not leave the bench, though, but sat, turning her grieved mouth toward Stephen.

Stephen quivered with the terrors of the adventure before him, but he said boldly, "I'll make some lemonade. I'll get sugar and lemon and some ice and we'll have lemonade."

"Oh, I love lemonade," cried Frances. "I'd rather have lemonade than liquish."

"You stay right here," said Stephen, "and I'll get everything."

He ran around the house, and under Old Janet's window he heard the dry, chattering voices of the two old women whom he must outwit. He sneaked on tiptoe to the pantry, took a lemon lying there by itself, a handful of lump sugar and a china teapot, smooth, round, with flowers and leaves all over it. These he left on the kitchen table while he broke a piece of ice with a sharp metal pick he had been forbidden to touch. He put the ice in the pot, cut the lemon and squeezed it as well as he could—a lemon was tougher and more slippery than he had thought—and mixed sugar and water. He decided there was not enough sugar so he sneaked back and took another handful. He was back on the porch in an astonishingly short time, his face tight, his knees trembling, carrying iced lemonade to thirsty Frances with both his devoted hands.

A pace distant from her he stopped, literally stabbed through with a thought. Here he stood in broad daylight carrying a teapot with lemonade in it, and his grandma or Old Janet might walk through the door at any moment.

"Come on, Frances," he whispered loudly. "Let's go round to the back behind the rose bushes where it's shady." Frances leaped up and ran like a deer beside him, her face wise with knowledge of why they ran; Stephen ran stiffly, cherishing his teapot with clenched hands.

It was shady behind the rose bushes, and much safer. They sat side by side on the dampish ground, legs doubled under, drinking in turn from the slender spout. Stephen took his just share in large, cool, delicious swallows. When Frances drank she set her round pink mouth daintily to the spout and her throat beat steadily as a heart. Stephen was thinking he had really done something pretty nice for Frances. He did not know where his own happiness was; it was mixed with the sweet-sour taste in his mouth and a cool feeling in his bosom because Frances was there drinking his lemonade which he had got for her with great danger.

Frances said, "My, what big swallows you take," when his turn came next.

"No bigger than yours," he told her downrightly. "You take awfully big swallows."

"Well," said Frances, turning this criticism into an argument for her rightness about things, "that's the way to drink lemonade anyway." She peered into the teapot. There was quite a lot of lemonade left and she

The Downward Path to Wisdom

was beginning to feel she had enough. "Let's make up a game and see who can take the biggest swallows."

This was such a wonderful notion they grew reckless, tipping the spout into their opened mouths above their heads until lemonade welled up and ran over their chins in rills down their fronts. When they tired of this there was still lemonade left in the pot. They played first at giving the rose bush a drink and ended by baptizing it. "Name father son holy-goat," shouted Stephen, pouring. At this sound Old Janet's face appeared over the low hedge, with the tan, disgusted-looking face of Frances' nurse hanging over her shoulder.

"Well, just as I thought," said Old Janet. "Just as I expected." The bag under her chin waggled.

"We were thirsty," he said; "we were awfully thirsty." Frances said nothing, but she gazed steadily at the toes of her shoes.

"Give me that teapot," said Old Janet, taking it with a rude snatch. "Just because you're thirsty is no reason," said Old Janet. "You can ask for things. You don't have to steal."

"We didn't steal," cried Frances suddenly. "We didn't. We didn't!"

"That's enough from you, missy," said her nurse. "Come straight out of there. You have nothing to do with this."

"Oh, I don't know," said Old Janet with a hard stare at Frances' nurse. "*He* never did such a thing before, by himself."

"Come on," said the nurse to Frances, "this is no place for you." She held Frances by the wrist and started walking away so fast Frances had to run to keep up. "Nobody can call *us* thieves and get away with it."

"You don't have to steal, even if others do," said Old Janet to Stephen, in a high carrying voice. "If you so much as pick up a lemon in somebody else's house you're a little thief." She lowered her voice then and said, "Now I'm going to tell your grandma and you'll see what you get."

"He went in the icebox and left it open," Janet told Grandma, "and he got into the lump sugar and spilt it all over the floor. Lumps everywhere underfoot. He dribbled water all over the clean kitchen floor, and he baptized the rose bush, blaspheming. And he took your Spode teapot."

"I didn't either," said Stephen loudly, trying to free his hand from Old Janet's big hard fist.

"Don't tell fibs," said Old Janet; "that's the last straw."

"Oh, dear," said Grandma. "He's not a baby any more." She shut the book she was reading and pulled the wet front of his pull-over toward her. "What's this sticky stuff on him?" she asked and straightened her glasses.

"Lemonade," said Old Janet. "He took the last lemon."

They were in the big dark room with the red curtains. Uncle David walked in from the room with the bookcases, holding a box in his uplifted hand. "Look here," he said to Stephen. "What's become of all my balloons?"

Stephen knew well that Uncle David was not really asking a question.

Stephen, sitting on a footstool at his grandma's knee, felt sleepy. He leaned heavily and wished he could put his head on her lap, but he might go to sleep, and it would be wrong to go to sleep while Uncle David was still talking. Uncle David walked about the room with his hands in his pockets, talking to Grandma. Now and then he would walk over to a lamp and, leaning, peer into the top of the shade, winking in the light, as if he expected to find something there.

"It's simply in the blood, I told her," said Uncle David. "I told her she would simply have to come and get him, and keep him. She asked me if I meant to call him a thief and I said if she could think of a more exact word I'd be glad to hear it."

"You shouldn't have said that," commented Grandma calmly.

"Why not? She might as well know the facts. . . . I suppose he can't help it," said Uncle David, stopping now in front of Stephen and dropping his chin into his collar, "I shouldn't expect too much of him, but you can't begin too early—"

"The trouble is," said Grandma, and while she spoke she took Stephen by the chin and held it up so that he had to meet her eye; she talked steadily in a mournful tone, but Stephen could not understand. She ended, "It's not just about the balloons, of course."

"It *is* about the balloons," said Uncle David angrily, "because balloons now mean something worse later. But what can you expect? His father —well, it's in the blood. He—"

"That's your sister's husband you're talking about," said Grandma, "and there is no use making things worse. Besides, you don't really *know*."

"I *do* know," said Uncle David. And he talked again very fast, walking up and down. Stephen tried to understand, but the sounds were strange and floating just over his head. They were talking about his father, and they did not like him. Uncle David came over and stood above Stephen and Grandma. He hunched over them with a frowning face, a long, crooked shadow from him falling across them to the wall. To Stephen he looked like his father, and he shrank against his grandma's skirts.

"The question is, what to do with him now?" asked Uncle David. "If we keep him here, he'd just be a—I won't be bothered with him. Why can't they take care of their own child? That house is crazy. Too far gone already, I'm afraid. No training. No example."

"You're right, they must take him and keep him," said Grandma. She ran her hands over Stephen's head; tenderly she pinched the nape of his neck between thumb and forefinger. "You're your Grandma's darling," she told him, "and you've had a nice long visit, and now you're going home. Mama is coming for you in a few minutes. Won't that be nice?"

"I want my mama," said Stephen, whimpering, for his grandma's face frightened him. There was something wrong with her smile.

Uncle David sat down. "Come over here, fellow," he said, wagging a forefinger at Stephen. Stephen went over slowly, and Uncle David drew him between his wide knees in their loose, rough clothes. "You ought to be ashamed of yourself," he said, "stealing Uncle David's balloons when he had already given you so many."

"It wasn't that," said Grandma quickly. "Don't say that. It will make an impression—"

"I hope it does," said Uncle David in a louder voice; "I hope he remembers it all his life. If he belonged to me I'd give him a good thrashing."

Stephen felt his mouth, his chin, his whole face jerking. He opened his mouth to take a breath, and tears and noise burst from him. "Stop that, fellow, stop that," said Uncle David, shaking him gently by the shoulders, but Stephen could not stop. He drew his breath again and it came back in a howl. Old Janet came to the door.

"Bring me some cold water," called Grandma. There was a flurry, a commotion, a breath of cool air from the hall, the door slammed, and Stephen heard his mother's voice. His howl died away, his breath sobbed and fluttered, he turned his dimmed eyes and saw her standing there. His heart turned over within him and he bleated like a lamb, "Maaaaama," running toward her. Uncle David stood back as Mama swooped in and fell on her knees beside Stephen. She gathered him to her and stood up with him in her arms.

"What are you doing to my baby?" she asked Uncle David in a thickened voice. "I should never have let him come here. I should have known better—"

"You always should know better," said Uncle David, "and you never do. And you never will. You haven't got it here," he told her, tapping his forehead.

"David," said Grandma, "that's your—"

"Yes, I know, she's my sister," said Uncle David. "I know it. But if she must run away and marry a—"

"Shut up," said Mama.

"And bring more like him into the world, let her keep them at home. I say let her keep—"

Mama set Stephen on the floor and, holding him by the hand, she said to Grandma all in a rush as if she were reading something, "Good-by, Mother. This is the last time, really the last. I can't bear it any longer. Say good-by to Stephen; you'll never see him again. You let this happen. It's your fault. You know David was a coward and a bully and a self-righteous little beast all his life and you never crossed him in anything. You let him bully me all my life and you let him slander my husband and call my baby a thief, and now this is the end. . . . He calls my baby a thief over a few horrible little balloons because he doesn't like my husband. . . ."

She was panting and staring about from one to the other. They were all standing. Now Grandma said, "Go home, daughter. Go away, David. I'm sick of your quarreling. I've never had a day's peace or comfort from either of you. I'm sick of you both. Now let me alone and stop this noise. Go away," said Grandma in a wavering voice. She took out her handkerchief and wiped first one eye and then the other and said, "All this hate, hate—what is it for? . . . So this is the way it turns out. Well, let me alone."

"You and your little advertising balloons," said Mama to Uncle David. "The big honest businessman advertises with balloons and if he loses one he'll be ruined. And your beastly little moral notions . . ."

Grandma went to the door to meet Old Janet, who handed her a glass of water. Grandma drank it all, standing there.

"Is your husband coming for you, or are you going home by yourself?" she asked Mama.

"I'm driving myself," said Mama in a far-away voice as if her mind had wandered. "You know he wouldn't set foot in this house."

"I should think not," said Uncle David.

"Come on, Stephen darling," said Mama. "It's far past his bedtime," she said, to no one in particular. "Imagine keeping a baby up to torture him about a few miserable little bits of colored rubber." She smiled at Uncle David with both rows of teeth as she passed him on the way to the door, keeping between him and Stephen. "Ah, where would we be without high moral standards," she said, and then to Grandma, "Good night, Mother," in quite her usual voice. "I'll see you in a day or so."

"Yes, indeed," said Grandma cheerfully, coming out into the hall with Stephen and Mama. "Let me hear from you. Ring me up tomorrow. I hope you'll be feeling better."

"I feel very well now," said Mama brightly, laughing. She bent down and kissed Stephen. "Sleepy, darling? Papa's waiting to see you. Don't go to sleep until you've kissed your papa good night."

Stephen woke with a sharp jerk. He raised his head and put out his chin a little. "I don't want to go home," he said; "I want to go to school. I don't want to see Papa, I don't like him."

Mama laid her palm over his mouth softly. "Darling, don't."

Uncle David put his head out with a kind of snort. "There you are," he said. "There you've got a statement from headquarters."

Mama opened the door and ran, almost carrying Stephen. She ran across the sidewalk, jerking open the car door and dragging Stephen in after her. She spun the car around and dashed forward so sharply Stephen was almost flung out of the seat. He sat braced then with all his might, hands digging into the cushions. The car speeded up and the trees and houses whizzed by all flattened out. Stephen began suddenly to sing to

The Downward Path to Wisdom

himself, a quiet, inside song so Mama would not hear. He sang his new secret; it was a comfortable, sleepy song: "I hate Papa, I hate Mama, I hate Grandma, I hate Uncle David, I hate Old Janet, I hate Marjory, I hate Papa, I hate Mama . . ."

His head bobbed, leaned, came to rest on Mama's knee, eyes closed. Mama drew him closer and slowed down, driving with one hand.

This child's sudden terror for the safety of her widowed mother suggests unconscious currents of hostility, along with the unreasoning, insatiable demands so frequent in children.

ELIZABETH BOWEN

Coming Home

ALL THE WAY HOME from school Rosalind's cheeks burnt, she felt something throbbing in her ears. It was sometimes terrible to live so far away. Before her body had turned the first corner her mind had many times wrenched open their gate, many times rushed up their path through the damp smells of the garden, waving the essay-book, and seen Darlingest coming to the window. Nothing like this had ever happened before to either her or Darlingest; it was the supreme moment that all these years they had been approaching, of which those dim, improbable future years would be spent in retrospect.

Rosalind's essay had been read aloud and everybody had praised it. Everybody had been there, the big girls sitting along the sides of the room had turned and looked at her, raising their eyebrows and smiling. For an infinity of time the room had held nothing but the rising and falling of Miss Wilfred's beautiful voice doing the service of Rosalind's brain. When the voice dropped to silence and the room was once more unbearably crowded, Rosalind had looked at the clock and seen that her essay had taken four and a half minutes to read. She found that her mouth was dry and her eyes ached from staring at a small fixed spot in the heart of whirling circles, and her knotted hands were damp and trembling. Somebody behind her gently poked the small of her back. Everybody in the room was thinking about Rosalind; she felt their admiration and attention lapping up against her in small waves. A long way off somebody spoke her name repeatedly, she stood up stupidly and everybody laughed. Miss Wilfred was trying to pass her back the red exercise-book. Rosalind sat down again thinking to herself how dazed she was, dazed with glory. She was beginning already to feel about for words for Darlingest.

She had understood some time ago that nothing became real for her until she had had time to live it over again. An actual occurrence was nothing but the blankness of a shock, then the knowledge that something had happened; afterwards one could creep back and look into one's mind and find new things in it, clear and solid. It was like waiting outside the hen-house till the hen came off the nest and then going in to look for the egg. She would not touch this egg until she was with Darlingest, then they would go and look for it together. Suddenly and vividly this afternoon would be real for her. "I won't think about it yet," she said, "for fear I'd spoil it."

The houses grew scarcer and the roads greener, and Rosalind relaxed a little; she was nearly home. She looked at the syringa-bushes by the gate, and it was as if a cold wing had brushed against her. Supposing Darlingest were out . . . ?

She slowed down her running steps to a walk. From here she would be able to call to Darlingest. But if she didn't answer there would be still a tortuous hope; she might be at the back of the house. She decided to pretend it didn't matter, one way or the other; she had done this before, and it rather took the wind out of Somebody's sails, she felt. She hitched up her essay-book under her arm, approached the gate, turned carefully to shut it, and walked slowly up the path looking carefully down at her feet, not up at all at the drawing-room window. Darlingest would think she was playing a game. Why didn't she hear her tapping on the glass with her thimble?

As soon as she entered the hall she knew that the house was empty. Clocks ticked very loudly; upstairs and downstairs the doors were a little open, letting through pale strips of light. Only the kitchen door was shut, down the end of the passage, and she could hear Emma moving about behind it. There was a spectral shimmer of light in the white panelling. On the table was a bowl of primroses; Darlingest must have put them there that morning. The hall was chilly; she could not think why the primroses gave her such a feeling of horror, then she remembered the wreath of primroses, and the scent of it, lying on the raw new earth of that grave. . . . The pair of grey gloves were gone from the bowl of visiting-cards. Darlingest had spent the morning doing those deathly primroses, and then taken up her grey gloves and gone out, at the end of the afternoon, just when she knew her little girl would be coming in. A quarter-past four. It was unforgivable of Darlingest: she had been a mother for more than twelve years, the mother exclusively of Rosalind, and still, it seemed, she knew no better than to do a thing like that. Other people's mothers had terrible little babies: they ran quickly in and out to go to them, or they had smoky husbands who came in and sat, with big feet. There was something distracted about other people's mothers. But Darlingest, so exclusively one's own. . . .

Darlingest could never have really believed in her. She could never have really believed that Rosalind would do anything wonderful at school, or she would have been more careful to be in to hear about it. Rosalind flung herself into the drawing-room; it was honey-coloured and lovely in the pale spring light, another little clock was ticking in the corner, there were more bowls of primroses and black-eyed, lowering anemones. The tarnished mirror on the wall distorted and reproved her angry face in its mild mauveness. Tea was spread on the table by the window, tea for two that the two might never. . . . Her work and an open book lay on the tumbled cushions of the window-seat. All the afternoon she had sat there waiting and working, and now—poor little Darlingest, perhaps she had gone out because she was lonely.

People who went out sometimes never came back again. Here she was, being angry with Darlingest, and all the time. . . . Well, she had drawn on those grey gloves and gone out wandering along the roads, vague and beautiful, because she was lonely, and then?

Ask Emma? No, she wouldn't; fancy having to ask *her!*

"Yes, your mother'll be in soon, Miss Rosie. Now run and get your things off, there's a good girl—" Oh no, intolerable.

The whole house was full of the scent and horror of the primroses. Rosalind dropped the exercise-book on the floor, looked at it, hesitated, and putting her hands over her mouth, went upstairs, choking back her sobs. She heard the handle of the kitchen door turn; Emma was coming out. O God! Now she was on the floor by Darlingest's bed, with the branches swaying and brushing outside the window, smothering her face in the eiderdown, smelling and tasting the wet satin. Down in the hall she heard Emma call her, mutter something, and slam back into the kitchen.

How could she ever have left Darlingest? She might have known, she might have known. The sense of insecurity had been growing on her year by year. A person might be part of you, almost part of your body, and yet once you went away from them they might utterly cease to be. That sea of horror ebbing and flowing round the edges of the world, whose tides were charted in the newspapers, might sweep out a long wave over them and they would be gone. There was no security. Safety and happiness were a game that grown-up people played with children to keep them from understanding, possibly to keep themselves from thinking. But they did think, that was what made grown-up people— queer. Anything might happen, there was no security. And now Darlingest—

This was her dressing-table, with the long beads straggling over it, the little coloured glass barrels and bottles had bright flames in the centre. In front of the looking-glass, filmed faintly over with a cloud of powder, Darlingest had put her hat on—for the last time. Supposing all that had ever been reflected in it were imprisoned somewhere in the back of a looking-glass. The blue hat with the drooping brim was hanging over the corner of a chair. Rosalind had never been kind about that blue hat, she didn't think it was becoming. And Darlingest had loved it so. She must have gone out wearing the brown one; Rosalind went over to the wardrobe and stood on tip-toe to look on the top shelf. Yes, the brown hat was gone. She would never see Darlingest again, in the brown hat, coming down the road to meet her and not seeing her because she was thinking about something else. Peau d'Espagne crept faintly from among the folds of the dresses; the blue, the gold, the soft furred edges of the tea-gown dripping out of the wardrobe. She heard herself making a high, whining noise at the back of her throat, like a puppy, felt her swollen face distorted by another paroxysm.

"I can't bear it, I can't bear it. What have I done? I did love her, I did so awfully love her.

"Perhaps she was all right when I came in; coming home smiling. Then I stopped loving her, I hated her and was angry. And it happened. She was crossing a road and something happened to her. I was angry and she died. I killed her.

"I don't know that she's dead. I'd better get used to believing it, it will hurt less afterwards. Supposing she does come back this time; it's only for a little. I shall never be able to keep her; now I've found out about this I shall never be happy. Life's nothing but waiting for awfulness to happen and trying to think about something else.

"If she could come back just this once—Darlingest."

Emma came half-way upstairs; Rosalind flattened herself behind the door.

"Will you begin your tea, Miss Rosie?"

"No. Where's mother?"

"I didn't hear her go out. I have the kettle boiling—will I make your tea?"

"No. *No.*"

Rosalind slammed the door on the angry mutterings, and heard with a sense of desolation Emma go downstairs. The silver clock by Darlingest's bed ticked; it was five o'clock. They had tea at a quarter-past four; Darlingest was never, never late. When they came to tell her about *It*, men would come, and they would tell Emma, and Emma would come up with a frightened, triumphant face and tell her.

She saw the grey-gloved hands spread out in the dust.

A sound at the gate. "I can't bear it, I can't bear it. Oh, save me, God!"

Steps on the gravel.

Darlingest.

She was at the window, pressing her speechless lips together.

Darlingest came slowly up the path with the long ends of her veil, untied, hanging over her shoulders. A paper parcel was pressed between her arm and her side. She paused, stood smiling down at the daffodils. Then she looked up with a start at the windows, as though she heard somebody calling. Rosalind drew back into the room.

She heard her mother's footsteps cross the stone floor of the hall, hesitate at the door of the drawing-room, and come over to the foot of the stairs. The voice was calling "Lindie! Lindie, duckie!" She was coming upstairs.

Rosalind leaned the weight of her body against the dressing-table and dabbed her face with the big powder-puff; the powder clung in paste to her wet lashes and in patches over her nose and cheeks. She was not happy, she was not relieved, she felt no particular feeling about Darlingest, did not even want to see her. Something had slackened down inside her, leaving her a little sick.

"Oh, you're *there*," said Darlingest from outside, hearing her movements. "Where did, where were—?"

She was standing in the doorway. Nothing had been for the last time, after all. She had come back. One could never explain to her how wrong she had been. She was holding out her arms; something drew one towards them.

"But, my little *Clown*," said Darlingest, wiping off the powder. "But, oh—" She scanned the glazed, blurred face. "Tell me why," she said.

"You were late."

"Yes, it was horrid of me; did you mind? . . . But that was silly, Rosalind, I can't be always in."

"But you're my mother."

Darlingest was amused; little trickles of laughter and gratification ran out of her. "You weren't *frightened*, Silly Billy." Her tone changed to distress. "Oh, Rosalind, don't be cross."

"I'm not," said Rosalind coldly.

"Then come—"

"I was wanting my tea."

"Rosalind, *don't* be—"

Rosalind walked past her to the door. She was hurting Darlingest, beautifully hurting her. She would never tell her about that essay. Everybody would be talking about it, and when Darlingest heard and asked her about it she would say: "Oh, that? I didn't think you'd be interested." That would hurt. She went down into the drawing-room, past the primroses. The grey gloves were back on the table. This was the mauve and golden room that Darlingest had come back to, from under the Shadow of Death, expecting to find her little daughter. . . . They would have sat together on the window-seat while Rosalind read the essay aloud, leaning their heads closer together as the room grew darker.

That was all spoilt.

Poor Darlingest, up there alone in the bedroom, puzzled, hurt, disappointed, taking off her hat. She hadn't known she was going to be hurt like this when she stood out there on the gravel, smiling at the daffodils. The red essay-book lay spread open on the carpet. There was the paper bag she had been carrying, lying on a table by the door; macaroons, all squashy from being carried the wrong way, disgorging, through a tear in the paper, a little trickle of crumbs.

The pathos of the forgotten macaroons, the silent pain! Rosalind ran upstairs to the bedroom.

Darlingest did not hear her; she had forgotten. She was standing in the middle of the room with her face turned towards the window, looking at something a long way away, smiling and singing to herself and rolling up her veil.

A mother teaches her son the difference between cruelty and the skill and courage needed to fight for survival in a Negro slum.

RICHARD WRIGHT

from *Black Boy*

ONE MORNING my brother and I, while playing in the rear of our flat, found a stray kitten that set up a loud, persistent meowing. We fed it some scraps of food and gave it water, but it still meowed. My father, clad in his underwear, stumbled sleepily to the back door and demanded that we keep quiet. We told him that it was the kitten that was making the noise and he ordered us to drive it away. We tried to make the kitten leave, but it would not budge. My father took a hand.

"Scat!" he shouted.

The scrawny kitten lingered, brushing itself against our legs, and meowing plaintively.

"Kill that damn thing!" my father exploded. "Do anything, but get it away from here!"

He went inside, grumbling. I resented his shouting and it irked me that I could never make him feel my resentment. How could I hit back at him? Oh, yes . . . He had said to kill the kitten and I would kill it! I knew that he had not really meant for me to kill the kitten, but my deep hate of him urged me toward a literal acceptance of his word.

"He said for us to kill the kitten," I told my brother.

"He didn't mean it," my brother said.

"He did, and I'm going to kill 'im."

"Then he *will* howl," my brother said.

"He can't howl if he's dead," I said.

"He didn't really say kill 'im," my brother protested.

"He did!" I said. "And you heard him!"

My brother ran away in fright. I found a piece of rope, made a noose, slipped it about the kitten's neck, pulled it over a nail, then jerked the animal clear of the ground. It gasped, slobbered, spun, doubled, clawed

from *Black Boy*

the air frantically; finally its mouth gaped and its pink-white tongue shot out stiffly. I tied the rope to a nail and went to find my brother. He was crouching behind a corner of the building.

"I killed 'im," I whispered.

"You did bad," my brother said.

"Now Papa can sleep," I said, deeply satisfied.

"He didn't mean for you to kill 'im," my brother said.

"Then why did he *tell* me to do it?" I demanded.

My brother could not answer; he stared fearfully at the dangling kitten.

"That kitten's going to get you," he warned me.

"I'm going to tell," my brother said, running into the house.

I waited, resolving to defend myself with my father's rash words, anticipating my enjoyment in repeating them to him even though I knew that he had spoken them in anger. My mother hurried toward me, drying her hands upon her apron. She stopped and paled when she saw the kitten suspended from the rope.

"What in God's name have you done?" she asked.

"The kitten was making noise and Papa said to kill it," I explained.

"You little fool!" she said. "Your father's going to beat you for this!"

"But he told me to kill it," I said.

"You shut your mouth!"

She grabbed my hand and dragged me to my father's bedside and told him what I had done.

"You know better than that!" my father stormed.

"You told me to kill 'im," I said.

"I told you to drive him away," he said.

"You told me to kill 'im," I countered positively.

"You get out of my eyes before I smack you down!" my father bellowed in disgust, then turned over in bed.

I had had my first triumph over my father. I had made him believe that I had taken his words literally. He could not punish me now without risking his authority. I was happy because I had at last found a way to throw my criticism of him into his face. I had made him feel that, if he whipped me for killing the kitten, I would never give serious weight to his words again. I had made him know that I felt he was cruel and I had done it without his punishing me.

But my mother, being more imaginative, retaliated with an assault upon my sensibilities that crushed me with the moral horror involved in taking a life. All that afternoon she directed toward me calculated words that spawned in my mind a horde of invisible demons bent upon exacting vengeance for what I had done. As evening drew near, anxiety filled me and I was afraid to go into an empty room alone.

"You owe a debt you can never pay," my mother said.

"I'm sorry," I mumbled.

"Being sorry can't make that kitten live again," she said.

Then, just before I was to go to bed, she uttered a paralyzing injunction: she ordered me to go out into the dark, dig a grave, and bury the kitten.

"No!" I screamed, feeling that if I went out of doors some evil spirit would whisk me away.

"Get out there and bury that poor kitten," she ordered.

"I'm scared!"

"And wasn't that kitten scared when you put that rope around its neck?" she asked.

"But it was only a kitten," I explained.

"But it was alive," she said. "Can you make it live again?"

"But Papa said to kill it," I said, trying to shift the moral blame upon my father.

My mother whacked me across my mouth with the flat palm of her hand.

"You stop that lying! You knew what he meant!"

"I didn't!" I bawled.

She shoved a tiny spade into my hands.

"Go out there and dig a hole and bury that kitten!"

I stumbled out into the black night, sobbing, my legs wobbly from fear. Though I knew that I had killed the kitten, my mother's words had made it live again in my mind. What would that kitten do to me when I touched it? Would it claw at my eyes? As I groped toward the dead kitten, my mother lingered behind me, unseen in the dark, her disembodied voice egging me on.

"Mama, come and stand by me," I begged.

"You didn't stand by that kitten, so why should I stand by you?" she asked tauntingly from the menacing darkness.

"I can't touch it," I whimpered, feeling that the kitten was staring at me with reproachful eyes.

"Untie it!" she ordered.

Shuddering, I fumbled at the rope and the kitten dropped to the pavement with a thud that echoed in my mind for many days and nights. Then, obeying my mother's floating voice, I hunted for a spot of earth, dug a shallow hole, and buried the stiff kitten; as I handled its cold body my skin prickled. When I had completed the burial, I sighed and started back to the flat, but my mother caught hold of my hand and led me again to the kitten's grave.

"Shut your eyes and repeat after me," she said.

I closed my eyes tightly, my hand clinging to hers.

"Dear God, our Father, forgive me, for I knew not what I was doing . . ."

from *Black Boy*

"Dear God, our Father, forgive me, for I knew not what I was doing," I repeated.

"And spare my poor life, even though I did not spare the life of the kitten . . ."

"And spare my poor life, even though I did not spare the life of the kitten," I repeated.

"And while I sleep tonight, do not snatch the breath of life from me . . ."

I opened my mouth but no words came. My mind was frozen with horror. I pictured myself gasping for breath and dying in my sleep. I broke away from my mother and ran into the night, crying, shaking with dread.

"No," I sobbed.

My mother called to me many times, but I would not go to her.

"Well, I suppose you've learned your lesson," she said at last.

Contrite, I went to bed, hoping that I would never see another kitten.

✸ ✸ ✸

Hunger stole upon me so slowly that at first I was not aware of what hunger really meant. Hunger had always been more or less at my elbow when I played, but now I began to wake up at night to find hunger standing at my bedside, staring at me gauntly. The hunger I had known before this had been no grim, hostile stranger; it had been a normal hunger that had made me beg constantly for bread, and when I ate a crust or two I was satisfied. But this new hunger baffled me, scared me, made me angry and insistent. Whenever I begged for food now my mother would pour me a cup of tea which would still the clamor in my stomach for a moment or two; but a little later I would feel hunger nudging my ribs, twisting my empty guts until they ached. I would grow dizzy and my vision would dim. I became less active in my play, and for the first time in my life I had to pause and think of what was happening to me.

"Mama, I'm hungry," I complained one afternoon.

"Jump up and catch a kungry," she said, trying to make me laugh and forget.

"What's a *kungry*?"

"It's what little boys eat when they get hungry," she said.

"What does it taste like?"

"I don't know."

"Then why do you tell me to catch one?"

"Because you said that you were hungry," she said smiling.

I sensed that she was teasing me and it made me angry.

"But I'm hungry. I want to eat."

"You'll have to wait."

"But I want to eat now."

"But there's nothing to eat," she told me.

"Why?"

"Just because there's none," she explained.

"But I want to eat," I said, beginning to cry.

"You'll just have to wait," she said again.

"But why?"

"For God to send some food."

"When is He going to send it?"

"I don't know."

"But I'm hungry!"

She was ironing and she paused and looked at me with tears in her eyes.

"Where's your father?" she asked me.

I stared in bewilderment. Yes, it was true that my father had not come home to sleep for many days now and I could make as much noise as I wanted. Though I had not known why he was absent, I had been glad that he was not there to shout his restrictions at me. But it had never occurred to me that his absence would mean that there would be no food.

"I don't know," I said.

"Who brings food into the house?" my mother asked me.

"Papa," I said. "He always brought food."

"Well, your father isn't here now," she said.

"Where is he?"

"I don't know," she said.

"But I'm hungry," I whimpered, stomping my feet.

"You'll have to wait until I get a job and buy food," she said.

As the days slid past the image of my father became associated with my pangs of hunger, and whenever I felt hunger I thought of him with a deep biological bitterness.

My mother finally went to work as a cook and left me and my brother alone in the flat each day with a loaf of bread and a pot of tea. When she returned at evening she would be tired and dispirited and would cry a lot. Sometimes, when she was in despair, she would call us to her and talk to us for hours, telling us that we now had no father, that our lives would be different from those of other children, that we must learn as soon as possible to take care of ourselves, to dress ourselves, to prepare our own food; that we must take upon ourselves the responsibility of the flat while she worked. Half frightened, we would promise solemnly. We did not understand what had happened between our father and our mother and the most that these long talks did to us was to make us feel a vague dread. Whenever we asked why father had left, she would tell us that we were too young to know.

One evening my mother told me that thereafter I would have to do the shopping for food. She took me to the corner store to show me the

from *Black Boy*

way. I was proud; I felt like a grownup. The next afternoon I looped the basket over my arm and went down the pavement toward the store. When I reached the corner, a gang of boys grabbed me, knocked me down, snatched the basket, took the money, and sent me running home in panic. That evening I told my mother what had happened, but she made no comment; she sat down at once, wrote another note, gave me more money, and sent me out to the grocery again. I crept down the steps and saw the same gang of boys playing down the street. I ran back into the house.

"What's the matter?" my mother asked.

"It's those same boys," I said. "They'll beat me."

"You've got to get over that," she said. "Now, go on."

"I'm scared," I said.

"Go on and don't pay any attention to them," she said.

I went out of the door and walked briskly down the sidewalk, praying that the gang would not molest me. But when I came abreast of them someone shouted.

"There he is!"

They came toward me and I broke into a wild run toward home. They overtook me and flung me to the pavement. I yelled, pleaded, kicked, but they wrenched the money out of my hand. They yanked me to my feet, gave me a few slaps, and sent me home sobbing. My mother met me at the door.

"They b-beat m-me," I gasped. "They t-t-took the m-money."

I started up the steps, seeking the shelter of the house.

"Don't you come in here," my mother warned me.

I froze in my tracks and stared at her.

"But they're coming after me," I said.

"You just stay right where you are," she said in a deadly tone. "I'm going to teach you this night to stand up and fight for yourself."

She went into the house and I waited, terrified, wondering what she was about. Presently she returned with more money and another note; she also had a long heavy stick.

"Take this money, this note, and this stick," she said. "Go to the store and buy those groceries. If those boys bother you, then fight."

I was baffled. My mother was telling me to fight, a thing that she had never done before.

"But I'm scared," I said.

"Don't you come into this house until you've gotten those groceries," she said.

"They'll beat me; they'll beat me," I said.

"Then stay in the streets; don't come back here!"

I ran up the steps and tried to force my way past her into the house. A stinging slap came on my jaw. I stood on the sidewalk, crying.

"Please, let me wait until tomorrow," I begged.

"No," she said. "Go now! If you come back into this house without those groceries, I'll whip you!"

She slammed the door and I heard the key turn in the lock. I shook with fright. I was alone upon the dark, hostile streets and gangs were after me. I had the choice of being beaten at home or away from home. I clutched the stick, crying, trying to reason. If I were beaten at home, there was absolutely nothing that I could do about it; but if I were beaten in the streets, I had a chance to fight and defend myself. I walked slowly down the sidewalk, coming closer to the gang of boys, holding the stick tightly. I was so full of fear that I could scarcely breathe. I was almost upon them now.

"There he is again!" the cry went up.

They surrounded me quickly and began to grab for my hand.

"I'll kill you!" I threatened.

They closed in. In blind fear I let the stick fly, feeling it crack against a boy's skull. I swung again, lamming another skull, then another. Realizing that they would retaliate if I let up for but a second, I fought to lay them low, to knock them cold, to kill them so that they could not strike back at me. I flayed with tears in my eyes, teeth clenched, stark fear making me throw every ounce of my strength behind each blow. I hit again and again, dropping the money and the grocery list. The boys scattered, yelling, nursing their heads, staring at me in utter disbelief. They had never seen such frenzy. I stood panting, egging them on, taunting them to come on and fight. When they refused, I ran after them and they tore out for their homes, screaming. The parents of the boys rushed into the streets and threatened me, and for the first time in my life I shouted at grownups, telling them that I would give them the same if they bothered me. I finally found my grocery list and the money and went to the store. On my way back I kept my stick poised for instant use, but there was not a single boy in sight. That night I won the right to the streets of Memphis.

A young father does his best to explain to two young children the reasons for his impending divorce from their mother.

HERBERT GOLD

from *Love and Like, Part 4*

PAULA, who was six, said to her father, "Mommy says you don't love her any more."

Her father, who was thirty-two, replied, "No, but I like her."

"But, but," said Cynthia, who was just four. "But can I go out and find Gary?"

"Why don't you stay with me for a little while?" her father asked. Dismayed by his querulousness, he repeated the remark in another voice. "Stay here with me. I have to go back soon. Anyway," he added, "it's almost bedtime."

"Okay," said Cynthia, resigned. She was a very small child, pouting and serious, with overbusy limbs. She paced back and forth on the long, low, especially constructed, "contemporary" couch which her mother had bought partly because her father didn't want it.

"But *why* don't you love Mommy any more?" Paula insisted. "You always told me you did."

"That was b-b-before." Her father stammered for an explanation, dulled by knowing that there could be no valid one for Paula. "I tried—we did—I wanted to. We just weren't happy together. You know how that is, Paula."

"No," she said flatly and firmly.

"We have to live separately. It's like when you and Cynthia are tired and quarrel. We put you in separate rooms until you feel better."

"When are you and Mommy going to feel better?"

"It's not exactly that way with grownups." The sly innocence of Paula's question brought his hand out to touch her pleadingly; he wiped away the smudge of dirt on her cheek. She always made herself up with a stroke of dust as soon as possible when her mother washed her face.

Cynthia, humming to herself, was listening with a smudge of prying watchfulness across her eyes. With a premature false security, the two girls frowned for serious discussion. The children of the divorced are engaged too soon in love as a strategy. Joy recedes before strategy; these children are robbed of their childhood. The huge brooding of possibility which human beings have at their best comes of the long passionate carnival of childhood; no fear of cost down this midway, just another and another breath-taking joyride on the great rollercoaster! and another quiet gathering-in of food and rest—it should be. It should be a storing of unquestioned certainties for the infinite risks of being a person. But instead, instead. Heavily Shaper touched the two girls as if to make them child animals again. It was not right that a father should feel this hopeless pity, and this need to enlist his daughters in the harried legions of rationality: "Here's how it is with grownups—"

"You mean Mommy and you?"

"Yes. Yes. Now listen. We feel better living in separate places. We're going to stay like that. But we like each other, Paula, and we love you and Cynthia. We both do."

"But, but, but, but," Cynthia sang, carefully wiping her feet on the pillows. "But heigh-ho, the derry-oh, the farmer takes a wife."

"Cynthia," said her father, "you shouldn't. Take off your shoes if you're going to play on the couch. It wasn't made for children."

Cynthia looked at him silently and, scraping the fabric, slid down beside him. Paula pulled between his knees, fighting to get closer than her sister. She began to suck her thumb. Her father pressed his lips together, resisted the temptation to remove her thumb from her mouth, and instead lit a cigarette. He decided that perhaps his silence would oblige her to remove the thumb and speak. It did not. At last he said, "I want you to understand. Mommy wants you to understand, too. Even though I'm not going to be Mommy's husband anymore, I'll always be your father. I couldn't change that even if I wanted to, and besides, I would never want to. Don't you want always to be my daughters?"

Sucking busily, Paula said nothing.

Cynthia announced with a grin, "But I want a daddy who loves my mommy. I think maybe Uncle Carl, he loves Mommy—" The look on her father's face told her that he was not enjoying her joke. "But I *know* you're my daddy for real."

"I am. For real."

"Okay," she said, bored with the discussion.

Paula looked at her wet and slippery thumb, considered putting it back, had another idea. "Why doesn't Mommy say hardly anything to you no more?"

"*Any* more," her father said. "I already explained. Because we don't get along—just like we don't let you and Cynthia talk to each other when

from *Love and Like*, Part 4

you don't get along—"

"But we do anyway! But that's only for a few minutes! But it's not, not, *not* the same thing, Daddy!"

"No," he said, "you're right. It's really not."

"Then *when?*"

"When what?"

"When are you coming to sleep here again?"

"I told you, I already explained. Mommy and I—"

"When you went away you said you'd come back to live here in a few days."

"Well, we thought maybe. I hoped. But it's worked out this way instead. Now listen to me, girls, it's not really so different. I see you very often. We go out together for milk shakes. We're just like before."

Silence from Cynthia. From Paula, coldly, suddenly with her mother's precise articulation: "It's not the same, and you know it."

"Okay, you're right, it's not." Her recognition of his hollow heartiness made him flush. She cut right through what he said. She remembered very well that he had been a part of the life of the house and she did not like her new sense of the house. He said, "I guess you're right, Paula, but that's how it is. That's all. We don't have to talk about it."

Silence. Then:

"So you really don't love Mommy any more." But she was a child again. The moment when she spoke with her mother's voice had passed. "Daddy," she said.

He resolved to go through it patiently once more. "No," he said, "and she doesn't love me. But we like each other, and we love and like you, both together, and we always will. You understand that, Cynthia?"

"Okay," said Cynthia.

Paula was sucking her thumb again. Her mouth was pulled around, working and bothering, as if she were trying to pull the skin off. She might be learning to bite the nail.

From the back of the house her mother walked toward the living room where the two children and their father were talking. She said hello, picked up a book, and returned to the bedroom. This meant that she would like him to notice that his time was up. A brisk, dark young woman, she was freshly showered and very pretty, although too thin. She wore a housecoat, but a girdle under it, stockings, and high heeled shoes. Obviously she wanted to get the girls to bed early because she was going out.

He began to say goodbye to his daughters. He reminded them that he would come to see them at noon tomorrow. Cynthia threw her arms around his neck, laughing, and demanded: "Bring me something, maybe a surprise!"

"If you like," he said. He had a sick lonely weakness in his stomach of something not yet done, not possible.

"Do you like me, Daddy?"

"I like you and love you, Cynthia kid."

Paula was rubbing her face against his hand, the thumb still in her mouth. He lifted her to kiss her, saying, "And Paula too. Now goodbye until tomorrow."

As he started down the stairs, Paula stood with her swollen thumb dripping and shouted after him: "Oh how I'm sick of those words love and like!"

A young girl caught in a conflict of loyalties to her divorced parents senses that the gulf between her and her "occasional" father is widening.

ASTRID MEIGHAN

Shoe the Horse and Shoe the Mare

LOOKING BACK, she could see the Avenue stretching down to Thirty-fourth Street, and the long vista of quiet Sunday streets seemed sad and dreamlike. Taxicabs slid leisurely in and out of parking spaces, and pigeons, circling over the roofs of buildings by the East River, were chalk-white against the gray sky.

There was no bus in sight and she started to walk, watching the solid, upright figure of the fourteen-year-old girl marching along beside her in the shop windows, as though the girl in the reflections were a stranger. Nice, she thought, as she stopped, coming face to face with her against a background of elaborately draped stockings. The tweed coat really did look nice, much better than the heavy winter coat. She had tried on first one, then the other, before leaving home, but the winter coat had a permanent hump in the back from hanging on a hook in the school cloakroom, and she and her mother had agreed it was better to look well than to be warm. A symphony in brown, she thought comfortably, looking down at the smooth, chocolate-colored suede of her gloves. They were her Christmas present to her mother, and when they had been brought out, beautiful and new, still wrapped in tissue, she had accepted them without a protest, knowing it was for her mother's pride she was to wear them.

Standing still, she felt the air raw and cold at her back, and she started to walk again as briskly as she could. Then suddenly a bus came rushing up and passed her. She raced it, running along the street, her coat flapping open in the wind, and caught it at the next corner.

Sitting in the bus, she went over in her mind all the things she must remember to say to her father. Her mother had written on a piece of paper the amounts paid each month and the amounts due, and at the bottom of the paper the columns were added up and the two hundred dollars he owed them was so clearly visible that even her father would have to admit her mother was right.

'He has the money and legally he has to pay it. Tell him that. Tell him I can't get along on a little bit this month and then a little bit next month and never knowing how much I'll have to do with. Really, Ann, make him see that I'm only asking for what is due.'

When the bus reached Fifty-seventh Street she said to herself, 'Now I've thought of it. I don't have to think of it again until I get there.' She opened her handbag to make sure her poem hadn't been crumpled. It was on a sheet of her mother's best notepaper, folded and in an envelope, like a letter. She took it out and read it again. It looked beautiful, neatly typed on the thick white paper, like something somebody else might have written. She had worked all morning, typing it over and over, but no matter how slowly she'd gone she couldn't get through it without a mistake, and in the end her mother had copied it for her.

At Eightieth Street she got out and walked east to the apartment building where her father lived. She hoped his wife wouldn't be there. Before her, Ann always was very careful not to suggest there had ever been any other time than the present, and it was only when she and her father were alone that they talked about the old times and said, 'Remember the Christmas when such-and-such happened?' or 'Do you ever see So-and-So now?' and he still would ask her how Bantam, the dog they used to have, was, and when she'd tell him again how Bantam was dead his voice would sound embarrassed and suddenly hushed—oh yes, that was right, he'd forgotten. It was going to be awkward to speak to him about the money if his wife was there, and, she thought, if I expect her to be there, maybe she won't be. If I think surely she'll be there, maybe it will work and she'll be out. And as she walked, she said to herself, stepping in time to her words, 'Of course she's there, of course she's there, of course she's there,' all the way to the apartment house.

After she got out of the elevator, she stood for a moment outside the door of the apartment and made sure her hat was on straight and her hair smooth before she rang the bell. The moment she stepped into the hallway she knew he was alone. She could see that the stiff, formal living room at the end of the hall, where he would have been sitting if his wife had been home, was empty, and, as she gave the maid her hat and coat, she saw him sitting at the desk in the study, reading a book.

He got up as she came into the room and leaned down and kissed her on the cheek. He always seemed shy at any gesture of affection, and she tried to help him by making their greeting as perfunctory as possible, as though a kiss were no more than a handshake.

When they sat down he wanted to know, how she was and what she'd been doing, and she tried to tell him things he might be interested in. She'd gone to a concert and she described the program. She had seen an

English movie that was very exciting and he would love it. His answers seemed absent-minded, and after she had said all the things she could think of, the conversation stopped. He sat drumming softly on the desk with his fingers, his legs crossed and his foot swinging, and she was quiet, watching the light gleaming on the polished leather of his shoe. It was a very beautiful shoe, long and narrow and with a kind of masculine elegance, and it was polished so that it shone softly, like dark satin. She sat and stared at it gravely and then, suddenly, she leaned down and touched it gently with her fingers. Instantly it was still and she looked up into her father's startled face.

'What good-looking shoes those are!' she said.

'I'm afraid it's going to be hard getting any more like them for a while,' he said. 'I had them made in England.'

They both looked down at his feet, and after a moment he said, 'How's your mother?'

'She's really quite well, although of course she still feels a little weak from the flu.' This was the time to do it, she thought desperately. 'Daddy, there was something she wanted me to speak to you about.' She was angry at herself for being so embarrassed by the subject of money. After all, it wasn't as though her mother wasn't in the right. 'You still haven't made up the money missing in the payments since August, and she really needs it, Daddy, you know, with Christmas and everything.' She was getting the paper with the columns of figures on it out of her handbag.

'What's that about Christmas? Why, I sent fifty dollars extra in December. What are you talking about?'

'Yes, I know, but that fifty dollars was only half of what you owed from October.' Why couldn't he understand that getting fifty dollars extra when the fifty dollars had been owed to you and you'd gone without it before wasn't getting anything extra at all? 'See, it's all written down here.'

'Let me see that,' he said angrily, and almost snatched it from her hand. 'Two hundred dollars! Why, that's ridiculous! My God, what does your mother think I am—a machine? After all, I have to make this money. How would she like it if she had to work?'

He was going over the figures. Ann knew they were correct, and she knew the less fault he could find with them the more indignant he'd become. For every time he had sent extra money there had been a time when he'd been short, and always the amounts owed were more than the amounts paid back.

Suddenly he crumpled the paper and threw it down on the desk. 'My God, what am I supposed to do—pay alimony the rest of my life? I'd like to know just what does your mother think I am—a work horse? What if I should die—how would she like that?'

'Oh, Daddy!' she called out, shocked, and then was silent, feeling the old helplessness of trying to explain to him anything about her mother.

He sat and glared threateningly at the floor.

'Really, Daddy, Mother doesn't like having to take alimony. She's said lots of times that if she could get a job that would pay enough she'd be glad never to take anything more from you. She doesn't even approve of alimony, but—' Her voice stopped as she thought, but if we don't get money from you, where will we get it?

'It's a wonder she doesn't try to poison your mind against me.'

It was such an unreasonable thing for him to say that she knew he couldn't believe it himself.

'No,' she said, 'that's not true! Why, she wants me to come and see you more often, and she always asks about you.' She could feel her voice tightening, and just as it started to waver the maid came in with a tray of tea things.

She poured herself a cup of tea and ate a sandwich while the maid went back and forth getting her father a Scotch-and-soda.

When the maid left the room Ann remembered the poem. She took it out of her bag and looked at her father, who was sitting separate from her, sipping his drink, his face angry and lowering.

'By the way, Dad, I won a prize in school.' She waited a minute. 'In Literature. I thought you might like to read it—the poem, I mean.' She held it out to him, and after a second he seemed to see it, and he put his drink down and took it from her.

After he had read it he looked up, and suddenly she felt all right again as she saw his face. 'Why, Ann,' he said, 'did you write this? It's really very good. I didn't know you could write like this.'

'Oh, I've written lots of poems, but that really is the best. They're going to publish it in the school paper. If you like, you can keep it. I know it by heart, so I don't need a copy.'

'Thanks. Yes, I'd like to have it. It's really very good.'

He started to read it again, and she wandered over to the window and looked out as she ate another sandwich.

'The prize was quite nice. I mean usually they're no good and you don't care about getting them or not, but this one is quite nice.' She waited for a moment, then she heard the doorbell.

'That must be Marian,' her father said, and as he got up to go to the door she said hurriedly, 'It was a volume of Keats, in leather.'

Her father and his wife came into the room together and he had his arm around her. Ann put her hand out and said, 'Hello, Marian,' but before she could think of how to avoid it her stepmother had kissed her, enveloping her in an embrace that was fresh and cold from the outdoors, and fragrant with perfume and furs.

'Ann, we haven't seen you for so long! Where have you been keeping yourself?' She took off her hat and coat and threw them on the couch beside Ann. 'My, it's getting cold out. Are you having a drink, dear?' she said to her husband. 'I think I'll have one, too.'

As her stepmother talked, Ann sat looking at the flat, rippling curls of the fur coat. The heavy satin lining looked soft, as though her fingers could sink deep down into it.

'It's awfully dark in here,' her father's wife said. 'Why didn't you put a light on? Ann, dear, will you have some hot tea?'

Ann said she thought it was getting late and she'd better start home. She excused herself for a moment and, going through the bedroom to the bathroom, stopped to look at herself in the large mirror at the dressing table. She loved to see herself in it. It was such an enormous mirror that it wasn't like looking at herself at all; it was like looking at a large room in the middle of which a girl stood. The low dressing table was covered with objects that glittered and sparkled. There were rows of perfume bottles and atomizers and silverbacked toilet articles, and the lamps at either end were made of crystal balls. It looked like a display of Christmas gifts in a shop window, and she stood looking down at it for quite a while.

When she came back to the study her father was talking to someone on the telephone. She waited for a few minutes, and then, feeling a sudden urgency to leave, she went over and kissed him on the cheek as he talked, whispering, 'Daddy, please don't forget what we talked about.'

He put his hand over the mouthpiece of the phone. 'Goodbye, dear,' he said, and then, 'Oh, wait a minute. Isn't this yours?' and he picked up her poem from the desk and handed it to her. For a second she stood there, not knowing what to do with it. Her father was talking into the phone again, and she stuffed the piece of paper into her handbag.

Her stepmother went to the door with her, helping her find her hat and coat. Through the hall she could see her father still sitting in the light at the desk with the telephone in his hand.

It was much colder than it had been when she arrived, and she walked quickly up to the bus corner and stood hunched up miserably, her muscles tense with the cold. It was dark. It must be almost six o'clock, she thought, and all the way home, as she sat in the bus, sometimes seeing her reflection in the window and sometimes looking past it out at the street, she had a feeling of wanting to hurry home, as though she might be late for something, as though she would never get there.

When she got to the house she ran up the two flights of stairs, and before she could get her key out her mother had the door open.

'My goodness, darling,' her mother said, 'what's the rush? I could hear you coming up the stairs like a herd of elephants.'

'Nothing special, only it's cold out. I think it's going to snow.'

'Look out! My stitches!' her mother cried, holding up a sweater on a pair of knitting needles as Ann hugged her around the waist. 'It's almost finished. You just have to try it on once more to see if it goes over your head all right!'

'Oh, Mums, I can wear it tomorrow. Doesn't it look kind of short, though?' She dumped her hat and coat in a chair, but when her mother said, 'Ann!' reproachfully, she picked them up and went to her room and hung them in the closet.

When she turned around she looked at her mother standing in the doorway and wished her hair wouldn't fall so untidily over her forehead.

'You have a run in your stocking, Mother.'

'I know it, dear.' Her mother's voice sounded surprised. 'I'm not going out. . . . Well,' she said after a pause, 'how was your father?'

'He was all right,' Ann said. 'He wanted to know how you were and was awfully sorry about your being sick.'

'Was she there?'

'No, she was out today. She was busy or something.'

'What did he say about the money?'

'Well, at first he was sure he couldn't owe us that much; then, when he added up the figures, he could see they were right and he promised to try and make it up.'

Her mother looked at her steadily, then she said, 'When?' and Ann knew it was no good, knew that her mother could guess everything he had said.

'I really think he will this time, Mother,' she said judiciously, as though she had some special information, but her mother asked fiercely, 'Why this time? Why any time? Oh, I'm so sick of fighting! How does he expect me to pay your school bills? And you need a new coat. Did he see how light that coat you had on was on a day like today?'

Suddenly remembering the coat, Ann could feel a rushing sensation going up her nose into her forehead and the muscles of her face pull up. She started to cry. Why, she thought, he never even saw it. I might just as well have worn the old warm one. I might just as well have looked awful. He never even saw it.

'Ann!' her mother said. 'Oh, Ann, don't cry. Everything will be all right. We'll manage. We can manage anything—a new coat, anything.' She went across the room and tried to put her arms around her. 'Baby, don't cry!'

Ann twisted away violently and threw herself face down on the bed, pulling in her breath in little gasping sobs. 'Can't you leave me alone?' she shouted. 'Can't anybody ever leave me alone?' She lay feeling the soft wetness of her tears where her cheek pressed against the counterpane.

This selection from a full-length novel begins the morning after the father of Rufus and Catherine has been killed in an automobile accident. A host of relatives are gathering. As Rufus goes out of his house into the morning sunlight he feels "gravely exhilarated as if this were the morning of his birthday."

JAMES AGEE

from *A Death in the Family*

WHEN BREAKFAST was over he wandered listlessly into the sitting room and looked all around, but he did not see any place where he would like to sit down. He felt deeply idle and empty and at the same time gravely exhilarated, as if this were the morning of his birthday, except that this day seemed even more particularly his own day. There was nothing in the way it looked which was not ordinary, but it was filled with a noiseless and invisible kind of energy. He could see his mother's face while she told them about it and hear her voice, over and over, and silently, over and over, while he looked around the sitting room and through the window into the street, words repeated themselves, He's dead. He died last night while I was asleep and now it was already morning. He has already been dead since way last night and I didn't even know until I woke up. He has been dead all night while I was asleep and now it is morning and I am awake but he is still dead and he will stay right on being dead all afternoon and all night and all tomorrow while I am asleep again and wake up again and go to sleep again and he can't come back home again ever any more but I will see him once more before he is taken away. Dead now. He died last night while I was asleep and now it is already morning.

A boy went by with his books in a strap.

Two girls went by with their satchels.

He went to the hat rack and took his satchel and his hat and started back down the hall to the kitchen to get his lunch; then he remembered his new cap. But it was upstairs. It would be in Mama's and Daddy's room, he could remember when she took it off his head. He did not want to go in for it where she was lying down and now he realized, too, that he did not want to wear it. He would like to tell her good-bye before he

[431]

went to school, but he did not want to go in and see her lying down and looking like that. He kept on towards the kitchen. He would tell Aunt Hannah good-bye instead.

She was at the sink washing dishes and Catherine sat on a kitchen chair watching her. He looked all around but he could not see any lunch. I guess she doesn't know about lunch, he reflected. She did not seem to realize that he was there so, after a moment, he said, "Good-bye."

"What-*is*-it?" she said and turned her lowered head, peering. "Why, Rufus!" she exclaimed, in such a tone that he wondered what he had done. "You're not going to *school*," she said, and now he realized that she was not mad at him.

"I can stay out of school?"

"Of course you can. You must. Today and tomorrow as well and—for a sufficient time. A few days. Now put up your things, and stay right in this house, child."

He looked at her and said to himself: but then they can't see me; but he knew there was no use begging her; already she was busy with the dishes again.

He went back along the hall towards the hat rack. In the first moment he had been only surprised and exhilarated not to have to go to school, and something of this sense of privilege remained, but almost immediately he was also disappointed. He could now see vividly how they would all look up when he came into the schoolroom and how the teacher would say something nice about his father and about him, and he knew that on this day everybody would treat him well, and even look up to him, for something had happened to him today which had not happened to any other boy in school, any other boy in town. They might even give him part of their lunches.

He felt even more profoundly empty and idle than before.

He laid down his satchel on the seat of the hat rack, but he kept his hat on. She'll spank me, he thought. Even worse, he could foresee her particular, crackling kind of anger. I won't let her find out, he told himself. Taking great care to be silent, he let himself out the front door.

The air was cool and gray and here and there along the street, shapeless and watery sunlight strayed and vanished. Now that he was in this outdoor air he felt even more listless and powerful; he was alone, and the silent, invisible energy was everywhere. He stood on the porch and supposed that everyone he saw passing knew of an event so famous. A man was walking quickly up the street and as Rufus watched him, and waited for the man to meet his eyes, he felt a great quiet lifting within him of pride and of shyness, and he felt his face break into a smile, and then an uncontrollable grin, which he knew he must try to make sober again; but the man walked past without looking at him, and so did the next man who

from *A Death in the Family*

walked past in the other direction. Two schoolboys passed whose faces he knew, so he knew that they must know his, but they did not even seem to see him. Arthur and Alvin Tripp came down their front steps and along the far sidewalk and now he was sure, and came down his own front steps and halfway out to the sidewalk, but then he stopped, for now, although both of them looked across into his eyes, and he into theirs, they did not cross the street to him or even say hello, but kept on their way, still looking into his eyes with a kind of shy curiosity, even when their heads were turned almost backwards on their necks, and he turned his own head slowly, watching them go by, but when he saw that they were not going to speak he took care not to speak either.

What's the matter with them, he wondered, and still watched them; and even now, far down the street, Arthur kept turning his head, and for several steps Alvin walked backwards.

What are they mad about?

Now they no longer looked around, and now he watched them vanish under the hill.

Maybe they don't know, he thought. Maybe the others don't know, either.

He came out to the sidewalk.

Maybe everybody knew. Or maybe he knew something of great importance which nobody else knew. The alternatives were not at all distinct in his mind; he was puzzled, but no less proud and expectant than before. My daddy's dead, he said to himself slowly, and then, shyly, he said it aloud: "My daddy's dead." Nobody in sight seemed to have heard; he had said it to nobody in particular. "My daddy's dead," he said again, chiefly for his own benefit. It sounded powerful, solid, and entirely creditable, and he knew that if need be he would tell people. He watched a large, slow man come towards him and waited for the man to look at him and acknowledge the fact first, but when the man was just ahead of him, and still did not appear even to have seen him, he told him, "My daddy's dead," but the man did not seem to hear him, he just swung on by. He took care to tell the next man sooner and the man's face looked almost as if he were dodging a blow but he went on by, looking back a few steps later with a worried face; and after a few steps more he turned and came slowly back.

"What was that you said, sonny?" he asked; he was frowning slightly.

"My daddy's dead," Rufus said, expectantly.

"You mean that sure enough?" the man asked.

"He died last night when I was asleep and now he can't come home ever any more."

The man looked at him as if something hurt him.

"Where do you live, sonny?"

"Right here"; he showed with his eyes.

"Do your folks know you out here wandern round?"

He felt his stomach go empty. He looked frankly into his eyes and nodded quickly.

The man just looked at him and Rufus realized: He doesn't believe me. How do they always know?

"You better just go on back in the house, son," he said. "They won't like you being out here on the street." He kept looking at him, hard.

Rufus looked into his eyes with reproach and apprehension, and turned in at his walk. The man still stood there. Rufus went on slowly up his steps, and looked around. The man was on his way again but at the moment Rufus looked around, he did too, and now he stopped again.

He shook his head and said, in a friendly voice which made Rufus feel ashamed, "How would your daddy like it, you out here telling strangers how he's dead?"

Rufus opened the door, taking care not to make a sound, and stepped in and silently closed it, and hurried into the sitting room. Through the curtains he watched the man. He still stood there, lighting a cigarette, but now he started walking again. He looked back once and Rufus felt, with a quailing of shame and fear, he sees me; but the man immediately looked away again and Rufus watched him until he was out of sight.

How would your daddy like it?

He thought of the way they teased him and did things to him, and how mad his father got when he just came home. He thought how different it would be today if he only didn't have to stay home from school.

He let himself out again and stole back between the houses to the alley, and walked along the alley, listening to the cinders cracking under each step, until he came near the sidewalk. He was not in front of his own home now, or even on Highland Avenue; he was coming into the side street down from his home, and he felt that here nobody would identify him with his home and send him back to it. What he could see from the mouth of the alley was much less familiar to him, and he took the last few steps which brought him out onto the sidewalk with deliberation and shyness. He was doing something he had been told not to do.

He looked up the street and he could see the corner he knew so well, where he always met the others so unhappily, and, farther away, the corner around which his father always disappeared on the way to work, and first appeared on his way home from work. He felt it would be good luck that he would not be meeting them at that corner. Slowly, uneasily, he turned his head, and looked down the side street in the other direction; and there they were: three together, and two along the far side of the street, and one alone, farther off, and another alone, farther off, and, without importance to him, some girls here and there, as well. He knew the faces of all of these boys well, though he was not sure of any of their names. The moment he saw them all he was sure they saw him, and sure that they knew. He stood still and waited for them, looking from one to another of them, into their eyes, and step by step at their several distances, each of them at all times looking into his eyes and knowing, they came silently nearer. Waiting, in silence, during those many seconds before the first of them came really near him, he felt that it was so long to wait, and be watched so closely and silently, and to watch back, that he wanted to go back into the alley and not be seen by them or by anybody else, and yet at the same time he knew that they were all approaching him with the realization that something had happened to him that had not happened to any other boy in town, and that now at last they were bound to think well of him; and the nearer they came but were yet at a distance, the more the gray, sober air was charged with the great energy and with a sense of glory and of danger, and the deeper and more exciting the silence became, and the more tall, proud, shy and exposed he felt; so that as they came still nearer he once again felt his face break into a wide smile, with which he had nothing to do, and, feeling that there was something deeply wrong in such a smile, tried his best to quieten his face and told them, shyly and proudly, "My daddy's dead."

Of the first three who came up, two merely looked at him and the third said, "Huh! Betcha he ain't"; and Rufus, astounded that they did not know and that they should disbelieve him, said, "Why he is so!"

"Where's your satchel at?" said the boy who had spoken. "You're just making up a lie so you can lay out of school."

"I am not laying out," Rufus replied. "I was going to school and my Aunt Hannah told me I didn't have to go to school today or tomorrow or not till—not for a few days. She said I mustn't. So I am not laying out. I'm just staying out."

And another of the boys said, "That's right. If his daddy is dead he don't have to go back to school till after the funerl."

While Rufus had been speaking two other boys had crossed over to join them and now one of them said, "He don't have to. He can lay out cause his daddy got killed," and Rufus looked at the boy gratefully and the boy looked back at him, it seemed to Rufus, with deference.

But the first boy who had spoken said, resentfully, "How do *you* know?"

And the second boy, while his companion nodded, said, "Cause my daddy seen it in the paper. Can't your daddy read the paper?"

The paper, Rufus thought; it's even in the paper! And he looked wisely at the first boy. And the first boy, interested enough to ignore the remark against his father, said, "Well how did he get killed, then?" and Rufus, realizing with respect that it was even more creditable to get killed than just to die, took a deep breath and said, "Why, he was . . ."; but the boy whose father had seen it in the paper was already talking, so he listened, instead, feeling as if all this were being spoken for him, and on his behalf, and in his praise, and feeling it all the more as he looked from one silent boy to the next and saw that their eyes were constantly on him. And Rufus listened, too, with as much interest as they did, while the boy said with relish, "In his ole Tin Lizzie, that's how. He was driving along in his ole Tin Lizzie and it hit a rock and throwed him out in the ditch and run up a eight-foot bank and then fell back and turned over and over and landed right on top of him *whomph* and mashed every bone in his body, that's all. And somebody come and found him and he was dead already time they got there, that's how."

"He was instantly killed," Rufus began, and expected to go ahead and correct some of the details of the account, but nobody seemed to hear him, for two other boys had come up and just as he began to speak one of them said, "Your daddy got his name in the paper didn he, and you too," and he saw that now all the boys looked at him with new respect.

"He's dead," he told them. "He got killed."

"That's what my daddy says," one of them said, and the other said, "What you get for driving a auto when you're drunk, that's what my dad says," and the two of them looked gravely at the other boys, nodding, and at Rufus.

"What's drunk?" Rufus asked.

"What's drunk?" one of the boys mocked incredulously: "Drunk is fulla good ole whiskey"; and he began to stagger about in circles with his knees weak and his head lolling. "At's what drunk is."

"Then he wasn't," Rufus said.

"How do *you* know?"

"He wasn't drunk because that wasn't how he died. The wheel hit a rock and the other wheel, the one you steer with, just hit him on the chin, but it hit him so hard it killed him. He was instantly killed."

"What's instantly killed?" one of them asked.

"What do *you* care?" another said.

"Right off like that," an older boy explained, snapping his fingers. Another boy joined the group. Thinking of what instantly meant, and how his father's name was in the paper and his own too, and how he had got killed, not just died, he was not listening to them very clearly for a few moments, and then, all of a sudden, he began to realize that he was the center of everything and that they all knew it and that they waited to hear him tell the true account of it.

"I don't know nothing about no chin," the boy whose father saw it in the paper was saying. "Way I heard it he was a-drivin along in his ole Tin Lizzie and he hit a rock and ole Tin Lizzie run off the road and thowed him out and run up a eight-foot bank and turned over and over and fell back down on top of him *whomp*."

"How do *you* know?" an older boy was saying. "*You* wasn't there. Anybody here knows it's *him*." And he pointed at Rufus and Rufus was

from *A Death in the Family* [437]

startled from his revery.

"Why?" asked the boy who had just come up.

"Cause it's his daddy," one of them explained.

"It's my daddy," Rufus said.

"What happened?" asked still another boy, at the fringe of the group.

"My daddy got killed," Rufus said.

"His daddy got killed," several of the others explained.

"My daddy says he bets he was drunk."

"Good ole whiskey!"

"Shut up, what's *your* daddy know about it."

"Was he drunk?"

"No," Rufus said.

"No," two others said.

"Let *him* tell it."

"Yeah, *you* tell it."

"Anybody here ought to know, it's him."

"Come on and tell us."

"Good ole whiskey."

"Shut your mouth."

"Well come on and tell us, then."

They became silent and all of them looked at him. Rufus looked back into their eyes in the sudden deep stillness. A man walked by, stepping into the gutter to skirt them.

Rufus said, quietly, "He was coming home from Grampa's last night, Grampa Follet. He's very sick and Daddy had to go up way in the middle of the night to see him, and he was hurrying as fast as he could to get back home because he was so late. And there was a cotter pin worked loose."

"What's a cotter pin?"

"Shut up."

"A cotter pin is what holds things together underneath, that you steer with. It worked loose and fell out so that when one of the front wheels hit a loose rock it wrenched the wheel and he couldn't steer and the auto ran down off the road with an awful bump and they saw where the wheel you steer with hit him right on the chin and he was instantly killed. He was thrown all the way out of the auto and it ran up an eight-foot emb—embankment and then it rolled back down and it was upside down beside him when they found him. There was not a mark on his body. Only a little tiny blue mark right on the end of the chin and another on his lip."

In the silence he could see the auto upside down with its wheels in the air and his father lying beside it with the little blue marks on his chin and on his lip.

"Heck," one of them said, "how can *that* kill anybody?"

He felt a kind of sullen stirring among the others, and he felt that he was not believed, or that they did not think very well of his father for being killed so easily.

"It was just exactly the way it just happened to hit him, Uncle Andrew says. He says it was just a chance in a million. It gave him a concush, con, concush—it did something to his brain that killed him."

"Just a chance in a million," one of the older boys said gravely, and another gravely nodded.

"A million trillion," another said.

"Knocked him crazy as a loon," another cried, and with a waggling forefinger he made a rapid blubbery noise against his loose lower lip.

"Shut yer Goddamn mouth," an older boy said coldly. "Ain't you got no sense at all?"

"Way I heard it, ole Tin Lizzie just rolled right back on top of him *whomp*."

This account of it was false, Rufus was sure, but it seemed to him more exciting than his own, and more creditable to his father and to him, and nobody could question, scornfully, whether that could kill, as they could of just a blow on the chin; so he didn't try to contradict. He felt that he was lying, and in some way being disloyal as well, but he said only, "He was instantly killed. He didn't have to feel any pain."

"Never even knowed what hit him," a boy said quietly. "That's what my dad says."

"No," Rufus said. It had not occurred to him that way. "I guess he didn't." Never even knowed what hit him. Knew.

"Reckon that ole Tin Lizzie is done for now. Huh?"

He wondered if there was some meanness behind calling it an old Tin Lizzie. "I guess so," he said.

"Good ole waggin, but she done broke down."

His father sang that.

"No more joy rides in that ole Tin Lizzie, huh Rufus?"

"I guess not," Rufus replied shyly.

He began to realize that for some moments now a bell, the school bell, had been weltering on the dark gray air; he realized it because at this moment the last of its reverberations were fading.

"Last bell," one of the boys said in sudden alarm.

"Come on, we're goana git hell," another said; and within another second Rufus was watching them all run dwindling away up the street, and around the corner into Highland Avenue, as fast as they could go, and all round him the morning was empty and still. He stood still and watched the corner for almost half a minute after the fattest of them, and then the smallest, had disappeared; then he walked slowly back along the alley, hearing once more the sober crumbling of the cinders under each step, and up through the narrow side yard between the houses, and up the steps of the front porch.

from A Death in the Family

In the paper! He looked for it beside the door, but it was not there. He listened carefully, but he could not hear anything. He let himself quietly through the front door, at the moment his Aunt Hannah came from the sitting room into the front hall. She wore a cloth over her hair and in her hands she was carrying the smoking stand. She did not see him at first and he saw how fierce and lonely her face looked. He tried to make himself small but just then she wheeled on him, her lenses flashing, and exclaimed, "Rufus Follet, where on earth have you been!" His stomach quailed, for her voice was so angry it was as if it were crackling with sparks.

"Outdoors."

"Where, outdoors! I've been looking for you all over the place."

"Just out. Back in the alley."

"Didn't you hear me calling you?"

He shook his head.

"I shouted until my voice was hoarse."

He kept shaking his head. "Honest," he said.

"Now listen to me carefully. You mustn't go outdoors today. Stay right here inside this house, do you understand?"

He nodded. He felt suddenly that he had done an awful thing.

* * *

"Come, now," their mother whispered, and, taking them each by the hand, led them through the Green Room and into the living room.

There it was, against the fireplace, and there seemed to be scarcely anything else in the room except the sunny light on the floor.

It was very long and dark; smooth like a boat; with bright handles. Half the top was open. There was a strange, sweet smell, so faint that it could scarcely be realized.

Rufus had never known such stillness. Their little sounds, as they approached his father, vanished upon it like the infinitesimal whisperings of snow, falling on open water.

There was his head, his arms; suit: there he was.

Rufus had never seen him so indifferent; and the instant he saw him, he knew that he would never see him otherwise. He had his look of faint impatience, the chin strained a little upward, as if he were concealing his objection to a collar which was too tight and too formal. And in this slight urgency of the chin; in the small trendings of a frown which stayed in the skin; in the arch of the nose; and in the still, strong mouth, there was a look of pride. But most of all, there was indifference; and through this indifference which held him in every particle of his being—an indifference which would have rejected them; have sent them away, except that it was too indifferent even to care whether they went or stayed—in this self-completedness which nothing could touch, there was something else, some other feeling which he gave, which there was no identifying even by feeling, for Rufus had never experienced this feeling before; there was perfected beauty. The head, the hand, dwelt in completion, immutable, indestructible: motionless. They moved upon existence quietly as stones which withdraw through water for which there is no floor.

The arm was bent. Out of the dark suit, the starched cuff, sprang the hairy wrist.

The wrist was angled; the hand was arched; none of the fingers touched each other.

The hand was so composed that it seemed at once casual and majestic. It stood exactly above the center of his body.

The fingers looked unusually clean and dry, as if they had been scrubbed with great care.

The hand looked very strong, and the veins were strong in it.

The nostrils were very dark, yet he thought he could see in one of them, something which looked like cotton.

On the lower lip, a trifle to the left of its middle, there was a small blue line which ran also a little below the lip.

At the exact point of the chin, there was another small blue mark, as straight and neat as might be drawn with a pencil, and scarcely wider.

The lines which formed the wings of the nose and the mouth were almost gone.

The hair was most carefully brushed.

The eyes were casually and quietly closed, the eyelids were like silk on the balls, and when Rufus glanced quickly from the eyes to the mouth it seemed as if his father were almost about to smile. Yet the mouth carried no suggestion either of smiling or of gravity; only strength, silence, manhood, and indifferent contentment.

He saw him much more clearly than he had ever seen him before; yet his face looked unreal, as if he had just been shaved by a barber. The whole head was waxen, and the hand, too, was as if perfectly made of wax.

The head was lifted on a small white satin pillow.

There was the subtle, curious odor, like fresh hay, and like a hospital, but not quite like either, and so faint that it was scarcely possible to be sure that it existed.

Rufus saw these things within a few seconds, and became aware that his mother was picking Catherine up in order that she might see more clearly; he drew a little aside. Out of the end of his eye he was faintly aware of his sister's rosy face and he could hear her gentle breathing as he continued to stare at his father, at his stillness, and his power, and his beauty.

He could see the tiny dark point of every shaven hair of the beard.

He watched the way the flesh was chiseled in a widening trough from the root of the nose to the white edge of the lip.

from *A Death in the Family*

He watched the still more delicate dent beneath the lower lip.

It became strange, and restive, that it was possible for anyone to lie so still for so long; yet he knew that his father would never move again; yet this knowledge made his motionlessness no less strange.

Within him, and outside him, everything except his father was dry, light, unreal, and touched with a kind of warmth and impulse and a kind of sweetness which felt like the beating of a heart. But borne within this strange and unreal sweetness, its center yet alien in nature from all the rest, and as nothing else was actual, his father lay graven, whose noble hand he longed, in shyness, to touch.

"Now, Rufus," his mother whispered; they knelt. He could just see over the edge of the coffin. He gazed at the perfect hand.

His mother's arm came round him; he felt her hand on the crest of his shoulder. He slid his arm around her and felt her hand become alive on his shoulder and felt his sister's arm. He touched her bare arm tenderly, and felt her hand grapple for and take his arm. He put his hand around her arm and felt how little it was. He could feel a vein beating against the bone, just below her armpit.

"Our Father," she said.

❋ ❋ ❋

As they came back with Mr. Starr, Rufus noticed that a man who went past along the sidewalk looked back at his grandfather's house, then quickly away, then back once more, and again quickly away.

He saw that there were several buggies and automobiles, idle and empty, along the opposite side of the street, but that the space in front of the house was empty. The house seemed at once especially bare, and changed, and silent, and its corners seemed particularly hard and distinct; and beside the front door there hung a great knotted bloom and streamer of black cloth. The front door was opened before it was touched and there stood their Uncle Andrew and their mother and behind them the dark hallway, and they were all but overwhelmed by a dizzying, sickening fragrance, and by a surging outward upon them likewise of multitudinous vitality. Almost immediately they were drawn within the darkness of the hallway and the fragrance became recognizable as the fragrance of flowers, and the vitality which poured upon them was that of the people with whom the house was crowded. Rufus experienced an intuition as of great force and possible danger on his right, and glancing quickly into the East Room, saw that every window shade was drawn except one and that against the cold light which came through that window the room was filled with dark figures which crouched disconsolately at the edge of chairs, heavy and primordial as bears in a pit; and even as he looked he heard the rising of a great, low groan, which was joined by a higher groan, which was surmounted by a low wailing and by a higher wailing, and he could see that a woman stood up suddenly and with a wailing and bellowing sob caught the hair at her temples and pulled, then flung her hands upward and outward: but upon this moment Andrew rushed and with desperate and brutal speed and silence, pulled the door shut, and Rufus was aware in the same instant that their own footstep and the wailing had caused a commotion on his left and, glancing as sharply into the sunlit room where his father lay, saw an incredibly dense crowd of soberly dressed people on weak, complaining chairs, catching his eye, looking past him, looking quickly away, trying to look as if they had not looked around.

"It's all right, Andrew," his mother whispered. "Open the door. Tell them we'll be in, in just a minute." And she drew the children more deeply into the hallway, where they could not be seen through either door, and whispered to Walter Starr, "Papa is in the Green Room, and Mama. Thank you, Walter."

"Don't you think of it," Walter said, as he passed her; and his hand hovered near her shoulder, and he went quietly through the door into the dining room.

"Now, children," their mother said, lowering her face above them. "We're all going in to see Daddy, just once more. But we won't be able to stay, we can just look for a moment. And then you'll see your Grandma Follet, just for a minute. And then Mr. Starr will take you down again to his house and Mother will see you again later this afternoon."

Andrew came toward her and nodded sharply.

"All right, Andrew," she said. "All right, children." Reaching suddenly behind the crest of her skull she lowered her veil and they saw her face and her eyes through its darkness. She took their hands. "Now come with Mother," she whispered.

There was Uncle Hubert in a dark suit; he was very clean and pink and his face was full of little lines. He looked quickly at them and quickly away. There was old Miss Storrs and there were Miss Amy Field and Miss Nettie Field and Doctor Dekalb and Mrs. Dekalb and Uncle Gordon Dekalb and Aunt Celia Gunn and Mrs. Gunn and Dan Gunn and Aunt Sarah Eldridge and Aunt Ann Taylor, and ever so many others, as well, whom the children were not sure they had seen before, and all of them looked as if they were trying not to look and as if they shared a secret they were offended to have been asked to tell; and there was the most enormous heap of flowers of all kinds that the children had ever seen, tall and extravagantly fresh and red and yellow, tall and starchy white, dark roses and white roses, ferns, carnations, great leaves of varnished-looking palm, all wreathed and wired and running with ribbons of black and silver and bright gold and dark gold, and almost suffocating in their fragrance; and there, almost hidden among these flowers, was the coffin, and beside it, two last strangers who, now that they had entered the room, turned away

from *A Death in the Family*

and quickly took chairs; and now a stranger man in a long, dark coat stepped towards their mother with silent alacrity, his eyes shining like dark jelly, and with a courtly gesture ushered her forward and stood proudly and humbly to one side; and there was Daddy again.

He had not stirred one inch; yet he had changed. His face looked more remote than before and much more ordinary and it was as if he were tired, or bored. He did not look as big as he really was, and the fragrance of the flowers was so strong and the vitality of the mourners was so many-souled and so pervasive, and so permeated and compounded by propriety and restraint, and they felt so urgently the force of all the eyes upon them, that they saw their father almost as idly as if he had been a picture, or a substituted image, and felt little realization of his presence and little interest. And while they were still looking, bemused with this empty curiosity, they felt themselves drawn away, and walked with their mother past the closed piano into the Green Room. And there were Grandpa and Grandma and Uncle Andrew and Aunt Amelia and Aunt Hannah; and Grandma got up quickly and took their mother in her arms and patted her several times emphatically across the shoulders, and Grandpa stood up too; and while Grandma stooped and embraced and kissed each of the children, saying, "Darlings, darlings," in a somewhat loud and ill-controlled voice, they could see their grandfather's graceful and cynical head as he embraced their mother, and realized that he was not quite as tall as she was; and their Aunt Amelia stood up shyly with her elbows out. As their mother led them from the room they looked back through the door and saw that the man in the long coat and another strange man had closed the coffin and were silently and quickly screwing it shut.

* * *

In intense quietness, Catherine stole through the open door opposite Aunt Hannah's door, and hid herself beneath her grandparents' bed. She was no longer crying. She only wanted never to be seen by anybody again. She lay on her side and stared down into the grim grain of the carpet. When Aunt Hannah's door opened she felt such terror that she gasped, and drew her knees up tight against her chest. When the voices began calling her, downstairs, she made herself even smaller, and when she heard their feet on the stairs and the rising concern in their voices she began to tremble all over. But by the time she heard them along the hallway she was out from under the bed and sitting on its edge, her back to them as they came in, her heart knocking her breath to pieces.

"Why *there* you *are*," her mother cried, and turning, Catherine was frightened by the fright and the tears on her face. "Didn't you *hear* us?"

She shook her head, no.

"Why how could you *help* but—were you asleep?"

She nodded, yes.

"I thought she was with you, Amelia."

"I thought she was with you or Mama."

"Why, where on earth *were* you, darling? Heavens and earth, have you been all *alone?*"

Catherine nodded yes; her lower lip thrust out farther and farther and she felt her chin trembling and hated everybody.

"Why, bless your little heart, come to Mother"; her mother came toward her stooping with her arms stretched out and Catherine ran to her as fast as she could run, and plunged her head into her, and cried as if she were made only of tears; and it was only when her mother said, just as kindly, "Just look at your panties, why they're *sopping* wet," that she realized that indeed they were.

Andrew had never invited him to take a walk with him before, and he felt honored, and worked hard to keep up with him. He realized that now, maybe, he would hear about it, but he knew it would not be a good thing to ask. When they got well into the next block beyond his grandfather's, and the houses and trees were unfamiliar, he took Andrew's hand and Andrew took his primly, but did not press it or look down at him. Pretty soon maybe he'll tell me, Rufus thought. Or anyway say something. But his uncle did not say anything. Looking up at him, from a half step behind him, Rufus could see that he looked mad about something. He looked ahead so fixedly that Rufus suspected he was not really looking at anything, even when they stepped from the curb, and stepped up for the curb across from it, his eyes did not change. He was frowning, and the corners of his nose were curled as if he smelled something bad. Did I do something? Rufus wondered. No, he wouldn't ask me for a walk if I did. Yes, he would too if he was real mad and wanted to give me a talking-to and not raise a fuss about it there. But he won't say anything, so I guess he doesn't want to give me a talking-to. Maybe he's thinking. Maybe about Daddy. The funeral. (He saw the sunlight on the hearse as it began to move.) What all did they do out there? They put him down in the ground and then they put all the flowers on top. Then they say their prayers and then they all come home again. In Greenwood Cemetery. He saw in his mind a clear image of Greenwood Cemetery; it was on a low hill and among many white stones there were many green trees through which the wind blew in the sunlight, and in the middle there was a heap of flowers and beneath the flowers, in his closed coffin, looking exactly as he had looked this morning, lay his father. Only it was dark, so he could not be seen. It would always be dark there. Dark as the inside of a cow.

The sun's agonna shine, and the wind's agonna blow.

The charcoal scraping of the needle against the record was in his ears and he saw the many sharp, grinning teeth in Buster Brown's dog.

from *A Death in the Family* [445]

"If anything ever makes me believe in God," his uncle said.

Rufus looked up at him quickly. He was still looking straight ahead, and he still looked angry but his voice was not angry. "Or life after death," his uncle said.

They were working and breathing rather hard, for they were walking westward up the steep hill towards Fort Sanders. The sky ahead of them was bright and they walked among the bright, moving shadows of trees.

"It'll be what happened this afternoon."

Rufus looked up at him carefully.

"There were a lot of clouds," his uncle said, and continued to look straight before him, "but they were blowing fast, so there was a lot of sunshine too. Right when they began to lower your father into the ground, into his grave, a cloud came over and there was a shadow just like iron, and a perfectly magnificent butterfly settled on the—coffin, just rested there, right over the breast, and stayed there, just barely making his wings breathe, like a heart."

Andrew stopped and for the first time looked at Rufus. His eyes were desperate. "He stayed there all the way down, Rufus," he said. "He never stirred, except just to move his wings that way, until it grated against the bottom like a—rowboat. And just when it did the sun came out just dazzling bright and he flew up out of that—hole in the ground, straight up into the sky, so high I couldn't even see him any more." He began to climb the hill again, and Rufus worked hard again to stay abreast of him. "Don't you think that's wonderful, Rufus?" he said, again looking straight and despairingly before him.

"Yes," Rufus said, now that his uncle really was asking him. "Yes," he was sure was not enough, but it was all he could say.

"If there are any such things as miracles," his uncle said, as if someone were arguing with him, "then *that's* surely miraculous."

Miraculous. Magnificent. He was sure he had better not ask what they were. He saw a giant butterfly clearly, and how he moved his wings so quietly and grandly, and the colors of the wings, and how he sprang straight up into the sky and how the colors all took fire in the sunshine, and he felt that he probably had a fair idea what "magnificent" meant. But "miraculous." He still saw the butterfly, which was resting there again, waving his great wings. Maybe "miraculous" was the way the colors were streaks and spots in patterns on the wings, or the bright flickering way they worked in the light when he flew fast, straight upwards. Miraculous. Magnificent.

He could see it very clearly, because his uncle saw it so clearly when he told about it, and what he saw made him feel that a special and good thing was happening. He felt that it was good for his father and that lying there in the darkness did not matter so much. He did not know what this good thing was, but because his uncle felt that it was good, and felt so strongly about it, it must be even more of a good thing than he himself could comprehend. His uncle even spoke of believing in God, or anyway, if anything could ever make him believe in God, and he had never before heard his uncle speak of God except as if he disliked Him, or anyway, disliked people who believed in Him. So it must be about as good a thing as a thing could be. And suddenly he began to realize that his uncle told it to him, out of everyone he might have told it to, and he breathed in a deep breath of pride and of love. He would not admit it to those who did believe in God, and he would not tell it to those who didn't, because he cared so much about it and they might swear at it, but he had to tell somebody, so he told it to him. And it made it much better than it had been, about his father, and about his not being let to be there at just that time he most needed to be there; it was all right now, almost. It was not all right about his father because his father could never come back again, but it was better than it had been, anyway, and it was all right about his not being let be there, because now it was almost as if he had been there and seen it with his own eyes, and seen the butterfly, which showed that even for his father, it was all right. It was all right and he felt as his uncle did. There was nobody else, not even his mother, not even his father if he could, that he even wanted to tell, or talk about it to. Not even his uncle, now that it was told.

"And *that* son of a bitch!" Andrew said.

He was not quite sure what it meant but he knew it was the worst thing you could call anybody; call anybody that, they had to fight, they had a right to kill you. He felt as if he had been hit in the stomach.

"That Jackson," Andrew said; and now he looked so really angry that Rufus realized that he had not been at all angry before. "*'Father'* Jackson," Andrew said, "as he insists on being called.

"Do you know what he did?"

He glared at him so, that Rufus was frightened. "What?" he asked.

"He said he couldn't read the complete, the complete burial service over your father because your father had never been baptized." He kept glaring at Rufus; he seemed to be waiting for him to answer. Rufus looked up at him, feeling scared and stupid. He was glad his uncle did not like Father Jackson, but that did not seem exactly the point, and he could not think of anything to say.

"He said he was deeply sorry," Andrew savagely caricatured the inflection, "but it was simply a rule of the Church."

"Some church," he snarled. "And they call themselves Christians. Bury a man who's a hundred times the man *he'll* ever be, in his stinking, swishing black petticoats, and a hundred times as good a man too, and 'No, there are certain requests and recommendations I cannot make Almighty God for the repose of this soul, for he never stuck his head under a holy-water tap.' Genuflecting, and ducking and bowing and scraping, and

from *A Death in the Family*

basting themselves with signs of the Cross, and all that disgusting hocus-pocus, and you come to one simple, single act of Christian charity and what happens? The rules of the Church forbid it. He's not a member of our little club.

"I tell you, Rufus, it's enough to make a man puke up his soul.

"That—that butterfly has got more of God in him than Jackson will ever see for the rest of eternity.

"Priggish, mealy-mouthed son of a bitch."

They were standing at the edge of Fort Sanders and looking out across the waste of briers and of embanked clay, and Rufus was trying to hold his feelings intact. Everything had seemed so nearly all right, up to a minute ago, and now it was changed and confused. It was still all right, everything which had been, still was, he did not see how it could stop being, yet it was hard to remember it clearly and to remember how he had felt and why it had seemed all right, for since then his uncle had said so much. He was glad he did not like Father Jackson and he wished his mother did not like him either, but that was not all. His uncle had talked about God, and Christians, and faith, with as much hatred as he had seemed, a minute before, to talk with reverence or even with love. But it was worse than that. It was when he was talking about everybody bowing and scraping and hocus-pocus and things like that, that Rufus began to realize that he was talking not just about Father Jackson but about all of them and that he hated all of them. He hates Mother, he said to himself. He really honestly does hate her. Aunt Hannah, too. He hates them. They don't hate him at all, they love him, but he hates them. But he doesn't hate them, really, he thought. He could remember how many ways he had shown how fond he was of both of them, all kinds of ways, and most of all by how easy he was with them when nothing was wrong and everybody was having a good time, and by how he had been with them in this time too. He doesn't hate them, he thought, he loves them, just as much as they love him. But he hates them, too. He talked about them as if he'd like to spit in their faces. When he's with them he's nice to them, he even likes them, loves them. When he's away from them and thinks about them saying their prayers and things, he hates them. When he's with them he just acts as if he likes them, but this is how he really feels, all the time. He told me about the butterfly and he wouldn't tell them because he hates them, but I don't hate them, I love them, and when he told me he told me a secret he wouldn't tell them as if I hated them too.

But they saw it too. They sure saw it too. So he didn't, he wouldn't tell them, there wouldn't be anything to tell. That's it. He told me because I wasn't there and he wanted to tell somebody and thought I would want to know and I do. But not if he hates them. And he does. He hates them just like opening a furnace door but he doesn't want them to know it. He doesn't want them to know it because he doesn't want to hurt their feelings. He doesn't want them to know it because he knows they love him and think he loves them. He doesn't want them to know it because he loves them. But how can he love them if he hates them so? How can he hate them if he loves them? Is he mad at them because they can say their prayers and he doesn't? He could if he wanted to, why doesn't he? Because he hates prayers. And them too for saying them.

He wished he could ask his uncle, "Why do you hate Mama?" but he was afraid to. While he thought he looked now across the devastated Fort, and again into his uncle's face, and wished that he could ask. But he did not ask, and his uncle did not speak except to say, after a few minutes, "It's time to go home," and all the way home they walked in silence.

An aging woman takes a journey, finds that her road lies forward and not back and that giving hostages to fortune is her inevitable destiny.

ROBIN WHITE

from *House of Many Rooms*

SHORTLY AFTER the oxcart had passed the first village along the southeast route across the tip of India to Meigudy, Mrs. Fisher saw the little boy come running after her through the early morning shadows. A heavy mist lay close upon the ground, muffling the rumble of wooden wheels and obscuring the river and paddy fields so that the banyan trees which lined the road seemed to be rising out of a vast gray marsh of silence, penetrated remotely by the hooting of monkeys and the hoarse, insolent call of myna birds and crows. Out of this silence the child emerged without warning as if, like some spirit of the dark hours, the figment of Mrs. Fisher's imagination, he had been conspiring to overtake her unawares.

Her immediate response was one of mild annoyance at the intrusion. The boy had broken so abruptly upon her entranced solitude as to startle her, and at first she turned stiffly to frown at him. Dressed in shorts of old and threadbare cloth, he might have been around six, Mrs. Fisher thought, although he looked to be not more than four. His hair was red-brown from the dust caked in it, his dark skin an ashy hue for need of a bath, and his features were pinched, almost distorted, by hunger and the wearing effects of having to fend for himself too early in life. Mrs. Fisher had learned to read these signs, and their meaning turned her surprise into sudden fear; for just by his appearance and the way he trailed her she could tell he was a stray—the dangerous type that would try, if possible, to become attached to her. Resolutely she turned away and focused her attention on her hands. Much as she loved children, strays were definitely not included in her plans for this trip.

By degrees mustering up courage, the boy moved in closer to the bandy. Mrs. Fisher knew he was not going to be easily shaken. She tried

[449]

not to look at him, but despite herself she was unable to keep from noticing how dreadfully stony and unchanging was the mask of his face. Her heart was torn with pity, as for all homeless, unwanted children, but she was afraid that if she revealed any of this the boy would use it to attach himself to her.

"Begone, child," she said in Tamil, waving the boy away. Immediately she realized that, unwittingly or by desire, she had made a mistake, done the very thing that would bring the boy to her. By showing that she had noticed him, she had openly acknowledged her concern. Taking heart, he pressed in close to the bandy.

He did not try to speak to her, and Mrs. Fisher knew this was another bad sign. If he had asked for food or money, it would have meant he was a beggar child who would leave as soon as he got what he wanted. So preoccupied was she with thinking about the boy that she did not see the man on horseback until he had overtaken the bandy and, unable to pass because of the narrowness of the road at that particular section, slowed to a pace behind. He was a well-dressed, middle-aged man, tall, strikingly handsome and arrogant-looking, and apparently Mohammedan, because he carried a prayer mat. Seeing Mrs. Fisher's anxious glance in the boy's direction, he reined back and drew his impatient, high-strung stallion around sideways to the bandy.

"Madame," he said in English, saluting, "is this filthy urchin causing you annoyance?"

"What? Oh, no, no," Mrs. Fisher said, collecting herself quickly. "Not really."

"Only permit me to be of service, Madame, and I shall gladly drive him off." He unstrung a bull whip from his saddle and turned as if to lash out at the child.

"Please," Mrs. Fisher said. "It's quite all right. Don't strike him." She raised her hand in protest, annoyed at having been put in the position of defending the boy. At the sight of the whip, the boy withdrew prudently just out of striking distance. "See," she said, "he doesn't want to cause any trouble."

"Very well, Madame, if you say." The Mohammedan curled the whip back into place. "But if I may be so bold as to advise, Madame would do well not to encourage him by any sign or word. It is the little ones like this who seek a home that are the most dangerous. They are filled with filth and vermin and all manner of worms and diseases, and for sheer persistence they cannot be excelled."

"I know," Mrs. Fisher agreed without enthusiasm. "One cannot be too careful."

"I see that Madame has been wisened by experience."

"Yes, I've taken in a few in my time," she said, thinking of the several stray children she had mothered in the past. Off and on over the years

from *House of Many Rooms*

she had taken in five homeless Indian children, one at a time, and each of them in turn had grown up and gone off—just as her own children had done. It seemed to her that her life could be measured out, divided into segments, by the children she had loved and lost. "The worst of it is, they all grow up and go away."

"Quite so, Madame, a completely worthless lot."

"I wouldn't say that exactly," Mrs. Fisher said. "It's just that they find lives of their own after a while, and for a person of my age it is difficult to live through fondness and departure."

"Then Madame is truly charitable," the Mohammedan said. "I myself cannot undertake to provide for more than my own."

"Do you have many children?" Mrs. Fisher asked, wondering at the man's almost militant self-interest.

"Five, Madame—all sons, praise be to Allah. And Madame?"

"Three," said Mrs. Fisher.

She smiled sadly, thinking of them again. Samuel had become a federal judge in New York, Barney had gone into the oil business in Texas, and Clare, after a brief fling at the stage, had settled down as the wife of a Boston research chemist. They all had children of their own now; they all seemed so right for the lives they had made for themselves. She wondered what Aaron would have become. Somehow she could never picture him as anything but just plain Aaron. In a way she wished at least one of her children had gone into the mission field, and yet she knew she could never wish that on anyone. There were too many heartbreaks; one had always to leave so much behind. She looked up at the Mohammedan. "Only three," she said. "I had four at one time—three boys and a girl. A sufficient average, I suppose. My eldest son was drowned in a flood, much like this." She nodded in the direction of the river, now plainly visible beyond the trees.

"My deepest sympathies, Madame."

"It's all right," Mrs. Fisher said. "I've lived with it a long time."

"And where are Madame's children now?"

"Oh, they've all grown up and gone to America. It wasn't so bad when my husband was still living. But now, sometimes I—well, I have my mission work, and that keeps me busy. I've lived in India so long I wouldn't know what to do in another country."

For a moment the Mohammedan studied her silently, taking in her sari and age. "May I ask where Madame travels dressed in Indian garb and riding in a bandy?"

"To Meigudy," she said. Then, seeing his questioning glance, she added, "It was my home for many years—and happy years they were, too. Mr. Fisher and I went there in a covered wagon like this, when we were first married, to reorganize the mission. It's always seemed like home to me because all our children grew up there."

The Mohammedan was instantly touched by this. "And now Madame is returning to recapture the old memories. Ah, such poetry, such significance: a pilgrimage to the scene of one's youth! I shall compose a poem about it the instant I reach home. I am a sometime poet, you know."

"How nice," said Mrs. Fisher. But somehow she didn't feel any poetry. It was as if by revealing the purpose of her trip, by putting the thought into words, the whole idea had suddenly taken on an unpleasant air, reminding her of a dream she often had of a house with many rooms. Every time the dream occurred, she would find herself, fully aware that she was asleep, entering a house with the familiar, almost useless feeling that she had seen it all before, knew every crack and cranny of the place; yet to her amazement every time she passed through the house, she would discover new and more beautiful rooms. And when she would finally awaken, it would be with the lonely, thwarted sense of having been cut off from an unfinished task. Restlessly now, her eyes wandered from the nose of the Mohammedan's horse to the little boy, trailing at a distance.

Overjoyed by the thought of the poem, the Mohammedan began composing lines of it in snatches and out loud, explaining to Mrs. Fisher what a success it would be among some of his friends who were artists of the first order. He even went so far as to offer Mrs. Fisher his protection for the rest of the trip, saying that it was dangerous for women to travel alone in these parts. But she told him that she had often traveled alone before along this road and that it would be a shame to hold him up unnecessarily. To this the Mohammedan agreed, and after he had thanked Mrs. Fisher for his pleasant conversation with her, he saluted and rode ahead, giving a final brandish of the whip in the boy's direction.

Presently the bandy lurched down a short embankment to ford a shallow channel, the brown, swiftly-moving flood water surged against the wheels, and the oxen came to a standstill. The driver, who had nearly fallen from his seat, leaped up to prod some life into the oxen, jabbing them with his whip handle, biting their tails and crying, "Haaaai! Hai! Eeeeeeya!" As they came up onto the far bank, the first rays of the rising sun penetrated and divided the mist into patches like flocks of sheep. On either side of the road clusters of low thatched huts appeared, and Mrs. Fisher knew they had reached the second village.

Here the bandy overtook a group of Hindu women. Mrs. Fisher could hear their loud early-morning laughter long before the slow-moving oxcart caught up with them, and from listening to their conversation she knew they were headed for a wedding. Even had she not been able to hear what they said, she would have known where they were going; for they were all dressed in their best saris, their hair washed and combed and braided with gay white and yellow flowers; and their laughter betrayed them. The only time village women were free from work and

from *House of Many Rooms*

had time to be happy was on a wedding day.

As the bandy slowly overtook and passed them, the women stopped talking momentarily until they caught sight of Mrs. Fisher. Of one accord they quickened their leisurely holiday pace to keep up with her, while maintaining a discreet distance. Their immediate presence directly behind the bandy would, under any other circumstances, have been a source of delight for Mrs. Fisher. She had always enjoyed the frank and unassuming manner of village women when their husbands were not around. But moving in such numbers and so close to the bandy, they blocked her view of the little boy, thus heightening her concern for him. She did not want to be the center of attention: she did not want to have to strike a pose. And all at once she felt irritated by their laughter.

Not realizing that she spoke Tamil, the women began conversing freely about Mrs. Fisher, wondering why she was dressed in a sari and why she rode in a bandy instead of taking the bus or train.

"Maybe she speaks Tamil," someone suggested.

"Never," replied another, loudly. "White ladies can't. Their tongues aren't made right for it. Too stiff. Haven't you noticed how they always speak with their teeth. They prefer to bite words. It comes from eating meat."

"You never can tell about these white ladies," someone else said. "They do many peculiar things, like appearing in public with strange men. It's all on account of education. That's what I say."

There was a unified murmur of agreement from the group, and the conversation branched out into a general discussion and condemnation of the sinful ways of modern educated city women.

"After all," someone remarked, "what else is there in life but hard work mixed in with weddings, births, funerals, and maybe a good fight or two. One can only accept these things and appease the gods. Give a woman a book and she goes to pot."

Accept? Mrs. Fisher said to herself. Was that where the answer lay? Accept? Accept what? Loneliness? Confusion? Defeat? Where then was there room for hope? It seemed to her that she had accepted so much that she was at cross-purposes with herself. She did not even know these women, and yet, whether she accepted them or not, they had insinuated themselves into her life, and their presence frustrated her by cutting her off from the little boy. She kept straining to see over their heads and finally, thinking that he had dropped out of sight altogether, she called impatiently for the women to step aside. They complied readily enough, surprise registering on their faces, and Mrs. Fisher heaved a sigh of relief. The boy was still following.

Far from being embarrassed by the discovery that Mrs. Fisher spoke Tamil, the women now pressed around her, anxious to please, anxious to learn the answers to their questions. With a renewed sense of humor,

Mrs. Fisher yielded to them, explaining her reasons for riding in the bandy and wearing a sari. When they asked how old she was, they were amazed to learn that she was nearly sixty. Why, she was a grandmother, they exclaimed, calling her respectfully, "Parti." She was older than anyone in the group, yet, see, she looked to be not more than forty at the most.

Their words buoyed Mrs. Fisher up, and for a while she was cheered to the point of laughter. Then they noticed her nylon stockings and, after asking permission to touch them, each in turn placed a rough forefinger on Mrs. Fisher's legs, uttering exclamations of awe and amazement. How far up did they go, they asked, all the way?

Mrs. Fisher was fortunately spared further interrogation and exploration by the oxcart's timely arrival at the third village, where the wedding was being held. The women abruptly bid her farewell and rushed ahead to join the throng gathered outside one of the huts, where a pavilion of thatch had been erected. Because of the crowd, the oxcart was unable to get through, and the driver had to climb out onto the yoke to break passage. Although Mrs. Fisher leaned out, she was unable to catch a glimpse of the bride and groom, and when the oxcart finally left the village, she sat back again, thinking about the women. She wondered how they could be content to live simply on the basis of accepting life and relieving its hardship by the amusement of social functions. The very thought of it had a disquieting effect on her. Now, although she tried, she could no longer make herself feel the desperateness of purpose that had forced her on this journey. Instead, thinking about the little boy, she searched the road for some sign of him. He would probably give up following her, she thought, for the more promising prospects of the wedding and handouts of food. But she found no joy in that.

By degrees the rising sun forced Mrs. Fisher farther back under the shade of the wagon cover. Traffic had increased along the road, and from time to time the bandy was slowed by encounters with herds of cattle, long lines of coolies, and the caravans of oxcarts laden with great bales of hemp and cotton. In the open stretches she could look on the fields where people worked in bunches, women bent over planting, men cultivating with wooden plows drawn by lethargic black water buffalos, boys running treadmills that raised the water from one irrigation ditch to another. Then there were the monkeys that chased each other along the ground, and in the distance flocks of teel dipped and soared over the fields, or alighted nervously upon clumps of trees. Sometimes the road would be flooded and boys would be swimming in the brown water. In other places it would skirt the edges of vast groves of coconut and palmyra palms, and the sudden deep shade with its accompanying hollow silence would come as a cool refreshing drink to Mrs. Fisher.

There had been a time when the cumulative effect of this changing landscape filled her with peace and a sense of belonging. But now the monotony of sound and movement made her feel lonely and dissatisfied, and all at once she knew she could not go on like this, not knowing what was happening to the boy. Frantically she called for the driver to stop and pull over. It was time for lunch anyway, she argued.

Stiffly she unfolded herself from the bandy and got down while the driver unhitched the oxen and led them over to the side of the road to graze. Taking her tiffin carrier in one hand, she sat down on a large hump formed by the root of a banyan tree. On the right the road was edged by a dense shola of palm trees, and on the left the land dipped sharply down to the river. As Mrs. Fisher opened her tiffin carrier and spread a linen napkin on the grass, she was startled to discover that her spot was shared by a sannyasi sitting on a reed mat near the banyan and contemplating infinity. Now there, she thought, looking at him, was freedom, real freedom. And yet it occurred to her that withdrawal was not exactly freedom, and avoidance was not exactly happiness. It only created an effect, and even the sannyasi had to make concessions to life: he had to eat and breathe, and someday he had to die.

The more she thought about it, the more it disturbed her. She tried to eat, but the food would not go down readily, and after a while she began putting it back in the tiffin carrier. Her worry for the little boy nauseated her, and when he appeared, walking up the road in her direction, she felt such a tightness in her stomach that she thought she was going to be sick.

At the sight of the food, the little boy abandoned caution and came within a yard of Mrs. Fisher. He squatted on his hams and watched her, and she, resigning herself to the inevitable, held out a brass tumbler of milk to him. He took it and downed it swiftly, furtively. The least I can do, she thought, is feed him. If I give him food, perhaps he will be satisfied and go his way. She handed a package of sandwiches and a cupcake to him, trying not to watch as, in his eagerness for the food, he ate the cake with the paper on it.

"What are you called, child?" she asked when he had finished.

"Krishnan," the boy said, in a voice that sounded dead and old.

"Are you from around these parts?"

The boy shrugged and Mrs. Fisher could not keep from asking, "Have you no relatives to look after you, no home to go to?" Even before he gave it, she knew the answer.

"No, Amma."

"No brothers? Sisters?"

"I am alone, Amma."

Alone? So alone then, little boy? The words seemed to rise up in her despite her fierce suppression of them. She was yielding unnecessarily. If this went on she would go too far and be unable to keep herself from becoming involved. And if she lost her will to shut him out, would he then not become a part of her life and grow up and leave her like all the others? Like all that she had ever cared for and loved? In that moment she admired the Mohammedan's ability to take what he wanted and drive off what he did not without suffering the agony of doubt; she admired the village women and envied their yielding ability to accept what came to them; she even admired the old sannyasi for his complete indifference. Anything, she said to herself, would be better than what I now feel.

Abruptly she rose, thinking that now the child would go and leave her in peace, free of the responsibility of making a decision about him. Yet in a way she almost hoped that he would force the decision on her. As if he knew what she was thinking, he rose and followed her over to where the driver was hitching up the oxen. With a final show of determination, Mrs. Fisher stepped on the footrail to get in, but even as she did so, her knees weakened under her and she knew she did not have the strength to let the boy walk on those spindly worn legs of his. He was so young, so frail, so alone, so innocent, and in his very weakness too strong for her.

"Oh, damn! Oh, damn you, sannyasi!" she said, trying to pinch back the words with one hand across her mouth. "Well, get in, boy. You will ride with me." She stepped back and motioned for him to climb up without touching her. She did not want him to touch her, for somehow the very thought of actual contact made her afraid.

The boy did as he was told, and Mrs. Fisher climbed in after him, telling herself that she was taking him with her only because he was so small, and that she would turn him over to the mission orphanage the moment she got back to the city. They were overcrowded at the orphanage already, she knew, but she would take some of her savings and make a little fund for his care. That was as far as it would go. He was not going to push his way into her life—not under any circumstances would she go through all that again. At her age she just couldn't bear it. And as if to make certain of this she said, "I want no misunderstanding, child. I'm taking you with me to Meigudy, and when we return to the city, I will put you in the orphanage where they'll educate, feed and clothe you. But that's all, mind, that's as much as I can do." Then she realized that he had said nothing, made no demands of her, and that her words had been spoken only for her own benefit. It was as if, having taken some action with the boy, she was now finding the reasons for it. I simply had to do something, she thought. With him trailing me like that, I was constantly distracted. Now I won't have to worry or think about him. "And just don't touch me," she added sharply, "because you're filthy and I won't have it, you hear?" But try as she would, she could not shut out the smell of his body or the soft sound of his breathing, and even with distance between them she could almost feel his presence.

Within minutes after the bandy got under way the boy fell asleep, exhausted, on the straw cushioning. Only then did Mrs. Fisher feel actually free to turn and study him, as if, had he been conscious and known she was looking, it would have harmed or weakened her in some way.

Then quite suddenly the oxcart was overtaken by a student on a bicycle. He came riding impetuously around a curve after them, nearly bumping into the bandy before he saw it. Mrs. Fisher could tell he was a student because he wore his vashti in what was called the "Rumba Regent" style. The style was popular on campuses around South India and involved knotting the vashti on the side instead of in front and twisting the belt off center, too. The young man was perspiring heavily and took this chance encounter with the bandy to slacken his pace. Mrs. Fisher could see that he was anxious to catch onto the side of the bandy and so rest without stopping, but seeing that a white lady rode within, he was not quite sure what to do. Mrs. Fisher nodded and smiled, and instantly his left hand snapped out to catch the side of the bandy. He back pedaled fancily, like a young acrobat giving out with the footwork before actually stepping on the tight wire. Then he released his hold of the handle bars and performed a flashy series of one-handed maneuvers with cigarette and match. Inhaling, he peered boldly into the bandy at Mrs. Fisher. He eyed her sari, her tali; he peered at the slumbering little boy; and finally, after he had made certain with deliberate and affected casualness that there was no more to be seen, he asked, "Madame is married to an Indian man?"

"No," Mrs. Fisher said.

He was visibly disappointed. "Perhaps Madame is only married in form to a European and is having an affair with an Indian."

Mrs. Fisher shook her head, in doubt as to whether she should be amused or annoyed.

"I do not understand," the young man said. "Why do you ride in a bandy? Where are you going dressed in this manner? And why is your son so Indian-looking?"

Mrs. Fisher explained.

"Oh, a missionary lady," he said, dejected. "Such a wretched business. I had thought for a moment that you were one of us."

"And what might that be?" asked Mrs. Fisher.

"One of the new set," the young man replied. "We believe in complete abolition of all social, moral and religious bonds due to the fact that they are largely invented by pettifoggers to hinder and restrict the free movement of the intellectual. I am a proponent of pure freedom, you see, Madame. I feel that man should be free to behave exactly as he pleases. For instance, have you ever thought of the daily tragedy of many men and women who are kept from meeting each other and making love by such trite restrictions as decorum? Absence of free love is a tragedy. Absence of free anything is a tragedy. A crime, Madame. Have you ever thought of that? People should be able simply to meet, make love, and separate without attachment. We live in a terrible world of rules, Madame, truly terrible, you know? And every generation adds more to the list."

The young man had not given himself time to catch his breath completely, and as he spoke with an amazing machinelike rapidity he was soon winded to the point of speechlessness. Mrs. Fisher frowned and turned to look at Krishnan. She wanted to ask the young man where there was room in his philosophy for children, but he anticipated her.

"Take this stray urchin, for instance. You do not really want him along, but you have picked him up out of charity. And what is charity? A foolish manifestation of social coercion. You feel obligated to do what you have done. You do not *want* to do it. What good does it do the boy, I ask you? Now he will lose that precious freedom that was his."

"Freedom from what!" Mrs. Fisher almost shouted. But the student did not hear her. At that moment they passed a young woman standing beside the road and drying her sari. She had apparently just come from washing her sari in the river and, it being her only garment, she was drying it, the way village women did, by tying one end to a post and wrapping the other tightly about her body. The sun, however, had made her slightly dozy, and as the bandy rolled past, a sudden breath of hot air caught the sari from her relaxed grasp and whipped it away from her, revealing, for one instant before she could recover her senses and snatch the cloth modestly around her, all the warm, sensual contours of her ripe young body.

"There!" the student shouted excitedly. "That is what I mean exactly! Here for a moment we have a brief glimpse of beauty in its essence, pure, unposed beauty—the ultimate in life—and what happens? She jumps like one possessed in order to cover it up. Why? Because the rules say that she must do so. Because of the rules, she deprives the world of one moment of ultimate realization and makes of it a thing of shame. She covers herself up."

"And so would I," Mrs. Fisher snapped.

The young man shrugged. "Ah, well. It is to be expected. But for a moment I had thought that perhaps you were one of us and that you had cast off societal bonds and taken up with an Indian."

"I'm sorry to have disappointed you," said Mrs. Fisher.

"Quite all right," the young man said, overlooking her sarcasm and brushing her words aside as if he were bestowing a favor. "We can't hope for everyone to be saved. New tricks cannot be learned to an old dog, you know." He paused and looked around for a new approach. "Why does Madame not take the bus or train?"

"For the same reason you don't," she said.

"Are you also penniless and unemployed?"

"I simply wish to ride this way," she said. "When I first came to Meigudy as a young woman, I went by oxcart. And now that I'm going back I want to do it the same way." She wished she hadn't said that. She didn't owe him an explanation, and his reply stung her.

"Such a trite sentiment utterly, Madame," he said. "I exhort you to purge yourself of these feelings. One must never become attached to the past because it constitutes a hindrance to the present. Simply because you are along in years is no excuse to let yourself be shackled by sentimental attachments to the past or to the nuisance of that child. Strike them off, Madame, while there is time."

Before Mrs. Fisher could hurl back an indignant reply, the young man pedaled off without taking his leave. Mrs. Fisher's hand went to her mouth. "But it's all I've got," she said, choking back the words. "It's all I've got."

From the changing landscape, she could tell they were at last nearing Meigudy, and her irritation at the young man gave way to a mounting tension of nervous anticipation. On the outskirts of town, the bandy passed an old woman struggling along the road. Mrs. Fisher took compassion on her, perhaps through some association of age, and, stopping, invited her to ride with them. The old woman climbed into the bandy gratefully and cupped her tired feet in her hands. The flesh had withered on her arms and legs, and her face was heavily seamed with wrinkles that puckered the flesh about her toothless old gums as if at one time the lips had been sewn together like a wound. There was no luster in evidence about the old woman's person. She wore a faded sari, her white hair looked quite lifeless, her eyes devoid of any curious gleam. Mrs. Fisher tried to picture herself that old, wondering what answer so many years of living had taught her.

"Do you go to Meigudy?" Mrs. Fisher asked in Tamil.

"Even so," the old woman replied. "My youngest son lives there with his children, and my old bones have an ache to see him again."

"I suppose you live nearby—I mean near enough to make the walk once in a while."

"Yes, I live in the city," the old woman said.

"In the city!" Mrs. Fisher exclaimed. "That's a good thirty miles from Meigudy."

"A good thirty," the old woman said. "In my younger days I could make it from sunrise to sunset. Now, alas, the weight of years is upon me and I must start a day in advance."

"But is it worth all that?"

"Worth? Worth? Amma, when I have an ache to see my son and his children, the question of worth does not come into my mind. What else is there to life but children? Family and children. That's all that counts, I say. And you, Amma, do you go to Meigudy?"

Mrs. Fisher nodded.

"To visit family, or friends?"

"Neither," said Mrs. Fisher.

"But if you go not to visit with someone and have no family with you, what is the purpose of your trip?"

"I make a pilgrimage," Mrs. Fisher explained, "to my old home."

"And no family lives there?"

"No."

The old woman shook her head. Mrs. Fisher tried to explain, but the old woman was unable to fathom her reasoning. "All that sort of thing is beyond me, Amma. It is unnatural for one to be attached to a place where no relatives live."

Her words drew Mrs. Fisher's mounting frustration out to a fine, biting edge. "It's the most natural thing in the world to me," she said.

"Forgive me, Amma," the old woman said. "I am an ancient fifty years of age, and the why and wherefores no longer matter to me. I have only an ache to see my children and my children's children before time is upon me and carries me down with its weight."

Mrs. Fisher opened and closed her mouth several times without a word. She was thunderstruck to learn that this old woman was actually younger than herself. Somehow she had looked upon her as older and more wise, forgetting how many village women were aged so early by hard work, and the realization of this bore down on her like a great stone on the back of her neck.

At the bridge the old woman uttered thanks and left. Mrs. Fisher was still too stunned to think. With dreadful slowness the bandy crept through the streets of Meigudy, past the bazaars and market square, the familiar places crowded with strange young faces, and across town to the old mission compound. Mrs. Fisher was afraid to look out at Aaron's grave as they swung right over the little bridge and up through the gate to the drive that meandered under tamarinds and margosas past the girls' school and the untended gardens to the bungalow. Every turn, every rut, every bump in the road, now had the painful touch of familiarity, and Mrs. Fisher could feel her heart quickening to a pounding, unbearable crescendo. Then the bandy came to a stop, the bullocks snorting from the final sprint the driver had put them through, and Mrs. Fisher's throat went dry and her limbs weakened as she turned to climb out.

It had been her plan to dismiss the bandy and stay overnight in the bungalow, returning the next day by train or bus. But somehow the moment of fulfillment was as far away as ever, and she knew it had been too

from House of Many Rooms

late and too hopeless from the start. As she looked up at the bungalow, she could see that everything about it had changed. While it remained much the same in outline—the spacious verandas, the red tiled roof, the arched porticoes—the insidious fingernails of time had picked mercilessly over everything, pulling down the vines and trellises, defacing the line of the windows and verandas, scratching off the plaster, breaking in the shutters, pulling off tiles, shredding woodwork. Deadness and ruin lay over the place, exuding the stifling oppression of heat.

Almost mechanically Mrs. Fisher forced herself to climb the steps and enter the front room. The key she had taken the trouble to secure from the mission secretary in the city was quite useless to her and she left it in her pocket because the doors were in such bad repair that it had been an easy thing for someone to break in before her arrival. In mounting torment she passed through one room after another. How well she knew these rooms. They had been the scenes of birth and death, happiness and sorrow and anger. All that meant anything to her had been encompassed by these crumbling walls. And yet in a way she did not know them and they were strange to her. The life that had once filled and made real this empty deserted shell had long since fled. Remembering the plaque she had had inscribed with the 127th Psalm, she went into the library and dusted away the wall where it was, nearly obliterated with age:

> Lo, children are an heritage of the Lord,
> And the fruit of the womb Man's reward.
> As arrows in the hands of a warrior,
> So are the children of one's youth.
> Happy is he that hath a quiver of them;
> For he shall not be put to shame
> When he meets with his enemies in the gate.

The sight of it drew from Mrs. Fisher a sharp cry of anguish and, crushed by her own loneliness, she turned and fled from the house. She would never be able to bear the feeling of this place overnight; for as it was now it had no attachment for her. In haste she gathered the awakened little Krishnan up into the bandy and told the surprised driver to take them to the station at once. He complied, bewildered, and in a moment they were on the road again.

Mrs. Fisher sat with her head bowed and looked down on the road unfolding slowly beneath her like a gravel ribbon from a spool that was the axle of the bandy. And all at once it seemed to her, looking at the road, that all this time it was not really the road but her own life that had been unfolding beneath her. She had been riding not into the past, as she had supposed, but away from it. She had started out a young woman, young in hope—from somewhere—and now, unsuspectingly, her own age had crept up on her to strike its heavy blow. Feeling Krishnan's hand on her arm, she turned to him sharply.

"Well, what is it, boy, what is it?"

"Recess, Amma," he said.

Almost hatefully she called for the driver to stop while the boy got out and went to the bathroom. Apparently the call had been quite urgent, and Mrs. Fisher was annoyed that he had not spoken sooner. "Well, hurry up, hurry up!" she snapped furiously as he came back to the bandy. Her anger made him hesitate, afraid to get in. Suddenly all the pain and futility seemed to sweep to the fore of Mrs. Fisher's mind, focusing on the boy. If the trip had been a failure, she could blame it on him, she thought; yes, she could blame every last bit on him because it was his fault.

"Oh, for heaven's sake, child, get in," she yelled. He stood crouching to one side, still afraid, and for the first time his somber face crumpled to reveal emotion: silently he wept.

Mrs. Fisher looked at him in surprise as if she had not really seen him before. His pants were wet slightly where he had not gone to the bathroom soon enough because she had not thought to let him go. At the sight, her anger melted away as if it had never been, and she was crushed with tenderness for him. Gathering him up into her arms, she held him in a maternal embrace, his sweat and tears intermingling with her own. After a while she sat him on the straw beside her, his small brown hand, so smooth-skinned with youth despite the wearing effects of early labor, enclosed in her own time-callused hands. Despite the fact that she knew he would some day grow up and leave her, as the others had done, she could not deny his need for her and her need for him to shield her from her loneliness. All that was and would be she accepted now unquestioningly at face value, along with the ultimate bitterness that would be her lot— that was the lot of all mothers—when he grew up. She just couldn't help herself. And if there was any mystery in that, then the mystery was also its own answer.

"Come, Krishnan," she said, as the bandy rolled out of the compound on its way to the station, and the town and the fields began circling again slowly about some distant, immobile spot on the horizon and the place that had held such promise and emptiness for her, "I will tell you the story of a young woman who once lived in a house of many rooms filled with the long-ago laughter of boys and girls."